MACROECONOMICS
THEORY, EVIDENCE, AND POLICY

second edition

FRANK C. WYKOFF

Pomona College

PRENTICE-HALL, INC., Englewood Cliffs, NJ   07632

HB
171.5
.W94
1981

Library of Congress Cataloging in Publication Data

Wykoff, Frank C.
   Macroeconomics.

   Includes bibliographies and index.
   1. Macroeconomics.   I. Title.
HB171.5.W94 1981   339   81-513
ISBN   0-13-543967-1   AACR2

Editorial/production supervision and interior design
by Natalie Krivanek
Cover design by Carol Zawislak
Manufacturing Buyer: Edward O'Dougherty

Printed in the United States of America

10   9   8   7   6   5   4   3   2   1

Prentice-Hall International, Inc., *London*
Prentice-Hall of Australia Pty. Limited, *Sydney*
Prentice-Hall of Canada, Ltd., *Toronto*
Prentice-Hall of India Private Limited, *New Delhi*
Prentice-Hall of Japan, Inc., *Tokyo*
Prentice-Hall of Southeast Asia Ptd. Ltd., *Singapore*
Whitehall Books Limited, *Wellington, New Zealand*

To Victor and Elisabeth

Preface ix

I
MACROECONOMICS IN PERSPECTIVE: POLICY AND MEASUREMENT 3

1 The Scope of Macroeconomics   *3*
2 Measuring Economic Performance   *18*
3 Comparing Economic Performance   *36*

II
THE FOUNDATIONS AND POLICY IMPLICATIONS OF KEYNESIAN THEORY 51

4 Keynes and the Classics: The Beginnings of a Great Debate   *53*
5 Keynesian Income-Expenditure Models   *73*
6 Theory of Fiscal Policy   *87*
7 Discretionary Policy Versus Automatic Stabilizers   *104*

III
PERSONAL CONSUMPTION EXPENDITURES 117

8 The Keynesian Consumption Anchor: Theory and Evidence   *119*
9 Advanced Consumption Analysis   *137*

Contents

IV
PRIVATE DOMESTIC
INVESTMENT EXPENDITURES   163

10   Investment: From Keynes to Metzler and Tobin   *165*
11   Jorgenson's Neoclassical Investment Model and Tax Policy   *183*

V
MONEY, NATIONAL INCOME
DETERMINATION, AND STABILIZATION
POLICY   205

12   The Need for a Money Market: The *IS* Curve   *207*
13   Money in a Macromodel   *223*
14   Stabilization Policy   *243*

VI
MONETARY THEORY AND
THE GREAT DEBATE   255

15   The Supply of Money   *257*
16   The Demand for Money   *273*
17   Keynes and the Monetarists   *287*

VII
FLEXIBLE PRICES, AGGREGATE
SUPPLY, AND THE LABOR MARKET:
NEOCLASSICAL AND NEO-KEYNESIAN
THEORIES AND POLICIES   301

18   Wage-price Flexibility: The Three Sector Models   *303*
19   Neoclassical and Neo-Keynesian Income Determination   *325*
20   The State of Macroeconomic Theory: Short-run Dynamics   *344*

VIII
INFLATION FROM PHILLIPS
TO RATIONAL EXPECTATIONS 367

21   Inflation I: A Theoretical Appraisal of its Causes   *369*
22   Inflation II: Wage-price Dynamics and Consequences   *389*

IX
GROWTH, TRADE, AND MACRO
POLICY ANALYSIS 419

23   Long-run Economic Growth   *421*
24   International Trade and Domestic Stabilization   *450*
25   Macroeconomic Policy in Action   *475*

Index   *511*

Since I wrote the first edition of this text, changes in the economy and in macroeconomic theory have been remarkable. The most important changes in the economy, in my judgment, have been (1) the persistence of accelerating inflation, (2) the worsening of inflation-unemployment conditions, (3) the deterioration of international monetary relations, and (4) the slowdown in the rate of productivity increase. Changes in economic analysis have more than kept pace: (1) our increased interest in aggregate supply, (2) new work on the labor market, (3) new research on short-run dynamics, (4) development and application of adaptive and rational expectations, and (5) reinterpretation of the ideas of Keynes are among the major areas of innovation.

I have tried to do justice in this edition to the changing environment and to our changing thinking. In order to do so I have virtually rewritten major portions of the book. The chapters on Keynes (4), investment (10 and 11), the labor market and short-run dynamics (20), inflation (21 and 22), and policy (25) are completely new. In addition, there are major additions in consumption (Clower's dual decision hypothesis), growth and productivity, modeling of aggregate supply, and international monetary activity. Despite these additions, the organization of the material is basically the same. However, fiscal behavior in a one-sector model now precedes detailed analysis of consumption and investment, and I introduce the IS-LM model before covering monetary theory in detail because some users like to cover IS-LM fairly early in their courses.

Accommodation of so much new material has its costs. The book is long and reasonably difficult when taken as a whole. It is probably not wise to try to cover all the material in a first intermediate theory course covering one quarter. Especially if students have not had a full quarter of macro principles under their belts, this much theory is hard to absorb. My strategy has been to put all important material in the text and to develop the ideas in the context in which they were brought out in the profession. But each instructor is, of course, free to select topics and to even choose the order of topics. The organization is flexible. One can delete detailed material on consumption, investment, government, money, and labor without loss of continuity. One can present IS-LM very early by, for example, for Covering chapters 1, 4, 12, and 13. A quarter course in macro might include Chapters 1, 4-5, 12-14, 17-19, 21, 22B, and 25 with 6, 10, 23, and 24 optional. In my intermediate undergraduate course I do not cover all the material in one semester. I leave

Preface

advanced consumption, investment, monetary theory, labor, and growth to a more advanced course. But the material in these areas is there if one wants to cover it; thus each instructor has the flexibility to cover as much material as he feels his students can handle.

Many very useful suggestions have been given to me by friends in the profession. I am very grateful for help from Bob Clower, Dale Jorgenson, David Laidler, and Keizo Nagatani. Especially detailed and valuable suggestions were made by Craig Swan and Stephen A. Meyer. Of course, I accept all responsibility for errors. Jeanette Magee cheerfully helped with various reproductions along the way for which I am grateful.

Frank C. Wykoff

MACROECONOMICS IN PERSPECTIVE: POLICY AND MEASUREMENT

part I

The suddenly-idle hands blame themselves, rather than society. True there were hunger marches and protestations to City Hall and Washington, but the millions experienced a private kind of shame when the pink slip came. No matter that others suffered the same fate, the inner voice whispered, "I'm a failure."

Studs Terkel, *Hard Times,* 1970.

It is really supreme folly for a nation which is arming against the threat of invasion from without to let this invader, inflation, bring ruin from within.

Senator Paul Douglas, February 22, 1951, before the U.S. Senate.

Ill health of the economic organism is perhaps the most persistent and perplexing political issue confronting modern industrial societies. A sick economy can bring down a government as effectively as a coup d'etat; yet even political leaders and astute citizens remain muddled and confused by such phenomena as spiraling inflation, productivity, frictional unemployment, stagflation, slumpflation, and the like. Can you envision a world in which we all understand exactly the economic options facing society so that we can make sensible decisions with relatively predictable outcomes? Consider a world in which leaders and citizens can communicate clearly about economic problems without the veils of rhetoric and shibboleth. You are embarking on an effort to strengthen and enrich your own understanding of the functioning of the economic system. After completing this effort, you will, it is hoped, not only make wiser judgments but will also help others to better understand and evaluate issues so that they too may make decisions which best reflect their priorities and beliefs.

Part I of this book has two primary objectives. Chapter 1 is designed to reacquaint you with the substantive issues of macroeconomics. It is unnecessary to understand all the issues raised in this chapter. If you can understand the nature of aggregate economic issues, you will be well equipped to pursue the subsequent portions of the book.

Chapters 2 and 3 are quite different from Chapter 1. Chapters 2 and 3 deal in detail with the logic, structure, and substance of social economic accounts. Economic accounts consist of the factual information, or data, employed in economic analysis and policy. Although not the most exciting topic in macroeconomics, measurement of economic performance is absolutely essential to both policy making and scientific inquiry. One can, of course, lie with statistics. Consequently, it is important to understand the conceptual bases of the social accounts to avoid being fooled. Their organization helps you answer certain questions accurately, but the data are also limited; the user of social accounts must appreciate these limitations. Finally, Chapters 2 and 3 contain many numbers about the actual performance of the U.S. economy. Memorizing numbers is nonproductive. However, the numbers do provide information—the relative magnitudes of various types of economic activity, the rates of growth of the economy over time, rates of change of prices, and so on. You should try to be selective in retaining the essentials rather than try to memorize numbers indiscriminately.

After having completed Part I, you should have a feeling for macroeconomics; you should understand the logic of social accounts and should appreciate the general organization of economic activity. With an understanding of the relative magnitudes involved, you are prepared to study the theories and models of aggregate economic activity which follow.

A ● Macroeconomics in Action

Inflation: The 1970s were a decade of inflation. Since the years of Lyndon Johnson in the late 1960s, Presidents Nixon, Ford, and Carter each came to view inflation as "Public Enemy Number 1." From 1960 to 1964 consumer prices were rising at a trivial rate of 1.2 percent per year, but by the middle and late 1970s, these prices were rising at annual rates between 5 and 12 percent. Figure 1 illustrates these inflation rates. As one can see from the diagram, price level increases have been erratic and generally accelerating. Their erratic nature made them difficult to anticipate, and if one cannot anticipate the economic environment, then it is difficult to plan for the future.

1

The Scope
of Macroeconomics

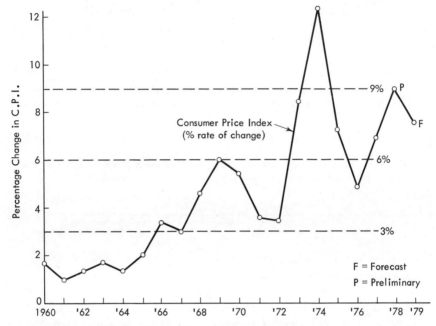

FIGURE 1   Inflation: 1960s and 1970s (percent change from preceding period)

Sources: 1960-1977—*Economic Report of the President*, January 1979; *Monthly Labor Review*, November 1978.

The corrosive effect on incomes of such rapid inflation is startling. A family earning $10,000 in 1967 was poorer in 1978 unless its income had reached $20,000. Of course, some jobs provided big salary and wage increases over the decade, and many assets provided larger dollar rates of return as well, but some people found their incomes unable to keep pace, so that inflation induced an income redistribution away from those individuals whose incomes were relatively fixed. Inflation erodes fixed incomes and deflates increases in money incomes.

The Board of Governors of the U.S. Federal Reserve System, to combat the seemingly persistent inflation, imposed temporary contractionary monetary policies in 1966, 1969, 1971, 1973, and 1975. Figure 2 shows the rate of monetary increase in these five periods, as well as the rates of monetary expansion over the entire period. The years of contraction, 1966, 1969, 1971, 1973, and 1975, were known as periods of "credit crunch." While inflation continued, credit availability was severely cramped.

Policies to influence aggregate economic behavior are not confined to actions of the central monetary authorities. The executive branch of the government can recommend, and the Congress can enact, a variety of fiscal measures to alter the course of the economy. The executive branch of government was not idle in the late 1960s and the 1970s. At the recommendation of the President's Council of Economic Advisors (the CEA), a tax surcharge was imposed in 1969 to slow

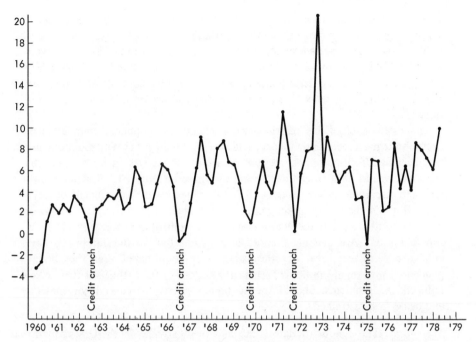

FIGURE 2   Monetary Policy—Cash Plus Commercial Demand Deposits: Rate of Change*

down and cool off the economy. It was frankly stated by the CEA that a slowdown was a necessary elixir to the economy.

Two years later, concluding that traditional monetary and fiscal tools were inadequate for dealing with the stubborn inflation, President Nixon, in August of 1971, imposed a direct wage and price freeze on the U.S. economy. This action was the first such dramatic measure taken in the peacetime U.S. Seventeen months after imposition of these price control measures, the CEA in 1973 announced: "By the end of 1972 the American anti-inflation policy had become the marvel of the rest of the world." Six months after that statement, prices were rising in the U.S. at a phenomenal annual rate of over 25 percent.

President Ford, Nixon's successor, attacked inflation by driving the federal budget into a substantial surplus. The result was the deepest and longest recession since the Great Depression of the 1930s. Alas, the inflation rate in the last half of the 1970s averaged well over 7 percent per year. Evidently the Ford anti-inflation program was also a failure. President Carter, unwilling to sustain another major recession as a means of slowing the rate of inflation, tried to gradually slow the rate of price increase by introducing a voluntary system of wage-price guidelines in 1978. Unfortunately, such measures seemed to please

*Data source: *Federal Reserve Bulletin*, December 1970-July 1972.

no one, neither business nor labor, and even advocates of such programs projected only modest improvements in the rate of inflation.

The large, erratic price level increases of the late 1960s and of the 1970s were widely agreed to have serious social consequences. Contractionary monetary policies, contractionary fiscal policies, direct wage-price controls, and voluntary wage-price guidelines were all employed to control inflation. Yet inflation continued.

Our brief sketch of this inflationary episode raises a number of complex questions about macroeconomic theory, evidence, and policy: (1) Why did monetary and fiscal authorities impose certain measures? What was their "view of the economic world" that lead them to impose these measures? (2) Did the monetary and fiscal authorities have as their sole objective the curtailment of inflation? How do they settle upon goals? Are the goals always complementary, or do they conflict? (3) If the goal was indeed to control inflation why did inflation continue? Are existing theories inadequate? (4) Do the authorities have enough control measures? Are they adequately coordinated? Can they be implemented in a timely fashion? Perhaps the actions of the authorities themselves induced the problems. Should the economic activity of central governments and banks be constrained?

Stagnation: Throughout the late 1950s and very early 1960s the U.S. economy seemed to suffer from two chronic and apparently distinct problems: "creeping" inflation—prices rising gradually at rates around 3 percent and "stagnation"—sluggish growth of output around 2 1/2 percent with a relatively large rate of unemployment, 6 to 7 percent of the labor force. Somewhat like pre-Keynesian classical economists, many people believed this general malaise to be the wave of the future. Books and articles sprang up on the Cybernetic Revolution—the replacement of man by machine. A new word entered the economic vocabulary: "Stagflation." Many economists predicted unemployment would plague the society indefinitely.

Consider, for example, the following 1963 comments by economist Robert Theobald:

> Unemployment rates must therefore be expected to rise in the sixties . . .
> no conceivable rate of economic growth will avoid this result.

The annual rate of unemployment in the U.S. from 1960 to 1979 is reproduced in Figure 3.

From 1960 through 1969, the labor force continued to grow, requiring increased employment in every year just to maintain a constant level of unemployment. Nevertheless, shortly after Theobald's prediction of increasing unemployment, the unemployment rate began to fall and reached a low of 3.5 percent in 1969. As is clear from the diagram, the decade of the 1970s was a period of rising unemployment, and we shall have more to say about this later in the text.

In November 1969, the former chairman of the Council of Economic Ad-

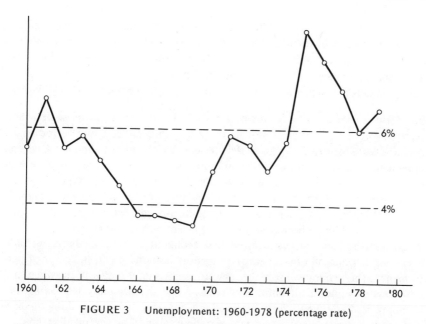

FIGURE 3   Unemployment: 1960-1978 (percentage rate)

Source: *Economic Indicators,* U.S. Government Printing Office, Washington, D.C., November 1978.

visers, under President Lyndon Johnson, proudly proclaimed:

> As of this writing, the nation is in its one-hundred-and-fifth month of un-paralleled, unprecedented, and uninterrupted economic expansion.
>
> Arthur Okun (1970)

Okun, and others, pointed with pride to a number of economic stabilization measures introduced by economists in the Kennedy and Johnson administrations to stimulate the economy. Rather than accept stagflation as a natural state of the economy, Kennedy introduced legislation to stimulate private domestic investment. The President actively "jawboned" for wage-price guideposts at 3 percent per year. President Lyndon Johnson later, in 1964, engineered the first major federal income tax cut for economic stabilization purposes in U.S. economic history. These measures have been widely credited with the boom period of the 1960s.

Other economists provide an entirely different interpretation of the economic events of the sixties. Monetarist economists tend to discount the impact of the above fiscalist actions and point instead to the generally smooth expansive nature of monetary policy throughout the sixties. In fact, some blame the activist fiscal measures for the subsequent period of extreme price instability.

This second episode in U.S. economic activity also suggests a number of questions about economic theory evidence and policy: (1) Why are economists in such disagreement about the effects of policy actions and of economic episodes? Are their theories different? Their evidence? Their ideologies? (2) Is unemployment an economic problem amenable to policy resolution? Can policy effectively lower unemployment or will attempts merely result in inflation? (3) Do economic models allow prediction to be accurate, or are economists usually wrong?

The Okun Diagram: In order for economic policy makers to propose fiscal and monetary actions, they must be able to evaluate actual economic performance. Arthur Okun, former chairman of the President's Council of Economic Advisors, developed a method of measuring and judging the economic performance of a system over time. His technique illustrates the problems confronted by central authorities in formulating economic policy. In order to evaluate the economy, Okun needed a norm against which he could measure success or failure. One possibility would have been to utilize the concept of business cycles.

Economists have long recognized that economic activity tends to fluctuate over long periods of time in roughly cyclical fashion. As an indicator of performance, the economy might be viewed as successful while on upswings and unsuccessful while on downturns. That is, when the economy is growing, the economy is doing well; when the economy is not growing, it is doing poorly. The implicit norm of cycles is zero economic growth as the dividing line between success and failure. Okun found such a norm unacceptable.

Rather than some cyclical norm, Okun settled on a measure of the economy's productive potential as a yardstick of performance. Okun developed the concept of *potential gross national product.* Though no single measure can adequately reflect economic performance, GNP is the most comprehensive single indicator of the level of economic activity. GNP measures the value of all final goods and services produced by the economy in a year. Okun theorized that, in any year, an economy was capable of attaining a given level of productive potential. To achieve this potential the economy would have to be operating at relatively full utilization of its resources.

The concept of potential GNP is not a static one, for over time a society's population grows and its labor force expands. As an economy grows, so does its capital stock. Over time, an economy enjoys technological advances. Consequently, productive potential, Okun reasoned, could be expected to grow over time. Finally, since changes in the factors upon which potential GNP depends would tend to be small compared to initial values, one would expect potential GNP to grow smoothly and gradually. Okun viewed potential GNP as growing at a constant annual rate of 4 1/2 percent per year. (We are not concerned now with how Okun measured potential GNP, except to note that he viewed it as rising at a steady rate.)[1] Figure 4 depicts the potential growth path of GNP.

[1]We abstract for simplicity from several complications: Technology cannot be expected to grow gradually, though its application to the economy may. A constant growth rate requires a nonlinear growth path.

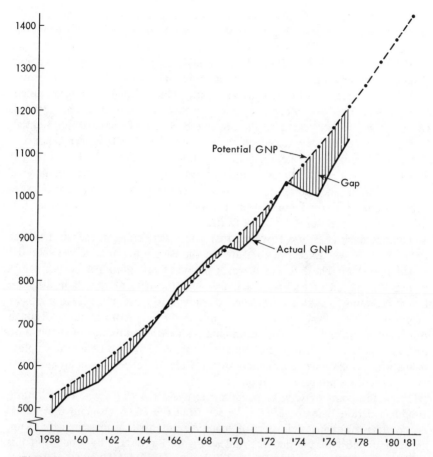

FIGURE 4   The Okun Diagram—U.S. Economy 1952-1981. Actual and Potential
Gross National Product

Okun used potential GNP as the norm against which he could evaluate performance. The difference between actual and potential GNP serves as the index
of economic performance. The jagged curve in Figure 4 represents the actual
growth path of the U.S. economy from 1952 to 1973. The index, potential
GNP minus actual GNP, is a much more stringent one than the zero growth
rate norm embodied in the business cycle approach. From 1955 to 1965 the
economy was growing in every year, except briefly from late 1957 to early
1958, yet the economy was not performing up to its potential over most of
the period. A business cycle norm would cause one to interpret the 1955 to
1965 period, except 1957-1958, as successful expansion. The potential GNP
norm indicates, however, that a good deal of productive output was lost as a
result of inadequate economic growth. The shaded area in Figure 4 measures
the loss in output. The 1958 to 1965 period is now seen as one of varying

degrees of success. In the main, a large gap exists between actual and potential output; however, from 1962 to 1965 the gap is being closed by economic growth.

The period of the late 1960s is quite interesting. From Figure 4 it appears that the economy was outperforming its potential. In fact, however, potential GNP is not a measure of output by an economy in "full steam." Rather, potential GNP characterizes an economy at reasonably low levels of unemployment. Okun allowed for an element of slack in an economy performing at its potential. The fact that actual GNP exceeded potential in the late 1960s indicates that very little slack was in the economy. To maintain production at such high levels, and growth at such a rapid rate, an economy must have strong pressures on material resources, labor, and capital inputs. These pressures could be expected to cause strong competition for factors of production which would, in turn, induce factor and subsequently product prices to rise.

Looking back at Figure 1, we see that prices were rising in the late 1960s at rather rapid rates. Excessive pressure on the economy's productive potential pulled prices up. The late 1960s was a period of inflation. The upshot of observing this period of economic activity, with the help of the Okun diagram, is that economic growth can be either too slow or too fast. The excessive growth of the late 1960s, from 1965 to 1969, produced a period of inflation. Although this may not have been sound economic policy, the result was predictable by orthodox economic theory: Inadequate economic growth produces unemployment, whereas excessive economic growth, while it reduces unemployment and increases output, produces inflation.

From the point of view of economic analysis, the 1970s was a much more troubling period than the 1960s. We see from the Okun Diagram that actual economic performance fell short of economic potential, as measured by Okun, throughout most of the decade. And as Figure 3 attests, a by-product of this inadequate production was a period of high unemployment. However, if we look back at Figure 1 in which the inflation rate for the U.S. is illustrated, we see that inflation was also unusually high in the 1970s. This combination of high unemployment and high inflation which typified the 1970s was most unusual by historical standards for the U.S. economy.

If possible traditionally we had learned to worry either about high unemployment as a social problem or about high inflation, but we did not expect to see periods in which inflation and unemployment were serious problems simultaneously. We can illustrate this new dilemma with an additional diagram. Figure 5 depicts the combinations of unemployment and inflation rates for the U.S. economy from 1960 through 1979. Each point in this diagram represents one year's combination of inflation and unemployment, and each point is dated. The points for the 1960s fall roughly on an arc of values which represent either relatively high unemployment and low inflation or relatively high rates of inflation and low levels of unemployment or various combinations in between. The points for the 1970s all lie above and to the right of the points for the 1960s. Thus the 1970s were a period of both higher inflation and higher unemployment

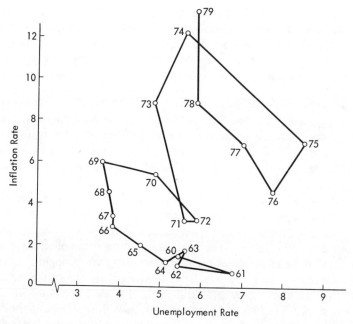

FIGURE 5   The Relation between Inflation and Unemployment for the U.S.
Economy 1960-1978

Sources: See Figures 1 and 3.

than were typical in the previous decade. High unemployment or stagnation, combined with the high rates of inflation, has come to be called *stagflation,* and the resolution of the problem of stagflation is probably the most difficult policy problem we shall attempt to analyze in this book.

The broad objective of this book is to provide the student with the theoretical tools to understand and interpret aggregate economic events and policies. He may be unable to definitively answer each of the questions raised, but he should feel confident in his understanding of theories of economic behavior with which events can be interpreted, and he should be capable of identifying the general areas in which economists can be expected to disagree on scientific grounds. Finally, the student should feel equipped to go on to more advanced topics. Though we use policy to motivate theory and measurement, the primary concern of this text is with positive economics. Our approach is a serious effort at eclectic nonnormative aggregate economics.

B ● Two Views of the World:
The Quantity of Money Theory vs. The Income Expenditure Theory

To study the complexity of aggregate economic activity, economists have developed a number of conceptual frameworks, or theories, which simplify the economic world to a manageable level. Regardless of their different models, all economists are ultimately concerned with the types of economic problems we illustrated above—inflation, unemployment, economic stagnation, and so on. However, the suitable framework for dealing with problems of macroeconomic activity is a subject of rather deep disagreement. Different views can be symbolized with the help of a simple, flexible model: the circular flow of income.

A Simple Model: Consider an economy which consists of two groups of economic units: households and firms. (The society will have no government and will not interact externally with other systems.) The primary activities of firms are (1) to produce goods and services employing factors of production provided by households and (2) to sell the final goods and services produced to either other firms or to households.

The primary economic activities of households are (1) to provide to firms factor services, such as labor, capital, and land, in the production process for which households receive income payments, and (2) to use this income from factor payments to either save for future consumption or to purchase goods and services from firms in the current period. We depict these economic activities of the two economic groups by two flows between them. In Figure 6 the inner circular flow between households and firms is a clockwise flow of physical goods and services. The lower portion of this inner flow represents the flow of final goods and services from firms to households and the upper portion of the loop is the flow of factor services—labor, land, capital—to be used in production by firms.

The outer loop in Figure 6 depicts the counterclockwise flow of dollar payments made in exchange for the various goods and services. The lower portion represents payments to firms for final goods and services purchased by households, and the upper portion represents dollar payments to households in exchange for use of their factor services.

The circular flow of income model is useful for a number of purposes. It illustrates that production of goods and services generates income for the owners of factors (households) and that households, in turn, use their income to acquire new goods and services by purchasing them from firms. Firms, after selling goods and services, then generate new factor income and more production. In short, economic activity is depicted as a circular flow of income and production. The rate of circulation, the amount of income generated in a year, is the dollar value of goods and services produced in a year. To understand aggregate economic activity, the level of production, the level of employment associated with production, and the level of output, we must understand the nature of the generation of income.

Savings and Investment: As a rule, of course, households do not pass all income on in the circular flow to firms. Some household income is saved and is, therefore, at least temporarily withdrawn from the circular flow. Similarly, firms often retain some of their income which is not circulated on into the flow. Furthermore, many firms carry on expenditures in excess of the income they

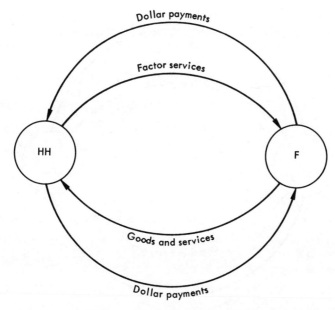

FIGURE 6   The Circular Flow of Income

are currently receiving from household expenditures. These excess spendings by firms are viewed as injections into the circular flow because they add dollar income to the flow which did not originate from households. Let us define investment as expenditures by firms which add to their stock of physical capital. All investment spending by firms will be considered net injections into the flow. (While, in fact, some investment expenditures are financed out of current income, one cannot, as a rule, identify particular investments by the source of revenue. Furthermore, current sources of funds which finance current investment will be treated both as withdrawals in the form of business savings and as injections of new investment expenditures.) Figure 7 elaborates the model, first depicted in Figure 6, by allowing for private saving, S_p, business saving, S_b, and investment expenditures, I.

To illustrate different approaches to macroeconomic analysis with the new circular flow model, it is first helpful to consider a physical analogue. Figure 8 depicts a circular pipe, made of a flexible material, through which water is circulating in a counter-clockwise direction. (This physical model might represent a closed system water fountain.) In the economic model of the circular flow of income, we are interested in the volume of the flow of income which passes through the circle over a period of time—say, a year. In the physical example the analogue to income is the volume of water swirling through the pipe over a period of time. In this latter case, one can compute the volume of water which passes through the pipe over a period of time—say, one hour—if the quantity of water in the system at any moment and the velocity of the water are both

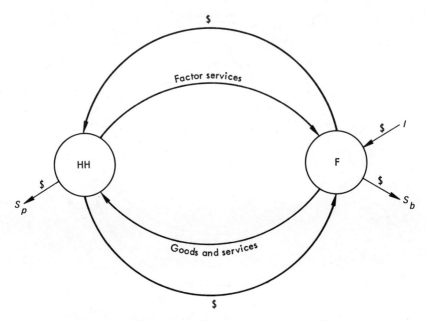

FIGURE 7   Circular Flow of Income with Saving and Investment

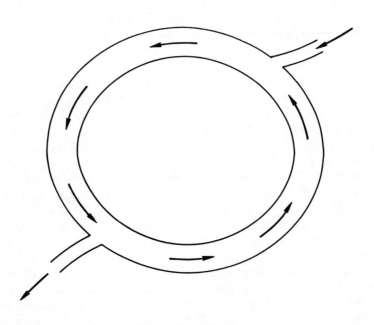

FIGURE 8   Water Pipe Analogy

known. The product of the quantity of water times the velocity of water per hour is the amount which passes through the pipe (crosses a marker) in one hour. It is not adequate to know only the quantity of water in the pipe. One must also know the speed with which it is moving through the system.

Corresponding to the quantity of water in the pipe at a point in time is the quantity of money in the circular flow at a moment in time. Knowing only the amount of money in circulation is inadequate to computing the flow of income over a year just as knowing the number of gallons of water in the pipe was inadequate to calculating the amount that passed through the pipe over a period of time. However, if, in addition to the quantity of money, one also knows its velocity through the economy, one can compute the level of income. Income, over a year, is the product of the quantity of money in circulation and the velocity of the money per year as it is exchanged for final goods and services.

The Quantity Theory of Money: One major approach to studying the level of income in an economy is called the quantity theory of money, and this approach concentrates on measuring the quantity of money, the income velocity of money (that is, the speed with which money changes hands in generating income), and the level of income. The link between the quantity of money, M, and the level of income, Y, is the velocity of money, V, which is defined as:

$$V \equiv Y/M \qquad\qquad (1)$$

From equation (1) it should be clear that if velocity is constant or very stable, changes in income will be closely related to changes in the quantity of money. Furthermore, policies which change the quantity of money will be important policies in determining the level of income, and policies which do not change the quantity of money will either be comparatively unimportant or will have to induce changes in velocity.

The quantity theory of money approach to income determination is the theoretical framework used today by modern *monetarists*. Economists of the nineteenth and early twentieth centuries, classical economists, held views somewhat similar to those of modern monetarists. These views had been in disrepute for many years, due, in large part, to the success of the Keynesian revolution in the 1930s and to the *apparent* failure of pre-Keynesian classical economics to deal with the Great Depression. In recent years, however, monetarism has made a significant and substantial revival—some say a counterrevolution.

The usefulness, and success, of the monetarist approach to income determination would seem to depend rather heavily upon the stability of the velocity of money. If velocity is constant, then, indeed, any other approach would seem to be circuitous and misleading. However, if velocity is not constant, then the monetarist approach would be less helpful. If velocity were not even stable, but rather unstable and unpredictable, then the quantity theory of money approach would be cumbersome and awkward.

The Income-Expenditure Theory: The possibility that the income velocity of money is not constant, and that it may not even be stable, suggests an alternative approach to income determination. The alternative approach is to concentrate directly upon the behavior of economic agents. This view is to study the behavior of households as they make expenditure-saving choices and the behavior of firms as they make investment-production decisions and so on.

Figure 6 depicts the outcomes of decisions by households, resulting in a consumption-saving mix, and of decisions by firms, determining retained earnings and investment spending. Analogous to the water pipe model, the level of the circular flow of income will be constant if the amount of expenditures entering the flow, injections, equals the amount leaving the flow—withdrawals. Given an initial constant flow of income, an increase in the rate of investment spending will result in a larger flow of income. As income is pushed up by the increased injections of investment spending, the amount withdrawn in saving will be likely to rise as well. In fact, saving will rise until the level of withdrawals, saving, just offsets the new higher level of investment spending. Notice that the level of income has been seen to rise as a result of an autonomous increase in investment spending by firms, even though the quantity of money has not increased, per se.

The income-expenditure approach is based on the work of Lord John M. Keynes and was largely developed by his followers, particularly Alvin Hansen. The income-expenditure approach concentrates upon the behavior of households in their consumption-saving choices and the behavior of firms in making their investment decisions. The quantity of money is not ignored by Keynesians, but its effect is indirectly felt through its altering the behavior of economic agents.

These two very different approaches to studying income, production, employment, and price level are both widely employed today. The student of macroeconomics would be well served if he learned a variety of views and approaches, the nature of the theoretical and empirical evidence on which they rest and the policy implications which derive from them. He must then determine which approach is most suitable for analysis.

STUDY QUESTIONS

1. Suppose you were asked to develop economic stabilization policies for the U.S. today. Without studying actual market data, comment on how you would organize your staff for dealing with this problem

2. Present a circular flow model in which you can compare the quantity of money and the income-expenditure approaches to income determination. On what issues do you think the debate hinges? Do you think these issues are empirical, theoretical, or political?

3. Construct the circular flow of income model. Does government economic activity influence this flow? How?

4. Comment on potential GNP as a device for evaluating economic performance.

5. List the years since 1975 when prices increased faster than 5 percent per year. Which of these do you believe can be explained by excess demand in the economy? (Hint: When is actual GNP larger than potential?)

6. Utilizing figures from this chapter, plot a scatter diagram in which the rate of change of the consumer price index is on the vertical axis and the rate of unemployment on the horizontal axis. Draw a curve approximating the scatter of points. At what rate of unemployment is the price level stable? At what rate of change of prices will the unemployment rate be zero? Can you select a point on the line you have drawn which you would accept as a target for economic policy?

REFERENCES

Anderson, Leonall C., "The State of the Monetarist Debate," *Federal Reserve Bank of St. Louis Review*, September 1973.

————, "An Explanation of Movements in the Labor Force Participation Rate, 1957-76," *Federal Reserve Bank of St. Louis Review*, 1978.

Clower, Robert W., "Monetary History and Positive Economics," *Journal of Economic History*, September 1964.

Council of Economic Advisors, *Economic Indicators*. Washington, D.C.: U.S. Government Printing Office, 1977.

Economic Report of the President. Washington, D.C.: United States Government Printing Office, 1973.

Economic Report of the President. Washington, D.C.: U.S. Government Printing Office, January 1979.

Feldstein, Martin, "The Economics of the New Unemployment," *The Public Interest*, No. 32 (Fall, 1973), pp. 3-43.

Finegan, T. Aldrich, "Improving Information on Discouraged Workers,"*Monthly Labor Review*, U.S. Labor Department, Washington, D.C., September 1978.

Friedman, Milton, *Essays in Positive Economics*. Chicago: The University of Chicago Press, 1953.

Lovati, Jean M., "The Growing Similarity Among Financial Institutions," *Federal Reserve Bank of St. Louis Review*, October, 1977, pp. 2-11.

Okun, Arthur M., "Upward Mobility in a High Pressure Economy," *Brookings Papers on Economic Activity*, No. 1 (1973), The Brookings Institution, Washington, D.C., pp. 210-221.

————, *The Political Economy of Prosperity*. New York: W.W. Norton, 1970.

Perry, George, "Potential Output and Productivity," *Brookings Papers on Economic Activity*, No. 1 (1977), The Brookings Institution, Washington, D.C., pp. 11-60.

Samuelson, Paul, *Economics*, 9th ed. New York: McGraw-Hill, 1973.

U.S. Labor Department, *Monthly Labor Review*. Washington, D.C.: U.S. Government Printing Office, November 1978.

> While there is some surface plausibility in the view that empirical and theoretical research are best carried out in isolation from each other, this view is seriously incomplete.
>
> Dale W. Jorgenson (1967)

Whether one is ultimately concerned with economic science or policy, an essential phase of study is the measurement of economic performance. From the scientific point of view, theories and hypotheses meet their ultimate tests when confronted with empirical evidence. Formulation of economic policy requires an understanding of the ordering of social preferences, a knowledge of the productive potential of an economy, and complete information about economic performance. To measure aggregate economic performance, we must develop an accounting framework which depicts the essential elements of economic activity. Accurate measurement of economic activity then forms the basis for evaluation of economic performance.

2

Measuring
Economic Performance

Suppose, for example, that one wished to evaluate productivity of the factor inputs in two different economies. Essential to comparison would be comparable data on the inputs of factors and on their ouput. Changes in factor inputs and on product outputs provide a basis for comparisons of changes in productive efficiency and economic growth. Consider questions relating to the distribution of income. Necessary information for dealing with such questions is data on the returns to factors of production. Factor returns provide, in addition to data on input returns, the basis for evaluation of distribution across other subsets of society. Finally, the use of output is often of interest to students of social studies, and a prerequisite to studying output by use is data about expenditure of final product: consumption, capital formation, public expenditure, and so forth.

The examples above illustrate the uses of data on the measurement of economic activity. In this chapter we develop the national income, expenditure, and product accounts for the U.S. economy as these accounts are the main source of empirical evidence for evaluation of economic performance in the U.S. Part A contains the conceptual basis for a comprehensive accounting framework and a brief discussion of the price-quantity separation necessary for intertemporal comparisons. Part B consists of the actual U.S. accounts in current price for 1978 with comments on conceptual problems encountered in interpreting the data.

A • Conceptual Basis for National Accounts

The rudiments of economic activity can be described with the use of an abstract model. Consider a society to begin a year with a stock of initial endowments. These initial endowments would include labor (a variety of skills, ages, education, etc.), capital (accumulated from previous periods), land (minerals, timber, water, etc.), and financial resources (money accumulated from previous periods plus some financial assets and liabilities). With a given technology, the society combines its initial endowment in two processes—production and exchange—culminating in output. Some output will consist of unchanged endowments; for example, some labor will be maintained in the form of leisure. The exact configuration of the outputs will depend, in a very complex way, on a wide variety of factors: the absolute and relative quantities of various endowments, the state of technological knowledge, the nature of social and economic organization, the social preferences of the members, the political organization, and so on.

Outputs, including nontransformed initial endowments, will be distributed to the members of the society. As in the case of choice of outputs, the allocation of final products to ultimate uses by society will depend upon a complex set of factors. Nevertheless, ultimately outputs are either consumed in the current period or accumulated for endowment in subsequent periods. The next period similarly begins with a set of initial endowments and the processes of economic activity continue. These rudiments of economic activity can be depicted in a simple flow diagram (Figure 1).

Given a particular type of economic and social organization, one can elaborate upon this model. Consider a market economy. Initial endowments are provided in the production process by factors of production in exchange for factor income payments. Similarly, output is allocated to its various uses in exchange for expenditures or is accumulated via saving and investment for future endowments. These elaborations are illustrated in Figure 2.

Figure 2 provides a useful point of departure for studying the structure of national accounts. Corresponding to each stage of economic activity in the model is a system of accounts. These accounts first organize all the relevant economic magnitudes valued at current prices. The account corresponding to initial endowments is a *wealth account* containing total values of labor, capital, land, and financial assets. The actual formation of a comprehensive wealth account has proved extremely difficult. Measurement of the values of capital, land, and labor involves some very complicated conceptual and practical problems. For example, measurement of the value of labor, or human capital, involves estimation of the present and future productivity of labor. In a society in which human capital per se is generally not marketed, its valuation is difficult. Consider also measurement of the value of the stock of tangible capital assets. Some economists argue that it is meaningless to talk of a unit of capital in the sense of a measurable quantity. Even if we accept the concept of a measurable capital stock, however, its actual valuation is impeded by inadequate data on capital asset prices. Nevertheless, a complete system of social accounts includes a balance sheet of national wealth.

The production process consists of employment of factor inputs—flows of labor, capital, land, and financial services—in the generation of final products. In an advanced industrialized economy many firms and industries are primarily involved in production of intermediate products—goods to be used in the current

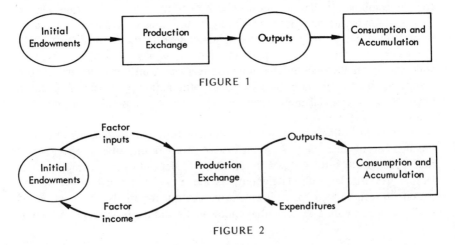

FIGURE 1

FIGURE 2

period as inputs in the production of other goods. In fact, some products are used both as intermediate products in some industries and as final products elsewhere. The *national income account* measures the value of final goods and services according to the remuneration of factor inputs.

The next stage in economic activity consists of the allocation of outputs to uses. These activities are measured in the *national product and expenditure accounts*. In the broadest terms, uses of output consist of personal consumption expenditures by households, gross private domestic investment by firms, net exports of goods and services to foreigners, and government purchases of goods and services.

Finally, to link accounts across time periods we must establish a connection between economic activity in one period to that in the next. The link is established by connecting the flow accounts, describing economic activities of income, production, and expenditure during the period, to the stock account, wealth, in the subsequent period. The link is the *accumulation account*. The accumulation account contains the values of saving, derived from the income and expenditure accounts, of capital formation and of asset revaluations. Just as the wealth account involves difficulties in compilation, so does the accumulation account. Definitions and valuations of endowments must be consistent with those of investments, savings, and revaluations.

Historical accident and severe measurement problems seem to have combined to retard the development of comprehensive, consistent social accounts for the U.S. economy. The areas of most difficulty, and perhaps of least historical interest, have been the wealth and accumulation accounts. We have already commented upon some of the difficulties. The historical causes relate to the timing of the development of national income, expenditure, and product accounts. Publication of these accounts for the U.S. coincided with the Keynesian revolution. National accounts were first available in 1934 and Keynes' *General Theory of Employment, Interest and Money* was published in 1935. Keynesian economists focused attention on flows of economic activity. They argued, in general, that the linkages in economic activity between stocks (money, capital, portfolio structure, and so on) and flows (consumption, investment, savings, etc.) were obscure and elusive. Their attention was on the determination of income and on its distribution between consumption and investment. Consequently, priority efforts have gone into development of accounts for the flows—national income, expenditure, and product accounts.

As mentioned in Chapter 1, the late 1950s and the 1960s witnessed the groundswell of a counterrevolution in economic theory. With it came a demand for improved national statistics on certain types of assets—monetary assets. The vanguard of the counterrevolution was lead by Milton Friedman and the "Chicago School." The approach was not the income-expenditure approach of Keynesians but the quantity theory of money—the modern offspring of the pre-Keynesian classical quantity theory. In contrast to the Keynesian obsession with flows, the Chicago School emphasized the importance of stocks. One particular stock was most important, the stock of money. Thus economists are once again focusing upon the linkage between stocks and flows, and renewed interest in monetary statistics is a by-product. Of course, one need not be a Chicago monetarist to study stocks. In point of fact, postwar developments in macro-economic theory across the board have been to emphasize stock-flow relations. We turn our attention now to the construction of and conceptual problems associated with the national accounts.

B ● National Income, Expenditure, and Product Accounts

Study of the national accounts begins with the definition of gross national product. According to the U.S. Commerce Department,[1] *GNP* is the gross value, measured at market prices, of all final goods and services produced in the U.S. in one year. GNP is the most commonly used single measure of the productive per-formance of an economy. GNP, and changes in its level over time, serve as con-cise indicators of economic performance. Table 1 contains GNP in current prices, GNP in constant prices, and the GNP deflator for the U.S. economy in some select years from 1929 through 1979.

The technical procedures for decomposing money GNP into a quantity com-ponent, real GNP, and a price component, the GNP deflator, are the main subjects of Chapter 3. It may be helpful to note at this time that the unit of measure, the dollar, changes over time, so that intertemporal comparisons of GNP, each year's measured in its own current prices, are not accurate reflections of economic production and output. Consequently, column 2 of Table 1 con-tains GNP in each year measured in the same units: 1972 prices. Column 3 measures the ratio of each year's prices to those of 1972. The prices are

TABLE 1

Gross National Product in Current and Constant Prices, Select Years 1929-1974

YEAR	GNP CURRENT PRICES	GNP CONSTANT PRICES	GNP DEFLATOR
1929	103.4	314.6	32.9
1933	55.8	222.1	25.1
1940	100.0	348.3	29.1
1945	212.3	560.0	37.9
1955	399.3	654.8	61.0
1965	688.1	925.9	74.3
1970	982.4	1075.3	91.4
1972	1171.1	1171.1	100.0
1975	1528.8	1202.3	127.2
1979	2368.8	1431.6	165.5

[1] *Survey of Current Business*, March 1975 and July 1980 and *Economic Report of The President*, January 1979.

TABLE 2

GNP by Major Use in Select Years (billions of 1972 dollars)

ITEM	1929	1933	1945	1965	1979
GNP	314.6	222.1	560.0	925.9	1431.6
C	215.6	170.7	271.4	558.1	924.5
I	55.9	8.4	104.1	150.1	215.2
X-M	2.2	0.2	− 4.5	4.7	17.6
G	40.9	42.8	265.3	150.9	274.3

weighted by their relative importance in GNP in 1952. These two series will aid our discussion of U.S. economic performance.

GNP in 1979 was $2.4 trillion. This is about a 450 percent increase, in constant prices, over GNP in 1929. It is fiarly clear that the U.S. economy has been very productive over this period. It is equally clear that the performance of the economy in 1933 was quite poor compared to 1929. GNP, measured in constant prices, decreased by nearly 30 percent. GNP, measured in current prices, overstates changes in output over the years, because prices changed considerably as well. For example, the GNP deflator indicates that the price level fell from 1929 to 1933 over 20 percent; from 32.9 to 25.1. The GNP deflator increased over the decade 1955 to 1965 by less than 25 percent. In the next 5 years, 1965 to 1970, the price level, as measured by the GNP deflator, increased at over twice the rate of the previous decade: over 4.5 percent per year. Over 1979 the price level increased 9 percent. Meanwhile, real output rose $32.4 billion, down from the real growth of $196.9 billion in 1978. These casual, general observations point up the grossest broad aspects of economic activity, but for adequate evaluation of economic performance, much more detail is necessary.

GNP may be detailed either from the point of view of income generated to the factor inputs in the course of production or from the point of view of the allocation of output to competing uses. We shall start analyzing the latter. Table 2 contains the major components of GNP by use in several select years.

We may make several observations about GNP and its uses from Table 2. First, the largest single component of GNP is consumption expenditures on final goods and services by households. Consumption varies in nonwar years between 65 and 80 percent of GNP. Since consumption expenditures are the major element of GNP, their determination will be quite important in the determination of GNP.

Private domestic investment expenditures are, on the other hand, rather small, ranging from 4 to 18 percent of GNP. Theories of investment behavior, nevertheless, play a very important role in economics. To some economists, investment expenditures are the engine of economic fluctuations. In percentage terms, they are quite volatile; from 1929 to 1933, for example, they fell 85 percent. Furthermore, unlike the other elements of GNP, investment spending is for future production and consumption. Consequently, its level is dependent upon anticipations of uncertain future events. The fact that businesses anticipate the future and invest billions of dollars on the basis of their expectations suggests the importance of investment to the pace of economic activity.

The contribution to final product of the foreign sector is very small, between 0 and 2 percent of GNP. However, its size understates its importance. Gross exports are often about half as large as domestic private investment, and the impact of foreign economic activity upon domestic governmental policies is extremely important. Furthermore, specific commodites play a vital role in the U.S. economy.

Perhaps the most striking aspect of the figures is the increasingly important role of government in GNP. Calvin Coolidge once said "business is the business of America." Today some say government is becoming the business of America. Prior to the 1930s, nondefense spending by government accounted for about 1 percent of GNP. In 1979 government expenditures absorbed about 20 percent of total GNP. Now that its role in the economy is so large, variations in government fiscal activity can have substantial impacts on the economy.

One can gain considerable insight into the nature and significance of national income accounting and aggregate economics as one explores the actual measurement practices of the U.S. Commerce Department in compiling data for GNP. A number of interesting conceptual problems are encountered as well. Table 3 contains more detail of the components of GNP for the year 1979 valued in current 1979 prices.

TABLE 3
Gross National Product 1979 (billions of dollars)

Personal consumption expenditures			1509.8
Durable goods		213.0	
Nondurable goods		596.9	
Services		699.8	
Gross private domestic investment			387.2
Fixed investment		369.0	
Nonresidential		254.9	
Structures	92.6		
Producers' durable equipment	162.2		
Residential structures		114.1	
Change in business inventories		18.2	
Net exports of goods and services			−4.6
Exports		257.5	
Imports		262.1	
Government purchases of goods and services			476.4
Federal		166.6	
National defense		108.3	
Other		58.4	
State and local		309.8	
Gross national product			2368.8

PERSONAL CONSUMPTION EXPENDITURES

Personal consumption expenditures[2] "consists of the market value of purchases of goods and services by persons and nonprofit institutions and the value of food, clothing, housing, and financial services received by them as income in kind." [U.S. Commerce Department (1973).] Three categories of consumer products are identified: durable goods, nondurable goods, and services. Durable goods, such as automobiles, refrigerators, and furniture, are products which provide services to consumers beyond the period of purchase. Nondurables are generally products which provide their services during the purchase period: food, clothing, and so on. Services represent consumer expenditures for which no tangible product is exchanged. Though these descriptions provide the general flavor of the categories, in actual practice it has been necessary to deviate from these broad concepts.

For measurement purposes economic accounting is tied to market activity, yet not all economic activity of consumers involves markets. Perhaps the largest single allocation of a scarce resource by the household sector which is excluded from the national accounts is home services. It has been estimated by J. K. Galbraith that these services may be as large as 25 percent of GNP. Within the home numerous goods and services are produced and consumed, cleaning, cooking, sewing, repairing, do-it-yourself construction, education, and so on. Yet, none of these economic activities undertaken by the family is included in GNP; this exclusion is mainly because these nonmarket goods and services are not explicitly priced and are therefore difficult to value accurately.

The market orientation of the production account has other implications for analysis. Students of economic behavior must recognize that when such economic behavior deviates from market activity, adjustments in the accounting data are likely to be necessary for careful analysis. Some economic activities of households are internalized, for example, and market accounts are inadequate descriptions of these activities. Consider the purchase and consumption of durable goods. The accounts provide the level of expenditures on durable goods. Durables provide a flow of services over a number of years to the owner. The rate of consumption of this flow of services is not evident from market data and inferences must be made to understand this activity. The market data are not a complete description of consumer behavior, in this case.

The treatment of housing, especially owner-occupied housing, is unique in the national accounts. Of course consumers buy homes. In fact, purchases of homes are a significant factor in the allocation of family income. Consumer purchases of houses are excluded from the consumption term. Instead, housing enters the accounts in two ways. The construction of new houses is included, as

---

[2] All accounting *definitions* are those employed by the U.S. Commerce Department, and appear in the July issues of *The Survey of Current Business*, U.S. Department of Commerce. The figures are from the July 1980 issue.

acquisition of physical capital goods, in the gross private domestic investment component of GNP under the heading residential construction. For houses or apartments which are rented, rental expenditure is included in the services component of personal consumption expenditure. For owner-occupied housing, the value of the housing services provided by the owner to himself is *imputed* and is included as a consumer expenditure on services. In one sense, this imputation of housing services seems inconsistent with the market nature of the accounts. However, from the point of view of measuring the consumption of housing services when they occur, this imputation is very useful indeed. In fact, a purist might argue that such imputations should be undertaken for all durable goods, not just housing. From a theoretical point of view such imputations would be quite useful but from a practical point of view probably rather inaccurate.

GROSS PRIVATE DOMESTIC INVESTMENT

Gross private domestic investment "consists of the net acquisitions of fixed capital goods by private business and nonprofit institutions; including commissions arising in the sale and purchase of new and existing fixed assets, principally real estate; and the value of the change in the volume of inventories held by business. It covers all private dwellings including those acquired by persons for their own occupancy." [U.S. Commerce Department (1973).]

The term "gross" in gross private domestic investment requires explanation. GNP measures only final goods and services. Many goods and services produced in the economy are intermediate products to be used as inputs in the subsequent stages of production of other goods. In a broad sense, one might view all investment as the production of intermediate goods on the ground that capital goods are used either in subsequent production by firms or to provide future services to households. The logical extreme of this argument is that all goods and services are intermediate to the production of human happiness.

However, the inclusion of investment in GNP is perfectly consistent with the concept of final goods and services. For GNP measures final product in the current period, not final consumption. Capital goods produced in the current period may be intermediate in the future, but they are also final product in this period. Now, along with this explanation, one must recognize that current production uses up capital goods, and, therefore, accurate measurement of final product should allow for this consumption of capital. The term "gross" serves as a signal that no deduction has been made from GNP for the consumption of capital goods during the current period. Consequently, we can view gross private domestic investment as consisting of two parts: net private domestic investment and replacement investment.

The deduction from GNP of capital consumption allowances results in net national product. Unfortunately, actual measurement of capital consumption is extremely difficult. How much of a machine, which lasts say 10 years, is used up after 1 year: 10 percent, none, 20 percent? It is usually difficult to tell.

Accountants simply settle upon arbitrary accounting schemes, such as straight line and double declining balance, to allocate the loss in value of a machine over its economic life. These schemes, often based upon tax treatment of income from capital, form the basis for the Commerce Department measurement of capital consumption allowances. These allowances are, therefore, an unreliable indicator of loss in economic value.

The isolation of final product, as distinct from intermediate product, though seemingly clear enough in the abstract, is rather difficult and somewhat arbitrary in actual practice. The technique employed by the Commerce Department is the "value added" approach. The value added approach is designed to measure the origins of final product, and the contributions of all the various sectors to final product, and to insure against "double counting." Double counting occurs when one includes the value of a product more than once in final product and would serve to misrepresent final product. The "value added" approach to measuring GNP can best be illustrated by a simple example. Consider the production process of a shirt occurring in four distinct stages: agricultural production of cotton, manufacture of cloth, fashioning of a shirt, and finally the retail sale of the product.

	PRICE	*VALUE ADDED*
Cotton	2	2
Cloth	3	1
Shirt (wholesale)	6	3
Final product	10	4
Final value	$10	$10

Each stage of production consists of utilizing a material input, adding to its value, and producing a new output. The value of the output at each stage consists of the sum of the initial value of the material input plus the value added by that stage of production. Clearly, measuring only the value added at each stage results in a final value equivalent to the sale price of the product and avoids double counting. The "value added" approach has the additional advantage that it elucidates details of the production process.

NET EXPORTS OF GOODS AND SERVICES

Net exports of goods and services "measures the balance on goods and services, excluding transfers under military grants, as reported in the U.S. balance of payments statistics." [U.S. Commerce Department (1973).] The inclusion of exports in GNP is straighforward. Exports are goods and services produced in the U.S. in the current period sold abroad. The subtraction of imports from exports in measuring GNP occurs because the other major components, consumption, government, etc., include purchases of goods and services from foreigners. In the measurement of consumption, for example, it is simply not feasible to identify the source of the product and include only those originating domestically. Therefore, we must measure total imports and deduct them at once from the sum of all other components to obtain a measure of U.S. output.

GOVERNMENT PURCHASES OF GOODS AND SERVICES

Government purchases of goods and services "consists of the net purchases of goods and services by general government and of the gross investment of government enterprise." [U.S. Commerce Department (1973).] Government expenditures are partitioned into two elements: Federal includes all U.S. government expenditures on final goods and services, and state and local measures the same expenditures for these governments. Federal purchases are further broken down into national defense and other.

The level of expenditures, included in GNP, by both the federal and the state and local governments is considerably smaller than their respective budgets. For example, in 1979 the federal component of GNP was $166.6 billion while its budget was $509.0 billion. Governments undertake large volumes of spending for which they directly receive no goods or services in return. The federal government, in 1979, paid out $209.8 billion in transfer payments to persons and $80.4 billion in grants-in-aid to state and local governments. The transfer payments include such items as social security payments to the elderly. Since these payments, and others, are not for final product, they do not represent use of final product by the government and are not included in the government component of GNP.

Nonpublic GNP has been partitioned into consumption and investment components. A use of this data will be to study social choices between current consumption of final product and capital accumulation. The government use of GNP includes elements both of consumption and investment, yet the government element is not partitioned according to these uses. Clearly, government spending on new highways and on dams should be viewed as capital goods acquisitions. Some government activities are somewhat ambiguous, however. Does one include space exploration as investment or not? When one considers GNP data to study social choices, caution in the treatment of government expenditure is warranted.

NET NATIONAL PRODUCT AND NATIONAL INCOME

Other measures of the magnitude of economic activity are useful as well as GNP. It has already been shown that the deduction from GNP of capital consumption allowances results in net national product (NNP). Conceptually, these two magnitudes, NNP and GNP, indicate the productivity of the U.S. economy. They differ only in that NNP excludes consumption of capital goods in the course of current production. Since capital consumption allowances are somewhat artibrary, however, NNP is not generally considered to be a superior measure to GNP of final product. From NNP, though, we can derive other aggregates of economic activity.

The derivation of national income from GNP is illustrated in Table 4. National income is a measure of the total value of the earnings of the factors of production in the generation of final output. Deductions from the market value of final product, as measured in NNP, must be made to obtain national income. In general, any element of market value which is not an earning of some factor input must be deducted from NNP to obtain rational income, NI. The largest single element deducted from NNP is *indirect business tax and nontax liability*. This deduction, $189.5 billion in 1979, consists of "tax liabilities and other general government revenues paid by business, except employer contributions for social insurance and corporate income taxes." Such items as sales, excise, and property taxes are included as well as fines, penalties, regulatory fees, and so forth. Business transfer payments are payments to persons, usually in monetary form, for which no services are rendered. Businesses receive some subsidies from government and government enterprises can obtain receipts in excess of costs. These latter items are usually relatively small. Finally, since the actual measurement of GNP according to use yields a different numerical result than that obtained by adding up from national income through NNP to GNP, a statistical discrepancy occurs.

TABLE 4

GNP, NNP, and National Income 1979 (billions of dollars)

Gross national product		2368.6
Capital consumption allowances	243.0	
Net national product		2125.9
Business transfer payments	10.2	
Indirect business tax and nontax liability	189.5	
Less: Subsidies less current surplus of government enterprises	−2.3	
Statistical discrepancy	3.7	
National income		1924.8

National income represents factor earnings and may be measured according to the "factor approach" rather than by the "value added" approach utilized above. The 1979 earning of the factors of production are reproduced in Table 5.

The most important point to observe about national income is that the "factor approach" yields precisely the same value as that obtained by utilizing the "value added" approach after the appropriate charges are made against GNP. Payment of market price for final product is distributed to factor earnings. Production generates income and the two methods of measuring national income, aside from statistical discrepancy due to practical measurement errors, yield the same magnitude: $1924.8 billion.

TABLE 5

1979 National Income (billions of dollars)

Compensation of employees		1459.2
Wages and salaries	1227.4	
Supplements to wages and salaries	231.8	
Proprietors' income		130.8
Rental income of persons		26.9
Corporate profits and inventory valuation adjustment		178.2
Profits before tax	194.9	
Inventory valuation adjustment	−41.8	
Net interest		129.7
National income		1924.8

Most of the factor payments are self-explanatory; however, several do warrant comment. The corporate profits and inventory valuation adjustment term is largely in accord with federal income tax regulations. It does not, therefore, correspond to economic profit. For example, the Internal Revenue Service permits deductions for depreciation of capital, which in recent years have exceeded the actual depreciation firms report to their stockholders. These large deductions cause profits to appear to be smaller than they in fact are. Again the student is cautioned about use of national income statistics.

Proprietors' income, unlike other terms in Table 5, does not correspond to a particular factor. Individual proprietorships, partnerships, and cooperatives are often incapable of distinguishing payments to various factors. The income of a general store, for example, includes wages and salary, profit, and so on. The proprietor's income, then, represents payments in the noncorporate sector to all factors other than rental income on property.

PERSONAL INCOME AND DISPOSABLE INCOME

Just as national income measures the earnings of factors of production, personal income measures the total income received by persons. Table 6 contains the derivation of personal income from national income with 1979 figures. The definitions of national and personal income explain the derivation of the latter from the former. For example, we deduct corporate profits and inventory valuation adjustment, then add back dividends. Dividends are the only part of corporate profits distributed in the current period to persons. Except for inventory valuation adjustment, the remainder of corporate profits is titled "undistributed corporate profits" and is allocated to two components: corporate profit taxes and retained earnings.

A substantial, and growing, deduction from factor earnings is the "contribution for social insurance." Most terms in the national accounts are self-explanatory, but the expression "contribution for social insurance" is a misnomer. First, the term "contribution" suggests choice, but of course social security payments are compulsory deductions from payroll income. In fact, these payments would

TABLE 6

1979 Personal Income from National Income (billions of dollars)

National income		1924.8
Less:		
Corporate profits and inventory valuation		
adjustments	178.2	
Net interest	129.7	
Contributions to social insurance	189.8	
Wage accruals less disbursements	−.2	
Plus:		
Government transfer payments	241.9	
Interest paid by government (net) and by		
consumers	192.1	
Business transfer payments	10.2	
Equals:		
Personal income		1924.2

more accurately be called payroll taxes for the social security fund. Second, the program is not an insurance program in the sense that one receives insurance benefits in return for particular payments. The benefits of the social security system are determined, to a large degree, independently of contributions. To illustrate, wage income of individuals over the age of 65, who are already receiving social security benefits, is still subject to the payroll tax for social security. Yet, no additional benefits accrue these individuals as a result of these additional payments.

A significant source of personal income is direct transfers of money from government to persons. The largest single transfer system is the social security system. Businesses also transfer income directly from their receipts to persons. These two transfers are not factor payments but are personal income.

Finally, the "interest paid by government (net) and by consumers" would appear to belong in factor payments. However, the bulk of this interest is payment on the national debt, and, since the national debt was largely incurred in the past, payment on it is not considered to be return for currently produced goods and services. Thus "interest paid by government (net) and by consumers" is excluded from NI and must be added in to obtain personal income.

From personal income, individuals are required to pay personal income taxes. The remainder from personal income, after deduction of these taxes, is disposable income: the income which persons may dispose of as they wish. Disposable income is allocated to either personal outlays or to savings. Personal outlays, in turn, consist of three components: (1) personal transfer payments to foreigners, (2) interest paid by consumers, and (3) personal consumption expenditure. These magnitudes for 1979 are recorded in Table 7.

The choice between outlays and saving by persons has important consequences. The savings of persons, along with business savings and charges against capital consumption, form the major sources of funds for capital accumulation

TABLE 7

Disposable Income: Derivation and Allocation 1979 (billions of dollars)

Personal income		1924.2
Personal income taxes	299.9	
Disposable income		1624.3
Personal outlays	1550.5	
Personal consumption expenditures 1509.8		
Interest paid by consumers	39.6	
Personal transfer payments to		
foreigners	1.1	
Personal saving		73.8

by firms. The savings-investment account illustrates the major sources and uses of gross savings. It is presented as Table 8. This account is a close approximation of the accumulation account discussed in part A of this chapter. It is, however, deficient as a complete, consistent accumulation account in several aspects. First, no allowance is made for accumulation by households in the form of durable goods acquisition, and no charge is imputed against durable goods consumption. Second, the capital consumption allowances are recorded from accountant book practices which, as we have seen, do not correspond perfectly to the economic concept of capital consumption. These, and other, shortcomings of the accounts should not discourage their use. They simply point up to us the necessity of caution in utilizing economic data.

TABLE 8

Saving and Investment 1979 (billions of dollars)

Gross private savings		349.6
Personal saving	73.8	
Undistributed corporate profits	32.9	
Corporate inventory valuation adjustment	−41.8	
Corporate capital consumption allowances	147.7	
Noncorporate capital consumption allowances	95.3	
Wage accruals less disbursements	0.0	
Government surplus (+) or deficit (−)		13.2
Federal	−11.4	
State and local	24.6	
Capital grants received by U.S.		1.1
Gross investment		367.6
Statistical discrepancy		3.7

STUDY QUESTIONS AND PROBLEMS

1. "GNP is the market value of all final goods and services produced in a year."

How does this definition compare with the actual practices of the Commerce Department?

2. Define GNP, NNP, and NI. Derive NI from GNP.

3. "GNP is a measure of human happiness. Relative prices represent the relative values afforded commodities by the individuals which comprise the society and are used as weights in adding commodities together to obtain GNP. Since these relative prices represent social preferences, GNP represents social welfare." Discuss carefully.

4. Explain the conceptual role of capital consumption allowances in the derivation of final product. How are capital consumption allowances actually constructed?

5. Comment on the use of national income accounts in the formulation of economic policy.

6. What kinds of adjustments would you make in the national accounts data if you were studying:

    (a) Consumption behavior?

    (b) Capital accumulation?

7. How does "government purchase of goods and services" as a major use of GNP differ from government budgets?

8. An accumulation account links flow accounts with wealth accounts. What modifications would you suggest in the savings-investment account for construction of an idealized accumulation account?

9. How do National Income and Personal Income differ? What will happen to the magnitude of the difference during an economic boom?

10. List the terms in the derivation of national income utilizing the "factor approach." Why must this approach yield essentially the same answer as the "value added" approach after suitable charges against GNP?

11. What problem does the "value added" approach to measuring GNP resolve? Explain. Does this approach serve any other purpose?

12. Which of the following would you include as final product as opposed to intermediate product in computation of GNP?

    (a) A hammer sold by a hardware store.

    (b) The manufacture of cloth sold to a shirt producer.

    (c) Production of machine tools, unsold in the current period.

    (d) Overalls sold to a carpenter.

    (e) A saw sold to a carpenter.

    (f) Nails sold to a carpenter.

    (g) Construction of a new computer to replace an obsolete one.

    (h) Payment of unemployment insurance.

    (i) The commission of a real estate broker on the sale of a used house.

    (j) Payments to the bank on a mortgage by a home-owner.

13. Consider the following table of data for an economy:

ITEM	AMOUNT
Capital consumption allowances	45
Compensation of employees	325
Gross private domestic investment	80
Subsidies less current surplus of government enterprises	1
Business transfer payments	2
Net exports of goods and services	− 1
Personal consumption expenditures	350
Disposable income	400
Corporate profits and inventory valuation adjustments	35
Government purchases of goods and services	125
Personal income taxes	80
Indirect business tax and nontax liability	43

Compute the values of GNP, NNP, NI, and PI.

14. List the major uses of GNP. Discuss the importance of each of these components. Which do you believe to be most important from the point of view of macroeconomic analysis? Why?

15. The following table contains some select data for a hypothetical economy. Compute GNP, NI, and PI.

ITEM	AMOUNT
Dividends	5.2
Compensation of employees	140.0
Government transfer payments	19.0
Net national product	210.0
Net private domestic investment	14.3
Corporate profits and inventory valuation adjustment	18.0
Contributions to social insurance	14.7
Business transfer payments	.9
Interest paid by government (net) and by consumers	6.5
Rental income of persons	4.8
Wage accruals less disbursements	−.1
Capital consumption allowances	20.3
Net interest	9.2
Disposable income	158.0
Personal income taxes	28.4

REFERENCES

Britton, John, *The Payroll Tax for Social Security*. Washington, D.C.: Brookings Institution, 1972.

Christensen, Laurits and Dale W. Jorgenson, "Measuring the Performance of the Private Sector of the U.S. Economy, 1929-1969," *Review of Income and Wealth*, 1973.

Friedman, Milton, *A Theory of the Consumption Function*, A Study by the National Bureau of Economic Research. Princeton: Princeton University Press, Princeton, 1957.

Goldsmith, Raymond, *The National Wealth of the United States in the Postwar Period*, National Bureau of Economic Research. New York: Columbia University Press, 1962.

Jorgenson, Dale W., "The Theory of Investment Behavior," in *Determinants of Investment Behavior*, Robert Ferber (ed.), National Bureau of Economic Research. New York: Columbia University Press, 1967.

Jorgenson, Dale W., Zvi Griliches, and Edward F. Denison, *The Measurement of Productivity*, Reprint 244. Washington, D.C.: Brookings Institution, 1972.

In addition to the national income, expenditure, and product accounts, valued at current prices, which were studied in Chapter 2, students of macroeconomics utilize a wide variety of data sources. For example, a variety of price indexes are used to indicate changes in the cost of living. The consumer price index and the indexes used to convert national income accounting magnitudes into constant prices, such as the GNP deflator, are among the most popular. Employment and unemployment statistics are also prime sources of information about economic performance. The uses to which unemployment statistics are often put have come into question in recent years because of dramatic changes in the behavior of labor markets. Substantial increases in the participation rates of women and of teenagers in particular have caused a need to reexamine unemployment data. Economists employ, in addition, balance of payment statistics, flow of funds data, input-output *arrays,* interest rate series, *ad infinitum.* Furthermore, in addition to the basic data on which economists rely, a number of special analytical series are constructed which indicate what economic activity might have been, as opposed to what it actually was, i.e., calculations of full employment budget surpluses, of potential GNP, of real rates of interest, and so on.

3

Comparing
Economic Performance

This chapter contains two parts. The technical aspects of separating changes in economic values, like money GNP, into price and quantity components are discussed in some detail in Part A. Part B contains a brief description, and comment about, unemployment statistics and analytic series.

A • Index Numbers

Evaluation of economic performance involves comparisons either over time or across groups of economic agents. For example, if we wish to say that the standard of living has improved from one year to the next, we are comparing the physical quantities of goods and services consumed or produced over the two years. Similarly, if we wish to make statements about changes in the cost of living, we are making intertemporal price comparisons. In order to make such comparisons, we must be able to separate changes in dollar magnitudes, such as GNP, into separate components for changes in the physical quantities of goods and services produced and changes in the prices of those goods and services. The solution to this problem involves selecting or constructing a set of index numbers. Two of the most commonly employed index numbers are the Laspeyres and the Paasche indexes, named after their respective authors.

LASPEYRES AND PAASCHE INDEX NUMBERS

GNP, it will be recalled, is the sum over commodities produced of the product of quantities and prices. GNP, in current prices, can be considered the weighted sum over all commodities of the quantities produced. The quantity of each good is weighted by its respective price. From the point of view of economic theory, prices are natural weights for goods, since relative prices represent the ratios at which goods can be exchanged for one another in the market. For example, suppose good x sells for $1.50 and good y sells for $.50. To purchase one unit of x, a consumer forgoes, in effect, 3 units of y: the opportunity cost of x is 3 units of y, and the price ratio p_x/p_y is 3. Thus, as we add x and y together, we select current dollar prices per unit as weights. Good x is given three times the weight, in GNP, as good y, because 3 is the rate at which y may be substituted, in the market, for x.

Consider the problem of selecting a measure to indicate percent changes in quantities produced of final goods and services from one year to another. A natural method of comparing changes in quantities over time is to assume that the weights, employed in one given year, say year t_0, maintain in all other years and in each year to add the quantities together by weighting them with the period t_0 market prices. (We shall assume that the same type of goods are produced in each period. The problems of new goods and changes in quality of goods will be discussed subsequently.) Now, every year's quantities are measured in the same units, and the resultant totals could be used to compare the different quantities produced in various periods. For purposes of comparison, percent changes are convenient. Consequently, it is useful to devise a system of index numbers in which the base year number has the value 1.00 (or 100.0). Thus, if the year $t + x$ index number is 1.05, one will immediately observe that production has increased 5 percent over year t. To achieve these index formulas simply divide each year's GNP, measured in year t_0 prices, by year t_0 GNP. The results are *Laspeyres quantity index numbers.*

The Laspeyres index, in addition to being an intuitively natural index formulation, has several valuable properties. First, the t_0 index value is 1.00, so that percent comparisons with the base period are immediately obvious. Second, the weights of commodity quantities are fixed over years. The only components allowed to change over time are the actual quantities. Consequently, quantity comparisons may be made between any years in a sequence utilizing Laspeyres indexes. The Laspeyres index is referred to as a fixed weight index. Third, the Laspeyres index attaches exactly the same relative weights to each commodity as those which prevailed as prices in the base year market. Thus Laspeyres weights represent base year marginal rates of substitution between commodities.[1]

The third property of Laspeyres index numbers creates certain difficulties. While fixed weights, which reflect relative market prices in the base period, are useful, they become somewhat less important as the year currently under consideration becomes more distant from the base. After a decade or so has elapsed, taste and other changes are likely to have occurred which have caused relative market prices of commodities to change. The selection of current year weights, rather than those associated with the base year, would seem useful.

The Paasche index is one in which current year relative prices form the basis for weights. The quantities of goods produced in both the current and the base period are weighted by current year prices and then summed. Both values are then divided by the base year value, so that the base period index value is always set equal to 1.00. For each current year, the weight attached to each good is associated with that good's relative price in the current year. The Paasche index is a variable weight index, and consequently output comparisons can only be made between the base and each current year.

The distinct advantage to Paasche indexes is that comparisons between the current year and the base are always couched in terms of current year price weights. The relative rates of substitution which currently prevail are those utilized by the Paasche scheme. The Paasche index has several disadvantages, however, which are indeed severe enough to limit its use. First, a new set of weights is required for every year under observation. Consequently, study of many time periods involves considerable effort. Second, unless relative weights remain unchanged, comparisons can only be made, utilizing Paasche indexes, between the current year and the base. Attempts to directly compare any other

[1] Theoretical and statistical analysis of index numbers is presented elsewhere. Microeconomics texts, such as Ferguson (1972), present the theoretical foundations for employing relative prices as weights, whereas economic statistics texts, such as Yamane (1973) derive the formulas in detail.

period to the current year will be nonsensical, because changes in prices and quantities over the two years will be hopelessly entangled.

Corresponding to Laspeyres and Paasche quantity indexes are indexes for observing changes in prices: price indexes. In the case of the Laspeyres price index, the fixed weights are the quantities produced relative to total value in the base period. The Paasche price index weights are also relative quantities, but those which prevail in the current period. The advantages and disadvantages of Paasche and Laspeyres quantity indexes discussed above apply similarly to the respective price indexes.

THEORY OF INDEX NUMBERS

Comparison of the mathematical properties of Laspeyres and Paasche indexes is ordinarily undertaken in microeconomic theory courses. Consequently, here we shall only go into nonmathematical evaluation of the economic properties of Paasche and Laspeyres price indexes. Consider a simple index number problem: An economic agent faces a change in one commodity price. He reallocates his expenditures in response to the price change. The price index number question is: Given the new set of prices, how much income is now required to make this agent indifferent between his new state and that defined by the income held and prices faced in the previous period? The answer will give us the change in the cost of living.

Let us assume that the individual's tastes are unchanged. The Paasche and Laspeyres index schemes place different interpretations upon the above question. Consider the Laspeyres index method. The Laspeyres method is to weight prices by base period quantities. As a result the Laspeyres index implicitly prohibits the individual from changing his consumption pattern in response to a relative price change. Microeconomic theory, however, suggests that an economic agent will in fact attempt to reduce the proportion of his income devoted to the good whose relative price has increased. Since the Laspeyres weighting scheme rigidly restricts the individual to the original consumption pattern, after a relative price change, it overweights those goods whose relative prices have increased and underweights those goods whose relative prices have fallen. Consequently, Laspeyres price indexes can be said to have an upward bias, e.g., to overstate price increases.

The weights of Paasche price indexes are current period relative quantities. In selecting current quantities, the economic agent has presumably allowed for the change in relative prices. If, after the price change, the individual's income had increased exactly enough to compensate him for the price rise, the quantity weights would correspond exactly to those quantities economic theory tells us he will consume. However, the Paasche base weights differ from those quantities he was originally consuming. The Paasche base year index will underweight commodities whose prices have increased the most. Consequently, the Paasche index will imply a smaller change in prices than in fact occurred, thus it can be said to have a downward bias, e.g., to understate price changes. Neither price index method, then, is a perfect cost of living index. However, the Laspeyres and Paasche indexes are upper and lower limits, respectively, on the true index.

Since neither the Laspeyres nor the Paasche index is a true index, perhaps we should ask if a better one could be found. Or can we make a choice between the two? Economists have long attempted to devise an ideal index number procedure. However, no particular index has stood out for all purposes. Fisher (Yamane, 1973), for example, proposed the square root of the product of the Laspeyres and Paasche indexes as an ideal price index; however, its economic content is unclear. A method of constructing indexes, called *chain-link indexes,* has gained favor among some economists in recent years. For example, the Bureau of Economic Analysis of the Department of Commerce, the agency which constructs the deflators used in the national income accounts, supplements their deflator for personal consumption expenditures with a chain price index.

The chain price index is designed to produce rates of price change which are built around current quantities but are still based on a fixed weight method. The chain price index, constructed by BEA, is designed in the following way. In each period a new Laspeyres index is constructed, the previous period's quantities being used as weights. The rate of price change in each period is calculated on the basis of these fixed previous period quantities as weights. Thus in essence a new set of weights is used in each period, but the rate of change calculated for each period is based on a fixed set of weights. Because the rates of change are calculated by using fixed weights while new weights are employed in each subsequent period's rate of change calculation, the index method is called the chain link price index. The advantage to the chain price index is obviously that the rate of inflation calculated in each period is based on fixed weights and yet is not grounded in weights which were developed in a base year very distant in time from the period in question. However, with the base itself continually changing in the construction of these chain price indexes, the meaning of accumulated price changes over several periods is unclear. We must observe that no particular price index method is superior for all economic uses. We shall turn now to several practical and theoretical problems encountered in the construction of price indexes.

TASTE CHANGES AND QUALITY CHANGES

Over time, individuals are likely to change their tastes. In the preceding evaluation of the Laspeyres and Paasche indexes, however, the economic agent was assumed to have possessed the same tastes in each period. If, however, tastes are allowed to change, the meaning of the two index methods is altered. The Paasche index can be shown to be superior to the Laspeyres for answering most crucial questions about the cost of living. A taste change means that the preferences of the individual between any two commodity bundles are different in one period from the next. Since the Laspeyres price index utilizes base period quantities as weights, it is anchored in the old base period tastes. If one wishes to ask cost of living questions such as: "How much income, given new relative prices, is required to make the agent indifferent, given current tastes, between his new state and his original budget constraint?" then the obsolete Laspeyres weights are misleading.

The superiority of the Paasche index derives from its reliance on current period weights and tastes. Most interesting cost of living and standard of living questions are likely to be those pertaining to current period tastes. In other words, in making comparisons, today's tastes would ordinarily seem more relevant than yesterday's tastes. Thus the Paasche index, while still an approximation given current tastes of actual price changes, seems more meaningful than the Laspeyres. One must caution, however, that this conceptual advantage of Paasche indexes must be balanced against their practical costs compared to Laspeyres indexes.

An important corollary to the above analysis is that certain uses to which index numbers are often put are inappropriate. The following question typifies an improper use of index numbers: "How much income, given current prices, is necessary to make an individual better off today than he was yesterday?" Because such questions suggest comparison of tastes over time, they are as inappropriate as attempts to compare tastes across individuals. Appropriate, and answerable, questions compare intertemporal budget constraints, not tastes.

Another practical problem associated with calculation of price indexes is called the "quality change" problem. Suppose crackers are priced by the box and the number of crackers per box is doubled for marketing purposes, but the price per box is not changed. Clearly, the correct treatment of cracker prices for index purposes is to reduce the new box price in half, because boxes of crackers have undergone a quality improvement. Though the cracker example is simple, quality change problems are often complex and subtle. Consider the case of an automobile. From one year to the next, an automobile's price might increase by $200. At the same time the new model might have a new safety bumper, higher gas mileage, and a narrower wheel base. How does one separate out of, and deduct from, the $200 price increase a component for improved quality?

The solution generally employed by the Bureau of Labor Statistics, which constructs the consumer price index, is called: "price hedonics." Some quality changes are so completely novel they must be treated as new goods; however, many changes are improvements over already existing characteristics. In the automobile example, mileage and wheel base are illustrations of already existing features. The BLS essentially attempts to decompose the car's price into components for the various features which comprise the car. Then, if a given characteristic is seen to increase by some percent, the fraction of the price associated with that aspect of the car is reduced accordingly. Obviously this problem is quite complicated, and economists disagree as to the success of BLS in resolving it.

We shall end this section with a comparison of two different index constructions of the rates of change of U.S. consumer goods' prices from 1970 to 1978.

One is the deflator used for personal consumption expenditures and is a Paasche style index. The second is the consumer price index, which is constructed by the Bureau of Labor Statistics. Figure 1 compares the deflator and the CPI from 1970 to 1978. As one can see by observing the figure, the general sweep of price movement is very similar regardless of the price index method employed. The closeness of the BEA and the BLS indexes for consumer goods prices occurs even though the two agencies' indexes are designed to apply to different definitions of consumers and even though the two agencies also employ different treatment of some specific goods and services. Partly for these reasons and partly because of the differences in index methods, some periods witness rather substantial differences in the rates of inflation according to different indexes. For example, in 1977, the deflator registered an annual rate of inflation in the second quarter of 5.7 percent, whereas the consumer price index indicated an inflation rate of 8.8 percent. Anyone emphasizing a price index in his studies should be aware of the definition of the group covered by the index and of the index method employed.

B ● Employment Statistics, Monetary Statistics, and Analytic Series

Employment and Unemployment: The Unemployment Act of 1946 states, "The Congress declares that it is the continuing responsibility of the federal government to . . . promote maximum employment, production and purchasing power." Full employment has become a widely accepted social and economic goal in the U.S. Full employment is set as a goal partly because of the social significance of employment itself and partly because high unemployment is symptomatic of other social problems.

Work, in a market economy, is the primary source of income for many individuals, and if people are unable to find work, then poverty, a personal sense of failure, and even deep social alienation can be the result. Unemployment is usually accompanied by underemployment as well. Consider your professor working as an unskilled dishwasher! While that particular prospect may actually appeal to you, the inability of workers in general to find jobs in which they can obtain meaningful training and skills clearly results in both inadequate use of their abilities and in inadequate preparation of their skills for future productivity. Unemployment and underemployment are both personal tragedies and failures by the society to fully utilize its human resources.

As mentioned above, unemployment is an indicator of deeper social problems. High unemployment is usually associated with immobility of those who are unemployed. Advancement and promotion are slow, and job mobility is risky and therefore rare. Firms are less willing to invest resources either in training younger workers or in training older workers who are interested in changing careers or entering the labor force later in life. Unemployment is, therefore, the

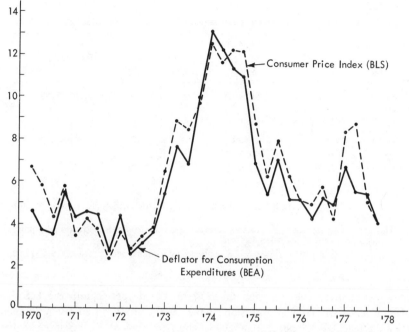

FIGURE 1   Comparison of different Indices of Consumer Goods Prices*

tip of an iceberg. Below the water line are social discontent and economic costs which influence us all, not simply those actually unemployed. As a consequence, the unemployment statistics are carefully studied and watched by economists, government agencies, businesses, and others concerned with the course and pace of economic activity.

How reliable are the employment and unemployment statistics available to us as indicators of the various social problems discussed above? We shall now study the unemployment and employment statistics that play such a major role in evaluating this aspect of our economic performance. In Table 1 we present statistics on the size of the U.S. labor force, the level of civilian employment, the unemployment rate, and the rate of participation in the labor force during some select years since World War II. Several interesting aspects of U.S. economic performance over these years are indicated by the figures in the table. For example, the 25 years from 1950 to 1975 witnessed a very large increase in the U.S. labor force. Over 30 million new workers entered the labor force over that time, for an increase of nearly 45 percent. The civilian employment figures indicate that 27 million new workers were absorbed by the labor force over this period.

A less pleasing feature of U.S. performance is indicated by the unemploy-

*Data Source: Bureau of Economic Analysis, U.S. Department of Commerce, "Reconciliation of Quarterly Changes in Measures of Prices Paid by Consumers," *Survey of Current Business,* March 1978, pp. 6-8, 24.

TABLE 1

Employment and Unemployment (thousands) of persons, 16 and older

YEAR	LABOR FORCE	CIVILIAN EMPLOY- MENT	UNEMPLOY- MENT RATE [1]	PARTICIPATION RATE [2]
1950	63,858	58,920	5.3	59.9
1960	72,142	65,778	5.5	60.2
1970	85,903	78,627	4.9	61.3
1974	93,240	85,936	5.6	61.8
1975	94,793	84,783	8.5	61.8
1976	96,917	87,485	7.7	62.1
1977	99,534	90,546	7.0	62.8

[1] The unemployment rate refers to the percentage of the civilian labor force which is unemployed.
[2] The participation rate refers to the percentage of the total noninstitutional population who are in the labor force.
Source: *Monthly Labor Review* U.S. Labor Department, select issues, 1977-1978, Washington, D.C.

ment rate figures. The recession of 1974-75, the deepest slump the U.S. had suffered since the Great Depression of the 1930s, produced an unemployment rate that reached 8.5 percent in 1975. The employment figures indicate that even though the labor force grew in 1975, the employment rate fell. Furthermore, it appears that the recession sustained itself for several more years, because the 1977 unemployment rate was still at 7 percent. Even by 1978 the unemployment rate had fallen only to 5.9 percent. These unemployment figures suggest that the recession which began in 1974 continued at least through 1977 and perhaps into 1978.

Many economists, however, are suspicious of the unemployment rate statistic as a reliable indicator of the performance of the economy. The rate of growth of output, as indicated by GNP, measured in constant prices, while negative in 1974 and 1975 (−1.4 percent and −1.3 percent, respectively), had reached 5.7 percent in 1976 and 4.9 percent in 1977. In other words, while the unemployment figures suggest that the recession lasted through 1977, growth in the economy indicates that the recession ended in late 1975. Are we to conclude that the unemployment figures are misleading as a "tip of the iceberg?" Two distinct questions arise with respect to the value and use of unemployment figures: First, are the unemployment statistics reliable measures of unemployment? Second, is unemployment a reliable indicator of the overall performance of the economy?

Concerned with the first question raised above, President John F. Kennedy in the early 1960s established the Committee to Appraise Employment and Unemployment Statistics. This blue ribbon committee was chaired by Robert A. Gordon, Professor of Economics at the University of California. The main thrust of the Gordon Committee's recommendations was to specify clear objective criteria for distinguishing members of the labor force, employed persons, and unemployed persons. The Bureaus of the Census and of Labor Statistics adopted the Gordon Committee criteria in 1967 as a basis for the current population survey.

The definitions on which the statistics are now based may therefore be clearly stated and unambiguously understood. For example, *employed persons* are those who performed any services during the specific week interviewed, either as paid employees, as self-employed individuals or professionals, or as unpaid workers (who worked fifteen hours or more) in a family enterprise. Those temporarily absent from their jobs or businesses due to such matters as illness, bad weather, vacations, labor-management disputes, and so forth, are also included in the employed. The *unemployed* include all persons over the age of 15 who did not work at all during the survey week and (1) had engaged in some specific job-seeking activity within the past four weeks, such as going to an employment service or applying to an employer, or (2) were waiting to start a new job within thirty days, or (3) were waiting to be called from layoff. The *labor force* is the sum of the employed plus the unemployed.[2]

Despite improvements in the quality of unemployment statistics which resulted from application of the Gordon Committee recommendations, the published figures still fail to capture some aspects of unemployment. Perhaps the most important group of unemployed excluded from the figures are those who are considered to be **"discouraged workers."** "Discouraged workers" are those individuals who have stopped looking for work either because the jobs available to them are unattractive or because they have just given up hope of finding a job. In the first quarter of 1978, a U.S. population survey suggested that there were perhaps as many as 900,000 discouraged workers in the U.S. economy. Unfortunately, we do not have adequate statistics to analyze this group.

Even more complicated and perhaps more serious problems arise when we attempt to use the unemployment figures as indicators of the pace of economic activity. We saw above that, judging from unemployment figures, the recession of 1974-1975 appeared to have lasted until 1978. However, figures in the last column of Table 1 on the participation rate of the adult population indicate a change in the nature of U.S. labor markets. From 1950 to 1975 the participation rate increased from 59.9 to 61.8 percent. This trend continued through 1977. In fact, we normally expect the participation rate to decline during economic slowdowns, because laborers tend to leave the labor market when jobs become less available and to reenter the market when the economy comes out of a slump. However, in the recession of 1974-75 even though the unemployment rate increased substantially and the employment rate fell, the participation rate remained high.

This increase in participation in the labor force will be better understood if we study details beneath the level of aggregation in Table 1. In particular, the in-

---

[2] We can add to this civilian labor force members of the armed forces to obtain the total labor force as in the above table.

crease in labor force activity comes primarily from women and teenagers. The unemployment rates for these two groups of workers tend to be considerably higher than the unemployment rate for adult men. In part, then, the high unemployment figures in the late 1970s reflect changes in the composition of the U.S. labor force. In other words, because teenagers and women represent a larger share of the labor force in the late 1970s and because these two groups traditionally have had relatively high unemployment, the average aggregate rate of unemployment under similar economic circumstances is higher in the late 1970s than it would have been in earlier years. To deal with this problem, George Perry constructed a "weighted unemployment rate" in which he weights the unemployment rates of different subgroups of the labor force according to estimates of their relative productive potential (as measured by their relative wage rates) in order to obtain a better measure of the degree of average tightness in labor markets than the usual aggregate rate would indicate. Perry's "weighted new unemployment rate" suggests that perhaps 1-1½ percent of the aggregate national unemployment statistic can be explained purely by changes in the composition of the labor force away from highly employable adult males towards teenagers and women. With his analysis, Perry attempts to salvage the unemployment rate as an indicator of Okun's gap between actual and potential GNP.

Other economists believe that unemployment itself is a very poor indicator of the level of macroeconomic activity. Martin Feldstein, for instance, argues that while the level of economic activity does have some influence on the rate of unemployment, the primary explanation for high unemployment rates in the U.S. lies in the specific nature of the details of various sectors of the American labor market. For example, Feldstein, noting that 40 percent of total teenage unemployment consists of new entrants into the labor force, argues that this high teenage unemployment can be explained in large part by the absence of any youth employment service to help young people who leave school. Feldstein and other economists also argue that much of the unemployment in the U.S. is voluntary in nature. In particular, they claim that workers with nearly no skills who operate in a "secondary labor market" often refuse available jobs or rotate from job to job fairly frequently with long intervals of leisure time. These long durations of unemployment, which can run from eight to sixteen weeks, according to Feldstein, help to produce a comparatively high average unemployment rate. Perhaps economists can utilize the ideas of Feldstein, Perry, and other economists to distinguish between those individuals who are voluntarily unemployed and those who are unemployed involuntarily. With this information at hand we could then construct more useful statistics on the status of the U.S. labor force.

Analytically Constructed Measures: Some statistical series which one may encounter when studying macroeconomics are more than collected data of observed economic activity. At times the construction of a statistical series involves rather elaborate theoretical assumptions. Before using analytically constructed data, one should be clear as to the nature of the theoretical assumptions involved. In this section, we shall discuss a specific example of an analytically constructed measure.

In Chapter 1 we presented the concept of potential GNP, and we discussed, earlier in this chapter, the relationship between the level of unemployment and the gap between actual and potential GNP. Arthur Okun, the author of the potential GNP concept, based his definition on the belief that an unemployment rate of around 4 percent was compatible with relative price stability in the U.S. economy. Given a benchmark level of potential GNP, Okun then estimated that for every 1 percent increase in the rate of unemployment above the 4 percent benchmark level, the economy would lose 3 percent of its potential GNP. This result, called *Okun's Law,* is extremely useful, because it indicates the social costs, in terms of forgone output, of each 1 percent of unemployment above the 4 percent base. Unfortunately, later analysis by Okun himself and by his colleague, George Perry, indicates that the relationship between unemployment and potential GNP may well have changed rather substantially. In 1978, Perry argued that the level of unemployment at potential GNP had become 4.7 percent rather than 4 percent. Okun's law that a loss of 3 percent in GNP was caused by each 1 percent of unemployment (above the new base) was still valid according to Perry. Some, however, argue that the GNP loss is 2 percent of unemployment.

STUDY QUESTIONS AND PROBLEMS

1. "The Laspeyres price index overstates the true price increase while the Paasche price index understates it." Discuss carefully.

2. New goods can be included in price indexes only for the year after the new goods exist. True or false? Why?

3. The following table contains prices and quantities of three goods produced in three different years:

COMMODITY	1970 PRICE	1970 QUANTITY	1971 PRICE	1971 QUANTITY	1972 PRICE	1972 QUANTITY
Nondurables	.87	12	.95	13	.98	14
Durables	1.30	10	1.24	12	1.20	15
Housing	5.00	4	6.00	4	7.00	5

(a) Compute, from figures above, the Laspeyres price index numbers, base 1970.

(b) Compute Paasche price index numbers for 1971 and 1972.

4. Evaluate the relative values of Laspeyres and Paasche price indexes for measuring the cost of living impact of a sudden, dramatic, large increase in oil prices and food prices.

5. Why is the Paasche index superior to the Laspeyres index of prices after a taste change has occurred?

6. Comment on the following use of the Paasche index numbers: The Paasche quantity index, base 1968, for 1973 was 112.0; therefore, people are better off with this budget in 1976 than they were in 1968.

7. Explain why the official U.S. unemployment statistics are a misleading guide to the employment performance of the U.S. economy.

8. Define and explain the significance of each of the following:

Discouraged workers
Capital consumption allowances
Chain link price index

9. Does potential GNP measure actual observed economic activity? Discuss.

10. Perry's weighted unemployment rate changes our perception of the unemployment statistics. Why is this so?

REFERENCES

Board of Governors of the Federal Reserve System, *Bulletin,* select issues. Washington, D.C.

Feldstein, Martin, "The Economics of the New Unemployment," *The Public Interest,* No. 33 (Fall 1973), pp. 3-42.

Ferguson, C. E., *Microeconomic Theory,* 3rd ed. Homewood, Ill.: Richard D. Irwin, Inc., 1972.

Fisher, Franklin M., and Karl Shell, *The Economic Theory of Price Indices.* New York: Academic Press, 1972.

Friedman, Milton, and Anna Jacobson Schwartz, *A Monetary History of the United States, 1867-1960.* National Bureau of Economic Research, Princeton: Princeton University Press, 1963.

————, *Monetary Statistics of the United States.* National Bureau of Economic Research, New York: Columbia University Press, 1970.

Gordon, Robert Aaron, *The Goal of Full Employment.* New York: John Wiley & Sons, Inc., 1967.

Griliches, Zvi (ed.), *Price Indexes and Quality Change.* Cambridge, Mass.: Harvard University Press, 1971.

Jorgenson, Dale W., *Measuring Economic Performances.* Conference on Measurement of Economic and Social Performances, Princeton University, 1971.

Lovati, Jean M., "The Growing Similarity Among Financial Institutions," *Federal Reserve Bank of Saint Louis Review,* October 1977, pp. 2-11.

Okun, Arthur M., *The Political Economy of Prosperity.* New York: W.W. Norton, 1970.

Perry, George L., "Changing Labor Markets and Inflation," *Brookings Papers on Economic Activity,* Vol. 3 (1970), pp. 411-441.

————, "Slowing the Wage-Price Spiral: The Macroeconomic View, *Brookings Papers on Economic Activity,* Vol. 2 (1978), pp. 259-299.

Samuelson, Paul Anthony, *Foundations of Economic Analysis.* Cambridge, Mass.: Harvard University Press, 1963.

U.S. Commerce Department, Bureau of Economic Analysis, "Reconciliation of Quarterly Changes in Measures of Prices Paid by Consumers," *Survey of Current Business,* Vol. 58, No. 3 (March 1978), pp. 6-9, 24.

U.S. Labor Department, *Monthly Labor Review,* select issues, 1977-78, Washington, D.C.

Usher, Dan, *The Price Mechanism and the Meaning of National Income Statistics.* Oxford: Clarendon Press, 1968.

Yamane, Taro, *Statistics: An Introductory Analysis,* 3rd ed. New York: Harper & Row, 1973.

Yohe, William P., and Denis S. Karnowsky, "Interest Rates and Price Level Changes, 1952-69," *Federal Reserve Bank of Saint Louis Review,* December 1969.

THE FOUNDATIONS AND POLICY IMPLICATIONS OF KEYNESIAN THEORY

part II

The foundations of modern economics are in the ideas of the early classical writers and of Lord Keynes. Their ideas are vital ingredients to understanding today's world, and many of our current theoretical and political debates traverse the same quarrels as between Keynes and the classics. This part begins with an examination of the classical dichotomy, which characterized pre-Keynesian thinking, and continues with a discussion of Keynes' break with the classics.

Classical economists divided their analysis into two distinct parts—supply and demand for goods and services on one hand, and money and the price level on the other. French engineer Leon Walras' general equilibrium analysis typified classical views of the "real" side of the dichotomy, and the quantity theory of money was applied to the "money" side. The Chapter 4 discussion of the dichotomy, especially of Walrasian analysis, includes some difficult material.

Keynes believed the classical dichotomy to be inappropriate, and he tried to integrate the two sides: monetary and nonmonetary. In so doing, he rejected the classical faith, á la Adam Smith, of self-correcting economies and argued that adjustments to large exogenous shocks took too long to make classical general equilibrium analysis very useful.

The rest of this part contains a few relatively simple Keynesian-style income expenditure models of the type you should have seen in principles courses. The models are built in Chapter 5 by using some fairly straightforward algebra. These models are then used to analyze Keynes' famous policy recommendation for dealing with depressions: fiscal policy.

Government spending in the U.S. now accounts for about 20 percent of GNP. The macroeconomic consequences of government spending and taxing plans are important—often the engine of government budgetary decisions. Some people regard the federal government as the central force for social change and economic stability. They advocate activist fiscal policy. Others view government as inefficient, unreliable, and untrustworthy. They prefer minimal government fiscal policy. Chapters 6 and 7 use the Keynesian income-expenditure models to evaluate the effects of discretionary fiscal policies and of built-in automatic stabilizers.

From the standpoint of pure theory, the most fundamental issue raised by Keynes in [*The*] *General Theory* lay in his attack on the traditional separation of monetary and value theory, the "classical dichotomy" as it has come to be called, according to which relative prices are determined by the "real" forces of demand and supply and the absolute price level is determined by the quantity of money and its velocity of circulation.

Harry G. Johnson (1962)

Alfred Kahn, one of President Carter's anti-inflation specialists, was fond of telling his audiences that if you lined all economists up end to end, they would point in every direction. The notion that you can find an economist to support any position derives in no small measure from the legendary disagreements between monetarists and Keynesian economists. The purpose of this chapter is to develop the rudiments of both the early classical and the Keynesian macroeconomic systems which form the underpinnings of the more sophisticated modern models. The student must be warned at this point that economists disagree both about the way in which the economy works and about exactly what it is they are disagreeing about. Consequently, at times we will be forced to merely report evident differences of opinion.

Keynes and the Classics: The Beginnings of a Great Debate

In recent years a number of different schools of thought have emerged, among them the neoclassical, the rationalists, and the (British) Cambridge neo-Keynesian. Nevertheless, the vast majority of economists fall into one of two major camps: monetarist and Keynesian. The roots of modern monetarism can be found in the classical system of economic analysis, especially in the quantity theory of money. To quote Milton Friedman (1956), the father of modern monetarism:

> Chicago was one of the few academic centers at which the quantity theory continued to be a central and vigorous part of the oral tradition throughout the 1930s and 1940s, where students continued to study monetary theory and to write theses on monetary problems.

While modern monetarism is in many respects much more sophisticated than classical economics, especially in terms of its empirical evidence and the specifics of policy recommendations, the classical ancestry of modern monetarism is undeniable.

The ancestry of modern Keynesian economics is similarly unmistakable. It is found, of course, in *The General Theory* of Lord John Maynard Keynes. Considerable disagreement, however, persists about the relationship between the mainstream Keynesian interpretation of Keynes' analysis and the actual analysis of Keynes himself. Some economists, most notably Axel Leijonhufvud, have gone so far as to argue that modern Keynesians failed to capture the central ideas expressed by Keynes himself. While this issue is still an open one, the legacy of Keynes' great work is undeniably recognized by modern Keynesians. Consider the following recognition of Keynes' great book by James Tobin (1972): "To begin with *The General Theory* is not just a ritual piety economists of my generation owe the book that shaped their minds."

We can most easily compare classical to Keynesian economics with the help of the most useful tool in the economist's tool kit, a diagram illustrating supply and demand curves. In Figure 1, supply and demand curves are shown with the price level P on the vertical axis and the quantity of real output Q on the horizontal axis. We may think of the price level P as indicating some measure of the level of prices such as the consumer price index, and we may think of output Q as a measure of total production, say GNP (measured in constant prices.) Students may recall from their study of microeconomics that a downward sloping demand curve and an upward sloping supply curve are derived from the respective reactions of consumers and producers to changes in the relative prices of commodities.

For example, an increase in the price of apples results in the reduction in the quantity of apples demanded, both because this price increase makes apples more expensive relative to substitute goods such as oranges and because the price increase reduces the purchasing power of one's income. We must be very cautious in applying this type of reasoning to a supply and demand model for an aggregate economy, because a change in the level of prices is not the same as a

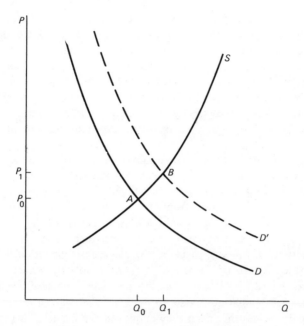

FIGURE 1   Aggregate Supply and Demand

change in the relative price of one good. In macroeconomics, we ordinarily assume that when the price level increases all commodity prices increase at the same rate and, furthermore, the money income of consumers increases at that rate as well. Consequently, the shapes of the supply and demand curves illustrated in Figure 1 cannot be justified with the same logical arguments upon which the micro curves were based. In fact, we will not be able to justify the shapes of these demand and supply curves, even though they are intuitively appealing, until much later in the course. Here we must just accept them as a convenient device for understanding the classical and Keynesian models.

In order to compare classical and Keynesian economics with the use of Figure 1, consider a simple experiment in which some exogenous shock causes an increase in the demand for goods and services. Supply and demand analysis tells us to express an increase in demand by a rightward shift in the demand curve from D to D'. As we can see from the figure, this increase in demand shifts the equilibrium from point A to point B, with the result that the level of prices is increased from P_0 to P_1 and the level of output is increased from Q_0 to Q_1. When we think of this experiment in terms of simple aggregate demand and aggregate supply curves, such as we have done here, the result is that both the level of prices and level of output will increase. This result seems pretty obvious.

However, neither classical (monetarist) economists nor Keynes (Keynesian economists) believed this proposition to be generally correct. In fact, classical and monetarist economists tend to believe that increases in demand produce, under most circumstances, increases in prices and only modest increases in the level of output. In terms of our supply and demand model, we may say that classical and monetarist economists tend to believe that the aggregate supply curve is vertical, so that shifts in demand produce only price changes and no quantity changes. Keynesian economists, at the other extreme, on the basis of the Great Depression analysis by Keynes, may be viewed as assuming that the aggregate supply curve is perfectly horizontal. In this Keynesian case, then, increases in demand will produce increases in output and no changes in the level of price.

These two schools of thought may appear to be rather unrealistic and extremist when viewed in terms of aggregate demand and aggregate supply curves. However, the student should again be warned that aggregate supply and demand curves cannot be derived from the principles of microeconomics which lead to such schedules for individual markets. In Part A of this chapter, an introduction to the classical system, the classical dichotomy, is presented. As the term *classical dichotomy* suggests, the classicalists dichotomized the economy. or divided it into two separate parts. A completely separate model was employed to describe each part. On the one hand, classicalists employed a Walrasian general equilibrium model to describe what was known as the "real" economy, and on the other hand they employed the quantity theory of money to describe the performance of the "nominal" economy.

The great and disastrous depression precipitated in 1929 and lasting throughout the decade of the 1930s produced a critical reexamination of economic analysis. In 1936 the British economist, Lord Keynes, published his greatest work, *The General Theory of Employment, Interest and Money*. The critical analysis in *The General Theory* of the classical dichotomy generated a heated debate among economists, many of the issues of which are still unresolved today. In Part B of this chapter we shall examine some of the ideas of Lord Keynes and compare them to the ideas of the classicists. His model, which dominated macroeconomic thinking from the 1930s through much of the postwar period, still comprises a central element of most macroeconomic models.

A ● The Classical Dichotomy[1]

The Walrasian General Equilibrium Model: The macroeconomic theory of classical economics was derived as a logical extension of microeconomic analysis. Recall from microeconomics that we begin with the analysis of an individual economic agent. When that economic agent is a consumer, we assume that he makes his consumption plans rationally by trying to get as much utility as he

---

[1]This section contains some very subtle and complicated historical material on the work of Walras, Say, and Keynes. I have tried to be faithful to the profession's understanding of the ideas of these great economists. Robert Clower, Keizo Nagatani, Hans C. Palmer and Stephen Meyer all helped me clarify this chapter. I am very grateful to them. Of course, I finally had to settle on the definitions and interpretations, and I may not have satisfied everyone.

can out of his given budget. When the economic agent is a producer, we assume that he tries to generate as much profit as he can subject to the constraints of his production process. In each case we have a rational economic agent whose market activity is derived from a plan. When we wish to study the performance of an individual market, we generally add up the plans of consumers to determine demand conditions in this market, and we sum up the plans of the producers to determine supply conditions in this market. From these market supply and demand schedules, we are then able to determine the quantity that will be produced and the price at which the goods will be produced.

Numerous other conclusions may be derived from this result. If we wish to determine the total quantity of all goods produced and the prices at which each is produced, then we should be able to logically sum up the results of supply and demand in each of the individual markets. The outcome of logically extending these microeconomic decisions would include the level of what is produced of all goods and services, the consumption level of all of these goods and services, the relative market prices of all goods and services, and even the distribution of all goods and services between all the various economic agents. If each economic agent is allowed to achieve his plan, as is assumed when we use orthodox microeconomic analysis, then the outcome for the market as a whole must be consistent with these individual plans.

The most famous attempt to determine the aggregate implications of microeconomic analysis was undertaken by a great nineteenth-century French economist named León Walras. Walras' objective was to build a model of the economy in which the aggregate outcome was consistent with the microeconomic assumption that the quantities demanded and supplied by each individual were consistent with that individual's carefully developed rational plans. In other words, Walras asked, if all our plans are satisfied, then what will be the nature of the equilibrium solution? Walras had to deal with several problems that are not noticed in a partial equilibrium framework but which become serious in his general equilibrium framework. First of all, when analyzing a competitive economy, we assume that each individual producer and consumer acts as if the market price is set by someone else. Well, who is it that sets the prices to which all economic agents react? Walras' answer was an *auctioneer*. Walras' auctioneer would announce prices. Economic agents would then react to these prices by expressing the quantities of various goods which they would demand and supply. The auctioneer himself would not be a trader, so that Walras would be maintaining the assumption that all economic agents act as price takers. Walras envisioned an auction environment in which the auctioneer would announce a set of prices for all goods and services and then the various economic agents would express the quantities of each they would demand and the quantities of each they would supply.

A second and more severe problem now becomes extremely important. Suppose the auctioneer announces a set of prices for all the goods. Each economic agent, considering this set of prices, then determines how much of each good he owns which he is willing to supply and which goods and services he is willing to demand. Walras and other economists assumed that economic agents would not express supplies and demands on the basis of inconsistent budgets. This assumption is called *Say's Principle*. That is, the economic agents would not attempt to spend more in their demands than they were able to earn in their supplies when facing this particular set of prices. Suppose now that economic agents begin to trade on the basis of their various plans. What would happen if one of these individuals let us say a consumer named Bob, finds himself unable to sell the supply of labor that he had planned to sell. What is Bob now to do? He had planned on selling a certain quantity of labor which, because of other people's plans, he now is unable to sell. But his demands, in turn, were based on his planned labor supply. By selling his labor, he would have wage income to spend. Bob's whole plan has been frustrated by the market place. Evidently the set of prices announced by the auctioneer is not an equilibrium set, because Bob is unable to sell the quantity of labor he wishes to at that particular wage rate. Since we required that the aggregate outcome be consistent with each individual's plans, we must not allow Bob to trade at a point at which his plan is frustrated.

One may argue that excess supplies, such as Bob's excess labor supply, or excess demands, could be solved if the auctioneer would announce a new set of prices modified in response to the surpluses and shortages announced after the first set. Such a process of groping toward an equilibrium set of prices was called by Walras a *tâtonnement* process. (Tâtonnement is French for "groping.") However, if trading is allowed to occur during the tâtonnement process, then the general equilibrium outcome may depend on the particular sets of prices announced as the auctioneer attempts to locate the equilibrium set. In other words, if trading is allowed to occur at disequilibrium prices, then plans are frustrated and new decisions must be made. These new decisions may be inconsistent with the plans that are assumed to determine the microeconomic outcomes. The equilibrium solution ultimately attained, therefore, may be inconsistent with the plans that are assumed to determine the microeconomic outcomes. The equilibrium solution ultimately attained, therefore, may be inconsistent with the microeconomic decisions developed earlier, and Walras will not have achieved his objective of finding the macro system consistent with micro analysis.

This problem is a very important one, and it bothered classical economists greatly. They came up with a number of possible solutions. The basic idea behind all of their solutions, though, was that trading was not allowed to occur until an equilibrium set of prices was attained. Walras, for example, assumed that the auctioneer would announce a set of prices, and all producers and consumers would announce their quantities supplied and demanded at that set of prices. The auctioneer would check his balance sheets to see which markets were in excess supply and which were in excess demand. But no actual exchange or trading would take place. If there were markets with surpluses or shortages, the auctioneer would announce a new set of prices designed to reduce the shortages and the surpluses. Given the new set of prices, economic agents would announce a new set of plans. Again, no trading would take place and the auctioneer would evaluate the new set of prices. Only when a set of prices which is equilibrium is announced do economic agents actually begin to undertake transactions and to trade. If attaining an equilibrium set of prices seems to be too much for an auctioneer, we may note that he has been replaced in recent years by a high-speed computer, which can solve quickly for the general equilibrium price set.

Another way of thinking about the way in which the Walrasian system worked as it moved toward equilibrium is to think of each individual in the economy as writing a set of contractual arrangements as each set of prices is announced. In other words, we each contract for certain quantities supplied and certain quantities demanded. These contracts are to be based on rational plans and to obey Say's principle. But if the prices announced turn out to be disequilibrium prices, then we may all void our contracts and establish a new set of contracts when the new set of prices is announced. Thus, implicit in the Walrasian tâtonnement process and all general equilibrium analysis is the assumption that all decisions may be recontracted and that no trading occurs at disequilibrium. (Walras himself did not speak of recontracting. Walras believed that well-organized markets *approximately* achieved an equilibrium *as if* guided by an auctioneer. The term *recontracting* came from a later economist, Francis V. Edgeworth.)

A number of important results follow from the Walrasian general equilibrium analysis described above. A most important result has to do with the outcome of a Walrasian general equilibrium. First, by definition of Walrasian equilibrium each market must clear:

$$\overline{p_i}\overline{D_i}(\overline{p}) - \overline{p_i}\overline{S_i}(\overline{p}) = 0 \qquad \text{all } i = 1, 2, \ldots, n$$

where p_i is the price of good i, p represents all n prices, D_i and S_i are the quantities of goods i demanded and supplied, respectively. The overbar represents an equilibrium value. Second, the nature of Walras' economy requires the following identity, known as *Walras's Law:*

$$\sum_{i=1}^{n} p_i D_i(p) - \sum_{i=1}^{n} p_i S_i(p) \equiv 0$$

This identity holds at all sets of prices, not just the equilibrium set. The n goods included in this identity are everything that is tradable, including any goods that may serve as media of exchange or stores of value (i.e., including money, bonds, and other financial assets). Using Walras's Law and the equilibrium requirement that each market must clear, we can determine whether a given set of prices is an equilibrium set by inspecting only $n - 1$ markets. If all

$n - 1$ markets clear for some set of prices, then that set is an equilibrium, because by *Walras's Law,* the nth will have to clear as well.

[*Historical note:* If one good is called money and if we index that good as good n, then we may rewrite Walras's Law as:

$$\sum_{i=1}^{n-1} p_i D_i(p) - \sum_{i=1}^{n-1} p_i S_i(p) \equiv p_n S_n(p) - p_n D_n(p)$$

The left-hand side of this expression need not be identically zero under Walras's Law. However, J. B. Say, another French economist, argued at times that the left-hand side of this expression was identically zero:

$$\sum_{i=1}^{n-1} p_i D_i(p) - \sum_{i=1}^{n-1} p_i S_i(p) \equiv 0$$

This last expression is called Say's Law or "supply creates its own demand." Because Say was quite ambiguous in his analysis, economists do not all agree on exactly what he believed. However, if the last identity is viewed as an outcome which holds at all sets of prices, rather than a planning rule as in Say's Principle, then it is rejected by most economists. If, of course, an nth good does not exist, then Walras's and Say's Laws are equivalent and both are correct.]

Let $\bar{p}_1, \bar{p}_2, \ldots, \bar{p}_{n-1}$ be a set of $n - 1$ prices for which equilibrium is attained: then the Walrasian solution yields these $n - 1$ "relative" prices and the equilibrium trading quantities of the $n - 1$ goods. That is, the set of equilibrium prices attained by the Walrasian system tells us the rate at which each good can be exchanged for each other good. In yet other words, we know the price ratios between every pair of goods. The nature of the Walrasian tâtonnement process, in which no actual exchange occurs until an equilibrium set of prices is announced, clearly can apply to an economy in which goods are (at equilibrium) traded one directly for another. That is, the Walrasian system does not require any good to serve as a medium of exchange. In fact, we must admit that no meaningful method of transactions takes place at all in this type of economy. All decisions are made and all plans are seen to work out, and all markets are cleared before any actual transactions occur. Once transactions begin to occur, then no more planning is done or needed.

The implications of Walras's equilibrium for two particular markets are especially interesting in light of subsequent ideas developed by Keynes. First of all, we have made no explicit mention yet of the relationship between withdrawals from current consumption and the expenditures for goods and services to be used for future production, i.e., between saving and investment. Just as the markets for all current consumption goods must clear, so must the market for loanable funds, within Walras's Law. The price through which classical economists were assured that savings and investment would be exactly offsetting, in equilibrium, was the interest rate. Persons save for future consumption at the expense of current consumption. The quantity of future consumption available for each dollar saved depends upon the interest earned from (or rate of return on) saving. Conversely, the rate of interest also measures the rate of return on an investment expenditure. The interest rate essentially is the price, which the auctioneer announces to elicit the volume of saving and the volume of investment which economic agents are willing to undertake. He must see that this market clears, as do all the others before attaining an equilibrium. The second market deserving special comment is the labor market. Obviously, at equilibrium, the labor market must clear. By clearing we mean that the equilibrium quantity supplied must equal the equilibrium quantity demanded. This result means that no individual willing and able to supply a certain volume of labor services will be unable to find work when the economy is at equilibrium.

Walras was not the only classical economist to deal with general equilibrium problems, and other classical economists developed different mechanisms for the workings of their economies. Marshall, for example, argued that prices, when the economy is at disequilibrium, instantaneously adjust to the equilibrium prices. Edgeworth, as mentioned above, developed the idea of "recontracting" to describe one of the conditions necessary for movement between equilibrium points. As noted earlier, another French economist played a very important role in the development of macroeconomic thinking, particularly with respect to the differences between Keynes's ideas and those of the classics: J. B. Say developed many ideas which are closely related to the concepts we discussed above in the Walrasian system. Clower in 1967 argued that Say's Law is formally equivalent to Walras's Law; however, Patinkin in 1965 specified two completely different laws.

Without involving ourselves deeply in this doctrinaire debate, we note that it is fairly clear from Keynes's *General Theory* and certainly from the writings of subsequent Keynesian economists, that Keynesians felt that Say's Law was, while similar to Walras's Law, a statement of a causal mechanism which described how a competitive economy achieved a general equilibrium without relying strictly on Walras's auctioneer, whereas Walras's Law is an outcome of his general framework. Say's Law, as it is generally understood by most economists, and again we must remind the student that there is some disagreement on this point, states that supply creates its own demand. Given this interpretation, *Say's Law* is that economic agents supply goods and services for the purpose of demanding other goods and services (rather than merely accumulating money).

Classical economists tended to assume that prices and wages would change quickly in response to excess supplies and excess demands in individual markets. By assuming flexibility of wages and prices, classical economists were able to argue that prices would adjust so as to eliminate surpluses and shortages. The classical economist argued, therefore, that the economy would tend to gravitate toward an equilibrium. At this equilibrium, savings would have to equal investment because interest rates are also flexible and this flexibility assures that we can have neither permanent surpluses of savings nor shortages of savings. We also have no permanent surpluses or shortages in the labor market nor in any product markets, because again wages and prices are flexible. Thus the flexibility of wages and prices, combined with Say's Law, led the classical economists to a solution in which total output is determined by relative prices and interest rates and in which the labor market clears at full employment.

To sum up, the Walrasian general equilibrium system determined the level of output, the level of employment, the level of investment and saving, the interest rate, and all relative prices. What is left for the remainder of the classical dichotomy to determine? The answer is that, although relative prices are determined by the Walrasian system, the absolute level of these prices is not. Put another way, the actual units in which prices are expressed has not yet been determined. And, provided that the price ratios between various goods stay the same, any set of prices (French francs, German marks, American dollars in 1972, or American dollars in 1984) will satisfy the same set of equilibrium conditions. All that is left to be determined in the remainder of the classical dichotomy is the price level, and it is the quantity theory of money which the classical economists employed to determine the price level.

Before we discuss the quantity theory of money, two potentially confusing points about thinking of classical economists should be cleared up. First, the notion that supply creates its own demand, popularly known as Say's Law, is a concept that pertains to the aggregate system and not strictly to each individual market. For example, a decision by individuals to work in shoe production need not generate an equivalent level of demand for shoes. Such a result would not follow from Say's Law. Only in the aggregate is it that the level of demand equals the level of supply. It is, nevertheless, true that at Walrasian equilibrium, each and every market must clear so that aggregate demand must equal total production at full employment.

The second point of possible confusion has to do with the existence in the economy of unemployment. It would be naive for us to reject classical analysis on the ground that unemployment exists in the economy. Classical economists recognized the presence of unemployment. However, they did not believe that involuntary unemployment would exist at equilibrium in a fully competitive economy. It may be that individuals are unwilling to work at existing wages, so they are unemployed voluntarily. Furthermore, the economy may have unemployment because it is not in equilibrium, so temporary surpluses of labor may exist in certain markets. Classical economists attribute such temporary unemployment to various shocks which hit certain markets, shocks such as new inventions that require automation, other technological changes, or changes in taste that produce shifts in demand. Finally, classical economists were well aware of various impediments which prevent the flexibility of prices. Such impediments prevent the appropriate reactions of economic agents and of prices to changes in economic circumstances. Thus it would be unfair for us to imply that classical economists were not aware of monopolies, cartels, labor unions, minimum wage laws, government interference, and the like. Nevertheless, classical economists did believe that the economy behaved in the main as if a Walrasian-type general equilibrium system were operating. Therefore, the classical macroeconomic paradigm focuses primarily on the macroeconomic version of a laissez-faire economic system, i.e., one which operates within a competitive equilibrium environment.

The Quantity Theory of Money: The equation of exchange is central to the second part of the classical dichotomy. This equation has appeared in many forms, often to the frustration of economists. Sir John Hicks (1935) wrote:

> This equation crops up again and again, and it has all sorts of ingenious little arithmetical tricks performed on it. Sometimes it comes out as $MV = PT$; and once, in its most stupendous transfiguration, it blossomed into $P = E/O + (I' - S)/R$.

A relatively simple version will suffice here. Define M as the quantity of the monetary unit in circulation at a moment in time and V as the speed with which the monetary unit is exchanged in transactions on final product (the income velocity of money). If Y represents the value, at current prices, of all final goods and services produced in a year (at this level of abstraction, no distinction need be made between GNP, NNP, and NI), then the following relation is an identity:

$$MV \equiv Y \tag{1}$$

Equation (1) is the equation of exchange. It can be viewed as a definition of the income velocity of money and can be used to calculate V from Y and M.

The classical economists utilized the equation of exchange to develop their theory of the determination of the level of prices. Two distinct approaches were employed to study the nature of V, income velocity. Different forms of the equation were employed and different types of velocity were considered, but the flavor of the two approaches can be appreciated by using equation (1). The *Fisherian* approach to the study of V, associated with Irving Fisher, focused on money as a means of production. Money was viewed as an input to the production of transactions. The processes of transactions and exchange are determined by particular institutional settings and factors. Consequently, velocity, in the short run, is likely to be constant. Institutional factors change only slowly.

The Cambridge school of thought, associated with Alfred Marshall, studied the equation of exchange, often called the Cambridge equation, from a very different point of view from the Fisherians. The Cambridge school considered the velocity of money from the point of view of the individual economic agents and their choices. Decisions by economic agents to hold money were dependent on opportunity costs and constraints just like decisions to hold and use other commodities. The general conclusion about velocity derived by the Cambridge school was the same as that of the Fisherians: Velocity is constant in the short run. Thus two quite different approaches transformed the identity equation (1) into a theory about the relation between M and Y, because they both drew the same conclusion about velocity. Imposing the restriction on equation (1) that V is constant creates a theory about economic activity: the quantity theory of money. The theory is embodied in equation (2):

$$MV_0 = Y \tag{2}$$

Given the restriction that velocity is a constant, increases in Y are associated with increases in M. Thus, the classical quantity theory of money concludes that changes in income are proportional to changes in the quantity of money.

Classical Dichotomy: The Walrasian general equilibrium system and the quantity theory of money may be combined to formulate the classical dichotomy. First, one further refinement of equation (2) is necessary. Y measures total income, at current prices. Income can be viewed as the sum of the quantities of goods and services, each weighted by its relative price:

$$Y = \sum_{i=1}^{n} p_i q_i \equiv P \cdot Q \tag{3}$$

It is clear from our discussion in Chapter 3 that money income may be viewed as the product of a price term and a quantity term: Changes in income are partitioned into changes in the level of prices and changes in the level of output. Combining equations (2) and (3), we have:

$$MV_0 = PQ \tag{4}$$

Recall that the outcome of the real system was that the level of output was determined at full employment. In equation form:

$$Q = Q^* \tag{5}$$

where Q^* is that level of Q associated with full employment. Substituting Q^* for Q in equation (4) yields the classical quantity theory of money conclusion that, after allowance for output determination from the real system:

$$MV_0 = PQ^* \tag{6}$$

Given Q^* from the real world and given $V = V_0$ from the quantity theory of money, equation (6) states that increases in M induce proportionate increases in P, the level of prices.

The classical dichotomy outlined above can be better understood when illustrated in terms of supply and demand. The real sector of the dichotomy implies that equilibrium occurs only at full employment output. As indicated earlier, we may interpret this result as implying an aggregate supply curve which is vertical at the level of production Q^*, output associated with full employment. Figure 2 illustrates the classical theory in terms of supply and demand. Regardless of the position of the demand curve, output occurs at Q^*. Suppose, for example, that the money supply is increased. An increase in M may be thought of as generating an increase in demand. Demand shifts from D to D'. In Figure 1, presented earlier, with normally shaped supply and demand curves, the new equilibrium at B was characterized by a higher price level, and a higher output level. However, now, given the Walrasian general equilibrium solution and market clearing wages and prices, we see that the increase in demand merely produces an increase in the price level while leaving total output the same.

In conclusion, the quantity theory of money on the one hand and Walrasian general equilibrium (or Say's Law and market clearing flexible prices) on the other comprise the classical dichotomy. The economic system is viewed in two separate, and independent, parts. In the real market, the level of output, the mix of output, relative prices and wages, and interest rates are all determined. In the money market and the quantity theory of money, the absolute values of all commodities, in terms of the monetary unit, that is, the price level, are determined. In other words, whereas relative prices, ratios of prices of any pair of

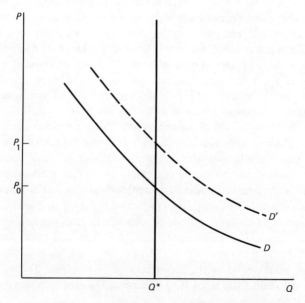

FIGURE 2   Classical Theory of Aggregate Economics

commodities, are determined in the real system, the level of these prices in terms of the monetary unit is set by the quantity theory of money. The determination of all underlying variables of the theory of value took place in the real system without regard to the existence in the economic system of money. Money was viewed as a veil over an economic system which was otherwise exactly like a barter economy.

The classical model was not without problems, and for some time economists had various reservations about several aspects of classical economics. Classicists had a difficult time reconciling hoarding by individuals (that is, holding money for reasons other than to undertake transactions) with the necessity of savings and investment to equilibriate in the loanable funds market. While many accepted the tendency for velocity to be relatively constant over a long time period, others questioned its rigidity in the short run. The proportionality between the level of prices and the money supply seemed difficult for many to reconcile with the apparent total independence of relative prices with respect to monetary phenomena. In fact, the concept that money was a veil on a system which in all important particulars was exactly the same as a barter system was subject to considerable disagreement. That the economic system could be divided into a neat dichotomy, free of interaction, bothered many. Some went so far as to suggest that the dichotomy was not a consistent model. Some argued that the quantity theory of money was inconsistent with Say's Law.

This theoretical discontent and these bothersome observations erupted abruptly to the surface in the 1930s as a result of two phenomena: The world economy underwent the Great Depression starting in late 1929, and, in 1936, John Maynard Keynes wrote *The General Theory of Employment, Interest and Money.* As when Adam ate the apple, there was no turning back. The classical model was an artifact, and new ways of studying an economy in the aggregate took hold. Debate has raged for many years over the exact role of Keynes in economic thought and over the validity of the views of classical economists. Was Keynes original? Was the classical dichotomy valid? How did Keynes and the classicists differ? Was the Great Depression understood by classicists? These and many other questions continue to bother historians of economic thought. However, several points can be agreed upon. Walras's general equilibrium system and the classical macroeconomic analysis in general are not well suited as theoretical tools for studying an economy with large levels of unemployment and with substantial and sustained reductions in output. While unemployment is consistent with classical analysis, unemployment essentially occurs because the model differs in some way from the economy itself or because the unemployment is only temporary. Given the depth and stubbornness of the Great Depression in the 1930s, to interpret unemployment and underproduction as "temporary" seems quite inadequate. Second, the issues on which many economists focused attention after the appearance of *The General Theory* were quite different in the main from what they had been. We now turn to a discussion of Keynes and Keynesian economics.

B • *The General Theory* of Lord Keynes

The General Theory of Employment, Interest and Money by Lord Keynes is the most famous twentieth-century book written in economics. Published in 1936, following five years of severe economic depression, *The General Theory* revolutionized macroeconomic thought. Many points Keynes made had been made before, some of what he said is confused, some is contradictory and some is, indeed, wrong. Nevertheless, this book transformed modern economic theory and may well have salvaged western economic thought. Keynes stressed the prefix *general* in his title and said, "I shall argue that the postulates of the classical theory are applicable to a special case only and not to the general case, the situation which it assumes being a limiting point of the possible positions of equilibrium." At an abstract theoretical level, economists still argue about how Keynes disagreed with the ideas of the classicists.

While Keynesian economists began to develop different models and use a whole new set of tools, virtually ignoring many of the ideas developed by the classical economists, some people have argued in recent years that these new approaches by Keynesian economists failed to capture the central themes which Keynes himself was expressing in *The General Theory*. Robert Clower (1965) and Axel Leijonhufvud (1968) argue eloquently that the body of economic theory which is known as Keynesian analysis differs from the actual analysis of Keynes; i.e., Keynesians, it is argued, misinterpreted the master. Clower and Leijonhufvud argue that Keynes's dispute with the classics ran deeper than his followers realized. Clower and Leijonhufvud argue that Keynes was rejecting Walras's Law as a relevant tool of analysis for economic activity and was focusing instead on economic processes at disequilibrium. Other economists do not share the Clower and Leijonhufvud reintepretation of Keynes. Grossman (1972), for example, argues that the traditional Keynesian interpretation of *The General Theory* is accurate. We are not yet equipped with adequate tools to evaluate this exegis issue in economic thought (i.e., this debate over the true interpretation of Keynesian "scripture"); however, we will return to this issue after we have developed better theoretical analysis.

Keynes set for himself the immediate practical task of building a model which would characterize the depression and from which he could derive resolutions to the economic hardship. *The General Theory* provides a theoretical framework in which one can analyze involuntary unemployment. Furthermore, *The General Theory* suggests new policy tools for eliminating this unemployment. Keynes believed that an advanced industrialized economy could suffer from massive unemployment and from severe underproduction which could last for a long period of time. In fact, he believed that a private, capitalist economy would be unable to rid itself of this unemployment unless it were bailed out by an active government fiscal intervention. The success that Keynes enjoyed can be fully appreciated only after one realizes the political unpopularity of his conclusions at the time.

Marxists, for example, had hoped that capitalism would collapse from its own weight. Keynes, however, suggested that government fiscal actions could avoid this end. Despite his suggested solution for salvaging capitalism, today some Marxist economists attempt to argue that Keynes himself was a Marxist. Their claim rests on the fact that Keynes attacked the relevance of general equilibrium analysis to modern economies. The mainstream economists in Keynes's day, as well as many business and political leaders, thought that capitalist economies were strong enough to support themselves with little or no government intervention. While the classicists may not have believed completely in a laissez-faire system, their analysis did suggest that a market economy would self-correct when driven from equilibrium by exogenous shocks. Keynes's analysis implies that this outcome is unlikely. In other words, Keynes rejected both the conventional wisdom of his day (classical doctrine) and the primary radical alternative (Marxism).

Involuntary unemployment, in the Keynesian sense, occurs when persons, both willing and able to work at existing wages, cannot find jobs and the market does not function to lower the wage. Keynes developed a model in which involuntary unemployment is possible, indeed in which full employment is "a limiting point of the possible positions of equilibrium." This Keynesian result is remarkable: large numbers of capable, willing workers might be unable to find jobs for an extended period of time. Furthermore, the economic system could not cope with this problem on its own. A model in which unemployment is the rule, not the exception, could explain the kinds of massive unemployment that characterized the Great Depression. Essentially, the Keynesian model was built as a depression model which could reconcile, with economic theory, large levels of involuntary unemployment.

Assumptions of Income-Expenditure Models: The models we will develop in Chapter 5 will be seen to be components of a very general theoretical framework embodying the analysis of both monetarist economists and Keynesian economists. Nevertheless, when viewed as simple Keynesian income-expenditure models, they contain two important implicit assumptions. Since we shall treat them first as complete Keynesian models, we shall first examine these two assumptions in some detail. We shall see that awareness of these two assumptions will help us understand the difference between Keynesian and classical economics. The first assumption is that unemployed and underutilized resources (including labor) are assumed to exist.

Supply and demand analysis can be used to illustrate the assumptions of the Keynesian income-expenditure approach. In the Keynesian model, the assumption of the existence of unemployed resources permits an increase in demand to induce an increase in real output. In other words, production is capable of increasing in response to an increase in demand. The second assumption, that the price level does not increase, is violated in the demand increase depicted earlier in Figure 1. Now, within the Keynesian depression analysis, the price increase is disallowed. Only one supply curve permits an increase in demand to result in an increase in only Q and not in P. Such a supply curve is horizontal. The new supply and demand diagram which represents these two implicit assumptions of the Keynesian depression analysis is Figure 3. In Figure 3 initial equilibrium is at the intersection of the demand curve D and the supply curve S. Equilibrium price and quantity are P_0 and Q_0, respectively. An increase in demand, which shifts D to D', increases real output from Q_0 to Q_1 and leaves the price level fixed at P_0. Comparing Figure 2, which depicts the classical model, and Figure 3, which depicts the Keynesian depression model, both with Figure 1, we now see that both classical and Keynesian economics are special different cases of supply and demand.

**Conclusion:** We shall conclude this chapter with a comparison of the early ideas of the classical economists and Keynes with the ideas of modern monetarists and Keynesians. The material in this chapter was not presented only as historical and academic exercise. Rather, the ideas of modern monetarists follow very closely the theoretical framework established by the classical economists several hundred years ago. Recall that the classical model consists of a dichotomy. In half of the dichotomy the general equilibrium analysis of Walras led to a solution for all the real variables in the economic system. The remaining half of the dichotomy consisted of the quantity theory of money in which it was the quantity of money supplied by some central monetary authority which determined the nominal or money values of all economic variables. In a very famous speech on policy, titled "The Role of Monetary Policy," the father of modern monetarism, Professor Milton Friedman, clearly established the linkages between his modern theories and the work of the classicists. While classicists argued that the economy

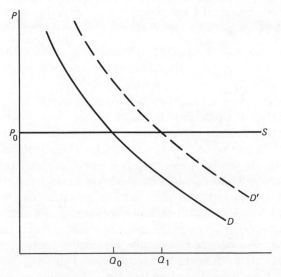

FIGURE 3   Keynesian Depression Model

would come to equilibrium at full employment, the modern monetarists argue that Walras's general equilibrium system works to bring the economy to a natural rate of unemployment. The major difference between the classicists and the monetarists on this point seems to be recognition on the part of the latter that today's economies are not strictly speaking competitive. Nevertheless, the outcome for the economy is a fixed level of output and a fixed level of unemployment. In Professor Friedman's own words:

> The "natural rate of unemployment," in other words, is the level that would be ground out by the Walrasian system of general equilibrium equations, provided there is imbedded in them the actual structural characteristics of the labor and commodity markets, including market imperfections, stochastic variability in demands and supplies, the cost of gathering information about job vacancies and labor availabilities, the cost of mobility, and so on.

That the economy is characterized by a dichotomy in which money and the monetary authorities influence only the money values of economic magnitudes is undeniably argued in this same volume by Professor Friedman:

> To state the general conclusion still differently, the monetary authority controls nominal quantities—directly the quantity of its own liabilities. In principle, it can use this control to peg a nominal quantity—an exchange rate, the price level, the nominal level of national income, the quantity of money by one or another definition—or to peg the rate of change in nominal quantity, the rate of inflation or deflation, the rate of growth or decline in nominal national income, the rate of growth of the quantity of money. It cannot use its control over nominal quantities to peg a real quantity—the real rate of interest, the rate of unemployment, the level of real national income, the real quantity of money, the rate of growth of real national income, or the rate of growth of the real quantity of money.

These two passages from Professor Friedman clearly indicate a system in which real and nominal magnitudes are dichotomized into two separate and distinct parts.

Just as modern monetarists have maintained the essence of classical doctrine, modern Keynesians reject their doctrines on the same grounds with which Keynes rejected the ideas of the classics. In another famous article, Professor James Tobin of Yale University indicates to us the modern relevance, in his view, of Keynes. In his article "How Dead is Keynes?" which, like the Friedman article, was an invited address to a major economic association, Professor Tobin identified four major propositions which are central to *The General Theory*. First, "In modern industrialist capitalist societies, prices and wages respond slowly to excess demand or supply, especially slowly to excess supply." Second, ". . . economies like ours (are vulnerable to) lengthy bouts of involuntary unemployment." Third, "Capital formation depends on long run appraisals of profit expectations and risks and on business attitudes toward bearing the risks. These are not simple, predictable functions of current and recent economic events." Fourth, "Even if money wages and prices were responsive to market demands and supplies, their flexibility would not necessarily stabilize monetary economies subject to demand and supply shocks. This was Keynes' challenge to accepted doctrine that market mechanisms are inherently self-correcting and stabilizing." What, in Tobin's judgment, is the relevance of these Keynesian propositions for today's modern economies? On this point he is unambiguous:

> I submit that none of these four central Keynesian propositions is incon-
> sistent with the contemporary economic scene here or in other advanced
> democratic, capitalist countries. At least the first three fit the facts ex-
> tremely well. Indeed, the middle 70s followed the Keynesian script better
> than any postwar period except the early 60s.

Many other implications of these models will be discussed in later chapters. We are about to develop the elements of macroeconomic analysis used by both monetarists and Keynesian economists, and we will begin with the simple Keynesian income-expenditure models.

STUDY QUESTIONS AND PROBLEMS

1. Define and discuss briefly the validity of:

   Walras's Law
   Say's Principle
   Tâtonnement
   Involuntary unemployment
   "Supply creates its own demand"
   Walrasian auctioneer

2. Discuss the relationship between each item of the following pairs:

   a. *The General Theory*   The Great Depression
   b. The quantity theory of money Barter economy
   c. General equilibrium analysis Price takers
   d. Savings   Investment
   e. Recontracting   Walrasian equilibrium

3. State whether each proposition below is true or false and explain:

   a. The unemployment of the 1930s is proof of the invalidity of the classical model.
   b. An increase in savings leads to an increase in income.
   c. Say's Law and Walras's Law are compatible.
   d. Money is needed in Walras's model in order to achieve equilibrium.

4. Can you reconcile the quantity theory of money proposition that an increase in M will lead to a proportionate increase in P with the classical view that relative prices are independent of M?

5. Utilizing supply and demand curves, compare and contrast the classical model with the Keynesian income-expenditure approach.

6. What role do interest rates play in the classical theory?

7. What proposals would you make, if you were a proponent of the classical dichotomy, to resolve unemployment? What would you suggest to stop an inflation?

8. Explain carefully the relationship between the following two expressions:

  a. $MV \equiv PQ$, the equation of exchange

  b. $MV_0 = PQ$, the quantity theory of money

9. Two assumptions were employed in the Keynesian model discussed in this chapter: Prices are stable, and unemployed resources exist. Illustrate these assumptions with supply and demand curves. Are these assumptions realistic? Are they useful? Explain.

REFERENCES

Clower, Robert W., "The Keynesian Counterrevolution: A Theoretical Appraisal," in F. H. Hahn and P. P. R. Brechling, eds., *The Theory of Interest Rates,* London, 1965.

Fisher, Irving, *The Purchasing Power of Money* (revised). New York: Macmillan, 1911.

Friedman, Milton, "The Quantity Theory of Money—A Restatement," *Studies in the Quantity Theory of Money,* Milton Friedman (ed.). Chicago: University of Chicago Press, 1956.

————, "The Role of Monetary Policy," *American Economic Review,* vol. 58, March 1968.

Hansen, Alvin H., *A Guide to Keynes.* New York: McGraw-Hill, 1953.

Hicks, John, "A Suggestion for Simplifying the Theory of Money," *Economica,* 1935, reprinted in American Economic Association, *Readings in Monetary Theory.* Homewood, Ill.: Irwin, 1951.

Johnson, Harry G., "Monetary Theory and Policy," *American Economic Review,* No. 3 (June 1962).

Keynes, John Maynard, *The General Theory of Employment, Interest and Money,* New York: Harcourt, Brace and World, 1965 (originally 1936).

Klein, Lawrence, *The Keynesian Revolution.* New York: Macmillan, 1961.

Leijonhufvud, Axel, *On Keynesian Economics and The Economics of Keynes.* New York: Oxford University Press, 1968.

Laidler, David E. W., *The Demand for Money: Theoretical and Empirical Evidence,* Scranton, Pa.: International Textbook Co., 1969.

Lange, Oskar, *Papers in Economics and Sociology* (translated by P. F. Knightsfield). London: Pergamon Press, 1970, Part III, pp. 149-170.

Lerner, Abba, *The Economics of Employment.* New York: McGraw-Hill, 1951.

Patinkin, Don, *Money, Interest and Prices,* 2nd ed. New York: Harper & Row, 1965.

Samuelson, Paul, *Economics,* 9th ed. New York: McGraw-Hill, 1973.

Tobin, James, "Inflation and Unemployment," *American Economic Review,* March 1972.

Wicksell, Knut, *Lectures on Political Economy, Vol. II, Money.* London: Routledge & Kegan Paul Ltd., 1967 (originally 1935).

The objective of this chapter is to present a simple, rudimentary model in the spirit of Keynesian models first popularized by his followers Alvin Hansen, Abba Lerner, and Paul Samuelson. These simple models form the core of macroeconomic theory of modern Keynesians and have also been incorporated into the work of modern monetarists. This latter point must not be underemphasized. While we shall present the models here as Keynesian models, the same models under slightly different assumptions will be used subsequently as components of more general theoretical frameworks.

Keynesian Model One: The allocation of GNP by use in Chapter 2 showed that final goods and services are utilized by four sectors: households (personal consumption expenditures); firms (gross private domestic investment); government (government purchases of goods and services); and the rest of the world (net exports of goods and services). First, we shall depict demand for goods and services by households.

5

Keynesian
Income-Expenditure Models

A major point at which Keynes took issue with the classical model was in its treatment of household financial decisions. Keynes focused on consumption expenditures, rather than saving, and believed that income was the main determinant of the level of consumption expenditures. The simplest Keynesian assumption one can make about consumption activity is that consumption is a linear function of income. Thus:

$$C = C_0 + bY \tag{1}$$

Equation (1) states that aggregate consumption, C, is a linear function of total income, Y; C_0 and b are algebraic constants.[1] A linear consumption function with intercept C_0 and slope b is depicted in Figure 1. Note that C_0 is a positive constant and that b is positive and less than one.

The simplest assumption one can make about private domestic investment expenditures is that they are exogenous. Equation (2) below sets private domestic investment, I, equal to an algebraic constant I_0.

$$I = I_0 \tag{2}$$

Figure 2 illustrates equation (2). Since I is exogenous, its level is invariant across changes in income. The restriction that I is fixed may appear absurdly confining. However, as a point of departure perhaps it can be motivated. First, theories about investment are likely to be very complicated. One will have to allow for technological change, uncertainty, anticipated profits, business finances, and so

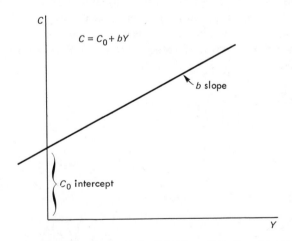

FIGURE 1   Consumption as a Linear Function of Income

[1] Standard notation to be utilized here will be to treat uppercase letters ($C, Y, R, \ldots$) as variables, and lowercase letters ($a, b, f, g, \ldots$) and uppercase letters with zero subscripts ($C_0, I_0, \ldots$) as algebraic constants.

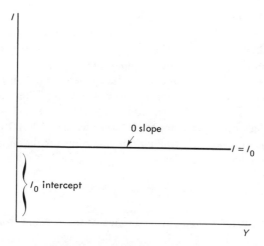

FIGURE 2   Exogenous Investment

forth. Rather than treat I as a simple function as if we understand its determination, it might be less misleading if we simply admit that its determinants are unknown; therefore, it is exogenous. Second, suppose I depends upon economic factors but those projected well into the future on the basis of very long-run trends. In this case, I is unlikely to vary as a result of short-run fluctuations in economic activity and is, in a short-run model, best treated as exogenous. Third, many students will recall from their course on principles of macroeconomics that interest rates play a role in investment expenditures. We could express investment as an inverse function of interest rates: $I = I_0 - vR$, where v is a constant and where R is the interest rate. Some readers may wish to replace our $I = I_0$ equation with $I = I_0 - vR_0$. However, for now we treat R as exogenous and constant. We will drop this restriction in Chapter 12, and endogenous models of investment will be studied carefully and incorporated into a more complex theory.

Government and the foreign sector will, purely for simplicity, be assumed not to exist. Given only a domestic private market economy, total demand for final goods and services produced in the economy is the sum of consumption expenditures and investment expenditures. Defining AD as aggregate, or total demand, we have

$$AD = C + I \tag{3}$$

Equation (3) states that AD is the sum of C, which depends on income, and I, which is exogenous. Consequently, AD depends on income. Replace C in equation (3) with the right-hand side of equation (1) and I in equation (3) with the right-hand side of equation (2):

$$AD = C_0 + bY + I_0 \qquad (4)$$

Figure 3 depicts equation (4). The aggregate demand curve drawn in Figure 3 is simply the consumption line shifted up by the exogenous level of investment.

Income, as we have seen from national income accounting, is generated in the process of production. The level of income can be viewed then as the total value of production or of supply. The equation $Y = AD$ means that income (or total production) equals aggregate demand. In other words, $Y = AD$ means that supply equals demand. Thus, the equilibrium condition for the model will be that supply equal demand:

$$Y = AD \qquad (5)$$

Finally, savings by households, S, is defined as the residual from income after consumption:

$$S \equiv Y - C \qquad (6)$$

Since consumption is a linear function of income, from equation (1), savings can be considered a function of income:

$$S = Y - C$$

$$S = Y - C_0 - bY \qquad (7)$$

$$S = -C_0 + (1 - b)Y$$

Diagrammatically, see Figure 4. Equation (6) is the definition of savings. Equation (7) embodies the theory of consumer behavior that consumption, and therefore the residual saving, is a function of income. Consequently equation (6) is an identity and equation (7) an equality.

The simple model developed so far has five variables, C, I, AD, Y, and S, and five equations:

$$C \quad = C_0 + bY \qquad (1)$$

$$I \quad = I_0 \qquad (2)$$

$$AD = C + I \qquad (3)$$

$$Y \quad = AD \qquad (5)$$

$$S \quad \equiv Y - C \qquad (6)$$

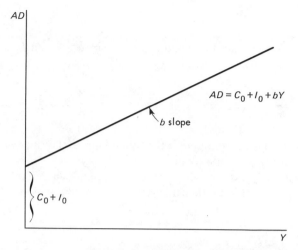

FIGURE 3   Aggregate Demand

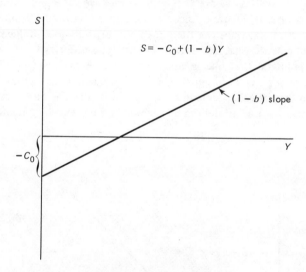

FIGURE 4   Savings Schedule

Solutions to the Model: This system of equations may be solved algebraically for the unknown equilibrium values of the variables. To solve for equilibrium values, impose the equilibrium condition, $Y = AD$, on the system of equations:

$$Y = C + I \qquad\qquad\qquad (8)$$

In equation (8), AD is replaced by the right-hand side of equation (3). Next C may be replaced by equation (1) and I by equation (2):

$$Y = C_0 + bY + I_0 \tag{9}$$

Equation (9) contains only one unknown, Y, since C_0, b, and I_0 are algebraic constants. Equation (9) is next solved for the value of Y at equilibrium:

$$Y(E) = \frac{C_0 + I_0}{1 - b} \tag{10}$$

Since equation (10) is the solution for the equilibrium level of income, income is labeled $Y(E)$ for the equilibrium value.

It is now relatively easy to solve for the equilibrium values of other variables. For example, given $Y(E)$, we find that $C(E)$, the equilibrium level of consumption, is

$$C(E) = C_0 + bY(E) \tag{11}$$

Geometry, as well as algebra, can be used to solve for equilibrium values of unknown variables. In Figure 5, income is measured on the horizontal axis and AD on the vertical axis, both in the same units, say billions of dollars. A 45-deg line, which bisects the space, is drawn. The analytic property of the 45-deg line is that any point on that line is equidistant from each axis; i.e., distance OA equals distance OA', and OB equals OB'. Figure 6 combines Figures 3 and 5 by drawing both the aggregate demand curve and the 45-deg line on the same figure.

Figure 6 can be used to determine the equilibrium level of income. Suppose

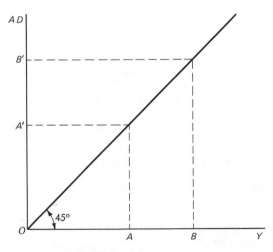

FIGURE 5   Forty-five-degree Line

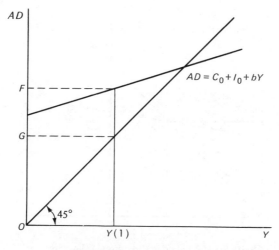

$$AD = C_0 + I_0 + bY$$

FIGURE 6   Keynesian Cross

income is at level $Y(1)$. With income at $Y(1)$, aggregate demand, which depends on income, will be equal to distance OF. According to the 45-deg line, income is equal to distance OG. OG is less than OF. In other words, income is less than aggregate demand at $Y(1)$. Consumers and firms are jointly demanding more goods and services than are, in the aggregate, being produced. Producers would, under these circumstances, observe undesired depletions of their inventory stocks. Since the economy is assumed to have unused resources and since demand exceeds production, firms, seeing their inventories depleted, can be expected to try to increase production. To increase output, firms must employ more resources. As they employ more resources, firms increase income, and income will continue to rise until AD no longer exceeds income.

In Figure 7, income equals aggregate demand at income level $Y(E)$, because at $Y(E)$ the aggregate demand curve cuts the 45-deg line, and, therefore, both $Y(E)$ and AD equal distance OD. $Y(E)$ is equilibrium, because when $Y = AD$, firms, in the aggregate, will be producing exactly that amount which other firms and consumers are willing and able to buy. Firms, when total production and income equal $Y(E)$, will in the aggregate have no tendency to alter the level of output. The reader can check his understanding of the equilibrium condition that $Y = AD$ by considering how firms would react if income were at level $Y(2)$ illustrated in Figure 7. (*Hint*: What will be happening to stocks of inventories?) Since consumption can be drawn as a function of income, as in Figure 1, the equilibrium level of consumption can be determined geometrically by measuring the level of C associated with $Y(E)$. Solutions to the equilibrium values of the other variables can be found in a similar fashion.

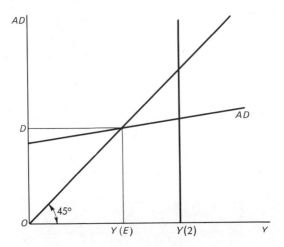

FIGURE 7   Keynesian Cross Equilibrium Income

Keynesian Investment Multiplier: Economics is a study of changes. What is the effect of a corn blight? How will a consumer react to a new sales tax? Will the economy grow faster if the government cuts taxes? How does an investment boom influence the economy? The income-expenditure model developed above is a useful vehicle for studying the macroeconomic effects of simple changes. For example, suppose that investment should increase, for unknown reasons, from I_0 to I_1. What will be the effect on the economy? Starting at equilibrium, i.e., $C = C(E)$, $Y = Y(E)$, and so on, a change in I will induce a multiplied change in Y. Keynesian multipliers can be used to calculate the effect on equilibrium income of a change in investment.

A *multiplier* is defined as the ratio of the change in equilibrium income over the change in an exogenous variable. The investment multiplier is $\Delta Y(E)/\Delta I$, where Δ represents "a change in." Equation (10) can be rewritten in a more helpful form:

$$Y(E) = \frac{C_o}{(1 - b)} + \frac{1}{(1 - b)}\, I \tag{12}$$

Equation (12) states equilibrium income as a linear function of investment with a slope $1/(1 - b)$. The investment multiplier for this simple model is the slope of equation (12):

$$\Delta Y(E)/\Delta I = 1/(1 - b) \equiv k_I \tag{13}$$

The investment multiplier k_I is seen to depend upon b, the slope of the consumption function. In more complex models the multiplier formula will be different. Keynes called b the marginal propensity to consume, MPC, and he assumed that MPC was less than one. The relationship between MPC and K_I can be illustrated with numbers. Table 1 lists some values for k_I associated with values for MPC:

TABLE 1

Relation Between MPC and k_I

MPC	k_I
0.9	10
0.8	5
0.75	4
0.5	2

Ceteris paribus, the larger MPC, the larger k_I.

The simple Keynesian model outlined above has a number of interesting implications. First, the model suggests that equilibrium income can occur at whatever level aggregate demand cuts the 45-deg line. This income level need not be the one associated with full employment. In fact, full employment income would appear to be a "limiting point of the possible positions of equilibrium." (This implication is not a proven result but follows from the restrictions imposed on aggregate supply and demand.) Second, an increase in investment leads to a multiplied increase in the equilibrium level of income. Third, the size of the multiplier depends upon the marginal propensity to consume.

It is important to realize that the formula for "the" multiplier given in equation (13) is only an example of multiplier analysis and that this equation applies only to this simple model. Later, we will build more complex models which will have different multiplier formulas. Consequently, memorization of a particular multiplier formula is a mistake—understanding its derivation is better.

The marginal propensity to consume, MPC, is the parameter upon which the investment multiplier is based. If $k_I = 10$, a $1 increase in investment induces a $10 increase in the equilibrium level of income. The model in which k_I was studied is a *comparative static model*. A comparative static model is one in which an economy is assumed to be in equilibrium, an exogenous change is imposed such as an increase in investment, and a new equilibrium is attained. Comparative statics consists of comparing two or more equilibria. *Dynamics*, distinct from comparative statics, consists of studying movements between equilibria. Thus, dynamic analysis will give us some insight into how an economy moves from one static equilibrium to another. Several dynamic questions about multipliers are of interest. How does an economy adjust to a change? What paths do the variables take between equilibrium values? How long does the economy take to move from one equilibrium to another?

A Dynamic Income-Expenditure Model: Perhaps the simplest dynamic model is one in which the economy responds to changes in demand with a delay—a lagged response. Lags in response to exogenous changes occur at several stages of the economic process.

Consider an increase in investment spending which induces an increase in incomes. First, a lag may occur between an increase in income and an increase in spending by the individuals whose incomes have increased—an *expenditure lag*. Second, once expenditures have increased, demand will have increased. The response by markets to increases in demands will be varied. Firms will observe inventory depletions, and, after they are sure the new demand is not temporary, they will place new orders. Once new orders are placed, manufacturers will lay the foundations to begin increased production. The time between an increase in expenditures and an increase in production is thought to be long and is subsumed under the heading *production lag*. Increases in production require the employment and utilization of additional factors of production. It is in the generation of new production that increased income occurs. However, a period of time exists between the increase in production and the actual payments to factor inputs of new income—the *earnings lag*.

A simple dynamic model, incorporating a production lag, can be examined. Far more complicated lag structures are, of course, possible; however, a relatively simple structure is a useful model with which to start. Production will be assumed to instantaneously generate income which, in turn, instantaneously generates demand. Production, however, will respond with a one-period lag to demand increases. Other than this simple one-period production lag, the model will correspond to the Keynesian comparative static income-expenditure model with the addition of explicit time subscripts. Four equations comprise the model:

$$C_t = C_0 + bY_t \tag{14}$$

$$I_t = I_0 \tag{15}$$

$$AD_t = C_t + I_t \tag{16}$$

$$Y_t = AD_{t-1} \tag{17}$$

Equilibrium in the static model simply required that income equal aggregate demand. Now, however, the economy must, to be in equilibrium, be at rest over time as well, so income must remain a constant over consecutive periods: $Y_{t+1} = Y_t = Y_{t-1}$. If income is constant over consecutive periods, so is consumption, $C_{t+1} = C_t = C_{t-1}$. The equilibrium values of consumption and income may be computed by simply setting $Y_t = Y_{t-1}$, $C_t = C_{t-1}$, $I_t = I_{t-1}$. Combining equations (16), (17), and dynamic equilibrium, we have

$$Y_t = C_t + I_t \tag{18}$$

Substituting from (14) and (15), we obtain

$$Y_t = C_0 + bY_t + I_0 \tag{19}$$

Therefore,

$$Y_t = (C_0 + I_0)/(1 - b) \tag{20}$$

Observe that this equilibrium result for the dynamic model is the same as the comparative static equilibrium solution, equation (10), found earlier.

Replacing algebraic constants with hypothetical numerical values, one can gain insight into the workings of this dynamic model: Equations (14) and (15) may be replaced with equations (14') and (15'), respectively:

$$C_t = 50 + 0.8\,Y_t \tag{14'}$$

$$I_t = 150 \tag{15'}$$

Equilibrium occurs in period t if: $Y_t = 1000$, $C_t = 850$, and $I_t = 150$. The reader may confirm that these values are equilibrium by computing Y_{t+1} from C_t and I_t, using equations (16) and (17): $Y_{t+1} = C_t + I_t$. All variables are constant over consecutive periods, and thus we have an equilibrium.

This model may now be used to examine dynamic reactions to an exogenous shock. Consider an increase in I of 50. Start at time period $t = 0$, in which income is equilibrium, $Y_0 = 1000$. Table 2 contains the disequilibrium sequence of events which follow an exogenous sustained[2] increase in I from 150 to 200. In period 1, aggregate demand increases by 50 over the period 0, equilibrium, level of demand. Y_1, however, remains at 1000, because period 1 production depends upon period 0 demand. In period 2 production will increase over that in period 1, because

$$Y_2 = AD_1$$

$$Y_2 = C_1 + I_1$$

$$Y_2 = 50 + 0.8\,Y_1 + 200$$

$$Y_2 = 50 + 0.8(1000) + 200 = 1050$$

Using $Y_2 = 1050$ from above, one can now compute C_2:

$$C_2 = 50 + 0.8\,Y_2$$

$$C_2 = 50 + 0.8(1050)$$

$$C_2 = 890$$

[2]The reader might wish to examine the sequence of events which follow a one-period increase in I of 50 followed by I's falling back to its original value of 150.

TABLE 2
Dynamic Model: Production Lag

VARIABLE	0	1	2	3	4	NEW EQUILIBRIUM
Y	1000	1000	1050	1090	1122 ...	1250
C	850	850	890	922	947.6 ...	1050
I	150	200	200	200	200 ...	200
$\Delta Y / \Delta I$*	—	0.0	1.0	1.8	2.44	5

*ΔI here is the original exogenous increase in I of 50.

Note that $C_2 + I_2 = 1090$, and this number is greater than production level 1050. The economy is clearly not in equilibrium. How can $C_2 + I_2$ be greater than production level Y_2? Y_2 represents the realized level of period 2 production: 1050. $C_2 + I_2$ represents the sum of *planned* demands by consumers and producers: 1090. The key to reconciling $C_2 + I_2 = 1090$ to $Y_2 = 1050$ is to realize that since actual period 2 production was 1050, investment plans were not realized. One way of explaining how the economy may work when these plans are not realized is to say that production is $C_2 + I_2 + IU_2$, where IU_2 is unplanned inventory changes in period 2. If plans call for 1090 of demand and if production is only 1050, then unplanned inventory changes are -40. In period 2 production equaled consumption plus realized investment, where *realized investment* is the sum of planned investment plus unplanned inventory change. The latter in general may be positive or negative.

Since production does not equal planned demand, period 2 is not equilibrium. $C_2 + I_2 > Y_2$. Therefore, period 3 production will exceed Y_2: $Y_3 = 1090$, and the economy will continue to move toward the new equilibrium depicted in the last column of Table 2. Several observations about this dynamic model are useful. First, the concept of multipliers must be reexamined. The multiplier developed earlier was a comparative static one:

$$k_I = \text{change in equilibrium income/change in investment}$$

The dynamic model illustrates that the full impact on income of an exogenous change is distributed over time. While the comparative static multiplier is 5, the change in Y four periods after a \$1 change in I is 2.44. One may not only wish to compare static multipliers, for various models, but also dynamic multipliers. The dynamic multiplier, after four elapsed periods, is

$$k_{I_4} \equiv \left(Y_4 - Y_0 \right) / (I_4 - I_0)$$

The speed with which the economic system adjusts to an exogenous change can now be seen to depend upon two factors: (1) the dynamic multiplier after a given number of periods has elapsed and (2) the length of each period. The bottom row of Table 1 contains the dynamic multipliers for respective periods. The length of each period would depend upon the time producers take to react to changes in demand. Of course, this model is extremely simple and little would be gained by trying to measure the lag.

At this point we must note that central to the income determination and multiplier analysis of a depression is the Keynesian consumption function. Thus, a central feature of Keynesian economics was his hypothesis about personal consumption expenditures. It is, consequently, quite important to study Keynes's consumption theories and to study actual consumption expenditures. However, as we shall see, the non-Keynesian economists of the modern day also place great importance on the nature of consumption behavior.

STUDY QUESTIONS AND PROBLEMS

1. a. Draw each of the following schedules:

   (1) $C = 50 + 0.75Y$
   (2) $I = 100$
   (3) $AD = C + I$
   (4) $S = -50 + 0.25Y$

   b. Locate in the diagrams above the equilibrium level of income. Explain why income level 200 is not equilibrium. Why not income level 1000? (*Hint:* Give an intuitive explanation of why, when $Y = 200$, or $Y = 1000$, the economy will not be at a point of rest.)

   c. Change the problem by setting $I = 200$. What is the new equilibrium level of income? How much has income changed? What are the new equilibrium levels of saving and consumption?

2. a. Solve, with algebra, for equilibrium income, consumption, and saving, given the following model:

   (1) $C = 200 + 0.9Y$
   (2) $I = 150$

   b. Suppose that, at each level of income, consumption fell by 100; i.e., $C = 100 + 0.9Y$. Calculate the new equilibrium level of income. Since C has fallen by 100 at each level of Y, S has increased by 100 at each level of Y. What has been the effect on equilibrium Y of the decision to save more at each level of Y?

   c. Consider the classical model of economic activity. Recall that savings and investment depended upon the rate of interest. Suppose that the economy is in equilibrium and, at each interest rate, people decide to save more. Compare the new equilibrium, after this shift in saving behavior, to the original equilibrium.

   d. Compare the economic effects of an increase in saving in the classical model to the effects of a similar increase in the Keynesian income-expenditure model.

3. Solve for the equilibrium levels of income, saving, and consumption in each of the following models:

a. $C = 200 + 0.8Y$
$I = 100$

b. $C = 200 + 0.8Y$
$I = 150$

c. $C = 0.8Y$
$I = 250$

d. $C = 14 + 0.7Y$
$I = 5$

e. $C = 0.95Y$
$I = 20$

f. $C = 50 + 0.95Y$
$I = 20$

4. For each model a-f in Question 3,
   a. Calculate the investment multiplier.
   b. Calculate, using multipliers, the new equilibrium income level when:
      (1) I doubles.
      (2) I decreases by 5.
      (3) Saving increases by 5 at each level of income.

5. a. Compute equilibrium income, saving, and investment:

$C = 250 + 0.75Y$

$I = 150$

b. If full employment income were $Y = 2000$, how much must I increase from 150 to bring about full employment income?

6. Explain intuitively the following lags in response to an exogenous shock to the economy: expenditure lag, production lag, earnings lag. Can you suggest qualitative (as opposed to quantitative) evidence that one might consider in estimating their respective lengths?

Is the close correlation of activist fiscal policy and strong expansion—which has brought our economy into the narrow band around full employment—a matter of accident or causation?

Walter Heller in Heller and Friedman (1969)

Prior to President Franklin D. Roosevelt's New Deal in the 1930s, nonmilitary economic activity of the U.S. federal government was very small, less than 1 percent of GNP. From the 1930s to the present, federal expenditures have played an increasingly important role in the economy. Since World War II, large increases in federal expenditures have been associated with the Cold War, the Arms Race, and the Great Society. In 1978, 7 percent of GNP consisted of federal expenditures and 35 percent of that was for nondefense purposes. Furthermore, federal budget outlays were 22 percent of GNP in 1978 with income security programs accounting for 7.2 percent and national defense 5.1 percent.[1] When government economic activity was small, changes in government fiscal actions had relatively minor effects on the pace of national economic activity. Today, however, the multibillion dollar government budget can have a substantial impact on GNP, employment, prices, and other aspects of the national economy.

In addition to influencing the economy through its expenditure policies, the federal government can alter the capabilities for private spending by its tax policies. A number of major changes in the tax laws have been implemented in recent years which have altered tax rates, relative tax burdens, and the level of taxation. The effects on private economic deci-

[1] 1979 *Economic Report of the President.*

The Theory of Fiscal Policy

sions and consequently on the level of economic activity have been substantial. In fact, in the 1960s and early 1970s major changes in federal tax revenues were legislated three times by Congress at the request of the executive branch in order to change the level of economic activity. In 1964 a major cut was instituted in the personal income tax. The purpose of the cut was to stimulate the economy. In 1968 a large tax increase was imposed on personal income to slow the economy. In 1975 tax rebates and investment tax credits were passed to stimulate the economy.

A number of other interventionist government actions were undertaken in the 1970s to influence the economy—the wage-price freeze, import surcharges, and price and wage controls. These non-traditional fiscal policy actions will be discussed independently in later chapters.

The purpose of this chapter is to examine the macroeconomic effects upon the level of income of government expenditures on goods and services, transfer payments, and taxes. The framework is the Keynesian income-expenditure approach developed in Chapter 5. Government fiscal action will be incorporated into the income-expenditure model in successively more complex versions. First, the only economic activity allowed the government is spending on goods and services. Specifically, in the first model, the government will not be allowed to tax. How, one might ask, can the government spend without collecting tax revenues?

The answer is that the government can borrow funds from the public. One must be cautious to note that government expenditures financed by borrowing will have two types of effects on spending: the government spending will have an effect and the borrowing will have an effect. The purpose here is to examine the government expenditure effect on income. The effect on private spending of government borrowing will be assumed to be negligible. The rationale for this assumption is based upon the assumption of unemployed resources. The funds borrowed by the government are assumed to have been idle. In other words, had the government not borrowed these funds, they would not have been used to carry on expenditures. In later chapters the details of government borrowing to carry on expenditures will be studied carefully.

The second version of the income-expenditure model in this chapter will include taxes and transfer payments. The primary source of revenue for government spending is taxation. The decision to tax is distinct from the decision to spend, and each process of government fiscal activity is treated separately. The actual nature of the taxation process in the U.S. is exceedingly complex. However, for purposes of understanding the macroeconomic effects of taxation, relatively simple tax functions are sufficient. Taxes are treated at first as if they were exogenous to the economic system.

The reasons for assuming that government expenditures, G, and taxes, T, are exogenous are somewhat different from the justifications for exogenous investment spending. While it is, of course, easier to model G and T as exogenous than to develop an endogenous equation, or system, to describe them, exogeneity is maintained to a large degree even in relatively complex models. Unlike consumption and investment, G and T are directly determined by public decisions. Public representatives, the executive and Congress, determine G and T within the political process. The purpose here is to evaluate the effects of G and T upon the economic system. Furthermore, alternative values of G and T will be shown to have different impacts upon the economy. One of the key factors considered by the executive in proposing budgetary policies is the macroeconomic effect on the economy. In short, G and T are viewed, here, as exogenous because they are viewed as *control variables*. One of the functions of economic advisers to the executive and Congress is to provide estimates of the effects on the economy of various tax and expenditure proposals, and for this purpose, G and T are control variables.

In fact, many elements of government expenditures are not controllable in the short run by government executive branch policy makers such as the CEA. Congress mandates many programs for continued growth, often in excess of inflation, and reductions in these programs require an act of Congress. For example, social security benefits are now indexed to the consumer price index so that benefits increase automatically. In the 1979 Economic Report to the President, the CEA noted that "existing legislation mandates continued real growth in some programs, such as health care and Social Security . . ." (p. 93). Such programs often include entitlement clauses in which any individual satisfying certain characteristics (age, race, job status, and so forth) is entitled to benefits. The costs of these programs grow automatically with the growth of entitled persons, and the executive branch must meet the commitments of these programs. In the fiscal 1981 budget (October 1980-September 1981) the executive estimated that 75 percent of the budget was uncontrollable by the executive.

Taxes, of course, are not purely exogenous either. Most sources of federal tax revenues are income based—personal income taxes, corporate income taxes, payroll taxes, sales taxes, excise taxes. All of these taxes fluctuate automatically with the level of economic activity. Tax revenues from each of these sources increase and decrease as income and production increase and decrease. In Chapter 7 the endogenous nature of taxes is examined.

A ● Government Expenditures

The only fiscal activity undertaken by the government in this model is the purchase of goods and services. Government spending is assumed to be exogenous. From the simple comparative static income expenditure model in Chapter 5. linear consumption and exogenous investment equations are reproduced:

$$C = C_0 + bY \tag{1}$$

$$I = I_0 \tag{2}$$

The equation for government spending is

$$G = G_0 \tag{3}$$

In the model in Chapter 5 the private sector was the sole source of demand for final goods and services: consumption expenditures and private domestic investment. In this model the government is a new source of demand because G consists of the total value of goods and services purchased by government. Aggregate demand is

$$AD = C + I + G \tag{4}$$

It is important to note that G does not comprise the federal government budget. Around half of the federal budget consists of outlays for which no goods and services are received by government in return. These federal outlays are transfer payments and are excluded from this version of the model.

Equilibrium requires that aggregate demand equal the final value of total production or income, thus the equilibrium condition is

$$Y = AD \tag{5}$$

Finally, saving is defined as the residual from income after consumption:

$$S \equiv Y - C \tag{6}$$

Equations (1)-(6) comprise the model.

Figure 1 depicts the aggregate demand curve and a 45-deg line. In this model the aggregate demand curve is the sum of the consumption line, exogenous investment and exogenous government spending. AD here differs from that in Chapter 5 only in that G has been added to $C + I$. In other words the old $C + I$ curve has been shifted upward by G_0. The slope remains b; the intercept is $C_0 + I_0 + G_0$.

Equilibrium income, $\overline{Y}$, is that level at which aggregate demand equals income. Of course, at the previous equilibrium level of income, Chapter 5, where G was zero, demand is greater than income because public demand G now has been added to private demand $C + I$.

Equations (1)-(6) can be solved for the equilibrium level of income. First, replace AD in (5) with (4):

$$Y = C + I + G \tag{7}$$

Next replace C, I, and G with their respective equations:

$$Y = C_0 + bY + I_0 + G_0 \tag{8}$$

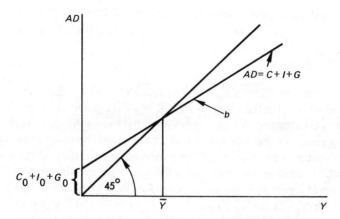

FIGURE 1   Income Determination—Government Spending Model

Solve (8) for $\overline{Y}$:

$$\overline{Y} = \frac{C_0 + I_0 + G_0}{1 - b} \tag{9}$$

The symbol $\overline{Y}$ replaces Y because $\overline{Y}$ represents the numerical (algebraic) value of Y at equilibrium.

The Government Multiplier: The government expenditure multiplier is the ratio of the change in equilibrium income over a change in government spending. Suppose equilibrium income $\overline{Y} = Y(1)$ when $G = G_1$. If government expenditure increases to G_2, the new equilibrium income $Y(2)$ would be

$$Y(2) = \frac{C_0 + I_0 + G_2}{1 - b} \tag{10}$$

The change in equilibrium income is $Y(2) - Y(1) \equiv \Delta Y$. Solve for ΔY:

$$\Delta Y = Y(2) - Y(1) = \left(\frac{C_0 + I_0 + G_2}{1 - b} \right) - \left(\frac{C_0 + I_0 + G_1}{1 - b} \right) \tag{11}$$

$$\Delta Y = \frac{G_2}{1 - b} - \frac{G_1}{1 - b} \tag{12}$$

$$\Delta Y = \frac{1}{1 - b} (G_2 - G_1) \tag{13}$$

$G_2 - G_1$ is the change in government spending ΔG. Divide (13) by ΔG:

$$\frac{\Delta Y}{\Delta G} = \frac{1}{1-b} \tag{14}$$

The government multiplier, k_g or $\Delta Y/\Delta G$, is $1/(1-b)$. k_g, the government multiplier, depends upon the *MPC*. In fact, $k_g = k_I$, the government and investment multipliers are identical. We must stress here that the multiplier formulae depend upon the nature of the model and that as the models become increasingly complex the multiplier expressions will change. Nevertheless, the multiplier formulae here, such as equation (14), do capture the spirit of multiplier analysis.

The similarity of an increase in I and G in their effect upon income is illustrated in Figure 2. The shift from AD to AD' of $100 could have occurred either from an exogenous $100 increase in federal government spending or an increase of $100 in private domestic investment expenditures. Thus any injection of new demand, public or private, will result in a multiple increase in equilibrium income. Keynes, in a somewhat humorous vein, made this point most effectively:

> If the Treasury were to fill old bottles with banknotes, bury them at suitable depths in disused coalmines which are then filled up to the surface with town rubbish, and leave it to private enterprise on well-tried principles of *laissez-faire* to dig the notes up again (the right to do so being obtained, of course, by tendering for leases of the note-bearing territory), there need be no more unemployment and, with the help of the repercussions, the real income of the community, and its capital wealth also, would probably become a good deal greater than it actually is. It would, indeed, be more sensible to build houses and the like; but if there are political and practical difficulties in the way of this, the above would be better than nothing.   *The General Theory*

B • Taxes and Transfers

One of the few unavoidable realities of modern living is that we must pay taxes. Let us introduce this rather unpleasant aspect of federal fiscal action into the income-expenditure model. *Taxation* consists simply of the extraction of income from the private sector. *Transfer payments* are the negative of taxes as transfers are the issuance of income to the private sector.

Federal government transfer payments have become a very large and important element of our economy. In 1978 these payments totalled $185.4 billion, or 40 percent of the government budget. This compares to $1.5 billion in 1930 and 22 percent of the federal budget. Furthermore, the federal budget was small relative to the economy in 1930 compared to today: 3.6 percent of GNP vs. 22 percent of GNP in 1978.

The New Model: A distinction must be made between income which is earned in production and, therefore, corresponds to the level of output, and income

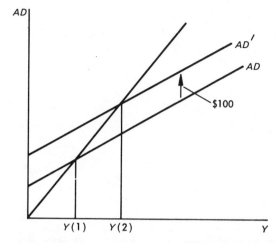

FIGURE 2   *AD* Shift: $100 Increase in Exogenous Expenditures

which is received and retained by persons for their own use. The symbol Y will continue to represent earned income. Y_d, disposable income, will consist of earned income minus taxes plus transfer payments. Consequently,

$$Y_d = Y - T_x + T_r \tag{15}$$

where T_x and T_r are taxes and transfers, respectively.

The conceptual difference between G and T_r is important. The total government budget consists of the sum of G and T_r. G is government expenditure on goods and services and is a component of aggregate demand along with C and I. T_r, on the other hand, is a government outlay for which no products or services are exchanged. T_r is not a component of demand. In the case of G, production occurs to generate the goods and services purchased by the government. In the case of T_r, no production occurs because the government does not receive any goods or services in exchange for the transfers. T_r will result in direct additions to persons' incomes, and those individuals may well increase their expenditures, but such increases appear in the C component of demand.

T_x is a government extraction of income and is not a component of aggregate demand. Like T_r, T_x alters income received by persons. If T_x increases, disposable income will decrease. Since C depends upon disposable income, C will be indirectly influenced by T_x and T_r.

The model, including exogenous taxes and transfers, consists of nine equations:

$$C = C_0 + bY_d \tag{16}$$

$$Y_d = Y - T_x + T_r \tag{17}$$

$$I = I_0 \tag{18}$$

$$G = G_0 \tag{19}$$

$$T_x = T_{x_0} \tag{20}$$

$$T_r = T_{r_0} \tag{21}$$

$$AD = C + I + G \tag{22}$$

$$Y = AD \tag{23}$$

$$S \equiv Y_d - C \tag{24}$$

The several distinctive features of this model compared to previous models must be emphasized. First, in (16) consumption depends upon disposable income, not upon total income. The reason for this consumption equation is that it is only the after-tax income over which persons have discretion between consumption and saving. Second, taxes and transfers are exogenous, (20)-(21). Aggregate demand, equation (22), is unchanged. Aggregate demand is the sum of demand by consumers, businesses, and government. Third, the definition of saving differs in this model from that in previous ones. In (24) saving is the residual from disposable income after consumption. This last point is important and often confused.

The nine equations, (16)-(24), may now be solved for the nine unknowns: $C, I, G, T_x, T_r, S, AD, Y_d$, and Y. As in solving the previous models, start with the equilibrium condition, equation (23). Replace AD by equation (22):

$$Y = C + I + G \tag{25}$$

Next, replace C, I, and G with their equations:

$$Y = C_0 + bY_d + I_0 + G_0 \tag{26}$$

Replace Y_d, disposable income, by its value in equation (17):

$$Y = C_0 + b(Y - T_x + T_r) + I_0 + G_0 \tag{27}$$

T_x and T_r are given by equations (20) and (21), respectively:

$$Y = C_0 + b(Y - T_{x_0} + T_{r_0}) + I_0 + G_0 \tag{28}$$

Equation (28) contains one unknown variable, Y. The equilibrium level of income is that value of Y, $\overline{Y}$, which is the solution to (28):

$$\overline{Y} = \frac{C_0 - b(T_{x_0} - T_{r_0}) + I_0 + G_0}{1 - b} \tag{29}$$

$\overline{Y}$ is the equilibrium level of income in this model. The geometric solution to $\overline{Y}$ corresponding to the above algebraic solution requires that the consumption line be adjusted to allow for the dependence of C upon disposable income rather than total income. First, disposable income is replaced in the consumption equation (16) with its value in equation (17):

$$C = C_0 + b(Y - T_x + T_r) \tag{30}$$

Since both transfers and taxes are exogenous, consumption only varies with income:

$$C = C_0 - b(T_{x_0} - T_{r_0}) + bY \tag{31}$$

Equation (31) illustrates that taxes and transfers change the intercept of the consumption line but not the slope. T_x shifts the intercept down; T_r shifts it up. Equation (31) states that an increase of \$1 in taxes will reduce C by \$$b$. Since the MPC is less than one, consumption will decline by less than \$1 when taxes increase by \$1. The remainder of the increase in taxes, $(1 - b)$, will come out of saving. Thus, in general, a \$1 increase in taxes is paid by reducing consumption by \$$b$ and saving by \$$(1 - b)$. A transfer payment is a negative tax, so that an increase in transfers of \$1 increases C by \$$b$ and S by \$$(1 - b)$.

Figure 3 depicts the consumption function, equation (31). $T = T_x - T_r$ is taxes minus transfers or net taxes. The consumption line is shifted downward by MPC times net taxes. Exogenous investment and government expenditures may be added to the consumption function by merely shifting the C line upward by $I_0 + G_0$ to obtain aggregate demand. AD is in Figure 4. The intercept of the AD curve is $C_0 - bT_0 + I_0 + G_0$ and the slope is b. The equilibrium level of income, $\overline{Y}$, is at the intersection of the AD curve and the 45-deg line.

Having solved for $\overline{Y}$ with algebra and geometry, we can compute the other unknowns easily. For example, solutions for equilibrium disposable income, $\overline{Y}_d$, and consumption, $\overline{C}$, are

$$\overline{Y}_d = \overline{Y} - T_0 \tag{32}$$

$$\overline{C} = C_0 + b\overline{Y}_d \tag{33}$$

T_0 is simply T_{x_0} minus T_{r_0}, and equation (32) follows from (17) and $\overline{Y}$.

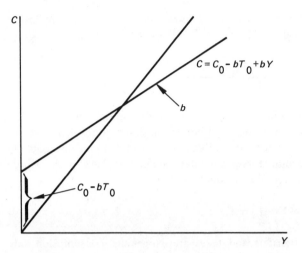

FIGURE 3   Consumption: Taxes and Transfers Exogenous

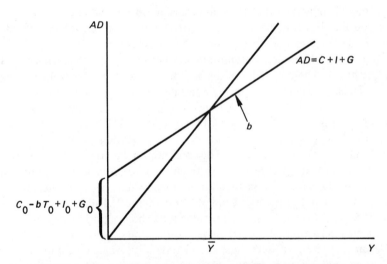

FIGURE 4   Income Determination—Government and Net Taxes Model

Multipliers: Of course, the most interesting questions about government fiscal actions and the macroeconomy relate to the effect on equilibrium income of changes in government fiscal policies, spending, transfers, and taxes. These questions can be dealt with by utilizing multipliers. First, consider taxes by rewriting the equilibrium income solution, equation (29), so that taxes are isolated from the other variables:

$$\overline{Y} = \frac{C_0 + bT_{r_0} + I_0 + G_0}{1 - b} + \frac{-b}{1 - b}T_x \qquad (34)$$

$\overline{Y}$ is written as a linear function of taxes with a slope $-b/(1 - b)$. The tax multiplier for this model, k_{T_x} or $\Delta Y / \Delta T_x$, is the slope:

$$k_{T_x} = \frac{-b}{1 - b} \qquad (35)$$

The transfer and government expenditure multipliers for this model are clearly:

$$k_{T_r} = \frac{b}{1 - b} \qquad (36)$$

$$k_g = \frac{1}{1 - b} \qquad (37)$$

The tax, transfer, and government multipliers may now be compared. The tax multiplier is negative, indicating that an increase in taxes will reduce income. From Figure 3 one can readily see that an increase in taxes will shift the consumption line downwards. Consequently, the aggregate demand curve will fall and equilibrium income will fall. Thus the negative sign for the tax multiplier is not unexpected. However, the magnitude of the tax multiplier, as opposed to the sign, is not immediately obvious. The tax multiplier is, in magnitude, smaller than the government multiplier:

$$k_{T_x} = \frac{-b}{1 - b} = -b\frac{1}{1 - b} = -bk_g$$

Ignoring the sign, we see that k_{T_x} is equal to k_g times MPC, and since $MPC < 1$, $k_{T_x} < k_g$. For example, if $b = 0.9$, $k_g = 10$, and $k_{T_x} = -9$. An increase of government expenditures of $1 billion, if $b = 0.9$, will induce an increase in equilibrium income of $10 billion. A decrease in taxes of $1 billion will also increase income, but by $9 billion.

Transfer payments are, in the model, the equivalent of a negative tax. An increase in transfers increases equilibrium income, but the transfer multiplier is smaller than that for government expenditures.

Perhaps the difference between k_{T_r} and k_g can be explained intuitively. Consider two government fiscal actions, one a transfer payment and one a government expenditure. The transfer may consist of a $100 payment in social security benefits to an aged person. The government expenditure may be a Labor Department purchase of a $100 typewriter. Both fiscal actions are government budget outlays. Both also increase someone's disposable income. The transfer increases the old person's income, and the expenditure increases income of typewriter producers, owners, and workers. In both cases, because disposable income is increasing, consumption expenditures could be expected to rise. Consumption rises because income has increased. The rise in consumption, in each case, will induce a subsequent increase in consumption, and so on. The chain of reactions in disposable income and consumption will be the same in both cases. However, the outcome will differ because of the different effects of transfers and expenditures on goods and services on aggregate demand and production.

In the case of the typewriter purchase, aggregate demand, and therefore production, has increased by $100, because $100 is the new demand by government for typewriters. In the transfer case, however, an individual's income has been increased by $100, but not in exchange for a good or service. The government has not increased demand, in this case, by $100. After incomes have increased by $100, the transfer and government expenditure allocations have similar effects. It is just the initial effect that differs. Thus,

$$k_{T_r} = k_g - 1$$

The transfer multiplier equals the government multiplier minus the initial increase in production equal to the change in government outlays. k_g can be replaced by its formula:

$$k_{T_r} = \frac{1}{1-b} - 1$$

Therefore;

$$k_{T_r} = \frac{1}{1-b} - \frac{1-b}{1-b}$$

Collecting terms yields:

$$k_{T_r} = \frac{1-1+b}{1-b} = \frac{b}{1-b} = bk_g$$

Thus, the transfer multiplier is b times k_g.

The simple analysis above indicates that government fiscal decisions have an impact on the equilibrium level of income. $\overline{Y}$ can be increased by an increase in government spending, an increase in transfers, or a decrease in taxes. Given the MPC, one can compute, from an income-expenditure model, the various fiscal multipliers. *Fiscal policy* consists of setting government expenditures, transfers, and taxes so as to determine the level of economic activity. With the use of the income-expenditure model, one can estimate the impact on $\overline{Y}$ of various tax, transfer, and expenditure programs, provided, of course, the model is a suitable description of the economy. The model presents a method of predicting the direction of the effect on $\overline{Y}$ and the magnitude of the effect on $\overline{Y}$ of various fiscal measures. The model does not indicate the speed with which multiplier effects of fiscal actions occur.

A Balanced Budget Multiplier: The above analysis considers tax and government expenditure actions to be taken independently, and, indeed, a good deal of evidence suggests that revenue and expenditure levels do not strictly coincide. Nevertheless, an interesting fiscal policy problem is to determine the effect upon $\overline{Y}$ of an increase in G financed by an equal increase in T_x. The ratio of the change in $\overline{Y}$ to a change in the budget, k_B, is the balanced budget multiplier. The problem, then, is: What is k_B when $\Delta G = \Delta T_x \equiv \Delta B$? $\Delta \overline{Y}$ will be the sum of the effect upon $\overline{Y}$ of ΔG and that of ΔT. The effect of ΔG is, if the multiplier is utilized,

$$\Delta \overline{Y}_{\Delta T=0} = k_g \ \Delta G$$

The joint effect on $\overline{Y}$ of ΔG and ΔT, if the multiplier is utilized, is

$$\Delta \overline{Y} = k_g \Delta G + k_{T_x} \Delta T_x \tag{38}$$

where

$$k_g = \frac{1}{1-b} \quad \text{and} \quad k_{T_x} = \frac{-b}{1-b}$$

Replacing both ΔG and ΔT_x with ΔB, we find that equation (38) may be written as:

$$\Delta \overline{Y} = \frac{1}{1-b} \Delta B + \frac{-b}{1-b} \Delta B$$

$$\Delta \overline{Y} = \frac{1-b}{1-b} \Delta B = \Delta B \tag{39}$$

$$\frac{\Delta \overline{Y}}{\Delta B} = 1$$

k_B, in this simple income-expenditure model, is one. An increase on G financed by new tax revenue will increase $\overline{Y}$ by the size of change in the budget.

Conclusion: Though the income-expenditure models employed in this chapter are relatively simple, they do suggest that government fiscal decisions can have a substantial impact on the economy. Whether intended or not, large changes in government expenditures and changes in transfers and taxes can alter the course of the economy. Government can add stimulus or mandate restraint. A controversial issue of political economy is whether fiscal policy should be actively used to direct the economy. The debate has often involved a blend of positive economics and normative judgments.

Those who reject active discretionary policy seem to do so on two grounds: It does not work, and it should not be used. The first set of arguments are clearly positive statements about fiscal policy. They include the following: (1) Economists do not understand the economy well enough to tinker with it. (2) Fiscal policy is slow to influence the economy, and the effects of actions are likely to occur at unexpected and undesired times. (3) Government leaders are not responsible enough to tinker with the budget. They should always attempt to balance it. (4) Fiscal policy which calls for tax cuts and expenditure increases, that is, deficits, are always easier than tighter budgets. Consequently, fiscal policy always has a built-in bias toward overexpansion. The normative arguments against discretionary policy are usually some variation on the theme that government economic activity is bad. Either the government is interfering with private activity, is inefficient and wastefully using resources, or is undertaking unneeded activities.

Fiscal activists support their beliefs by a corresponding set of subjective and objective arguments. On the positive side, they claim: (1) Discretionary policy is effective, and as it is employed economists learn more about the economy and fiscal policy itself. (2) While fiscal policy operates with lags, they are short enough to warrant stimulative policies to offset major recessions and contractionary measures to stem inflationary booms. (3) If government leaders prove irresponsible, they will not be maintained in office. The electoral process allows for public evaluation of the budgetary decisions of leaders. (4) Activist fiscal policies can be applied in both expansionary and contractionary directions. It is the task of political leaders to implement responsible programs even if they may seem unpopular. Fiscal activists also rely upon normative arguments. For example, public programs are usually starved. Programs for dealing with poverty, health care, education, rapid transit, environmental pollution, and so on, are not adequately handled by the private sector and require government economic activity.

Several observations may be made about the fiscalist debate. Issues may be organized into three categories: (1) normative statements about the role of government in a mixed industrial society; (2) philosophical judgments about the use to which limited knowledge of fiscal policy should be put; and (3) positive statements about how fiscal policy actions influence the economy. The first type of statement can, and probably will, be argued for the rest of time. The choice of public-private mix is an open and complex issue. The only point one may wish to make here is that fiscal policy is flexible enough so that a given stimulus can be instituted either by increasing government activity or decreasing tax activity. Such a choice would depend, presumably, on these normative issues.

Philosophical judgments about the appropriate use of fiscal policy, given limited information, should be recognized for what they are. When either Milton Friedman or Allan Greenspan argues against fiscal policy because our knowledge of the economy is limited, their views, in part, reflect a conservative political philosophy. Each individual must decide about his position of philosophy. When Walter Heller or Charles Schultze favors trying fiscal policy on the basis of the best guess, the opinion surely reflects a liberal leaning.

The positive statements about the workings of fiscal policy are those to which we address ourselves here. How does fiscal policy work? How much time must elapse before its effects are felt? The pursuit of such questions will continue in Chapter 7. Let us stress here that whether one leans toward fiscal activism or not, fiscal decisions are made—tax reforms, new programs, defense budget cuts, new transfer systems—which do have an impact on the economy. The objective of positive economics is to understand them.

We note that empirical estimates of fiscal multipliers for the U.S. economy suggest that they are around 1.5 to 2.5. Edward Gramlich in 1971, for example, reported estimates based upon five macroeconometric models. The consensus judgment was around +2.7 for government expenditures and around −1.7 for taxation. The primary reason that these multipliers are small, relative to MPC values of around 0.9, is the presence in the U.S. economy of a great many large built-in automatic stabilizers, such as Social Security payments and taxes, unemployment compensation, other income support programs, federal grants-in-aid, and the like. Automatic stabilizers tend to cushion the economy by serving as buffers to personal disposable income fluctuations. These built-in fiscal measures will be analyzed in the next chapter.

STUDY QUESTIONS AND PROBLEMS

1. Consider the following model of an economy:

$C = 50 + 0.85 \ Y_d$

$I = 120$

$G = 40$

 a. If taxes are 20 and transfers zero, what is the equilibrium level of income?
 b. If the government wishes to lower income to 1100, how much must it alter government expenditures? Transfers? Taxes?
 c. If government increases spending by 40 and finances half the increase by taxes, how much will income change?

2. Compute Y, C, and S for each of the following problems:

 a. $C = 100 + 0.8 \ Y_d$ b. $C = 2000 + 0.9 \ Y_d$
   $I = 50$ $I = 40$
   $G = 100$ $G = 200$
   $T = 50$ $T = 150$

   c. $C = 40 + 0.85\ Y_d$
     $I = 50$
     $G = 20$
     $T = 20$

3. What are the investment, government, and tax multipliers for Problems 2a, b, and c above?

4. In each part of Problem 2 above, calculate the effect on $\overline{Y}$ of:

  a. Balancing the budget without changing G.
  b. Balancing the budget without changing T.
  c. Increasing each budget by 50 without changing the deficit.

5. The economy is in the second quarter of continued slowdown in rate of growth of GNP. What issues would fiscal activists and fiscal conservatives debate?

6. Consider the following economic model:

$C = 220 + 0.75\ Y_d$

$I = 80$

$G = 50$

$T = 40$

  a. Compute $\overline{Y}, \overline{Y_d}, \overline{C},$ and $\overline{S}.$

  b. Suppose that full employment income is 2500. What fiscal action can the government undertake under the following constraints?

    (1) Only G can be increased.
    (2) Only transfers can be increased.
    (3) The budget must be balanced.
    (4) The deficit must neither increase nor decrease.

7. "Transfer payments have never played an important role in the U.S. economy." Discuss.

8. "In fact, the multiplier for fiscal actions by the federal government is around 10 to 15." True or false? Explain.

REFERENCES

Economic Report of the President, Washington, D.C., January, 1979.

Heller, Walter W. and Milton Friedman, *Monetary vs. Fiscal Policy: A Dialogue.* New York: W. W. Norton, 1969.

Macrae, Norman, *The Neurotic Trillionaire.* New York: Harcourt, Brace & World, 1970.

Okun, Arthur M., *The Politicial Economy of Prosperity.* New York: W. W. Norton, 1970.

Okun, Arthur M., and George L. Perry, *Brookings Papers on Economic Activity*, select issues, 1969-1973. Washington, D.C.: Brookings Institution.

Peckman, Joseph A., *Federal Tax Policy*, revised, New York: W. W. Norton, 1971.

Shultze, Charles L., Edward R. Fried, Alice M. Rivlin, and Nancy H. Teeters, *Setting National Priorities, the 1973 Budget*. Washington, D.C.: Brookings Institution, 1972.

One can compile a long list of discretionary policy actions during the postwar era that helped to stabilize the economy—the tight fiscal policy of the late forties, the accord of fiscal-monetary policy in 1951, the tax increases of 1950-51, the decision to allow taxes to be reduced in 1954, the antirecession fiscal and monetary program of 1958, the Kennedy recovery program in 1961, the series of tax cuts and the supportive monetary policy in 1962-65, and the variety of restraining actions taken during the Vietnam period.

Arthur Okun (1969)

And then I went on, "Political pressures to 'do something' in the face of either relatively mild price rises or relatively mild price and employment declines are clearly very strong indeed in the existing state of public attitudes. The main moral to be drawn . . . is that yielding to these pressures may frequently do more harm than good. There is a saying that the best is often the enemy of the good, which seems highly relevant."

Milton Friedman in Heller and Friedman (1969)

The policy thrust of Chapter 6 is clear—if the economy is in a recession, increases in government spending, decreases in taxes, and increases in transfers could all be employed to stimulate the economy. One must be cautious, of course, in drawing real world policy implications from an abstract model. The particular models considered above only indicate the direction of fiscal action effects upon income and the comparative static

7

Discretionary Fiscal Policy Versus Automatic Stabilizers

size of the multipliers. The comparative static model does not provide information about the speed with which fiscal policy might be expected to operate on the economy. The issue of the speed of fiscal policy effects is not a simply a refinement of a generally accepted technique. Rather, the speed of fiscal policy is a crucial issue bearing on its use as a stablizing device.

Suppose the economy is thought of as a system of relatively stable relations which is subject to random shocks from time to time. These shocks might be exogenous fluctuations in investment spending, changes in savings rates, shifts in technology, and so on. Because it is subject to shocks, the economy fluctuates. At times it may be in recession, at times boom. Given this interpretation of economic activity, one may well support the use of countercyclical fiscal policies to stabilize the economy. If, however, the lags between a random shock which warrants new countercyclical fiscal action and the actual impacts of such actions are long, then the policies designed to stabilize the economy may well be destabilizing.

Lags in Fiscal Policy: The lags between the need for an action and the effects on the economy of the resultant action may be studied with a variety of methods. Perhaps the logical place to start is to discuss the practical nature of fiscal policy actions. Let us consider, in general, the chain of events which might follow a random shock to the economy through to the effects of fiscal policy actions. Each phase of events will involve a lag. The first problem confronted by a policy maker is in recognizing the need for an action—the *recognition lag*. Suppose the policy maker bases decisions on the level of income. The process of collection, refinement, and synthesis of income data usually requires at least three months before the policy maker can observe income. If the shock gradually affects income, three months may not be enough time. The policy maker may have to delay his decisions until he is convinced that the problem is not transitory. Policy makers do have available to them a number of tools to help them anticipate problems without waiting for data. For example, economic theory assists the policy maker in anticipating the effects upon income of major shocks. He need not wait for three months to confim that income will fall. Models, such as the income-expenditure models, are tools for anticipating the need for a change in fiscal policies.

Once a problem has been recognized, policy makers must decide upon a course of action—the *decision lag*. This lag could be of varying lengths depending upon the political circumstances. If a broad political consensus is reached quickly about the nature and scope of the problem, decisions may be made rather quickly. In the U.S., however, the decision lag can be very long, and, to the economists involved, somewhat frustrating. In early 1966, the Council of Economic Advisors recognized the need to begin slowing the economy down with contractionary fiscal policies. It was necessary first to convince the President that a tax increase or a spending cut was required. A spending cut was out of the question, because the war on poverty and the war in Vietnam were in full flower. The C.E.A. suggested a tax increase. The President, for political considerations, was unable to recommend a tax increase to Congress. Finally, in 1967, President Johnson decided, late in the year, to urge a tax increase to Congress. The decision lag already absorbing 1966 and 1967 was not completed. It was not until the summer of 1968 that Congress passed a tax surcharge. In this example, the decision lag absorbed about three years. Perhaps this episode is an extreme example, but the decision lag for fiscal policy requires a professional economic judgment, a Presidential decision, and a Congressional decision.

Though one may be tempted to conclude that the U.S. political system is hopelessly inefficient for dealing with economic stabilization, the President and the Congress are *elected*, and as such it is their responsibility to carry out the public mandate and also to determine fiscal policy. It is the job of economists to recommend courses of action consistent with sound economics, but not, of course, to dictate decisions to elected officials.

After the government has decided on a course of action, the action must be taken—the *action lag*. How long does it take for an action once passed to be implemented? A decision to reduce the personal income tax will result in lower withholding as soon as the tax change is implemented. A decision to increase government expenditures will often take some time. One of the major political proposals of Keynesian economics for dealing with the Great Depression was to utilize public works. New public works programs would increase government spending and therefore income by a multiple amount, reduce unemployment, and create public projects which are of social value. These public works would appear to be excellent stabilization devices. However, even after they are legislated, rather long lags are necessary for their implementation. Some researchers have concluded that the action lag could be as long as a year for public works.

The recognition, decision and action lags comprise the *inside lag* of fiscal policy actions. At the completion of the inside lag, the flow of government expenditures, transfers, or taxes is occurring. The *outside lag* deals with the length of time required once the fiscal action has occurred, the tax cut, expenditure increase, etc., for the economy to respond. The outside lag may also be decomposed into several parts: the *expenditure lag*, the *production lag*, and the *earnings lag*. These three lags were discussed in Chapter 5. Here let us simply note that the expenditure and earnings lags are likely to depend upon patterns of shopping, payments of factor inputs, and the like. These elements can be expected to be comparatively small and stable. The large outside lag is in the delay between an increase in demand and an increase in production—the production lag.

A natural question of fiscal policy is: Can these lags be reduced? The lags can be greatly reduced in several ways. First, the recognition lag can be reduced by improved economic policy tools. Better models, improved forecasts, and so on can reduce the recognition lag. Second, the decision lag can be reduced by changing the political budgetary decision process. For example, it has been suggested that the President be given budgetary leeway to, within limits, increase or decrease expenditures or taxes. Alternatively, Congress could introduce a certain range of expenditures to be implemented on the basis of the state of the economy. Of course, these types of changes in federal decision making should be considered with caution, because the ramifications exceed the economic arena. Third, stand-by programs can be legislated to be undertaken only after a vote of the Congress. Some of these devices have been suggested by many economists, and some have been enacted. However, the major method of shortening the lags is the method of built-in automatic stabilizers.

The increased importance of automatic stabilizers to the U.S. economy can be seen by studying transfer payments in the national income accounts. During the Great Depression transfers were unimportant. In 1930, transfers were only 1.3 percent of national income, so when national income fell, transfers were barely large enough to hold personal income up. (In 1930 national income was $75.7 billion and personal income $76.9 billion.) Even after Roosevelt became president, transfers were small—3.2 percent of national income in 1935.

When President Ford engineered the 1974 "made in Washington" recession to combat oil price increases and inflation, transfers played a major role. The slowdown in the economy was reflected by the slowdown in real GNP from 1973 of $1235.0 billion to $1217.8 in 1974 and $1202.3 in 1975, a total reduction of $32.7 billion. In 1976 real GNP increased $68.7 billion. The compressing effect of the recession on personal incomes was buffered, however, by a huge system of built-in federal transfer payments. Transfer payments, which by 1965 had become 6.6 percent of national income, were 11.9 percent of national income in 1974, 14 percent in 1975, 13.5 percent in 1976. When the economy is in a slump, personal income tends to rise *relative* to national income because taxes automatically fall and because transfers automatically rise. As a result of the 1974-75 recession, personal income rose above national income and stayed there through 1978. Consequently, while national income, a measure of the factor earnings, fell, personal income, which persons receive (before personal income taxes), rose above it. This continued through 1978, even though the recession technically ended in 1976.

Automatic Stabilizers: The essential nature of automatic stabilizers can be understood with the aid of a simple elaboration on the previous model. Taxes, and transfers, can be written as functions of income. Let $T = T_x - T_r$, net taxes. The new income-expenditure model is

$$C = C_0 + bY_d \tag{1}$$

$$Y_d = Y - T \tag{2}$$

$$I = I_0 \tag{3}$$

$$G = G_0 \tag{4}$$

$$T = T_0 + tY \tag{5}$$

$$AD = C + I + G \tag{6}$$

$$Y = AD \tag{7}$$

$$S \equiv Y_d - C \tag{8}$$

This model differs from the previous one only in that net taxes are endogenous. From equation (5), T_0 is the exogenous component of taxes and t is the constant marginal rate at which taxes increase with income. Equation (5) should not be confused with a progressive income tax, because the change in taxes is a constant fraction of a change in income. Under a progressive tax system, the marginal tax rate increases as income increases.

The effect of endogenous net taxes on the economy can be illustrated by comparing consumption with endogenous taxes to consumption without endogenous taxes. Starting with the consumption function (1), replace Y_d by equation (2) and T by equation (5):

$$C = C_0 + b(Y - T_0 - tY) \tag{9}$$

or

$$C = C_0 - bT_0 + b(1 - t)Y \tag{10}$$

Equation (10) illustrates that net taxes change both the intercept and the slope of the consumption function. The exogenous component of net taxes, T_0, shifts the consumption line down by $-bT_0$, and the endogenous component of net taxes, $-tY$, reduces the slope from b to $b(1 - t)$. The effect of net taxes upon consumption is depicted in Figure 1. Clearly, the slope of the consumption line is reduced by the endogenous tax function, and since the fiscal multipliers depend upon the slope of the consumption function, endogenous taxes will reduce the multipliers. This result may be confirmed by solving for equilibrium income and calculating multipliers.

The first step in solving for equilibrium income is to set income equal to aggregate demand. From equations (6) and (7):

$$Y = C + I + G \tag{11}$$

C, I, and G are next replaced by the consumption function, equation (10), and I_0 and G_0 respectively:

$$Y = C_0 - bT_0 + b(1 - t)Y + I_0 + G_0 \tag{12}$$

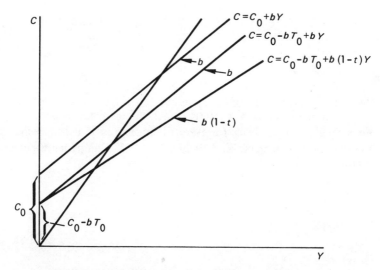

FIGURE 1   Consumption with Endogenous Taxes

Equation (12) contains one unknown Y and may be solved for the equilibrium level of income $\overline{Y}$:

$$\overline{Y} = \frac{C_0 - bT_0 + I_0 + G_0}{1 - b(1 - t)} \tag{13}$$

$\overline{Y}$ is the equilibrium level of income for the model [equations (1)-(8)]. Given $\overline{Y}$, other unknowns in the model may be determined. For example, net taxes:

$$\overline{T} = T_0 + t\overline{Y}$$

The multipliers for each exogenous component may now be calculated by expressing $\overline{Y}$, from (13), as a linear function of the given exogenous component. The investment, government expenditure, and net tax multipliers are

$$k_I = \frac{1}{1 - b(1 - t)} \qquad k_T = \frac{-b}{1 - b(1 - t)}$$

$$k_g = \frac{1}{1 - b(1 - t)} \qquad k_T = k_{T_x} = -k_{T_r} \tag{14}$$

Each of the multipliers above may be compared to its counterpart in the more primitive model without endogenous taxes. Consider the government expenditure multiplier:

NET TAXES EXOGENOUS   NET TAXES ENDOGENOUS

$$k_g = \frac{1}{1-b} \qquad\qquad k_g = \frac{1}{1 - b(1-t)} \qquad\qquad (15)$$

The marginal propensity to consume out of Y is b if taxes do not fluctuate with income. If the marginal tax rate is t, then the marginal propensity to consume out of Y is $b(1-t)$. Thus, for every \$1 increase in Y, net taxes increase by \$$t$, thus the induced increase in C is b of $(1-t)Y$. Comparing the denominators of (15), we have

$$b(1-t) \quad < b$$

$$1 - b(1-t) > 1 - b$$

Therefore,

$$\frac{1}{1 - b(1-t)} < \frac{1}{1-b}$$

Mathematically, it has been shown that the multipliers are smaller with endogenous net taxes than without them. The reader may wish to compare the impact on $\overline{Y}$ of an exogenous change in net taxes under the two different models to confirm that endogenous net taxes which fluctuate positively with income reduce the multipliers.

An *automatic stabilizer* may now be defined as an endogenous variable which reduces the size of the multipliers. Recall the policy implications of the multiplier analysis above—fiscal policy could be employed to dampen booms and stimulate the economy in recession. However, it was argued above that discretionary fiscal policy might take quite some time to be effective. In particular, the recognition, decision, and action lags could be long. The model containing endogenous net taxes illustrates a method of eliminating the entire inside lag of fiscal policy. If some fiscal actions by government are built in to fluctuate automatically with the pace of the economy, one need not wait for lengthy recognition, decision, and action lags to occur. The federal fiscal apparatus can respond automatically to fluctuations in the economy.

In fact, the U.S. federal budget contains a number of mechanisms which automatically help to stabilize the economy: progressive income taxes, excise taxes, property taxes, corporate profits taxes, all fluctuate with income. In addition, unemployment insurance, social security payments, and other transfers fluctuate inversely with income, so that in a recession federal taxes fall off automatically while transfers increase automatically. Note once again that the marginal tax rate is a constant in the model, which rules out a progressive income tax. Under a progressive income tax regime, upswings in economic activity are accompanied by even greater tax increases than would be the case under a constant marginal tax rate.

Automatic stabilizers dampen wide fluctuations in economic activity, automatically stabilizing the economy, and avoid the inside lag of discretionary fiscal policy. They would seem to be an ideal method of employing fiscal policy. However, automatic stabilizers are not without difficulties. First, suppose that despite automatic stabilizers the economy is following an undesired path—say the economy is heading for a recession. Discretionary fiscal policy is called for. However, automatic stabilizers reduce the multipliers. Consequently, the automatic stabilizers vitiate the impact of discretionary fiscal policy. One's views on the relative value of discretionary fiscal policy and built-in mechanisms depend in part upon one's attitude toward the economic sense of elected officials and upon one's view of how well fiscal advisers understand the economy. Some economists prefer almost a complete absence of discretionary fiscal policy; others prefer a very activist policy.

Historically, as the U.S. economy has grown, the automatic increases in tax revenues have provided the federal government with a *fiscal dividend*. Federal fiscal planners expended effort to find uses for these funds. In the 1960s Walter Heller, chairman of the Council of Economic Advisers, popularized the term *fiscal drag* to point to the problem that if unspent the fiscal dividend would serve as a drag on the economy. However, Charles Shultze of the Brookings Institution pointed out that fiscal drag was a problem much earlier than the 1960s. As early as the 1920s, fiscal drag from automatic stabilizers was recognized as a potential problem. Director of the Bureau of the Budget, General H. M. Lord, lamented in 1927:

> Despite persistent efforts to reduce revenue by cutting taxes to a point barely sufficient to meet our actual demands we seem helpless in the face of the country's continuing prosperity. Reduction in taxes has come to be almost synonymous with increase in revenue. At the end of each year we are called upon to determine what to do with surplus millions.[1]

Nevertheless, as we noted earlier, the automatic stabilizers by the late 1970s had become a truly dominant feature of the U.S. economic landscape by accounting for over 10 percent of national income and for as much as 13 percent of personal income. These transfers have many positive social advantages. They provide income for the poor, the aged, and the needy. They cushion the loss in income from loss of employment. They help children whose families are unable to provide adequate care. At the same time these programs have costs. Martin Feldstein in 1976 illustrated the nature of one problem—the disincentives to work created by our current unemployment compensation program. When one is laid off, one's federal income, social security, and state taxes fall, and because one receives unemployment compensation, the actual loss in income can be very

[1] Taken from Schultze, et al. (1972).

small. Conversely, the reinstitution of these taxes plus the loss in compensation if one returns to work imposes, in effect, a marginal tax rate of as high as 93 percent. In other words, for every dollar one earns, an effective tax of 93¢ is imposed, so that one keeps only 7¢ of the extra earned dollar. The incentive to stay out is obviously quite high. Feldstein and others propose structural reforms of our transfer system to maintain income security without placing such huge marginal tax rate barriers to returning to work.

Dynamics: The nature of the outside lag of fiscal policy can be examined by utilizing a dynamic model like the one employed in Chapter 5. As a starting point consider a model with exogenous government expenditure and taxes. The model under consideration here will be very simple. It will contain a one-period expenditure lag in the consumption function. The model is

$$C_t = 50 + .9Y_{d,t-1} \tag{16}$$

$$I_t = 100 \tag{17}$$

$$G_t = 100 \tag{18}$$

$$T_t = 100 \tag{19}$$

$$Y_t = C_t + I_t + G_t \tag{20}$$

The initial equilibrium income is determined by assuming all variables are constant over time so that $Y_t = Y_{t-1}$, $Y_{d,t} = Y_{d,t-1}$ and so on. $\overline{Y} = 1600$. The initial equilibrium values are reproduced in Table 1, column 1. In period 1 government expenditures are assumed to increase, exogenously, to a level of 150, and maintain at that level. In period 1 consumption is computed, from equation (16) and period 0 disposable income, to be 1400. Y_1 is $C_1 + I_1 + G_1$ or 1650. $Y_{d_1} = Y_1 - T_1 = 1550$. Period 2 consumption is calculated, with (16), from period 1 disposable income. $C_2 = 1445$, and so on. After four periods 34.4 percent of the government multiplier has occurred in this model. These results may be compared to the impact on the economy of a 50-unit cut in taxes. Start at the same initial equilibrium and decrease taxes to 50 in period 1. Since C_1 depends upon Y_{d_0}, C_1 is unchanged by the period 1 tax cut. G_1 and I_1 are exogenous, so Y_1 which equals C_1 plus G_1 plus I_1, is unchanged by the tax cut. The period 1 tax multiplier is 0 compared to the period 1 government expenditure multiplier of 1. The sequence of events which follow the exogenous tax cut is presented in Table 2. The reader should have no difficulty calculating the steps to confirm the numbers in the table.

The sequence of reactions, and the comparative static results, of the 50-unit tax cut in period 1 may be compared to the reactions of the 50-unit government expenditure increase. The last two rows of numbers in each table contain infor-

TABLE 1

Government Multiplier Expenditure Lag Model $\Delta G = 50$

			TIME PERIOD			NEW EQUILIB-RIUM
VARIABLE	0	1	2	3	4	
Y	1600	1650	1695	1735.5	1771.95	2100
Y_d	1500	1550	1595	1635.5	1671.95	2000
C	1400	1400	1445	1485.5	1521.95	1850
I	100	100	100	100	100	100
G	100	150	150	150	150	150
T	100	100	100	100	100	100
k_{g_t}	—	1.00	1.90	2.71	3.44	10
$\%k$	—	10%	19%	27%	34.4%	100%

TABLE 2

Tax Multiplier Expenditure Lag Model $\Delta T = -50$

			TIME PERIOD			NEW EQUILIB-RIUM
VARIABLE	0	1	2	3	4	
Y	1600	1600	1645	1685.5	1721.95	2050
Y_d	1500	1550	1595	1635.5	1671.95	2000
C	1400	1400	1445	1485.5	1521.95	1850
I	100	100	100	100	100	100
G	100	100	100	100	100	100
T	100	50	50	50	50	50
k_{T_t}	—	0.00	−.90	−1.71	−2.44	−9
$\%k$	—		10%	19%	27%	100%

mation about the dynamic and comparative static multipliers. k_{g_t} are 1.00, 1.90, 2.71, 3.44, ... , 10, and k_{T_t} are 0.00, −.90, −1.71, −2.44, ... , −9. The tax multipliers are all negative, and, in each period, the tax multiplier is just one less than the government multiplier. The percentage of the total multiplier which has occurred after a given number of periods is always smaller for the tax multiplier. For example, after four periods, 27 percent of the comparative static tax multiplier has occurred and 34.4 percent of the total government spending multiplier has occurred. Thus government expenditures have a larger and a faster impact on income according to this model.

To examine the effect of automatic stabilizers, the dynamic model may be modified by replacing the exogenous tax equation (19), by:

$$T_t = 100 + .1Y_t$$

(21)

For comparison purposes, start at $\overline{Y}$, in which $Y_{t+1} = Y_t = Y_{t-1}$, and consider an increase in G of 50 in period 1. Table 3 contains the initial equilibrium values and the sequence of reactions. The initial equilibrium differs from that in the previous model, because the comparative static solution to this model is different from the exogenous net tax model. Nevertheless, the reader may confirm the initial equilibrium by computing period 1 values for the variables assuming no change in G. The period 1 values will be exactly the same as the period 0 values.

TABLE 3

Government Multiplier Expenditure Lag Model with Automatic Stabilizers $G = +50$

VARI-ABLE	TIME PERIOD					NEW EQUILIB-RIUM
	0	1	2	3	4	
Y	842.08	892.08	932.58	965.39	991.96	1105.24
Y_d	657.87	702.87	739.32	768.85	792.76	894.71
C	642.08	642.08	682.58	715.39	741.96	855.24
I	100	100	100	100	100	100
G	100	150	150	150	100	150
T	184.21	189.21	193.26	196.54	199.20	210.52
k_{g_t}	—	1.00	1.81	2.47	3.00	5.263
$\%k$	—	19%	34.4%	46.9%	57%	100%

Consider period 1, given an increase of 50 in G. C_1 depends upon Y_{d_0} and will not change, thus $C_1 + G_1 + I_1$ will have increased by ΔG to 892.08. The increase in Y from period 0 to 1 of 50 will increase tax revenues in period 1 by .1 × 50, or 5. Thus, $T_1 = 189.21$. This tax increase, induced by the increase in Y, must be deducted from the new level of Y to compute period 1 disposable income. $Y_{d_1} = 702.87$. Period 2 consumption depends upon Y_{d_1}: $C_2 = 682.58$. The period 1 government multiplier is 1.00, exactly the same as in the exogenous tax case, Table 1.

In period 2, however, income is $C_2 + I_2 + G_2$. While I_2 and G_2 are still at 100 and 150, respectively, C_2 has increased to 682.58. C_2 has increased 40 over period 1 consumption. This compares to a period 2 consumption increase of 45 in the Table 1 model. Thus $Y_2 = C_2 + I_2 + G_2 = 932.58$. $k_{g_2} = 1.81$. The smaller increase in consumption in this model means a smaller multiplier. The smaller rise in consumption has occurred because the automatic increase in tax revenues has dampened the increase in disposable income. Thus, $k_{g_2} = 1.81$ with endogenous taxes and $k_{g_2} = 1.90$ without endogenous taxes.

The comparative static impact of $\Delta G = +50$ in Table 3 is an income increase of 263.16 for a comparative static multiplier of 5.263. The automatic stabilizer has reduced the comparative static government expenditure multiplier from 10 to 5.263. Each period multiplier is smaller as well. For example, k_{g_4} has fallen from 3.44 to 3.00. However, note that the percentage of the total comparative static multiplier which has occurred after a given number of periods is larger under automatic stabilizers. Without exogenous taxes, after four periods, 34.4 percent of k_g has occurred, while Table 3 indicates 57 percent of the total k_g occurs after four periods given automatic stabilizers. This result is not intuitively obvious: automatic stabilizers reduce the multipliers but exogenous changes occur more rapidly.

While illustrating an exogenous change in taxes in the model with stabilizers would be redundant, we should note that the meaning of a tax multiplier must now be refined. k_T, defined as the change in Y over a change in T_0, does not account for the endogenous reaction of T to a change in Y. Furthermore, the tax rate may be considered to change as well. These and other elaborations will be discussed in subsequent chapters on fiscal policy after more sophisticated treatment of other elements of the economy is introduced.

STUDY QUESTIONS AND PROBLEMS

1. Let an economy be characterized by the following model:

$C = 100 + 3/4Y_d$

$I = 60$

$G = 80$

$T = -20 + 0.10Y$

   a. What is the investment multiplier? What is equilibrium income?

   b. How will $\overline{Y}$ change if:

      (1) G increases by 20?

      (2) T_0 increases by 20?

      (3) T increases by 20?

2. How might the following measures influence the stabilizing nature of government fiscal behavior?

   a. An increase in family exemptions.

   b. A decrease in the income tax rate.

   c. The tying of corporate tax deductions to business investment spending. (If I increases, tax revenues fall.)

3. Make a list of built-in automatic stabilizers for the U.S. economy. Could you suggest additional measures to stabilize the economy?

4. Comment on the costs and benefits of automatic stabilizers and discretionary fiscal policy.

5. Discuss the inside lag in fiscal policy. Without resorting to automatic stabilizers, how might this lag be shortened? Do you believe your suggested measure should be implemented?

6. Solve the following model for $\overline{Y}$:

$$C_t = 1000 + 0.9Y_{dt-1}$$
$$I_t = 500$$
$$G_t = 2000$$
$$T_t = 500 + 0.05Y_t$$
$$Y_t = C_t + I_t + G_t$$

Trace the effects of the following actions on the economy:

a. G_t decreases by 1000 in one period, then resumes its level of 2000.

b. G_t decreases by 1000 permanently.

7. What was the effect of transfer payments for the relation between personal income and national income in the 1974-1975 recession?

8. How do you think the Great Depression experience might have been different had automatic stabilizers been a larger fraction of national income, as they are today?

9. Why do you think President Ford's economic advisors recommended a recession policy to him in 1974-1975? Build a model to illustrate the effectiveness of a "made-in-Washington" recession with and without transfer payments.

REFERENCES

Ando, Albert, E. Cary Brown, and Ann F. Friedlaender, *Studies in Economic Stabilization*, Studies of Government Finance. Washington, D.C.: Brookings Institution, 1968.

Brookings Papers on Economic Activity, Arthur Okun and George L. Perry (eds.), select issues, 1969-1973. Washington, D.C.: Brookings Institution.

Feldstein, Martin, "Temporary Layoffs in the Theory of Unemployment," *Journal of Political Economy*, Vol. 84, No. 8 (October 1976), pp. 937-957.

Heller, Walter W., and Milton Friedman, *Monetary vs. Fiscal Policy: A Dialogue*. New York: W. W. Norton, 1969.

Okun, Arthur M., *The Political Economy of Prosperity*. New York: W. W. Norton, 1970.

Peckman, Joseph A., *Federal Tax Policy*, revised. New York: W. W. Norton, 1971.

Shultze, Charles L., Edward R. Fried, Alice M. Rivlin, and Nancy H. Teeters, *Setting National Priorities, the 1973 Budget*. Washington, D.C.: Brookings Institution, 1972.

Smith, Warren L., and Ronald L. Teigen, *Readings in Money, National Income, and Stabilization Policy*, 3rd ed. Homewood, Ill.: Richard D. Irwin, 1974.

PERSONAL CONSUMPTION EXPENDITURES

part III

Fiscal policy multipliers make evident the importance to Keynesian analysis of the marginal propensity to consume. Indeed, the stable consumption function formed a central pillar of Keynes's *General Theory*. However, when placed in the crucible of econometric scrutiny, Keynes's consumption hypothesis, built upon psychological laws, gave way to an empirical enigma. Chapter 8 is an analysis of the nature of this early search for the true consumption function.

Many attempts were made to explain the consumption evidence discovered by researchers. Three major hypotheses have stood out. In Chapter 9 we explore one hypothesis in some detail: Milton Friedman's permanent income hypothesis (PIH). In his PIH, Friedman pulled up the stable consumption anchor and set modern fiscal policy adrift. He accomplished this result with a blend of theory, empirical evidence, and policy analysis which still stands as a model of scientific inquiry. In part for this work, Professor Friedman was awarded a Nobel Prize in economics.

The consumption story does not stop with Friedman, for his model also was placed in the crucible of research. Chapter 9 also studies the other two major hypotheses: Duesenberry's relative income hypothesis and Modigliani's life cycle hypothesis. The three all reject Keynes's simple view that consumption expenditures are a function of current disposable income. Theoretician Robert Clower of UCLA, however, rejuvenates Keynes's thinking by challenging the new views. Detailed analysis of durable good expenditures and of time series studies points to some of the expected areas for research over the next decade.

Personal consumption expenditures by households are the largest component of U.S. GNP, ranging during this century, in nonwar years, from a low of 62 percent (1968) to a high of 81 percent (1932). Keynes used his theory of the "propensity to consume" to shatter the interest rate linkage between saving and investment which had assured the classical outcome of full employment. Keynes argued that the severity of economic instability, generated by random shocks in investment spending, depends upon the marginal propensity to consume. Thus, the determination of consumption expenditures is central to Keynesian macroeconomic theory.

Consumption will be discussed in two parts in this chapter. In part A, the Keynesian consumption theory is presented in detail with a brief discussion of its importance to the Keynesian system. Part B contains empirical evidence on the Keynesian model. In part B, apparent inconsistencies in the evidence are revealed.

The Keynesian Consumption Anchor: Theory and Evidence

A • A Testable Theory

An essential property of a viable theory is that it be possible to devise a test the results of which could reject the theory. Keynes's consumption theory was viable, and economists lost little time in subjecting the Keynesian consumption hypothesis to empirical evidence. The results were mixed and led to a remarkable variety of imaginative refinements and innovations. Keynes stated his theory of consumption expenditures in four explicit propositions:

> 1. Aggregate consumption is a stable function of aggregate disposable income: "We are left, therefore, with the conclusion that in a given situation the propensity to consume may be considered a fairly stable function, . . ."
> 2. The marginal propensity to consume is positive and less than one: "The fundamental psychological law, upon which we are entitled to depend with great confidence both *a priori* from our knowledge of human nature and from the detailed facts of experience, is that men are disposed, as a rule and on the average, to increase their consumption as their income increases, but not by as much as their income."
> 3. As income increases, the average propensity to consume declines: ". . . it is also obvious that a higher absolute level of income will tend, as a rule, to widen the gap between income and consumption."
> 4. As income increases, the marginal propensity to consume declines: "The marginal propensity to consume is not constant for all levels of employment, and it is probable that there will be, as a rule, a tendency for it to diminish as employment (income) increases; . . ."

The first three of Keynes's propositions can be illustrated with the linear consumption function introduced in Chapter 5:

$$C = C_0 + bY \tag{1}$$

Consider the term "stable." It is not very precise, but the idea Keynes was expressing is that factors on which consumption might depend, other than income, change slowly, have offsetting effects on consumption, or have no substantial effects on consumption at all. Thus, income dominates interest rates, wealth, demography, expectations, and other factors as determinants of consumption.

The marginal propensity to consume, *MPC,* corresponds to b in equation (1), so that proposition 2 is that $0 < b < 1$. Keynes placed great importance on this "fundamental psychological law." Since he felt b was less than one, Keynes believed that increases in income toward full employment would have to be accompanied by exogenous increases in investment to insure that demand would rise enough to meet the higher level of income. If *MPC* were greater than or equal to one, the nature of the multiplier, $1/(1 - b)$, would endanger the stability of the system.

The third proposition is that as income increases, the average propensity to consume (*APC*) decreases. To understand the implication of this proposition it is first necessary to study the relationship between marginal values and average values. The relation between *MPC* and *APC* can be illustrated with the linear function. *APC* is C/Y, and from equation (1):

$$C/Y = C_0/Y + b \tag{2}$$

or

$$APC = C_0/Y + MPC \tag{3}$$

As Y increases, *APC* will decrease if and only if C_0 is positive. Thus, the third Keynesian proposition is consistent with (1) if C_0 is positive. Note also that $APC = C_0/Y + MPC$ and that $C_0/Y > 0$; therefore, $APC > MPC$. This relation between *APC* and *MPC* is quite important, for a declining *APC* is the main proposition challenged by confrontation with empirical evidence. The relation between *APC* and *MPC* also raised new views about consumption behavior.

Figure 1 of the linear consumption function can be used to illustrate the relation between *MPC* and *APC*. The slope of the consumption line is *MPC*. *APC* can be measured at each point on the consumption line. For example, at point A a ray is drawn to the origin. The vertical distance AB from the point to the horizontal axis measures the level of consumption at A. The horizontal distance OB along the axis from the origin to the vertical line AB measures income. The ratio of these two sides AB/OB is average consumption, $C(A)/Y(A)$ or *APC*. This ratio is also the *slope* of the ray. The slopes of rays from points on the consumption line to the origin always exceed the slope of the consumption function itself, because C_0 is positive. Consequently, $APC > MPC$. It is also clear from the figure that as Y increases and we move from left to right along the consumption

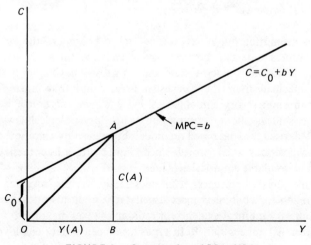

FIGURE 1   Consumption: $APC > MPC$

line, *APC* declines, since the slopes of the rays become flatter. The relationship between *MPC* and *APC* implied by proposition 3 has now been illustrated both with geometry and algebra.

The fourth proposition of the Keynesian hypothesis, that *MPC* declines as income increases, cannot be illustrated with the linear consumption function, because straight lines have constant slopes. However, a relatively simple nonlinear function, a second-degree polynomial, may be employed to illustrate proposition 4. Consider the following:

$$C = 506 + 0.92Y - 0.000014Y^2 \tag{4}$$

(These parameter values were actually estimated by Ralph Husby in 1971.) Calculation of the marginal propensity to consume yields:

$$MPC = 0.92 - 0.0028Y \tag{5}$$

MPC is a linear function of income and as income increases *MPC* declines. Figure 2 illustrates this consumption function. Keynes believed *MPC* would tend to decline during a boom and rise during slowdowns for two reasons. First, during a boom as employment increases relative to available capital, diminishing returns to labor set in. Income to property, relative to labor, increases. Keynes felt that entrepreneurs, whose relative share of income would rise, tend to have a low marginal propensity to consume. Consequently, aggregate *MPC* would decline during booms. Second, during downturns in the cycle transfer payments are relatively high, and the propensity to spend such income by unemployed and those on public relief would be high, in Keynes's view.

B ● Empirical Evidence

Keynes's consumption hypothesis was central to his general theory—it broke the classical interest rate link between saving and investment, it was the key stable relation in Keynes's macrosystem and, as we saw in Chapter 6, it was the transmission mechanism of the Keynesian fiscal solution to unemployment. Upon what consumer theory and empirical evidence was this crucial hypothesis based? Keynes's ideas about consumption were "psychological laws," rather than carefully devised theories based on models buttressed by empirical evidence. These four propositions, then, provided economists with a hypothesis requiring confirmation by available empirical evidence.

Unlike some physical sciences, economics rarely has the advantage of controlled experiments. Economists must usually rely upon historical evidence to test their theories. Empirical evidence in economics takes one of two forms: (1) cross section or (2) time series. Both types have been widely employed to ex-

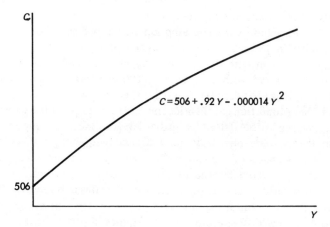

FIGURE 2   Nonlinear Consumption Function—*MPC* Declines as *Y* Increases

plore Keynes's theory. Cross-section data usually consist of the economic behavior of different groups, usually families but also cities, races, or countries, at a point in time. Researchers attempt to explain differences in consumption expenditures as a result of differences in other factors—income, family size, age of family, social characteristics, and so on. From observed differences, inferences are drawn about the effects on consumption of changes in the other variables. Cross-section studies in which consumption behavior is the issue are, for obvious reasons, called *budget studies.*

Time-series studies focus on the economic activity of groups, usually aggregates, over time. An observation of a typical consumption time-series study, for example, would be total U.S. consumption, income, and other aggregate variables for a given year. The time period need not be a year; it could be a month, a quarter (three months), or a decade. The economic unit need not be a country; it could be a city, ethnic group, etc. The essential feature of time-series data and their principal advantage over cross section, is that actual changes are observed rather than differences. The difficulty with time series, however, is that numerous changes occur from one period to the next, and it is quite difficult to sort out the separate effects.

Budget Studies: Typical of the many budget studies undertaken is the Bureau of Labor Statistics—Wharton School of Finance Study using a 1950 sample survey of 12,500 U.S. families collected by the Michigan Survey Research Center. Rather than treating each family as an observation, researchers grouped families according to their income. A single observation consists of the average consumption and average income of families in a given income range, i.e., $4000 to $4999. Each observation can be represented by one point in a diagram measuring average consumption on the vertical axis and average income on the horizontal axis. These points are depicted in Figure 3. The curve, sketched through these points, characterizes the consumption-income averages from cross-section data of families in 1950. All four Keynesian propositions about consumption behavior are consistent with the grouped budget study evidence: (1) Consumption is closely tracked with income. (2) *MPC* estimates, across a number of budget studies, range between 0.6 and 0.8. (3) Groups with low average incomes consume higher proportions of their incomes. (4) The slope of the curve through the points seemed to be flatter for higher levels of income. Supporters of the Keynesian theory were obviously quite pleased with budget study evidence. Fairly reliable estimates of the marginal propensity to consume were obtained, and from these *MPC* estimates, the multipliers could be calculated.

Despite such early successes, proponents of the consumption hypothesis had several reasons to be cautious about cross-section evidence in general and about the results of several different cross-section studies in particular. First, Figure 3 depicts only the average levels of consumption associated with each income group. In fact, rather wide variations in consumption expenditures were observed within each group. Clearly these wide variations within the groups could not be explained by income variations. Variations in factors other than income must have caused variations in consumption and the hypothesis does not explain these variations.

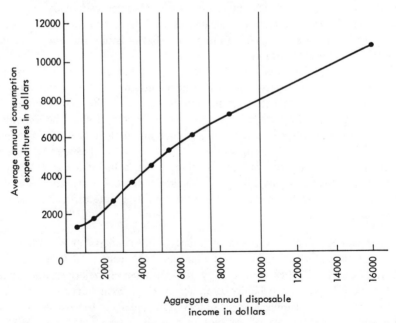

FIGURE 3   Cross-section Consumption Evidence—1950 Michigan Research Study

Source: Gardner Ackley, *Macroeconomic Theory* (New York: The Macmillan Co., 1961), p. 222 © 1961 by Gardner Ackley.

Consider a factor which may go unnoticed by budget studies. Young families can be observed undertaking expenditures for cars, washers and dryers, refrigerators, and so on in excess of their current income. Older couples are known to spend above their current earnings, because they have saved while in their earning prime. If the population of a society undergoes substantial demographic changes, consumption patterns might well change as a result. Again, a budget study, without careful attention to demographic factors, might not account for such changes.

A conceptual difficulty with cross-section evidence has to do with the fact that economists are interested in changes in consumption and in how these changes are induced by changes in other variables. Yet cross-section data consists of different observations at a point in time and we infer, from these differences, changes. An example will illustrate the nature of the problem. Suppose we observe two families, C and D, both with 1950 incomes of \$20,000. In 1949 Family C earned \$15,000 and D \$25,000. Given this knowledge of their 1949 incomes, would we expect identical expenditure behavior in 1950? Probably not. Family C, whose income has increased, will find \$20,000 comfortable. Family D, whose relative income has fallen, may well overspend the \$20,000. In general, consumption in 1950 may depend on income relative to other years rather than simply the absolute level of income in 1950. In a very interesting study, reexamining cross-section evidence, James Duesenberry (1949) made this point very effectively.

Finally, a difficulty with budget study results pertains to comparisons across a number of such studies, each taken at a different time. Table 1 contains summary results of five budget studies. Each study is a cross section; in comparing them we are studying time series.

Despite widely varying circumstances and a range of five decades the results

TABLE 1
Summary of Five Cross-section Budget Studies in U.S.

YEAR	SAMPLE*	AVERAGE INCOME	MPC	APC	AVERAGE CONSUMPTION AT INCOME OF \$2000
1888-90	Wage earners	682	0.67	0.90	1610
1901	Wage earners	651	0.68	0.92	1565
1917-19	Wage earners	1513	0.78	0.91	1735
1935-36	Nonfarm	1952	0.73	0.89	1880
1941	Urban	2865	0.79	0.92	1930

*Wage earners: select wage-earner families; nonfarm: nonrelief, nonfarm families; Urban: urban families.

Source: Milton Friedman, *A Theory of the Consumption Function* (Princeton: National Bureau of Economic Research, Princeton University Press, 1957), p. 45.

are remarkably similar. The *MPC* ranges from 0.67 to 0.79 and the *APC*, incredibly stable, from 0.89 to 0.92. *MPC* < *APC* in each case. (We shall discuss the procedure for estimating these parameters shortly.) Though these facts alone are strongly supportive of Keynes's views they contain an apparent enigma. *MPC* < *APC* means *APC* is falling as income increases. Yet as income increases the *APC* figures are virtually constant. Why do not the *APC* figures decline as income increases? The answer can be found by observing *APC* at a fixed income level for all studies. For *Y* = $2000, average consumption is recorded in the last column of Table 1. Average consumption, at *Y* = $2000, is increasing as average income increases. In other words, while each budget study appears to reveal the same stable *MPC*, predicted by Keynes, the absolute consumption level seems to be shifting upward.

Figure 4 depicts a consumption line for each budget study. As we consider successively higher budget lines along the line for which *Y* = $2000, it is clear that the *APC*s (slopes of rays to the origin) increase. Consumption behavior is apparently not as stable as we had thought. How can these upward drifting lines be explained? A number of possibilities have been suggested.

One suggestion was that each consumption line represented a stable, short-run relation between income and consumption and that the line drifted upward slowly over time. Arthur Smithies presented the view that over short-run cyclical fluctuations in income, consumption responded in a Keynesian fashion. Over long-run secular increases in income, other demographic factors caused an upward drift in the level of consumption associated with each level of income. Many felt major causes of this secular "drift" of the consumption function were new consumer goods and urbanization. In fact, cross-section budget comparisons of farm and nonfarm families revealed a higher urban *APC*. In any case, these issues raised by budget studies could be resolved only by time series evidence.

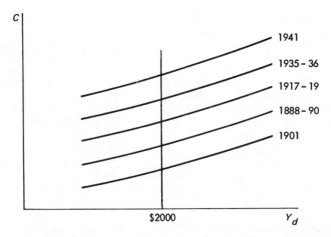

FIGURE 4   Intertemporal Comparison of Budget Studies: 1880-1941

Annual Time Series: Though rudimentary income accounts were developed in the 1930s, comprehensive national product accounts, with GNP allocated by use, only became available in 1942. Accounts compiled to aid war-planning agencies covered the years 1929-1941. One of the first uses to which these data were applied by economists was study of consumption activity. The first difficulty faced by researchers is that over time a great many changes occur and they must be sorted out. Utilizing techniques similar to the index number solutions discussed in Chapter 3, researchers isolated changes in "real" income and in "real" consumption from corresponding nominal changes. Employing revised data, Figure 5 depicts aggregate annual consumption expenditures and aggregate annual disposable income, each in constant 1958 prices, for the years 1929-1941. Each point in Figure 5 represents total consumption and total disposable income in the U.S. for a given year, in constant 1958 prices. The scatter diagram in Figure 5 clearly indicates that increases in consumption expenditures are highly correlated with increases in disposable income, in the aggregate. In fact, from the scatter, this positive correlation appears to be very precise.

It is useful to be more explicit about the correlation between consumption and income than simply observing that the scatter of points is very close to a pattern. A technique called *ordinary least squares* has been developed to give more precision to study of economic hypotheses and to estimation of parameters, like *MPC*, than merely observing scatter diagrams. A heuristic explanation of the ordinary least squares technique will be helpful to our study of consumption.

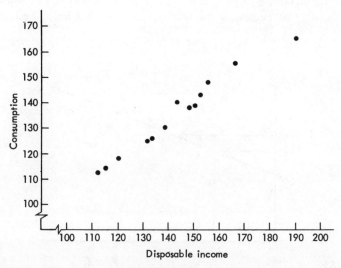

FIGURE 5   Annual Aggregate Consumption Evidence 1929-1941 (billions of 1958 dollars)

Least-squares Method: The objective of the least-squares method is to select the "best" line, from all possible lines, to describe a scatter of points. The least-squares method is restricted to consider only linear representations of the scatter of points. More elaborate nonlinear techniques are available, but they go beyond our scope here. The least-squares method can be illustrated by considering the use to which such a line might be put. Consider Figure 6, in which a line is drawn through a scatter of observations. Suppose the line is used to predict consumption from income. At income level Y_0, an actual observation appears in which consumption was quantity $C(a)$. Had $C(a)$ not been known and had the line been used to predict consumption at income level Y_0, it would have predicted level $C(p)$. The difference, $C(a) - C(p)$, could be thought of as the extent to which the actual level of C deviates from the predicted level, or $C(a) - C(p)$ could be called the "error." In a heuristic sense, the best line is one which is closest to the scatter of points. The "errors" should, in some sense, be as small as possible. A natural way in which one might select the best line would be to select the one for which the sum of all deviations between actual and predicted consumption, $C(a) - C(p)$, is smallest. Unfortunately, this method will not result in a unique line. It can be shown that any line through the point of average consumption and average income has the property that the sum of the deviations is zero.

The least-squares method is to square each error, then sum them and select the line for which the sum of the squared errors is a minimum—least squares.

Economists find it useful to be able to evaluate the accuracy of the least-squares line through a scatter, for while the least-squares line can be shown to have certain optimal properties, how good is this "best" line? In other words, to evaluate the hypothesis that C and Y are linearly correlated, one would like to have a method of evaluating the least-squares line. Similarly, the least-squares

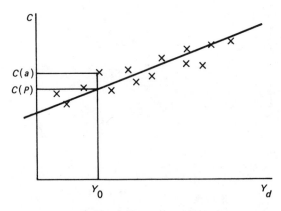

FIGURE 6   Ordinary Least Squares

method provides estimates of parameters; for example, estimates of the marginal propensity to consume. How accurate is the least-squares estimator?

Figures 7(a) and (b) illustrate the accuracy of a least-squares line in two different hypothetical samples. In each figure an ordinary least-squares line is drawn through a scatter of points. In Figure 7(a) the line, though the best, does a rather poor job of describing the scatter of points. In Figure 7(b), on the other hand, the line is very close to all the points. If both figures are measured in the same units one would not hesitate to say that the hypothesis tested in (b) is consistent with the data drawn in the scatter; however, (a) does not represent a very useful hypothesis for predicting C from Y.

From Figure 7 one could simply conclude that "(b) is a good fit" and "(a) is a bad fit." However, to obtain more precision in evaluation of hypotheses econometricians and statisticians have developed statistics which quantify the relative accuracy of least-squares lines. The rationale, development, and properties of these statistics form the core of the field of econometrics and would be inappropriate here. However, since we do wish to explore the empirical evidence about consumption behavior, it is useful to comment on two statistics: the coefficient of determination and the standard error of a coefficient.

The hypothesis that consumption is a stable function of income is a statement about the relationship between variations in consumption and variations in income. Heuristically, the hypothesis is that variations in consumption can be "explained" by variations in income. Variations in a variable may be given precise meaning. Consider a problem with thirteen observations on consumption and income. If one computes average consumption, then for any observation its variation is the difference between its level of consumption and average consumption.

The *coefficient of determination* is a statistic, i.e., a variable with known properties, based upon the ratio of the proportion of variation in the dependent variable (consumption) explained by the hypothesis (variations in disposable in-

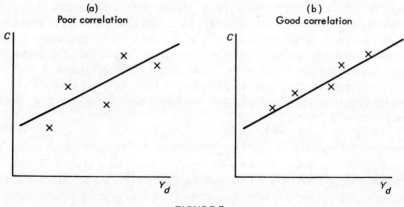

FIGURE 7

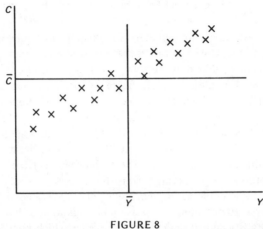

FIGURE 8

come and the consumption line) to the total amount of variation in consumption in the data. In the consumption function example illustrated in Figure 8, a least-squares line sketched through the scatter could explain some of the variations in consumption as a result of variations in income. However, some proportion of the variation in consumption would remain unexplained by the consumption function line. The more of the variation in C unexplained by the line, the less supportive of the hypothesis are the data. The coefficient of determination, symbolized by R^2, takes value from 0 to 1. R^2 values approach 1 as the proportion of the variance in C unexplained by the hypothesis (i.e., variations in Y and the consumption line) approaches zero. R^2, then, is a statistic which can be used to judge the overall accuracy of the hypothesis. In the consumption case, R^2 will indicate the proportion of total variation in C, explained by the hypothesis that C is a linear function of disposable income.

A note of caution is in order about the use of coefficients of determination. A common error is often made when R^2 statistics for two competing models are used for comparison. Unless the dependent variables are exactly the same, comparative R^2's can be quite misleading. R^2 is based upon the explained proportion of variation in the dependent variable, and if dependent variables in competing models differ, the total variation differs so that the R^2's are not necessarily comparable. A second warning about interpretation of the coefficient of determination is that whereas a high value for R^2 means high correlation, it does not necessarily indicate the causation embodied in the hypothesis. Consequently, in principle no amount of evidence can confirm a theory; evidence can only be used to reject a theory.

Just as the coefficient of determination is a statistic for evaluating the hypothesis, the *standard error of a coefficient* is used to evaluate a single parameter estimate. For example, one may wish to judge the accuracy of the *MPC* estimate associated with a least-squares consumption line. Again, the actual computation of the standard error is a subject of econometrics; however, we can consider an example to illustrate the use of the standard error. Suppose $\hat{b} = 0.75$ and the standard error is 0.05. We know $\hat{b}$ is an estimate of the *MPC*, a statistical guess, but how confident can we be in 0.75? The standard error can be used to compute a range of values around 0.75 such that we can have a fixed level of confidence that the true value of *MPC* is within the range. (These properties of $\hat{b}$ and the standard error depend upon certain restrictive assumptions about the nature of the model and the data.) For example, consider the range 0.75 ± 0.05, 0.70 to 0.80. One can state, with 67 percent confidence, that β is between 0.70 and 0.80. Consider the range 0.75 ± 0.1, 0.65 to 0.85: one can state, with 95 percent confidence, that β is between 0.65 to 0.85. Finally, suppose one wished to compare two coefficient estimates, as to accuracy. Both estimators are 0.75. One has a standard error of 0.002, the second of 0.2. The first is a more precise estimate, because its standard error is much smaller, relative to the size of the coefficient, than the first. Though these various statistical concepts have only been described in very general terms, they will be helpful for discussing empirical evidence, like time-series consumption data.

Annual Time Series Continued: Figure 9 superimposes on the scatter diagram of annual time-series observations on aggregate consumption and disposable income the least-squares line computed from the observations.

The equation for the least-squares line in Figure 9, with some useful statistics, is

$$C = 31.4 + 0.73 \ Yd \qquad R^2 = 0.97 \qquad n = 13$$
$$(5.2) \quad (0.04)$$

(6)

The numbers in parentheses are the standard errors of their respective coeffi-

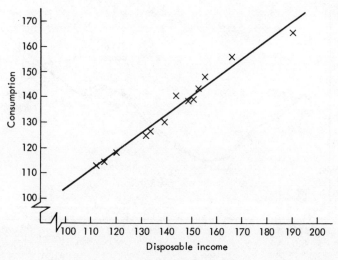

FIGURE 9   Consumption Evidence 1929-1941—Least-squares Line (billions of 1958 dollars)

cients, and n is the number of observations. The *MPC* is 0.73 and *APC* at average Y is 0.94. Annual time-series data were clearly supportive of the Keynesian hypothesis:

> 1. Consumption appeared to be a highly stable function of income. The $R^2 = 0.97$. Figure 10 plots the path of aggregate consumption expenditures from 1929 through 1941 along with the predicted values. No predicted value was more than 3.3 percent off the true value. For nine of the thirteen observations predicted consumption was within 2 percent of actual consumption. The predicted values track the actual values reasonably well in Figure 10.
> 2. The estimator of the *MPC* is 0.73 with a standard error of 0.04, so one can be reasonably confident that *MPC* over the period was between 0.65 and 0.81.
> 3. The intercept is 31.4 with a standard error of 5.2; therefore, with reasonable certainty, the true value of the intercept can be said to be within the range 21 to 41.8.

A positive intercept means that *APC* declines as income increases. In fact, *APC* calculated for 1933, when income was low, is 1.005; and *APC* for 1941, when income was relatively high, is 0.87. In conclusion, the first three Keynesian consumption hypotheses were not rejected by the evidence. Indeed, the short-run time-series evidence appears to be quite supportive of these hypotheses.

Despite the supportive evidence from the short-run time-series and grouped cross-section data, the long-run stability of the Keynesian consumption function was doubtful for several reasons. First, budget lines, computed from studies taken in different decades, appeared to drift upward. Second, it is illogical for a consumption function with *MPC* < *APC* to have remained in place, over a long

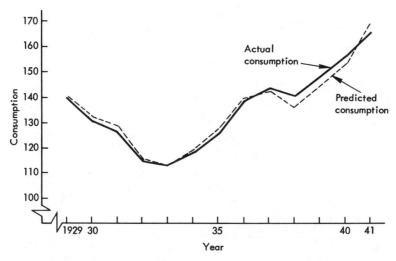

FIGURE 10   Actual and Predicted Consumption 1929-1941 (billions of 1958 dollars)

period of time: The corollary to the property that APC falls as income increases is the property that APC increases as income falls. Tracing income back in time, one should reach a level of aggregate income at which $APC > 1$. But it is impossible for C to exceed disposable income except for temporary periods of time.

Third, the consumption function estimated on 1929-1941 data used to predict post-war consumption patterns from postwar incomes failed quite badly. Disposable income (1958 prices) in 1947 was $218 billion. Substituting this value into equation (6), we find that predicted consumption is $189.66 billion. Actual consumption in 1947 was $206.3 billion. The full impact of the puzzle of the consumption hypotheses, however, was not appreciated until a truly herculean effort to compile aggregate U.S. data for a long period of time, 1869 to 1938, was undertaken successfully by Nobel Laureate Simon Kuznets. The Kuznets data formed the basis for a long-run empirical evaluation of consumption.

Long-run Time Series: Kuznets, in 1946, produced aggregate national income and product figures for overlapping decades from 1869 to 1938. His findings are presented in Table 2. The remarkable difference between Kuznets's findings and the results from cross-section and short-run time series is that the long-run APC is constant, between 0.84 and 0.89, until per capita income actually falls in the 1930s, while the short-run APC falls as income increases. Figure 11 depicts the

TABLE 2

National Income and Consumption Expenditure, in 1929 Prices, 1869-1938

DECADE	NATIONAL INCOME (BILLIONS OF DOLLARS) (1)	CONSUMPTION EXPENDITURES (BILLIONS OF DOLLARS) (2)	APC (3)	NATIONAL INCOME PER CAPITA (DOLLARS) (4)
1869-78	9.3	8.1	0.86	215
1874-83	13.6	11.6	0.86	278
1879-88	17.9	15.3	0.85	326
1884-93	21.0	17.7	0.84	344
1889-98	24.2	20.2	0.84	357
1894-1903	29.8	25.4	0.85	401
1899-1908	37.3	32.3	0.86	458
1904-13	45.0	39.1	0.87	502
1909-18	50.6	44.0	0.87	517
1914-23	57.3	50.7	0.89	546
1919-28	69.0	62.0	0.89	612
1924-33	73.3	68.9	0.94	607
1929-38	72.0	71.0	0.99	572

Source: Columns (1) and (2) are from S. Kuznets, *National Product Since 1869* (National Bureau of Economic Research, 1946), p. 119. Columns (3) and (4) are from *idem., National Income: A Summary of Findings* (National Bureau of Economic Research, 1946), pp. 53 and 32.

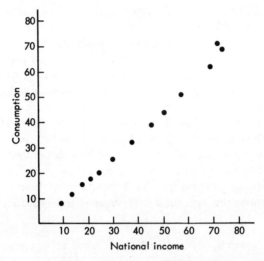

FIGURE   11   Long-run Time Series Consumption Evidence (billions of 1929 dollars)

Kuznets observations. *APC* appears to be constant and *APC* = *MPC*. In other words, over long periods, income and consumption are proportional, but over the short run, consumption's relation to income is nonproportional. Algebraically, the long-run consumption line is

$$C = gY \tag{7}$$

where $0.84 \leqslant g \leqslant 0.89$. The short-run line is

$$C = C_0 + bY \tag{8}$$

where $C_0 > 0$ and $0.6 \leqslant b \leqslant 0.8$. The two lines, (7) and (8), are drawn in Fig. 12.

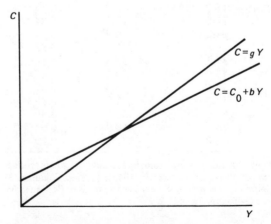

FIGURE 12   Long-run Consumption Line vs. Short-run

The problem confronting economists was that empirical evidence seemed to point to two consumption relations with income. Both lines cannot represent, it would seem, the underlying behavioral causational relation between consumption and income. Some reconciliation between the two types of evidence was necessary. Faced with this apparent enigma, economists devised a number of interesting hypotheses to reconcile the evidence. The outcome has been a more sophisticated understanding of personal consumption expenditures. In the next chapter, several attempts to reconcile consumption evidence are discussed.

STUDY QUESTIONS AND PROBLEMS

1. Classical economists believed saving was dependent upon interest rates. Keynes argued that consumption was a stable function of disposable income. Are these views incompatible with one another?

2. Suppose an economy is at full employment equilibrium income. Consider an exogenous increase in saving. How will the economy be affected (a) if it is represented by the income-expenditure model and (b) if it is represented by the classical model?

3. What were the results of the cross-section evidence on the Keynesian consumption hypothesis? Why might one be suspicious of cross-section consumption evidence?

4. Keynes stated four psychological laws about consumption behavior. What were they? Explain each and illustrate it geometrically.

5. Define, and illustrate with an example or a picture, each of the following:
    ordinary least squares
    cross-section budget studies
    marginal propensity vs. average propensity to consume
    coefficient of determination
    proportional consumption function

6. Comment briefly on the contributions to consumption theory and evidence of each of the following:
    John Maynard Keynes
    Simon Kuznets
    Arthur Smithies

7. "As long as consumption depends upon income in a reasonably stable way, it does not matter which is the correct function." Comment.

8. Compare the results of short- and long-run time-series evidence on consumption behavior. How might the apparent differences be reconciled?

REFERENCES

Ackley, Gardner, *Macroeconomic Theory*. New York: Macmillan, 1961.

Duesenberry, James S., *Income, Saving and the Theory of Consumer Behavior* Oxford: Oxford University Press, 1967; New York: 1949.

Husby, Ralph D., "A Nonlinear Consumption Function Estimated from Time Series and Cross Section Data," *Review of Economics and Statistics,* February 1971.

Keynes, John Maynard, *The General Theory of Employment, Interest and Money.* New York: Harcourt, Brace & World, Inc., 1932.

Kuznets, Simon, *National Income, A Summary of Findings,* NBER, New York, 1946.

———, *National Product Since 1869*, NBER, 1946.

Mikesell, Raymond F., and James E. Zinser, "The Nature of the Saving Function in Developing Countries: A Survey of the Theoretical and Empirical Literature," *Review of Economic Literature*, March 1973.

> It does seem to me that economists have been continually peeling away one after another layer of mystery or misunderstanding about consumer spending only to find another, denser one below.
>
> Gardner Ackley (1971)
>
> But part of the job of economics is weeding out errors. That is much harder than making them, but also more fun.
>
> Robert Solow (1969)

A great deal of research, undertaken in recent years, has improved our understanding of consumer spending. The micro-foundation of aggregate consumer theory was cautiously reexamined from a number of perspectives. Careful attention was given to the process of aggregation from the behavior of individual consumers to aggregate consumption spending. Considerable empirical evidence, from cross-section surveys and cross-section samples of large groups of households to quarterly, annual, and even decade-long time series data, was collected and examined to test various aspects of consumer behavior. Detailed studies of specific commodity markets were undertaken, including studies of the markets for housing services and for various types of durable goods. Despite all of these efforts, the lead quote of this chapter from Gardner Ackley indicates that confidence in our aggregate consumption models has progressively deteriorated. The purpose of this chapter is to incorporate some of the major innovations into our understanding of consumer behavior and to point out some of the key unresolved issues.

Advanced Consumption Analysis

We saw that Keynes believed consumption to be dependent on disposable income. Disposable income is a measure of what economists call the constraint variable: the variable which limits the level of consumer spending. Other economists have suggested different constraint variables: permanent income, past peak income, nonhuman wealth, and so on. Keynes himself thought that certain types of income might be associated with different marginal propensities to consume. For example, he thought that income from transfer payments would produce high marginal consumption responses. One of the most interesting and important ideas was the permanent income hypothesis (PIH) of Milton Friedman in which he proposed permanent income as the appropriate constraint variable. The PIH reconciles the apparent inconsistencies in empirical evidence on consumption which were discussed in the previous chapter. In a *tour de force* Friedman challenged the central thesis of Keynesian theory and policy—the stability of the marginal propensity to consume. The PIH is a classic illustration of the interplay between theory and empirical evidence within the scope of positive economics.

Section A of this chapter contains an analysis of the PIH. In Section B a review of other major approaches to the constraint variable is presented including an attack by Robert Clower on the PIH and other models. Section C of this chapter briefly examines some recent work in durable goods consumption and expenditures. Consumption of durable goods occurs over many periods, and it is therefore necessary to modify consumption analysis to allow for the distinct treatment of both durable goods' consumption and expenditures. We shall see that some interesting ideas have been proposed for the analysis of consumer durables. One of the most important results to follow from this line of research has been the reemphasis in the consumption function of interest rates.

We know that the economy may be slow to react to exogenous changes. Consumers, for example, may react with a considerable lag to changes in their budget constraints. In Section C, the speed of consumers' reactions to parameter changes is also studied. It is shown that lagged responses are closely related to the development of expectations about future events. Professor Friedman's permanent income concept is seen to be a special type of lagged response.

A ● The Permanent Income Hypothesis

We shall begin our discussion of the Friedman consumption function with the nature of the model in terms of decision making. Consumption by households is the outcome of an intertemporal decision-making process. Families receive a flow of receipts over time and they allocate these receipts to a flow of consumption expenditures over time. If, in any period, the consumption flow exceeds the receipts, the family is said to dis-save. If consumption is less than receipts, the family is said to save. The theoretical problem is to explain how families determine the sequence of consumption expenditures from the sequence of receipts.

Friedman resolved the problem by arguing that consumption has two components, a permanent planned component based upon habits, budget planning, and current needs, and a transitory capricious component based upon whim, chance occurrence, and random phenomena. The permanent consumption component is a constant fraction of the family's "permanent income" while the transitory component fluctuates randomly about a value of zero. The keys to the hypothesis are the concept of permanent income and the proportionality between permanent consumption and permanent income.

Permanent income is defined as the amount one can spend while leaving wealth intact. This magnitude, not disposable income, constrains the economic agent in his consumption-saving choice. Permanent income takes into account a longer horizon than current receipts and recognizes that the central mass of consumption is based upon planned behavior. Letting $C(P)$ represent permanent consumption and $Y(P)$ permanent income, Friedman argues that:

$$C(P) = g Y(P) \tag{1}$$

Consumption is proportional to permanent income. Two questions arise: Why proportionality and what determines the value of g, the factor of proportionality?

Proportionality between consumption and permanent income derives from Friedman's microeconomic analysis. If the consumption equation (1) were not proportional, then this would suggest that the level of permanent income has an influence upon the proportion families allocate to different periods. Friedman did not feel this supposition to be reasonable.

The actual fraction of permanent income to be consumed by families depends on three factors—one's preferences for future as opposed to current consumption, the opportunity cost of current consumption, and one's uncertainty about future needs and wants. Note that the concept of consumption as an allocation to one period of permanent income rather than to another differs from consumption expenditures. For example, consumer expenditures on durable goods are expenditures to own goods which will yield a flow of services over time. It is the future flow of services which will be consumed. In other words, consumption of durable goods' services are included in consumption while expenditures on durable goods are included in savings.

Statistical Properties: The permanent income and consumption concepts developed above are *ex ante* concepts; that is, concepts about planned behavior rather than actual behavior. Desired permanent consumption is said to be proportional, under specific assumptions, to desired permanent income. To utilize economic data to study consumption, however, one must be careful to recognize that observed actual consumption and income are *ex post* in nature. That is, the actual data one observes is the product of both decision making and unplanned occurrences of the past. Consequently, measured magnitudes are not *ex ante* and do not correspond to the theoretical concepts discussed above.

Permanent income has been defined as that which can be spent without depleting wealth. However, wealth, the present value of one's future income stream, is not at any point in time known with certainty. In fact, the farther one projects into the future to determine receipts, the hazier is the picture. Given uncertainty, permanent income can be thought of as the income one can expect to allocate to each period without depleting wealth—*expected income*. Expected income is the income one normally expects to earn on wealth. The length of time into the future which one projects to decide expected income is called the *horizon*. The horizon may be three years, a lifetime, or longer. Measured income consists, in part, of unexpected receipts—windfall gains and unexpected short-falls. Friedman partitions measured income into two components, permanent income and transitory income:

$$Y = Y(P) + Y(T) \tag{2}$$

Transitory income, $Y(T)$, may be positive or negative, so that measured income may overstate or understate permanent income. Permanent income is the magnitude upon which decisions are based.

The actual measurement of permanent income depends in part upon theory and part upon empirical evidence. Individuals, at any time, can only develop expected values from current and past information. Expected income depends upon current and past levels of income. In fact, permanent income is a weighted average of current and past income levels. The farther from the present, the lower the weights assigned to past levels of income:

$$Y_t(P) = \sum_{i=0}^{H} w_i Y_{t-i} \qquad w_i > w_{i+1} \text{ for all } i \tag{3}$$

H is the length of the horizon. Equation (3) simply states that permanent income in period t is a weighted sum of current and past incomes, in which the weights, w_i, decline into the past. The actual values of the weights are determined by empirical procedures rather than theory.

The concept of transitory income can also be elaborated. If one were to trace aggregate income over time, certain fluctuations would be observed. Some of these fluctuations may not be viewed as permanent. For example, suppose a particularly bad crop year causes farm incomes to fall. To some extent the reduction in incomes is a transitory loss; transitory income has become negative.

Reconciliation of Evidence: The PIH may now be employed to reconcile the empirical evidence. The PIH states that the behavior of consumers in determining their consumption choice is represented by the proportional line observed by the long-run Kuznets data:

$$C = gY \tag{4}$$

The short-run time-series and cross-section data reveal a line which is nonproportional,

$$C = C_0 + bY \qquad (5)$$

and according to the PIH, this line is a statistical artifact. Measurement errors in C and Y, which occur in the short run or cross section, generate a nonproportional line that does not characterize behavior.

Figure 1 depicts the two consumption lines. The proportional line represents, according to the PIH, consumption behavior. The other line is an artifact. The long-run evidence coincides with the permanent consumption function because transitory errors in C and Y cancel one another out over the very long run. Thus Y measures $Y(P)$. The slope of the line, $MPC = APC$, is g, the factor of proportionality.

Since the PIH states that the proportional line represents the behavioral relation, how does it explain the nonproportional line? First, observe that the two lines intersect at average consumption and average income, because measured income and consumption equal their permanent counterparts on average. The two equations state that $C = \overline{C}$ when $Y = \overline{Y}$. The two may be compared at $Y = Y_0$. At Y_0, measured income is above average. In the short run, when $Y > \overline{Y}$, measured income is above average partly because transitory income is positive. Consequently, permanent income is less than Y_0 when measured income is Y_0. Consumption is based upon permanent income $Y_0(P)$, not measured income. Thus measured income at Y_0 overstates permanent income. C_0 was caused by $Y_0(P)$, but the latter is unobserved because of the error in measurement of income.

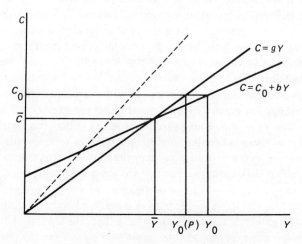

FIGURE 1   Permanent Income Hypothesis

In conclusion, errors in measured income overstate $Y(P)$ when income is large and understate $Y(P)$ when income is small. Overstatements of $Y(P)$ when Y is large cause APC to appear small, and understatements of $Y(P)$ when Y is small cause APC to appear large. Therefore, measured income makes APC appear to decline as income increases. Friedman shows that once one adjusts properly for transitory components, APC is seen to be constant. The reader may test his understanding of the PIH by reconciling points on the two observed lines, below $\overline{Y}$.

Policy Implications and Reservations: The theoretical and policy implications of the PIH are far-reaching. Friedman has shown that current measured income may not correspond to the income concept upon which consumers base their decisions. A change in measured income may not completely correspond to a change in permanent income. If a measured income change is viewed by individuals as transitory, the marginal propensity to consume will be zero. If the measured income change is viewed as permanent, then MPC will be large. Thus MPC in response to an income change will depend upon the perception of the individual about the nature of the income change. MPC is not stable. The stability of MPC was a central reliable feature of behavior in Keynesian theory and thus the PIH dealt this relation a severe blow.

Because permanent income takes time to change, the PIH may suggest that the Keynesian multipliers operate more slowly than previously believed. This result is extremely damaging to Keynesian macroeconomic policy. A primary policy use of the Keynesian analysis would be to induce countercyclical variations in measured income in order to cause countercyclical variations in consumption spending. In other words, dampen disposable income and therefore consumption during booms and stimulate these magnitudes during slowdowns. Because of the multipliers, small exogenous changes could be utilized to generate large consumption and income changes. However, if consumption responds only slowly to income changes, the impacts of the multipliers may be occurring later than expected. In fact, seemingly countercyclical measures, designed to dampen economic fluctuations and stabilize the economy, may end up being procyclical and destabilizing!

Just as the Keynesian consumption hypothesis came under considerable scientific scrutiny, Friedman's PIH has come under the gun of scientific examination. A number of reservations must be observed. First, the conclusion that expected income changes are the only income changes which result in increases in consumption raises the issue of what happens to transitory changes in income? The answer is that they are saved, but this answer is not wholly adequate. Recall that consumption excludes purchases of durable goods in the current period. If an increase in income results in an increase in durable goods expenditures, the PIH treats this expenditure as a saving! It is, from a theoretical point of view, correct to distribute the expense on durable goods purchases over the periods during which the goods' services are actually consumed. It is correct, then, to treat purchases of durables as mainly saving for future consumption. However, from the point of view of evaluating multipliers one must account for expenditures on durables, not consumption of services.

One must be cautious about drawing conclusions about dynamic multipliers from the PIH. The PIH is about one behavioral equation of the model, and the dynamics of multipliers will depend upon many factors. The speed of reactions to an exogenous variable will depend upon the nature of the entire model and not merely upon any one equation. The PIH may suggest slower reactions but the speed of reactions depends upon the other elements of the model as well as the nature of expected income.

Methodologically, the PIH exemplifies positive economics. The analysis began with a consumption hypothesis. When confronted with empirical evidence, inconsistencies were observed. A new hypothesis was developed to reconcile the inconsistencies, and our understanding of consumer behavior improved.

B ● Income or Wealth?

We saw in the previous section that conflicting empirical evidence on aggregate consumption spending led Professor Friedman to introduce the permanent income concept. Another economist, Professor James Duesenberry of Harvard University, utilized a very different approach to the same problem.

Past-Peak Income: James Duesenberry in 1949 proposed a very imaginative approach to consumption behavior. Unsatisfied with cross-section consumption evidence, Duesenberry reasoned that while a relation such as the Keynesian consumption function may appear stable from short-run evidence, other factors on which consumption depends may not have changed over the short period under observation. Once outside the observed short-run period, these alternative factors may suddenly change, thus violating what had appeared to be a stable relationship. Duesenberry argued that the early tests of the consumption function were undertaken in an aberrant period of time in which some important alternative factors were fixed. Specifically, the 1930s and early 1940s were unusual, because much of the period was spent in a depression, and the income of many families was below what it had been in the past. Duesenberry explains how this aberrant period led to a misspecification of the consumption function.

Cross-section evidence on consumer behavior failed to account for the direction of the change in income *vis-à-vis* the initial standard of living. Duesenberry believed that consumers would respond differently to income increases than to income decreases. His view was that income decreases would be difficult to adjust to, because families have a difficult time lowering their standard of living. For example, if your income last year was $20,000 and it fell this year to $15,000, then you may attempt to maintain your former relatively high standard of living even though your realized income has become only $15,000.

Another family with an income of $15,000 who had never before had such a high income is likely to have a different spending pattern than yours, even though your current measured incomes are the same. In order to deal with this phenomenon, Duesenberry postulated his *relative income hypothesis* (RIH) in which consumption depends both upon current income and upon the highest income attained by the consumer in the past. If one's income exceeds the previous peak level of income, then no downward adjustments in living standards are necessary, and consumption will adjust to income according to a proportional relationship. (In other words, in this case, consumption will be related to income, as it was discovered to be by Kuznets in his long-run consumption function.) If, however, income has fallen below one's previous peak income, then one's consumption will react more gradually to the change in income. In this case, consumption will fall less than proportionately to the reduction in income, producing a flatter consumption line than the one observed in the long-run Kuznets data.

To illustrate this relative income hypothesis consider consumption responses to increases in income from an initial level Y_0 to Y_1. If it is assumed that income is rising so that at each point in time current income is also past-peak income, consumption may increase along a path according to the following formula:

$$C_t = 0.9Y_t \tag{6}$$

Figure 2 illustrates such a response as path *a*. Suppose income now begins to fall from peak Y_1; consumption will fall but along a different path. Consumption will not only respond to Y_t but also Y_1. Consider formula (7):

$$C_t = 0.95Y_t - 0.05Y_t^2/Y_p \tag{7}$$

where Yp is past-peak income. Whenever $Y_t = Y_p$, that is, when current income is the peak, (7) is equivalent to (6). When, however, income has fallen from a past peak, (7) will differ, and C_t will move on a different path from that described in (6). Suppose, for example, that $Y_1 = 20,000$ and income falls to 18,000, 15,000, and 10,000 in successive periods. Consumption will fall to 16,290, 13,687.5, and 9,250, respectively. These values for consumption compare to those, according to path *a* and the corresponding income values, of 16,200, 13,500, and 9,000. Path *b*, that according to (2) given past peak $Y_p = Y_1$, is depicted in Figure 2.

In general, consumption's response to changes in income depends upon the circumstances in which the changes occur. As income once again increases from 10,000 back to 20,000, equation (7) will continue to hold. As income exceeds 20,000, however, current income again becomes past peak and (7) degenerates into (6). Should income fall again somewhat later, for example at Y_2 in Figure 2, consumption will decline subject both to Y_t and to Y_2, because Y_2 is the new past-peak income. Since the consumption line looks like a ratchet and since

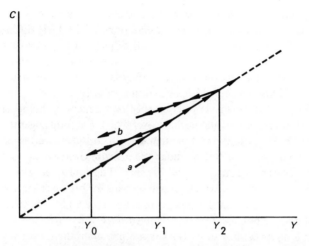

FIGURE 2   Relative Income Hypothesis

consumption is, in a sense, being ratcheted upward, the effect expressed in (7) is called a *ratchet effect*.

Duesenberry attributed his consumption theory to the idea that consumer preferences were interdependent and irreversible. Habits of consumption depended in part upon others' consumption, thus interdependence; and the consumption path taken if income fell would differ from that which consumption had taken when income was rising, thus irreversibility. This hypothesis, like Friedman's, explains why the *APC* was large in the 1930s even though *APC* may, over the long run, be constant. Furthermore, the Duesenberry model may well explain why consumption seems to react slowly to tax increases and reductions in disposable income as seemed to be the case in 1968 when a tax surcharge was imposed on the U.S. economy.

Duesenberry's RIH has not had the lasting impact of the permanent income hypothesis, nor of the life cycle hypothesis to be examined next. The reason for this is no doubt the fact that the RIH only explains nonproportional consumption when income is below past peak coupled with the fact that U.S. personal income has not fallen for any length of time below past peak since the Great Depression. Nevertheless, a valuable lesson from the RIH is that history can produce distorted experiments and these distortions may become evident only when outside the sample period. Furthermore, Duesenberry reminds us that economic behavior can be asymmetrical and intertemporally dependent. Duesenberry's ratchet effect gives us some idea of how to deal mathematically with such problems.

Wealth and Wage Income: One of the most important and influential theories of consumption behavior was developed by three economists, Modigliani, Ando, and Brumberg. The Modigliani, Ando, and Brumberg (MAB) theory is called the life cycle hypothesis (LCH). MAB, like Friedman and Duesenberry, build their consumption function from microeconomic analysis of the behavior of individual consumers. The underlying micro foundations in the LCH differ, however, from those of Duesenberry and Friedman. Whereas Duesenberry considered consumer preferences to be interdependent and irreversible, and thus essentially rejected the traditional microeconomic analysis of consumer behavior, both Friedman and MAB developed their consumption functions from traditional economic theory. Friedman views consumer preferences as homogeneous and symmetrical, but argues that the horizon over which economic agents make their decisions can be determined from data. MAB also consider intertemporal preferences to be homogeneous, but consider the horizon over which consumers are making their choices to consist of the life span. The consumer takes as given his initial assets and the wage at which he will be paid for his labor services. In other words, all of his initial wealth, except his own labor ability, is taken as given. His *wage income* is not assumed to be given until the consumer decides when and for how long he wishes to work. The lifetime plan, then, involves determining simultaneously a stream of labor services he will provide and a lifetime consumption stream. The LCH planner receives utility for consumption and disutility from the time spent working. He maximizes his utility over his lifetime, given his stock of nonhuman wealth and given the wage he expects to be offered from the labor he decides to supply. While we shall not undertake the actual mathematics to derive a consumption pattern, we can examine some of the aspects of this life cycle model.

One important aspect of the LCH is that the Keynesian constraint variable, disposable income, is replaced by a wealth constraint. This wealth constraint, unlike permanent income, reflects the value only of nonhuman assets. Most important, the consumer simultaneously determines his wage income and his consumption pattern so that consumption does not depend upon income.

It is the dependence of consumption on wealth which produces long-run proportionality in the traditional consumption function. The argument for proportionality is as follows: In the long run, income tracks wealth closely. In the long run, realized income is congruent with expected income, and expected income is proportional to wealth. (The reason for this proportionality is that expected income is the expected return on wealth and the rate of return in the long run on wealth is probably relatively constant.) Over the long run, then, the return on nonhuman wealth plus labor income, which comprise expected income, grow at some steady secular trend rate. Consumers making life cycle plans will spend in proportion to these steady secular trend values.

Of course, over the short run wage income is procyclical, and unexpected changes take place in nonwage wealth. The procyclical wage income fluctuations produce the counter cyclical swings in the average propensity to consume (*APC*) due to the more stable life cycle consumption plans. Similarly, unexpected changes in nonhuman wealth, such as sudden changes in equity prices, produce alterations in the life cycle plans. Like Friedman's permanent income hypothesis, then, the LCH reconciles the long- and short-run empirical evidence of consumption spending by rejecting the short-run nonproportional line as an indicator of planned consumption behavior.

A second element of the LCH is that since consumers are making an intertemporal spending decision, their consumption patterns will be influenced by the rate of return they could earn on income not spent, and by the rate they would be charged if they had to borrow. Of course, these rates are measured by interest rates. Thus the LCH reintroduces interest rates into the consumption decision. The interest rate measures the rate at which the consumer can substitute one dollar of current consumption for future consumption. Given his personal rate at which he prefers to substitute current for future consumption, an increase in the rate of interest would ordinarily reduce current consumption and increase saving for future consumption.

The spirit of the LCH is that families, recognizing that their wage earnings and perhaps their property income streams will fluctuate over their lifetimes, attempt to smooth out these fluctuating streams so that their consumption patterns are relatively stable. Figure 3 depicts the spirit of the life-cycle hypothesis. We see, from the lightly dashed line in Figure 3, that income, earned by labor, rises to a peak at mid-life of the earning unit of the family and then declines at retirement. If one were to calculate the present value of income earned at each period of time in the future for this individual family, then the life cycle of income is dampened somewhat, as illustrated by the solid income stream labeled "discounted Y." The consumption paths in Figure 3 are seen to be considerably smoother than the income streams, rising only gradually in actual terms and being even smoother when calculated in present value terms. Notice that the LCH as depicted in Figure 3 suggests that younger families will be consuming above their income. (The consumption lines are above the income lines in the early years of the family's life.) Similarly, we see that retired families are consuming above their incomes. Families in middle life are "overearning" in terms

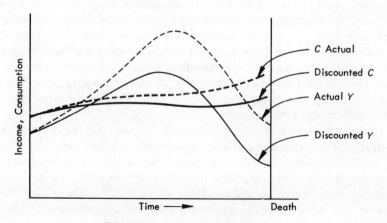

FIGURE 3   Life-cycle Hypothesis

of their current consumption, because they are paying off debts incurred in early life and they are saving for retirement. This pattern indicates that the age composition of the population may have an influence on the relationship between consumption and income.

The life-cycle hypothesis is obviously a very rich and detailed analysis of consumer behavior. It brings together a number of important influences, including wealth, wage income, interest rates, and demographic characteristics, while within the framework of a carefully specified theoretical model. In addition to providing a specific measure of the relationship between aggregate consumption and other economic variables, this model has proved to be a very useful tool for analyzing a number of economic questions in which consumer behavior plays a role. Nevertheless, some of the ideas expressed by Keynes may well have been lost in this model in which careful planning takes place in a relatively certain environment.

Real Cash Balances: The role of wealth in the consumption function is central to the LCH, just as long-run expected income was central to the PIH. It should be clear by now that at any point in time, consumers base their consumption-savings choice on an intertemporal plan allowing, in some fashion, for their long-run command over resources. The PIH stressed expectations in constructing the constraint variable. The RIH emphasized the highest living habits which prevailed when a decision was made. The LCH, we have now seen, focused upon the long-run nature of consumer planning. Still other models concentrate on the form in which wealth is held by households.

A. C. Pigou and others, mainly monetarists, emphasize both wealth and the form in which wealth is held in the portfolio, especially the monetary assets held by households. Their analysis contains two distinct arguments. First, increases in wealth, *ceteris paribus*, induce increases in consumption expenditures. Pigou and his followers utilized the role of wealth as a counterattack on Keynes's consumption thesis. They argued that in a depression, while income flows were declining, the accompanying reduction in commodity prices was increasing the purchasing power of monetary wealth held in household portfolios. As the value of wealth was increased, consumption, Pigouvians argued, was increased as well. This effect is called the *Pigou wealth effect*. While it is somewhat premature to fully consider the Pigou effect, recall that in fact commodity prices fell substantially during the Great Depression and therefore increases in monetary wealth were likely to have occurred.

The second element of the Pigou position is based upon the composition of wealth rather than its size. In particular, given wealth, consumption may depend on the proportion of wealth held in cash form. Given wealth, an increase in the proportion held in cash balances, rather than other types of assets, will increase consumption expenditures, because portfolios are more liquid. The positive relation between real balances in the wealth portfolio and consumption is called the

Pigou real balance effect. Since cash balances are readily exchanged for commodities and since other assets are ordinarily more difficult to exchange, consumption may increase with the change in wealth *composition.*

Liquidity Constraints and the Dual Decision Hypothesis:

At this point a brief summary of the development of consumption analysis since Keynes may be useful. Remember, Keynes believed that consumption depended upon the current flow of earned income which he measured with disposable income. However, inconsistencies in empirical evidence produced throughout the 1940s and 1950s led economists to the development of new consumption models based upon established microeconomic theory. This established, or orthodox, theory produced two important and widely used consumption hypotheses; the permanent income hypothesis and the life-cycle hypothesis. One very important theme is common to both of these hypotheses. That theme is reliance on a theory in which rational economic agents derive their consumption expenditures from carefully laid plans in which they optimize the utility from a consumption flow subject to a constraint measure of their long-run command over resources. Implicit in both models is the assumption that economic agents are able to consume from their long-run command over resources *exclusive* of their actual current receipts. For example, in both models, if a consumer is confronted with a temporary reduction in actual earned income, he is still capable of borrowing on the basis of future expected income.

Thus both theories imply not only that consumers are rational but also that the economic environment is sufficiently certain to allow them to act on the basis of meaningful long-run plans. Furthermore, financial markets are sufficiently well developed, and the environment is sufficiently certain, to allow consumers to borrow when their plans call for consumption in excess of their current receipts. Remember back in Chapter 4 the difference between the ideas of Keynes and those of the classical economists depicted by Walras. Remember that Walras's analysis had economic agents making careful plans in a completely certain environment. Keynes, on the other hand, argued that the environment was uncertain and suggested that economic agents may be unable to act as they were assumed to act in the Walrasian system.

Keynes in 1937 wrote:

> By "uncertain" knowledge, let me explain, ... The sense in which I am using the term is that in which the prospect of a European war is uncertain, or the price of copper and the rate of interest twenty years hence, or the obsolescence of a new invention, or the position of private wealthowners in the social system in 1970. About these matters there is no scientific basis on which to form any capable probability whatever. We simply do not know.[1]

[1] "The General Theory of Employment," *Quarterly Journal of Economics*, 1937, pp. 209-223.

Are Keynes's ideas wrong? Do current flows of income matter? Can agents, in our uncertain world, act on the basis of carefully laid plans? Some analysis in recent years suggests that as elegant as they may be, these new theories of consumption behavior assume that the world works better than it actually does. We shall consider two of these arguments.

James Tobin and Walter Dolde (1971) argue that since households' future incomes are uncertain, the consumption patterns derived from a long-run plan such as in the LCH may not be an accurate description of consumer behavior. Specifically, they argue that many households may be constrained not simply by their command over resources, but also by the relative liquidity of their assets. For example, consider a young family who would like to consume in the current period more than their current receipts. In the LCH, this young family could borrow on the basis of its future earning power and its nonhuman wealth. However, to what extent can one really borrow on the basis of one's future earning power? Will banks lend large sums of money to college students just because the students expect some day to have a higher level of income? It may be that in many situations borrowing on one's future earning power is extremely difficult. Even when borrowing is permitted, the rates charged for borrowing may be quite high compared to rates available for lending.

Given the nature of financial markets, one may wish to consider consumption to be constrained by the liquidity power of one's wealth rather than by its eventual command over resources. Though by today's vigorous modeling standards his notions may have been somewhat primitive, Keynes's idea was that disposable income would represent the liquidity of the portfolio rather than its command over resources. Thus the analysis of Tobin and Dolde suggests that once we take into account the liquidity restraints on households, we no longer find that consumption depends only on very slow-moving variables like wealth or expected income. One important implication of the Tobin-Dolde analysis, in addition to the suggestion that Keynes's consumption ideas are revitalized, is the idea that policy measures may operate in the short run on the marginal propensity to consume by changing the liquidity nature of the portfolio.

A second important attempt to revitalize the Keynesian consumption hypothesis was undertaken by Robert Clower in 1969 in which he asks: How do these consumers respond when the market fails to allow them to satisfy their carefully laid plans? To quote Clower,

> Specifically, imagine that we have a strong wish to satisfy our champagne appetites but that the demand for our services as economic consultants does not in fact allow us to gratify this desire without doing serious damage to our household finances. How do we communicate our thirstiness to producers of champagne; how can they be made aware of our willingness to solve their market research problems in exchange for copious quantities of their excellent beverage?
>
> The answer is that we do so indirectly. We offer more favorable terms to potential buyers of our services (these may include some champagne merchants), leaving it to the market to provide us more employment and

income and, in due time, more booze. Do we also signal our craving directly by drawing on money balances and savings accounts and sending our children out to work? In short, do we drink more even before we work more? Or do we become, at least temporarily, involuntarily abstemious and postpone our satisfaction to financially more propitious times?

Clower goes on to develop the dual decision hypothesis in which the first decision is the type of consumption decision based on a LCH model and the second decision is a new one which takes into account the inability, if such should occur, of the economic agent to fulfill his plans. Special emphasis is on one's inability to sell the planned quantity of his labor services. The second decision, also an optimization decision, differs from the first because now the consumer is able to earn only as much income as would currently be bought by the market. If that level of income is less than the amount called for in his plan, then he must optimize his consumption subject to an income constraint imposed by the market. Clower shows that in this second decision the level of consumption will depend upon the level of current measured income which is mandated to the consumer by the market. An interesting implication of Clower's analysis is that consumption demand produced by the dual decision hypothesis will be the same as the LCH consumption demand only in the special case in which the market allows consumers to sell the amount of labor services which they had planned to sell. In other words, the solution to the planned decision is a special case of the more general dual decision hypothesis. Recall that Keynes himself had argued that his theory was a general one of which the classical theory was but one special case.

C ● Durable Goods and the Speed of Adjustment

The authors of the permanent income hypothesis and the life-cycle hypothesis both distinguish between durable goods expenditures and durable goods consumption. The national income accounts distinguish between residential construction, or housing starts, and consumption of housing services. Residential construction is included as a component of private domestic investment, and consumption of housing services is included in the service component of consumption expenditures. Neither durables nor housing services are small elements of national economic activity. Residential construction, for example, has been estimated to account for a quarter to a third of gross private domestic investment. Alan Hess has shown that durables expenditures are the third most volatile component of GNP, after inventory investment and federal government expenditures. Consequently, durable goods expenditures fluctuate rather violently so that "most modern theories give it a key role in causing and/or exacerbating business fluctuations," according to Harberger. In this section, these important elements of consumption, placed into the background until now, are the main focus of attention.

Both durables and housing confront the economist with similar and difficult problems. While expenditures on durables and housing are market activities, consumption of the services is ordinarily extramarket activity. In some cases houses are rented, and, more rarely, durables are rented. When rented, the rents charged the consumer correspond to the price of the service being consumed. However, homes are usually owner-occupied and durables are ordinarily consumed directly by the owner. Imputations are required to measure and evaluate these extra-market activities.

Implicit Service Prices: A useful tool in understanding durable goods consumption is the concept of the *user-cost* or *implicit rental price* of a durable. One may define the user cost as the cost (implicit or explicit) of the services provided by the durable as opposed to the cost or price of owning the asset. While some durable goods are leased, consumer durables are usually purchased and then used by the owner over a period of time. Thus user-costs are rarely observed market prices. It is helpful in developing the user-cost concept to view ownership of a durable as consisting of the rights to the future flow of services from the durable good. Durables deteriorate as they age and therefore provide both a lower quality and a lower quantity of services. Used durables also become obsolete relative to newer models that are issued. Consequently, the services provided by a durable when old are likely to be worth less than those it provided when new. It is necessary, therefore, in determining the user-cost of a durable to identify services by age. Since technology, prices, and other things change over time, it is also necessary to distinguish between dates when identifying the user-cost. Let the symbol $C(s, t)$ signify the value to a user of a durable age s at time t. A new durable good at time t is going to yield a future flow of services, and corresponding to this flow of services is a sequence of future implicit values to the user which may be respresented as:

$$C(0, t), C(1, t + 1), C(2, t + 2), \ldots, C(s, t + s), \ldots \tag{8}$$

The present value of this future flow of implicit user values is the present discounted value of the above sequence. We can gain insight into the nature of these user values if we can establish a relationship between the user values of the durable services and the price one pays to purchase the durable. While in fact the above sequence of user values cannot actually be known in advance of purchasing a new durable good, one does know that a durable will provide a future flow of services and that associated with this flow of services will be an implicit flow of future values. Precisely how long the durable will provide services, what type of maintenance and repair expenses will be incurred, how rapidly the durable will deteriorate and so forth cannot be known *a priori*. It is, nevertheless, useful for us to analyze the relationships between purchase prices and user values. In order to do so, let us make assumptions that make this relationship as simple as possible. Specifically, assume that we have perfectly competitive durables markets, perfect financial markets, and individuals with perfect foresight. Under these conditions, in order to receive the ownership rights to a durable asset, one would pay exactly the present value of the above sequence of user values.

$$p(0, t) = \sum_{s=0}^{n} \frac{C(s, t + s)}{(1 + R)^s} \tag{9}$$

where n is the age of the durable good when it will perish. Under the same restrictive assumptions, similar reasoning will yield an expression for the present value of a one-year-old asset at time $t + 1$ related to its present and future service values:

$$p(1, t + 1) = \sum_{s=1}^{n} \frac{C(s, t + s)}{(1 + R)^{s-1}} \tag{10}$$

It is convenient to write (9) as:

$$p(0, t) = C(0, t) + \frac{1}{1 + R} \sum_{s=1}^{n} \frac{C(s, t + s)}{(1 + R)^{s-1}} \tag{11}$$

The sum on the right-hand side of equation (11) is equation (10); therefore,

$$p(0, t) = C(0, t) + p(1, t + 1)(1 + R) \tag{12}$$

While a market price for a durable asset usually can be observed, the service value flow, $C(0, t)$ cannot be directly observed. However, we may equate at the margin the market price to the present value of the future service flow. Thus, we can solve equation (12) for $C(0, t)$ in terms of $p(0, t)$ and $p(1, t + 1)$ which depict the acquisition prices of new and used assets respectively and in terms of the discount rate R:

$$C(0, t) = \frac{Rp(0, t) + p(0, t) - p(1, t + 1)}{(1 + R)} \tag{13}$$

$C(0, t)$ is defined as the *user-cost* of the services from a new durable in period t, i.e., equation (13) expresses this implicit rental price of the durable, the price of the period t flow of services from the durable to the user, in terms of the durable's rate of return R and acquisition prices.

As we mentioned above, durable goods are ordinarily purchased and then used by the owner for a long period of time. Consequently, the user-cost is rarely an observed market price. Rather, one must infer the user-cost from other market information that may be available. One of the values of equation (13) is that this unobserved user-cost of the durable services is seen to be related to an interest rate R which may be represented by a market rate of interest and an acquisition price p which may be represented by the market prices of assets when they are bought and sold. In other words, equation (13) may be employed to impute from market acquisition prices and interest rates implicit user-costs.

When the assumptions of competition and perfect foresight are relaxed, the problem of relating the user-cost to the acquisition price becomes more complex. For example, one may not know the rate of interest which will be forgone in holding an asset until after the period has occurred. In addition, one does not know whether capital gains or losses will occur in the future. Different assumptions about the organization of markets and the extent of information about the future will lead to different methods of constructing a user-cost type equation. A good deal of economic research is currently being undertaken to analyze how economic agents, operating in uncertainty, develop expectations about prices in the future. We shall have something to say about this later in the book.

Speed of Adjustment: Our discussion of the speed of adjustment begins with the work of L. M. Koyck. Though economists had long recognized that consumption spending may respond to changes in exogenous variables only after a lengthy delay, barriers to estimation of these lags were believed to be intractable. Suppose a household's income increases. Its consumption spending may react gradually over time to its new standard of living if persons are slow to adjust their habits and plans to accommodate exogenous changes, i.e., consumption spending may react with a distributed lag to a once and for all change in income. Koyck developed a simplifying technique to measuring the lag process even though the response of a dependent to an independent variable may be distributed over time. Koyck worked on investment behavior, which is the subject of later chapters, but his work is applicable to consumer lag reactions also.

Suppose a household's income, after having remained in equilibrium for a long period of time, is subject to a once and for all increase. A number of reactions to this shift in the budget constraint are possible. Figure 4 depicts several paths consumption spending might take in response to a once and for all increase in income. This wide range of possibilities indicates the complexity of the lag problem. It may indeed seem impossible to actually measure the nature of the lag process.

Utilizing some fairly straightforward mathematics, however, Koyck greatly simplified the problem of measuring the lag process. Consumption may respond over time to a change in income with a *distributed lag*. Consumption spending in any time period, then, consists of responses to current and past levels of incomes. C_t is reacting to y_t, y_{t-1}, y_{t-2}, and so on. Defining a_i as the reaction of C_t to y_{t-i}, we can write

$$C_t = a_0 y_t + a_1 y_{t-1} + a_2 y_{t-2} + \ldots \tag{14}$$

The Koyck restriction of the a_i, which facilitates measurement of lags, is

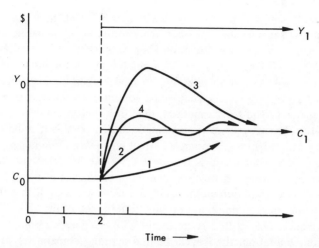

FIGURE 4   Consumption Paths in Response to a Step Change in Income

that each a_i is a constant fraction of the previous a_{i-1}. Therefore $a_1 = \lambda a_0$, $a_2 = \lambda^2 a_0$, $a_3 = \lambda^3 a_0$, and so on. Equation (14) may be replaced by (15):

$$C_t = a_0 \sum_{i=0}^{\infty} \lambda^i y_{t-i} \tag{15}$$

Suppose a once and for all, or step, change in income has occurred. What will the total long-run multiplier be? Suppose the income change has occurred long ago so that $y_{t-i} = \overline{y}$ for all i, and equilibrium is attained. Equation (15) becomes

$$C_t = \overline{y} a_0 \sum_{i=0}^{\infty} \lambda^i \tag{16}$$

The sum $\sum_{i=0}^{\infty} \lambda^i$ is a geometric sum whose solution is $1/(1 - \lambda)$.[2] Equation (16) becomes

$$\overline{C}t = \overline{y} a_0 / (1 - \lambda) \tag{17}$$

[2] Consider the sum up to a number n:

$$s_n = 1 + \lambda + \lambda^2 + \lambda^3 + \ldots + \lambda^n$$

$$\lambda s_n = \lambda + \lambda^2 + \lambda^3 + \ldots + \lambda^{n+1}$$

Subtracting (2) from (1) gives

$$(1 - \lambda)s_n = 1 - \lambda^{n+1}$$

$$s_n = (1 - \lambda^{n+1})/(1 - \lambda)$$

As n becomes large, λ^{n+1} approaches zero, as $\lambda < 1$ and $s_n = 1/(1 - \lambda)$.

The full multiplier will be $a_0/(1 - \lambda)$ where a_0 is called the *impact multiplier*.

Let us now examine some possible values of a_0 and λ to evaluate the nature of the Koyck assumption in Equation (14). Suppose $a_0 = 0.1$ and $\lambda = 0.6$. The full multiplier is $0.1/(1 - 0.6)$ or 0.25. Equilibrium consumption, corresponding to $\overline{C_1}$ in Figure 4, is determined by $\overline{y}_1$, the new equilibrium income, and the full multiplier. Since $\lambda < 1$, each succeeding consumption increase is less than the previous increase. The Koyck method, then, rules out a number of possible reaction paths. The Koyck restriction on the coefficients a_i may be represented graphically as in Figure 5. The largest effect on consumption in period t is from current period t income and is represented by the impact multiplier, a_0. The impacts of more distant incomes on consumption decline at a constant rate, λ. Thus the Koyck restriction on the a_is is equivalent to assuming that they decline according to a constant deterioration function. In fact, of the paths illustrated in Figure 4 above, only path 2 is consistent with the Koyck assumption. Despite this obvious limitation, the Koyck method permits comparatively useful measurement of the lag within a broad range of possibilities. Figure 6 depicts some possible lag patterns consistent with the Koyck framework.[3]

The Koyck simplification can be shown to allow estimation of λ and a_0, and thus both the size and speed of multipliers, from very little data. Equation (15), expressing consumption as a distributed lag function of income, can be simplified as follows:

$$C_t - \lambda C_{t-1} = [a_0 y_t + \lambda a_0 y_{t-1} + \lambda^2 a_0 y_{t-2} + \ldots]$$
$$- [\lambda a_0 y_{t-1} + \lambda^2 a_0 y_{t-2} + \ldots] \tag{18}$$

or

$$C_t - \lambda C_{t-1} = a_0 y_t$$

Solving for C_t, we obtain

$$C_t = \lambda C_{t-1} + a_0 y_t \tag{19}$$

Equation (19) may be used to estimate from time series data on y and C both the speed of adjustment λ and the impact multiplier a_0.

The Koyck lag itself can be derived from economic ideas. Suppose one postulates that individuals formulate expectations about their incomes from their past incomes and that consumption is proportional to expected income; then

[3] A note of caution: the numerical and algebraic analysis is somewhat simpler with time periods and the figures are simpler with smooth curved paths. In fact the smooth paths come from analysis of continuous time.

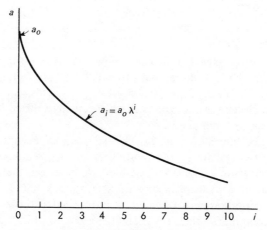

FIGURE 5   Koyck Restriction on Lag Terms

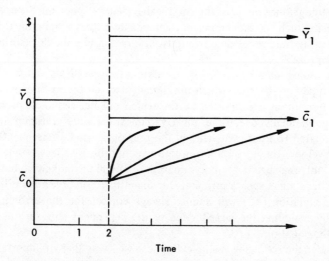

FIGURE 6   Possible Consumption Paths Under Koyck Restriction

$$C_t = \alpha Y_t^e = \alpha \sum_{i=1}^{\infty} \lambda^i y_{t-i} \tag{20}$$

where α is the proportionality factor. Equation (20) is the same form as (15) which imposes the Koyck restriction on the distributed lag. Thus the Koyck lag distribution may be interpreted as an *adapted expectation* mechanism on income. Furthermore, these expressions for expected income are very similar to equation (3) in part A expressing permanent income, according to Professor Friedman, as a weighted average of past levels of measured income:

$$Y_t(P) = \sum_{i=0}^{H} w_i Y_{t-i}$$

Permanent income or expected income is now seen as very simple adaptive expectation variable. Each w_i corresponds to $a_0(1 - a_0)^i$. In fact, if $a_0 = 0.33$, the w_i sequence is 0.33, 0.218, 0.144, 0.095, 0.063, ... This sequence of weights truncated at an eleven-year horizon is the one actually utilized by Friedman in the permanent income hypothesis.

Because it is so convenient, the Koyck restriction has been widely employed by economists to estimate impact multipliers and the sequence of effects of exogenous variables on endogenous variables. We have seen that implicit in the construction of the permanent income variable, for example, is a Koyck distributed lag. An important *caveat* should be introduced at this point concerning the Koyck restriction. Consider equation (19) above in which the lagged effects on consumption of income are estimated by expressing consumption as a function of income and of lagged consumption itself. This type of specification can be misleading. Since much of the empirical evidence supporting the consumption hypotheses, such as the permanent income hypothesis, rely on this type of analysis using time series data, we must briefly consider the difficulties inherent in this approach.

When doing empirical studies of economic hypotheses, researchers study various types of statistics which are designed to tell the researcher whether or not the hypothesis is supported by the evidence. Since economic processes tend to change gradually over time, most variables, certainly consumption, will be closely related to their own value in the previous period. Consequently, even if, as we develop a theory of consumption expenditures, we leave some important variable out, the specification in equation (19) will be unlikely to indicate to us that we have made such a mistake. Our inability to observe error is because the form of equation (19) will almost always correct for the error in the next period by including the lagged value of the dependent term on the right-hand side of the equation.

Consider the following example. Suppose we know that an important variable has been left out of our model to describe consumption. Suppose we then estimate our model, which is knowingly incorrect, using a specification such as equation (19). Specification (19) will probably produce results that will not indicate to us that errors have been made in our hypothesis. Specification (19) will perform well because consumption tends to move gradually over time, and by including last period's consumption on the right-hand side of equation (19) in estimating current period's consumption, we will have automatically eliminated error from the right-hand side of the equation to the extent that the left-out variable took on the same value as in this period. In other words, specifications such as equation (19) are treacherous in that they have a tendency to obscure exactly those errors which the usual empirical tests are designed to identify.

STUDY QUESTIONS AND PROBLEMS

1. What role do interest rates play in consumption-saving choices? Consider, in particular, the following: borrowing, lending, saving, discounting, wealth, permanent income, and opportunity cost.

2. Define and illustrate each of the following terms:

transitory income
ex ante and *ex post*
permanent consumption

What role does each of the above terms play in the permanent income hypothesis?

3. Compare the theory of the permanent income hypothesis to Keynes's psychological laws of consumption.

4. Why do individuals save according to the permanent income hypothesis? What factors might change the average propensity to save?

5. How do the permanent income hypothesis and Keynesian consumption hypothesis differ in terms of their policy implications?

6. Compare the policy implications of each of the following theories of consumption behavior:

a. The permanent income hypothesis.
b. The relative income hypothesis.
c. The life cycle hypothesis.

7. Consider the reaction of consumption to a step increase in income, subsequently sustained, in each of the following models:

a. $C_t = C_{t-1} + .4(C_t^* - C_{t-1})$ where $C_t^* = .9Y$
b. $C_t = C_{t-1} + 1.5(C_t^* - C_{t-1})$ where $C_t^* = .9Y$

8. Define and illustrate the use of each of the following expressions in consumption theory:

ratchet effect
distributed lag
Koyck transformation
implicit rental price
expected income
real balance effect

9. How does Koyck restrict distributed lags? Are there any benefits to be gained by this restriction?

10. Utilizing the following Duesenberry-style consumption function,

$$C_t = 0.85Y_t - .1\frac{Y_t^2}{Y_p}$$

where Y_p is past-peak income, compute and diagram consumption for the following sequence of income values. (Assume at $t = 0$, past-peak income is 1000).

t	Y_t
0	1000
1	1500
2	2000
3	3000
4	5000
5	4000
6	3000
7	4000
8	5000
9	6000
10	8000
11	7000
12	5000
13	9000
14	8000
15	10000

11. Evaluate the life-cycle hypothesis in light of the dual decision hypothesis.

12. What is the appropriate choice variable for a LCH consumer? a RIH consumer? a Clower consumer? Which consumer most closely behaves as a Keynesian consumer?

13. "User-cost concepts require used asset markets to make any sense." True or false? Discuss.

14. Can Keynes's consumption function exist in a Walrasian world? (*Hint*: Reread Part A of Chapter 4.)

REFERENCES

Ackley, Gardner, Discussion, *Consumer Spending and Monetary Policy: The Linkages*, Proceedings of a Monetary Conference, Nantucket Island, Massachusetts, June 1971; sponsored by The Federal Reserve Bank of Boston, Boston, Mass.

Agarwala, R., and J. Drinkwater, "Consumption Functions with Shifting Parameters Due to Socio-Economic Factors," *Review of Economics and Statistics*, February, 1972.

Ando, A., and Franco Modigliani, "The 'Life Cycle' Hypothesis of Saving: Aggregate Implications and Tests," *American Economic Review*, March 1963.

Bhatia, Kul B., "Capital Gains and the Aggregate Consumption Function," *American Economic Review*, December 1972.

Clower, Robert W., "The Keynesian Counter-Revolution: A Theoretical Appraisal," *The Theory of Interest Rates*, P. H. Hahn and F. Brechling (eds.). New York: MacMillan, 1965, Chapter 5.

Duesenberry, James S., *Income, Saving and the Theory of Consumer Behavior*. Oxford: Oxford University Press, 1967, New York: 1949.

Evans, Michael K., "The Importance of Wealth in the Consumption Function," *Journal of Political Economy*, August 1967.

Farrell, M. J., "The New Theories of the Consumption Function," *The Economic Journal*, December 1959.

Friedman, Milton, *A Theory of the Consumption Function*. NBER, Princeton: Princeton University Press, 1957.

Harberger, Arnold C., *The Demand for Durable Goods*. Chicago: University of Chicago Press, 1960.

Hess, Alan C., "Household Demand for Durable Goods: The Influences of Rates of Return and Wealth," *Review of Economics and Statistics*, February 1973.

Houthakker, H. S., and Lester Taylor, *Consumer Demand in the United States: Analyses and Projections*, 2nd ed. Cambridge: Harvard University Press, 1970.

Kaldor, Nicholas, "Marginal Productivity and the Macro-Economic Theories of Distribution: Comment on Samuelson and Modigliani," *Review of Economic Studies*, October 1966.

Koyck, L. M., *Distributed Lags and Investment Analysis*. Amsterdam: North Holland Publishing Co., 1954.

Landsberger, M., "The Life Cycle Hypothesis: A Reinterpretation and Empirical Test," *American Economic Review*, March 1970.

Modigliani, Franco, and R. Brumberg, "The 'Permanent Income' and 'Life Cycle' Hypotheses of Savings Behavior: Comparison and Tests," in I. Friend and R. C. Jones (eds.), *Consumption and Saving*, Vol. 2, Philadelphia: 1960.

_____, "Utility Analysis and the Consumption Function: An Interpretation of Cross Section Data," in K. Kurihara (ed.), *Post Keynesian Economics*. New Brunswick: Rutgers University Press, 1954.

Motley, Brian, "Household Demand for Assets: A Model of Short Run Adjustments," *Review of Economics and Statistics*, August 1970.

Nerlove, Marc, *Distributed Lags and Demand Analysis*, Agriculture Handbook No. 141, USDA, Washington, D.C., 1958.

Patinkin, Don, *Money, Interest and Prices*, 2nd ed. New York: Harper & Row, 1965.

Pigou, A. C., "Economic Progress in a Stable Environment," *Economica*, 1947.

Poole, William, "The Role of Interest Rates and Inflation in the Consumption Function," *Brookings Papers on Economic Activity*, No. 1, 1972.

Solow, Robert, in "The Explanation of Productivity Change," by Dale W. Jorgenson and Zvi Griliches, *Review of Economic Studies*, July 1967.

Taylor, Lester D., "Saving out of Different Types of Income," *Brookings Papers on Economic Activity*, No. 2, 1971.

Tobin, James, and Walter Dolde, "Wealth, Liquidity and Consumption," *Consumer Spending and Monetary Policy: The Linkages*, Proceedings of a Monetary Conference, June 1971; sponsored by The Federal Reserve Bank of Boston, Boston, Mass.

Webber, Warren E., "The Effect of Interest Rates on Aggregate Consumption," *American Economic Review*, September 1970.

Wykoff, Frank C., "A User Cost Approach to New Automobile Purchases," *Review of Economic Studies*, July 1973.

————, "A Deflator for Consumer Durable Services in Theory and Practice," 1979, forthcoming.

Zellner, A., D. S. Huang, and L. C. Chan, "Further Analysis of the Short-Run Consumption Function, with Emphasis on the Role of Liquid Assets," *Econometrics*, July 1965.

PRIVATE DOMESTIC INVESTMENT EXPENDITURES

part IV

From revolutionary Karl Marx to Lord Keynes economists have long been intrigued with the role of capital accumulation in the dynamics of capitalist economies. Capital accumulation, defined as the production of machinery and equipment, the construction of structures, residential as well as industrial and commercial, and additions to stocks of inventories, is the subject of Chapters 10 and 11.

The decisions by entrepreneurs to commit vast sums of money to the purchase and production of capital goods in order to gain some distant wealth is one of the least understood of economic activities. Imagine planning to spend millions of dollars because you think, or hope, that consumers will demand, years from now, a product you will then have the capacity to produce. Successful decisions of such magnitude under uncertainty take guile, vision, planning, courage, and luck.

In Chapter 10 we see the inherent complexity of investment analysis as it was presented in a famous critique by the great English communist from Cambridge, Ms. Joan Robinson. We then build from Keynes to his modern apostle, James Tobin. Tobin's q-theory carries the spirit of Keynes's investment model: It has a rational planner's core but is subject to the external and unpredictable vagaries of the stock market. Then a dynamic model of inventory cycles was developed by Lloyd Metzler.

Chapter 11 presents, examines, applies, and assesses the major investment model of our day: the model of optimal capital accumulation by Harvard econometrician and John Bates Clark Award winner, Dale Jorgenson. Jorgenson's work is complex, and we develop it carefully and sequentially. It pulls together central ideas from the theory of production functions, market equilibrium conditions, the accelerator and distributed lags. Jorgenson's investment analysis has done more for the integration of economic theory and empirical investigation than any other modern work. The model is ideal for the study of tax policy, and we end this part with a study of tax policy and investment spending. Of course, this model too requires critical evaluation, and we probe and dissect this model as well.

Private domestic investment, expenditures by firms to build new physical capital equipment, though often small in comparison to consumption and government expenditures, is perhaps the most important component of GNP. In a capitalist economy, the decision to acquire new capital is a private choice dependent in large part upon the motive to make money. Those who risk large sums of money to undertake investment projects are among the highest-paid members of society. Those who decide on investment plans for major corporations earn incomes far in excess of those earned by U.S. senators, judges, brain surgeons, and nuclear physicists. Even the President of the United States earns far less than the leading entrepreneurs. While their high incomes may be attributed to many causes, these entrepreneurs provide a very important and difficult social service: They project the future and back their expectations with large sums of money. While the risks are high, the benefits to them and society can be great.

Investment:
From Keynes to Metzler and Tobin

Joseph Schumpeter, the great economic historian-philosopher, placed the investment decisions of leading entrepreneurs at the center stage of cyclical economic activity. Schumpeter believed that booms in business activity are initiated by a few profit-motivated entrepreneurs who take great risks to implement new technologies in new capital investment. The poor guessers, marginal firms, and weak planners are all eliminated by the unexpected downturns in economic activity. Only the healthy, robust firms remain. In the depths of the slump, the entrepreneurs begin again to plan for the future.

Sir Roy Harrod, the famous Keynesian economist, placed great emphasis upon the role of investment in the stability of economic growth. Investment, Sir Roy argued, plays a dual role in the economic system. Investment expenditures create demand, and they also add to the capital stock and therefore increase supply. Sir Roy showed that excessive investment could lead to further excessive investment and an unstable economic boom.

Although many, including Schumpeter and Harrod, argue that volatile investment expenditures play a dominant role in determining the pace of economic activity, there is little agreement on the determinants of investment spending. Some place great importance upon the ability of firms to obtain financing for investment projects. Investment expenditures may be financed either internally, through retained earnings, or externally. External finance includes selling stocks or bonds and borrowing from financial institutions. The relationship between investment expenditures and corporate finance can be complex and subtle. In many large firms, these decisions are made by entirely different agencies within the firm. Nevertheless, in explaining variations in the rate of investment, one may discover that financial considerations are crucial.

Other economists emphasize the importance of sales and profits in determining investment. Again, profits and sales can be related to the ability of a firm to obtain financing for future investment. But, in addition, sales and profits may be related to anticipated future returns. If sales and profits are rising, investors may be more optimistic about the future and may acquire new capital. Furthermore, new capital is necessary to support higher sustained levels of sales.

Interest rates play a dominant role in most theories of investment. Interest rates are a cost to firms who borrow funds to finance investment. For firms who finance investment projects from retained earnings, interest rates represent the opportunity cost of the internal funds, because the firm could have lent the money to earn interest. If market interest rates rise, firms can earn relatively more from financial loans, and thus viable projects must provide a higher rate of return. Similarly, firms who borrow have to pay more, if interest rates rise. Clearly, the relation between investment and interest rates is complex.

Some Complexities in Investment Analysis: National product accounts identify three major categories of investment expenditures: (1) fixed business investment, (2) changes in inventories, and (3) residential construction. Most economic theorists apply different models to each of these three categories.

Residential construction is ultimately for use by homeowners. Consequently, residential construction depends upon the difference between the demand for homes and the supply of homes. The bulk of the supply of homes is, of course, the existing stock of housing. When families wish to buy new homes, they must borrow large sums of money in order to do so. The I.O.U. they sign which carries the financial terms of the loan is called a mortgage. While the long-run demand for homes will depend upon factors such as the number of families and the standard of living, short-run fluctuations in the demand for homes are heavily influenced by the financial terms available on home mortgages. Consequently, the most volatile short-term influence on new residential construction is the state of financial markets for mortgages. The federal government has long been greatly interested in mortgage finance and has had a tremendous amount of influence in this industry. A variety of financial institutions, private and quasi-public, buy and sell home mortgages. Furthermore, a number of regulatory agencies influence this market as well, including the Federal Reserve Board, the Federal Deposit Insurance Corporation, and the Federal Home Loan Bank Board.

The most important type of private financial institution which makes mortgage loans is the savings and loan association. Throughout the 1960s and much of the 1970s, the ability of savings and loan associations to attract deposits in order to make mortgage loans was a crucial factor in determining the rate of residential construction. In the 1930s, the U.S. Federal Reserve System was given the power to establish ceilings on the interest rates commercial banks could offer on their deposits of various types. These *Regulation Q* ceilings for savings accounts were, until the early 1960s, above market rates and thus Regulation Q had little actual impact. However, as interest rates rose in the 1960s, savings and loans, with most of their earnings from mortgages made earlier at lower rates, argued that they could not pay higher deposit rates. As a result, Regulation Q was extended to cover the deposit rates which savings and loan associations were allowed to pay. To some extent, these rate ceilings were an advantage to savings and loans, because competition in the form of higher deposit rates was eliminated. Thus they were, in effect, protected against having to offer higher rates to their depositors. However, as rates of interest on other unregulated market securities, particularly government bonds, increased, customers became less willing to place their funds in low-yielding deposits which were restricted by rate ceilings.

Under these particular institutional arrangements, the market for new residential construction proved very sensitive to even minor fluctuations in market interest rates. Whenever the Federal Reserve tried to slow the pace of economic activity by reducing the money supply and raising market interest rates, the first and most substantial shock to the economic system was a sudden withdrawal of deposits from financial institutions which ordinarily made mortgage loans. The collapse of the market for new housing was so devastating that eventually the Federal Reserve System was compelled in each of these instances to reverse its tight monetary policy and allow interest rates to go back down.

Variations in the acquisition of business inventories is an investment category that is likely to be determined by yet another set of factors. Changes in inventories do not depend on the ability of a small home owner to obtain finance, because they are undertaken by businesses who in general have access to much broader financial capital sources. Furthermore, unlike new plant and equipment, changes in the stocks of inventories are a rather short-run activity. Inventories seem to serve as a buffer against unexpected variations in the sales of goods and services. This buffer activity is likely to depend upon the current pace of economic activity and to respond sensitively to short-run variations in sales. Of the three components of investment spending, changes in inventories are the most volatile. Analysts of business cycles tend to devote considerable energies to studying fluctuations in inventories as indicators of the nature of general economic fluctuations. The most famous work undertaken on inventory investment was by Lloyd Metzler. Metzler produced a number of models which both explain the volatility of inventory expenditures and which show how inventory fluctuations can be the cause of business cycles leading to what is now known as the Metzler inventory cycle.

Finally, almost every student of investment emphasizes the dominance of uncertainty. Entrepreneurs operate in a highly uncertain environment. How do they make decisions in this risky venture of investment planning? Do they make their best guess about the future and then take actions as if they were certain about their best guess? Do they attempt to forecast the economy over a long horizon? Do they merely try to predict how others predict the future, relying on a kind of mass psychology approach? Do investors hedge their bets by accounting for a range of possible future outcomes? Some economists have placed so much emphasis on uncertainty that they prefer to describe investment spending by purely exogenous models. And, in terms of stimulating investment activity, models incorporating stochastic random terms seem to have most success.

Joan Robinson's Query: To many economists analysis of the investment decision is the most complex in all of economics. To help us appreciate this complexity we shall briefly review some of the ideas of the caustic, articulate, and famous Cambridge economist, Ms. Joan Robinson. Investment consists of adding to some stock of physical capital, but Ms. Robinson warns us to think carefully at the outset of what we mean by "capital." We could simply list all of the items which belong in the capital stock. Our list would consist of things such as fork lifts, blast furnaces, lathes, shovels, and so on. But when we consider additions to the capital stock, we analytically think in terms of acquiring capital while holding all other factor inputs fixed. As Ms. Robinson points out, when we change the quantity of one factor input (capital), while holding the others (labor) constant, we have to consider a possible change in the type of capital that the labor will be using. In other words, even if we assume a given state of technological knowledge, as we change the ratios of the factor inputs we will change the items in the list of capital. In order to maintain some coherent measure of the quantity of capital as a change in the rate of investment is considered, we must be able to sum up the items in the list into some aggregate measure of the quantity of capital. To derive such a quantity, we must be able to weight the various elements in the list for purposes of aggregation.

After remembering from our discussion of index numbers in Chapter 3 that economists usually select as weights the prices of the goods being added together, we would naturally think of using the relative prices of different capital goods as we add them together. However, here Ms. Robinson points to a very sticky problem indeed: Dealing with a capital good, which lasts for several periods, we must ask what is the meaning of the price of this good? Obviously, the answer cannot rest on the particular units in which we are accounting, that is, on whether or not we are using 1982 American dollars, German marks, or Japanese yen, but it must rest on a deeper meaning of price. Do we mean by price the cost of producing the capital good? Or do we mean by price that which one would pay to obtain the future services of the capital good? In either case, Ms. Robinson points out that we need to have information in order to obtain this price, which only becomes available after we know how much investment there will be in this period. And yet we need this information before we can make the investment decision.

The neoclassical solution to this problem is to assume that the economy is in equilibrium so that the market price or the past costs, or the future return on the asset will all yield the same value. Ms. Robinson, however, goes on to attack the concept of equilibrium as itself being untenable. To quote Ms. Robinson:

> The neoclassical economist thinks of the position of equilibrium as a position towards which an economy is tending to move as time goes by. But it is impossible for a system to *get into* a position of equilibrium, for the very nature of equilibrium is that the system is already in it, and has been in it for a certain length of past time.

In order to make any headway in the analysis of investment behavior, it is obviously necessary to disentangle this complex philosophical maze with the use of simplified models of behavior. As with consumption theory, our point of departure will be the work of John Maynard Keynes. In Part A of this chapter, we will deal with the Keynesian model of investment spending. In Part B, we shall show how several economists since Keynes tried to fill in the disequilibrium aspects of Keynes's analysis with the ideas of the accelerator and the coefficient of expectations.

A • Keynes's Investment Theory

The Marginal Efficiency of Capital: Keynes avoided the Joan Robinson dilemma by dealing with the short run: a time period which he described as being short enough so that the capital stock would be a part of the environment which did not change over the course of the analysis. Second, Keynes viewed investment as a disequilibrium process. That is, investment expenditures exceed those needed to replace wearing out capital only because the economy has been thrown into disequilibrium; thus Keynes avoids the equilibrium analysis which Robinson felt was a trap.

Keynes analyzes investment expenditures as follows: The production of a physical capital asset involves costs. Costs are associated with the prices of factor inputs utilized in the production process. Keynes considered the costs of producing new capital to be a crucial element of the investment decision. Keynes called this cost the *supply price of capital*, which he defined to be "the price which would just induce a manufacturer newly to produce an additional unit" of the asset. In other words, the supply price of capital is the replacement cost of a unit of capital, and the replacement cost of a unit of capital is a market price over which the investor has no direct control.

Firms do not usually acquire capital goods just to look at them. When a firm acquires a new unit of capital, it acquires ownership to a future flow of productive potential. An owner of new capital anticipates an expected flow of returns from that capital throughout the future. The Keynesian investor is then confronted with the following problem: Does it make sense to pay p_k, the supply price of capital, in order to receive this sequence of anticipated net returns? To answer this question, Keynes views investors as calculating, for any potential investment project, a rate which Keynes called the *marginal efficiency of capital*. The marginal efficiency of capital is the rate, r, which discounts the future net stream of earnings of the capital asset so that the resultant discounted sum will exactly equal the supply price of capital.

It is important to note that the computation of MEC for each capital asset is a subjective internal process undertaken by each potential investor for each potential piece of capital equipment. For each unit of capital one considers its probable economic life, its depreciation pattern, and its probable obsolescence. Also, one accounts for expected tax treatment of the product and the factors required in the production process. Furthermore, general economic stability as well as future demand for the products must be taken into consideration. None of the above factors is known with certainty when capital acquisition is considered. However, the MEC calculation does not depend upon interest rates. The marginal efficiency of capital is a discount rate which equates a future flow of expected net returns to an initial cost of replacing a capital asset, and the MEC is an internal rate of return calculated by the firm. It is not the interest rate.

Suppose MEC calculations were undertaken at a point in time for all possible capital asset projects. If one ranked projects according to their MEC values from highest to lowest, and then computed the amount of capital associated with each MEC value, one could derive a schedule relating MEC to the stock of capital. Let K represent the stock of capital for which MEC is at least as large as a given level. Figure 1 depicts the relation between MEC and K. If, for example, one considers projects with MEC values at least as high as 10 percent, the stock of such assets will be K_0. At MEC of 6 percent, more projects can be considered, so K increases to K_1.

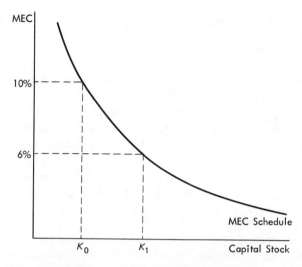

FIGURE 1   Marginal Efficiency of Capital

Interest Rates: The MEC schedule forms the basis for the decision to invest. Before we establish the relation between investment and the marginal efficiency of capital, however, it is helpful to establish several other subsidiary ideas. First, the concept of investment needs to be related to the concept of the stock of capital. Gross investment is a flow which consists of expenditures on the production of new physical capital. Ignoring the subtle problems of Joan Robinson, we let the change in the stock of capital from one period to the next, $K_t - K_{t-1}$, be defined as:

$$K_t - K_{t-1} = I_t - D_t \qquad (1)$$

where I_t is the period t flow of gross investment and D_t is replacement requirements as a result of depreciation of existing capital. The relation between gross investment and capital stock is obtained by solving equation (1) for I_t:

$$I_t = (K_t - K_{t-1}) + Dt \qquad (2)$$

Gross investment has two components: first, additions to the capital stock, or net investment, and second, replacement investment to make up for depreciation of existing capital.

It has been shown that quite a bit of information enters the MEC calculations. However, yet one additional piece of information is required by an investor, within the Keynesian model: In Keynes's model there was only one interest rate, but of course, at any moment in time, numerous market interest rates can be observed. Rarely are any of these interest rates equal to one another. Interest rates vary for a variety of reasons including default risk, period to maturity and legal limitations.

While the assumption that market rates can be represented by one rate is obviously a simplification, it may not seem too farfetched once one understands the idea of *arbitrage*. Suppose two otherwise identical bonds bear different interest rates. Rational economic agents holding the bond bearing the lower interest would sell and buy the high-yielding bond. The process of transacting between two bonds for purposes of earning income on the interest rate differential is arbitrage. As financiers try to sell a low-yielding bond in order to buy the high, market pressure would drive the latter's price up and the former's down. Since each bond is a fixed money contract, the price changes will result in reducing the interest rate differential. More generally, arbitrage will tend to bring interest rates on various assets into some sort of alignment in which interest rate differentials reflect risk, maturity, tax differences, and so on. As long as risk, maturity, etc. do not change, most interest rates will tend to move up and down together because of arbitrage. As an example of this line of reasoning, economists developed the idea of the *term structure of interest rates*. This approach attempts to explain observed differences in interest rates on securities of similar risk and tax status but different maturities as the result of arbitrage, which keeps some type of alignment between rates. This is not the only approach to interest rate differentials by any means, but it is consistent with the Keynesian notion that the market can be represented by one rate of interest.

In any case, Keynes assumed one market rate of interest. In evaluating capital projects as potential investments, a producer compares the marginal efficiency of capital to the market interest rate. Whether the firm borrows to finance capital or utilizes internal finance, the opportunity cost of a capital project is the market interest forgone in undertaking the capital project. If the MEC exceeds the opportunity cost, the project should be undertaken.

Suppose the market rate of interest is 8 percent. Suppose further that this rate has prevailed for some time so that the stock of capital consists of those projects which historically had an MEC of at least 8 percent. This stock of capital could be, say, 5000 units. If replacement requirements are 5 percent of the capital stock, replacement investment would be 250 units. In this case, net new investment will be zero unless either MEC or the interest rate changes.

If the interest rate now falls to 4 percent, capital projects whose MECs are from 8 to 4 percent are suddenly worth undertaking. The reduction in the rate of interest generates a gap between the desired and actual stocks of capital which could equal say 500 units. The problem now confronting firms is how quickly to close the desired capital stock gap.

Replacement requirements are for 250 new units of capital, and firms wish to add 500 units to the total stock. These combine to a total of 750 units of new capital demand. Capital-producing industries observe an increase in demand for capital-producing goods. They may be unable to produce all these goods at once.

Capacity in the industry may be only 600 units. In fact, as capital goods production increases, the costs of production are likely to rise, driving up the supply price of capital. Thus, given the MEC schedule, another schedule must now be considered—the *marginal efficiency of investment* schedule. The MEI schedule illustrates the inverse relation between investment and the interest rate. As the rate of investment increases, the supply price of capital rises and the marginal efficiency of investment (MEI) declines. The level of investment expenditures, which requires the flow of actual capital production in response to the gap between desired and actual capital, will depend upon the relation between the market rate of interest and the marginal efficiency of investment. These relations are depicted in Figure 2.

Investment in the first period, in response to the reduced interest rate, is 350 units of new capital, 250 replacement, and 100 net additions. In the next period, actual K will have increased to 5100. The lowest MEC in the new capital stock will be below 8 percent because of the net additions and the downward sloping MEC. Furthermore, replacement requirements will have increased to 255 units. The desired stock remains short of actual capital, and additional net new investment will be undertaken in the future.

A number of phenomena can generate changes in the MEC schedule itself, thus creating a gap between desired and actual capital stocks:

1. *Expectations*: Schumpeter stressed the expectations of entrepreneurs. Keynes emphasized expectations as well:

The most important confusion concerning the meaning and significance of the marginal efficiency of capital has ensued on the failure to see that it depends on the *prospective* yield of capital, and not merely on its current yield. (*The General Theory*, p. 141.)

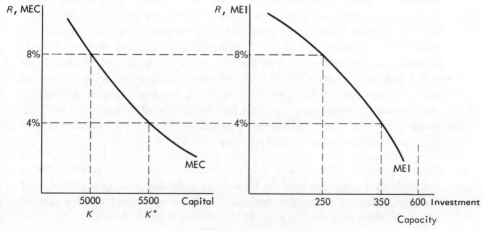

FIGURE 2   MEC and MEI Schedules

2. *Technological change and innovation*: Technological change consists of the implementation of inventions and innovations in the production process and may be expected to reduce costs of production. In a competitive industry lower costs will lead to lower prices and can lead to expanded output from increased demand. However, technological changes can also alter the relative prices of factor inputs and lead firms to use a different mix of capital and labor. If the change is capital saving, substitution away from capital may occur thus reducing the desired stock of capital. Technical change can expand industry output then without expanding the desired capital stock. If, however, technological change reduces capital costs relative to other factor costs, the MEC schedule will shift rightward, generating an increase in K^*.

3. *Income-output level*: At a given state of technological development, output can be generated by various combinations of factor inputs. Generally, an increased level of output can be sustained, under competitive conditions and fixed factor prices, only by expanding the quantities of each factor. Thus, an increase in production can generally be expected to lead to an increase in desired capital.

4. *A change in income level*: While higher output levels will lead to new capital requirements due to constraints of the production function technology, changes in the level of economic activity may have an additional independent effect on capital demand. An increase in income can suggest to producers subsequent increases in economic activity. Expansion can lead to expectations of subsequent expansions. Thus the expected flow of returns to a capital project may rise as income is increasing.

In summary, entrepreneurs expect a future flow of net receipts from a capital project. They consider that rate which discounts the flow to exactly equal the supply price of capital. The resultant rate is the marginal efficiency of capital. MEC can change if expectations, technology, output, or the rate of change in income change. Given MEC, entrepreneurs select those capital projects whose MEC rates are at least as high as the market rate of interest, to determine the desired capital stock. The rate of investment, the rate at which new capital for replacement and net capital increases will be produced, then depends upon comparison in capital-producing industries between the market rate of interest and the marginal efficiency of investment. As investment increases, two factors cause MEI to decline: (1) as capital production occurs, and some investment opportunities are used up, the prospective yields on further projects will begin to fall and, more importantly, (2) the cost of reproducing the capital, the supply price, will rise. Reason (1) is a reflection of the downward sloping MEC schedule. Reason (2) shows why the MEI falls below the MEC schedule. The final result is that the rate of investment is inversely related to the interest rate—the functional relation being the MEI schedule.

Tobin's q-theory: James Tobin and his colleagues at the Cowles Foundation for Research in Economics at Yale University, following the spirit of Keynes's marginal efficiency of capital analysis, have developed the idea of a variable labeled q which measures the ratio of two different values of the same asset. The numerator (top) of the ratio is the market's value of existing assets. In other words, the market valuation would be the going price on the open market for exchanging existing assets. For example, the numerator might consist of the price of an existing home in the case of considering residential construction investment. The denominator is a measure of the costs of newly producing this type of asset, which is what Keynes had called the supply price of capital. In the case of residential construction, the denominator would consist of the construction costs of new homes and in the case of an automobile the denominator of q would consist of the price of a newly produced car while the numerator would be the price of an existing current vintage car. For business investment projects the denominator is the replacement cost of a firm's capital stock, while the numerator might be the price of all its stocks and bonds.

Under perfectly competitive equilibrium conditions, the market valuation for exchanging existing assets and the replacement costs of producing new assets would be equal, so the value of q would be 1. However, just as Keynes was interested in disequilibrium analysis, Tobin's q-theory is a disequilibrium theory of investment behavior. In disequilibrium q can be greater than one or less than one, and this will lead to more or less investment. Consider again, for example, the housing market. Suppose the monetary authorities raise interest rates and make it difficult for savings and loan associations to provide loans to potential homeowners. The result is a reduction in the demand for existing housing so that the market value for existing homes falls. Given the replacement cost of newly produced homes, the value of q would fall below one, and Tobin would argue that investment in new housing would be discouraged so that residential construction would begin to slow down. Conversely, if mortgage borrowing were made easier and the demand for housing were to increase, raising the value of existing homes, then q would become greater than one and residential construction would be stimulated.

While Tobin's q-theory explained in terms of single asset such as a house is comparatively straightforward, the theory is much more complex and tenuous when applied to investment in producers' durable equipment or nonresidential structures. Tobin and his colleague at the Cowles Commission, William Brainard, pointed out in 1977 that when capital is used in the production process it is combined in a very complex technology with a wide variety of types of capital and with specialized types of labor and other kinds of inputs such as raw materials. Consequently, markets tend not to value individual pieces of capital used in business enterprises but rather to value the entire businesses. At times small firms may be valued by brokers and actually sold on open markets, but for larger firms such transactions rarely take place. Rather, the firm's assets are valued through the issuance of ownership rights in the form of stocks or through borrowing by the firm through the issuance of bonds. Thus in the case of corporations the estimate of q which indicates whether or not investment is stimulated involves a ratio between the market value of the business as a whole as indicated by the stock and bond markets and the replacement cost of all the items in the firm's balance sheet in addition to its physical capital. Again, Tobin is following closely in the footsteps of Keynes. Tobin and Brainard quote Keynes's *General Theory* as saying, "The daily revaluations of the Stock Exchange, though they are primarily made to facilitate transfers of old investments between one individual and another, inevitably exert a decisive influence on the rate of current investment."

In Tobin's judgment investment is depressed when q is less than one; that is, when the market value of the firm is less than the present value of the future flow of net receipts discounted by the market interest rate. Why should one invest by purchasing new capital when a superior return could be obtained by purchasing ownership rights in the existing firm?

Conversely, investment is stimulated when market values exceed the replacement cost of capital. It is now cheaper to expand by buying new capital goods.

According to Tobin, investment, as we use the term to mean additions to physical units of capital, is greatly influenced by financial market conditions, i.e., by interest rates, the availability of loans, the nature of bonds, and the risk involved in these markets. All of these influences are summarized in the value of a firm's stock, and they affect investment through their influence on the numerator of q. However, attempts by Tobin and Brainard and by others to actually measure q involve a number of qualitative judgments which are difficult to support on purely theoretical grounds.

It is important to observe that Tobin distinguishes between his q-theory and the marginal efficiency of capital theory developed by Keynes. While the spirit of the q-theory is quite clearly Keynesian, the q-ratio is not the same as the difference between MEC and the market rate of interest which Keynes had his investors comparing. Roughly speaking, the MEC of Keynes is based on the supply price of capital at replacement cost and corresponds roughly to the denominator of Tobin's q. The present value of the flow of net receipts discounted by the exogenous interest rate for the Keynesian investor corresponds roughly to the numerator of Tobin's q, the market value of the business as a whole. Nevertheless, the appropriate market discount rate which the Keynesian investor should compare with the MEC is not really observable in the open market. The market does provide interest rates on bonds, but rates of return on bonds are not the same as market evaluation rates would be on physical capital. While there is some relationship between bond rates and the rates of return on physical capital, bond rates are closely influenced by financial market considerations such as the ability of the lender to pay and other types of risk factors in financial markets, whereas the rate of return on physical capital will be more closely influenced by technological and physical conditions: expected future changes in technology, expected utilization rates and labor costs, and so on. Tobin argues that whereas MEC and the bond rate in Keynes's analysis are not observable, his q term is. Nevertheless, some of the reasons why the appropriate market discount rate for the Keynesian investor and the MEC for the Keynesian investor are not observable also apply to some of the judgments by Tobin and Brainard in measuring q.

For Tobin the q term is central to analysis of macroeconomic behavior, because q is the point at which financial market considerations influence investment decisions. While Tobin and his predecessor, Keynes, have provided us with a theory of how a variety of factors can stimulate or discourage investment spending, neither is a complete theory of investment behavior. In particular, neither spells out the complete process by which investment expenditures and the economy as a whole would move as a result of a new stimulus to a new equilibrium. Nonetheless, employing Keynes's investment and consumption theories, other economists have worked toward developing intertemporal models to illustrate paths upon which an economy can move from an investment shock towards a new equilibrium. We shall turn now to the analysis of one such economist, Lloyd Metzler.

B ● The Accelerator and Inventory Cycles

Whereas Keynes's investment theory emphasized the uncertainty of business investors and Tobin's emphasized the interaction between financial markets and the evaluation of physical capital, the problem we shall now analyze deals with the effect of a change in investment spending on the movement of an economy away from one equilibrium towards another. The central notion in this type of analysis is the idea of the *accelerator*. The simple accelerator postulates that a given quantity of capital is required to support any given level of output:

$$K_t = \beta Y_t \tag{3}$$

If this ratio is assumed to be constant, then any change in output will require a change in the capital stock:

$$K_t - K_{t-1} = \beta(Y_t - Y_{t-1}) \tag{4}$$

The left-hand side of equation (4) is net investment, I_n:

$$I_t = \beta(Y_t - Y_{t-1}) \tag{5}$$

β is the simple, or naive, accelerator.

The accelerator is an interesting idea. However, the simple accelerator model does not seem particularly plausible, since it is based on a constant capital-output ratio. Nevertheless, more sophisticated investment theories, such as the one developed in the next chapter, are based on a flexible accelerator, and we will be able to see that a very interesting model of inventory fluctuations can be built on the same general analytic framework.

Metzler's Inventory Cycles: Lloyd Metzler in 1947 developed an analysis of inventory fluctuations. Inventories serve as the buffer for firms against unexpected fluctuations in sales. Fluctuations in inventories in turn provide signals to the firm about the pace of economic activity. Let us turn now to Metzler's analysis of inventories.

First, consider an equation which expresses production for consumption demand as a constant fraction of lagged income. Metzler thinks of this equation as representing the production of consumption goods:

$$C_t = \alpha Y_{t-1} \tag{6}$$

Equation (6) contains a production lag. The accelerator equation, (5), may be written:

$$I_t = \beta(C_t - C_{t-1}) \tag{7}$$

and is viewed by Metzler as representing an adjustment in inventory production by firms in response to fluctuations in sales. In other words, equation (7) represents the production of consumption goods for accumulations of inventories. The central idea of this model is that inventories are accumulated in response to the difference between current production for consumption and production for consumption in the previous period. The β term in equation (7) is what Metzler calls "the coefficient of expectation." β can range from zero to one. (If $\beta = 0$, then an increase in the demand for consumption goods from period $t - 1$ to period t would be expected to have occurred only once and not to continue. If $\beta = 1$, then the trend in consumption demand would be expected to continue into the next period.) Equations (6) and (7) yield:

$$I_t = \alpha\beta[Y_{t-1} - Y_{t-2}]$$

Letting I_0 represent exogenous investment demand, production in period t will, in equilibrium, be:

$$Y_t = C_t + I_t + I_0 \tag{8}$$

Solving for Y_t, we have:

$$Y_t = I_0 + \alpha(1 - \beta)Y_{t-1} - \alpha\beta Y_{t-2} \tag{9}$$

Given values for α and β and for I_0 along with starting period values for Y, equation (9) may be solved for the time path of inventory production. Equation (9) is what mathematicians call a difference equation. To solve for the mathematical properties of (9) is a difficult mathematical task beyond our scope here. Income paths Y_t, Y_{t+1}, Y_{t+2}, ... may be generated which converge, diverge, or cycle, depending mathematically on the values of α and β.

Metzler elaborates on this analysis because the above equations are too restrictive in that they assume that inventories are accumulated only as a passive factor of adjustment to trends in consumption. Metzler assumes that producers are more sophisticated than the above model implies, and that they attempt to maintain their stock of inventories at a constant level in the face of current sales and of expectations for future expansions in sales. This elaboration means that in addition to production in equation (6) and production in equation (7), production takes place in order to build up "stocks" in a given period. This third source of production is equal to the "unintended inventory loss of the preceding period."

It is perhaps easiest at this point to simply replace (6) and (7) with two new equations. Equation (10) will depict production for purposes of current sales including sales which are expected as a result of past trends. Equation (11) will depict investment for purposes of maintaining inventory stocks intact or the difference between *actual t* − 1 sales and *expected t* − 1 sales.

$$C_t = \alpha Y_{t-1} + \beta[\alpha Y_{t-1} - \alpha Y_{t-2}] \tag{10}$$

$$I_t = \alpha Y_{t-1} - \{\alpha Y_{t-2} + \beta[\alpha Y_{t-2} - \alpha Y_{t-3}]\} \tag{11}$$

We may solve this new system of equations (10)-(11) along with equation (8) in order to obtain a solution similar to equation (9) above.

$$Y_t = (2 + \beta)\alpha Y_{t-1} - (1 + 2\beta)\alpha Y_{t-2} + \beta\alpha Y_{t-3} + I_0 \tag{12}$$

The behavior of an economy subject to a difference equation, equation (12), can be best illustrated with an example. Figure 3 is taken from Metzler's famous analysis of inventory cycles and illustrates the nature of these cycles under the assumption that the marginal propensity to produce for consumption, α, is 0.6 and the coefficient of expectations is 1. Notice that attempts by firms to anticipate changes in sales and to try to maintain their constant level of inventories result in a cyclical pattern for the economy. Metzler goes on to several elaborations in which he shows that he can reintroduce the accelerator, and that interaction between the accelerator and his inventory cycles can produce a rather unstable economy, an economy whose fluctuations are exacerbated by the need to frequently replace inventories.

The Metzler analysis of inventory cycles has greatly enriched our understanding of how exogenous shocks affecting investment move through an economy to cause intertemporal fluctuations. However, we must at the same time recognize that these models, as general descriptions of all capital formation, have certain limitations. First, as we noted above, this simple accelerator, which is based on a constant capital-to-output ratio, is a rather strong simplification of reality. At times income may rise before capital does. A careful planner will surely forecast and prepare for random eventualities. A planner could be expected to maintain some slack in his production process in order to cushion his enterprise against cyclical increases in demand. The possibility of varying the utilization level of existing capital depends upon such factors as entrepreneurs'

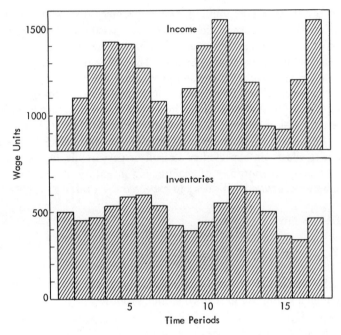

FIGURE 3   Income and Inventory Movements as Described by Data in Table 2

Source: Lloyd A. Metzler, "The Nature and Stability of Inventory Cycles," in R. A. Gordon and Lawrence Klein (eds.), *Readings in Business Cycles*. George Allen and Unwin, 1966, pg. 119.

attitudes toward risk, the nature of the production process, attitudes of potential product purchasers toward shortfalls of output demand, and so on. Potential variation in utilization of capital greatly diminishes the likelihood of a constant capital-output ratio. Second, the inventory cycle process we described above is symmetrical: Increases in income generate the same level of responses as decreases in income. This symmetry seems unrealistic, because firms are not likely to destroy capital in the face of demand contractions.

Third, lags are likely to inhibit immediate responses in investment to changes in demand. If a change in demand is expected to be temporary, then firms may respond by more intensive use of their existing capital stock, by Saturday work, night shifts, etc. If a change in demand is expected to be maintained over time, then firms would probably place new capital orders, but this does not necessarily mean that changes in production can occur instantly. Capital goods production and deliveries may be delayed for some length of time, depending upon the nature of the production process in capital goods industries.

Fourth, empirical attempts to describe investment expenditures utilizing the simple accelerator model have been of only limited success. Accelerator estimates are unreliable, and a large element of investment remains largely unexplained. Furthermore, the calculated accelerators, from these investment studies, are far smaller than those implied by the capital-output ratio. Simon Kuznets has reported annual accelerators less than one from investment studies and around 2.5 from capital-output ratios.

A number of difficult problems remain to be cleared up about investment behavior. First, little direct emphasis has been put on the relation between the choice of labor and capital in the production process and the decision to invest. Second, little has been developed about replacement investment. The latter is not insignificant. According to the national accounts, replacement requirements absorb approximately half the total gross private domestic investment every year. Third, no attempt has been made to compare competing theories of investment behavior. What is the *relative* importance of profits, finance, output, interest rates, and so on? Many other topics have not been examined carefully: speed of adjustment processes, the relation between underlying objectives of the firm and investment decisions, and the effect on investment of tax policy are three. In the next chapter, Chapter 11, we develop a more powerful and flexible model of investment behavior with which we may examine some of these questions. That model, the neoclassical theory of optimal capital accumulation, has dominated investment research in the last several decades. The neoclassical theory we will be studying has the important advantage of being derived in large part explicitly from micro foundations of the theory of the firm.

STUDY QUESTIONS AND PROBLEMS

1. What is the relationship between Keynes's MEC and MEI concepts?

2. How did Regulation Q affect housing markets in the 1960s and 1970s?

3. Discuss the kinds of factors a business executive would consider in evaluating an investment project if he were to utilize Keynes's MEC approach.

4. Compare and contrast Tobin's q to Keynes's MEC.

5. Use supply and demand curves to illustrate the effect on loans of Regulation Q.

6. Comment upon the relative importance of interest rates, output, and liquidity as determinants of investment expenditures in each of the following theories:

   a. Metzler's inventory cycle model
   b. Keynes's MEC-MEI theory

7. Give some examples to show that you understand the difference between the numerator and denominator of Tobin's q.

8. Reconcile apparent differences in market interest rates with the assumption that all rates can be represented by one market rate.

9. Define and illustrate:

   Metzler's coefficient of expectations
   Tobin's q
   Keynes's p_K supply price of capital

10. Why are different models used to describe changes in inventories and changes in housing construction?

11. Select several sets of value for α and β and use a calculator to general Metzler inventory cycles, using equations (10)-(12).

REFERENCES

Chiang, Alpha C., *Fundamental Methods of Mathematical Economics*. New York: McGraw-Hill, 1967.

Christ, Carl, and others, *Measurement in Economics*. Stanford: Stanford University Press, 1963.

Eisner, Robert, *Factors in Business Investment*, NBER General Series No. 102, Ballinger Publishing Co., Cambridge, Mass., 1978.

Eisner, Robert, and Robert H. Strotz, "Determinants of Business Investment: The Theoretical Framework," in *Impacts of Monetary Policy* by the Commission on Money and Credit. Englewood Cliffs, N.J.: Prentice-Hall, 1963.

Evans, Michael K., *Macroeconomic Activity: Theory, Forecasting and Control*, Chaps. 4 and 5. New York: Harper & Row, 1969.

Fisher, Irving, *The Theory of Interest*. New York: Macmillan, 1930.

Harrod, Roy, *Towards a Dynamic Economics*. London: Macmillan, 1948.

Keynes, John Maynard, *The General Theory of Employment, Interest and Money*. New York: Harcourt, Brace & World, 1936.

_____, "The General Theory of Employment," *Quarterly Journal of Economics*, Vol. 51, 1936, pp. 209-223.

Kuznets, Simon, *Capital in the American Economy*. Princeton, N.J.: Princeton University Press, NBER, 1961.

Meltzer, Lloyd A., "The Nature and Stability of Inventory Cycles," *Review of Economics and Statistics*, February 1947.

_____, "The Nature and Stability of Inventory Cycles," in *Readings in Business Cycles*, Robert A. Gordon and Lawrence R. Klein (eds.). New York: Richard D. Irwin, 1966.

Robinson, Joan, "The Production Function and the Theory of Capital," *Review of Economic Studies*, 1953-4. Reprinted in *Capital and Growth*, G. C. Harcourt and N. F. Laing (eds.). London, England: Penguin, 1971.

Samuelson, Paul A., "Irving Fisher and the Theory of Capital," in *Ten Economic Studies in the Tradition of Irving Fisher*, William Fellner, et al. New York: John Wiley & Sons, Inc., 1967.

Schumpeter, Joseph A., *History of Economic Analysis*. Oxford: Oxford University Press, 1954.

Swan, Craig, "Homebuilding: A Review of Experience," *Brooking Papers on Economic Activity*, No. 1, 1970, pp. 48-76.

Tobin, James and William Brainard, "Asset Markets and the Cost of Capital," Cowles Foundation Monograph No. 440, 1977.

Neoclassical economics is a methodology in which decision makers are viewed as maximizers of some objective function subject to constraints. For example, neoclassical theory views a consumer as a utility maximizer constrained by a budget and a competitive firm as a profit maximizer. The engine of neoclassical doctrine is marginalism. The consumer equates marginal rates of substitution to price ratios; the producer, marginal costs to marginal revenue, and so on. If these terms sound familiar to the student, it is because they play a central role in the mainstream orthodox analysis of modern economics. Although neoclassical economics is the dominant mode of analysis used by American economists today, it has come under severe attack by many critics. Recall the views of Joan Robinson discussed in Chapter 10 in which she attacked the central tool of neoclassical economics, equilibrium analysis. Despite its drawbacks, neoclassical economics has been found by most students of economic problems to be an enormously enlightening device for understanding how economic agents, when behaving rationally, in a relatively certain environment will behave. Conse-

11

Jorgenson's
Neoclassical Investment Model
and Tax Policy

quently, the neoclassical model is perhaps the most highly developed aspect of modern economic thought. And furthermore, perhaps the most precise area of neoclassical theory is the model of firm behavior. On a theoretical level economists can state with great precision the nature of decision making by a profit-maximizing firm under certainty. Therefore, despite the complexity of intertemporal decision making, the neoclassical theory of capital has been refined to a high degree of clarity. Nevertheless, in addition to the radical assaults of Marxist economists, the neoclassical theory had long met with considerable resistance from conventional analysts as a source of explanation for business investment decisions.

Leaving aside the radical philosophical assaults, resistance to neoclassical theory rested on three factors. First, nonquantitative, subjective evidence in the form of business opinion surveys had indicated that "marginalist" concepts were irrelevant to investment decisions. Almost without fail, business respondents would denigrate marginalist factors and interest rates as determinants of their investment decisions. However, William H. White (1956) carefully evaluated five major opinion surveys of the type in question and found their methodologies so weak, even by the standards of sample surveys, that the evidence was actually useless. White concluded: "In view of their defects, no definite conclusion can be drawn from the surveys of business attitudes toward capital costs."

Second, early attempts to examine investment theory from a neoclassical point of view with aggregate data were somewhat unsuccessful. It is true that relatively primitive versions of neoclassical theory were unable to support strong interest rate effects on investment expenditures. However, Jorgenson (1967) has argued that these studies failed to adequately allow for the lengthy lagged responses he believes to exist. Koyck's important geometric distributed lag concept, discussed in Chapter 9, particularly the transformation allowing estimation of the lag parameter, permitted more sophisticated examination of investment's response to neoclassical forces.

The third objection to the neoclassical theory as a foundation for investment decisions questioned the linkage between capital theory and the investment flow. The objection was stated succinctly by Haavelmo in 1960:

> Demand for a finite addition to the stock of capital can lead to any rate of investment, from almost zero to infinity, depending on the additional hypothesis we introduce regarding the speed of reaction of capital users.

This chapter contains the neoclassical theory of optimal capital accumulation which finds its antecedents in the early writings of Irving Fisher in the 1920s but which has been extensively redeveloped and very successfully revitalized in recent years by Dale W. Jorgenson and his colleagues at the University of California and Harvard University. While many aspects of Jorgenson's investment theory are quite controversial, his general framework is now the dominant mode of examination of investment behavior. The singular advantage to Jorgenson's methodology is that from specific postulates of business behavior it develops a model of investment spending which incorporates interest rates, output, capital prices, and existing stocks of capital goods into a coherent framework. Furthermore, this framework has been shown by Jorgenson to be amenable to empirical investigation. Finally, Jorgenson has had considerable success in comparing, empirically, his formulation of the neoclassical theory with competing hypotheses of investment behavior. Jorgenson and his followers have applied this neoclassical framework to the evaluation of a number of tax policies designed to stimulate investment spending. The neoclassical framework of Jorgenson was actually the basis for a number of tax policy decisions designed to stimulate investment spending employed in the 1960s and 1970s, including the use of investment tax credits and revisions in business tax deductions for depreciation.

In Part A of this chapter the neoclassical theoretical framework is developed. The capital accumulation model presented here is a simple version based upon standard comparative static profit maximization. More elaborate versions are those in which an intertemporal net worth stream is maximized. An advantage of Jorgenson's formulation of the neoclassical approach is that it links maximization of the present value of the firm to the concept of the accelerator. The outcome is called the "flexible accelerator." The central theoretical feature of neoclassical capital theory is the *user-cost-of-capital* concept. Recall that the idea of the user-cost of a durable good was developed in Chapter 9. The user-cost of a capital good is the price of the services provided by the capital. Put another way, the user cost of capital plays the same role for the services of capital as the wage rate plays for labor services. One important difference is that the wage rate is an observed market price which firms pay for labor services; however, since capital services are ordinarily obtained by purchasing machines and buildings, user costs are generally unobserved. Nevertheless, implicit user costs are very important to firm investment decisions, and interest rates and taxes will be shown to influence investment through this user-cost expression.

Part B contains a discussion of empirical comparisons of competing theories of investment. Before competing theories may be compared, they must be placed on equal footing. Comparison of hypotheses in economics is a treacherous business, and a good deal of effort has been devoted to developing valid criteria for comparison. In particular, the problem of selecting the appropriate distributed lag structure for each investment theory has received quite a bit of attention. The Koyck geometric lag may be extended to other less restricted lag specifications.

Actual empirical evidence may be organized about several criteria. Studies tend to compare competing theories. Various versions of the neoclassical model have been compared to (1) the simple and generalized accelerator model, (2) liquidity or cash flow theories, and (3) expected profit or value of securities approaches. Alternatively, evidence may be examined according to the investment data to be explained: investment decisions by individual firms, investment by industry, investment by type—fixed plant and equipment, nonresidential structures, residential structures, changes in inventories, aggregates in investment, replacement investment and net new investment, or gross private U.S. investment. After examining several studies, the methodology becomes strikingly similar so our emphasis is on the particular models, evidence, and the actual results.

In the concluding section, Part C, the implications of modern investment theory for fiscal policy will be examined. In particular, the effect on the user cost of capital of various changes in the tax code are studied, and the subsequent effect upon investment of these changes is illustrated. As investment is widely believed to be a major force for growth and a key source of instability, these fiscal implications are not without considerable importance. We will complete this chapter with a discussion of some critical analysis of Jorgenson's model. Many of these issues are as yet unresolved, and considerable research is being undertaken to clear them up.

A • From Capital Theory to Investment Theory

Profit Maximization: While profit maximization is a problem ordinarily dealt with in microeconomics, aggregate investment schedules can be derived in neoclassical fashion from this process. A firm is assumed to maximize profits at each point in time and is constrained by certain technological relations between its inputs and outputs. These technological constraints are expressed by a production function in which additions to output from additional units of any input, given the other input quantities fixed, will decline as quantities of the variable input increase. In other words, production is characterized by diminishing marginal physical products.

We indicated earlier that the investment decision is very complicated and subtle, causing economists a great deal of difficulty. In order to reduce this complicated problem to a manageable level, it is necessary to make some rather strong assumptions about the relationship between various vintages of capital. (We use the term *vintage of capital* here in the sense that you may use the term when thinking of vintages of wine. Each year produces a unique flavor of wine based upon that year's climate. Similarly, we may think of each year's machinery being unique to that particular year or vintage.) To understand the nature and significance of these restrictive assumptions, consider the nature of the investment decision in the following light. Suppose that you are trying to decide whether or not to produce or buy a new piece of capital. You would like to know what return you will receive on this piece of capital throughout its life. The essence of capital is that it produces goods and services over a long period of time, and this fact means that you would like to know what its productivity will be in the future. To know the output of a piece of capital in the future, one must know the nature of the environment in which the capital will be producing in the future. In other words, we must have foresight into the future, and an important part of that foresight will be the nature of the capital and the technology which will operate with the asset you are considering buying.

Specifically, in neoclassical terms, one would like to know the marginal rates of substitution between factor inputs in future periods when one is considering acquiring a new piece of capital. But the productivity three years hence of a capital good produced today will depend in part upon the quantity of capital available three years hence. This means that we would have to know how much capital is to be acquired next year and the year after that and in the third year itself before we can know the productivity, three years hence, of a piece of capital which we are going to acquire this year. In other words, if a rational planner with foresight is to make an investment decision today, he must also simultaneously make his investment decision for next year and the year after and the year after that and so on. In other words, all future investment decisions must be made simultaneously. Unfortunately, this prospect is not only terribly complex but seems somewhat implausible as a description of investment behavior.

How does Jorgenson cut this Gordian knot and maintain a theory of rational behavior that does not depend on all future decisions being made simultaneously? Basically Jorgenson assumes that the relative productive efficiencies of new and used capital can be represented by a stationary process. In other words, he assumes that if the productivity of one new drill press is worth two five-year-old drill presses in 1950, then the same will be true in 1980. Given this underlying anchor of a constant, or stationary, relationship between new and used capital regardless of the vintages in question, Jorgenson is able to free his investor from being overly concerned with future periods when making today's investment decision. He can simply study the marginal value of an additional unit of capital in the current period as opposed to one future period. The result is that the firm can be seen to behave as if it is maximizing profits in the current period subject to the costs of the flow of capital services. We now proceed to the derivation of the Jorgenson model.

Profits are the difference between revenues and costs. Revenues are straightforward: the product of price and quantity produced. Costs are defined here in a special sense. For a firm using two inputs, capital and labor, costs are the sum of the costs of labor *services* and those of capital *services* employed in the current production of output. Labor costs are, of course, the wage rate w times the quantity of labor L. Capital costs are the product of the cost of capital services c and the quantity of capital services K. Let p represent product price and Q output; profits Z are

$$Z = pQ - wL - cK \tag{1}$$

The profit maximizer will select quantities of labor and capital up to the point at which the value of marginal product just equals the price of the factor. The value of the marginal product is the product price times the marginal physical product. Let MPP_L and MPP_K represent the marginal physical products of labor and capital, respectively. As is familiar from microeconomics, necessary conditions for maximization of profit will be

$$pMPP_L = w$$

$$pMPP_K = c$$

(2)

Consider intuitively the actions of the maximizer. He adds capital input to production, and as he does so the value at which output rises decreases. He continues to add capital until the value of output added by the last capital unit employed is just exactly offset by the cost of hiring that capital unit. He can at this point neither increase nor decrease his profit. Notice that if c, the cost of capital, should rise, then, because the marginal physical product declines as output rises, the profit-maximizing condition requires that capital services employed in production decline. The profit-maximizing conditions may be rewritten in more convenient form by dividing equation (2) by the product price:

$$MPP_L = \frac{w}{p}$$

$$MPP_K = \frac{c}{p}$$

(3)

Levels of capital and labor inputs are chosen such that marginal physical products are equated to the ratio of respective service prices to the product price.

The User Cost of Capital: Let us turn now to the meaning of c, the price of a unit of capital services. Capital, unlike labor, is ordinarily purchased and services are consumed by its owner. Consequently, we rarely observe the costs of using capital in production and the implicit price must be imputed from available information. If the user of capital is a rational profit maximizer, as we have assumed him to be, then he will act as if he were renting the capital to himself and make decisions that reflect the implicit charges of using the capital. In simple models the implicit cost, sometimes called the _shadow price_, of using capital has three terms: the opportunity cost of using capital plus depreciation of the capital over the period of use minus any capital gains received by the owner over the period. (The major item missing here is tax effects on investment decisions. They are considered in Section C.)

The opportunity cost term will be the interest lost in holding command over resources in the form of the capital asset and is the product of the rate of interest and the price of the asset. Depreciation is more complicated as it is the loss in value of the capital due to deterioration and obsolescence. A number of possible depreciation patterns may occur for assets. If a capital asset behaves like Robert Frost's famous "one-hoss shay" then it would, as long as it were operating, provide exactly "like new" services. A light bulb might be such an asset—not deteriorating until the last moment. However, most machinery is probably better characterized by a decaying pattern, as most machinery depreciates while in place. Consider, as an example, a block of dry ice evaporating in the open air. As evaporation is related to the square of the surface, it occurs at a steady rate. Capital will be assumed to depreciate, as a block of evaporating dry ice, at a constant rate over time. Under this assumption of *geometric* decay, the depreciation term is the product of the constant depreciation rate and the price.

Even though capital depreciates from use, prices in general change over time, and these changes can result in capital gains or losses to asset-owners. If capital gains occur, the cost of capital is reduced by the change in asset price whereas capital losses result in larger capital costs. Thus the third term in the shadow price of capital services is the negative of capital gains, the percentage time rate of change of the capital price. Letting r and δ represent the rates of interest and depreciation, respectively, and letting q represent the acquisition price of the capital asset and $\dot{q}$ its percent capital gain (loss), the user cost of capital may be written as:

$$c = (r + \delta - \dot{q})q \qquad (4)$$

The marginal condition for hiring the capital factor in profit maximization, from equation (3), may be rewritten:

$$MPP_K = \frac{(r + \delta - \dot{q})q}{p} \qquad (5)$$

Equation (5) illustrates that in addition to product price p and the purchase price q of the capital factor, the interest rate r enters into the decision to acquire capital.

Cobb-Douglas Production Function: The objective of this section is to use the result about the user cost to derive an expression for the demand to acquire capital on the part of a rational producer. A specific demand function can be derived if the production function is exactly specified. A simple and now very famous function is the Cobb-Douglas production function:

$$Q = AL^{\alpha}K^{\beta} \qquad (6)$$

where A, α, and β are constants. Given this simple functional relation between the labor and capital inputs on the one hand and the level of output on the other, one can derive the marginal physical products utilizing calculus by differentiating (6) partially with respect to both L and K. Our interest here is with the capital factor:

$$MPP_K = \frac{\beta Q}{K} \qquad (7)$$

β can be shown to have an interesting economic interpretation. Q/K is the average product per unit of capital, AP_K, and β is, therefore, the ratio of MPP_K over AP_K. This ratio, recall from microeconomics, is the elasticity of output with respect to the capital input.

If production is characterized by a Cobb-Douglas function, then the general profit-maximizing condition (5) may be combined with the specific expression for MPP_K (7):

$$\beta Q/K = \frac{(r + \delta - \dot{q})q}{p} \tag{8}$$

Solving (8) for the quantity of capital to be demanded by rational producers yields:

$$K = \beta p Q/[(r + \delta - \dot{q})q] \quad \text{or} \quad K = \frac{\beta Q}{c/p} \tag{9}$$

In words, the optimal level of capital, the equilibrium value demanded by profit-maximizing producers, is equal to the output elasticity of capital times the value of output divided by the user cost of capital. The optimal level of capital will be determined by the production function, product price, output level, and the user cost. Equation (9) provides a specific form in which these factors can be combined to determine K. Of course, the Cobb-Douglas production function is quite restrictive, but it does permit the derivation of an exact expression for optimal capital holdings dependent only upon one parameter—the elasticity β of output with respect to the capital input. A different production function would change the exact form of (9). Labor's wage might be included, for example. But that would not change the important message that the optimal level of capital will be determined by the production function, product price, output level, and user cost.

The Flexible Accelerator: If, as variables on the right-hand side of equation (9) shift, capital accumulation responds instantly and completely, then investment is determined wholly from the analysis above. It would seem more plausible, however, to allow for gradual reaction of actual investment outlays to changes in the optimal level of capital. First, recall the Keynesian marginal efficiency of investment arguments that the supply price of capital is likely to rise as the rate of production in the capital goods industries increases. Increases in the reproduction costs of capital were seen to slow the rate of investment. In addition, the development of plans, market research, financing, placing of orders, and hiring of new factors will all contribute to a production lag.

To illustrate the investment delay response to changes in the optimal level of capital, suppose K_{t-1} represents the actual stock of capital at the beginning of time period t and K_t^* represents the stock desired at the end of time t derived from the maximization processes discussed above. The actual rate of capital accumulation can be thought of as adjusting toward K_t^* from K_{t-1}, so that

$$K_t - K_{t-1} = (1 - \gamma)(K_t^* - K_{t-1}) \tag{10}$$

According to (10), net additions to the capital stock will be proportional $(1-\gamma)$ to the gap between desired and actual capital. Equation (10) contains an adjustment process for investment in which the Koyck assumption of a geometrically declining distributed lag can be shown to be imposed. Forms different from (10) can be derived which do not depend upon the Koyck lag process but are not derived here.

A theory of replacement demand can be added to (10) to obtain a complete theory of gross investment expenditures. From the discussion above about depreciation, replacement requirements will be proportional to the capital stock with the rate of depreciation δ serving as the factor of proportionality:

$$R_t = \delta K_{t-1} \tag{11}$$

Since gross investment I_t is the sum of net new investment and replacement, (10) and (11) may be combined:

$$I_t = (1 - \gamma)[K_t^* - K_{t-1}] + \delta K_{t-1} \tag{12}$$

Equation (12) is useful for estimating the rate of investment if K_t^*, the desired stock of capital, is known. Equation (12) expresses the *flexible accelerator* model. Investment responds to the gap between K_t^* and K_{t-1} much as the naive accelerator suggested I_t would respond to changes in Q. In fact, if $\gamma = 0$, $K_t^* = \beta Q_t$ and $\delta = 0$, then equation (10) would yield the simple accelerator. However, the formulation here is much more flexible than the rigid accelerator because (1) it adapts gradually to deviations between actual and desired capital, (2) it explicitly considers replacement requirements and allows them to be filled faster than new demand, and (3) it can be combined with any possible specification of K_t^*.

The Complete Model: The neoclassical maximization process and the flexible accelerator can now be combined to derive the optimal rate of capital accumulation. K^* is derived from profit maximization. In the special case of Cobb-Douglas production technology, K^* is

$$K_t^* = \beta[p_t Q_t / c_t] \tag{13}$$

Substituting equation (13) into the flexible accelerator, we find that equation (12), yields the *optimal rate of capital accumulation*:

$$I_t = (1 - \gamma)[\beta p_t Q_t / c_t - K_{t-1}] + \delta K_{t-1} \tag{14}$$

where

$$c_t = (r_t + \delta - \dot{q}_t)q_t$$

Equation (14) expresses the neoclassical theory of investment spending.

This model of investment behavior may be used to test the neoclassical theory and to estimate parameters, such as the output elasticity of capital β, the lag coefficient γ, and the depreciation rate δ. After examining empirical evidence about the neoclassical model, we will modify equation (14) to include terms for the taxation of income from capital in order to evaluate the effects of tax policy on investment.

B • Empirical Evidence

A number of ideas about investment have now been examined: the accelerator, marginal efficiency of capital, financial constraints, expected profits, and the neoclassical framework. The purpose of this section is to illustrate the nature of empirical investigations into investment spending. Research in this area has been very active, and the evidence can only be sampled. The objectives of this research have been to test competing theories, to measure parameters, to explain investment behavior, to estimate the nature of the lag, and to evaluate economic policies which operate through investment. The evidence to be presented here is illustrative and should not be interpreted as definitive.

Competing Theories: The flexible accelerator model developed above [equation (12)] may be used as a framework in which to compare competing models of the determinants of K^*. The neoclassical model, with a Cobb-Douglas production function, yields:

Neoclassical: $K_t^* = \beta\, p_t Q_t / c_t$ where $c_t = (r_t + \delta - \dot{q}_t)q_t$

If assumptions about expectations of capital gains are made, then the $\dot{q}$ term can be included in the model. Otherwise, it is often deleted by empirical investigators. Thus two versions of the neoclassical model may be considered, one with $\dot{q}$ and one without. In fact, if alternatives to the Cobb-Douglas production function are allowed, still more neoclassical versions may be possible.

A model of K_t^* discussed in Chapter 10 was the accelerator in Metzler's inventory cycles theory. A constant ratio of capital to output formed the basis for for this model, and K^* may be written as:

Accelerator: $K_t^* = \alpha Q_t$

where α is the desired capital-output ratio. When it is combined with the flexible accelerator, the result is called the generalized accelerator; it can be shown that the accelerator model leads to a high level of investment when the output to capital ratio is low and vice versa. Consequently, this version of the accelerator is sometimes called the *capacity utilization theory* or generalized accelerator.

The next model under consideration derives in part from Keynes and from Tobin's q theory. It is the expected profits theory. Realized profits undoubtedly provide a major source of funds for many firms; however, they are probably a rather poor representation of expected profits. As a market indicator of expected profits, perhaps a better variable would be the market value of outstanding stocks plus the book value of debt. This corresponds to the numerator of Tobin's q. This measure serves as an approximation of the discounted value of expected future cash flow:

Expected profits: $K_t^* = \alpha V_t$

α here is the desired ratio of capital to the market value.

Finally, the theory that investment opportunities may be constrained by financial opportunities is a candidate. It was argued above that actual profits are a poor indicator of expected profits; however, realized profits may correspond rather closely to the firm's ability for internal finance. The theoretical notion here is that when internal funds become exhausted, the cost of obtaining additional funds rises sharply. Profits after taxes and dividends serve as a proxy for liquidity:

Liquidity: $K_t^* = \alpha L_t$

In summary, four theories will be compared within the context of the flexible accelerator model: neoclassical, accelerator, expected profit, and liquidity.

Econometric Model: A great number of empirical studies have been undertaken to examine the competing models. Eisner and Strotz in (1963) discuss earlier studies, and Jorgenson, in a survey of econometric studies of investment behavior (1971), studies the scope of research up to then.

To illustrate empirical investment studies, the work of Jorgenson and Siebert (1968) is selected as they compare the four competing models using one body of data. JS examine the investment behavior of fifteen of *Fortune Magazine's* five hundred largest U.S. corporations. Most firms' behavior is studied for the 1949 to 1963 period and many firms for the 1937 to 1941 period as well.

The JS basic strategy is to replace K^* in an equation like (12) by each of the competing theories discussed above. Gross investment spending for each of the fifteen corporations is then estimated by each model and the results are compared. Though the exact measurement problems encountered by JS are too detailed for our purposes here, the problem of selecting a lag pattern for the flexible accelerator deserves comment.

Evaluation of competing hypotheses would clearly be meaningless if the lag structure selected favored any one model. Starting with a form such as (12) above, JS derive an equation in which the lag distribution is more flexible than the Koyck geometric distribution which is included as a special case. They called the form a general Pascal distributed lag function because Jorgenson (1966) derived it from a Pascal probability distribution. The final form of the lag will not be derived here but is closely related to (12), since it contains a distributed lag of changes in K^* and lagged values of net investment, $I_{t-x} - \delta K_{t-1-x}$, and replacement. Rather than select the number of lag terms in the equation *a priori*, JS include, for each model and each firm, as many lagged terms as are statistically warranted. Consequently, each model is allowed the framework of its best flexible accelerator within a broad class of lag patterns.

Empirical Results: JS estimate investment spending for each of the fifteen firms utilizing the following five models: neoclassical I, which includes the capital gains term; neoclassical II, without $\dot{q}$; accelerator; expected profits; and liquidity. The nature of the results is illustrated in Figure 1, which contains the estimate for General Motors investment from 1949 to 1963. Each model is identified along the vertical axis.

JS wished to measure the performance of various models. To do so, they selected three criteria for evaluation. First, to measure the overall explanatory power of each model, JS used the coefficient of determination, R^2. Second, since the different theories are each contained in the ΔK_t^* terms, the number of these terms which contribute to explaining the variations in investment is a basis for evaluation. Third, while it is important to explain overall variations in investment, it is at least equally important to be able to explain changes in direction of investment spending. Consequently, the number of correctly estimated turning points of actual investment is the third criterion.

Table 1 contains a sampling of R^2 statistics for the competing models. Four firms are selected as illustrations: General Motors, Standard Oil of New Jersey, General Electric, and U.S. Steel. The neoclassical models have higher R^2 terms than the other three, and the liquidity model has the smallest R^2 terms. It was also shown that more ΔK_t^* terms enter the neoclassical equations and more enter significantly than in the competing models. The liquidity theory has fewer terms and fewer significant terms.

TABLE 1
R^2 by Model and Firm, 1949-1963 Investment Behavior*

	FIRM			
MODEL	*GM*	*SO*	*GE*	*U.S. STEEL*
Neoclassical I	.70	.86	.72	.51
Neoclassical II	.89	.86	.85	.50
Accelerator	.62	.69	.58	—**
Expected profits	.64	.75	.71	.69
Liquidity	.61	.55	.71	.46

*Figures were taken from Table 3, pp. 702-3, Jorgenson and Siebert (1968).
**No ΔK_t^* terms entered the equation.

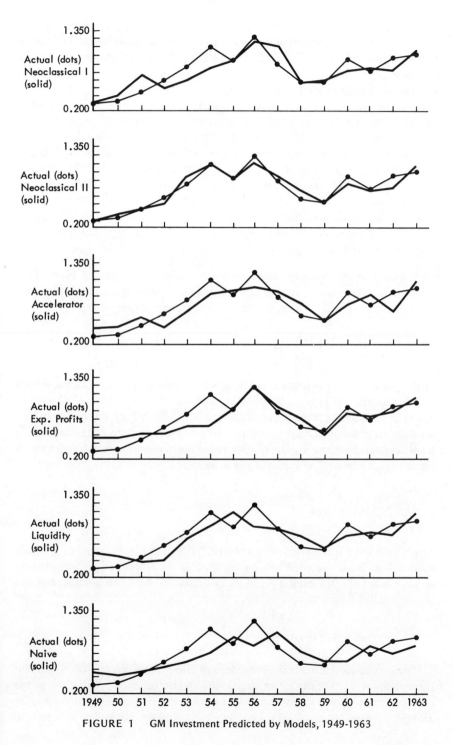

FIGURE 1   GM Investment Predicted by Models, 1949-1963

195

On the basis of the evidence JS draw three conclusions: (1) The liquidity theory can be "dismissed from serious consideration as an explanation of corporate investment behavior." (2) The expected profits and accelerator models "perform about equally well." (3) Most importantly, the two neoclassical models are "clearly superior" to the competitors.

The neoclassical model has been supported by a number of researchers, though some have used versions very different from those of Jorgenson-Siebert. Studying quarterly industry investment figures in manufacturing, 1949-1964, Jorgenson, Hunter, and Nadiri (1970a and b) settled upon the following ranking: (1) neoclassical, (2) accelerator, and (3) liquidity. Robert Coen (1971) has had considerable success employing a neoclassical framework. Charles Bishoff (1971), studying quarterly aggregate investment from 1953 to 1968 for purposes of projecting investment into the 1970s, ranks a more flexible version of the neoclassical model first, accelerator second, with expected profits and cash flow far behind.

The Putty Clay Model: The unique feature of the Bishoff version of the neoclassical model warrants special comment as it represents an interesting economic concept. The ΔK_t^* term utilized by Jorgenson and Siebert was

$$\Delta K_t^* = \left[\frac{p_t Q_t}{c_t} - \frac{p_{t-1} Q_{t-1}}{c_{t-1}} \right]$$

In this formulation the desired capital stock's response to output changes were exactly the same as changes in the ratio of product to factor price p/c. Suppose, however, that capital-labor proportions and hence desired capital can change in response to p/c only for new machines. In other words, before machines are in place, capital-labor and capital-output ratios are variable; once machines are in place, they are fixed. The Bishoff form is similar to

$$\Delta K_t^* = \frac{p_t}{c_t} [Q_t - Q_{t-1}]$$

This allows for a differential response of K^* depending upon whether Q or c/p is changing. Because capital can be adjusted in its proportion to labor before in place but not after, capital is like putty turned to clay when in place, and this model is called the *putty-clay* model.

C • Tax Policy and Investment

There remains considerable disagreement about many aspects of investment theory. Some economists claim the Cobb-Douglas production function is too restrictive and suggest that other less restrictive forms should be used (see, for example, Arrow, et al., 1961). Economists dispute the putty-clay approach to capital holdings. The role of financial considerations, perhaps not the dominant feature of investment behavior, is still controversial. The apparent imperfections of real world financial capital markets suggest that firms cannot be completely indifferent regarding internal and external finance. The treatment of replacement investment as proportional to existing capital stocks has been questioned by Feldstein and Rothschild (1974) and Hulten and Wykoff (1978) on the ground that replacement and modernization varies more than warranted by proportionality and the ground that replacement is mismeasured.

Nevertheless, a high degree of consensus has been achieved on a number of important points. First, investment expenditures react to changes in capital demand with a distributed lag along the lines of a flexible accelerator model. Second, capital demand and investment expenditure can be derived from an approach that stresses profit maximization. Third, the broad thrust of the neoclassical approach is strongly supported by both theoretical and empirical considerations. That is, maximization of a neoclassical production function, though not necessarily Cobb-Douglas, has performed well in describing investment expenditures by individual firms, industry groups, and the economy as a whole. Finally, the user cost of capital, incorporating interest charges, depreciation, and capital gains as well as acquisition costs, clearly plays a vital role in the investment decision.

Taxes and User Costs: The neoclassical model provides a useful framework in which to evaluate tax policy and its impact upon investment spending. Taxes may be introduced into the investment decision by considering their impact on the cost of capital. From equation (4) above, the cost of capital consists of the opportunity cost plus depreciation minus capital gains. At equilibrium these costs must equal the after-tax yield on capital. Three aspects of the federal tax code may be incorporated into the user-cost expression. First, we set the right-hand side terms for costs equal to the after-tax yield. If the marginal tax rate is u, then c is replaced by $(1 - u)c$. (These tax formulae become more complex if one allows for variations in the ratio of debt to equity finance, because debt and equity are treated differently in the tax code. We assume a constant debt-to-equity ratio here.) Second, to stimulate investment, at times the government permits a tax credit, say at a rate k, on total investment outlay q. Consequently, $(1 - k)q$ must be the actual acquisition cost of capital to firms. Combining these two tax provisions into (4) yields

$$(1 - u)c = (1 - k)[(r + \delta) - \dot{q}]q \qquad (16)$$

The third tax measure is a bit more complicated. The corporate tax rate u is designed to apply to the *income* from capital; consequently, a deduction is allowed for consumption of capital, or depreciation, which is incurred in the generation of income. Every year a deduction from the initial cost outlay $q(t)$ is allowed on a piece of capital, and income in this amount is not subject to the corporate income tax. The IRS determines the allowable stream of deductions by using various accounting schemes for depreciation. Thus the entire present value z of the depreciation stream on any $1 of investment can be predetermined from the nature of the accounting scheme. Thus, the acquisition behavior of the firm can be modeled as if it deducts from its gross outlay q both the investment tax credit k and the tax saving which results from the future stream of depreciation deductions uz. The q in equation (4) is replaced by $(1 - k - uz)q$. Thus c becomes

$$c = \frac{1 - k - uz}{(1 - u)} [r + \delta - \dot{q}] q \qquad (17)$$

Equation (17) illustrates that tax policy alters investment behavior by changing the user cost of capital. By combining (17) and (14) one may illustrate the tax impact on I in the optimal capital accumulation theory.

Qualitative Effects: Several qualitative effects of changes in tax policy can now be observed. These qualitative effects can be seen by partially differentiating (17). The investment tax credit k clearly reduces the user cost of capital and thus stimulates investment because it increases the desired capital stock. As long as capital gains do not exceed the sum of depreciation and opportunity costs, $[r + \delta - \dot{q}]q$ is positive and since u is less than one, the change in c with respect to k is negative:

$$\frac{\partial c}{\partial k} = - \frac{1}{(1 - u)} [r + \delta - \dot{q}] q < 0 \qquad (18)$$

An increase in k, the investment tax credit, reduces the user cost of capital. Similarly,

$$\frac{\partial c}{\partial z} = - \frac{u}{1 - u} [r + \delta - \dot{q}] q < 0 \qquad (19)$$

Increases in z, the present value of tax depreciation deductions, reduces user costs and stimulates investment. Since z is based on accounting practice, its exact form is determined by IRS rules for depreciation allowance. Historically, z has been very simple, allowing a fixed dollar amount of initial costs to be deducted each year over the estimated life of the asset.

In 1954, new accounting schemes were permitted under the tax code which increased z by *accelerating* the rate at which deductions could be taken. Then in a 1962 Treasury publication, the government shortened the lives on which deductions were calculated, again increasing z. Both measures were designed to stimulate investment spending.

Quantitative Effects: Hall and Jorgenson (1967) estimate the effects upon investment of these major changes in the tax code and of the 1962 adoption of the 7 percent investment tax credit. They compute user costs for manufacturing equipment and nonfarm, nonmanufacturing equipment from (17) before and after each of the tax code changes taken independently. Table 2 contains their before and after tax change user costs.

Hall and Jorgenson conclude that liberalization of depreciation deductions (shorter lives and accelerated rates) and the investment tax credit reduce capital user costs and stimulate net investment quickly and substantially.

TABLE 2
Impacts on User Costs of Various Tax Measures*

	Accelerated Depreciation		1962 Short Lives		Tax Credit	
	Before	After	Before	After	Before	After
Manufacturing equipment	.293	.267	.315	.307	.316	.297
Nonfarm, nonmanufacturing equipment	.375	.341	.384	.374	.383	.361

*Taken from numbers given by Hall and Jorgenson (1971).

Furthermore, subsequent permanent increases in replacement investment are required to sustain the higher level of desired capital holdings. Hall and Jorgenson state: "The effects of the investment tax credit of 1962 are quite dramatic and leave little room for doubt about the efficacy of tax policy in influencing investment behavior."

Critiques of Jorgenson's Investment Theory: With the possible exception of the Phillips curve, few modern theories have attracted as much criticism in recent years as the Jorgenson theory of investment behavior. An advocate and progenitor of Tobin's q theory, William Brainard, in comments on Hall (1977), said, for example: "If I ever find a corporation that behaves in the Jorgenson-Hall fashion, looking only one year ahead in making twenty year investments and responding only to the current bill rate, I'll sell short." Let us consider here three of the major criticisms of Jorgenson's investment theory. First, while more modest than the radical attack on the fundamental concept of equilibrium, a number of Jorgenson's critics complain about the use of equilibrium analysis in a model in which investors are seen to respond to changes in exogenous variables with a distributed lag. In particular, the critics ask if it is reasonable to suppose that the investors' world is deliberately balanced enough so that he can rely on underlying equilibrium relationships while moving with a lag under disequilibrium conditions. Wouldn't firms incorporate any lag relationship into their original optimization plans? Of course, while Tobin's q theory, the central competitor to the Jorgenson model, is itself a disequilibrium analysis of investment behavior, it is not a complete analysis of investment spending, for while the conditions for investment are described, the rate of investment is not.

Feldstein and Rothschild (1974) attack perhaps the central pillar of Jorgenson's analysis—the stationarity of the relationship between various vintages of capital. Hall and Jorgenson, in their analysis of tax policy, assume that the technological relationships between capital goods are predetermined. Yet Feldstein and Rothschild present a model in which an asset producer is shown to choose the durability of his capital on the basis in part of its *after-tax user-costs*. In other words, Feldstein and Rothschild argue that if we change the tax laws which influence the return to durable goods, then firms will change the underlying technological relationship between vintages of capital. If this were to be the case, then Jorgenson's investor would be unable to focus solely on the short-run time period by relying on the stationarity of capital in future periods. Finally, perhaps Jorgenson's most vocal and persistent critic, Robert Eisner of Northwestern University, has suggested that the choice of a Cobb-Douglas technology greatly exaggerates the capital demand elasticity with which the desired capital stock will respond to changes in the tax parameters. It can be shown that a Cobb-Douglas production function imposes a high degree of substitutability between labor and capital for a given level of output so that changes in the after-tax cost of capital, say brought about by tax changes, will produce large changes in the capital-labor ratio. Unfortunately, on all three of these important issues, the empirical evidence is extremely difficult to analyze and interpret. We can only conclude with the hope that these criticisms will, as criticisms have in the past, lead us to more refined and better analysis of the investment decision.

STUDY QUESTIONS

1. Compare and contrast neoclassical investment theory and the theory of consumers' durables from Chapter 9.

2. Are the Keynesian MEC-MEI theories and neoclassical investment theories incompatible? Explain.

3. Derive an expression for the optimal stock of capital from each of the following relations:

    a. $Q = AL^{+\frac{1}{2}}K^{+\frac{1}{2}}$
        $TC = wL + cK$
    b. $Q = AL^{\frac{1}{4}}K^{\frac{3}{4}}$
        $\delta = 0.2$
        $R = 10$ percent
        $\dot{q} = 0$

4. Define and relate each of the following pairs of concepts:

a. User cost of capital	supply price of capital
b. MEC	user cost of capital
c. MEI schedule	optimal rate of capital accumulation
d. Accelerator	flexible accelerator
e. Koyck distributed lag	stock adjustment model

5. Comment on the following simplifications of the neoclassical theory:

Cobb-Douglas production function
Constant rate of depreciation
Koyck lag restriction

How would one examine the validity of these assumptions?

6. Discuss the nature of empirical study of investment. Comment upon (a) sample surveys, (b) individual firm behavior, (c) tests of competing hypotheses, (d) measurement of variables.

7. Trace, as carefully as you can, utilizing the model developed in this chapter, the economic effects of:

a. The removal of an investment tax credit.

b. An increase in the marginal tax rate (u in the chapter).

8. Discuss the theoretical role of the following factors in modern investment models, including Keynes' theories and neoclassical theories:

a. The rate of interest

b. Expectations and uncertainty

c. Output

d. Product prices, including capital goods' prices

e. Lags

9. How will an investor respond to each of the following exogenous shocks?

a. An increase in his firm's stock prices

b. A reduction in the depreciation rate on new capital goods

c. An increase in energy prices

d. An increase in the rate of inflation

e. A reduction in the value of existing capital

f. An increase in the cost of producing new capital

Answer a-f for (1) a Keynesian investor, (2) a Tobin investor, and (3) a Jorgenson investor.

10. Compare and contrast Tobin's q theory and Jorgenson's model of optimal capital accumulations.

11. Assess Jorgenson's investment model in light of Eisner's criticisms.

REFERENCES

Arrow, K. J., H. B. Chenery, B. S. Minhas, and R. M. Solow. "Capital-Labor Substitution and Economic Efficiency," *Review of Economics and Statistics*, August 1961.

Bishoff, Charles, "Business Indicators in the 1970s: A Comparison of Models," *Brookings Papers on Economic Activity*, No. 1, 1971, Washington, D.C.

————, "The Effect of Alternative Lag Distributions," in G. Fromm (ed.), *Tax Incentives and Capital Spending*. Washington, D.C.: Brookings Institution, 1971.

Chenery, H. B., "Overcapacity and the Acceleration Principle," *Econometrica*, January 1952.

Coen, R. M., "The Effect of Cash Flow on the Speed of Adjustment," in G. Fromm (ed.), *Tax Incentives and Capital Spending*. Washington, D.C.: Brookings Institution, 1971.

————, "Effects of Tax Policy on Investment in Manufacturing, *American Economic Review*, May 1968.

Eisner, Robert, "Capital Expenditures, Profits and the Acceleration Principle," in *Models of Income Determination, Studies in Income and Wealth*, Vol. 28. Princeton: Princeton University Press, 1964.

————, "Econometric Studies of Investment Behavior: A Comment," *Economic Inquiry*, March 1974, pp. 91-104.

————, "Realization of Investment Anticipations," in J. Duesenberry, G. Fromm, L. R. Klein, and E. Kuh (eds.), *The Brookings Quarterly Model of the United States*. Amsterdam: North Holland, 1965.

————, and R. H. Strotz., "Determinants of Business Investment," in *Commission on Money and Credit, Impacts of Monetary Policy*. Englewood Cliffs, N.J.: Prentice-Hall, 1963.

Evans, M. K., "A Study of Industry Investment Decisions," *Review of Economics and Statistics*, May 1967.

Feldstein, Martin and Michael Rothschild, "Towards an Economic Theory of Replacement Investment," *Econometrica*, Vol. 42, No. 3 (May 1974), pp. 393-423.

Feldstein, M. S., and D. K. Foot. "The Other Half of Gross Investment: Replacement and Modernization Expenditures," *Review of Economics and Statistics*, February 1971.

Fisher, Irving, *The Theory of Interest*. New York: Macmillan, 1930.

Fromm, G., *Tax Incentives and Capital Spending*. Washington, D.C.: Brookings Institution, 1971.

Grunfeld, Y., "The Determinants of Corporate Investment," in A. C. Harberger (ed.), *The Demand for Durable Goods*. Chicago: University of Chicago Press, 1960.

Haavelmo, T., *A Study in the Theory of Investment*. Chicago: University of Chicago Press, 1960.

Hall, Robert E., "Investment, Interest Rates, and the Effects of Stabilization Policies," *Brookings Papers on Economic Activity*, No. 1, 1977, pp. 61-122.

Hall, R. E., and D. W. Jorgenson, "Tax Policy and Investment Behavior," *American Economic Review*, June 1967.

Hickman, B., *Investment Demand and U.S. Economic Growth*. Washington, D.C.: Brookings Institution, 1965.

Hulten, Charles R. and Frank C. Wykoff, "On the Feasibility of Equating Tax to Economic Depreciation," *1978 Compendium of Tax Research*, Office of Tax Analysis, U.S. Treasury Department, 1978.

Jorgenson, D. W., "Capital Theory and Investment Behavior," *American Economic Review*, May 1963.

————, "Rational Distributed Lag Functions," *Econometrica*, January 1966.

————, "The Theory of Investment Behavior," in Robert Ferber, *Determinants of Investment Behavior*. New York: NBER, 1967.

_____, "The Predictive Performance of Econometric Models of Quarterly Investment Behavior," *Econometrica*, March 1970.

_____, "Econometric Studies of Investment Behavior: A Review," *Journal of Economic Literature*, December 1971.

_____, J. Hunter, and M. I. Nadiri, "A Comparison of Alternative Econometric Models of Corporate Investment Behavior," *Econometrica*, March 1970.

_____ and C. D. Siebert, "A Comparison of Alternative Theories of Corporate Investment Behavior," *American Economic Review*, September 1968.

_____ and J. A. Stephenson, "Anticipations and Investment Behavior in U.S. Manufacturing, 1947-1960," *Journal American Statistic Association*, March 1969.

Keynes, John Maynard, *The General Theory of Employment, Interest and Money*. New York: Harcourt, Brace & World, 1935.

Koyck, L. M., *Distributed Lags and Investment Analysis*, Amsterdam: North Holland, 1954.

Kuh, E., *Capital Stock Growth: A Microeconometric Approach*. Amsterdam: North Holland, 1963.

Kuznets, S., *Capital in the American Economy*. Princeton: Princeton University Press, 1961.

Meyer, J., and R. Glauber, *Investment Decisions, Economic Forecasting, and Public Policy*. Boston: Division of Research, Graduate School of Business Administration, Harvard University, 1964.

Resek, R. W., "Investment by Manufacturing Firms: A Quarterly Time Series Analysis of Industry Data," *Review of Economics and Statistics*, August 1966.

Swan, C., "Labor and Material Requirements for Housing," *Brookings Papers on Economic Activity*, No. 2, Washington, D.C., 1971.

Tinbergen, J., "A Method and Its Application to Investment Activity," in *Statistical Testing of Business Cycle Theories*, Vol. I. League of Nations, Geneva, 1939.

Von Furstenberg, George M., "Corporate Investment: Does Market Valuation Matter in the Aggregate?" *Brookings Papers on Economic Activity*, No. 2, 1977, pp. 347-397.

White, William H., "Interest Inelasticity of Investment Demand," *American Economic Review*, September 1956.

Wykoff, F., "Capital Depreciation in the Post-War Period: Automobiles," *Review of Economics and Statistics*, May 1970.

MONEY, NATIONAL INCOME DETERMINATION, and STABILIZATION POLICY

part $\bigvee$

Monetary policy, undertaken by the central bank (the FED in the U.S.), and fiscal policy, undertaken by the government, are the two most important tools, without excessive direct intervention, for stabilization of the private market economy. The models we have studied so far bring together consumption, government expenditures, and investment, the three domestic sources of commodity demand. In the next three chapters the money market is brought together with the market for commodities to form the famous IS-LM model of Sir John Hicks. The IS-LM model has proven to be one of the most useful pedagogical tools for macroeconomic analysis: With it, one can illustrate, evaluate, and compare monetary and fiscal policies. It can be used to assess policy performance under different economic circumstances. And it can even be used to evaluate different theoretical views of economic analysis. The IS-LM model forms the core of the more advanced models to be studied later; consequently, it is vital to learn it carefully now.

The economic behavior of the three major sectors of the economy, households, government, and business, has been examined in detail. Let us now incorporate these behavioral relations into a comparative static model of the macroeconomy. To do so in a convenient framework will require considerable simplification of the behavior of each sector. However, even the rudiments of the models studied above will generate potentially radical new interpretations of economic interaction. The simple income-expenditure approach will be seen as entirely inadequate except under rather specialized circumstances. The full impact of the Keynesian-classical conflict will become more evident and economic policy will be seen to be considerably more complicated than has been apparent.

12

The Need
for a Money Market:
The *IS* Curve

In Section A, the behavior of business in formulating the investment decision will be simplified and introduced into the income-expenditure model. Equilibrium income will be derived, both geometrically and algebraically, in a linear comparative static model. However, equilibrium income will not in general be unique. The problem of determining a unique equilibrium income level will lead us to study money and monetary theory.

Section B consists of motivation for the study of money. The Keynesian interpretation of the Depression is compared to the monetarist reinterpretation. In the monumental book, *A Monetary History of the United States 1867-1960*, Milton Friedman and Anna Schwartz present detailed monetarist empirical evidence for the view that money was the central causative factor in creating the Great Depression. Friedman and Schwartz present massive empirical documentation to support their position that income determination, both cyclically over the short run, and secularly over the long run, is essentially a monetary phenomenon. Their view and the Keynesian position that money was a passive agent during the Depression are seen to derive from diametrically opposed interpretations of economic theory.

A • Endogenous Investment and the Income-Expenditure Approach

To develop a macroeconomic model incorporating the complex consumption and investment behavioral relations developed in Chapters 8, 9, 10, and 11 would be quite difficult. Indeed, given the dynamic properties of the neoclassical investment function and the flexible accelerator and of the permanent income and life cycle hypotheses of consumption behavior, the model would require a computer to derive a solution. Furthermore, the endogenous and complex tax schedules, the fiscal policy lags and the production, expenditure and earnings lags, not to mention uncertainty, would add considerably to our difficulties. It is clearly essential to boil down all these relations to their static certainty rudiments to derive a manageable theoretical framework.

First, the static features of investment behavior can be considered in a simple implicit function containing the variables, under certainty, on which investment depends:

$$I = I(c, p, Y, K) \tag{1}$$

Investment, I, depends upon the user cost c, product price p, income Y, and the stock of capital K. Equation (1) may be simplified in a number of ways. The capital stock changes very slowly because even when positive, net investment is likely to be small in any year compared to the size of the total capital stock. Thus capital shall be assumed to have no effect on I in the model. Product price, p, represents the price of goods produced, and since the economy is being viewed in the aggregate and the Keynesian price stability assumption is being maintained, p will be deleted from equation (1). Recall that the user cost of capital c is the sum of interest costs R, depreciation δ, and anticipated capital gains $\dot{q}$. Capital gains will be viewed as static so that $\dot{q}$ may be deleted, and let us assume δ is zero for simplicity. Finally q is the product price of capital and, as with p, changes in q will be set to zero. Now none of these assumptions is essential but all allow the considerable simplification of (1) to:

$$I = I(R, Y) \tag{2}$$

The essential characteristics of the investment schedule on which we wish to focus are its dependence upon interest rates and income. In other words, the two short-run variables which are likely to have the strongest impact upon investment expenditures are interest rates and income. Tax policy may be incorporated by replacing R with an after-tax capital cost $R/(1 - u)$, where u represents the tax rate on income from capital.

Consumption may be similarly simplified by ignoring the dynamic features of permanent income, wealth, and so on. Thus we shall view C as a function of after-tax income, bearing in mind that disposable income is only an approximation of the constraint variable. Thus, the following behavioral equations comprise the core of the model:

$$C = C(Y_d) \tag{3}$$

$$I = I(R, Y) \tag{4}$$

$$G = G_0 \tag{5}$$

$$T = T(Y) \tag{6}$$

To these four equations, one may easily add the familiar definitional equations of aggregate demand, disposable income, and saving, as well as the equilibrium condition equating income to aggregate demand. As they are all familiar equations, after Chapters 5, 6, and 7, they shall no longer be reproduced.

The model, equations (3)–(6), may be linearized for computational convenience:

$$C = C_0 + bY_d \tag{3'}$$

$$I = I_0 + fY - vR \tag{4'}$$

$$G = G_0 \tag{5'}$$

$$T = T_0 + tY \tag{6'}$$

Note that b, f, v, and t are all assumed to be positive constants. $\Delta I / \Delta R = -v < 0$ corresponds either to the negative slope of the Keynesian marginal efficiency of investment schedule or to the inverse relation between investment and the cost of capital in the neoclassical model.

Solving equations $(3')$–$(6')$ for the equilibrium level of income, we obtain

$$Y = C + 1 + G$$

$$Y = C_0 + bY_d + I_0 + fY - vR + G_0 \tag{7}$$

$$Y = C_0 + b(Y - T_0 - tY) + I_0 + fY - vR + G_0$$

Therefore,

$$\overline{Y} = \frac{C_0 - bT_0 + I_0 - vR + G_0}{1 - [b(1 - t) + f]} \tag{8}$$

Equation (8) is the solution to the equilibrium level of income for model equations $(3')$–$(6')$. Several observations may be made about the equilibrium level of income. The most important point, of course, is that $\overline{Y}$ is not unique. The equilibrium level of income varies if the interest rate varies. One must be cautious to observe that (8) is not, strictly speaking, a function. Rather, (8) is the solution to a system of simultaneous equations. The difficulty is that the solution is not unique. It is convenient to return to this point later. Let us, for the moment, assume that R is fixed exogenously, so that another special feature of (8) may be observed. Consider the government expenditure multiplier:

$$k_G = \frac{1}{1 - [b(1 - t) + f]} \tag{9}$$

For given values of b and t, k_G will be larger than in previous models, because f represents the marginal propensity to invest out of income which when added to the *MPC*, $b(1 - t)$, increases the overall marginal propensity to spend. The marginal propensity to spend shall be assumed to be less than one.

Return to the relation between $\overline{Y}$ and R. Rewrite (8) as

$$\overline{Y} = \frac{C_0 - bT_0 + I_0 + G_0}{1 - [b(1 - t) + f]} + \frac{-v}{1 - [b(1 - t) + f]} R \tag{10}$$

Equation (10) expresses Y as linear in R, where the intercept is

$$\frac{C_0 - bT_0 + I_0 + G_0}{1 - [b(1 - t) + f]}$$

and the slope is

$$\frac{-v}{1 - [b(1 - t) + f]}$$

The intercept of the relation, $\overline{Y}$ when $R = 0$, corresponds to the solutions to $\overline{Y}$ in models for which investment was assumed to be independent of interest rates.

Since the denominator of the slope of (10) is positive and since $-v$ is negative, the slope of the relation between $\overline{Y}$ and R is negative: Higher interest rates are associated with lower equilibrium income levels. Figure 1 illustrates equation (10). R is on the vertical axis and Y on the horizontal due to considerable tradition. However, since neither variable is dependent or independent, the line represents a locus of solutions to a system of equations rather than a function.

Figure 1 may also be derived with geometry as well as algebra. In previous models the key diagram was the Keynesian cross depicting the aggregate demand curve and the 45° line. The aggregate demand schedule was drawn as a line with a positive slope because demand was an increasing function of income. Aggregate demand consists of consumption plus investment plus government spending. Consumption is still dependent on income, and so is investment; however, the level of investment, from equation (4), is now also related to the interest rate. Consequently, while in previous models aggregate demand depended only on income, it is now inversely related to the interest rate as well. A single *AD* curve cannot be drawn because *AD* also varies with R. The Keynesian cross diagram

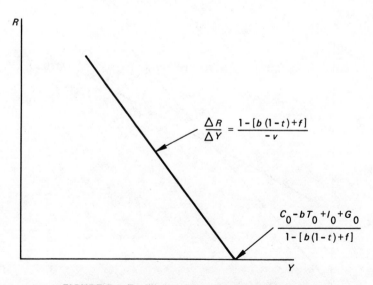

FIGURE 1   Equilibrium Income and the Interest Rate

with one AD curve is inaccurate. In fact, a different AD schedule is associated with each possible value of R. Consider some arbitrary rate of interest R_2. AD, given R_2, will be the following sum:

$$AD(R_2) = C(Y) + I(Y, R_2) + G$$

$AD(R_2)$ will be an increasing function of Y. Figure 2 depicts $AD(R_2)$. Now consider R_1, a rate of interest below R_2. Since $R_1 < R_2$, investment, at each income level, will be larger. The AD curve in Figure 2 shifts upward. That is, $AD(R_1)$ is another aggregate demand curve:

$$AD(R_1) = C(Y) + I(Y, R_1) + G$$

which depends upon income and is shifted vertically upward from $AD(R_2)$ by the amount investment demand increases due to the lower value of R. Figure 3 depicts several AD curves, each associated with a different interest rate.

Equilibrium income is that level at which AD equals income; in other words, equilibrium occurs where AD cuts the 45-deg line. If the interest rate is R_2, AD is $AD(R_2)$ which cuts the 45-deg line in Figure 4 at Y_2. If $R = R_1$, $AD(R_1)$ cuts the 45-deg line at Y_3. Equilibrium income can be Y_1, Y_2, or Y_3 depending upon R. Intuitively, suppose $R = R_2$ and $Y = Y_2$; then consider the consequences of an increase in R to R_3. If the interest rate rises, the cost of capital increases, the desired capital stock falls, and the optimal rate of capital accumulation falls: Investment declines. Since investment has fallen, the aggregate demand curve

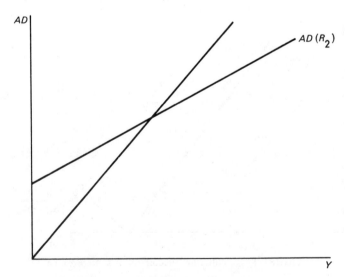

FIGURE 2   Aggregate Demand Schedule at R_2

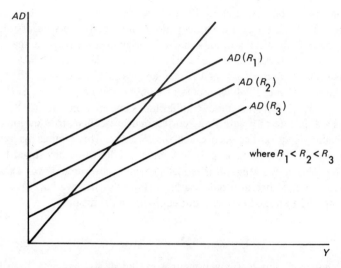

FIGURE 3   Aggregate Demand Curves

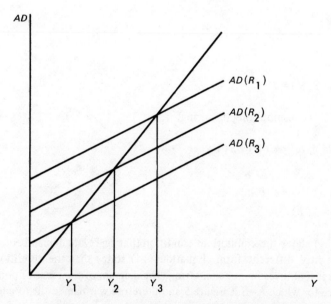

FIGURE 4   Equilibrium Income and Interest Rate Values

shifts downward to $AD(R_3)$. At $Y = Y_2$, given $AD(R_3)$, income exceeds aggregate demand and undesired inventory stocks build up: Income falls. The new equilibrium income is Y_1. In summary, an increase in the rate of interest decreases investment, which induces a multiple reduction in income.

Nothing has yet been said about interest rate determination. To illustrate the dependence of I on interest, the strategy has been to postulate arbitrary changes in R and trace their effects upon I and Y. The important result is that rather than a unique $\overline{Y}$, a locus of income levels is inversely related to the interest rate. The inverse relation between Y and R may be illustrated by drawing the various combinations of R and Y which represent equilibrium, i.e., $(R_1, Y_3), (R_2, Y_2)$, (R_3, Y_1). Figure 5 depicts these equilibrium combinations in (R, Y) space. Figure 5 is a duplicate of Figure 1 and corresponds, of course, to equation (8).

Historically, Figure 5 has been called the *IS* curve. This famous diagram was developed by Sir John Hicks as part of a larger model to be developed later in Chapter 13. Hicks, working on a model in which government was excluded, approached the equilibrium problem a bit differently than we have. His results can be compared to ours. Start with our equilibrium condition:

$$AD = Y$$

Since AD equals C plus I, if government is excluded, AD depends upon R and Y:

$$AD(R, Y) = Y \tag{11}$$

or

$$C(Y) + I(Y, R) = Y \tag{12}$$

Recall that Y is consumption plus saving:

$$C(Y) + I(Y, R) = C(Y) + S(Y) \tag{13}$$

Therefore;

$$I(Y, R) = S(Y) \tag{14}$$

Equation (14) states the equilibrium condition that aggregate demand equals income in slightly different form. Equation (14) states that the condition for equilibrium is that investment equal saving. The diagram of the locus of points in (R, Y) space for which $I = S$ is Figure 5 and therefore was named the *IS* curve by Hicks.

The models in which I was not dependent upon R can be shown to be special cases of Figure 5. Suppost investment is perfectly interest-*inelastic*, $v = 0$, thus:

$$I = I_0 + fY$$

I will not vary with R, AD will be independent of R, and $\overline{Y}$ will not vary with R.

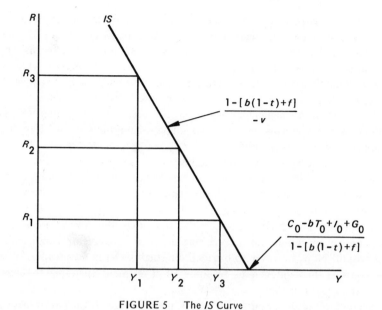

FIGURE 5   The *IS* Curve

The equilibrium level of income will be the intercept of the *IS* curve. The *IS* curve will be vertical and equilibrium income will be unique. Of course, on the basis of the investment theories and evidence examined in Chapters 10 and 11, it would seem incorrect to dismiss interest rate effects on investment, aggregate demand, and income.

In general, then, equilibrium income is not uniquely determined by the income-expenditure approach. This model is incomplete unless investment is perfectly interest-inelastic. The income-expenditure model is, at this stage, indeterminant. To determine unique values for the variables, equations dealing with interest rate determination will have to be introduced.

B • Why Study Money?

Depression Assumptions vs. a More Flexible Model: It is now useful to recall the underlying assumptions, stated in Chapter 4, of the income-expenditure approach when viewed as a depression model. (Of course, it was not necessary to view these earlier models as applying only to a depression, but the implicit restrictions of this model make more sense when applied to a depression than they otherwise would.) The two most important assumptions were (1) There exists unemployment and (2) The price level is fixed. These two assumptions imply a horizontal (perfectly elastic) aggregate supply curve. (The reader may wish to glance back at Chapter 4 to understand why this result is so.) Without these assumptions, when changes occur in the level of aggregate demand, either from fiscal policy or from exogenous shocks to investment or consumption demand, the resultant changes in income could be either changes in output (the standard of living) or changes in prices (the cost of living). Without restrictive assumptions on employment and the price level, we are unable to distinguish what type of change is implied when the level of money income changes in the above models. Because our interest was partly to develop a Keynesian-style depression model and was partly to begin building a general model, these assumptions seemed appropriate. Now, however, we relax these assumptions in order to focus on more general theoretical models.

First, until Chapters 10 and 11, investment in the models was exogenous. Now consider the response of investment demand to changes in interest rates or income. If, as Keynes stresses, investment expenditures depend heavily on expectations of future production, then during a depression, investment spending may not respond at all. Consequently, the exogenous investment assumption may be an approximation of the stagnation of investment spending during a depression. Now, however to broaden our analysis to nondepression situations, we consider the endogenous response of investment spending to changes in interest rates and income.

Second, recall the discussion of government finance. If the government undertakes deficit finance, its expenditures are not wholly financed from tax revenues. Since a depression environment was implicit, it was claimed that government could finance expenditures by selling bonds. The revenues generated by such borrowing could then be spent. The funds now being spent by the government were assumed to have been idle. This implicit assumption of idle funds, available to finance a government deficit, may well be warranted in a depression environment. In a depression, perhaps in a recession as well, funds are surely idle, since private spending, particularly investment spending, is low. These sources of private spending would ordinarily employ funds through private borrowing; however, in a depression the volume of private borrowing is probably quite small.

Consider, however, the opposite extreme of a depression situation—consider an economy operating at full employment capacity. Suppose the government borrowed to undertake deficit finance under these circumstances. It would seem obvious that no net increase in production and real income could result from a government deficit. Either aggregate demand must increase over productive potential, creating inflationary tendencies, or the increase in G must be offset by a corresponding decrease in private demand. In either case, the impact on the economy is surely quite different from that implied by the multiplier analysis embodied in the income-expenditure approach. In intermediate situations, recession, mild slowdown, gradual growth, etc., the results of government deficit finance may involve a blend of a net increase in aggregate demand and a partial reduction in private demand. Let us examine carefully the nature of federal deficit finance.

The reader will recall from introductory macroeconomics that the federal government borrows by selling U.S. government bonds. The purchaser of the bond is essentially lending money to the government. It is useful to distinguish two buyers of U.S. government securities, the U.S. Federal Reserve System and the general public. The Federal Reserve (the FED), it will be recalled, is a quasipublic agency which issues Federal Reserve Notes, and these notes are legal tender for all debts public and private. If the federal government sells U.S. government bonds to the FED, the FED purchases the bonds with Federal Reserve Notes. These notes are the legal tender, or currency, used by the government to undertake its deficit finance. In this case, the government deficit is accompanied by an increase in the volume of legal tender held by the public. The FED has issued currency to the government, and the latter has spent it.

Had the government sold U.S. government bonds to the public, then the currency is loaned to the government by the public. If the government then spends the currency, no net change in currency held by the public occurs. However, one may question what the public was doing with the currency before it was used to buy government bonds. Suppose the currency was idle. Then the government borrowed idle funds and put them to use. No corresponding reduction in private usage of funds need occur. If the currency was not idle, then the government is competing for funds with the private sector. Thus as we relax the depression assumption, a number of complex issues are raised. How is the economy influenced by a deficit when financed by borrowing from the FED? From the public? Are funds idle when borrowed? If not, what happens to private demand if the government runs a deficit? To answer these questions, it is essential to study deficit finance, and in particular the role of currency and the FED, explicitly.

In addition to helping us deal with specific questions about a nondepression economy outlined above, study of currency and the FED and more generally of money and monetary phenomena is useful for other reasons. First, an important and influential segment of economists believe money is central to income determination. Furthermore, they believe it is changes in the stock of money which most strongly determine the course of crucial economic variables, inflation, unemployment, economic growth, and so on. Third, the role of money in economic theory is controversial. Classical economists, it will be remembered, believed that money largely determined the level of income. Keynes, in *The General Theory*, argued that money was ineffective in influencing income. Post-Keynes neoclassical economists, led by A. C. Pigou, felt money was central once again. Today, two dominant groups of economists, neo-Keynesians and monetarists, differ strongly on the role of money in macroeconomics. Let us turn now to a discussion of the monetarist position to further motivate the study of money.

Monetarist Approach: The theoretical study of an aggregate economic model was begun formally in Chapter 4. In that chapter, we tried to compare rather carefully the analysis used by classical economists to the ideas developed by Keynes in the 1930s. After discussing the differences between the analysis of

Keynes and his predecessors, we used the strategy in Chapter 5 of developing the income-expenditure approach devised by Keynes's followers in the late 1930s, 1940s, and 1950s. An alternative strategy might have been to follow the classical model directly through to its modern lineage—modern monetarism. Many of the specific features of monetarism and Keynesianism can, and will, be synthesized to some degree. However, in the broadest sense, monetarism is an entirely different approach to economics. Monetarism differs from the approach utilized so far in methodology, theory, and policy.

Methodologically, the point of departure of modern monetarism is empirical evidence, not economic theory. The basic foundations of monetarism are not found in the microfoundations of the theory of consumer behavior or the theory of the firm. Rather, its underpinnings consist of massive empirical evidence of a high correlation between monetary activity and other aggregate economic activity—growth, stability, inflation. The empirical evidence consists of three types.

Historical case studies have been undertaken in which monetary actions of central authorities, such as the FED and of the banking community and others, during major economic disturbances and other important episodes are analyzed. The general conclusion drawn from these studies is that the central source of instability in the economy is the central monetary authority itself—the FED. The FED, in its attempts to stabilize and manage the economy, actually proves to be a destabilizing force. Friedman (1959) states the policy conclusion:

> What we need is not a skilled monetary driver of the economic vehicle continuously turning the steering wheel to adjust to the unexpected irregularities of the route, but some means of keeping the monetary passenger who is in the back seat as ballast from occasionally leaning over and giving the steering wheel a jerk that threatens to send the car off the road.

Probably the most interesting historical case study of monetarists is that of Friedman and Schwartz (1963) concerning the role of money during the great contraction from 1929 to 1933. Keynes and his followers had argued that the monetary authorities were impotent in the presence of a severe contraction. Keynes held the view that personal saving increases and investment stagnation combined to reduce demand severely. The refusal of the private sector to increase spending could not be counteracted by the helpless monetary authorities. Friedman and Schwartz (FS) (1963) argue just the opposite: "The contraction is in fact a tragic testimonial to the importance of monetary forces." FS depict the crisis as greatly exacerbated by the FED. Take the quantity theory of money, from Chapter 4, as the point of departure:

$$MV = Y \tag{15}$$

FS (1963) argue that contractions in the money supply were closely related to the contractions in money income:

Money income declined by 15 percent from 1929 to 1930, 20 percent the next year, and 27 percent in the next, and then by a further 5 percent from 1932 to 1933, . . . the money stock fell at a decidedly lower rate than money income—by 2 percent, 7 percent, 17 percent and 12 percent in the four years from 1929 to 1933, a total of 33 percent, or at a continuous annual rate of 10 percent. As a result, velocity fell by nearly one-third.

Friedman and Schwartz go on to make two major points. They state that:

. . . had a decline in the stock of money been avoided, velocity also would probably have declined less and thus would have reinforced money in moderating the decline in income.

Second, Friedman and Schwartz place the burden for monetary contraction squarely on the shoulders of the FED itself. The FED, Friedman and Schwartz claim, was remiss in not preventing bank failures which contributed substantially to the decline in the money supply. Furthermore, the FED failed to expand the money supply by open market operations. Whereas Keynesians had argued that the FED was largely a helpless and passive victim of the contraction, Friedman and Schwartz claim: "At all times, the (Federal Reserve) System was technically in a position to adopt the alternative policies."

The second type of empirical evidence to support the importance of money as a determinant of income is ordinary least squares regression analysis of time series economic magnitudes, believed, *a priori,* to be highly correlated. Andersen and Jordan (1968) utilize such a technique to compare the relative effectiveness of monetary and fiscal actions as determinants of the level of money income. Andersen and Jordan correlated changes in money GNP against current and lagged values of various money supply measures and government fiscal actions. Andersen and Jordan found changes in money GNP more closely correlated to monetary than to fiscal actions. From these results they concluded that monetary stabilization actions are "more certain than that of fiscal actions." A substantial, and influential, group of economists find this empirical evidence persuasive.

Finally, the third type of evidence consists of observed timing relations between the money supply measures and money income, particularly at turning points in business cycles. While Friedman suggests such results are treacherous due to the complexity of economic relations and "are by no means decisive," he concludes that money leads the level of economic activity and that the chain of causation is from money to the economy, not the reverse. These results are subject to considerable dispute. Nonetheless, many students of macroeconomics believe that money has a powerful and independent influence on the economy.

The monetarist approach, though heavily emphasizing empirical evidence, is certainly not without theoretical underpinnings. The classical quantity theory, equation (15) above, provides the point of departure for monetarist theory. Dividing both sides of (15) by V, the income velocity of money, we obtain

$$M = \frac{1}{V}Y \tag{16}$$

If the income velocity of money V is constant, then

$$M = kY \tag{17}$$

The money supply is proportional to money income. The conformation of (17) as a long-run proposition is a basic theme of monetarist economics. However, in its modern versions, monetarism deals more with the question of the stability of velocity rather than with its constancy.

One of the most interesting uses of the monetarist analysis has been in the study of economic episodes in which the rates of inflation have been extremely high and extremely volatile. These situations are periods of what economists call hyperinflation. Three of the most famous inflations which economists have studied using the monetarist paradigm have been the hyperinflation suffered by Germany between World War I and World War II, the hyperinflation suffered by the Confederacy toward the end of the Civil War in the United States, and the hyperinflations suffered in Latin American countries such as Brazil and Chile in the early part of this century.

Monetarists have drawn several conclusions from their observations of hyperinflation episodes. First, an extreme rise in prices depends almost entirely upon expansion of the quantity of money. Second, these monetary expansions, in turn, take place because governments, which are too weak to finance their expenditures out of taxes during troubled times (either immediately following wars or during war), find that printing money is the only means of collecting revenues. Third, once a currency *reform* is undertaken so that the money supply ceases to increase rapidly, the hyperinflation stops. These conclusions imply that hyperinflation is not a self-perpetuating process. We shall study carefully the theoretical underpinnings of monetarist inflation analysis in Chapter 21. A principal advantage of studying money and of integrating it formally into a general model of the economy is that we will be equipped to analyze inflation.

What determines the volume of money, M, and its relation to the level of prices, P, and output Q? Modern monetarism focuses on the market for money much as economists focus on any commodity market: supply and demand are identified. As is evident from the theme of *A Monetary History of the United States*, monetarists consider the money supply to be largely determined by central monetary authorities—the Federal Reserve System. The spirit of their argument is that even though changes in the supply of money can be initiated outside the FED, this institution can always maintain tight control over the supply by a variety of effective defensive measures. The stability of income velocity is a central issue in the debate between monetarists and Keynesians as to the relative value of their respective approaches. Before we analyze the money market in detail, it is useful to integrate the money market and the commodity market into a general framework which may be used to compare the monetarist and Keynesian ideas.

STUDY QUESTIONS AND PROBLEMS

1. What, according to Friedman and Schwartz, was the role of the Federal Reserve System in the great contraction from 1929-1933?

2. How does the Friedman-Schwartz interpretation of the Great Depression compare with that of Keynes?

3. a. Utilizing the following model, derive the equation for, and plot, the *IS* curve:

$$C = 50 + 0.9 Y_d$$

$$I = 25 - 50R$$

$$G = 50$$

$$T = 20 + 0.1 Y$$

b. If the market rate of interest R equals 10 percent, calculate the equilibrium level of income.

c. If R increases from 10 to 20 percent, how much does I change? How much does Y change?

d. Given $R = 20$ percent, compute the effect on $\overline{Y}$ of an increase in G of 5.

4. Consider the following three models:

I. $C = C_0 + bY$ II. $C = C_0 + bY_d$ III. $C = C_0 + bY_d$
 $I = I_0 - vR$ $I = I_0 + fY - vR$ $I = I_0 + fY_d$
 $G = G_0$ $G = G_0$ $G = G_0$
 $T = T_0 + tY$ $T = tY$

a. Derive both algebraically and geometrically the Hicksian *IS* curve.

b. Trace the effects on the consumption schedule, the investment schedule, and the *IS* curve of:

(1) An increase in G of ΔG.
(2) An increase in exogenous taxes of ΔT (models II and III only).
(3) A fall in exogenous I of ΔI.

c. Compute the following multipliers for each model:

(1) Government expenditure.
(2) Investment.
(3) Exogenous tax (models II and III only).

5. Derive the *IS* curve for each of the following models:

I. $C = 25 + 0.8 Y$ II. $C = 1000 + 0.75 Y_d$
 $I = 50 - 25R$ $I = 500 + 0.05 Y - 100R$
 $G = 100$ $G = 1000$
 $T = 100 + 0.1 Y$

6. Compute $\overline{Y}$ in the models in Problem 5 if $R = 10$ percent and $R = 15$ percent. Recompute these values for each model if $\Delta G = +10$.

7. Derive the income velocity of money if money supply is exogenous, money demand, M^d equals money supply and:

    a. $M^d = 0.9\,Y$

    b. $M^d = 0.9\,Y^{\frac{1}{2}}$

    c. $M^d = 0.9\,Y^{\frac{1}{2}}R^{-\frac{1}{2}}$

8. Comment on the nature of evidence which supports the monetarist emphasis on the role of money in income determination. How does this evidence compare to that of the income-expenditure approach?

9. How can a government finance an expenditure? In each case, trace the effects of the method of finance on (a) an economy in full employment, (b) an economy with unemployment.

REFERENCES

Anderson, Leonall, and Jerry Jordan, "Monetary and Fiscal Actions: A Test of Their Relative Importance in Economic Stabilization," *Federal Reserve Bank of Saint Louis Review*, November 1968.

Friedman, Milton, *A Program for Monetary Stability*. New York: Fordham University Press, 1959.

———(ed.), *Studies in the Quantity Theory of Money*. Chicago: University of Chicago Press, 1956.

———and David Meiselman, "The Relative Stability of Monetary Velocity and the Investment Multiplier in the United States 1897-1958," Commission on Money and Credit, *Stabilization Politics*. Englewood Cliffs, N.J.: Prentice-Hall, 1963.

———and Anna J. Schwartz, *A Monetary History of the United States 1867-1960*, NBER. Princeton: Princeton University Press, 1963.

Hicks, John R., "Mr. Keynes and the 'Classics'; A Suggested Interpretation," *Econometrica*, 1937.

> It will be admitted by the least charitable reader that the entertainment value of Mr. Keynes's *General Theory of Employment* is considerably enhanced by its satirical aspect. But it is also clear that many readers have been left very bewildered by this Dunciad.
>
> Sir John Hicks (1937)

In this chapter, a general macroeconomic model is developed in which the market for money is included as well as the market for commodities. It was shown in Chapter 12 that commodity market demand cannot be understood without examining the market for money: (1) Government deficits can be financed by changing the supply of money. (2) Investors compete with government for money to finance their expenditures. (3) Consumers provide money in loans to investors through financial institutions and consumers hold money themselves to undertake transactions, and so on. Every phase of activity in commodity markets is permeated with money. It was also shown that monetarists focus their study of income determination on the demand for money which they believe to be "stable." The monetarist model will later be applied to the study of hyperinflation in which it will be shown that the primary cause of hyperinflation is expansion of the money supply. Consequently, the role of money is quite important and yet is very controversial.

In Section A of this chapter the income-expenditure approach is shown to be part of a more general two-sector model: a commodity sector and a money sector. The model is developed algebraically and geometrically.

13

Money in a Macromodel

Just as investment and consumption schedules were greatly simplified to study the determination of income, the money market presented in Section A of this chapter will be a very simple version of more detailed analysis to appear later in Chapters 15 and 16. Section B consists of studying the effects on equilibrium income of change in various exogenous variables: government expenditures, investment, taxes, the money supply, and so on. Exogenous changes are seen to lead to interactive reverberations throughout the two sectors.

A ● The Money Market

The Model: Our first objective is to develop a simple model of the money market. As with any other single market, one can specify a demand function, a supply function, and an equilibrium condition. The reader undoubtedly recalls some aspects of the money market from introductory economics. Remember, the emphasis in introductory courses is on the U.S. Federal Reserve System. In the traditional approach to studying the money supply, emphasis is on the FED's control over the money supply: M_1, M_2 or some other measure. While fluctuations in the money supply can always be generated by private actions, such as changes in the ratio of cash to demand deposits, defensive open market operations, changes in reserve requirements, and adjustments of the discount rate can be employed by the FED to set M_1 and M_2 at the desired level. This theory of the money supply is strictly analogous to government control over government expenditures. The money supply is treated as an exogenous control variable:

$$M^s = M_0 \qquad (1)$$

M_0 represents the level at which the money supply is set by the Central Bank.

An alternative money supply approach focuses on the endogeneity of M. While the FED clearly has quite a bit of influence on the monetary base, its control of the money supply may be incomplete for several reasons. First, money may not simply consist of a fixed set of well-defined assets. It may be that the market for liquid assets is a complex one in which a wide variety of assets are relevant, assets over which the FED has little control. Second, the behavior of the monetary institutions which participate in the multiple expansion process of M may be considerably more complex than a mechanistic reserve-deposit ratio, such as studied in a principles course, would suggest. Third, the public cash-deposit ratio and demand deposit-time deposit ratio may be functionally related to the economy and thus endogenous. Finally, public behavior may be more difficult for the FED to predict than a simple formula suggests. An alternative to equation (1) is to consider M to respond endogenously to economic variables. For example, given the monetary base, banks may increase their loans if they can receive higher interest rates on their loans. Thus one might argue that the supply of money is positively related to the interest rate:

$$M^s = M_0 + uR \tag{2}$$

where M_0 is the exogenous component and u a constant representing the endogenous component of M^s.

Two basic approaches to money demand will be studied later in Chapter 16: the modern quantity theory of money employed by monetarist economists and the three motives approach to the demand for money developed by Keynes. While there are significant differences—for example, monetarists assert the stability of money demand while Keynesians believe it to be unstable—there is now considerable common ground. Theoretical evidence will be presented later which indicates that money demand depends upon income, either as a constraint variable or as a proxy for transactions. In addition, money demand appears to be inversely related to the interest rate. A word of caution—returns on bonds and equities, while they will enter the money demand function on theoretical grounds, do not in the view of monetarists play a major empirical role. The Keynesian analysis of money demand also leads to a demand equation depending upon income and the rate of interest. The simplest version of such an equation that we could consider would be the linear one:

$$M^d = kY - mR \tag{3}$$

where k and m are positive algebraic constants, where Y represents income and R the interest rate, and where M^d represents the demand for money. (If the reader feels uncomfortable studying the money market with the use of equations (1) and (3) without more detailed analysis, he could proceed directly at this point to Chapters 15 and 16. However, all that is necessary to read on here is a money supply equation, a money demand equation, and an equilibrium condition.)

If we consider first the exogenous money supply theory, the money market consists of three equations: equations (1) and (3) and the equilibrium condition:

$$M^s = M^d \tag{4}$$

These three equations contain four unknowns: M^d, M^s, Y, and R. In equation (4) replace M^s with equation (1) and M^d with equation (3):

$$M_0 = kY - mR \tag{5}$$

Equation (5) contains two unknowns, Y and R. Solve for Y:

$$Y = (M_0/k) + (m/k)R \tag{6}$$

Equation (6) is the solution to equations (1), (3), and (4). The pairs of Y and R which satisfy (6) are those pairs which are consistent with money market equilibrium. For each interest rate, a different income level yields money market equilibrium. Figure 1 depicts equation (6) in (R, Y) space. The slope is k/m, which is positive, and the Y intercept is M_0/k. Each point on the line in Figure 1 corresponds to an equilibrium solution to the money market. It may be helpful to derive Figure 1 geometrically.

First, money demand, equation (3), may be diagrammed. M^d depends upon Y and R. To diagram M^d in a two-space diagram requires development of a very useful geometric technique. First, fix Y at some arbitrary level $Y = Y(2)$; then the relation between M^d and R may be represented by one line in a two-space diagram. Figure 2 represents equation (7) below, in which $Y = Y(2)$.

$$M^d = kY(2) - mR \qquad\qquad (7)$$

Figure 2 depicts the inverse relation between R and money demand. Suppose now we wish to consider money demand at $Y(3)$, an income level greater than $Y(2)$. The intercept of the money demand schedule for $Y = Y(3)$ will be to the right of that for $Y(2)$ in Figure 2. If Y increases from $Y(2)$ to $Y(3)$ by ΔY, M^d will increase at each R by $k\Delta Y$. The money demand line will shift to the right. Three money demand schedules are depicted in Figure 3, each associated with a different income level.

Figure 3 is a convenient diagram for depicting the effect of two variables on a third in a two-dimensional diagram. Viewed another way, Figure 3 states that for each R, money demand will increase as Y increases. Next, money demand and supply can be combined to obtain the locus of money market equilibrium

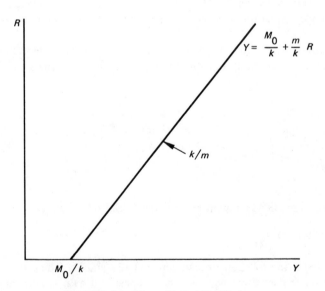

FIGURE 1   Money Market Equilibrium

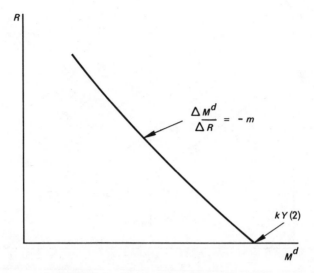

FIGURE 2   Money Demand Given $Y = Y(2)$

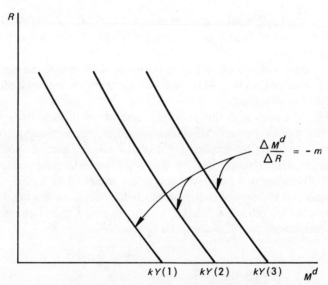

FIGURE 3   Money Demand Schedules

values. Figure 4 combines the money demand schedules from Figure 3 and the exogenous money supply, equation (1).

Equilibrium in the money market occurs when $M^d = M^s$. In Figure 4 a different equilibrium interest rate cccurs for each demand line; for each income level, $M^d = M^s$ at a given rate of interest. For $Y = Y(1)$, equilibrium interest is $R = R(1)$; for $Y = Y(2)$, $R = R(2)$; for $Y = Y(3)$, $R = R(3)$. The pairs of (R, Y) values

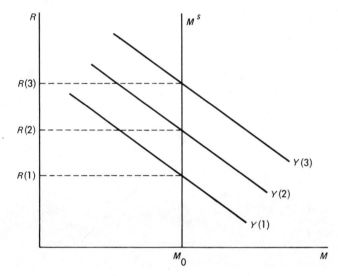

FIGURE 4   Money Market Equilibrium

which represent money market equilibrium $[R(1), Y(1)]$, $[R(2), Y(2)]$, $[R(3), Y(3)]$ may be mapped from Figure 4 into (R, Y) space. Figure 5 depicts these money market equilibrium pairs.

Figure 5, depicting the (R, Y) pairs consistent with money market equilibrium, is the same as Figure 1, which was derived from the algebraic solution to money market equilibrium.

It is important to note at this point that linearity of the liquidity preference schedule (or money demand schedule) suppresses some valuable concepts. Rather than specifying the explicit form of the money demand function, we could depict it with a simple implicit function representing the preference for "liquidity." Liquidity preference was a concept suggested by Keynes to represent the desire on the part of individuals to hold money assets while foregoing the higher return on other less "liquid" assets. We could, therefore, replace the linear expression with the following implicit equation:

$$M_d = L(Y, R) \tag{8}$$

As we shall explain in more detail in Chapter 16, Keynes felt that the liquidity preference schedule would become horizontal (very flat), and infinitely elastic at low rates of interest so that rather than a straight line demand function, the liquidity preference schedule may be better represented as a bowed line which flattens out at low rates of interest. See Figure 6. The equilibrium condition in the money market is $M^d = M^s$ or $L(Y, R) = M_0$. The locus of money market equilibrium points in (R, Y) space, developed by Sir John Hicks, is called therefore the *LM curve*.

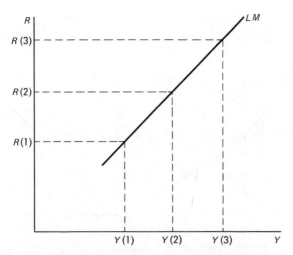

FIGURE 5   Money Market Equilibrium

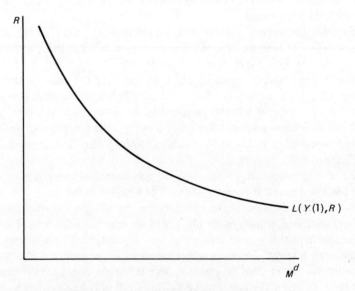

FIGURE 6   Liquidity Preference Schedule

Parameter Changes: The effect upon the _LM_ curve of exogenous change in the money market may be examined in much the same way as were the effects on _Y_ of changes in exogenous factors in the income-expenditure model. Figures 7(a) and (b) depict the money market: 7(a) contains the demand and supply curves for money and 7(b) the _LM_ curve. For graphic simplicity, only one of the locus of liquidity preference curves has been drawn in 7(a), that for _Y_ equals $Y(1)$. Since $Y(1)$ is selected arbitrarily, the effect upon the rate of interest

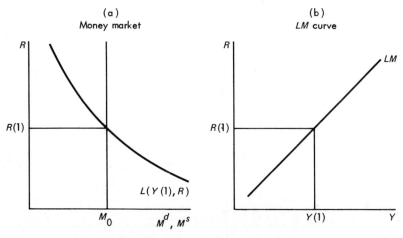

FIGURE 7   Monetary Sector

$R(1)$ associated with $Y(1)$ of an exogenous change will represent the effect on R associated with each Y.

Suppose the money market is in equilibrium at $[Y(1), R(1)]$ depicted in Figure 7(b). Consider the effects of an increase in M^s. The FED may increase M^s by purchasing U.S. Government securities from the public, by reducing the minimum legal reserve requirement, or by lowering the discount rate and thus encouraging bank borrowing of reserves. Money supply expansion, regardless of how the FED generates the increase in the monetary base, will take time as the multiple expansion process takes time; however, the comparative static effect is a rightward shift from M_0 to $M_0 + \Delta M$ or to $M(1)$. This M^s increase is illustrated in Figure 8.

At rate of interest R_1, after the FED increases the money supply to M_1, M_1 exceeds the demand for money at M_0. The FED has created a surplus of money. The quantity of money held by economic agents (M_0) is now less than the amount available in the system (M_1), and we may ask what would induce individuals to hold this greater amount of new liquidity in lieu of alternative assets which earn interest? In other words, what can now induce the public to hold quantity M_1 rather than the quantity M_0? If income does not fall below its original level Y_1, then the new money balances will only be absorbed by the public if the return on competing assets, such as bonds, is forced downward. This means that the new equilibrium rate of interest R associated with income level Y_1 must be below the old rate of interest R_1.

This reduced R holds for every income level. The reader can confirm this result by drawing the liquidity preference schedule for $Y = Y(2)$ and studying the effect of ΔM on $R(2)$. (A word of warning: though an increase in M has been shown to drive R down for each Y, the effects on the economy of an increase in M will depend not just upon this one *ceteris paribus* change. An increase in M

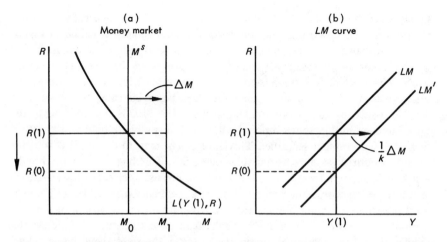

FIGURE 8   Money Supply Increase by FED

may eventually induce some change in Y as well as in R, but this issue requires a more complete exposition than the one we have just presented).

An increase in M^s will drive interest down at each income level. Figure 8(a) depicts R falling at $Y = Y(1)$. Figure 8(b) depicts R falling at each income level, the entire locus of equilibrium points in the money market shifts; LM shifts downward to the right from LM to LM'.

The algebraic description of the effect on money market equilibrium of a money supply increase is relatively easy. The equilibrium income solution in the linear illustration is

$$Y = \frac{M_0}{k} + \frac{m}{k}R \qquad (9)$$

An increase in M_0 to $M(1)$ simply increases the Y-intercept value of the LM curve by $(1/k)\Delta M$. Thus the numerical shift in the LM curve depends upon ΔM and the value k. Figure 8(b) shows the LM curve horizontal shift equal to $(1/k)\Delta M$.

(An exogenous money supply increase will shift the LM curve to the right even when the money supply is partly endogenous, as in equation (2): $M^s = M_0 + uR$. In this case the algebraic solution to the LM curve, corresponding to equation (9) for the exogenous money supply case, is

$$Y = \frac{M_0}{k} + \frac{(m + u)}{k}R$$

The exogenous component of the money supply, M_0, as in equation (9), enters the Y-intercept value of the LM curve, and thus exogenous money increases simply shift the schedule to the right, as in Figure 8(b). Geometrically, equation (2) produces an upward sloping nonvertical money supply schedule in Figure 8(a) rather than a vertical schedule at M_0. Otherwise, the model is the same.)

The reason an increase in M^s leads to a reduction in R can be explained intuitively. The Federal Reserve System injects new money into the economy, and this injection of new money generates subsequent increases the volume of deposits issued by the private banking system. The FED is able to bring about these increases in the money supply by inducing the public to hold money rather than U.S. Government securities. This inducement may force the FED to offer to buy securities at a comparatively high price. This higher price for bonds, which are contracts for a fixed money return, means, in effect, a lower rate of return. In other words, the process of monetary expansion coincides with downward pressure on market interest rates. Furthermore, the expansion of demand deposits by banks comes about as banks lend excess reserves. To induce the public to borrow additional funds, banks lower the rates they charge. Thus, again monetary expansion puts downward pressure on interest rates.

The LM curve has been shown to shift rightward when the money supply increases, and by analogy LM will shift to the left as the money supply is contracted. The LM curve can also be shown to shift in response to exogenous changes in money demand. Suppose that persons decide to hold fewer cash balances on average to undertake a given level of transactions. This reduction in transactions demand may come about if credit availability increases. A reduction in the preference for liquidity is represented in Figure 9(a). At income level $Y(1)$, reduced transactions demand for money has released money available in portfolios for other purposes. In competing for loans at $R(1)$, this surplus money drives interest rates down from $R(1)$. Since R must fall at each income level, the LM curve shifts down and to the right.

B ● The IS-LM Curves

The commodity market, evaluated in Chapters 5 through 11, may now be combined with the money market, developed in Chapter 12, here, and later in more detail in Chapters 15 and 16. First recall that the commodity market may be represented by five equations:

$$C = C_0 + bY_d \tag{10}$$

$$I = I_0 + fY - vR \tag{11}$$

$$G = G_0 \tag{12}$$

$$T = T_0 + tY \tag{13}$$

$$Y = C + I + G \tag{14}$$

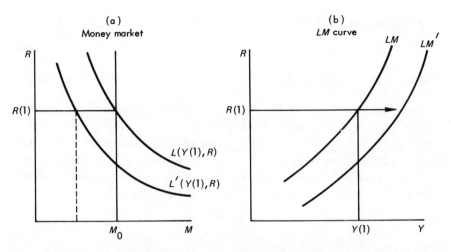

FIGURE 9   Decrease in Money Demand

Equations (10) through (13) represent the behavior of consumers, investors, and government. Equation (14) specifies the conditions for commodity market equilibrium. The commodity market can be conveniently summarized in Figure 10(a) by a modified Keynesian cross diagram. The equilibrium points in the commodity market are depicted as the *IS* curve in Figure 10(b). The algebraic solution to the commodity market, corresponding to the *IS* curve, is

$$Y = \frac{C_0 - bT_0 + I_0 + G_0 - vR}{1 - [b(1-t)+f]} \qquad (15)$$

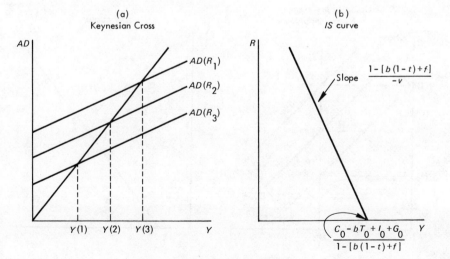

FIGURE 10   Commodity Market

The money market consists of three equations:

$$M^s = M^0 \tag{16}$$

$$M^d = kY - mR = L(Y, R) \tag{17}$$

$$M^s = M^d \tag{18}$$

Equations (16) and (17) represent money supply and demand theories, respectively, and (18) the money market equilibrium. Figure 11(a) represents the money market and Figure 11(b) the locus of money market equilibrium values. The algebraic solution to the money market corresponding to the *LM* curve is

$$Y = \frac{M_0}{k} + \frac{m}{k}R \tag{19}$$

Figures 10(b) and 11(b) are two loci of market equilibrium values in (R, Y) space. They may be drawn on the same diagram—Figure 12. The Hicksian *IS-LM* curve, Figure 12, contains in summary form the commodity market equilibrium pairs of interest and income derived from the modified Keynesian cross diagram and the money market equilibrium pairs of interest and income derived from the money supply and liquidity preference schedules. Equations (15) and (19) correspond to the *IS* and *LM* curves, respectively. Point A on both the *IS* and *LM* curves is common equilibrium in both markets. Any other point in the figure will represent at least one market in disequilibrium. The algebraic solu-

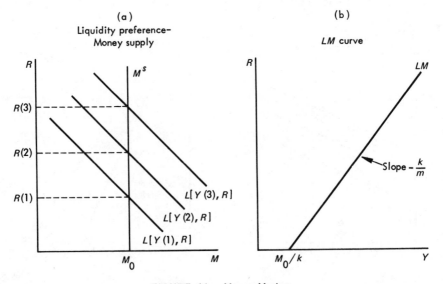

FIGURE 11   Money Market

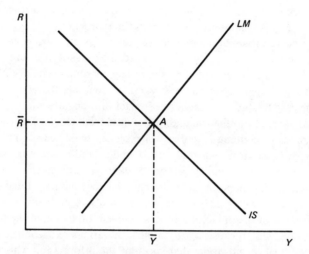

FIGURE 12   Hicks' *IS-LM* Diagram

tion, corresponding to A, is the pair of R and Y which are the joint solution to (15) and (19). Solve (19) for R:

$$R = -\frac{M_0}{m} + \frac{k}{m}Y \tag{20}$$

Substitute (20) into (15).

$$Y = \frac{C_0 - bT_0 + I_0 + G_0 - v\left[-\dfrac{M_0}{m} + \dfrac{k}{m}Y\right]}{1 - [b(1 - t) + f]} \tag{21}$$

Simplifying yields:

$$Y = \frac{C_0 - bT_0 + I_0 + G_0 + v(M_0/m)}{1 - [b(1 - t) + f]} + \frac{-vk/m}{1 - [b(1 - t) + f]}Y \tag{22}$$

Therefore;

$$\bar{Y} = \frac{C_0 - bT_0 + I_0 + G_0 + (v/m)M_0}{1 - [b(1 - t) + f] + vk/m} \tag{23}$$

Equation (23) is the algebraic solution for the equilibrium level of income in the model containing two markets, the commodity market [equations (10)-(14)], and the money market [equations (16)-(18)] . $\overline{Y}$, in equation (23), corresponds to $\overline{Y}$ in Figure 12. Given $\overline{Y}$, one can solve equation (20) for $\overline{R}$.

The *IS-LM* curve model developed above is perhaps the most useful diagram developed in macroeconomics. Its usefulness to the student of macroeconomics is like that of supply and demand curves in microeconomics. The *IS-LM* diagram may be used to compare classical to Keynesian economic theories. The *IS-LM* curves may be used to study the economic impact of monetary and fiscal policies and the *IS-LM* curves form the foundations of advanced neoclassical, monetarist, and neo-Keynesian economic theories. The reader must learn to utilize the *IS-LM* framework as it is essential to an understanding of macroeconomic theory, measurement, and policy issues. Without a firm grasp of the *IS-LM* framework, one has no hope of understanding macroeconomics. Furthermore, a firm grasp of the *IS-LM* model is the key to studying macroeconomics with ease. The workings of the model can best be understood by exploring the effects on the economy, with the use of the model, of various exogenous changes. It is important to realize, however, that most of the information which leads to the *IS-LM* curves is suppressed by them. The underlying consumption-money demand-investment relations are suppressed. One must always bear in mind the individual markets [Figures 10(a) and 11(a)] behind the *IS-LM* curves.

Let us examine the effect of an exogenous increase in private domestic investment expenditures on the *IS-LM* model. As a point of departure, suppose the economy is in equilibrium at $(\overline{R}, \overline{Y})$ in Figure 12. Investment is an element of the commodity market, so start with Figure 13, in which the initial equilibrium point is depicted. Only the *AD* curve for $\overline{R}$ is drawn; the others are implicit. An increase in exogenous investment will shift *AD* upward by the change in I:

$$\Delta AD(\overline{R}) = \Delta I_0$$

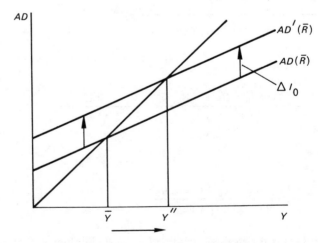

FIGURE 13   Increase in I:Commodity Market

According to the investment multiplier analysis, this upward shift in AD for rate R will increase commodity market income to $k_I \cdot \Delta I$. For each R, the level of I has increased and commodity market Y increases by $k_I \cdot \Delta I$. This increase in Y for each R in the commodity market is represented by a rightward shift in the IS curve by a distance $k_I \cdot \Delta I$. Figure 14 depicts the shift in the IS curve. If initially the interest rate remains unchanged, the economy would move from point A in Figure 14 to point B: Y would increase from $\overline{Y}$ to Y''.

However, from Figure 14, the new equilibrium point satisfying both markets is at point C, not B. The movement from A to C represents a smaller increase in income than the multiplier analysis had suggested. The investment multiplier tells the extent of the IS curve shift, but the final change in income is from $\overline{Y}$ to $\overline{Y}'$, not to Y''. The smaller increase in income is combined with an increase in the rate of interest. From the investment equation (11) it is clear that increases in R will dampen endogenous investment spending. It is necessary to examine the money market to understand why an exogenous increase in aggregate demand should cause the interest rate to rise and how the increase in R induces a subsequent reduction in I to partly offset the initial exogenous increase in I.

The key to the movement from A to C rather than to B is that the increased pressure on Y generates an increased transactions demand for money. Economic agents require more cash to undertake a higher level of expenditures. Put another way, at a higher level of income, Y'', the preference for liquidity at $\overline{R}$ increases from $L(\overline{Y}, \overline{R})$ to $L(Y'', \overline{R})$. Figure 15 depicts the shift to a higher liquidity preference schedule. At $R = \overline{R}$, the initial equilibrium rate of interest, money demand exceeds supply. The excess demand for cash increases competi-

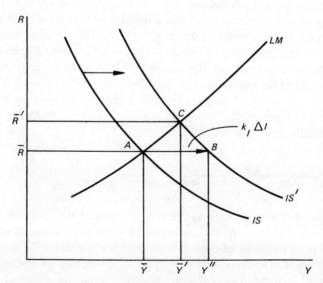

FIGURE 14   Exogenous Increase in Investment *IS-LM* Analysis

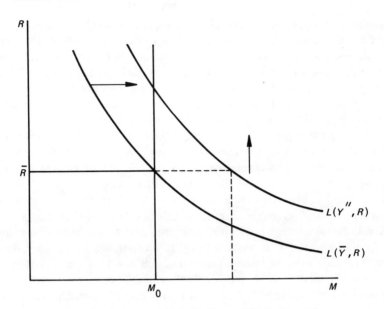

FIGURE 15   Increase in Y effect on Money Demand

tion for liquid assets as opposed to bonds, and interest rates are pressured upward. The scarce cash is bidding a higher interest charge. As interest rates start to rise the excess money demand is choked off. The increases in R will have feedback effects on investment.

As interest rates rise, endogenous investment falls. The increased competition for scarce funds drives up the user cost of capital by raising the interest term. The increased user cost reduces the desire to build up the capital stock. Thus the exogenously induced investment boom is partly choked off by an increase in R and by a limited availability of funds. Rather than income increasing to Y'', Figure 14, the economy can only move to $\overline{Y}'$, because R has increased and dampened part of the new excess aggregate demand.

The effect upon equilibrium income of the exogenous change in investment can be derived algebraically by computing the investment multiplier from the "global" equilibrium solution (23):

$$\frac{\Delta Y}{\Delta I} = \frac{1}{1 - [b(1 - t) + f] + vk/m} \tag{24}$$

The change in Y from ΔI in equation (24) includes all the feedback and interaction effects between commodity and money markets discussed above. The multiplier is no longer simply one over the quantity one minus the marginal propensity to spend. The denominator of equation (24) contains a new term: vk/m. Since $(vk/m) > 0$, the new multiplier is smaller than the commodity market multipliers studied in early chapters. This mathematical result corresponds to the graphic conclusion that $\overline{Y}$ increased to $\overline{Y}'$ not Y''. The new term vk/m represents the money market repercussions of the initial increase in income. The term k is the effect of the income increase on money needed for transactions. If k is large, less money is available to support loans and investment. m is the responsiveness of R to the reduced money available in money markets for loans. If m is large, the R response will be small and investment will not be greatly dampened. v represents the effect on endogenous I of a given change in R. A large v corresponds to a large cut in I, offsetting the initial demand increase.

The effects on income and the interest rate of other exogenous changes in the commodity market are strictly analogous to the above treatment of an investment boom. Whether personal consumption expenditures increase, government expenditures increase, or taxes are cut, the effects are identical to the above descriptions. The IS curve shifts, because each AD curve is shifted, horizontally by the market multiplier, for C_0, G_0, or T_0. Increased income requires additional transactions balances, interest rates rise, and the feedback effects through the money market on investment occur. The only qualitative difference between the change in I and other exogenous changes is that the repercussions through the monetary system back onto the commodity market always operate through investment. Consequently, any exogenous increase, in spending, G, C, or a cut in T, will cause a change in the GNP *mix* away from private investment.

Finally, consider the economic impact of an increase in the money supply. The LM curve will shift to the right horizontally by $(1/k)\Delta M$. Figure 16 depicts the shift. At the initial interest rate, $R(1)$, money market equilibrium is at point B. However, the increased supply of funds has driven down interest rates. The lower interest stimulates investment through the cost of capital, and income is

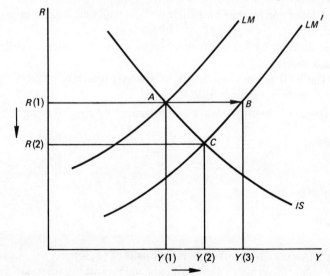

FIGURE 16   Money Supply Increase : *IS-LM* Analysis

driven upward. The new global two-market equilibrium is at C because the increased demand has subsequent feedback effects, requiring some excess money for transactions, and driving R back upward. The final effect is an increase in Y and a decrease in R. Compare Figure 16 to Figure 14. How does an increase in M^s compare, in its economic effects, to an increase in I?

Study the questions and problems at the end of this chapter carefully, as the ability to understand and manipulate *IS-LM* curves is essential to understanding subsequent material. After having a solid grasp of the *IS-LM* framework, one is well prepared to begin the study of stabilization policy.

STUDY QUESTIONS AND PROBLEMS

1. a. Construct an *LM* curve for the following equations:

    (1) $M^s = M_0$

    (2) $M^d = L(Y, R)$

    (3) $M^s = M^d$

   b. What is the effect upon the money market equilibria of each of the following:

    (1) A FED open market sale of U.S. government securities.

    (2) A technical improvement reducing transactions demand for money at each level of transactions.

    (3) A reduction by the Central Bank of the minimum legal reserve requirement.

    (4) A decision by bankers to hold larger volumes of nonrequired reserves in bank vaults.

    (5) The FED decides to adjust M to whatever level is required to maintain interest rates at a given level $R(1)$.

2. Assume that the money market is represented by the following linear relations:

   $M^s = M_0$

   $M^d = ky - mR$

   $M^s = M^d$

   a. Solve algebraically for the equilibrium pairs of (Y, R).
   b. Show that for each R, a decrease in M_0 will mean a lower level of income.

3. a. Diagram each of the following schedules:

(1) $C = C_0 + bY_d$

(2) $I = I_0 - vR$

(3) $G = G_0$

(4) $T = T_0 + tY$

b. Diagram the locus of equilibrium income values associated with R_1, R_2, R_3 where $R_1 < R_2 < R_3$.

c. Solve equations (1), (2), (3), and (4) and the equilibrium condition that $Y = C + I + G$ for Y. Plot the locus of equilibrium values.

4. Utilize the following system of equations:

$C = C_0 + bY_d$

$I = I_0 + vR$

$G = G_0$

$T = T_0 + tY$

$Y = C + I + G$

$M^s = M_0$

$M^d = kY - mR$

$M^s = M^d$

a. Diagram each relation in the model and construct the IS and LM curves. Derive the equation corresponding to each curve: IS and LM.

b. Compute from the above model the equilibrium levels of income and the interest rate.

c. Illustrate both algebraically and geometrically the comparative static effects upon $Y, R, I, C,$ and T of:

(1) An exogenous increase in I.
(2) An increase in government spending financed by public borrowing.
(3) A tax increase.
(4) A decrease in the money supply.
(5) A FED open market sale of U.S. government securities.

5. Consider models I, II, and III below.

I	II	III
$C = C_0 + bY_d$	$C = C_0 + bY_d$	$C = C_0 + bY_d$
$I = I_0 + fY$	$I = I_0 - vR$	$I = I_0 + fY_d - vR$
$G = G_0$	$G = G_0$	$G = G_0$
$T = T_0 + tY$	$T = T_0 + tY$	$T = T_0 + tY$
$Y = C + I + G$	$Y = C + I + G$	$Y = C + I + G$
$M^s = M_0$	$M^s = M^0$	$M^s = M^0$
$M^d = kY - mR$	$M^d = kY - mR$	$M^d = kY$
$Ms = M^d$	$M^s = M^d$	$M^s = M^d$

a. Solve in each model for commodity market equilibrium values of Y and R. Draw the *IS-LM* schedules in each model.

b. Compute the equilibrium values of $\overline{Y}, \overline{R}$ in each model.

c. What is the effect in each model upon $\overline{Y}$ of:

    (1) An increase in G of ΔG.

    (2) A decrease in taxes of ΔT.

    (3) A money supply increase of ΔM.

REFERENCES

Bailey, Martin J., *National Income and the Price Level: A Study in Macroeconomic Theory*, 2nd ed. New York: McGraw-Hill, 1971.

Hicks, John, "Mr. Keynes and the 'Classics'," *Econometrica*, April 1937, in Sir John Hicks, *Critical Essays in Monetary Theory*. Oxford: Clarendon Press, 1967.

Keynes, John Maynard, *The General Theory of Employment, Interest and Money*. New York: Harcourt, Brace & World, 1935.

McKenna, Joseph P., *Aggregate Economic Analysis*, 3rd ed. New York: Holt, Rinehart & Winston, 1969.

Smith, Warren, and Ronald L. Teigen, *Readings in Money, National Income and Stabilization Policy*, 3rd ed. Homewood, Ill.: Richard D. Irwin, 1974.

> The basic general eclectic principle that ought to guide us, as a first approximation, is that either fiscal or monetary policy can administer a required sedative or stimulus to economic activity.
>
> Arthur Okun (1971)

The U.S. economy, like most advanced industrialized systems, is a mixed market economy and two types of broad policies are available to central economic authorities who wish to stabilize the economy with a minimum of direct interference in private markets. The specific objectives of stabilization are not well defined though the magnitudes to which domestic stabilization goals refer are well known: high employment, price level stability, and balanced growth. Since the attainment of specific values of these goals may not always be compatible, policy makers must make choices and set priorities between the objectives. The selection of objectives and priorities involves value judgments and must evolve from the political process. However, given a set of policy objectives, the authorities have available two principal types of stabilization tools: fiscal policies and monetary policies.

Fiscal policy consists of selecting a federal budget, surplus, deficit, or balance, through the appropriate tax, transfer, and expenditure measures, for purposes of achieving the desired macroeconomic stabilization objectives. Given a specific objective, for example, 4 percent unemployment, a variety of fiscal measures may be employed. The actual policies chosen will depend upon a variety of normative and positive factors. Monetary policy consists of actions of the central monetary authority, for example,

14

Stabilization Policy

the decision to expand the money supply, in order to achieve some stabilization objective.

The purpose of this chapter is to discuss how fiscal and monetary policies work in a comparative static *IS-LM* framework and to use this foundation to evaluate these two sets of policies. Furthermore, fiscal and monetary policy will be shown to interact when certain types of actions are undertaken. The nature and implications of interaction will be discussed.

Pure Fiscal and Pure Monetary Policy: Organizationally the central monetary and fiscal authorities in the U.S. are two distinct, independent agencies. The fiscal authority is the U.S. government—the executive recommends and the Congress modifies and enacts fiscal legislation. The monetary authority is the Federal Reserve System. Created by Congress, the FED is nominally, and to some extent actually, subject to the control of Congress. However, the members of the Board of Governors of the Federal Reserve System, who primarily implement monetary policy, are appointed by the president for fourteen-year terms. The FED is consequently quite free to operate independently of the Executive Branch specifically and the government in general. In practice, then, two distinct independent agencies have responsibility for stabilization policies. The government implements fiscal policy, and the FED implements monetary policy. In most economies, however, the central bank is not as independent of the government as is the U.S. Federal Reserve System. Most advanced, industrialized countries have a central bank such as the Bank of England or the Bundesbank of Germany, which is more closely aligned with the government in power.

Of course, even in the U.S., the Board of Governors of the Federal Reserve System, our central bank, and the advisors on economic matters to the president interact on a regular basis. In addition the Chairman of the Board of the FED testifies before, and meets with, members of Congress. A certain degree of fiscal and monetary interaction is not uncommon. However, the FED and the government can, and often do, operate independently. At times they each pursue different policy objective priorities. Let us examine first, then, pure fiscal and pure monetary actions separately. Later the mix of fiscal and monetary actions shall be examined and the interaction of the agencies' decisions shall be studied.

A pure fiscal action can be defined as a change in the Federal Budget, generating a shift in the *IS* curve, with no change in the money supply. The government can finance an increase in expenditures in two ways which will not change the money supply and will, therefore, leave the *LM* curve in place. Increases in G can be financed by equal increases in taxes. Increases in G can also be financed by selling U.S. government securities to the public. Because the public purchases government securities, it provides the government with the money which the latter will spend. Neither method of government finance involves a net change in the money supply.

Suppose G is increased and financed completely by an equal increase in T. Let the increase in T, including the induced endogenous tax increase, equal the initial increase in G. From the discussion of fiscal policy in Chapters 6 and 7, the increase in aggregate demand will be ΔG minus any induced reductions in private spending from ΔT. The increase in income, at each rate of interest, will equal the government multiplier times the increase in government spending plus the tax multiplier times the increase in taxes. [It should be clarified that the term "multipliers" here refers to those developed in Chapters 6 and 7 in the income-expenditure model and not those which could be derived from the global solution, equation (23) of Chapter 15, to the two market equations.] In symbols:

$$\Delta Y \text{ [for } R = R(1)] = k_G \Delta G + k_T \Delta T$$

Since k_G exceeds k_T, the change in Y at each rate of interest is positive. The IS curve, as illustrated in Figure 1, shifts to the right by $k_G \Delta G + k_T \Delta T$. The comparative static effect is an increase in Y and an increase in R. If $k_G + k_T = 1$, then the income change from $Y(1)$ to $Y(3)$ would equal ΔG; however, income increases only to $Y(2)$ because increased interest reduces investment which partly offsets the increase in G.

Suppose the increase in G is financed by Treasury sales of U.S. securities to the public. $\Delta T = 0$ and $\Delta G > 0$. The IS curve shifts right by $k_G \Delta G$. Figure 2 depicts the expansionary effect upon Y and the increase in R. The change in Y from an additional dollar of government expenditures will be greater than when it was financed by taxes but less than k_G suggests because the change in R has induced reductions in I.

Figure 3 compares pure expansionary fiscal to pure expansionary monetary

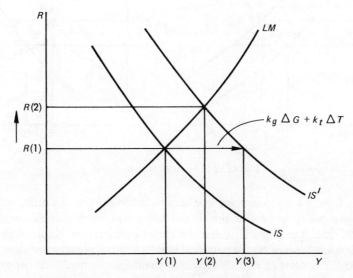

FIGURE 1   Pure Fiscal Expansion: $\Delta G = \Delta T > 0$

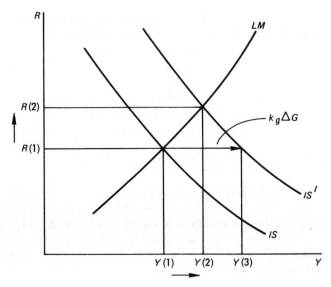

FIGURE 2   Pure Government Expenditure Increase

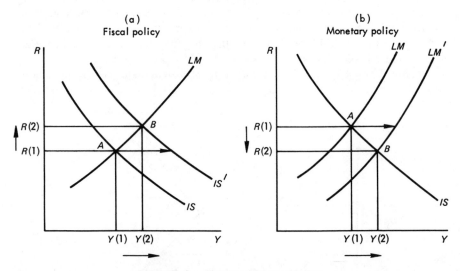

FIGURE 3   Fiscal vs. Monetary Policy

policy. Clearly a given increase in Y can be achieved either by utilizing fiscal or monetary policy as long as the IS and LM curves are neither infinitely elastic nor inelastic. The possibility that the curves have extreme elastic shapes raises the basic question of the fundamental effectiveness of monetary or fiscal policy. Chapter 17 is devoted to a discussion of the shapes of the IS-LM curves. Let us momentarily leave those possibilities for Chapter 17 and conclude: If the IS-LM

curves are neither perfectly elastic nor inelastic, then comparative static increases in Y can be accomplished either with fiscal or monetary policy alone.

Stabilization objectives are ordinarily more complex than setting a target for a particular goal: increasing Y from $Y(1)$ to $Y(2)$. The most obvious difference between fiscal and monetary policy seen from Figure 3 is that expansionary fiscal policy increases interest rates whereas expansionary monetary policy decreases interest rates.[1] Consider fiscal policy. If the objective is to stimulate the economy and R is driven upward, the rate of capital accumulation may decline. In a longer-run analysis, the capital stock can be shown to contribute to growth potential. Consequently, expansionary fiscal policy while it increases income, may constrain growth potential.

Monetary policy can increase income while driving interest rates down. Thus monetary policy stimulates private domestic investment. However, expansionary monetary policy is not without costs. While low rates of interest may encourage investment, financial capital may be induced abroad to the relatively higher foreign rates. Financial flows out of a country can weaken its balance of payments.

Resource Allocation: Monetary and fiscal policy both alter the allocation of resources. Fiscal expansion, while it increases total GNP also generates a reallocation away from private investment toward public expenditures. Monetary policy may reallocate resources between interest sensitive and nonsensitive industries. Consider a monetary policy contraction which increases interest rates. Higher interest rates across all industries would reduce all private investment plans at the margin. However in some industries, such as residential construction, output is quite sensitive to interest gyrations. The sensitivity of the housing and financial industries to interest rate changes may in large part be due to restraints on the rates paid to attract funds to these industries. As interest rates rise in general, rates on financial deposits are held down by legal limits. Funds available for mortgage loans dry up, and housing starts are curtailed.

Expansion or Contraction: Economists have long held the view that monetary and fiscal policies' effectiveness depends upon the direction of change in income that they are attempting to induce. Monetary policy operates through the expansion or contraction of the monetary base. Banks, with either increased or decreased reserves, alter their lending policies. Consider an increase in bank reserves designed to induce expansion. It has been historically argued that at low levels of income, monetary policy will be relatively ineffective because banks

[1] A warning on a subtle point which will be dealt with later in more detail. One rate of interest appears in the model. If inflation is expected to occur, then, according to the quantity theory of money, the rate of return on physical capital will diverge from that on bonds and two rates must be introduced to the model. Thus, the rate of anticipated inflation is not assumed to change here. See Chapter 22 for details.

will be unwilling to borrow. Monetary, unlike fiscal policy, operates indirectly through the banking system on spending. Indirect inducements to spend may not work. Advocates of this view refer to expansionary monetary policy as "pushing on a string."

In recent years, however, many economists have rejected the notion that monetary policy is less effective than fiscal policy in a recession. They point out that banks in recession do not hold excess reserves unless, as in the Depression, banks face the real fear of runs, unprotected by the central bank. The traditional argument was that banks faced with reduced reserves would have no choice but to contract loans and discourage spending. However, in recent years we have observed that banks, when faced with reduced reserves, will go to great lengths to try to replenish them. Even when the central bank is attempting to contract the money supply, banks will find sources to borrow funds and maintain their loans. The enormous volume of American dollars held by foreigners in Europe and Japan and in the Arab countries provides a tremendous amount of liquidity for bank borrowing which may allow U.S. banks to circumvent tight monetary policy. In addition, commercial banks and other financial institutions borrow funds from each other on a very short-term basis in what is called the federal funds market. Again, the federal funds market provides a mechanism by which banks can attempt to protect their lending policies from contractionary measures by the Federal Reserve System. Thus, banks will go to great lengths, even perhaps temporary losses, to avoid contracting loans to prime customers. Banks try to insulate themselves and therefore the economy from contractionary FED policies.

Lags in Monetary Policy: Chapter 7 contained a discussion of the inside and outside lags of fiscal policy. Monetary policy also incurs lags, and their lengths may well be long and varied. The inside lag of monetary policy, as opposed to fiscal policy, may be quite short, however. Recall from Chapter 7 the three divisions of the inside lag: recognition, decision, and action. These lags can be prohibitively large for discretionary fiscal policy stabilization due to the complexity of the political process. The recognition, decision, and action lags for monetary policy are surely short. Central banks have large staffs of economists with data, data gathering and synthesizing and analyzing tools to allow the recognition of economic problems every bit as quickly as the president's Council of Economic Advisors. Furthermore, the FED need not undertake a complex political process to determine a course of action. The actual committee of the Federal Reserve System which sets monetary policy, the Federal Open Market Committee, meets every few weeks and can be called into emergency sessions between regularly scheduled meetings. They have available to them information on the state of the economy and recommendations from their staff. Once they decide upon a course of action, the FED can instruct the manager of the desk in New York, the man who actually undertakes open market operations, to act. This inside lag can be very short indeed—just hours after the FED decision, the manager can take action.

The outside lag of monetary policy may be somewhat longer than that for fiscal policy. Monetary policy operates indirectly through the financial system on the incentive to invest and on the portfolios of individuals rather than directly on their incomes. New loans must be made, new deposits issued, and so on. Portfolio adjustments tend to be sluggish. Once a spending decision is made the economy must undergo the same outside lags as under fiscal policy action: production, earnings, and expenditures.

Empirical estimates of the whole monetary policy lag vary from three months to two-and-a-half years. However, such evidence is treacherous. Timing evidence in economics can be misleading. First, the public, particularly sophisticated bankers, financiers, and investors, may anticipate FED actions, so that causes actually precede the effect. Second, suppose monetary policy were so effective that it virtually eliminated any cyclical variations in income. To do so, monetary actions may have to vary considerably. Observing timing evidence, one would conclude that monetary actions never alter income; however, this conclusion is quite wrong. Monetary policy has, by assumption, stabilized income.

Mixed Policies: While it is fruitful to compare pure monetary and fiscal policies, one must also realize that fiscal and monetary policy can be and usually are, mixed. The government can finance an increase in expenditures by borrowing from the central bank. For example, the U.S. Treasury simply sells U.S. government securities to the Federal Reserve in exchange for Federal Reserve Notes— fiat money. The government then finances its expenditures by spending the money. In effect, the government, with the FED, increases G by printing money: ΔG will shift the IS curve to the right and ΔM will shift the LM curve to the right. Figure 4 depicts IS shifting by $k_G \Delta G$ and LM by $(1/k)\Delta M$: By increasing spending, government has increased competition for funds; however, it has also increased the money supply. Because more funds are available, interest rates need not rise. As a result, the induced reduction in private spending need not occur. In Figure 4 the IS-LM curves shift the same amount and $\Delta R = 0$; however, the change in R will in general be ambiguous.

The U.S. central bank, the FED, was not always as independent from the federal government as it is today. The FED achieved its independence only after a fight with the U.S. Treasury, which took place at the end of World War II. After the federal government had incurred a substantial debt financing World War II by deficit spending, the U.S. Treasury required that the FED freely buy all U.S. government securities at existing market prices so that interest charges to the government would not rise. At that time, until 1951, the FED was a relatively passive agent supporting new Treasury debt issues by buying them at existing interest rates. During the Korean Conflict President Truman pressured the Board of Governors to continue to support federal deficits at existing interest rates. The Federal Open Market Committee recalled:

> The President emphasized that we must combat Communist influence on many fronts. He said one way to do this is to maintain confidence in the government's credit and in government securities.

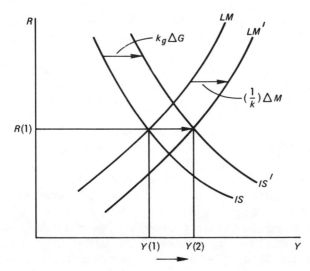

FIGURE 4   Government Expenditures Financed by Printing Money

It was the FED's view that the steady issuance of new money resulting from their passive continual purchase of government securities, while it supported low rates on government debt, was overly expansionary and inflationary. They wanted to set their own course. In March 1951, the FED and Treasury came to an "accord" which effectively reestablished the independence of the FED. However, it should be stressed that the Treasury and the FED both undertake similar actions—they both operate in the open market on a day-to-day basis to alter the size and composition of federal debt in the hands of the public. As a practical matter it is often difficult to distinguish the actions of these two agencies and to identify pure fiscal and pure monetary actions.

The Inflation-Unemployment Trade-Off: Two primary goals of domestic stabilization are price stability and high employment. Yet neither prices nor the level of employment appear directly as variables in the models we have so far developed. Furthermore, our models are comparative static models, meaning that from an initial equilibrium, the economy shifts to a new equilibrium after some parameter change. Once a new equilibrium is reached, variables are held constant. It would seem, therefore, that this model is not well designed to deal with problems of inflation and unemployment. In fact, it is useful to study the inflation-unemployment trade-off with a dynamic model rather than a comparative static model. The *IS-LM* model is deficient for two reasons: First, no explicit distinction is made between increases in prices and increases in quantities when money income is assumed to have increased. Second, if inflation is occurring, prices are rising and the economy is not in equilibrium, so a comparative static model is inadequate for analysis of the situation. In this section, in order to begin a more explicit study of inflation, a new theoretical framework, in addition to the *IS-LM* models developed above, will be introduced.

Recall that economic magnitudes, C, I, G, Y, T, are each measured in dollar units and consequently can in fact change, either because of a change in the price level or a change in quantity. Consider income Y. Y is the product of a price term and a quantity term. The *IS-LM* model, developed above, tells us how monetary and fiscal policies bring about changes in income, but it does not distinguish between price and quantity changes. To do this we must introduce an additional assumption either about prices or about quantities. In studying the depression, Keynesians assumed that prices were fixed so that when changes in Y took place they were always associated with changes in Q. Monetarists, when they study hyperinflations, assume that Q is fixed and that changes in Y are always associated with changes in prices. Serious analytic difficulties are encountered when one is dealing with less extreme economic situations in which both the level of prices and the level of output are changing at the same time.

One view of the relation between unemployment and the rate of inflation evolved in the 1950s and 1960s based upon empirical evidence and the work of A. W. Phillips. The spirit of this approach is that as money income begins to rise from a low level toward Y^* (full employment income), changes in output are gradually replaced by changes in prices. The thrust of the argument is that as $Y \rightarrow Y^*$ slack in markets is eliminated, unused resources are more difficult to place, markets tighten, workers who are still unemployed are more difficult to hire and perhaps less productive, and even before Y^* is reached prices start to increase. In fact, inflation occurs well before Y^* is attained and accelerates as Y approaches Y^*. In Figure 5 curve *PP* illustrates the Phillips curve theory of the inflation-unemployment trade-off.

Many economists are quite skeptical about the viability of Phillips curve theory. In recent years the rates of inflation associated with various levels of unemployment have been much higher than in the past, suggesting that the Phillips curve is not bow-shaped and that some other type of analysis must be used to describe the relationship between inflation and unemployment. Monetarist economists, for example, take the position that as a set of stable attainable points the Phillips curve does not look like curve *PP* at all. The spirit of the monetarist argument is based upon the view that a modified version of the classical theory is a relatively accurate description of the long run. Suppose that there exists some level of output, less than full employment, towards which the economy would naturally gravitate. The monetarists propose that the economy will gravitate towards a *natural rate of unemployment* regardless of the rate of inflation. Figure 5 depicts the natural rate hypothesis version of the relation between inflation and unemployment as the vertical line NRH. It will obviously be helpful to study in detail the theories and evidence upon which the Phillips curve and the natural rate hypothesis are based. First, however, since much of the dialogue depends on differences of analysis of monetary theory on the part of

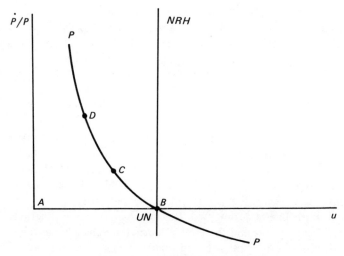

FIGURE 5   Phillips Curve Trade-off

Keynesian economists and monetarist economists, it is necessary for us to study the money market in much more detail than we have so far. The next two chapters are devoted to the supply and the demand for money.

STUDY QUESTIONS

1. You have been asked to make stabilization policy recommendations to deal with each of the following situations. What are your recommendations in each case? (Defend your recommendations, utilizing *IS-LM* curve analysis.)

  a. You are to reduce the level of unemployment, but without encouraging financial capital to flow abroad.

  b. The economy is "overheating." Slow the inflation, but avoid undue pressure on slowing residential construction.

  c. The economy is sluggish and needs impetus to grow, but you are not to alter the "mix" between private investment and government spending.

2. As a response to persistent threats of international instability, the monetary authority has pegged interest rates so as to discourage capital flows abroad.

  In the context of a carefully constructed two-sector model, explain the nature of constraints placed on *domestic* stabilization by the monetary authority. Can you predict the size of various multipliers?

3. Assume a two-sector (*IS-LM* curves) model in which all schedules have normal shapes (none are perfectly elastic nor perfectly inelastic), tax receipts depend on income with a positive marginal tax rate, and unemployment exists. Show, in each of the following cases the appropriate shifts in *IS-LM* curves and indicate

the effect upon income, interest rates, investment, consumption, and the government deficit.

a. The Central Bank sells U.S. government securities to commercial banks.

b. The government finances an increase in its expenditures by the sale of bonds to the public.

c. Households decide to increase their savings at each level of income.

d. The government finances an increase in its expenditures by printing money.

e. The government sells bonds to the Federal Reserve System and spends the proceeds.

f. Government transfer payments are increased and are financed by an exogenous (nonincome-related) increase in taxes.

4. Consider the *IS-LM* model to be a model of money income and suppose the economy has an unemployment level of 6 percent. The stabilization authorities believe the economy is characterized by a Phillips relation. They utilize expansionary measures to reduce unemployment by 2 percent at an expected cost of an additional 2 percent rate of inflation.

a. Show the measures the authorities might take and explain intuitively how they would work.

b. What will happen to inflation and unemployment if the economy is actually characterized by the natural rate hypothesis?

REFERENCES

Bach, G. L., *Making Monetary and Fiscal Policy*. Washington, D.C.: Brookings Institution, 1971.

Friedman, Milton, "The Role of Monetary Policy," *American Economic Review*, March 1968.

Heller, Walter J., *Perspectives on Economic Growth*. New York: Random House, 1968.

Maisel, Sherman, *Managing the Dollar*. New York: W. W. Norton, 1973.

Mayer, Thomas, *Monetary Policy in the United States*. New York: Random House, 1968.

Okun, Arthur, "Measuring the Impact of the 1964 Tax Reduction," in W. L. Smith, and R. L. Teigen, *Readings in Money, National Income, and Stabilization Policy*, 3rd ed. Homewood, Ill.: Richard D. Irwin, 1974.

_____, "Rules and Roles in Fiscal and Monetary policy," in W. L. Smith and R. L. Teigen, *Readings in Money, National Income, and Stabilization Policy*, 3rd ed. Homewood, Ill.: Richard D. Irwin, 1974.

Phillips, A. W., "The Relation between Unemployment and the Rate of Change of Money Wage Rates in the United Kingdom, 1861-1957," *Economica*, New Series, Vol. 25, November 1958.

Samuelson, Paul, and Robert Solow, "Analytical Aspects of Anti-Inflation Policy," *American Economic Review*, May 1960.

MONETARY THEORY
and
THE GREAT DEBATE

part VI

Does money matter? Monetarists will tell you that all major and most minor fluctuations in the pace of economic activity are the direct result of monetary forces. What of crop failures, steel strikes, oil embargos, construction slumps, and the like? Merely blips on the path dominated by money. Nonmonetarists, eclectics, are less sure. Money matters, but so do government fiscal policies, consumer choices, interest rates, and exogenous shocks to the system. In short, the role of money in the determination of income, the price level, and the rate of employment is the most controversial question in economics today. One point is, however, undeniable—money matters a good deal. Twenty years ago, many economists, judging by their texts and teachings, would have questioned this conclusion. Today few would.

This part of the text examines in detail the nature of money and its functions in a modern economic system. An even-handed attempt is made to present the two dominant views of the role of money. Economists long held the view that money played no role in determining the essentials of economic activity: production, employment consumption-investment mix, and so on. However, Keynes revolutionized thinking on the role of money and argued that monetized economies were qualitatively different from primitive barter systems and that the modern economy was subject to breakdown due in part to the unstable nature of the uncertain demand for money.

Monetarists counterattack these Keynesian notions arguing that the use of money in the economy is highly stable while the issuers are unreliably capricious. It is the Federal Reserve System, created to stabilize the economy, which has been the major source of instability—rapidly shifting its policies from expansion to contraction of the money supply. Chapters 15 through 17 examine the determinants of the supply and the demand for money to compare and contrast the monetarist and Keynesian ideas.

> "Money is but the fat of the Body-Politick, whereof too much doth as often hinder its agility as too little makes it sick." (William Petty, 1665)
>
> "Money is the vitale spirit of trade and if the spirits faile, needs must the body faint." (Edward Misselden, 1662)
>
> "Money is like Muck, not good except it be spread." (Thomas Manley, 1625)
>
> "Money is Muscle (specifically, the sinews of war)." (James Whiston, 1693)
>
> Alfred Martial in Gibson and Kaufman (1971)

The question "What is money?" would seem to have a perfectly straight-forward answer. Money is what one spends to purchase commodities—it is cash, dollar bills, coins, and so on. However, monetary theory is in such a state of flux that from every monetary economist, one will obtain a different definition of money. Milton Friedman and Anna Schwartz define money as cash plus demand deposits at commercial banks plus time deposits at commercial banks. Lester Chandler defines money as cash plus demand deposits at commercial banks. James Tobin seems to reject the very concept that a specific set of assets comprises the money supply. In addition to different definitions of money, economists distinguish many different types of money: high-powered money, inside money, outside money, bank money, ghost money, fiat money, full-bodied money, and so on. The first objective of this chapter is to answer the question "What is money?"

Even if two economists may agree on the definition of money, they may

15

The Supply of Money

still disagree about the determinants of its supply. Some economists emphasize the mechanical determinants of the money supply. Central monetary authorities, such as the Federal Reserve System in the U.S., control the money supply, and any variations in its quantity can be understood by examining these mechanical processes which link specific central authority actions to the total volume of money in circulation. Others argue that, in addition, one should consider the institutional and behavioral aspects of the private financial institutions in the economy rather than mechanical relationships. To some extent, behavior of economic agents have an effect on the money supply. Thus, the quantity of money is determined jointly by the actions of the monetary authorities and by the private financial institutions.

A ● What is money?

The Functions of Money: Suppose one were to consider a barter exchange economy in which each transaction undertaken between economic agents entailed the direct exchange of commodities. The terms of exchange would be determined in each transaction by barter. For example, a farmer may wish to exchange wheat for cloth. He would have to go to the market and find a cloth dealer willing to purchase wheat. The wheat-cloth exchange price would be hammered out by barter. Should the farmer next wish to obtain some goat's milk, he would have to find a shepherd willing to trade goat's milk for wheat. Again, a new price ratio would have to be ironed out by barter. In a very primitive system, barter exchange is possible; however, even in the most rudimentary society, some commodity is usually specified which serves some basic functions which facilitate exchange, contractual settlements, accounting practices, and so on. The commodities which provide these services comprise the money supply.

The primary abstract function provided by money, in a nonbarter economy, is *a unit of account*. Given a unit of account, such as a dollar, a yen, a guinea, or a peso, the price of each commodity may be specified in the account unit terms. The exchange price between any two commodities can easily be determined from their respective unit of account prices. The unit of account is often called the *numéraire*. The unit of account may, but need not, be the sole type of money in the economy.[1]

The second abstract function of money is a *medium of exchange*. With the possible exception of very primitive hunting and fishing societies, virtually all exchange economies require an asset which serves as an exchange medium. Table 1 contains a list of commodities that have served as media of exchange in various economies. Ranging from cows to paper, from shells to debt, the list is obviously quite varied. The dominant medium of exchange in the U.S. economy today is

[1] In fact, no asset corresponding to the unit of account need exist at all. The guinea can be utilized as a unit of account in England. Today, however, no actual guinea coin exists. Such nonexistent monies are called *ghost money*.

bank checking accounts, or demand deposits. Currency also serves as a medium of exchange; however, far fewer and much smaller transactions involve currency than involve demand deposits. Of course, many transactions involve a credit card. The card itself is not exchanged, rather claims on demand deposits are exchanged.

TABLE 1

Items Which Have Served as Money

Clay	Cattle	Salt	Paper
Cowry shells	Slaves	Beer	Playing cards
Wampum	Tea	Gold	Debts of governments
Whale teeth	Wool	Bronze	Debts of banks

Source: This list was extracted from Lester Chandler, *The Economics of Money and Banking*, 6th ed. (New York: Harper & Row, 1973), Table 1.1, p. 11.

Third, a barter economy suffers from not having available a *standard of deferred payment*. As an economy becomes more advanced and complex, the need for intertemporal arrangements in exchange increases. It is useful to have available a standard yardstick in which to establish terms for such intertemporal transactions. Loans, for example, can involve commitments in terms of payments in kind; however, terms specified in the monetary unit are far more common. An entrepreneur may arrange the payment of capital several years after revenues have been received. A large purchase for future delivery may involve payment on delivery. Speculation of the value of wheat several years into the future involves agreements based on future prices. Money is the standard utilized for such deferred payments.

Finally, a money economy utilizes some commodities as a *store of value*. Or, put another way, the assets which serve as media of exchange are also used as a store of value. Having available an asset whose value is stable in terms of other commodities and which is risk-free and nonperishable is very useful. A good many assets are used as a store of value in most economies; however, only a small number are riskless in terms of maintaining their value.

The Traditional Approach: Money, in any economy, can be defined as those assets which serve as a unit of account, a medium of exchange, a means of deferred payment, and a store of value. Commodities which provide these services of money may provide other types of services as well. Metals, for example, have historically been utilized in coins, and, of course, serve other industrial and ornamental purposes. Such types of money are called *commodity money*. If the exchange price of a commodity money as a money is the same as its price in other uses, it is a *full-bodied* money. However, it is neither necessary nor sufficient for an asset to have nonmonetary uses to serve the purposes of money. Paper currencies and bank demand deposits have no purpose other than as monies.

Until the 1970s, the assets which served as a medium of exchange in the U.S. economy were currency and demand deposits (checking accounts) issued by commercial banks. Currency in the U.S. consists of coins, which are in part commodity money because they contain some metals useful for other purposes, and paper issued by the Federal Reserve System called Federal Reserve notes. Federal Reserve notes and Treasury-issued coins are media of exchange by fiat. That is, the government decrees that Federal Reserve notes are "legal tender for all debts, public and private." Such money is called *fiat money,* as it has no industrial, ornamental, or commercial use except as a means of payment by government fiat. Federal Reserve notes are accepted as a medium of exchange because the Federal Government decrees it so, and because people, in the U.S., accept the legitimacy of the government's decree.

Until the 1970s, commercial banks were the only financial institutions allowed to issue liabilities that were negotiable and therefore payable on demand. It is these liabilities, demand deposits of commercial banks, which were the only form of nonfiat money in the U.S. economy. Money in the form of demand deposits can be created in the following way: An individual may deposit $1000 worth of Federal Reserve notes in his local bank. The bank would credit this individual's account with a $1000 deposit. The individual's $1000 demand deposit is a liability of the bank but an asset of this person which is payable to him, or, more importantly, to the legitimate bearer of his check, on demand. Unlike government fiat money, such as Federal Reserve notes and coins, demand deposits need not be accepted as a medium of exchange. That is, demand deposits are not legal tender but are widely accepted in the form of checks, as a means of payment. Economists who focus attention on the medium of exchange function of money have usually considered money to consist of money plus demand deposits. This magnitude is called M_1, so named because it represents the first definition of money.

In the 1970s the U.S. financial system underwent a number of structural changes which, among other things, have rendered the old measure of money, M_1, obsolete. For example, in 1972 a new type of account which one could open in savings and loan associations was introduced. These accounts, introduced in the New England states, were negotiable orders of withdrawal accounts, named NOW accounts. These NOW accounts, though issued by savings and loan associations rather than commercial banks, were virtually the same as bank demand deposits, because the deposits held in NOW accounts could be used as a medium of exchange, since they were negotiable and thus checkable. After a brief experimental period, a system of share drafts was introduced by credit unions in the United States. Members of credit unions could deposit their money in the credit unions and in doing so open share draft accounts. These share draft accounts were also checkable instruments and could, therefore, be used as a medium of exchange. Thus, the distinction between commercial bank demand deposits and some of the new liabilities of other financial institutions has become blurred. As a practical matter, an individual can spend his savings and loan NOW account, his share draft, and his commercial bank or mutual savings bank NOW account as easily as he can spend from his checking account. It seems clear that if we are to measure the volume of assets in the U.S. economy which serve as a medium of exchange, then the old magnitude M_1 must be broadened to include certain deposits in nonbank financial institutions. To accommodate these new assets, economists use other measures such as the measure M_1+: the old M_1 plus checkable deposits at nonbank thrift institutions. Figure 1 illustrates the relative magnitude of three components of M_1+ in select years: currency, demand deposits, and the rest: $(M_1+) - M_1$.

Keynes, in *The General Theory*, emphasized the nontransactions usages of money, and his ideas have suggested to many a different definition of money. Keynes argued that assets which served as a medium of exchange were also held as a temporary store of value. In fact, the somewhat capricious nature of the desire to hold money as a store of value plays a very important role in Keynesian monetary theory. For the purpose here, however, note that if one focuses on money as a store of value, the selection of assets becomes more difficult. Warren Smith (1970) argues that money includes time deposits of commercial banks, time deposits in savings banks, shares in savings and loan institutions,

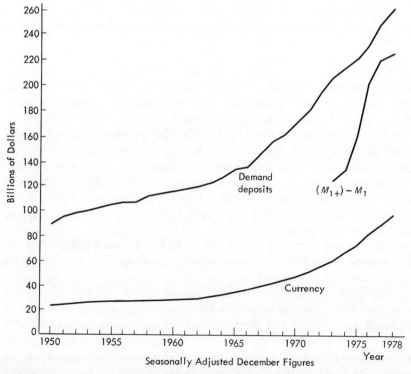

FIGURE 1   The Quantities of Demand Deposits and Currency in the U.S., 1950-1973

and so on. Milton Friedman, emphasizing money as "a temporary abode of purchasing power" often includes time deposits issued by commercial banks but not those issued by others. David Laidler (1969), utilizing an empirical approach to the definition, buttresses the Friedman definition of money as cash plus demand deposits plus time deposits issued by commercial banks. This definition of money is called M_2. Table 2 depicts the growth rates of M_1, M_1+, and M_2 as defined in this text for some select postwar years. While M_1 and M_2 tend to move together, their rates of change are quite different; M_1 has changed more slowly than M_2. Notice the relative explosion in M_1+ from 1974 to 1978.

TABLE 2

Money Supply Changes in Select Years (First quarter to first quarter annual percent rate of change)

YEAR	M_1	M_1+	M_2
1959-60	0.3%	–	0.6
1969-70	6.3	–	10.9
1974-75	4.7	5.4	7.2
1976-77	6.2	13.2	11.4
1977-78	7.9	8.4	9.3
1978-79	6.6	4.7	8.2

Just as the assets which comprise M_1 changed throughout the 1970s due to structural changes in financial markets, the distinction between M_1+ and M_2 also became blurred. In 1975, commercial banks were allowed to permit their customers to write checks in amounts which exceeded their demand deposit holdings as long as they did not exceed the holdings in the commercial bank savings account. In other words, the distinction between writing a check on one's demand deposit and writing a check on one's savings deposit became moot. Individuals could, in effect, keep their assets in savings accounts, which earn interest, and write checks on the basis of those interest-earning accounts. Similar provisions were introduced to allow individuals to earn interest on NOW accounts in some parts of the country. Consequently, the traditional primary difference between assets in the narrow money definition M_1 and the broad definition M_2 no longer existed. One could spend savings accounts, and one could earn interest on accounts which one could spend.

A final point should be made about changes in the structure of financial transactions which have an impact on the relationship between the supply of money and the economy. For some time, economists and others have suspected that the use of electronics and computer systems to undertake transactions could render our current method of using checking accounts obsolete. If, for example, one could purchase one's groceries by making an electronic transfer immediately from one's checking account to that of the supermarket, then why would it not be possible to make an electronic transfer from an account in which one is earning interest directly to one's supermarket? In other words, theoretically, consumers should be able to avoid holding deposits which bear no interest. The extent of the impact of such a technological change on financial intermediaries and on the economy is uncertain at this time. The speed with which the economy adopts new electronic methods, such as electronic funds transfer, depends upon the adaptability of our financial institutions, especially the regulators and the private financial institutions themselves, and upon the ability of various retail stores to learn how to utilize electronics methods.

An Alternative Approach: Not all monetary theorists consider a particular set of assets to comprise the money supply. An alternative approach is to consider the inherent property which many assets possess and which permits them to provide, in various degrees, the functions of money. This crucial property of assets is _liquidity._ Liquidity may be defined as the degree to which an object can be converted into a medium of exchange with no loss of value, quickly, at any time and place. Naturally, currency is quite liquid, as it is an acceptable medium of exchange by law. Demand deposits are somewhat less liquid than currency, since at times (notably Saturday nights) and at some places, usually far from home, one cannot exchange demand deposits. With the financial market innovations introduced in the 1970s, a number of other assets are very similar to demand deposits. Savings and loan shares which are in the form of NOW accounts and credit union shares both can serve as media of exchange and are, therefore, hard to distinguish from commercial bank demand deposits. Also, time deposits issued at commercial banks and savings accounts issued by other savings institutions, while not perhaps used directly as a medium of exchange, can be spent by the simple device of transferring from this form into a checking account, in some cases almost automatically. Thus, time and savings deposits are highly liquid and very close substitutes, especially for large investors, for checking accounts.

Savings in the form of life insurance policies are comparatively liquid assets in that under certain circumstances one can borrow on the basis of such policies and undertake expenditures. Certain types of commercial negotiable instruments, such as prime commercial paper, are highly liquid, because again they can be converted into a medium of exchange relatively quickly by large firms or by financial institutions. Somewhat less liquid assets are short-term U.S. government securities. In borrowing to finance its deficits, the government issues a variety of bonds. Short-term U.S. government securities include Treasury bills with maturity dates varying from sixty to ninety days. These short-term issues are basically immune to default risk and are highly stable in price because the maturity period is so short. Consequently, short-term U.S. government securities are highly liquid. For many institutions short-term U.S. government securities are nearly perfect substitutes for savings deposits. While the government securities may appear to be a bit less liquid, they bear a greater interest return.

One could continue to consider the relative liquidities of federal funds, long-term U.S. government securities, corporate bonds, stocks, physical equity, and so on. However, the thrust of this approach is that each of a wide variety of types of assets has, in varying degrees, liquidity, so that no fixed set of assets can be identified as "money" and studied to the exclusion of others. Rather, the entire spectrum of liquid assets is important and the course of the economy is influenced by the general level and nature of its liquidity rather than by the simple quantity of one small set of these assets called money. In other words, rather than a well-defined bundle of assets, the entire spectrum of liquid assets may serve from time to time as temporary abodes of purchasing power.

James Duesenberry (1963), a leading proponent of this approach, focused on the interactions between various financial institutions and various firms and persons in their holdings of liquid assets. Gail Pearson (1970) emphasized distinguishing between liquid assets held by financial institutions and those held by other firms in determining the course of the economy. Perhaps the most famous proponent of this approach is James Tobin. Led by Tobin and others at the Cowles Foundation at Yale University, economists have developed an analysis of financial markets that is based on a general equilibrium framework in which financial assets are viewed to be near but not perfect substitutes so that each asset has a demand schedule which depends upon its return and upon the returns of near substitutes. The emphasis of this approach is on the variety of financial assets and institutions. We turn now to the determinants of the money supply— the volume of assets defined as money in the hands of the public.

B ● Theories of the Supply of Money

Historically, analysis of the money supply has focused upon institutional and mechanical relationships. The economic impact of a noncommodity money issued by a monetary authority rather than a commodity money, such as gold, has received considerable attention. Consider fiat paper money, such as Federal Reserve notes. Clearly the issuing agency, the FED, has a good deal to do with the volume of such notes in the hands of the public. It can be shown that the volume of such money can be as tightly controlled as can the volume of commodity money—even more so. The problem of control over the money supply, however, becomes far more complex when private institutions, commercial banks, are granted rights to issue deposit liabilities which provide money services.

The money supply, narrowly defined, consists of two types of assets: bank deposits and fiat money in the hands of the nonbank public. Fiat money serves two purposes: circulating medium and bank-held reserves. Even though the central authority may still be able to closely control the volume of fiat money outstanding, it may be unable to control the mix between bank and public holdings. Furthermore, the relation between actions of the central authority and the volume of bank money is complex. The introduction of fractional banking, time deposits, and nonbank financial institutions further complicates the problem of determining the money supply. Nevertheless, the general thrust of the traditional analysis of the money supply focuses upon money's exogenous nature.

To illustrate the exogeneity of the money supply, consider a hypothetical simplified economy with a central bank authority, the FED, a private commercial banking system, a government, and the public. The government empowers the central bank authority to print fiat money which is legal tender, called Federal Reserve notes. The government may issue bonds to the central bank in exchange for paper money, which the government may then spend to finance deficits. Thus fiat money may become a circulating medium of exchange when the government finances deficits.

The central bank charters commercial banks allowing them to issue, in exchange for fiat money, deposit liabilities, payable on demand. Suppose, as a first approximation, banks may only issue demand deposits, dollar for dollar, in exchange for fiat money, and that the fiat money received must be held in reserve. Suppose the government has run $1000 of deficits financed by fiat money, so that $1000 has been issued to the public. Fiat money held by the public is $1000, and if none is deposited in commercial banks, the money supply will remain at $1000 of fiat money.

Now, let the public deposit $600 of its fiat money in commercial banks. The banks credit the depositors with demand deposits of $600 and place the $600 of fiat money in the bank vault. The money supply now consists of $400 fiat money in the hands of the public and $600 of demand deposits. The remaining $600 of fiat money is no longer circulating because it is held in reserve by the commercial banks. The total money supply is still $1000. The public choice between holding their money in the form of bank notes or Federal Reserve notes has had no effect upon the total volume of money. The money supply is completely determined by the two central authorities—the FED and the government.[2]

Let us now introduce fractional reserve banking. Suppose the FED permits banks to hold in reserve only a fraction of the fiat money deposited by customers. Suppose the FED sets a minimum legal reserve requirement on demand deposits, r_d, of 20 percent. Now, of the $600 deposited in banks, only 20 percent, or $120, is required to be held on reserve. The remaining $480 may be loaned to the public by the commercial banks. If the entire $600 always returns as reserves to the banking system and if banks always lend their excess reserves, then bank loans may be made and new deposits issued until the $600 becomes 20 percent of total deposits. Mathematically, defining R as total bank reserves and DD as demand deposits, their relation under a fractional reserve banking system is:

$$R = r_d DD \qquad (1)$$

Equation (1) states that reserves must be r_d percent of total demand deposits. If

---

[2]These authorities could be consolidated into one. However, for institutional realism two separate agencies are distinguished. In the U.S. the FED serves as central bank and the U.S. Treasury as the government's financial agency. Most countries have both a central bank and a government financial branch.

reserves are $600, demand deposits may, through bank loans, expand to $3000. The total money supply is the sum of demand deposits and public-held currency (fiat money). In this example, M equals $3000 demand deposits plus $400 fiat money, or $3400.

What is the effect on M of a public decision to alter its mix of fiat and bank money? Suppose the public wishes to hold $500 in fiat money rather than $400. The banking system reserves will have fallen by $100 to $500. Since reserves have fallen by $100, equation (1) states that deposits must fall by a multiple of $100 because these $100 reserves were supporting demand deposits of $500, given $r_d = 20$ percent. The decision by the public to hold $500 in fiat money rather than $400, given total fiat money issues by the FED of $1000, reduces demand deposits by $500 from $3000 to $2500. The total money supply is now $500 fiat money plus $2500 demand deposits, or $3000 compared to $3400 before. The public choice of mix between bank and fiat money has endogenously altered the total volume or supply of money!

The impact on M of the choice between demand deposits and fiat money may be clarified mathematically. Let c represent the ratio of currency C to demand deposits DD:

$$C = cDD \tag{2}$$

Defining HP as total outstanding Federal Reserve notes issued by the central bank, HP consists of public-held fiat money C plus commercial bank-held reserves, R, and is sometimes called high-powered money:

$$HP = R + C \tag{3}$$

Since R is a legal fraction r_d of DD, we have

$$HP = r_d DD + C \tag{4}$$

Substituting (2) into (4) yields

$$HP = (r_d + c)DD \tag{5}$$

From equations (5) and (2) we may derive the following relationship between M_1, which is cash plus demand deposits, and high-powered money:

$$M_1 = C + DD = \frac{c}{(r_d + c)} HP + \frac{1}{(r_d + c)} HP \tag{6}$$

or

$$M_1 = kHP \quad \text{where} \quad k = \frac{c+1}{(r_d + c)} \tag{7}$$

k may be thought of as the money multiplier, because it tells us the multiple by which the volume of high-powered money is converted into M_1. The money multiplier, k, is seen to depend upon two variables: r_d, the legal reserve requirement set by the central monetary authority, and c, the ratio of cash held by the public to demand deposits. In this model, if the public choice of the ratio c is fixed, then the central monetary authority can control the money supply through its control of the volume of high-powered money and through its required reserve ratio r_d. Furthermore, if c changes but can be predicted by the central authority, then they can offset, defensively, any undesired changes in the money supply brought about by changes in the cash-to-deposit ratio. An elaboration of this model would allow commercial banks to issue time deposits as well as demand deposits. Just as with cash and demand deposits, the public may exercise choice about the mix between demand and time deposits which would further complicate FED control of the money supply. Let t be the public choice of the ratio of time deposits TD to demand deposits and r_t the time deposit reserve requirement, and devise the new model. It will be employed subsequently.

Though the FED is reluctant to alter reserve requirements, considerable activity is undertaken in regard to the volume of high-powered money. In the example above, high-powered money reaches the public through federal deficits. In the U.S. economy, as a result of historical deficits, a very large volume of high-powered money is outstanding. In addition to selling its securities to the FED in exchange for fiat money, the U.S. Treasury borrows directly from the public to obtain money. Consequently, both the FED and the general public hold large volumes of U.S. government securities. The most common method employed by the FED to alter the volume of high-powered money held by the public is by buying and selling U.S. government securities to the public. These FED transactions with the public are called *open market operations.*

As suggested above, we can alter the equations to allow for a more complex model in which banks can borrow from the central bank at a discount rate, d, and in which banks can issue time deposits as well as demand deposits. The money multiplier, k, would in this case depend not only upon the two parameters c and r_d but also upon d, r_t, and t. The direction of the effect on M_2, which consists of M_1 plus time deposits, of an increase in each of these variables is indicated by the sign over the variable: + for an increase and − for a decrease:

$$M_2 = k(\overset{-}{r_d}, \overset{-}{r_t}, \overset{+}{t}, \overset{-}{c}, \overset{-}{d})HP \tag{8}$$

In summary, the FED can alter the volume of the monetary base by open market operations and by encouraging or discouraging bank borrowings of reserves. The monetary base, in turn, is a major determinant of the total money supply whether it be M_1 or M_2. The money supply can be altered by the FED if it changes the reserve requirements on bank deposits. Though public choices about the mix between cash, demand deposits, and time deposits can alter M_1 and M_2, the FED, if it can anticipate the changes in M_1 and M_2, can offset them by open market operations or by changes in reserve requirements or the discount rates. Thus the traditional approach leads to the conclusion that the money supply, whether M_1 or M_2, is predominantly determined by the Federal Reserve System.

Another approach to monetary theory focuses attention on credit and liquidity in the hands of the nonbank public rather than on monetary aggregates like M_1 and M_2. The proponents of this approach, associated with the "Yale school," deemphasize banks, demand deposits, and mechanical relations. They stress the general processes of financial markets and the behavior of the various financial institutions.

James Tobin (1963) pointed to a conceptual flaw in the traditional treatment of bank behavior. Consider the effect, through the multiple expansion process, upon demand deposits of a sequence of reductions in the minimum legal reserve requirements on demand and time deposits. In Table 3 the quantities of M_1 and M_2 are calculated from the model elaborated from equations (1)-(5) including time deposits.[3] The values of r_d and r_t vary in the table. The ratio t is 0.5 and c is 0.01. The idea that emerges from Table 3 is that the money supply, whether one measures M_1 or M_2, can expand to virtually any limit from a given monetary base as the legal reserve requirement approaches zero. The FED has available to it a "widow's cruse";[4] regardless of the volume of bank money, the FED can generate more by simply reducing reserve requirements. How far can this process be undertaken? The process of expansion itself involves bank loans being made with reserves held in excess of required reserves. The multiple expansion process rests upon banks' making loans with any excess reserves. However, why do banks make these loans? Banks are surely not mechanical robots who mindlessly increase their loans in response to excess reserves.

TABLE 3

M_1 and M_2 Under Various Reserve Requirements on Demand and Time Deposits
$c = .01, t = .5, HP = \$1000$

r_d	r_t	C	M_1	M_2
0.2	0.05	42.55	4,297.87	6,425.53
0.15	0.05	54.05	5,459.46	8,162.16
0.10	0.05	74.07	7,481.48	11,185.18
0.10	0.01	86.96	8,782.61	13,130.43
0.01	0.001	487.80	49,268.29	73,658.53
0.001	0.001	869.57	87,826.09	131,304.35

[3] r_t is the discount rate and t the ratio of time to demand deposits. The equations for computing demand deposits and time deposits are

$$HP = (c + r_d + r_t t)DD \quad \text{and} \quad TD = tDD.$$

[4] A vase with a never-ending supply of oil.

Bankers are in business to make profits. The profit-maximizing banker will attempt to make loans with new excess reserves if the new loans will increase the bank's profits. Bank profits, in this example, derive from the interest earned on loans minus the cost of running the bank. Net revenues from a loan can be viewed as the difference between the borrower's rate paid the bank and any bank payments to the depositor. The costs of the bank operation consist of all the bank services—check clearing, security, collection, accounting, market analysis, and so on, plus the opportunity costs of income forgone in the next best alternative.

If banking is competitive and bankers are profit-maximizers, they will expand bank assets and liabilities until economic profits are zero, not to an arbitrarily large level based upon central bank generated excess reserves. The profit maximization position may well entail banks' holding excess reserves even while interest rates are positive. As loans are expanded banks may have to offer lower interest charges to potential borrowers. While revenues accrue to the bank, free reserves would protect it from lack of solvency. Consequently, the desire to maintain solvency and the lower interest rate return from borrowers plus the fact that the last borrowers may be higher risks begins to balance the bank's preferences between free excess reserves and bank loans. Thus a factor influencing the level of bank deposits is the behavior of commercial banks.

The volume of bank money is not independent of the behavior of the public either. Consider the implications for the public portfolio of an injection of high-powered money into the economy. The multiple expansion process suggests that the public will be induced to hold a multiplied quantity of bank money via loans through banks. How can the public be induced to accept large volumes of new bank loans and new demand deposits? Clearly, interest rate reductions will have to be permitted to encourage public holdings of new loans.

What role do reserve requirements play in this view of the financial system? It has been shown that banks desiring to maintain solvency and maximize profits may hold free reserves. They will surely maintain a high degree of liquidity to insulate themselves against insolvency. Suppose, however, reserve requirements are large enough to exceed the reserve banks would be willing to hold were it not for requirements. In other words, suppose banks would like to expand loans but are constrained by the reserve requirements. In this case, banks would like to expand precisely because they are earning above normal profits, or above pure economic profits, and consequently would like to expand to take advantage of these profits. The reserve requirement, then, has the effect of protecting abnormal profits.

If, in the presence of an effective reserve requirement, i.e., one which protects above-normal bank profits, the central bank increases excess reserves, bank loans and deposits will expand just as predicted by the "widow's cruse" argument. The multiple expansion, however, is evidence that the central authority is, by its reserve requirement, constraining the industry from expanding to the point of zero economic profits. The multiple expansion process is not, however, immutable but rather occurs because of the underlying maximization motives of banks and the public. The apparent widow's cruse, which had appeared to single out commercial banks as a unique institution, derives mainly from controls and restrictions placed on the banking system by the FED.

The models developed above for money creation can accommodate various aspects of Tobin's approach. Rather than viewing the volume of high-powered money as being determined by a strictly mechanical process, we can think of the actions by the central bank as determining the supply of high-powered money and we could develop a demand for high-powered money on the part of the financial system. Furthermore, we could think of the expression in equation (8) for the money multiplier as representing a function in which the value of k is actually derived from supply and demand conditions for various types of commercial bank loans. The discussion in this section suggests that the rate of return on loans and the risk associated with these loans might be two variables which should be introduced into the money multiplier expression.

In conclusion, financial institutions, besides simply commercial banks, provide services to savers, primary lenders, and to investors, primary borrowers. These services of financial intermediation facilitate economic expansion by providing to potential investors funds at a lower rate than would be available from direct finance. Commercial banks, whose liabilities include a medium of exchange, are simply one such intermediary. The money supply expands and contracts both in response to central bank actions and to forces endogenous to the economy. Commercial banks compete with nonbank financial institutions for depositors and for loan customers. While reserve requirements are effective, commercial banks appear to react mechanically to FED actions; however, underlying behavioral equations are necessary to accurately describe bank behavior.

STUDY QUESTIONS AND PROBLEMS

1. What is money? Why is money given more importance in macroeconomics than any other single commodity?

2. Define and illustrate each of the following terms:
   Fiat money
   Numéraire
   Ghost money
   High-powered money
   Full bodied money
   Liquidity

3. How does the FED, in the traditional view, control the money supply? What factors which influence M_1 are outside FED control?

4. What are the functions of money? How well are these functions performed by cash, demand deposits, time deposits of commercial banks, Treasury bills?

5. What is the relation between money as a medium of exchange and credit cards?

6. Suppose the ratio of cash to demand deposits is 0.05 and the ratio of time to demand deposits is 0.2. If the minimum reserve requirement on demand deposits is 0.2 and that on time deposits is 0.1, compute C, M_1, and M_2, for a monetary base of $5000.

7. Given C, M_1, and M_2 from Problem 6, compute the effects on these monetary aggregates of an increase of $1000 in excess reserves over required money brought about by:

    a. A federal deficit of $1000.

    b. A reduction in the reserve requirement on demand deposits.

8. What defensive actions can the FED take to offset unwanted contractions in the money supply? Will these actions be as effective in offsetting contractions as expansions?

9. Compare the traditional approach to money with the Tobin's approach. What emphasis do these two approaches place upon:

    a. Stores of value?

    b. M_1?

    c. Credit availability?

    d. Nonbank financial institutions?

10. Are banks unique institutions deserving of intensive study in macroeconomics?

REFERENCES

Chandler, Lester V., *The Economics of Money and Banking*, 6th ed. New York: Harper & Row, 1973.

Duesenberry, James, "The Portfolio Approach to the Demand for Money and Other Assets," *Review of Economics and Statistics*, Supplement, February 1963.

Friedman, Milton, "The Quantity Theory of Money—A Restatement," in *Studies in the Quantity Theory of Money*, Milton Friedman (ed.). Chicago: University of Chicago Press, 1956.

————, "Letter on Monetary Policy: To Senator William Proxmire," *The Federal Reserve Bank of Saint Louis Review*, March 1974.

Gibson, William, and George Kaufman, *Monetary Economics Readings on Current Issues*. New York: McGraw-Hill, 1971.

Gurley, John, and Edward Shaw, *Money in a Theory of Finance*. Washington, D.C.: The Brookings Institution, 1960.

Laidler, David, "The Definition of Money," *Journal of Money Credit and Banking*, August 1969.

Martial, Alfred, "Biological Analogies for Money: A Crucial Breakthrough," in *Monetary Economics Readings on Current Issues*, William Gibson and George Kaufman. New York: McGraw-Hill, 1971.

Pierson, Gail, "Why Have Interest Rates Risen?" *Review of Economics and Statistics,* February 1971.

Tobin, James, "Commercial Banks As Creators of 'Money'," in W. L. Smith and R. L. Teigen, *Readings in Money, National Income, and Stabilization Policy.* Homewood, Ill.: Richard D. Irwin, 1974.

The essence of the method that I am proposing is that we should take the position of an individual at a particular point in time, and inquire what determines the precise quantity of money which he will desire to hold.

Sir John Hicks (1935)

The quantity theory is in the first instance a theory of the *demand* for money.

Milton Friedman (1956)

In the very famous landmark article, "The Quantity Theory of Money— a Restatement," written in 1956, Professor Milton Friedman established the theoretical foundations of modern monetarism. The quote at the lead of the chapter above is taken from Professor Friedman's famous article and expresses the central theme of modern monetarism: that the quantity theory is a theory of the demand for money. However, it is of historical interest to note that it was Sir John Hicks in 1935 who forcefully rejected the quantity theory of money as practiced by the classical economists. They had focused upon a constant value for velocity, but Sir John proposed shifting attention away from the study of velocity toward the study of the demand for money. Hicks's famous attack on the classical economists is also quoted at the lead to this chapter. While any given proposition about money demand can be shown to have a formal equivalent regarding the velocity of money, the shift in emphasis away from the classical aggregative and mechanical study of velocity toward the modern

16

The Demand for Money

marginalist demand and supply approach to money resulted in substantial advances in the analysis of monetary economics.

One of the major issues upon which Lord Keynes had broken with the traditional classicists was over the issue of the stability of velocity. Recall that the anchor to the classical relation between money and income was a constant value for velocity. (The reader may wish to review the discussion of the classical quantity theory of money in Chapter 4 at this point.) Keynes argued that velocity was not constant. He studied the demand for money rather than velocity directly and argued that money demand was not even stable. This Keynesian view that money demand and, therefore, velocity are unstable shattered the classical link between money and income. As a result, the Keynesian arguments about the demand for money became central points in the debate between classical and Keynesian economists about the true determination of income.

In his restatement of the quantity theory, Friedman focused on money demand and not on velocity. Arguing that the quantity theory was a continuing oral tradition at the University of Chicago throughout the 1930s, 1940s, and early 1950s (while monetarism was in disrepute elsewhere), Friedman views the revival of monetarism as deriving along a direct channel from the classical quantity theory. Even though Friedman seems to exaggerate the independence of the Chicago and monetarist approach to monetary activity as opposed to the Keynesian traditions, it is clear that the modern quantity theory provides a very different approach to money demand than the Keynesian.

Since the work of Keynes, money demand theory and evidence have advanced considerably. On the one hand, monetarists have followed the work of Friedman, concentrating on a demand for money function. On the other, Keynesian economists have studied money holdings along the framework set out by Keynes. Both approaches have tended toward viewing money as one of many assets in the portfolio and the choice of holding money as a portfolio choice. Baumol and Tobin view the demand for money in the context of an inventory problem facing the holder. Tobin, Markowitz, and others have also developed money demand theories under uncertainty.

Section A contains an overview of the modern quantity theory of money developed and applied by Friedman and many advocates of the Chicago approach. In Section B, Keynesian analysis forms the point of departure to the study of modern money demand theories.

A ● The Revitalized Quantity Theory of Money

As studied by Friedman and his followers, money is an asset held by individuals and by firms in their portfolios. The demand for money is analogous to the demand for any capital asset which provides capital services. Friedman lists a number of variables which might be expected to enter the demand equation for money. He includes wealth as a constraint variable, the price level as an indicator of the purchasing power of money, the returns on equities and bonds as these assets are close substitutes for money. Before examining each of these variables, let us note the relation between classical statements about income velocity and modern analysis of money demand.

Certain statements about the income velocity of money and about money demand can be shown to be formally equivalent if the supply of money is exogenous. Consider the proposition that income velocity is constant, expressed in equation (17) of Chapter 12. Suppose, after examining the demand for money as a function of the variables discussed in the previous paragraph and of others, we conclude that money demand is proportional to income:

$$M^d = kY \tag{1}$$

Setting the exogenous money supply M^0 equal to money demand yields

$$M^0 = kY \tag{2}$$

Equation (2) is structurally equivalent to equation (17) of Chapter 12. The statement that the demand for money is proportional to income is therefore equivalent to the statement that the income velocity of money is a constant, given the exogenous nature of money supply.

The proposition that income velocity is a stable function of income is equivalent to the proposition that money demand depends only upon income. Both are more flexible than the propositions examined in the preceding paragraph. Similarly, if the demand for money is dependent upon variables other than income or if the demand for money is unstable, then it follows that velocity is not a stable function of income. This latter possibility is a crucial question in macroeconomic theory. Considerable research has been devoted to the demand for money function as its form is a crucial determinant of the stability of the income velocity of money. The income velocity of money, or equivalently the demand for money, is the link between the volume of money and money income.

The Assets in the Portfolio: Money is an asset competing with others in the portfolio of economic agents. First, money provides services related to a medium of exchange, a store of value, and so on. A one-dollar unit of money provides one dollar of purchasing power over commodities. Over time this purchasing power service can change if commodity prices change. Suppose the dollar price of all commodities should increase; then the command over resources provided by the one dollar unit of money will have fallen, and therefore the service yield on money is inversely related to commodity money prices. Generally, an index of commodity money prices can be used to depict the value of the services, as money, which are provided by the monetary asset. This index is called the *price level.*

It should be noted that the price level is an abstract economic concept which, unlike the price of wine or bread, is not observed by economic agents either as consumers or as asset holders. The price level depicts the actual value of monetary asset services compared to the services provided by other assets. In fact, as was shown in Chapter 3 on index numbers, price level indexes are ambiguous measures of changes in the purchasing power of money. Price level indexes are approximations derived from separating changes in monetary magnitudes into price and quantity components.

The second type of asset in the portfolio is a bond consisting of ownership rights to a sequence of future fixed-dollar payments. Suppose only one type of bond exists, a consol. A *consol* is defined as the rights to a fixed nominal dollar payment in each year into perpetuity, i.e., forever. The nominal dollar payment each year is called the bond *coupon* value because, in fact, an actual coupon is clipped from the bond each year and is exchanged for the nominal dollar payment. Let the coupon equal \$1. If the bond holder does not anticipate any future changes in the value of his bond, then at time $t = 0$, the present value P of the consol is

$$P = \frac{1}{(1 + R)} + \frac{1}{(1 + R)^2} + \ldots = \sum_{t=1}^{\infty} \frac{1}{(1 + R)^t} \tag{3}$$

The present value of the bond, if no expected changes in bond prices exist, is the discounted sum of the future flow of dollars or coupon values. The right-hand side of equation (3) is a simple geometric sum, therefore:

$$P = 1/R \tag{4}$$

Suppose capital changes are expected. Since P is simply $1/R$, one will expect capital changes if and only if one anticipates interest rate changes. If R is expected to rise, then, *ipso facto*, P is expected to fall. The coupon return in each year is simply $\$1/P$, or R. The total yield on the consol, however, is the sum of the coupon return and the anticipated capital gain or loss on the asset. The expected capital value change can be represented by either the expected percent change in P or, since P and R are inversely related, by an expected percent change in R. If R is expected to rise then the capital value is expected to fall and vice versa. The total expected yield on a coupon is $E(Y)$:

$$E(Y) = R - \dot{R}$$

where $\dot{R}$ is the *expected* percentage change in R over the period.

The third type of asset in the portfolio, equities, differs in one important respect from bonds. While both are ownership claims to a future flow of returns, equities are not fixed in dollar amounts and are ownership rights to some economic activity. An equity may be ownership of commodities, a production process, or a firm. But in any case if the price level should increase, the effects on bond and money holdings will differ from those on equities. Consider a general increase in the price level. The purchasing power of money is eroded. The purchasing power of a \$1 return on bonds is also eroded, because bonds are fixed-dollar contracts. However, if all commodity prices rise in the same proportion so that all relative prices remain unchanged, then the equity claims' dollar value will rise in proportion to the price level. The difference, then, between equity claims on the one hand and bond and money claims on the other is that, in general, price level increases will increase the dollar yield on equity assets while leaving the dollar yield on bonds, and by definition money, unchanged. The expected dollar yield, then, on an equity will be the sum of three yields: the nominal interest return on the activity of which the equity is an ownership claim, the nominal return from expected price level changes, and any expected capital value changes analogous to that on bonds. In symbols the expected equity yield is

$$R_e + \dot{P} - \dot{R}_e$$

Where R_e is the expected rate of return on an equity claim corresponding to R, the bond rates of return, and $\dot{P}$ and $\dot{R}_e$ are anticipated percent price level and capital changes, respectively.

We should issue a warning at this point, that emphasis upon the expected yield of equities and upon their apparent insulation from loss of value due to price level changes abstracts from an important feature of price level changes. When the price level is expected to increase, one cannot be certain that the particular equity claim one holds will rise at the same rate as the price level. Individual equity claims entail a considerable degree of uncertainty. It may be inappropriate to consider the expected return on equities, including reevaluation from price level increases, apart from the risk associated with individual equity claims. Later, the problem of uncertainty will be examined directly.

Durable goods, or physical goods in general, held in the portfolio are not given great importance in the monetarist treatment of the demand for money. The yield on physical assets is not a dollar return but a flow of services. Service yields on durables have been examined earlier, Chapter 9, in the context of the user cost. However, the only element of the user cost relevant to money demand is the change in capital value from anticipated price level changes: $\dot{P}$.

The final asset in the portfolio to be considered is human capital. Money is one of many assets and the economic agent is assumed to select a distribution of assets in an optimizing fashion. Subject to the size of his portfolio, or to his wealth constraint, he compares expected service yields on assets. This approach presumes that economic agents can exchange asset types in the portfolio. Now surely economic agents can exchange money for bonds or bonds for equities and durable goods for each of the others. However, the ability to exchange human capital in the portfolio for other forms is much more limited. Human capital can be defined as the present value of one's future labor income stream. To exchange money holdings for human capital would require exchanging claims on one's human wealth for money. One may be able to borrow a modest amount on the basis of future earning power; however, in a nonslave society, persons can rarely sell claims to their human capital. A professional athlete can sign a contract in which he exchanges a claim on his physical services for a promise to pay a fixed dollar amount, but such contractual arrangements are somewhat rare in the economy as a whole. Consequently, at any point in time the ratio of human to nonhuman capital H/NH is relatively rigid, and only the form of the latter is discretionary.

The Demand for Money Function: The demand function for money will depend upon the variables discussed above: the constraint wealth, the service price of money, P, and the various opportunity costs. At this level of abstraction, however, the quantity theory is clearly very broad and general. It would, consequently, be quite difficult to distinguish this approach from any other very general specification of money demand. No precise hypotheses about the relation between money and other macroeconomic magnitudes, such as income, the price level, and interest rates have been stated. The demand for money function may be modified in order to develop monetarist hypotheses closely related to the classical quantity theory of money. Let us discuss these monetarist restrictions, the validity of which forms the subject matter of considerable debate.

First recall that income is the return on wealth. If we let R represent the rate of return on a dollar of wealth as well as the specific bond return; then W may be replaced by Y/R. Second, both the returns on bonds and equities include expected capital gain (or loss) terms. If one supposes that expected interest rates are stable, then these terms may be deleted. Third, if arbitrage occurs between bond and equity holdings, then the dollar rate of return on bonds must equal the sum of the dollar yield on equity plus the return on equity from price level changes. This proposition between nominal returns on bonds and equities is an important monetarist proposition. Thus, the demand for money may be written as

$$M^d = F(\overset{+}{Y}, \overset{+}{P}, \overset{-}{R}, \overset{-}{R_e}, \overset{-}{\dot{P}}, \overset{-}{H/NH}) \tag{5}$$

(The signs of the effect on money demand of increases in variables are represented over each variable.)

From the analysis of rational optimizing behavior, economic agents are not expected to alter their behavior if all product prices and income change in the same proportion. Thus, the real commodities and asset services demanded should be invariant if P and Y change in the same proportion. Mathematically, if P and Y both increase by a constant α then M^d must increase by α. This proposition about M^d states that money demand is *linear homogeneous.* Linear homogeneity is helpful to derive an alternative form of equation (5):

$$M^d/P = F(\overset{+}{Y/P}, \overset{-}{R}, \overset{-}{R_e}, \overset{-}{\dot{P}}, \overset{-}{H/NH})$$ (6)

Equation (6) states that the demand for "real" money holdings, in terms of purchasing power, is dependent upon real magnitudes only and is independent of the monetary unit. In other words, the demand for real cash balances rises with real income and declines with increases in the returns on competing assets, R and R_e, the expected rate of change of prices and the ratio of human to nonhuman wealth.

The modern quantity theory developed by Friedman is not the "atrophied and rigid caricature" of the classical quantity theory in which velocity is depicted as a constant. Several important observations about the modern quantity theory are important. First, to quote Friedman (1956) ". . . the quantity theorist need not, and generally does not, mean that the real quantity of money demanded per unit of output, or the velocity of circulation of money, is to be regarded as numerically constant over time." Second, velocity is a complex variable dependent upon real income, anticipated inflation, and, most important, the interest rate returns on nonmoney assets. The role of interest rates in the demand for money function has been a major issue of conflict among economists. Third, study of money demand, or income velocity, of the relative importance of the demand function variables, of the form of the function, of the elasticities, of the stability of money demand comprises a major effort in quantity theory activity. Fourth, according to Friedman (1956): "The quantity theorist accepts the empirical hypothesis that the demand for money is highly stable—more stable than functions such as the consumption function that are offered as alternative key relations." Subsequently, it shall be shown that many modern monetarists, but not all, believe that many of the classical propositions about money and income are essentially correct. Now, however, let us turn to the Keynesian approach to money demand.

B ● Keynes: The Demand for Money Motives

While the quantity theory of money appreciated a sudden revival in the late 1950s and early 1960s under the tutelage of Milton Friedman and the "Chicago school," a parallel development in money demand had been following the design laid out by Lord Keynes.

Keynes viewed money in the Hicksian demand fashion but went on to propose three distinct motives for holding money balances: The transactions demand, precautionary demand, and speculative demand. The essential feature of Keynes' argument is that money holdings depend upon factors other than income and that money is held in part, as a result of uncertainty about future events, for the liquidity it provides. Uncertainty suggests that the dependence of money holdings upon income will not be a constant or even a stable relation. Rather, money demand will vary as a result of expectations, which are not quantifiable. Just as the modern quantity theory differs from the classical model, modern Keynesian money demand has evolved from the work of Keynes.

The Transactions Demand: Keynes agreed with the classicists that money, the medium of exchange, was held in order to undertake transactions. However, both Keynes and the classicists held a rather mechanistic view of this relation. Typically, transactions were viewed as work which had to be undertaken by a machine—money. In the 1950s, William Baumol and James Tobin independently developed the "inventory-theoretic" approach to money demand. Suppose an individual can hold two types of assets in his portfolio: fiat money, which yields no interest, and interest-bearing bonds, which may not be used in transactions for commodities. Suppose, also, that he receives monthly income payments in the form of money and that he carries out transactions evenly throughout the month, exhausting his entire income on the purchase of commodities.

He faces a tension between the costs of holding bonds and the cost of not holding bonds. The larger his bond holdings the greater his costs will be in exchanging bonds for money to buy commodities. On the other hand, if he holds fewer bonds and more money in order to avoid the exchange costs, he forgoes the interest yield on bond holdings. Consequently, each individual holds the optimal amounts of bonds and money to minimize the conflicting opportunity cost of holding money and transaction costs of exchanging bonds for money.

The quantity of money the individual optimizer will decide to hold will depend upon his income—the higher his income, the more transactions he will undertake and the more money he will have to hold. However, the demand for money will rise less than proportionately to increases in income. The reason the transactions demand for money will be income-inelastic is that economic agents can take advantage of returns to scale in using money: The number of trips to the bank to exchange bonds for money may increase as income rises but the number of such trips is unlikely to rise as rapidly as income.

The transactions demand for money will also depend upon the opportunity cost of holding money—the interest forgone. *Ceteris paribus,* increases in R will reduce money holdings used for transactions purposes. If interest rates on bonds are very large, economic agents will go to great lengths to economize on the use of cash balances, and thus money demand will be small. This theoretical result that transactions demand for money is inversely related to the interest rate has important consequences for the monetarist-Keynesian debate: Since transactions demand does not depend upon income alone, income velocity is not a constant nor is it dependent only on income.

Speculative Demand: One of the most controversial theoretical concepts presented by Keynes in *The General Theory* was the speculative motive for the demand for money. Whereas economists had long accepted the notion that money balances would be held for transactions purposes, despite positive interest losses as opportunity costs, the idea that additional balances may be held, by rational economic agents, was alien. Keynes, however, himself a speculator of considerable success, suggested that speculators playing the market for profits would, at times, hold positive money balances for liquidity in lieu of interest-bearing securities. The volume of these speculative balances held by the public would depend upon expectations about the future. Dependent upon such subjective factors as expectations, speculative balances would be somewhat capricious and unstable. The speculative motive lends further theoretical evidence to the dependence of money demand on interest rates.

If interest rates rise while a speculator holds a bond, then the market sales price, inverse to the interest rate, will fall and capital losses will result. The anticipated yield is the sum of R plus anticipated gains or losses on capital value. At very low interest rates, the interest return is low and for many speculators capital losses are anticipated, because R is expected to rise. Consequently, speculators will hold money balances instead of bonds, until R rises. The speculative demand for money will be high when interest rates are low. The relation between speculative demand for money, as the demand for a riskless nonearning liquid asset rather than a risky interest-earning asset, is inversely related to the interest rate.

The most intriguing and controversial aspect of Keynes' liquidity preference function was his special case of speculative money demand balances when interest rates were particularly low. The flight from bonds would generate an infinitely elastic demand for money. Keynes called such a situation the *liquidity trap*. The speculative demand for money, with the liquidity trap, is depicted in Figure 1.

Both Keynesian and non-Keynesian economists now have reservations about the liquidity trap and about the speculative demand for money motive. The idea that money demand depends upon uncertainty and upon risk aversion from

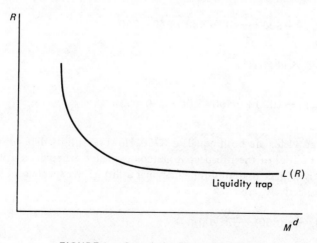

FIGURE 1   Speculative Demand for Money

capital losses is persuasive. However, after the Keynesian speculator develops his expectation, he acts as if it is a certainty: he holds the asset with the highest expected yield. He is a "plunger," all bonds or all money. Diversity of portfolios is not explained. Furthermore, if everyone expects rates to rise and tries to hold only money, how long will they maintain this expectation if rates fail to rise? Reservations about Keynes's speculative demand caused economists to reexamine the demand for money under uncertainty. While he seems to have set out to revive the Keynesian speculative motive, Tobin in 1958 developed a liquidity preference schedule, like Figure 1, which was actually based upon the third demand for money motive: precautionary demand.

Precautionary Demand: Though Keynes paid little attention to the precautionary motive, save to point out that individuals would hold money as a hedge against uncertain expenditures, this motive forms the basis for the most significant contribution to Keynesian money demand in many years. Tobin (1958) starts by assuming diminishing marginal utility from wealth: as wealth increases the additional utility from wealth declines.

Tobin extends diminishing marginal utility on wealth by applying it to prospective yields on assets under uncertainty. Consider two assets, A and B, the yields on which are uncertain. Each may bear the same anticipated yield; however, A may be relatively more certain than B. The spread of possible yields on A may be very narrow while that on B is quite broad. B is a riskier asset—chances of big losses but also chances for big gains.

For example, suppose the yields on assets A and B depend upon coin tosses. Heads means the yield on A is $800 and on B $1000. Tails, the yield on A is $700 and on B $500. The yield one could expect on A is, if the coin is fair, the average of the prospective yields

$$E\ (\text{yield}_A) = \frac{1}{2}800 + \frac{1}{2}700 = 400 + 350 = 750$$

The expected yield on B is

$$E\ (\text{yield}_B) = \frac{1}{2}1000 + \frac{1}{2}500 = 500 + 250 = 750$$

The expected yields are both equal to $750. However, utility depends upon the average of utilities of the prospective outcomes. Table 1 depicts a utility function which is subject to diminishing marginal utility. The expected utilities from A and B, respectively, are

$$E[u(A)] = \frac{1}{2}u(800) + \frac{1}{2}u(700)$$
$$= \frac{1}{2}245 + \frac{1}{2}230$$
$$= 237.50$$

$$E[u(B)] = \frac{1}{2}u(500) + \frac{1}{2}u(1000)$$

$$= \frac{1}{2}180 + \frac{1}{2}260$$

$$= 220$$

TABLE 1

Example of a Diminishing Marginal Utility Function

YIELD	UTILITY
250	100
500	180
700	230
750	240
800	245
1000	260

The expected utility from A, 237.50, exceeds that from B, 220.

The example above depicts utility as dependent upon prospective yield and upon the risk associated with that yield. In the example, two assets have the same expected yield but different spreads on prospective yields and, therefore different risks. The riskier asset, with the greater spread, provides less utility, because the additional utility gained from prospects of $1000 is not enough to offset the lower utility from the chance of obtaining only $500. Diminishing marginal utility causes a higher utility to be placed on the more certain asset. Other examples, in which assets have the same spread and different expected yields, or in which one asset has a greater expected yield and a lower spread resulting in the same level of utility as the other, could be devised. The point is, utility depends both upon expected yield and risk.

Suppose we let expected yield be represented by a number μ and risk by a number σ. μ is large if expected yield is large, and σ is large if risk is large. Since utility depends upon both μ and σ, it can be represented by a mapping of indifference curves in (μ, σ) space. Recall from microeconomics that each indifference curve represents all combinations of μ and σ which yield the same level of utility. Figure 2 contains three such indifference curves and shows assets A and B on curve $I(2)$ and $I(1)$, respectively. Since expected utility from A, with small risk σ_A, exceeds that from B, A is on a higher indifference curve. A is preferred to B. Of course, the indifference curves through A and B are upward sloping because greater risk, *ceteris paribus*, reduces utility. Such a utility function characterizes the preferences of a *risk averter*.[1] The idea is simple: Given diminishing marginal utility from expected income, a riskier asset will be worth less than a "sure thing."

Figure 2 may be employed to derive the precautionary demand for money.

---

[1] Technically, μ is the expected yield on an asset and σ the standard deviation of its probability distribution.

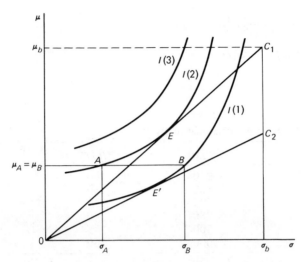

FIGURE 2   Utility Maximization and Portfolio Diversification

The risk averter may hold money or bonds. Money bears no risk, $\sigma = 0$, and no yield, $\mu = 0$; thus point zero represents the entire portfolio in money form. As the portfolio composition shifts from money to bonds, the expected yield increases, but so does risk. At C_1, his portfolio contains only bonds with expected yield μ_b and risk σ_b. Line $0C_1$ is his "budget constraint" or "portfolio constraint." Utility is maximized at the highest attainable indifference curve: $I(2)$ at point E. The significance of this result is that the optimizer selects a portfolio which will include money balances as a hedge, or precaution, against risk. The optimizer selects a diverse portfolio—holding interest-earning bonds and non-earning, riskless money simultaneously.

Interest rate decreases can be shown to lead to increases in money holdings for precautionary demand. If R falls, this corresponds to a fall in the expected yield on bonds in the portfolio. For a given portfolio distribution between bonds and money, and therefore a given σ, μ falls with R, so that a lower R is depicted by a rotation of $0C$, the portfolio constraint about the point 0 downward. The rotation of the line from $0C_1$ to $0C_2$ induces the individual to alter the structure of his portfolio by moving from E to E'. E' is characterized by a smaller expected yield and risk than E. Since the portfolio risk has fallen, money holdings as a proportion of the portfolio have increased. The precautionary demand for money by the risk averter is inverse to the interest rate.

If we were now to infer an implicit demand for money function from the Keynesian discussion above of transactions, speculative and precautionary motives, we would produce an equation very much like Friedman's money demand function, equation (6). From the Keynesian reasoning, money demand depends upon income, the return on money relative to competing assets in the portfolio such as bonds and stocks, and on the size of one's portfolio, represented perhaps by nonhuman wealth. Thus, at a theoretical level of abstraction, the monetarists and the Keynesians believe in very similar money demand schedules. When it comes to specific shapes of schedules, values of elasticities, measurement of variables, and stability of functions, however, much disagreement remains.

Monetarists argue that money demand is a reasonably stable function of money income, that increases in money supply will be controlled by the FED and transmitted to the economy through a stable demand for money function. Keynesians claim that money demand depends heavily upon interest rates, expectations, and risk. Keynesians doubt the ability of the FED to control the money supply and argue that the demand function is certainly not a very stable function of income. It remains now to develop a framework in which the policy implications of these two views may be compared.

STUDY QUESTIONS

1. Compare Tobin's precautionary to Keynes' speculative demand for money.
2. Define and illustrate the following:
   a. Transactions demand for money.
   b. Liquidity trap.
   c. Consol.
   d. Risk aversion.
3. Explain carefully the difference between a bond and an equity. How do they each influence money demand?
4. Utilizing a quantity theory approach, derive the general relation between the demand for money and the income velocity of money.
5. How does the modern quantity theory of money compare to (a) the classical quantity theory and (b) Keynes' liquidity preference theory?
6. Explain how a demand schedule for money as a function of the interest rate can be derived from an optimization procedure.
7. Assess each of the following money demand models:
   a. The quantity theory of money.
   b. The inventory-theoretic approach.
   c. The risk aversion model.
8. Why do individuals hold money?
9. Explain the role of the following terms in the modern quantity theory of money:
   a. Linear homogeneity of money demand function in price and income.
   b. Human to nonhuman wealth ratio.
   c. Anticipated inflation.
   d. Risks of capital losses on equity.
   e. Stability of money demand.

10. Suppose an individual enjoyed risk. Compare the "risk-lover's" preference ordering in (μ, σ) space to that of a "risk averter." Can you describe the risk-lover's portfolio mix between money and bonds?

11. Figure 2, depicts convex indifference curves, bowls containing water. Can you justify convexity on the basis of diminishing marginal utility? How would the economic agent distribute his portfolio if his preferences were represented by concave indifference curves?

12. Figure 2 illustrates the effect on portfolio distribution of an increase on bond rates, given risks. Can you separate an income and substitution effect from the rate change?

REFERENCES

Baumol, William J., "The Transactions Demand for Cash: An Inventory Theoretic Approach," *Quarterly Journal of Economics,* 1952.

Friedman, Milton, "The Quantity Theory of Money—A Restatement," in *Studies in the Quantity Theory of Money,* Milton Friedman (ed.). Chicago: University of Chicago Press, 1956.

Hicks, J. R., "A Suggestion for Simplifying the Theory of Money," *Economica,* 1935, reprinted in *Readings in Monetary Theory,* selected by a Committee of the American Economics Association. Homewood, Illinois: Richard D. Irwin, Inc., 1951.

Keynes, John M., *The General Theory of Employment, Interest and Money,* New York: Harcourt, Brace, & World, 1935.

Laidler, David E. W., "The Rate of Interest and the Demand for Money," *Journal of Political Economy,* December 1966.

Saving, Thomas, "Transaction Costs and the Demand for Money," *American Economic Review,* June 1971.

Tobin, James, "Liquidity Preference as Behavior Towards Risk," *The Review of Economic Studies,* Vol. 25, February 1958.

What is, it seems to me, distinctive about Keynesianism is the view that fiscal policy is capable of exerting very significant independent effects—that there are, broadly speaking, two instruments of stabilization policy, fiscal policy and monetary policy, and that the mix of the two is important.

Warren L. Smith (1969)

We do not know enough to be able to achieve stated objectives by delicate, or even fairly coarse, changes in the mix of monetary and fiscal policy. In this area particularly the best is likely to be the enemy of the good. Experience suggests that the path of wisdom is to use monetary policy explicitly to offset other disturbances only when they offer a "clear and present danger."

Milton Friedman (1968)

John Maynard Keynes in *The General Theory* (1935) challenged the classical orthodoxy of his day and in so doing initiated debate about the macroeconomic theory of income determination and about the workings of stabilization policies. John Hicks, in 1937, developed the *IS-LM* curves to compare Keynes to the classics. The *IS-LM* framework was employed in Chapter 14 to study the workings of monetary and fiscal policies. It was pointed out that the *IS* or *LM* curve may have an extremely elastic or inelastic shape. In this chapter, the *IS-LM* model will be used for its original purpose: to compare the theories and policies of ultramonetarists and ultra-Keynesians. The views of the vast majority of economists, including many who characterize themselves as monetarists and many who call themselves Keynesians, are moderate versions of the extremes

17

Keynes
and the Monetarists

outlined here. In subsequent chapters, the core of sophisticated modern models, neoclassical and neo-Keynesian, will be seen to be the *IS-LM* model.

Keynes challenged the classics at the outset of *The General Theory*:

> I have called this book the *General Theory of Employment, Interest and Money*, placing the emphasis on the prefix *general*. The object of such a title is to contrast the character of my arguments and conclusions with those of the *classical* theory of the subject, . . . I shall argue that the postulates of the classical theory are applicable to a special case only and not to the general case, . . . Moreover, the characteristics of the special case assumed by the classical theory happen not to be those of the economic society in which we actually live, with the result that its teaching is misleading and disastrous if we attempt to apply it to the facts of experience.

Lord Keynes clearly believed his theory to be both more general and more relevant than the classical orthodoxy. Both the Keynesian and monetarist positions contain special cases as extreme versions of a more general view. It may be argued that special cases are applicable under certain circumstances so that while the general view is broadly realistic the special cases suggested by Keynes and by the monetarists are also pertinent.

First, this chapter contains Keynes' Great Depression analysis. The practical problem Keynes was attempting to study in *The General Theory* was the problem of an economy in under-full employment. It was his view that under-full employment was a position for a market economy which could be sustained for a long period of time. Because he was writing in the 1930s his focus was on the unemployment situation. He suggested a number of possible cases which he believed were consistent with the Depression. The income-expenditure models studied in Chapters 5, 6, and 7 are derived from these special cases. The ultramonetarist position is also described with the *IS-LM* framework. As with Keynesianism, monetarism has a number of cases, but the one discussed here is the ultra version. Finally, a synthesis and brief review of the empirical evidence brought to bear on the monetarist-Keynesian debate will be examined.

A ● Keynes and Monetarism

The Liquidity Trap: It was Keynes' view that the Depression was caused by inadequate aggregate demand which pulled income below full employment potential. Aggregate demand was inadequate because private domestic investment fell and, because saving increased, consumption decreased. Monetary policy which under normal circumstances could be counted on to stimulate private demand was, in a severe depression, blocked. Keynes believed that monetary policy ordinarily operated through a complex channel of events on private demand. Expansionary monetary policy, either generated by the central authorities or by a general deflation of the monetary unit, operates through the banking system and demand for money function on interest rates. Increases in the money supply drive down interest rates, which then stimulate private demand for investment goods and durable goods. Keynes suggested two possible breaks in the chain linking monetary policy to aggregate demand.

The liquidity trap establishes one circumstance in which monetary policy cannot expand demand. Consider an economy in depression. Figure 1 depicts an economy in which the *IS-LM* curves intersect at income level $\overline{Y}$, less than full employment output Y^*. The economy might reach point A because consumers decide to "tighten their belts" and save more, investors are fearful of the future and cut their investment, government increases taxes and cuts expenditures, and so on. The classical view would have been that if the economy were at A, natural forces or a monetary authority would stimulate the economy to increase income. At A demand is below output and prices will be falling; as prices fall, the money supply held by the public automatically increases. Furthermore, a classical monetary authority could speed expansion along by increasing the supply of currency. An increase in M drives the *LM* curve to the right because at each Y, the excess money supply drives interest rates down. Lower R stimulates private aggregate demand. A does not remain equilibrium—the *LM* curve shifts right.

Keynes proposed that new cash balances, whether induced by an expansionist monetary authority or by a general deflation, would not in a depression drive interest rates downward. Keynes suggested that the economy may be in a liquidity trap. Recall Keynes' speculative demand for money. Speculators, when rates are below expected normal rates, anticipate capital losses. If losses are expected and if they exceed interest income, speculators will hold money in lieu of bonds.

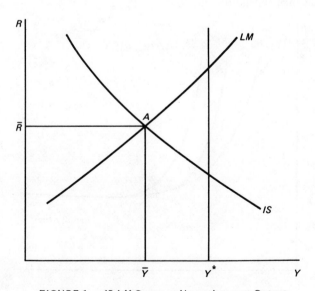

FIGURE 1   *IS-LM* Curves at Unemployment Output

In a liquidity trap, the demand for money becomes infinite at a positive rate of interest. Speculators will absorb any new cash without requiring lower interest rates. Figure 2 depicts the Keynesian liquidity trap. At $R = R_1$, all speculators anticipate capital losses because they expect rates to rise in the future. (The normal rate, in the subjective opinion of each speculator, is above R_1.) Capital losses are expected to exceed interest yields so that speculators will hold all the cash they can get.

Suppose the economy is in a liquidity trap and either the monetary authority increases M or the price level falls, due to low demand, and M increases. Figure 3 depicts the situation. The initial position of the economy is income at Y_1, below Y^* full employment income, and interest at R_1, a low liquidity trap rate. At R_1 the total demand for money is infinitely elastic so that adding transactions demand does not alter the shape of the schedule at R_1. The money supply is initially at M_0.

M increases from M_0 to M'. The increased money supply is purchased by speculators anxious to part with their bonds because the latter are expected to bear capital losses in excess of interest income. Interest rates are not bid down and the link to investment spending is broken. Equilibrium income remains at Y_1. Figure 3(b) illustrates the LM-curve shift to the right leaving (R_1, Y_1) as equilibrium. Monetary policy is ineffective in a depression according to the liquidity trap.

What about fiscal policy in a liquidity trap? Consider an increase in G financed by borrowing from the public. Aggregate demand will increase at each rate of interest. Since R is fixed in the liquidity trap, $\Delta Y/\Delta G$ can be determined from the simple income-expenditure models:

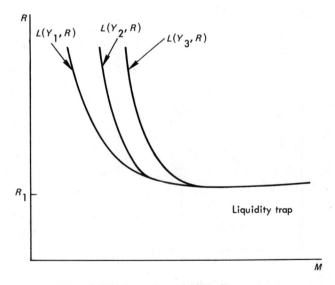

FIGURE 2   The Liquidity Trap

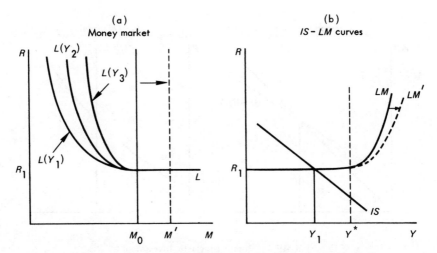

FIGURE 3   Expansionary Monetary Policy in the Liquidity Trap

$$\frac{\Delta Y}{\Delta G} = \frac{1}{1 - [b(1 - t) + f]}$$

Increased spending, both exogenous ΔG and induced ΔC and ΔI, increases the transactions demand for cash; however, in the trap, interest rates are fixed. Essentially, idle money held in cash balances is turned into active balances by government spending. The increased competition for money, to undertake the new higher levels of spending, need not drive R up and need not curtail private investment.

The liquidity trap case yields the simple Keynesian "income-expenditure" model. The policy implications of the liquidity trap are (1) monetary policy is ineffective in expanding income, and (2) fiscal policy is effective in increasing income and it can do so without raising interest rates.

Interest Inelasticity of Investment: A second break in the chain linking monetary policy to private demand occurs between a change in interest rates and a change in investment. Suppose the money market is not in a liquidity trap so that expansionary monetary policy may drive interest rates down. Keynes placed great emphasis on uncertainty and expectations. His theory of investment was based on computing a marginal efficiency of capital for each project on the basis of the supply price and anticipated returns on the project. Suppose expectations in a depression are such that anticipated returns are very low—potential investors are simply pessimistic. They will not produce new capital even if R falls. A perfectly inelastic investment schedule corresponds to an aggregate demand curve which does not depend upon R. Figure 4 depicts this second Keynesian

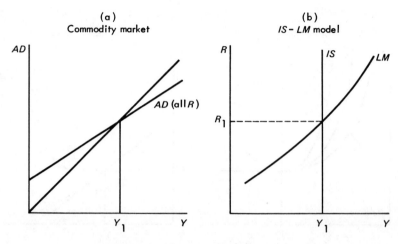

FIGURE 4   Interest Inelastic Investment

case of a depression. The IS curve is vertical because I is independent of R. The equilibrium level of income is Y_1 regardless of the value of R.

What are the effects, given the model in Figure 4, of monetary and fiscal policy? Expansionary monetary policy drives down interest rates, but investors uncertain and pessimistic about future business conditions do not respond by expanding investment expenditures. Equilibrium income remains at the depression level Y_1. Expansionary fiscal policy, on the other hand, increases income with multipliers derived in the one-market income-expenditure models. The effectiveness of fiscal policy is because the increased interest has no contractionary induced effect on investment.

Both Keynesian cases, the liquidity trap and interest inelastic investment, are similar in that the level of income determination is completely based upon the IS curve. The LM curve plays no role in income determination. In fact, the IS curve itself is unnecessary because in the liquidity trap case R never changes and in the investment rigid case I never responds to an R change. Only one aggregate demand curve is pertinent and the model is fully described by the Keynesian cross diagram. In other words, these two special cases suggested by Keynes are the basis of the Keynesian income-expenditure models illustrated by the Keynesian cross.

Monetarism: Monetarism, like Keynesianism, is a complex term referring to many different interrelated concepts. Monetarism, in the broadest sense, refers to a methodology, a subject matter and a political position. However, monetarism is also a set of conclusions about macroeconomics in general and stabilization policies in particular. These conclusions, which are a recurring theme of a great many economists who call themselves monetarists, are the subject of this section.

First we shall identify the main monetarist propositions and then develop a version of the *IS-LM* model consistent with these propositions. Monetarists distinguish between short-run transitory phenomena and long-run factors. Their short-run propositions are

1. Money is the dominant factor in setting the levels of money income, prices, employment, and output. Monetarist Leonall Andersen (1973) states:

The key proposition is that changes in money dominate other short-run influences on output and other long-run influences on the price level and nominal aggregate demand.

2. Neither monetary nor fiscal policy is a reliable tool of economic stabilization because the short-run effects are largely unknown and temporary. Fiscal policy is particularly ineffective in comparison to monetary policy.

Andersen states:

Monetarist theories and empirical studies point to a relatively quick, but short-lived, response of output to a change in money growth, with a longer time period required for prices to respond fully.

Andersen goes on to dismiss short-run fiscal policy:

Most monetarists, but not all, contend that the influence of [changes in federal government expenditures and tax rates] is transitory.

Friedman's statement at the beginning of this chapter buttresses this monetarist view of stabilization policies. While he stresses that all "fine tuning has been oversold," Friedman, like Andersen, rejects the effectiveness only of fiscal policy:

I come to the main point—in my opinion, the state of the [federal] budget by itself has no significant effect on the course of nominal income, on inflation, on deflation, or on cyclical fluctuations.

David Fand, a monetarist, supports the relative weakness of fiscal and strength of monetary policy (1971):

The Monetarist concludes that discretionary budget changes are not an efficient means for short run stabilization purposes, and that fiscal policy changes are likely to have permanent effects on the relative sizes of the private and public sectors. Monetarists believe that stable monetary growth is the most effective policy for stabilizing the economy, . . .

Monetarists are much more decisive about their long-run propositions of the workings of the economy, the relation between stabilization goals, and therefore the outcome of stabilization policies. The long-run monetarist position can be summarized in three propositions:

1. The economy is essentially self-stabilizing, settling on a long-run output path with a natural rate of unemployment independent of monetary policy.

Mr. Andersen:

Many economists now agree with the proposition of monetarists that the long-run influence of money is only on the price level, with no lasting impact on output.

Milton Friedman, in his famous 1968 discussion of the limits of monetary policy, tells us:

To state the general conclusion still differently, the monetary authority controls nominal magnitudes—directly, the quantity of its own liabilities. . . . It cannot use its control over nominal quantities to peg a real quantity— the real rate of interest, the rate of unemployment, the level of real national income, the real quantity of money, the rate of growth of real national income, or the rate of growth of the real quantity of money.

Again Mr. Andersen does not equivocate:

Monetarists contend that our economic system is such that disturbing forces, including even changes in money growth, are rather rapidly absorbed and that output will naturally revert to its long-run growth path following a disturbance.

2. Expansionary monetary policy increases only the price component of money income.

Fand argues:

[Monetarists] postulate, following Fisher, a sequence leading from monetary expansion to rising prices and high market rates; . . .

Friedman concurs:

What I and those who share my views have emphasized is that the quantity of money is extremely important for nominal magnitudes, for nominal income, the level of income in dollars—important for what happens to prices. It is not important at all, or, if that's perhaps an exaggeration, not very important, for what happens to real output over the long period.

3. The economy is characterized by a natural rate of unemployment and no trade-off exists between the rates of inflation and unemployment.

Friedman:

. . . there is always a temporary trade off between inflation and unemployment; there is no permanent trade off.

Andersen:

Monetarists, as well as many other economists, reject [the Phillips curve trade-off], contending that in the long run the 'normal' or 'natural' unemployment rate will eventually evolve regardless of the rate of inflation.

The stabilization policy thrusts of these monetarist propositions are

1. That fiscal policy does not alter the level of money income, either the price term or the output term. Rather, fiscal policy alters the public-private mix of income;
2. That monetary policy alters money income but in the long run only the price component can change.

Consider an *IS-LM* model in which the variables such as C, I, G, M, and Y are all assumed to represent dollar values and that changes in each can be changes in either the price or the quantity components. (In other words, drop the assumption that the prices are stable.) A special *IS-LM* version will be shown to lead to the monetarists' propositions listed above, although it is not the only model to do so. Let the demand for money be perfectly interest inelastic. Since money demand and supply are interest inelastic, the *LM* curve, locus of money market equilibrium, is vertical in (R, Y) space. Figure 5 depicts the *IS-LM* model characterizing the monetarist position.

Suppose expansionary fiscal policy were employed to increase money income from Y_1. The *IS* curve shifts right to *IS'*, as in Figure 5. However, how can G increase without a change in M or T_x? The government must borrow money from the public. However, idle money is not held by speculators, because no interest-elastic speculative money demand exists. Consequently, all money balances are active. The government must compete with private borrowers for active funds. Interest rates rise and private investment declines to accommodate increased government activity given equilibrium income at Y_1. The outcome? A change in the GNP mix from private to public, no increase in output or prices.

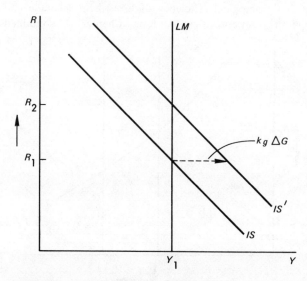

FIGURE 5   Expansionary Fiscal Policy in a Monetarist Model

Figure 6 depicts expansionary monetary policy. An increase in Federal Reserve notes and bank money generates an excess supply of money. The increased funds generate an increase in expenditures. (The transmission mechanism from an increase in M to an increase in Y will be discussed in a later chapter.) Equilibrium money income will rise. What of the output-price mix in money income? The monetarists argue that in the long run the real output term is fixed so that only the price component of Y is increasing. The short-run outcome is much less certain, and monetarists do not claim to be able to determine the output-price mix.

A crucial relation both for the Keynesian liquidity trap and the vertical LM curve monetarist model is the money demand equation. For if money demand is interest inelastic, or if interest rates do not change, then money demand depends only upon income. (Real money demand on real income and nominal money demand on nominal income.) If money demand depends only upon Y, then M and Y are related by a stable function and the LM curve is vertical. If, on the other hand, money demand depends on the interest rate in a stable way then the conventional IS-LM model, neither ultra-Keynesian nor ultramonetarist, is appropriate. Finally, if liquidity preference is an unstable relation due to speculators, then the liquidity trap may well be possible.

Synthesis and Evidence: The ultra-Keynesian and ultramonetarist models considered above seem quite extreme in light of the theoretical models of money demand and of investment behavior developed in earlier chapters. In Chapters 10 and 11 both the Keynesian and neoclassical theories of investment behavior indicated that investment decisions depended upon interest rates; Keynes through the marginal efficiency of investment schedule and neoclassicalists through the user-cost-of-capital term. Chapter 16 contained extensive

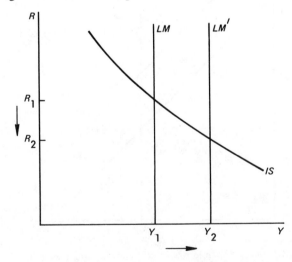

FIGURE 6   Expansionary Monetary Policy in a Monetarist Model

theoretical grounds for the responsiveness of money demand to interest rate changes; Baumol's transactions model, Keynes's speculative demand, and Tobin's precautionary demand each support the inverse relation between interest and money demand. Friedman's restatement of the quantity theory explicitly contains the returns on bonds in the money demand equation. Consequently, monetarists and Keynesians present theoretical evidence for *IS-LM* curves which are neither perfectly elastic nor perfectly inelastic.

Some economists, for example, Paul Samuelson, believe that the shape of the *LM* schedule is, as Keynes believed, horizontal at low levels of income and yet, as monetarists believe, vertical at high levels of income. Thus, in their view a synthesis of the two positions could be depicted as shown in Figure 7.

However, considerable room still remains for dispute. First, moderate versions of the Keynesian and monetarist positions are consistent with the theoretical evidence. Figure 8 contains moderate versions of each school of thought. None of the curves in Figure 8 is perfectly elastic or inelastic. However, the moderate Keynesian model [Figure 8(a)] suggests that investment is relatively nonresponsive to interest charges and that the money market's equilibrium locus is very flat so that money demand is quite interest elastic. Conversely, the monetarists [Figure 8(b)] depict the *LM* curve as very steep, indicating some responsiveness of money demand to interest rates but quite an inelastic relation. On the other hand, the *IS* curve is elastic, suggesting very responsive private demand to interest changes. An economist who believes the economy looks like Figure 8(a) would tend to favor fiscal policy because the multipliers are large and monetary policy is relatively ineffective. The Keynesian might also believe the *LM* curve is unstable, and this is indicated by the shady area about the *LM* curve. Monetary policy would not be reliable to him. An economist who thinks

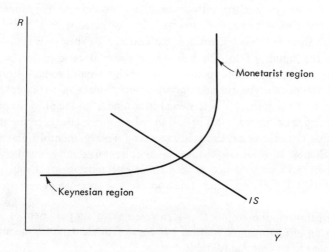

FIGURE 7   A Possible Synthesis of Keynes and Monetarist Views

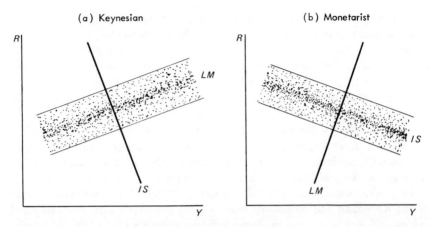

FIGURE 8   Moderate *IS-LM* Models

Figure 8(b) represents the economy would feel that fiscal policy has only minor, and unsure, effects upon income and that it mainly alters the public-private mix. Monetary policy, to the contrary, is effective in altering money income. Furthermore, the monetarist may believe that the *IS* curve is relatively unstable. (Recall Friedman's critique of Keynes' *MPC*.)

While one's views as to the relative validity of these moderate, and the extreme, *IS-LM* models depend in part upon theoretical considerations, empirical evidence is also quite important.

Despite difficulties in statistical research, a consensus has developed on several major aspects of money demand. Studies by Brunner and Meltzer (1964, 1968), Chow (1966), Heller (1965), Starleaf and Reimer (1967), Teigen (1970), and Goldfeld (1973) all support two important results: (1) Money demand is a function of income (or wealth) with an elasticity around one. (2) Money demand depends upon interest rates with an elasticity less than one.

Robert Crouch (1971) examined the extreme Keynesian version of money demand, the liquidity trap. The behavior of speculators suggested by Keynes is that they will always react to keep rates sticky around some historical norm. Thus, if Keynesian-type speculators are a major force in setting interest rates, rates should be sequentially determined over time. If in the previous period rates rise, then speculators react this period to reduce them, always trying to maintain the normal rate. However, Crouch, examining weekly, monthly, and annual lags of rate changes to prior rate changes in consols, consistently found only random movements with no evidence of sequential rate movements. Crouch found no evidence that speculators cause rates on consols to move as reactions to prior changes.

In conclusion, the empirical evidence seems to support neither a liquidity trap nor an ultramonetarist vertical *LM* curve. The demand for money function does appear to be reasonably stable.

STUDY QUESTIONS

1. Utilizing algebra, build a model in which an increase in government expenditures has no effect upon the equilibrium level of income. Consider an expansionary monetary policy. What will happen to income, interest rates, consumption, and investment?

2. Defend, utilizing empirical arguments and theoretical models, an ultramonetarist model of the economy.

3. How might a Keynesian economist evaluate the evidence on the ultramonetarist case?

4. Suppose the economy is in a liquidity trap. Show the effects of (a) expansionary fiscal policy and (b) expansionary monetary policy.

5. On what evidence have economists been skeptical of the liquidity trap?

6. Discuss the relative effectiveness of monetary and fiscal policy for dealing with:

   a. Depression.
   b. Mild recession.
   c. Inflation.

7. Construct a geometric model in which an increase in the money supply has no effect upon the equilibrium level of income. Compare the effectiveness of monetary and fiscal policies in your model with the standard *IS-LM* model.

8. What does the empirical and theoretical evidence suggest about the role of interest rates in money demand?

9. Compare and contrast Tobin's risk aversion model to Keynes' liquidity preference theory. Consider theory, empirical evidence, and policy.

REFERENCES

Andersen, Leonall C., "The State of the Monetarist Debate," *Federal Reserve Bank of St. Louis Review,* September 1973.

Brunner, Karl, and Allen Meltzer, "Some Further Investigations of Demand and Supply Functions of Money," *Journal of Finance,* May 1964.

———, "Liquidity Traps for Money, Bank Credit and Interest Rates," *Journal of Political Economy,* January-February 1968.

Chow, Gregory, "On the Long-Run and Short-Run Demand for Money," *Journal of Political Economy,* April 1966.

Crouch, R. L., "Tobin vs. Keynes on Liquidity Preference," *The Review of Economics and Statistics,* November 1971.

Fand, David, "Keynesian Monetary Theory, Stabilization Policy and Recent Inflation," *Journal of Money, Credit and Banking,* 1969.

———, "A Monetarist Model of the Monetary Process," in William E. Gibson and George G. Kaufman (eds.), *Monetary Economics: Readings on Current Issues.* New York: McGraw-Hill, 1971.

Friedman, Milton, "The Demand for Money: Some Theoretical and Empirical Results," *Journal of Political Economy*, August 1959.

————, "A Theoretical Framework of Monetary Analysis," *Journal of Political Economy*, March-April 1970.

————, "A Monetary Theory of Nominal Income," *Journal of Political Economy*, March-April 1971.

————and Anna Jacobson Schwartz, *A Monetary History of the United States, 1867-1960.* Princeton: Princeton University Press, 1963.

Goldfeld, Steven, "The Demand for Money Revisited," *Brookings Papers on Economic Activity*, Washington, D.C., No. 3, 1973.

Heller, H. R., "The Demand for Money: The Evidence from the Short Run Data," *Quarterly Journal of Economics*, May 1965.

Keynes, John M., *The General Theory of Employment, Interest and Money.* New York: Harcourt, Brace & World, 1935.

Laidler, David E. W., "The Rate of Interest and the Demand for Money," *Journal of Political Economy*, December 1966.

————, "Some Evidence on the Demand for Money," *The Journal of Political Economy*, February 1966.

Latané, Henry, "Cash Balances and the Interest Rate: A Pragmatic Approach," *Review of Economics and Statistics*, November 1960.

Meltzer, Allen, "The Demand for Money: The Evidence from the Time Series," *Journal of Political Economy*, June 1963.

Modigliani, Franco, "Liquidity Preference and the Theory of Interest and Money," *American Economic Review*, January 1944.

Samuelson, Paul, "The Simple Mathematics of Income Determination," *Income, Employment and Public Policy, Essays in Honor of Alvin H. Hansen.* New York: W. W. Norton, 1948.

Smith, Warren L., "On Some Current Issues in Monetary Economics: An Interpretation," *Journal of Economic Literature*, September 1970.

————, "A Neo-Keynesian View of Monetary Policy," in William E. Gibson and George G. Kaufman (eds.), *Monetary Economics: Readings on Current Issues.* New York: McGraw-Hill, 1971.

Starleaf, Dennis R., and R. Reimer, "The Keynesian Demand Function for Money: Some Statistical Tests," *Journal of Finance*, March 1967.

Teigen, Ronald, "The Demand for and Supply of Money," in *Readings in Money, National Income and Stabilization Policy*, Warren Smith and Ronald Teigen (eds.). Homewood, Ill.: Richard D. Irwin, 1974.

————, "A Critical Look at Monetarist Economics," *Federal Reserve Bank of St. Louis Review*, January 1972.

FLEXIBLE PRICES, AGGREGATE SUPPLY, AND THE LABOR MARKET: NEOCLASSICAL AND NEO-KEYNESIAN THEORIES AND POLICIES

part VII

A central theoretical issue in macroeconomics upon which economists disagree is on the relative magnitudes of price and quantity changes which occur when stabilization actions alter money income. To understand this basic conflict in macroeconomic theory, with its monumental policy implications, one must develop and examine models in which both the price level and output appear explicitly. To develop such models is an arduous and yet rewarding task. It is the task of Chapter 18. The outcome, a versatile three-market model which is built upon the *IS-LM* framework, provides the necessary theoretical construct to compare modern neoclassical and neo-Keynesian views.

Neoclassical and neo-Keynesian economists differ on a number of important issues. Fundamentally, neoclassicists take the view that markets clear in the sense of Léon Walras: all excess demands and supplies are eventually eliminated by the appropriate set of prices. Neo-Keynesians, on the other hand, take the position that a variety of factors—money illusion, segmented labor markets, administered prices, imperfect information, uncertainty, and so forth—impede the well-oiled Walrasion market-clearing auctioneer mechanism. Markets need not and do not clear. These issues are examined in Chapter 19.

While the neoclassicists argue that because markets clear the economy is basically self-stabilizing, neo-Keynesians claim that markets, and therefore the economy, are far from perfect. Different policies are implied by each view. If the economy is believed to be stable, activist policy is unnecessary. If the economy is believed to be self-corrective, yet is actually unstable, the source of the instability may well be the "stabilization" authorities themselves. Since neo-Keynesians believe markets are very slow to clear, stabilization policy is actively suggested as a means of speeding the clearing process.

In Chapter 20, we are concerned with the foundations of an economic system when markets fail to clear. Realization of the uniqueness of the labor commodity has led to study of the behavior of workers and firms when they are uncertain about relative wage offers. This literature into the job-search and job-acceptance behavior of the labor force has produced some choice–theoretic explanations for downward stickiness of wages in the presence of increases in the average unemployment rate. The interaction between markets when any one fails to clear is also examined in Chapter 20. This material is designed to try to reconcile the evident failure of markets to work well with the compelling belief on the part of economists that economic agents are rational.

The terms of the truce between the two factions (Revolutionary Orthodoxy and Neoclassical Resurgence) comprise two broad propositions: (1) the model which Keynes had the gall to call his "general theory" is but a special case of the Classical theory, obtained by imposing certain restrictive assumptions on the latter; and (2) the Keynesian "special case," while theoretically trivial, is nonetheless important because it so happens that it is a better guide in the real world than is the general (equilibrium) theory.

Axel Leijonhufvud (1968)

In Chapter 17 we studied an intense debate between monetarists and Keynesians over the relative effectiveness of fiscal and monetary policy. We concluded that the analytic distinction between their positions could be expressed by their differences over the appropriate shapes of the *IS-LM* schedules and over the relative elasticities of commodity market demand and money market demand. As seems to be the case with many debates in economic theory, this issue has dissipated, and the decibel level of the debate is now considerably reduced. Nonetheless, economists still enjoy a good fight, and today monetarists and Keynesians argue over yet another issue. This new issue, in the background throughout the earlier arguments, involves the relative effects of stabilization policies on the cost and standard of living.

Suppose we consider the standard *IS-LM* model in which no schedules are perfectly elastic or inelastic; then either monetary or fiscal policy can produce a change in income. The question is whether the policy-induced

Wage-price Flexibility:
The Three-sector Models

change in income is a change in the price level at which real income is measured or a change in actual output measured at a constant level of prices. Put another way, we may define money income as the product of two distinct variables, the price level and the output level. (Recall from our discussion of gross national product that money GNP can increase either because the prices at which all products are measured increases or because the quantity of products produced increases.) Which does stabilization policy change, P or Q?

In order to analyze this new debate, we must develop models in which the distinction between nominal income and real income is explicit. The development of comparative static models in which prices and quantities both appear explicitly will also prove helpful in understanding the theoretical foundations of the models which relate inflation to unemployment, the Phillips curve and the natural rate hypothesis.

The primary objective of Chapter 18 is to develop a comparative static macro-economic framework in which each variable measured in money terms will have both a price and a quantity component separately identified. Throughout this book we have been developing continually more complex models, and just as the introduction of the interest rate to the simple Keynesian cross model of Chapter 5 had the effect of making the commodity market solution indeterminate, the introduction now of the price level into the *IS-LM* models will be seen to make the two-market model also indeterminate. What we shall see is that the *IS-LM* model in which the price level is allowed to vary will produce not a unique solution to the economy but a downward sloping aggregate demand curve for the economy. In other words, when prices are allowed to vary, changes in aggregate demand brought about by either shifts in the *LM* curve or by shifts in the *IS* curve will produce changes in the level of aggregate demand rather than changes in the level of output. Thus, in order to complete the new model, it will be necessary to produce an aggregate supply schedule. In this chapter, the aggregate supply schedule will be derived from two new sets of equations: the labor market and the production function. The outcome of this chapter will be an aggregate demand and aggregate supply schedule for commodities based upon a model in which we have three submarkets: labor, money, and goods. We complete this chapter with analysis of the determination of aggregate income, output, and the price level. (A warning is in order here: Because this model is more complex than any studied so far, and because the *IS-LM* model is a major element of the new model, it is absolutely essential that students have a firm understanding of the *IS-LM* framework at this point. If one feels uncertain about the *IS-LM* framework, it is essential to return to Chapters 5, 12, and 15 in order to carefully review the *IS-LM* schedules.)

A • Price Level Changes in the *IS-LM* Model: Indeterminancy

Let us begin with the *IS-LM* model in which all relations are interpreted as occurring between variables measured in money terms and in which changes can be either price or quantity changes. Consumption, for example, is measured in dollars of consumption expenditures. The *IS-LM* model is thought of here as a model determining the money values of the variables: money income, money consumption, and so on. The problem is to distinguish for each variable price and quantity changes.

The price level will be allowed to change; however, the nature of such changes will be limited. In general when prices rise, not all prices rise in the same proportion. Some rise faster than others, and resources are reallocated from one product to another. Variations in relative prices and their impacts are the primary subject of microeconomics or price theory. Our interest in price level changes is not in the effects on resource allocation but in the effect on total production and on inflation itself. Furthermore, if relative price changes occur, one must consider the entire microeconomic system of equations. It will be assumed, therefore, that price level changes constitute changes in all prices in the same proportion. The implication of the assumption that all prices change only in the same proportion is that any variable expressed in money terms, such as consumption expenditures, also changes in proportion to the price level. The prices of all commodities change in exactly the same proportion whenever P changes.

Consider the variable Y, money income. Y contains two components which can change, a price component P and a quantity component y.

$$Y = Py \tag{1}$$

Y, money income, may be converted into y real income by dividing by P:

$$y = Y/P \tag{2}$$

The consumption and investment equations need now be respecified since prices can change. The theories and evidence discussed about consumption and investment in Chapters 8, 9, 10, and 11 were all based upon real consumption and real investment expenditures. The actual quantity of consumer expenditures on final goods and services depends upon the real purchasing power of income. If P increases, C increases, because C is dollar consumption expenditures. If the quantity of goods and services consumed is to remain fixed when P increases, then (C/P) is a constant. In other words, (C/P) represents the real quantity of goods and services consumed, whereas C represents money consumption expenditures.

At this point, in order to distinguish money variables from the real values of those variables, we must make a change in notation. We shall replace the expression (C/P) with a lowercase c. As we introduce the real values of variables, we shall adopt this procedure of replacing the uppercase letter with the lowercase letter, and the relationship will always be consistent with the practice that the lowercase variable will equal the uppercase divided by the price level. Consumer theory and evidence indicate that real consumption c is a linear function of real disposable income, y_d or (Y_d/P). The consumption equation now becomes

$$c = c_0 + by_d \tag{3}$$

$c_0 = C_0/P$. The algebraic constant C_0, like the variable Y_d, was measured in money units. c_0 is measured in constant dollars. One can think of P as a price index used to deflate all variables and constants measured in money terms. Equation (3) is analogous to the consumption equations studied above except that prices are now allowed to change. Equation (3) states that pure price level changes will not alter the relation between real consumption and real income. It does not follow, however, that pure price level changes will not change real disposable income y_d. The effect of changes in P upon endogenous variables will depend upon the nature of the full model.

Private domestic investment will maintain the same relation to R the rate of interest and y real income as in previous models:

$$i = i_0 + fy - v_0 R \tag{4}$$

where $i = I/P$, $i_0 = I_0/P$, $v_0 = v/P$ because the algebraic constants I_0 and v are also measured in money units. Equation (4) states that real investment is a positive function of real income and an inverse function of the interest rate. Note that R is a percent and is not measured in money units.[1] The relation between real additions to the capital stock and real income and the interest rate is independent of the level of prices.

Government and tax equations are also measured in money unit variables and must be transformed:

$$g = g_0 \tag{5}$$

$$\tau = t_0 + ty \tag{6}$$

where g is G/P, g_0 is G_0/P, τ is T/P, and t_0 is T_0/P. Government fiscal actions are independent of the price level.

The equilibrium condition in the commodity market is

$$y = \frac{C + I + G}{P} = c + i + g \tag{7}$$

Equations (3) through (6) involve new and important behavioral relations. It is assumed that real investment, consumption, and government fiscal decisions are made by economic agents free of *money illusion*. That is, given real command over resources, y_d, consumers determine real quantity of consumption c regardless of their level of money income. Similarly, for investors and fiscal planners real decisions are free of nominal units. Equilibrium condition (7) does not contain any new behavioral assumption.

---

[1] A subtle point: Prices are allowed to rise, but expectations will be assumed to remain static, so that no distinction need be made between nominal and real rates of return at this point. This complication is introduced in Chapter 22.

The commodity market solution to equations (3) through (7) is

$$y = \frac{c_0 + i_0 + g_0 - bt_0 - v_0 R}{1 - [b(1 - t) + f]} \tag{8}$$

Equation (8) states that the commodity market equilibrium level of real income y is inversely related to the market rate of interest R. The lowercase constants c_0, i_0, g_0, t_0 represent the exogenous levels of real consumption, investment, government expenditures, and taxes, respectively. The diagram corresponding to equation (8) is the usual IS curve except that y replaces Y on the horizontal axis. Under the assumptions that all prices change in the same proportion when the price level changes and that economic agents are free of money illusion, the locus of commodity market equilibria is independent of the price level. Thus commodity market equilibria are represented by an IS curve in (R, y) space.

The incorporation of price level changes into the money market is more complex than in the commodity market. Money is held because it provides command over resources. If prices change, the ability of a given quantity of money to purchase commodities changes. More important, if one expects prices to change in the future, this expectation will alter one's demand for money. For simplicity, price expectations will at first be assumed to be zero. Prices may change but expectations will always be that the current level of prices will maintain in the future.[2]

While the government can set the level of its real expenditures and taxes free of dollar units, the FED sets the nominal quantity of money in circulation. The FED can set the monetary base and can closely control the money multiplier to control M_1 and M_2. However, the FED cannot necessarily set the price level. Thus the money supply equation is

$$m^s = M_0 / P \tag{9}$$

where $m^s = M^s/P$. Note that we do not use the expression m_0 for the actual real money supply because the nominal quantity of money M_0 is controlled by Federal Reserve action and the denominator P is not; thus we must leave these two components separately identified. In other words, the monetary authority is assumed to control the nominal quantity of money but not the real purchasing power of that money. If the price level increases, the real purchasing power of M_0 declines and this change is outside the direct control of the FED.

In the absence of expected inflation, which has been assumed not to exist, the demand for real money balances; M^d/P or m^d will depend upon real income and the interest rate. All discussions of money demand were based upon real cash balances, real income and so forth:

___

[2]Since the model deals with *a priori* plans, R is the expected return in current dollars and is unchanged if the price level rises, *ceteris paribus*. However, the realized return in command over resources may change.

$$m^d = L(y, R) \tag{10}$$

or

$$m^d = ky - m_0 R$$

where $m_0 = m/P$ because the algebraic constant m is measured in dollar units. Equation (10) states that the quantity of purchasing power over commodities which economic agents are willing to hold in money form, m^d, will depend upon real income y and the opportunity cost of holding money R.

Money market equilibrium is

$$m^d = m^s \tag{11}$$

Solving for real income in the linear case of the money market yields

$$M_0/P = ky - m_0 R \tag{12}$$

$$y = \left(\frac{M_0}{k}\right) \frac{1}{P} + m_0 R \tag{13}$$

Equation (13) is the linear locus of money market equilibrium values, which indicates that money market equilibrium depends upon three variables: real income y, the price level P, and the interest rate R. Since the nominal money supply M_0 is exogenous, the equilibrium value of y in the money market depends upon P and R. Figure 1 depicts money market equilibrium for some arbitrary price level P_1. P_1 is arbitrary and yields a locus of money market equilibria in (R, y) space.

Consider a price level P_2 higher than P_1. At a price level above P_1 the money supply will have less purchasing power and M/P will be lower. Figure 2 depicts the outcome. At price level P_2 the money supply is smaller than at price level P_1 and the shortage of money will drive up interest rates at each real income level. For example, at real income level y_1, the rate of interest must rise to R'. Consequently the locus of money market equilibria in (R, y) space will shift upward to $LM(P_2)$ as in Figure 2. For each price level, a different locus of money market equilibria exists because a different real money supply exists. Thus, corresponding to the algebraic solution to the money market, equation (13) is an entire locus of LM curves.

The two-market model consists of eight equations, (3) through (7) and (9) through (11), and nine unknown variables c, i, y, g, τ, R, m^s, m^d and P. The commodity market solution is:

$$y = \frac{c_0 + i_0 + g_0 - bt_0 - v_0 R}{1 - [b(1 - t) + f]} \tag{8}$$

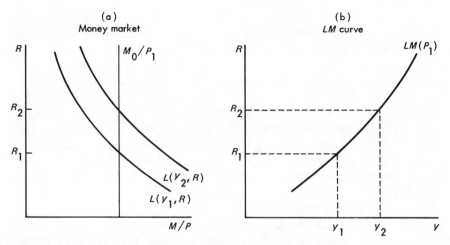

FIGURE 1   Money Market Equilibrium at P_1

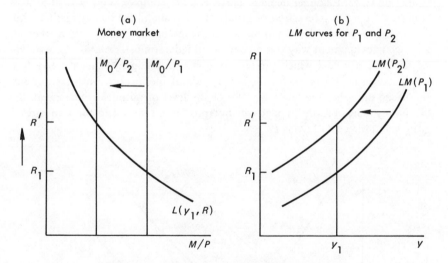

FIGURE 2   Price Levels P_1 and P_2 in Money Markets

Money market solution is

$$y = \left(\frac{M_0}{k}\right)\frac{1}{P} + m_0 R \tag{13}$$

If equation (8), the *IS* curve, and equation (13), the *LM* curves, are combined, two unknowns will remain. Figure 3 depicts the *IS* curve and the mapping of *LM* curves associated with various price levels. At each price level, for example P_2, equilibrium occurs at an (R, y) pair, (R_2, y_2).

The *IS-LM* diagram illustrated in Figure 3 is now rather awkward. Back in Chapter 12, when interest rates were introduced into the simple Keynesian cross model, the Keynesian cross diagram became awkward because rather than one unique aggregate demand schedule, a different schedule was associated with each rate of interest. Similarly, in this chapter, it is now awkward to deal with the *IS-LM* model because rather than one *LM* schedule we have a locus of *LM* schedules, a different one associated with each price level. We do not have a unique output-interest rate combination. As complex as this model must now seem, it may be converted into a very simple and useful form by simply illustrating the pairs of price and output levels associated with the intersections of the *LM* curves and the *IS* curve. Figure 4 depicts the pairs of P and y derived from Figure 3 which correspond to equilibrium in the money and commodity markets. We have labeled this schedule the *AD* schedule for aggregate demand. Notice that the lower price level P_1 is associated with a high level of output y_3, and a high price level is associated with a low level of output. In other words, we have produced a standard downward sloping demand curve. The analysis which leads to this downward sloping demand curve is quite complex, however, since it is produced from the interaction of supply and demand in the money market with the aggregate demand for commodities in the *IS* curve or commodity market. It now becomes apparent why this model has an indeterminate solution. In particular, we have a model which produces a downward sloping demand curve but which makes no provision for the supply side of the market. Until restrictions are placed on either the level of prices or the level of output or, in general, on the supply schedule, the model will not provide a solution to the standard of living y and the cost of living P.

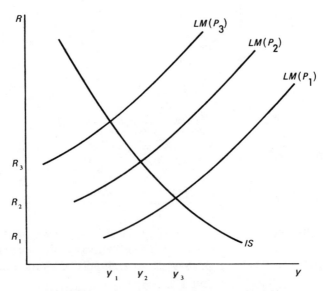

FIGURE 3   *IS-LM* Model with Price Level Variable

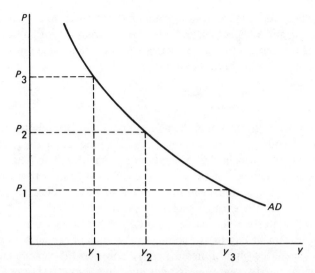

FIGURE 4   Downward Sloping *AD* Curve

In order to close the model represented in Figure 4 and derive a solution for either output or the price level, two very simple restrictions are possible. One is to assume that the price level is fixed. This assumption is equivalent to restricting the aggregate supply curve to a perfectly elastic schedule. Illustrated in Figure 3 of Chapter 4, it represents the Keynesian depression model. Alternatively, one could impose a restriction on aggregate output and assume that it is fixed. This restriction would correspond to a perfectly inelastic aggregate supply curve; it is represented in Figure 2 of Chapter 4. This restriction corresponds to the classical economists' model of the aggregate economy. The Keynesian restriction on the price level leads to the result that changes in demand generate changes in output, whereas the monetarist restriction on output leads to the result that changes in demand produce changes in the price level.

The student may wonder at this point what he is doing here, and why he did not major in journalism instead of economics. What advantages has he gained through the considerable analysis he has studied between Chapter 4 and this chapter? What we have achieved is that we no longer need to postulate these supply conditions, and we are now prepared to turn to a new market in which the determinants of aggregate supply can be studied. Only after developing a model of supply can one evaluate, judge, and study the bases for differences in the great debate between Keynesians and monetarists.

B ● The Production-labor Market

Our objective in this section is to derive an aggregate supply schedule for commodities. Supply or output in microeconomics is generally derived by studying the behavior of producers. In this chapter we will similarly derive a supply schedule for the aggregate economy by specifying a relationship between output and the factors of production, namely, labor and capital. We may think of this relationship as an aggregate production function. In symbols we represent the aggregate production function as

$$y = h(N, K) \tag{14}$$

Equation (14) states that real income y is a function of two inputs: the level of employment N and the stock of capital K. This production function will be assumed to satisfy the neoclassical properties of production functions.[3]

The analysis of stabilization policy is basically a short-run analysis, and therefore the production function shall be restricted to those production configurations consistent with the existing capital stock. K will be restricted to level K_0. The reader will note that the model permits positive net investment and that positive net investment consists of adding to the stock of capital. Consequently, the model contains a technical inconsistency. However, the capital stock is very large in comparison to year-to-year additions, and the effects on supply, or production, of year-to-year additions to K can be expected to be small. Of course, if the model were to be used for long-run analysis, the supply effects of investment could no longer be ignored. The advantage of this assumption is that a one-to-one relation remains between y and N.

Given the capital stock in the short run, additions to employment will increase output at a diminishing rate. Figure 5 depicts the short-run relation between N employment and y output. Associated with each level of employment, say N_1, is a level of output y_1. Increases in N result in increases in y.

It is now necessary for us to determine where the value of employment N_1 in Figure 5 comes from. Up until now in all of our analysis we have not really explicitly introduced the quantity of labor or the level of unemployment into our models. We have always implicitly assumed that a quantity of labor is producing output, but it is now necessary for us to actually construct the details of the market for labor. The labor market, like the money market, may be divided into two parts—a demand for labor and a supply schedule for labor. The demand for labor is not, of course, derived from a utility maximization schedule on the part of consumers but is a demand which is derived from the behavior of producers. Producers in competitive markets, who act to maximize profits, will hire labor until the value the last laborer adds to the firm exactly equals the cost of hiring that additional laborer. The value the laborer adds to the firm is the additional physical production from his labor, his "marginal physical product," times the product price paid for each new unit produced: $P \cdot MPP_N$. In competitive labor markets, the marginal cost of the laborer, given capital, is the wage the new laborer must be paid, W. Consequently, the producer equates $P \cdot MPP_N$ to W:

$$W = P \cdot MPP_N \tag{15}$$

[3]Recall the neoclassical production function discussed in Chapter 11.

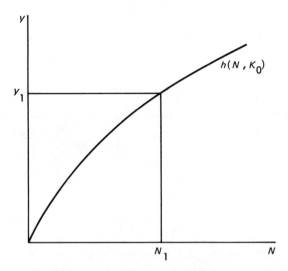

FIGURE 5   Production Function for $K = K_0$

Equation (15) may now be employed to derive the demand for labor. First, from Figure 5 the marginal physical product of labor is assumed to decline as N increases. Producers are assumed to behave as maximizers in competitive markets. They are, therefore, price takers. Suppose the wage and price they face results in a real wage of $(W/P)_1$, as depicted in Figure 6. Dividing both sides of equation (15) by the produce price, we see that the producer's decision rule is equivalent to equating W/P to MPP_N, the real wage is equated to the marginal physical product of labor, and this rule determines the profit-maximizing level of employment firms will be willing and able to hire. At $(W/P)_1$, firms will hire exactly N_2 units of labor, as shown in Figure 6. Consider their profits if firms were hiring N_1 units of labor. By increasing employment from N_1, firms add to their profits because $P{\cdot}MPP_N$ is greater than W; thus revenues rise faster than costs. Conversely, at employment levels such as N_3, firms will raise profits by reducing employment. Thus at $(W/P)_1$, N_2 units of labor will be demanded.

Real wage $(W/P)_1$ was selected arbitrarily as the real wage faced by price takers. For every real wage the maximizing competitive firms will equate W/P to MPP_N and hire the resulting quantity of labor. Thus the downward sloping marginal physical product of labor curve is the market demand curve for labor, and its equation is

$$N^d = D(W/P) \tag{16}$$

Ths supply of labor shall be assumed to depend upon the real wage rate W/P and to be upward sloping. This includes the assumption that laborers are not concerned solely with the money wage but with its command over resources. At high levels of real wages, labor may increase its demand for leisure so that the

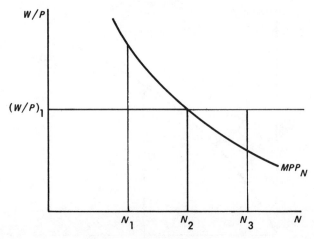

FIGURE 6   Derived Demand for Labor

supply curve may be backward bending. Figure 7 depicts the supply curve for labor with the demand curve. The supply equation is

$$N^s = S(W/P) \tag{17}$$

This model also assumes a competitive labor market and flexible wages as well as flexible prices and absence of money illusion.

Finally, labor market equilibrium is

$$N^s = N^d \tag{18}$$

Suppose the real wage were $(W/P)_1$ as in Figure 7. Laborers are willing to supply N_3 units of labor, yet firms are willing and able to employ N_1 units. $N_3 - N_1$ is the surplus of laborers willing and able to work at $(W/P)_1$ who are unemployed. These unemployed will offer their labor services at a lower wage and bid down the market wage rate until equilibrium is attained at real wage $(W/P)^*$ and N^*.

Involuntary unemployment and full employment may now be defined. *Involuntary unemployment* consists of persons out of work who are willing and able to work at the existing real wage rate. *Full employment* is the absence of involuntary unemployment. N^* in Figure 7 is full employment. Note that full employment does not imply that the entire labor force is employed or even that some given level of N is "the labor force."

With the production function and the labor market we have now introduced four new equations—the supply of labor, the demand for labor, the equilibrium equation for labor, and the production function. Under our current assumptions that wages and prices are flexible and given our assumptions about the demand

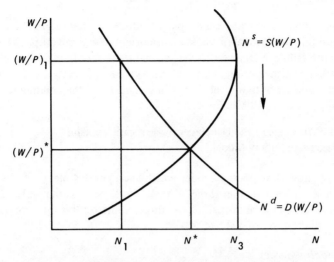

FIGURE 7   The Market for Labor

and supply schedules for labor, the three labor market equations determine the quantity of labor demanded, the quantity of labor supplied, and the real wage rate. In other words, since we have made assumptions that permit the labor market to clear, from the labor market we determine the quantity of employment N^* and the real wage rate, $(W/P)^*$. Given N^* and K_0, the production function determines the real level of output, y^*. In sum, the production function and the labor market determine real output, real employment, and the real wage rate.

Since output y^* is determined regardless of the price level, this corresponds to an aggregate supply curve that is vertical, as shown in Figure 8.

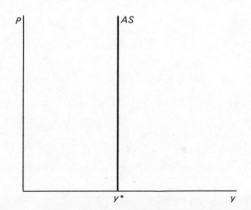

FIGURE 8   Aggregate Supply when Wages and Prices Are Flexible

Mapping the solution for real output y^* into the *IS-LM* diagram in (R, y) the production function and labor market equilibrium determine output at y^* which may be represented with a vertical line at that level of output. This model of the labor market and the production function leads to a perfectly inelastic aggregate supply curve at an output level that is independent of the commodity demand and money market equilibrium.

C ● The Workings of the Neoclassical Aggregate Demand and Aggregate Supply Model

We have now developed a model which incorporates many of the ideas of Keynes and which contains three distinct markets: a commodity market, a money market, and a labor market. We now summarize this three-market model with the equations derived above.

Commodity Market

$$c = c_0 + by_d \tag{3}$$

$$i = i_0 + fy - v_0 R \tag{4}$$

$$g = g_0 \tag{5}$$

$$\tau = t_0 + ty \tag{6}$$

$$y = c + i + g \tag{7}$$

$$y = h(N, K_0) \tag{14}$$

Money Market

$$m^s = M_0/P \tag{9}$$

$$m^d = ky - m_0 R \tag{10}$$

$$m^s = m^d \tag{11}$$

Labor Market

$$N^d = D(W/P) \tag{16}$$

$$N^s = S(W/P) \tag{17}$$

$$N^s = N^d \tag{18}$$

The twelve equations above comprise a three-market model. Each market could be solved for its equilibrium; however, it is convenient to solve for commodity market demand rather than for the commodity market equilibrium between demand and supply and to solve the labor market and inject this solution into the production function. We will have a better understanding of the workings of the model if we present the solutions in the following way:

Commodity Demand

$$y = \frac{c_0 + i_0 + g_0 - bt_0 - v_0 R}{1 - [b(1-t) + f]} \qquad (8)$$

Money Market

$$y = (M_0/k)(1/P) + m_0 R \qquad (13)$$

Production Function (given labor solution)

$$y^* = h[N^*(W/P)^*, k_0] \qquad (19)$$

As we noted earlier in Figure 8, equation (19) implies a vertical aggregate supply schedule. If we solve equations (8) and (13) for the solutions to the *IS-LM* schedules, then we have

$$y = \frac{c_0 + i_0 + g_0 - bt_0 + (v_0/m_0 k)M_0(1/P)}{1 - [b(1-t) + f] + v_0/m_0} \qquad (20)$$

Equation (20) may be thought of as the equation for aggregate demand, because it represents commodity demand y after allowing for the interest rate effects from the money market on commodity demand. Equation (20) shows that y is inversely related to P. The logic is that a higher price level means, *ceteris paribus,* a lower real money supply, higher interest rates, and, therefore, lower commodity demand. Thus we have a downward sloping aggregate demand curve. Figure 9 depicts these two schedules, aggregate supply for equation (19) and

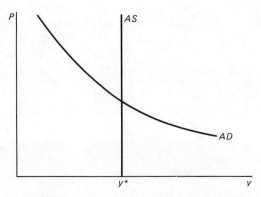

FIGURE 9   Aggregate Supply and Demand Schedule for Three-sector Model

aggregate demand for equation (20). To illustrate greater detail, Figure 10 depicts each market separately with the commodity market demand schedule and the production function shown separately as well. Figure 10 also combines all market solutions into the (R, y) space. The IS curve corresponds to equation (8), commodity market demand, and derives from Figure 10(a). The LM curves

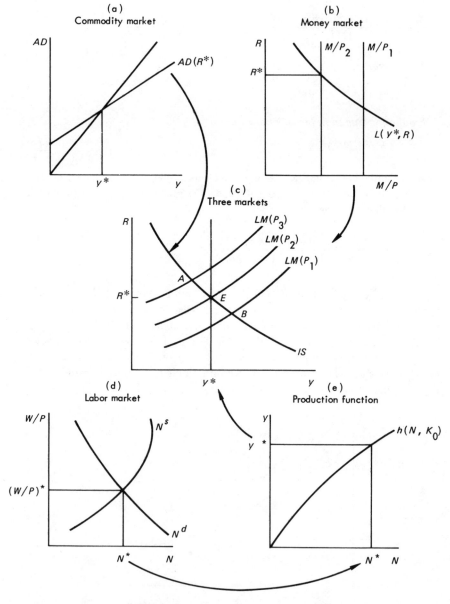

FIGURE 10   Three-market Model in Detail

correspond to equation (13), money market equilibrium, and the vertical line at y^* corresponds to the production function solution with the labor market equilibrium injected into it, which is represented in equation (19) above. For clarity of exposition, we represented only one commodity aggregate demand curve in Figure 10(a), but it clearly represents an entire mapping of AD curves inversely related to the interest rate. Similarly, only one liquidity preference schedule is shown in Figure 10(b), and it again represents an entire mapping of liquidity schedules, each associated with a different level of real income. Figure 10(c) in the middle of the diagram is derived from all other figures. The IS curve is from Figure 10(a); the LM curve from Figure 10(b), and the vertical line from Figures 10(d) and 10(e). The arrows illustrate these relationships. The particular schedules drawn in each figure are those associated with R^* and y^* in the commodity and money markets, and both are in equilibrium at point E. Furthermore, y^* is equilibrium from the production function and from N^* of the cleared labor market so that all schedules are drawn in such a way that each market is in equilibrium and all variables are determined: $(W/P) = (W/P)^*$, $N = N^*$, $y = y^*$, $R = R^*$, and $P = P_2$. However, can one be sure the economy will obtain an equilibrium such as E? The workings of this three-market model can be understood by assuming the economy is not at the convenient point E.

Let us suppose the price level is at P_3 so that real cash balances M_0/P_3 generate an LM curve to the left of $LM(P_2)$ and so that $LM(P_3)$ intersects the IS curve at a real income level below y^*. Figure 11 depicts such a possibility. The money supply when the price level is P_3 will, at real income level y_1, yield an interest rate of R_3 therefore aggregate demand $AD(R_3)$ will cut the 45-deg line at y_1, not y^*.

The money market is in equilibrium, and commodity demand appears to be in equilibrium; however, the aggregate demand curve produces income level y_1, which is below the level of output determined by the quantity of labor and the aggregate production function which produces output level y^*. The vertical distance between $AD(R_3)$ and the aggregate demand curve which cuts the 45-deg line at y^* is called the *deflationary gap*. Demand determined by the interaction of the money market with commodity demand at price level P_3 is below production, which is determined by the production function and the labor market. Since prices are now assumed to be variable, a deflationary gap will result in downward pressure on prices.

Inadequate aggregate demand at A in Figure 11 drives prices down. Since all prices are falling in the same proportion, real decisions of economic agents still depend upon real variables so that the IS curve does not move. However, falling prices increase the value of real cash balances. In Figure 11, the money supply, M_0/P, automatically begins to rise. The money market moves from $LM(P_3)$ toward $LM(P_2)$. At each real income level, for example y_1, the increased real money supply drives interest rates down and the aggregate demand curve moves to higher levels.

As long as a deflationary gap exists, the LM curve will continue to move right and the IS curve will stay the same, but the IS-LM intersection will move from A

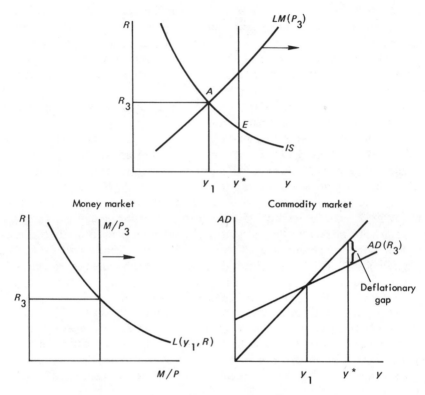

FIGURE 11   Disequilibrium in Three-market Model

toward E as the deflationary gap falls. Thus point A is not equilibrium in the three-market model. If the economy is at A, it will not stay there because deflation will occur. Equilibrium will occur only when prices have fallen sufficiently for the LM curve to intersect the IS curve at point E. The LM curve at point E is the one associated with price level P_2, the original equilibrium price level.

Suppose the price level is P_1 as in Figure 10. At P_1, the IS-LM curves intersect at B which is now shown in Figure 12. In words, interest rate R_1 and real income level y_3 represent the intersection of money supply M_0/P_1 and money demand $L(y_3, R_1)$, and $AD(R_1)$ cuts the 45-deg line at y_3. Production, from the production function and labor market, is at y^* less than aggregate demand at y_3; consequently, the economy is characterized by an inflationary gap. The reader should be able to explain why B, with an inflationary gap, is disequilibrium and how the increase in prices will move the economy away from B toward E.

The three-market model developed and studied above leads to very different implications from the two-sector IS-LM models discussed in earlier chapters. First, the level of real income, y, is determined in the production function and labor market. Labor market equilibrium determines the real wage rate and the

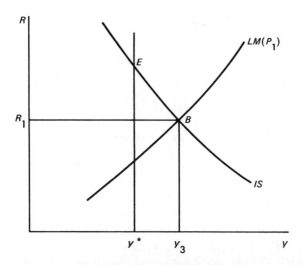

FIGURE 12   Inflationary Gap

level of employment. Real income is completely independent of the commodity aggregate demand schedule and the money market. Second, the commodity market IS curve combines with output y^* from the production function to determine the market interest rate. The interest rate, in turn, determines the mix among consumption, investment, and government expenditures, and is itself completely independent of the money market. In fact, the only variable that is influenced by the money market is the level of prices. This new three-sector model is clearly the antithesis of Keynesian macroeconomics, in which the demand for commodities determined the level of real output. Here output is predetermined before we even consider aggregate demand conditions. Figure 9 depicts this new three-sector model in terms of aggregate demand and aggregate supply schedules. Demand is downward sloping, and the supply schedule is perfectly inelastic at y^*, where $N = N^*$, full employment which clears the labor market. Demand determines only the price level and not real income. It now becomes apparent that the vertical aggregate supply curve associated with neoclassical economics derives from a model in which the labor market works in such a way as to clear and therefore determines a level of employment which, when combined with a given capital stock, produces a fixed level of output. We now have a far richer model than we had in earlier chapters and one in which the aggregate supply curve is not assumed to take on any particular shape but in which its shape is derived from assumptions about the workings of the labor market and the production function.

In the next chapter, stabilization policies will be examined in the context of this three-sector neoclassical model. However, as with those at the end of Chapter 15, the study questions here should be given careful attention. One can understand this complex model only after working with it carefully.

STUDY QUESTIONS AND PROBLEMS

1. Consider the following model:

(1) $C = C_0 + bY_d$ (6) $M^s = M_0$

(2) $I = I_0 - vR$ (7) $M^d = kY - mR$

(3) $G = G_0$ (8) $M^s = M^d$

(4) $T = T_0 + tY$ (9) $Y = P \cdot y$

(5) $Y = C + I + G$ (10) $P = P_0$

a. Trace the effects upon real income y, consumption c, investment i, and the interest rate R of expansionary fiscal policy.

b. Replace equation (10) with equation (11): $y = y_0$. Compare the effects of fiscal policy to those developed in the first model.

2. The economy is characterized by the following system of equations:

(1) $C = C_0 + bY_d$ (6) $M^s = M_0$

(2) $I = I_0 + fY$ (7) $M^d = kY - mR$

(3) $G = G_0$ (8) $M^s = M^d$

(4) $T = T_0 + tY$ (9) $Y = P \cdot y$

(5) $Y = C + I + G$ (10) $P = P_0$

Illustrate expansionary monetary policy in this model, and compare the results with those in the model of equations (1) through (10) in Question 1.

3. The following model represents the economy:

(1) $C = C_0 + bY$ (5) $M^d = kY$

(2) $I = I_0 - vR$ (6) $M^s = M^d$

(3) $Y = C + I$ (7) $Y = P \cdot y$

(4) $M^s = M_0$ (8) $y = y_0$

a. What are the effects upon y, c, i, P, Y of an increase in the money supply?

b. Compare monetary policy effects in the above model to those in a model in which equation (5) is replaced by $M^d = k - mR$.

4. a. Solve for commodity market equilibrium, given the following equations:

(1) $c = 100 + 0.8y_d$

(2) $i = 50 + 0.1y - 200R$

(3) $g = 100$

(4) $\tau = -50 + 0.1y$

b. Diagram commodity market equilibrium for equations (1) through (4).
c. Solve for the new commodity market equilibria if $g = +50$; if $c_0 = +50$.

5. a. Compute the money market equilibrium solutions for the following equations:

(1) $M^s/P = 200/P$

(2) $M^d/P = 0.8y - 100R$

(3) $M^s/P = M^d/P$

b. Plot the LM curve for $P = 1.00$; for $P = 2.00$.
c. If $P = 1.00$, what will happen to the LM curve?

6. Utilizing separate diagrams for each sector, construct a three-sector model: An IS-LM production labor sector diagram. Illustrate the initial effect upon each market of the following exogenous shifts:

a. An exogenous decrease in liquidity preference at each rate of interest.
b. A decrease in real government expenditures.
c. A decrease in the money supply.

7. Illustrate graphically an economy by a three-sector model. Assume that the economy is initially in equilibrium in all three markets.

a. Trace the effects of an exogenous tax increase of T_0.
b. Illustrate the effect of a decrease in the money supply of M.
c. What will happen if consumers decide to spend less at each level of income?

8. Consider the three-sector model developed in this chapter. Can any changes in the commodity or money markets change the equilibrium level of real income, employment, or the real wage rate? Explain your answer carefully.

9. Assume that after an initial equilibrium in the three-sector model, an inflationary gap occurs. Trace the effects intuitively through each sector of the increase in the price level.

REFERENCES

Bailey, Martin J., *National Income and the Price Level,* 2nd ed., Chaps. 1-42. New York: McGraw-Hill, 1971.

Brownlee, Oswald H., "The Theory of Employment and Stabilization Policy," *Journal of Political Economy,* Vol. 58, 1950.

Friedman, Milton, *A Theoretical Framework for Monetary Analysis,* NBER. New York: Columbia University Press, 1971.

Leijonhufvud, Axel, *On Keynesian Economics and the Economics of Keynes.* New York: Oxford University Press, 1968.

Modigliani, Franco, "Liquidity Preference and the Theory of Interest and Money," *Econometrica,* January 1944.

But why is the money wage so stubborn if more labor is willingly available at the same or lower real wage? Consider first some answers Keynes did not give. He did not appeal to trade union monopolies or minimum wage laws. He was anxious, perhaps overanxious, to meet his putative classical opponents on their home field, the competitive economy. He did not rely on any failure of workers to perceive what a rise in prices does to real wages. The unemployed take new jobs, the employed hold old ones, with eyes open. Otherwise the situation would be transient.

Instead, Keynes emphasized the institutional fact that wages are bargained and set in the monetary unit of account. Money wage rates are, to use an unKeynesian term, 'administered prices.' That is, they are not set and reset in daily auctions but posted and fixed for finite periods of time. This observation led Keynes to his central explanation: Workers, individually and in groups, are more concerned with relative than absolute real wages.

James Tobin (1972)

In the last chapter a three-market aggregate economic model was developed. In this chapter, income determination will be studied in the context of that model. A variety of assumptions about the various sectors will be employed to illustrate the essence of modern neoclassical and Keynesian "equilibrium analysis." In its present form, the model leads to classical propositions, non-Keynesian in their policy implications, and consequently this model is characterized "neoclassical." By making different assumptions

19

Neoclassical
and Neo-Keynesian
Income Determination Theories

about the workings of several markets, especially the labor market we will alter the model considerably and produce one which displays Keynesian policy implications. While these latter models will be Keynesian without relying on the assumptions that prices are rigid and that unemployment exists, these models will rely upon restrictive assumptions about the workings of various sectors. Keynesian results follow from restrictive assumptions on the neoclassical framework. Furthermore, the positions of rest in these new models, which we call *equilibrium points*, are only quasi-equilibria, because some markets are in disequilibrium. It is in the sense of these quasi-equilibria that the famous Keynesian conclusion, that "a monetary economy will come into equilibrium within a range of possibilities of which full employment is only one extreme" (Johnson 1967), will be seen to be correct. In Chapter 20 we will examine in more detail the essence of Keynes's disagreement with the classical paradigm, but our primary objectives in this chapter are to examine the policy implications of the neoclassical model and the implication of imposing various restrictions on markets in this model.

Stabilization policy considerations follow logically from one's assumptions about the structure of the economy. In Section A, we shall examine the monetary and fiscal policy implications of the neoclassical model. The neoclassical model will be seen to imply comparatively inactive policy. On the other hand, the Keynesian models, which rely upon different assumptions about behavior and market responses to exogenous changes, imply more active stabilization policies on the parts of both authorities. Section B of this chapter introduces these Keynesian versions of the three-market model.

A • Income Determination in Neoclassical Macroeconomics

Comparative Statics in the IS *Curve:* To study the effects on the economy of shifts in public or private demand, first assume that all markets are in equilibrium. Figures 1(a) and (b) illustrate the initial equilibrium in all three markets at interest rate R_2, real output level y_2^*, and price level P_2. An increase in demand can be initiated by consumers if c_0 increases, by producers if i_0 increases, or by government fiscal actions. Expansionary fiscal policy can consist of an increase in g_0, a decrease in t_0, or a net increase in the difference. In any of the above cases, the AD curve associated with the initial equilibrium, $AD(R_2)$, will shift upward. Figure 2 depicts the increase in demand brought about by the exogenous shock in several ways. Figure 2(a) depicts the Keynesian cross diagram, in which the initial upward shift in demand at interest rate R_2 occurs. The result of this upward shift in demand is a rightward shift in the *IS* curve, which is illustrated in Figure 2(b). Finally, the combined expansion of the *IS* curve and its interaction with the *LM* curve produces an increase in aggregate commodity demand relative to current production, and this increase is illustrated in Figure 2(c) as a rightward shift in aggregate demand. The next paragraph will discuss these various components of the expansion in demand step by step.

Figure 2(a) indicates first that an exogenous increase in demand induces, at

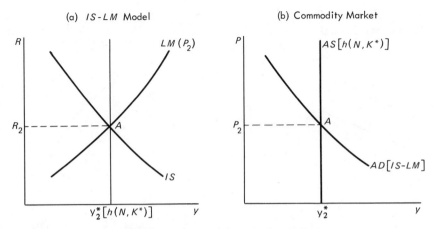

FIGURE 1   Full Employment Equilibrium

the initial rate of interest, a multiplied increase in real income from y_2^* to y_3. The rightward shift in the IS curve, illustrated in Figure 2(b), from point A to point B is equal to the old standard multipliers, taken from the earlier Keynesian cross models, times the magnitude of the initial demand shock. From our analysis of IS-LM curves in Chapters 12 through 14 it is clear that interaction between the money and commodity markets will move the economy from point B in Figure 2(b) to point C. Intuitively, the shift from point A to point C occurs because increased demand for commodities pulls cash balances out of portfolios to be used for expenditure purposes, and this shortage of liquidity will drive interest rates up, since money balances are scarce. As interest rates rise, the level of demand will fall back to some extent because of induced reductions in private investment. We have labeled the income level at which the new IS curve intersects the LM curve as income level y_4. The conditions of the money market having been taken into account, aggregate demand has increased above the original income level y_2^*. This shift in aggregate demand is illustrated in Figure 2(c) as a rightward shift from point A to point C. These points A and C correspond to the points A and C in the IS-LM diagram.

The economy from the point of view of the IS and LM curves would appear to be in equilibrium at point C, which is represented by output level y_4. However, production is still occurring at output level y_2^*. Consequently, what the shift in demand has created is a gap between demand and production, and this excess demand for limited goods and services will produce an increase in the level of prices. In familiar terms, the expansion in demand over and above current production has produced an inflationary gap, and inflation will be the result.[1]

How will the economy, in this model, respond to increases in prices induced

[1]The model is a comparative static one so that inflation will be transitory if equilibrium is again to be attained.

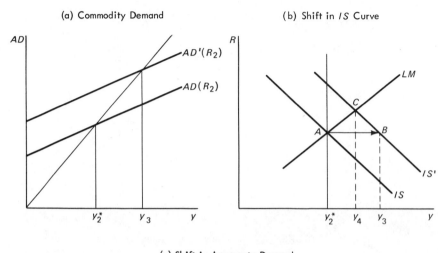

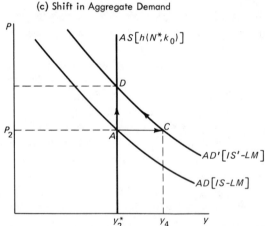

(c) Shift in Aggregate Demand

FIGURE 2   Exogenous Increase in Aggregate Demand

by excess demand? First, consider the labor market. An increase in product prices reduces the real wage rate. Figure 3 illustrates the labor market response. Initially the money wage is at W_2 and the real wage at (W_2/P_2). The increase in P drives W/P down to (W_2/P_3). How does the labor market react? Producers, finding increases in the value of marginal product because P is rising, increase their labor demand to N_3. Laborers meanwhile face product price increases and forgo labor since its real return, versus leisure, has fallen. Labor supply drops to N_1. $N_3 - N_1$ represents the excess demand for labor. Producers start competing for labor, and the money wage, W, starts to rise. Money wages will rise as long as a shortage of labor exists. The shortage will disappear only after W has increased exactly as much as P, because only then will the ratio W/P again equal $(W_2/P_2)*$ and only then will N^d equal N^s. Thus the labor market reaction to inflation is

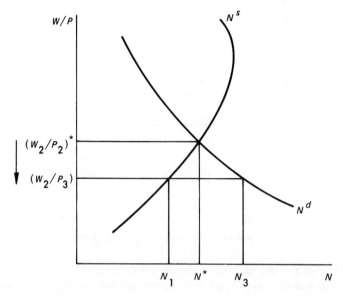

FIGURE 3   Labor Market Response to Price Level Increase

simply that wages are driven up in the same proportion as prices. The equilibrium level of employment remains at N^*. The production function, it will be
recalled from Chapter 18, provides the link between the labor market and the
commodity market. The production function implies that N^* and K_0 will combine to produce y_2^* level of output. Consequently, the aggregate supply schedule
which depends upon the labor market and the production function will remain
at output level y_2^* despite the increases in prices.

While the aggregate supply curve is not influenced by the inflation, money
market equilibrium will be altered by the increase in product prices. Inflation reduces the command over resources of the monetary unit and thus reduces the
real quantity of money, M_0/P. From the point of view of the money market an
increase in P is equivalent to a decrease in M_0, nominal cash balances. The preference for real cash balances depends upon real income, y, and the rate of return
on competing assets, R; this liquidity preference schedule is invariant to inflation. Of course, if economic agents had anticipated inflation, then they would
have expected their new cash balances to diminish in purchasing power and this
expectation would have reduced their real demand for money. However, inflation has been assumed not to breed expectations of inflation. The supply of real
cash balances therefore falls and the liquidity preference schedule remains intact.
Figure 4 shows the money market response to the price level increase. The
smaller quantity of cash balances drives the rate of return on loans upward. At
y_2, the rate of interest increases. The result, of course, is a leftward shift in the
LM curve.

To illustrate the economy's return to equilibrium after the initial shock to

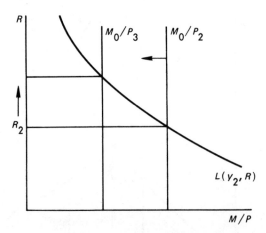

FIGURE 4   Inflation in Money Market

commodity demand, we reproduce Figures 2(b) and (c) in Figure 5, deleting the initial IS curve for clarity. Figure 5(a) illustrates the movement away from the initial LM curve $LM(P_2)$ as a result of the price level increase. Figure 5(b) illustrates that the increase in the level of prices reduces the inflationary gap by moving the economy away from disequilibrium, in which demand is at level C and production at level A, and moves the economy up to point D on the original aggregate supply curve and the new aggregate demand curve. While it is clear that production stays at level y_2^* and the money supply contracts, driving the LM schedule leftward from $LM(P_2)$, it is not quite so obvious that inflation leaves the IS curve stationary at IS'. After the initial shift in commodity market equilibria which induced the inflation to begin with, the locus of these commodity demand equilibria points does not shift. Nevertheless, the contracting money supply does drive up the interest rate above the original rate R_2, and this increased interest rate contracts aggregate demand by curtailing induced private investment. Since this contraction in demand is induced by increasing interest rates, it does not correspond to an IS curve shift. Rather, the LM curve is moving left along the IS curve IS', as shown in Figure 5(a). The new equilibrium point must occur at point D, because only at D will the inflationary gap be eliminated.

The comparative static effects of an exogenous increase in aggregate demand may now be summarized with the help of Figure 5. Figure 5(a) depicts the initial IS-LM equilibrium at point A. Equilibrium moved from point A to point D. Clearly, real income remained fixed at y_2^*. Had the initial rightward shift in aggregate demand been caused by an expansionary fiscal policy, then no increase in output would have occurred. The implication of this model should be clear: fiscal policy cannot permanently alter real output. However, point D does represent a higher rate of interest than point A; consequently, the expansionary fiscal policy has resulted in less private domestic investment. In other words, since total output is unchanged, private spending, consumption plus investment, must fall by exactly as much as real government spending has increased. In other words, we see in this neoclassical model that fiscal policy "crowds out" private investment. Furthermore, expansionary fiscal policy induces a once and for all increase in the price level.

We may conclude that in the neoclassical model expansionary fiscal policy has three permanent effects: (1) It replaces and crowds out private spending, especially private investment. (2) It raises interest rates and thus alters the mix of private spending away from capital accumulation toward current consumption. (3) It produces an increase in the price level. While many economists believe that these conclusions are correct, we should emphasize that these results depend very heavily upon the fact that the labor market must clear at one and only one level of employment and that, operating through the production function, this level of employment predetermines the level of real output in the economy without regard to conditions of aggregate demand. Consequently, in the context of this model, aggregate demand, whether it be public or private, has no sustained impact upon the level of real output.

Money Market Shifts: We have seen that fiscal policy has no real effects on the economy other than to alter the rate of interest and the mix of GNP between capital accumulation and current consumption. How will the economy react to exogenous shifts in monetary policy? To answer this question, let us suppose that the central bank reduces the nominal money supply. In the case of the U.S., the FED would sell U.S. securities on the open market. If it is assumed that the economy is initially in equilibrium, Figure 6 illustrates the effect on the money market.

The contraction of M_0 to M' shifts the locus of LM curves (only one, that associated with initial equilibrium price level P_2, is depicted) to the left. The reduced volume of money stimulates bidding for the remaining scarce balances

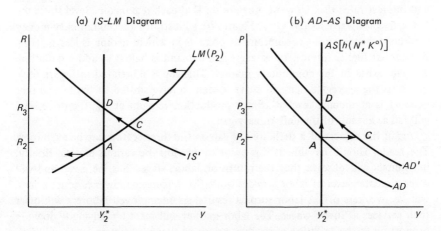

FIGURE 5   Price Level Increase in Three-market Model

(a) Money Market

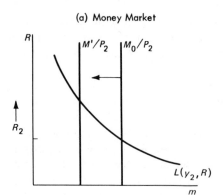

(b) Three Sector Model

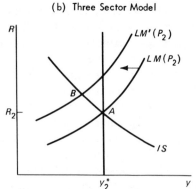

(c) Aggregate Demand – Aggregate Supply

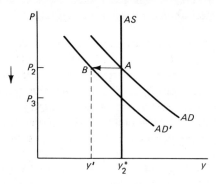

FIGURE 6   Contractionary Monetary Policy

and interest rates rise. Upward pressure on R at each real income level shifts the LM curve leftward to $LM'(P_2)$. Figure 7(b) illustrates the commodity-money markets achieving joint equilibrium at point B in which income is less than y_2. Because of higher interest rates, aggregate demand is below y_2 and a deflationary gap exists in the commodity market. This gap is illustrated in Figure 6(c), in which the aggregate demand curve is seen to have shifted to the left so that demand is at income level y'. Since production remains at y_2^*, the price level will fall as a result of the deflationary gap.

Again the effects of a deflationary gap on the three sectors can be examined. The reader should be able at this point to develop the various effects. Briefly, individuals will observe that the return on labor, wages, has increased and will offer a greater level of labor services while firms, receiving lower product prices, will lay workers off. A labor surplus results, so unemployed laborers will offer their services at lower wages. The labor market will react by driving W down in proportion to the deflation of product prices, so that W/P remains at the $(W/P)^*$, which clears the labor market at N^*, producing y_2^*.

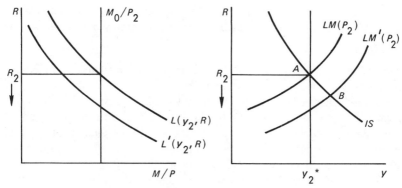

FIGURE 7   Exogenous Money Demand Shift

The money market is affected by deflation because price level reductions have the effect of increasing real money balances M'/P. Thus the LM' curve shifts back to the right. Since the IS locus is independent of the price level, it remains stationary and the deflationary gap is eliminated only after the LM curve returns to its intersection with the IS curve at point A. The real money supply must be exactly equal to the original M_0/P_2; consequently P has fallen exactly in proportion to M. If $M' = \lambda M_0$, then $P' = \lambda P_2$ so that $(M'/P') = (M_0/P_2)$ and the LM curve is back where it was originally.

In summary, the contraction of M by the monetary authority has induced a general deflation in money wages and product prices in proportion to the reduction in M. However, the real wage W/P, real income y, real consumption c, real investment i, the level of employment N, and the rate of interest R all remain unchanged. In a model with this outcome money is *neutral*: a change in the money supply has no influence on real economic variables.

The demand for money schedule can, like the money supply schedule, be subjected to exogenous shifts. Suppose, for example, the demand for money schedule shifts leftward. Figure 7 depicts the initial effect on the LM curve and money market. A reduction in the demand for money, an exogenous shift left in the schedule, at initial equilibrium, frees balances for money markets and at y_2 interest rates will be driven downward. Thus the LM curve will shift right, creating an inflationary gap. It should be clear that the comparative static effect will be to drive the price level upward until the LM curve returns from $LM'(P_2)$ to the original position, cutting the IS curve at A. The new and original equilibria differ only in that prices have increased. All real variables, W/P, N, y, R, c, and i remain fixed.

For purposes of presenting an intuitive flavor to the workings of the model, the sequential effects of parameter shifts were discussed above. It is important to note, however, that the three-market model is a comparative static model and that the process, or path, which the economy takes in moving from one equilibrium to another is not revealed. The above discussions about how the economy moves from an intial to a new equilibrium are really only intuitive scenarios and do not follow from the model. All the model reveals is the comparative static effects of shifts, not the process by which the economy moves between equilibria.

Implications of the Neoclassical Model: The neoclassical model developed in Chapter 18 and studied above has interesting implications for the workings of an economy which can be summarized in three main points: (1) The level of employment N^*, the real wage W/P^* (or, hereafter w^*) and the level of production y^* are determined in the labor market and by the production function independently of the money market and commodity demand. Equilibrium in the money market occurs only at full employment. If the positions of the labor market supply and demand curves are permanently altered by various types of market imperfections, then N^* and y^* may occur at a less than full employment level. We may summarize this result by saying that the model has the characteristic of a natural rate of unemployment associated with the point at which the labor market is assumed to clear. (2) The money market sets the level of prices, but the values of the real variables N, w, y, c, i, R, g, and τ are all determined outside the money market. This independence of all real magnitudes of the money market is the *classical dichotomy* introduced in Chapter 4. (3) The allocation of output y^* between c, i, and g is determined in the commodity market. Changes in aggregate demand such as private decisions to save more, or fiscal actions, will change the price level and the rate of interest but not total output y.

Let us stress two aspects of the neoclassical model: First, the *IS-LM* curves are neither perfectly elastic nor perfectly inelastic. Second, wages and prices are flexible. Several policy implications of this model are clearly classical in nature: Expansionary fiscal policy alters only the mix of real income, not the level, and monetary policy alters the level of prices in proportion to the change in the money supply, leaving all real magnitudes unchanged. It is important to note that these distinctly monetarist-classical results follow in a model containing a liquidity preference function in which the *LM* curve is not vertical and a stable consumption function in which *MPC* is a constant. In other words, the monetarists' propositions follow from a model which is much broader than the simple quantity theory of money model of Chapter 15.

The predictions for policy of this model deserve comment in light of the substantial inflationary pressures in the late 1960s, the 1970s and early 1980s especially in the U.S. economy. Inflation in this model results from excess aggregate demand. This excess demand can be induced either by expansionary fiscal or by expansionary monetary policy. Any attempts by policy makers to force the economy above output level y^* and employment level N^* would result only in inflation. As long as policy makers persist in expansionary measures, the level of prices continues to rise. The economy is characterized by a natural state y^*, N^*; any laborers willing and able to work who are unemployed must be so for reasons other than inadequate demand in the economy. The economy will naturally revert to y^* if driven off by exogenous shocks whether from policy or not. This model clearly implies that policy makers should not utilize government budgets for stabilization purposes and that monetary authorities should attempt to achieve monetary stability.

B ● Neo-Keynesian Income Determination

As the statement by James Tobin at the outset of the chapter suggests, Keynes did not share the classical view that markets cleared in a well-behaved competitive sense. Particularly, Keynes recognized that wage determination did not take the form of a perfect market in which the market-clearing wage was settled by a Walrasian auctioneer. Rather, wages are bargained and negotiated, and set in decentralized labor markets. Keynes focused attention on the problem that labor markets are unable to clear quickly. These markets fail in Keynes's view, in part, because wage earners provide services in response to the money wage and resist reduction in their money wage *vis-à-vis* that received by others. Keynes broke with the classical orthodoxy embodied in the neoclassical model above in many respects. However, one of the most important is that Keynes dropped the assumption that wages and prices are flexible. Recall (and perhaps even review at this point) our discussion in Chapter 4 in which we compared Keynes to the classical economists. We saw that the classical paradigm rests on the ability of markets when driven from equilibrium to adjust instantly, so that plans of decision makers are not disrupted. This instantaneous price adjustment assumption of the classical models is clearly extreme. In the models that follow we shall reverse this assumption and assume that certain prices, namely those of laborers, are extremely slow to adjust. As a plausible short-run assumption we shall assume that money wages are rigid downward. Although we will discuss this assumption in more detail in Chapter 20, at this point we simply note that employers realize that lower money wages are bad for morale; consequently, habit and custom force resistance to reductions in money wages. Also, laborers, often with limited information about the future and about wages in other areas, base their labor supply decisions on the money value of their wage. If a laborer receives a cut in money wages, he may well quit and seek employment elsewhere. Frequent mobility of labor may be something that both laborers and employers would like to avoid. There is some evidence that they may be willing to accept sticky wages as the cost of avoiding labor mobility. The stickiness of money wages may be based on money illusion on the part of labor, that is, on confusion about the real purchasing power of their wage, but it may also be based on the inability of the labor market to effectively clear in the short run as a result of imperfections in markets.

Sticky Money Wages: Let us study the three-market economy, assuming that money wages are sticky downward. Let W_2 represent the money wage level below which W will not fall. (W_2/P_2) or w_2 represents the real wage at which the labor market will clear at N_2^* (see Figure 8). For price levels below P_2, the real wage will be raised above W_2/P_2 to, for example, W_2/P_1. Because wage earners

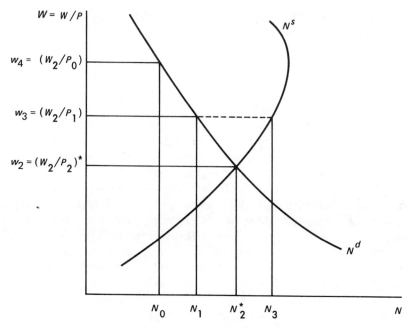

FIGURE 8   Sticky Wages in Labor Market

are unaware of the increase in their real wage or because they are responding only to relative money wages, they do not bid the money wage downward. Consequently, at (W_2/P_1) the demand for labor will be short of supply, $N_3 - N_1$; however, the labor market in disequilibrium will be unable to clear. The neoclassical model contained the assumption that wages were flexible and that W would, therefore, be driven downward by the unemployed. However, the assumption now is that the money wage fails to fall and clear labor markets:

> Money wages do not adjust rapidly enough to clear all labor markets every day. Excess supplies in labor markets take the form of unemployment, and excess demands the form of unfilled vacancies. *James Tobin (1972)*

At price level P_1, therefore, involuntary unemployment is $N_3 - N_1$. Employment at price level P_2 is N_2^*, at P_1, it is N_1, and at P_0 it is N_0 in Figure 9.

Because the labor market fails to clear due to wage rate stickiness downward, several levels of employment are attainable. According to the production function, a different level of output will be associated with each level of employment and therefore with each price level. Figure 9 illustrates the locus of real income levels compatible with each price level according to the labor market and the production function. At price level P_2, the real wage is w_2 and the labor market clears at N_2^*. N_2^* units of labor produce, given K_0, real income level y_2^*. At P_1 the real wage is $W_2/P_1 = w_3$. Since the labor market fails to clear, employment is N_1, which is less than N_2^*, and N_1 units of labor produce y_1 level of real income.

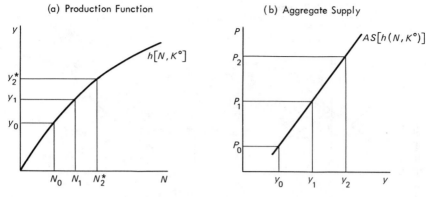

FIGURE 9   Keynesian Production and Aggregate Supply

The level of real income y is not determined uniquely in the labor market and production function.

Suppose initially the economy is in the position illustrated in Figure 10 at A. At price level P_1 the IS-LM curves interesect exactly at real income level y_1 so that all markets are compatible and the commodity and money markets are in equilibrium. Though the labor market is not in equilibrium, it fails to clear because the clearing mechanism, falling money wages, does not work.

Now let us examine the workings of this model, which differs from the neoclassical only in that we have assumed that wages are fixed. Suppose households decide to increase their savings at each level of real income. An increase in savings corresponds to an exogenous decrease in consumption expenditures, which can be represented by a leftward shift in the IS curve. This reduction in private demand is illustrated in Figure 10. Figure 10(a) illustrates the leftward shift in the IS schedule, and Figure 10(b) illustrates the leftward shift in aggregate demand which follows from the interaction of the money market and the reduction in commodity demand. How will this economy respond to the deflationary gap caused by a reduction in private demand? Let us consider the effects in each market of falling commodity prices.

Figure 11 depicts the effects of deflation on the money and labor markets. The money supply rises, causing the LM curve to move toward the right. Real wages rise, which reduces employment and consequently output. This simultaneous rightward shift of the LM curve and leftward movement of the level of employment and output as a result of falling prices closes the deflationary gap. The elimination of the deflationary gap is illustrated in Figure 10(b) as the economy moves from its initial equilibrium point A toward point C, the intersection of the new aggregate demand curve and the original aggregate supply curve. The reduction in private aggregate demand which started this process resulted in a reduction in real income from y_1 to y_0, a reduction in employment from N_1 to N_0, an increase in the real wage rate from w_3 to w_4, and a reduction in the price level from P_1 to P_0. The economy has come to rest be-

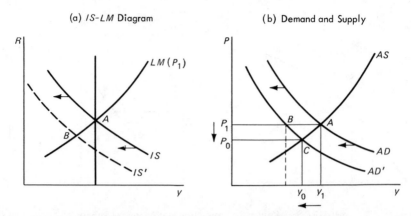

FIGURE 10   Initial Equilibrium and a Reduction in Demand

cause no forces in any market are inducing a movement away from point C in the aggregate demand and aggregate supply schedule illustrated in Figure 10(b). However, it is important to note that the labor market represented in Figure 11(b) is not cleared. Consequently, while the economy is at rest, one market is not at equilibrium; thus we should think of this as a quasi-equilibrium in which the economy has come to rest at less than full employment equilibrium.

What would be the impact of expansionary monetary policy from this quasi-equilibrium point illustrated in Figure 10? An exogenous increase in the nominal money supply M_0 would shift the LM curve to the right and create an inflationary gap at production level y_0. As the price level rises, the real wage falls, employment increases, and production increases as well. Of course, increasing prices will also erode the initial monetary policy expansion by contracting the real money supply m_0. The expansionary monetary policy would correspond

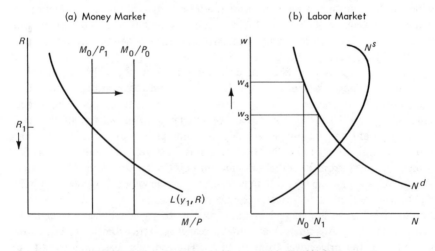

FIGURE 11   Deflation in Money and Labor Markets

to a rightward shift in the aggregate demand curve of Figure 10(b) back toward the original aggregate demand curve. At the expense of a period of rising prices, the level of employment and output could be increased.

The policy implications of this three-sector model in which wages are sticky downward in the short run are distinctly Keynesian: (1) Full employment is only one of a wide range of possible outcomes for the economy. Keynes, it will be recalled, claimed that the classical full employment case was but one special case of his "general theory." Note that, strictly speaking, the labor market is not in equilibrium even though the economy is at rest at unemployment positions. (2) Unemployment can be reduced by either fiscal or monetary policy. (3) The cost of reducing unemployment is that an inflationary gap must be created. Thus, the model suggests a trade-off between the level of unemployment and the level of prices. (4) Full employment and price stability seem attainable in this model. Of course, the model is a comparative static model and inflation is a dynamic process so that the model precedes study of a trade-off between the rates of inflation and unemployment. The model does show that when unemployment exists, a higher price level will be required to reduce the level of unemployment. (5) Unemployment and inflation can occur simultaneously. In fact, expansionary policies will induce inflation as a remedy for unemployment. What if the economy is at full employment? In this event, expansionary stabilization policies would drive prices up creating an excess demand for labor and and an increase in wages. Production cannot exceed y^*, the full employment level, and the only result is inflation. Of course, as in the previous neoclassical model, fiscal policy will alter the mix of GNP among consumption, investment, and government expenditures.

The Liquidity Trap: Keynes's analysis of the depression also included the concept of a liquidity trap. Discussed in Chapters 16 and 17, the liquidity trap may be integrated either into the neoclassical model or into the Keynesian model in which money wages are assumed to be rigid downward. In this latter context, the Keynesian analysis of the depression will contain a much more realistic description of what actually happened. Figure 12 depicts the three-sector model in a liquidity trap. Suppose initially the *IS-LM* curves intersect at point A, a real income level which is below full employment output level y^*. Point A may represent the economy in depression.

With aggregate demand at point A in Figures 12(b) and 12(c), demand is below full employment output. Initially this shortage in demand will result in a deflationary gap. It is important to remember historically that the Great Depression was accompanied by a 50 percent reduction in the aggregate price level. The substantial deflation throughout the early months and years of the depression can now be explained within the context of our models. Deflation, of course, automatically increases the purchasing power of money, which shifts the *LM* curve to the right. In a liquidity trap, new cash balances freed by deflation are automatically absorbed by speculators and those in the financial sector holding cash balances, because they have an infinite demand for money and no desire to

(a) Money Market

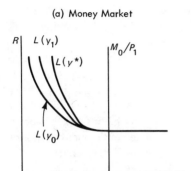

(b) IS-LM

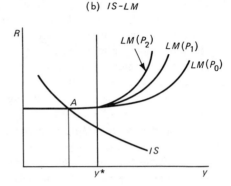

(c) Aggregate Demand — Aggregate Supply

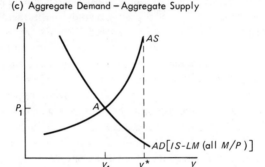

FIGURE 12   The Liquidity Trap

make loans. (It will be recalled that the banking system also collapsed during the Great Depression so that excess liquidity was absorbed immediately by people holding onto cash and unwilling to hold bank liabilities.) In Figure 12(b) the *LM* curve merely shifts right, but the *IS-LM* intersection remains at point A. What of the labor market and the production function? Of course, the reaction of the labor market and production will depend upon whether we assume that money wages are as flexible as other prices or if money wages are sticky downward. If, as Keynes thought, money wages are relatively sticky, so that we may view them as fixed throughout the course of the price deflation, then the deflation will drive the real wage upward and generate unemployment. The output level will fall to the *IS-LM* intersection at point A, and the economy will come to rest at a lower price level in a depression. This result is represented in Figure 12(c). If, on the other hand, wages are flexible downward, as neoclassical economists think, then wages will spiral downward with prices; the economy will fail to attain a point of rest, because production will steadily attempt to remain at output level y^* while demand remains at level A.

Regardless of whether money wages are sticky downward or not, however, monetary policy will be ineffective in offsetting the depressed demand. Increases in M_0 will act like decreases in the price level. Either the economy will remain in equilibrium at point A, as in Figures 12(b) and (c), or the economy will fail to stabilize at any equilibrium point. Fiscal policy, on the other hand, will shift the IS curve to the right and expand aggregate demand, reducing the deflationary gap. This in turn will move the commodity money market equilibrium toward full employment as the economy moves along the aggregate supply schedule toward y^*.

Interest–Inelastic Investment: Keynes, it will be recalled, also proposed that in a depression, private investors may be unwilling to produce new capital even if monetary policy is successful in reducing interest rates. We can visualize the interest inelastic schedule as a vertical IS curve. If the liquidity trap no longer maintains, then the LM curve would not be flat. An exogenous reduction in demand shifts the IS curve down and creates a deflationary gap. The effect on the money market of deflation is to increase cash balances. The resultant rightward shifts in the LM curve, however, will not increase real income, because the IS curve is vertical. Demand will remain below full employment income. The aggregate supply and aggregate demand curves associated with this Keynesian case are different from the one illustrated in Figure 12(c). Regardless of the price level, the IS curve produces equilibrium output. Consequently, the aggregate demand curve becomes vertical once the economy reaches a point of depression.

The effect of deflation in this case depends upon whether wages are sticky downward or flexible. If wages are sticky, then the deflation will raise real wages and reduce employment and output, and the economy will move into a depression state. If wages are flexible downward, then prices and wages will spiral downward, and the economy will have intermittent unemployment and no point of equilibrium.

Sticky Real Wages: Keynesian cases which depict the Depression have been outlined above, and the liquidity trap, interest-inelastic investment, and sticky money wages all suggest that the economy may not come to rest at the neoclassical model's full employment point. A final case, though not Keynesian in nature, is interesting, and some modern economists believe it to be quite relevant. Suppose labor and product markets operate so as to restrict real wages, w, to some level other than the market-clearing level w^*. Figure 13 illustrates this possibility. w' is the level below which real wages cannot fall. w' could come about if prices and wages were administered by concentrated market forces whose concern was not to clear the labor market but to achieve a given real return to employed labor. This model is a modification of the neoclassical model. Rather than the economy's naturally attaining N^*, it attains N_1. $N_3 - N_1$ is unemployment at w'. Let y_1 represent the level of output and real income produced by N_1 units of

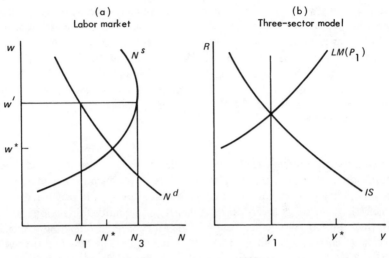

FIGURE 13   Sticky Real Wages

labor. Figure 13(b) depicts the commodity and money markets in equilibirum at output level y_1. While Keynes felt y_1 was attainable, in his models unemployment could be reduced and real income increased by expansionary fiscal policy. In this model, expansionary fiscal policy will shift the *IS* curve to the right, creating an inflationary gap. As prices rise, the money wage rises, keeping pace, and production remains at y_1. The rising price and wage levels drive down the real money supply and the *LM* curve moves left to eliminate the inflationary gap created by fiscal policy. The aggregate supply schedule is vertical at that level of output which N_1 units of labor are capable of producing. Expansionary fiscal policy raises prices and interest rates but leaves unemployment at the same level. Expansionary monetary policy also drives prices upward but fails to reduce the level of unemployment. This model suggests that if wages and prices can be administered effectively enough to maintain the real wage rate rigid, then the level of unemployment will be unchanged and technology will determine the level of output. Consequently, any attempt by stabilization authorities to reduce the unemployment rate will always fail and will instead generate spiraling inflation.

In conclusion, a number of models have been studied in this chapter. Which is the correct model of the economy? Unfortunately, an unambiguous answer to that question does not exist. Neoclassical economists believe stabilization authorities ought to think in terms of the wage-price flexibility model The economy is basically self-corrective, and authorities should not tinker with it. Keynes suggested, and neo-Keynesians believe, that sticky wages and other market imperfections explain unemployment. The economy, in their view, can be helped along by stabilization actions. Still other economists draw on a model close to the real-wage sticky version to base their policy recommendations.

1. Despite steady deflation and an aggressive, expansionary monetary policy, the economy is suffering from persistent unemployment. Construct a *three*-sector model, justifying your assumptions, consistent with this situation, and propose solutions for dealing with it.

2. Milton Friedman (1969): "What I and those who share my views have emphasized is that the quantity of money is extremely important for nominal magnitudes, for nominal income, for the level of income in dollars—important for what happens to prices. It is not important at all, or if that's perhaps an exaggeration, not very important, for what happens to real output over the long period."

Structure a three-sector macroeconomic model consistent with Friedman's statement. Discuss the policy implications of such a model for a dynamic, growing economy.

3. Answer the following within the context of a three-sector model: Recommend stabilization policies for dealing with inflation which will not alter aggregate private domestic investment. Specify the characteristics of your model clearly.

4. After World War II, the U.S. Treasury compelled the FED to support the price of U.S. government securities held by the public. Predict the effects of this policy on the economy with the aid of a three-sector model.

REFERENCES

Bailey, Martin J., *National Income and the Price Level*, 2nd ed. New York: McGraw-Hill, 1971.

Friedman, Milton, *A Theoretical Framework for Monetary Analysis*, National Bureau of Economic Research. New York: Columbia University Press, 1971.

_____ and Walter W. Heller, *Monetary vs. Fiscal Policy: A Dialogue.* New York: W. W. Norton, 1969.

Johnson, Harry G., *Essays in Monetary Economics.* London: George Allen and Unwin, 1967.

Ritter, Lawrence S., "The Role of Money in Keynesian Theory," in *Readings in Macroeconomics*, 2nd ed., M. G. Mueller (ed.). New York: Holt, Rinehart and Winston, 1971.

Samuelson, Paul A., "What Classical and Neoclassical Monetary Theory Really Was," *Canadian Journal of Economics*, February 1968.

Tobin, James, "Inflation and Unemployment," *American Economic Review*, March 1972.

> *... either Walras' law is incompatible with Keynesian economics, or Keynes had nothing fundamentally new to add to orthodox economic theory.* This may seem an unnecessarily brutal way to confront one sacred cow with another. But what other conclusion is possible?
>
> Robert N. Clower (1965)

The first objective of this chapter is to summarize the state of macroeconomic theory. In addition to developing a very general macroeconomic model, culminating in Chapters 18 and 19. The text so far has been devoted to specific components of these aggregate models. We studied consumption, investment, and government fiscal behavior in detail, and we also studied monetary phenomenon. The market that received the least attention is the labor market; thus the second objective of this chapter will be to study the workings of the labor market. As will become evident, the foundations of Keynesian economics are rather unsatisfactory. Thus the third objective of this chapter will be to review attempts to improve the microeconomics foundations of Keynesian economics.

We may summarize the state of analysis, as presented in Chapters 18 and 19, with the observation that most macroeconomic theorists seem to hold one of two basic positions about how an economy functions. The first view is the neoclassical; the second is the Keynesian. First, we shall review the neoclassical position. The analysis of neoclassicalists implies that an economy will attain a natural level of employment and a natural

The State of Macroeconomic Theory: Short-run Dynamics

level of output. These natural levels need not be constant over time but depend upon the underlying structure of various markets; the degree of competition and concentration, the presence of legal constraints, and the degree of governmental intervention and influence. Demand management policies, both monetary and fiscal, are unable, in the neoclassical view, to substantially alter the natural level of employment. Given the labor force, the tendency for the economy to come to rest at a given level of output and employment implies a natural rate of unemployment.

Illustrative of the neoclassical point of view is the analysis of Nobel laureate Milton Friedman. Table 1 contains some figures developed by Friedman of the relationship between the rate of monetary expansion and the rate of inflation.

TABLE 1

Money's Lagged Effect on Prices

PERIOD	% RATE OF MONEY INCREASE	PERIOD	% RATE OF INFLATION
12/71- 1/73	11.4%	12/73- 1/75	11.7%
1/73- 2/75	7.7	1/75- 2/77	6.2
2/75-10/77	10.1	2/77-10/79	7.10
10/77- 3/78	6.1	10/79- 3/80	?

Source: Milton Friedman, *Newsweek*, 1978.

Friedman argues that, given the natural rates of unemployment and output, the rate of monetary increase produces a commensurate rate of inflation. Thus, the table contains two sets of numbers: (1) the rate of monetary expansion as depicted by annual average percent increases in the quantity of money (M_2), and (2) the annual inflation rates as depicted by the rates of change of the consumer price index, lagged two years after the monetary increases. In theoretical terms, Friedman argues that the *LM* curve is relatively steep, that the *IS* curve is comparatively flat, and that the wage rate adjusts about as rapidly as the price level. Friedman further argues that about two years is required for a rate of monetary expansion to be fed through the economic system into a rate of increase in the level of prices. Therefore, the neoclassical model in which prices may rise but in which the real wage rate is fixed serves as an accurate comparative static model of Friedman's view of the workings of the U.S. economy. In this model, increases in the rate of expansion in the money supply produce, after a lag, nearly proportional increases in the rate of inflation. Of course, the length of the lag (two years) is not derived from the theoretical model but from empirical observation. Although the data presented in Table 1 are very simple and the lags are fairly crude, the experience of the 1970s with respect to the rate of change of M_2 and with respect to the rate of change of the consumer price index, as indicated in Table 1, appear to lend some support to Friedman's position.

Despite its ability to explain the correlation between the rate of monetary expansion and the lagged rate of inflation, Friedman's story is incomplete in one important respect. It fails to explain endogenously the employment and unemployment figures. In particular, the model does not explain where the natural rate of unemployment comes from nor why observed data indicate short-run fluctuations in the unemployment rate. Of course, a model in which the levels of production and employment, as well as the values of all real variables, are exogenous to monetary phenomena is a dichotomized model. But beyond that point, unemployment is explained outside the entire framework of the neoclassical model. At any point in time, the neoclassical model assumes that the economy has a natural rate of unemployment. This natural rate of unemployment is specified in some rather vague way by the structural conditions in the economy. The level at which the unemployment rate is assumed to be natural is determined by structural defects in the economy which prevent the labor market from clearing at the full employment point. While these defects are said to include concentration in the labor market, legal constraints (such as the minimum wage laws), and various forms of government intervention (such as unemployment insurance and unemployment compensation), how are these facts combined to produce a particular natural unemployment rate? And why does the observed unemployment rate appear to vary in the short term rather than to be a slow-moving constant?

The purpose of Keynesian economics was to explain short-term fluctuations in the unemployment rate. It was Keynes's view that unemployment was to a large extent involuntary, and his objective was to explain the presence of this involuntary unemployment in the context of an aggregate economic model. In other words, Keynes wanted to develop a model in which variations in the unemployment rate could be explained endogenously. Keynes recognized that economies went through periods in which involuntary unemployment could increase significantly and persist for a long period of time. To deal with these large persistent levels of unemployment, Keynes recommended expansionary stabilization policies. Two important points should be made about Keynes's analysis. One is a question of fact and the other a theoretical comment. First, even though we observe fluctuations in the statistics on unemployment, we cannot conclude from this fact alone that the unemployment we observe is *involuntary* in the sense of Keynes. Nor does it imply that this unemployment can most effectively be reduced by expansions in the level of aggregate demand. In a labor market as complex as that of the United States, undoubtedly there are elements of involuntary unemployment and elements of structural unemployment such as that discussed by neoclassical economists. Also, as we shall see, some unemployment in the U.S. may be a result of rational agreements between employees and employers, and unemployment may, therefore, have a voluntary component to it.

Perhaps a more important point is the theoretical one that the Keynesian model which explains involuntary unemployment endogenously was not achieved without considerable cost to the analytic framework which classical economists were employing. Keynes suggested, in addition to new stabilization policies, a change in the fundamental nature of aggregate economic analysis. In order for Keynesian economics to make any sense, we must reject the view that markets always work well enough to clear at some natural point. In theoretical terms, it is not possible for the economy to have long periods of involuntary unemployment if the labor market is always in Walrasian equilibrium. (It may be recalled by some readers that Chapter 4 contained a discussion of the conflict between Walrasian equilibrium analysis and Keynesian analysis of the aggregate economy. That discussion should make much more sense to the student now, and it would be extremely helpful to re-read the sections of Chapter 4 which deal with this issue.)

The Keynesian story may be briefly summarized as follows: The aggregate supply curve is not vertical, as in the neoclassical model, but is upward sloping. This slope is a result of the labor market's failure to clear at the full employment rate, but the unemployment rate attained depends upon the point at which the aggregate demand curve cuts the aggregate supply schedule. If the economy suffers a sharp depressive shock in aggregate demand, the downward movement in private demand produces a deflationary gap. As prices fall and the real wage is driven up, a reduction in the employment level and a reduction in output are produced. Even though a general deflation is taking place, the resultant expansion in the real purchasing power of money is not able to push aggregate demand back upward. In the neoclassical model, the channel through which a deflation and the resultant increase in the real purchasing power of money was able to push the economy back up was the interest rate channel. The increased money supply reduced interest rates, which stimulated private demand. In the Keynesian story, then, the economy can achieve a new *quasi-equilibrium*, (quasi because the labor market is in fact not clearing) at a lower level of production and at a lower price level. While expansionary monetary policy will not work in this situation, fiscal policy which operates directly on expenditures will.

While the Keynesian analysis clearly enriched our understanding of the macroeconomic system by providing both an explanation for involuntary unemployment and a resolution of the problem, we have not yet developed a sophisticated explanation of the inability of the labor market to operate efficiently. We merely attribute the failure of the labor market to the assumption that wages are sticky downward. We justify this assumption about sticky wages by referring to the habits of employers and employees of maintaining a fixed money wage and by referring to the idea that laborers, subject to money illusion, think that their money wage is worth more than it really is. Since neither of these explanations is very satisfying, a main objective of this chapter will be to develop more sophisticated stories in support of the notion that the labor market will fail to clear at some natural rate of employment.

In the late 1960s and early 1970s economists attempted to develop the micro foundations of the Keynesian macroeconomic analysis of the labor market. They argued that labor market failure was the result of limited information on the part of the suppliers of labor. The most famous book carrying this body of analysis was *Microeconomic Foundations of Employment and Inflation Theory*, edited by Edmund Phelps. This literature basically tried to describe how laborers would behave when uncertain about the wages available in other jobs or at other points in time. Thus the analysis attempted to describe how laborers would search for jobs in the presence of uncertainty about the set of wage alternatives available to them. We shall examine their theories in Section A of this chapter.

A ● Job Search and Employment Acceptance Analysis

The neoclassical model, developed earlier, is based upon the notion of a Walrasian tâtonnement process. In the Walrasian story of the functioning of an economic system, actions occur at only market clearing prices. Consequently, all decision making is undertaken before any exchanges actually take place. Once economic agents are prepared to undertake exchange, the economy has achieved its equilibrium. Although this model has elegance and describes the nature of an aggregate equilibrium, it suffers a number of important defects. First, in a neoclassical model, if wages are flexible there is really no need for any commodity to serve as money. Since the system is basically frictionless, money is not needed to lubricate the transactions process. No one is found stuck with a need for liquidity; no one is found in a position in which his plans are not satisfied. Since money does indeed exist, models not requiring it are probably defective.

Second, under neoclassical assumptions, starting at a position of equilibrium, a change in aggregate demand will have no permanent effect upon real variables. In other words, money is neutral and serves as a veil over an economy which is otherwise barter in character as long as full information is available to the economic agents. Apparently, it is necessary, in order to link fluctuations in aggregate demand to fluctuations in the level of employment, to introduce some type of frictions into the economic system. A frictionless Walrasian tâtonnement process is not compatible with the Keynesian notion that fluctuations in aggregate demand produce fluctuations in the level of output and employment. As the Keynesian model was developed in Chapter 19, Keynesian economics appeared to be merely a special case of the neoclassical system. Furthermore, this special Keynesian case is based upon simple *ad hoc* assumptions about the rigidity of wages or prices and has no real foundations in microeconomic theory.

Third, the structure of both the Keynesian and neoclassical models are in some sense incompatible with the core of modern microeconomic theory. In particular, central to both the Keynesian and neoclassical models developed above are the consumption equation and the investment schedule. We argue that consumption depends upon some measure of income and that investment depends upon some measure of output, yet in a truly general analysis of microeconomics, a household determines its consumption plan before it knows its income. In particular, in a life-cycle model, one thinks of a household decision maker planning his consumption pattern and his work pattern simultaneously. The implication of this decision process is that income is not known when the consumption plan is made. Put another way, demand depends upon prices and not upon quantitites. Similarly, the producer is usually viewed in microeconomics as constrained by a production function restricting the nature of the technological choices available to him and restricted by the set of prices for his inputs and for his product. Then he, as a profit maximizer, chooses his input combination and his output simultaneously. Once again, the producer does not know his output when he is making his investment decision. Now the key to these traditional micro analyses of decision making by consumers and producers is either the Walrasian tâtonnement process or some assumption such as Marshall's of instanteous price adjustment. Economic agents are assumed to develop their utility maximization or profit maximization plans subject to exogenous prices, wages, and the like, and the economic agents are able to exercise their plans because no actual action takes place until all markets are cleared at an equilibrium set of prices and wages. No Keynesian assumptions and no Keynesian results follow in such a framework. Thus, the problem being dealt with in this chapter is to examine the implications for aggregate decision making of various frictions in the model. In other words, which assumptions of the neoclassical are essential to the conclusion that the only possible equilibrium is associated with full employment? Can we develop a theoretical foundation for a model based upon rational economic decision making subject to constraints, in which the outcome links fluctuations in aggregate demand to fluctuations in employment?

Three very stringent assumptions underlie the neoclassical model based upon the Walrasian system: (1) All economic agents are *price takers*. Economic agents, both consumers and producers, select the quantities they will demand and supply on the basis of prices set for them by some outside agent. (2) Economic agents have *perfect information* about all wages and prices available in the current market and in the future. That is, economic agents know the prices that are announced as they are making their decisions. (3) Wages and prices are assumed to fluctuate, so that by the time the quantities chosen by economic agents are actually traded, the economy is in a *market clearing equilibrium*. The analysis presented in this section deals with the implications of relaxing the second assumption on perfect information. In particular, the *job search and employment-acceptance* literature deals with the implications of the suppliers of labor having inadequate information about the range of possible wages available to them.

In order to study this analysis, we shall greatly simplify the theoretical models developed earlier so that we may focus attention upon the relationship between the labor market and commodity demand. Before developing this model, which will then be modified under assumptions of limited information, we note that assumption (1), that economic agents are price takers, would not seem to be critical to the inability of these models to link the level of private demand to the employment level. Replacing the assumption that economic agents are competitive with a model in which there is some degree of monopoly power in either labor or commodity markets can be shown to produce the result that, while the equilibrium achieved depends on the degree of concentration, markets still clear and fluctuations in demand will not produce fluctuations in the employment level.

The bare bones model we shall develop to analyze frictions in the labor market will be one in which we have no explicit government fiscal and monetary actions. Fiscal and monetary actions will be represented only by an exogenous component to aggregate demand. Furthermore, we shall assume no investment spending and we shall assume that the production function is simply a conduit through which the quantity of labor employed determines aggregate supply. We shall first specify the labor market and second the commodity market. The labor market will be represented by a demand equation and a supply equation of the traditional type in which demand and supply both depend with the appropriate signs upon the real wage rate and in which the market clears. This market is represented by the following equation:

$$N^d(w) = N^s(w) = \overline{N} \tag{1}$$

The labor market is illustrated in panel (a) of Figure 1.

Commodity market demand will be the sum of two sources, consumption demand and exogenous policy demand. (We will not examine implications of fluctuations in interest rates for demand, because our attention is focused on the connection between the labor market and consumption demand.) Since we are assuming the Walrasian system, commodity demand does not depend upon income but upon the wage received by labor. (The implication is that as individuals confront given wages, the higher the wage rate, the greater will be the supply of labor and consequently commodity demand.) Equation (2) depicts the aggregate demand condition:

$$y^d = c(w) + e(m, g - \tau) \tag{2}$$

In equation (2) we simply depict aggregate demand as the sum of consumption demand which depends on the wage rate, $c(w)$, plus exogenous sources of demand from monetary policy and the government deficit, which are represented by the term, $e(m, g - \tau)$.

The commodity supply function is represented by a production function in which the capital stock is exogenous and in which the quantity of labor depends upon the wage rate and therefore determines the level of output. These relationships are expressed in equation (3):

$$y^s = h[N(w), k^*] \tag{3}$$

Equilibrium, of course, requires that aggregate supply equal aggregate demand. Equation (2) and (3) and the equilibrium condition are represented in Figure

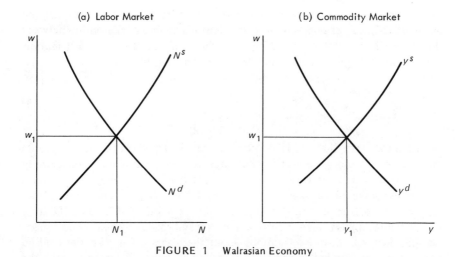

(a) Labor Market   (b) Commodity Market

FIGURE 1   Walrasian Economy

1(b). The model is depicted initially at equilibrium position 1 in which the labor market and commodity markets both clear.

If this economic system is hit with an exogenous increase in demand the new equilibrium must be at the original wage rate on the original aggregate supply schedule, because the labor market must return to the original employment level and wage rate and because the position of the aggregate supply curve does not change. Consequently, upward shifts in aggregate demand must be reduced by increases in prices so that the aggregate demand curve is returned to the original position. The mechanism by which this would take place would be an increase in the price level which reduces the real money supply, forcing the exogenous demand term, $e(m, g - t)$ to return to its original level. In other words, this simple version of the neoclassical model satisfies the result we were discussing earlier: Consumption demand is not linked to the level of employment and depends only upon the wage rate. All real economic variables—the employment level, the real wage, and the level of production as represented by the quantity of commodities which clear the commodity market—are independent of monetary and fiscal policy. Consequently, Keynesian results do not apply.

Let us now turn to the relaxation of assumption (2) above in order to study the implications of inadequate information on the part of laborers. In particular, it will be shown that if households have incomplete information as to the true array of possible wage offers, then a link between consumer demand and the employment level will exist. Assumption (2) will be replaced with two other assumptions: First, laborers form some expectation about the array of wages available. Furthermore, the wages which laborers expect to prevail will not change with changes in the actual distribution of wages. In other words, it will be assumed that laborers are aware of their own wage rate but that when this wage rate changes, they do not realize that it may be accompanied by changes in wages offered at other job opportunities. Second, the labor supply schedule, reflecting the decision to work, depends upon the relationship between the wage offer and the subjective expectation about the wage distribution. Specifically, the labor supply schedule is represented as follows:

$$N^s = \begin{cases} N^s(w) & \text{if } w \geq w^e \\ 0 & \text{if } w < w^e \end{cases} \tag{4}$$

Equation (4) states that the labor supply schedule depends upon the wage rate only as long as the wage is at least as large as that which workers subjectively expect to prevail. If, however, the wage offer falls below the expected wage, then workers would be unwilling to supply labor services. [The market labor supply schedule is actually more complicated than equation (4), because the story we are telling applies to an individual laborer, and each individual laborer specifies his own subjective expectations about the wages other than the realized wage he is receiving.] The aggregate labor supply schedule depends upon the array of expected real wages and upon the ratio of wage offers to expected wages:

$$N^s = N^s(w^e, w/w^e) \tag{5}$$

The first argument in the labor supply function, equation (5), is represented by the traditional labor supply schedule as in Figure 1(a). If the wage offer to some worker should drop below an initial equilibrium point on this labor supply schedule, then that laborer would cease to supply labor services and the quantity of labor supplied would drop to zero.

Two different stories about the lack of perfect information in the labor market may be told which are consistent with equation (5). However, the behavior of households when confronted with a lower wage offer differs according to the story told. The first assumption is that wage offers vary across jobs at a point in time so that when a wage earner is offered a low wage, he expects a higher wage to be available in other jobs at the same point in time. If the wage offer is small enough, then the laborer will quit and search for an alternative job. Thus, unemployment is created when workers are searching for alternative jobs because they are under the impression that the lower wage rate they have been offered represents only the offer from their current employer and not what may be available elsewhere. The alternative assumption is that wage offers are thought to vary over time. In other words, when a laborer is offered a low wage, he thinks that by staying out of the market for a time he will be able to find an alternative job later at a higher wage. In this case, the individual who stops working consumes leisure and waits until a better job arrives. In both cases, though, the new assumption about the lack of information in the labor market requires change in other parts of the model. For example, now that households are assumed to either be consuming leisure or to be searching for alternative jobs, it must be that a Walrasian auctioneer is not setting the wage at equilibrium at every point in time. Consumption demand, which was assumed to depend upon the wage offer, will now be seen to depend also upon the relationship between wage offers and the subjective expectation of an appropriate wage. Similarly, since a new rule is being undertaken on the part of employees about whether or not to accept jobs, it is not clear that profit-maximizing firms can adopt the same attitude towards wages and employment that they did before. Thus a new assumption in the labor market has implications for the commodity market as well. We now turn to respecifying the demand for commodities.

We begin with consumption demand. Suppose, now that there is uncertainty about the relation between the wage and the expected wage, that we adopt a consumption equation consistent with the notion that consumers have a horizon which exceeds the current period. In this case (consistent with the permanent income and life cycle hypotheses principles) we might begin by assuming that normal consumption demand depends upon the expected wage rather than the wage offer. If economic agents are unaware of wages offered outside the market for their own services then it may be reasonable to also assume that, as purchasers, households are unaware of the prices available on commodities elsewhere. In other words, we should make a distinction between the price offered consumers when they buy products and the prices which they expect to prevail. The consumption demand equation is analogous to the labor supply equation. In this case we specify the consumption demand equation as

$$c^d = c^d(w^e, p/p^e) \tag{6}$$

Equation (6) carries the two ideas that (1) the consumption demand and labor supply decision on the part of households depends upon the expected wage, and (2) consumption demand depends upon observed prices and expected prices. If the price offer exceeds the expected price, then consumption demand will fall, because consumers will either search for lower prices elsewhere, wait until prices fall, or consume any storage of goods they have until prices change later.

One other modification must be made in the general model. Because consumption demand declines with a price increase and because labor supply increases with a wage increase, firms must be confronted with downward sloping commodity demand equations and upward sloping labor supply schedules. Consequently, there is some degree of monopoly power available to firms. The labor demand schedule will have to be modified so that firms will employ the quantity of labor made available by households at each wage. Thus the profit maximizing rule will have to include a degree of concentration in the labor market. Unfortunately, we cannot construct a labor demand schedule as we did in the competitive case. Thus, if we begin at an initial equilibrium at which the actual wage and the expected wage are the same, then the level of employment will be determined by the labor supply schedule. If the wage rate then falls, labor supply will drop to zero. Thus we must replace Figure 1(a) with Figure 2(a), in which the labor supply schedule determines the employment level. Furthermore, the product supply line no longer depends upon the wage rate, but instead depends upon the actual quantity of labor employed. Suppose that we begin at an initial equilibrium in which the wage and the expected wage are equal so that the commodity supply is given from employment level $\hat{N}$, as depicted in Figure 2(b). The commodity demand and supply equations are represented as follows:

$$y^d = c^d(w^e, p/p^e) + e(m, g - \tau) \tag{7}$$

$$y^s = h[\hat{N}, K^*] \tag{8}$$

Consider the effects in this model of a reduction in exogenous demand, $e(m, g - \tau)$. Because commodity demand now depends upon prices, a reduction in demand will drive product prices down. Similarly, through profit maximization, firms will reduce the wage offers to labor. Because price offers are lower and wage offers are lower, consumer demand will rise and labor supply will fall. The effect of this negative shock to aggregate demand on the labor market is critical to this analysis. The reduction in the series of wage offers will cause a reduction in labor supply, because individuals find that their own wage rate has fallen, but they are unaware of the fact that the real wage may have stayed the same. (Product prices are falling as well.) In other words, while each laborer realizes that his own wage rate has fallen, he is unaware of the fact that wages in general have been depressed by a negative aggregate demand shock. Put another way, individual economic agents are only aware of the fact that their own wage is lower, and they are not aware of the fact that this is a result of a general marketwide reduction in wages. Thus, they respond to reduced aggregate demand by reducing

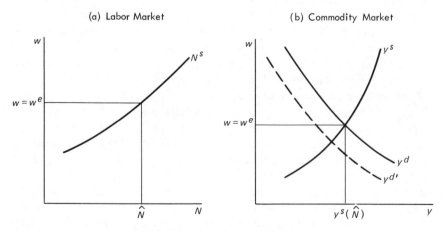

(a) Labor Market   (b) Commodity Market

FIGURE 2   Non-Walrasian Economy

their supply of labor—leaving work, searching for jobs, or consuming leisure. The result is that downward pressure on demand produces a reduction in the level of employment. This is the very conclusion which the job-search and employment-acceptance literature was designed to produce!

The value of this job-search and employment-acceptance friction literature is that it provides a logical foundation for the apparent empirical fact that the labor market fails to function as quickly and as efficiently as other markets, with the consequence that we observe long periods of high unemployment. This analysis has also proved useful for studying the nature of unemployment statistics and the working of various components of the aggregate labor market. However, from the point of view of salvaging the foundations of Keynesian economics, the job-search and employment-acceptance literature may not be entirely satisfactory. The idea that unemployment is created because workers are unaware of wage offers elsewhere and leave their jobs voluntarily may be a valuable one, but, alas, it does not yield the result that alterations in aggregate demand produce *involuntary unemployment*. In fact, it is *voluntary* unemployment which is explained in the job-search literature. Workers are refusing to accept jobs because they believe the wage offer is lower than what they could receive elsewhere. This is a voluntary decision. Data on the labor market suggests, however, that unemployment is to some degree involuntary. The search story suggests that *quits* should be a major factor in creating unemployment. However, we observe a high level of *layoffs* at fixed wages in many markets. For example, when a negative demand shock hits the automobile industry, it is not unlikely for substantial layoffs to take place with reductions in the wage rate.

Also, if wage earners are laid off, reflecting a reduction in the demand for labor, then we logically would expect consumption demand to decline. After all, households have had their sources of income cut off and their plans frustrated. However, in the example above, consumption demand actually increased in the presence of a reduction in employment. This result is perverse. Another strange feature of this model is that increases in exogenous demand produce price increases, which in turn produce reductions in private consumption demand. This result does not appear to make much sense. As a rule, we find that expansions in demand produce concomitant expansions in consumpton demand which feed on themselves.

One final difficulty with the implications of this search story should be mentioned. This last idea was emphasized by Grossman (1973). Grossman points out that implicit in the search-acceptance literature is the idea that if the economy is in a boom and employment rises, because the marginal product of labor will be declining (given that we are expanding the units of labor available to a fixed capital stock), wage offers should fall. In other words, this model suggests that when the economy is expanding in boom times, the wage rate should be declining, and that when the economy slumps, the wage rate should be rising. However, wages tend to move with the business cycle; i.e., they tend to be procyclical. Thus while the job-search and employment-acceptance stories are very useful for analyzing a number of aspects of the labor market, they may not have salvaged the foundations of Keynesian economics. We turn now to a different approach to studying the underlying conditions of Keynesian economics. This second approach alters assumption (3) of the Walrasian neoclassical model: that the economy always achieves equilibrium.

B • Keynesian Economics as Short-Run Disequilibrium Analysis

Patinkin's View of Keynes: One of the most important books on macroeconomic theory written since *The General Theory* is Don Patinkin's *Money, Interest and Prices*, 2nd ed., subtitled "An Integration of Monetary and Value Theory." In this monumental work, Patinkin codified the state of macroeconomic theory as of the mid-1960s. While most of the book is devoted to developing the foundations of a macroeconomic model similar in spirit to the neoclassical model developed in this text, the latter part of the Patinkin book is devoted to an analysis of the ideas of Keynes. Patinkin begins his analysis by defining involuntary unemployment. To Patinkin, unemployment is *involuntary* if it results from the inability of economic agents to supply the level of employment which results from their optimization plans at each set of wages and prices. In other words, if economic agents, when facing a given real wage, maximize their own utility and determine to supply a certain level of employment, then if they are unable to actually sell that volume of employment, they may be said to be "involuntarily unemployed." This definition of involuntary unemployment leads Patinkin to a very important result which he calls the "coexistence theorem": *Involuntary unemployment and flexible money wages cannot coexist at equilibrium.* In other words, if money wages are flexible, as Patinkin and many others believe them to be, then once equilibrium is achieved in the labor market, there must be no involuntary unemployment.

This leaves us with several possible interpretations of how Keynesian economics differs from the mainstream neoclassical paradigm: It is possible that Keynes was merely suggesting several special restrictions on the general neoclassical theory. That is, Keynes may have been arguing that investment could be interest inelastic, that the money market could be in a liquidity trap, or that wages could be sticky downward. However, if we believe that that is what Keynes was saying, then we must conclude that Keynes really did not produce a general theory and merely introduced a few special assumptions which result in special cases of the general neoclassical theory. However, other interpretations of Keynes may also be considered: Either Keynes had in mind a nonequilibrium situation, or he had in mind some fundamentally different ways in which economic agents act. Patinkin explores the possibility that Keynes had in mind a macroeconomic system in *disequilibrium.*

Let us examine the workings of the neoclassical model when driven from equilibrium. Suppose, for example, that some depressive shock strikes the aggregate demand schedule and forces aggregate demand down unexpectedly. We illustrate this situation in Figure 3 below. The economy is depicted as having originally been at equilibrium y^* but demand has fallen to output level $\hat{y}$. Now, the analysis of the neoclassical model will suggest that inadequate aggregate demand merely produces a deflationary gap. When prices fall, as we argued in Chapter 18, aggregate demand will be forced back upward and the economy will come to rest at the original equilibrium. However, in the real world it takes time for prices to fall and in the interval, before prices fall, economic agents must continue to undertake transactions. In the interval before the deflationary gap is closed, demand will be less than the level of production that firms had intended to achieve. Consequently, firms will be unable to execute their plans. In particular, the firms will be forced to accumulate inventories beyond those they had intended to accumulate. Because they are holding stocks of their commodities, they are not bringing in cash revenues from sales as they had planned. As a result, firms will find themselves with inadequate cash balances with which to pay their bills. One result is that the firms will be unable to pay the wage bill. What are firms to do? Will they reduce the wage rate in order to pay the number of workers that they had planned to employ originally, will they reduce their level of employment, or will they do some combination?

Firms had originally planned, as profit maximizers, to employ labor up to the point at which the marginal product of labor equalled the real wage rate. The resultant level of employment, the equilibrium level, is depicted as point A in Figure 4(a). Now, however, firms are unable to employ N^* units of labor at wage rate w^*. Because firms have unexpectedly low revenues, they must reduce the wage bill, which means that they are driven to the left of point A somewhere into the shaded region in the diagram. This result is depicted by the arrows' moving to the left from point A. Recall that because employment level N^* was the result of a rational plan on the part of a profit maximizing firm, quantity N^*

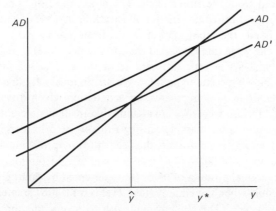

FIGURE 3   Downward Shock to Aggregate Demand

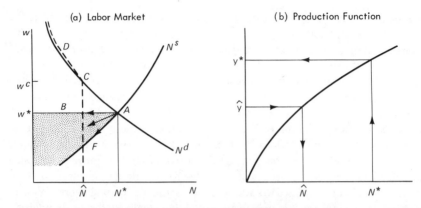

FIGURE 4   Patinkin's Disequilibrium Analysis

was seen, operating through the production function, to produce output level y^*. Now, at disequilibrium, the firm is unable to sell y^* units of output. Instead, buyers are buying only quantity $\hat{y}$. Consequently, it seem unlikely that the firm would employ the original quantity of labor to produce goods which the firm is unable to sell. Suppose that, immediately in the face of the reduced level of demand, firms maintain the wage rate at the original level w^* but reduce employment to that level needed to produce the level of goods and services actually demanded in the market. In other words, the direction of causation is reversed: Output level $\hat{y}$ operates through the production function to determine employment level $\hat{N}$. This idea is illustrated in Figure 4(b) by showing arrows leading from the output level $\hat{y}$ through the production function to the employment level $\hat{N}$. Notice that the direction of causation has reversed from one in which the labor market clears and determines the output level to a situation in which the output level produces the quantity of labor demanded. In this disequilibrium situation the quantity of labor demanded, $\hat{N}$, is not that quantity which is derived from the firm's plans. Therefore, the firm is not on its equilibrium labor demand schedule. In this illustration, in which we assume that the wage rate is fixed, the labor market moves from point A to point B in Figure 4(a) at which the wage rate is w^* and the employment level is $\hat{N}$.

Now this analysis is very different from the analysis of the labor market used to describe Keynesian economics. We are no longer arguing that disequilibrium in the labor market is created by a deflation which drives the real wage above the equilibrium wage. We are arguing that inadequate commodity demand *spills over* into the labor market, causing firms to be driven from their equilibrium point to hiring fewer workers than called for by profit maximization. Thus the wage rate does not fall, but workers are laid off. Furthermore, notice that at point B, the marginal product of labor (as represented by point C on the demand for labor schedule when the employment level is $\hat{N}$) is now greater than the wage being paid labor, w^*. (The student may wish to review the construction of the labor demand schedule in Chapter 18.) Heuristically, firms have laid off workers, without reducing the wage, so that the marginal product of workers has risen while the cost per unit of labor has remained the same. Thus, labor is now a comparatively inexpensive input. As we shall see shortly, when the wage bill is reduced, as it is in this example, this may in turn have an additional spillover effect back onto the commodity market. Labor is now earning less income, and aggregate demand may actually fall more.

The demand for labor schedule, in this disequilibrium situation with inadequate aggregate demand, is no longer the straight downward sloping schedule labeled N^d in Figure 4(a) but is now the dash line running from $\hat{N}$ on the horizontal axis through point B up to point C on the original demand schedule and then up along that schedule through point D. In other words, at any wage below wage w_c, the quantity of labor demanded will remain at level $\hat{N}$, because only that level of employment is needed to achieve the level of production required by market demand. If, naturally, the wage rate rises enough, that is, above point w_c, then the employment level will decline below $\hat{N}$.

One important policy implication of this disequilibrium interpretation of Keynesian economics is the effect on the economy of reducing the wage in order to eliminate unemployment. Recall that from traditional analysis, unemployment occurs because the real wage exceeds the market clearing wage. This traditional view is shown in Figure 5. In the traditional story, the shock which struck the labor market came from commodity market deflation of the deflationary gap. Falling product prices raised the real wage, which created unemployment. Stickiness of money wages prevent money wages from falling as rapidly as product prices, so the real wage increased from w^* to $\hat{w}$. To eliminate the unemployment, a natural solution is to reduce the real wage rate from $\hat{w}$ towards w^*. However, suppose the unemployment was brought about not by the deflation but by layoffs, as suggested in this disequilibrium analysis story told by Patinkin. Then the labor market is at point B in Figure 4(a), rather than at point E in Figure 5. Given the labor demand schedule, the dotted line in Figure 4(a), a reduction in the real wage from w^* will not increase the level of employment from $\hat{N}$, because firms are hiring $\hat{N}$ not as a result of a high wage rate but as a result of inadequate demand for their products.

In fact, this new analysis of the labor market suggests that a reduction of the real wage will not raise employment but will have several other effects. First, it will further reduce the wage bill so that labor income will fail; second, it will cause laborers to move down the supply schedule from point A toward point F [in Figure 4(a)]. Thus the first effect will be to reduce unemployment by driving laborers out of the labor market, not by increasing employment. Third, labor income is lower, because the wage bill is lowered by the reduction in the real wage. This lower wage income will result in a reduction in consumer demand as a result of lower income. However, the reduced real wage is not a result of lower revenues but of our exogenous policy recommendation. Consequently, the firm's revenues are the same; since its wage bill is lower, some other aspect of the firm's balance sheet must be adjusted. In particular, we may assume that the residual

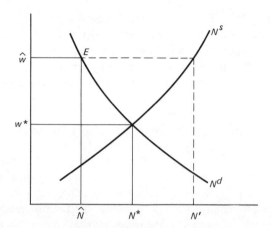

FIGURE 5   Traditional Labor Market Analysis

of revenue after costs increased. Thus, reducing the real wage from point B in Figure 4(a) does not increase employment but reduces the wage bill, contracts consumer demand, and increases profits.

How the economy will proceed from disequilibrium is not something that is fully understood in economic analysis yet. Before pointing out the difficulties one encounters when attempting to further analyze this situation, let us turn to another, related, attempt to analyze Keynesian economics as disequilibrium analysis.

Clower's Dual Decision Hypothesis Revisited: In Chapter 9 on consumption behavior, we discussed Clower's dual decision hypothesis as a rebuttal to the permanent income and life cycle hypotheses' attacks on the Keynesian notion that consumption in the short run depends upon disposable income. It turns out that the Clower dual decision hypothesis is similar in concept to the Patinkin disequilibrium analysis. While Patinkin showed that disequilibrium in the commodity market spills into disequilibrium in the labor market, Clower's dual decision hypothesis argued that disequilibrium in the labor market could spill into disequilibrium in the commodity market. In other words, both Clower and Patinkin point out that when an economic agent's plans are frustrated in one area, this frustration has spillover effects into their plans elsewhere. (One's understanding of this analysis will be enhanced considerably with review of the dual decision hypothesis in the advanced consumption chapter at this time.) Briefly, Clower argues that if a worker is unexpectedly driven off his labor supply schedule because there is inadequate demand for labor, then the worker will be forced to modify his consumption plan. In other words, if a labor unit is unable to sell the quantity of labor he had planned to sell, then he will be unable to buy the goods he had planned to buy. Thus, inadequate labor demand produces inadequate consumption demand. This is the converse of Patinkin's situation in which inadequate commodity demand produced inadequate labor demand. Figure 6 illustrates Clower's arguments. To summarize, households unable to supply the labor which they had planned to supply, do not receive the income they need to meet their original consumption plans. Consequently, a second decision must be undertaken on the part of households in which their consumption plan is restricted by the lower wage income they receive.

Barro and Grossman's Disequilibrium Analysis: A very interesting analysis of the macroeconomic system at disequilibrium is contained in the 1976 book, *Money, Employment and Inflation*, by Robert Barro and Herschel Grossman. Barro and Grossman observed the symmetrical nature of the Patinkin and Clower analyses outlined above. They put these two bodies of analysis together and produced a full model operating at disequilibrium. Barro and Grossman (BG) make several restrictive assumptions which allow them to derive a quasi-equilibrium in which the macro system may come to rest at below full employment. They begin by pointing out that the Walrasian model implicitly allows economic agents to avoid undertaking transactions until an equilibrium price vector is achieved; BG choose to made the extreme opposite assumption that economic adjustments take place before prices are able to move. In other words, BG assume that wages and prices are rigid throughout the course of their analysis. A second assumption which proves crucial is that inventories are not accumulated. All goods and services consist of perishable commodities. Third, BG assume that when suppliers and demanders disagree about the quantities they wish to exchange, the actual exchange which takes place will reflect the choice of the smallest offer in the market. For example, if laborers agree to supply a quantity which is larger than that which firms demand, then the quantity demanded will prevail in the market. Similarly, if commodity demand is less than supply, the quantity demanded will dominate and determine the level of commodity transactions. BG

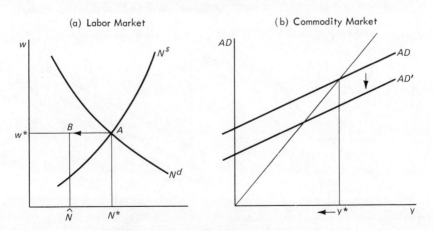

FIGURE 6   Clower's Dual Decision Analysis

defend this assumption on the grounds that only voluntary transactions are allowed in a market economy. Given these three assumption and putting the ideas of Patinkin and Clower together, BG produce an economy which will, when struck with certain kinds of exogenous shocks, appear to behave much in the way Keynes described an economy in slump.

Begin with an economy in which the commodity and labor markets are in equilibrium, as illustrated at points A in Figure 7. Suppose that this economy is struck with depressive shocks that hit both the labor and commodity markets simultaneously, so that a sudden reduction in commodity demand and a sudden reduction in labor demand initiate the process. In Figure 7 these depressive shocks are illustrated as driving the commodity market and labor markets from the original equilibrium points A to points B. According to Patinkin's analysis, the reduced commodity demand from point A to point B will spill over into the labor market and reduce the demand for labor. This spillover effect is illustrated by driving the labor market from point B farther to the left to point C. Clower's analysis, at the same time, implies that when the labor market is driven from equilibrium point A to point B, this will spill over into the commodity market by further reducing commodity demand from point B to point C. If we assume that these spillover effects are going to be dissipated somewhat by caution in the successive reactions of economic agents, then the shifts from points B to C will be smaller than the original demand shocks. However, each shift from B to C would produce another round of smaller spillover effects. By the assumption that the spillover effects become subsequently smaller and smaller, each subsequent shock to each market will become smaller and smaller, and the economy will appear to be spiralling downward from its original equilibrium in a *multiplier*like fashion. Could it be that this is the type of analysis which Keynes had in mind when he developed the concepts of the multipliers, the consumption function, and the like? Frankly, economists are not yet fully agreed as to whether this approach correctly captures Keynes's thinking. Nevertheless,

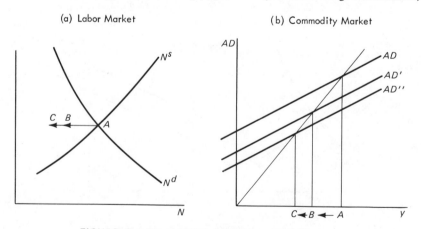

(a) Labor Market   (b) Commodity Market

FIGURE 7   Barro and Grossman Disequilibrium

it has pointed out an interesting aspect of aggregate economic behavior, namely, that the effects in one market in a non-Walrasian world may have important spillover effects in other markets.

Despite this major contribution of Barro and Grossman to integrating the ideas of Patinkin and Clower and to following the lead of these authors that one may be dealing with a non-Walrasian system when dealing with Keynes, the BG analysis seems to fall somewhat short of capturing the workings of an economy at disequilibrium. The shortcoming is in part a result of assumptions imposed by BG. Perhaps the most damaging assumptions are the perishable nature of all goods and the absence of inventory stocks. Although it may have been necessary to make these assumptions in order to achieve some kind of understanding of the movement of the economy at disequilibrium, they do fail to capture the importance which Keynes attributed to labor and to inventory holdings. Inventory behavior is an important difference between the labor market and the commodity market. When firms are stuck with inadequate demand, their inventories accumulate, and this accumulation implies that they may save these inventories for future demand. This result suggests that firms may reduce labor demand not only because there is inadequate demand currently, but because they are accumulating inventories which they may sell off later. Laborers, however, cannot store inventories of labor services when demand for their services is inadequate. A labor service not sold in one period may never be sold again. Because some commodities are storable and others are not, we must consider the possibility that economic agents utilize inventories of some goods as buffers against fluctuations in demand. However, the extent to which buffers can be constructed depends in part upon the technological characteristics of commodities. Does the presence of inventories, then, suggest that the macro-economy can insulate itself against these kinds of shocks, or does it suggest that, with various goods having various degrees of storability, the very structure of activity at disequilibrium is far more complex than that suggested by Barro and Grossman?

A second set of questions deals with the assumption by BG that, when economic agents' plans do not correspond to the same transactions level, the short side of the market—that is, the inadequate commodity demand or the inadequate labor demand—dominates the decision of what will actually be trans-acted. In order for BG to illustrate multiplier-type behavior, they find it neces-sary to assume that after an initial shock, economic agents refrain from actual exchange until they reach a new quasi-equilibrium. Over this time period, wages are rigid, no inventories are accumulated, and economic agents wait until they reach the new quasi-equilibrium. However, this assumption is very similar to the original Walrasian assumption in which recontracting is allowed until a true equilibrium set of prices is reached. Again, the actual processes undertaken in an economy in disequilibrium may be much more complicated than the BG analysis suggests, because both some quantity adjustments and some price adjustments occur simultaneously. Economists at this point are uncertain about which of these assumptions is most crucial and about how they should be modified to derive a richer understanding of the processes of economic movement at disequilibrium. We complete this discussion by simply pointing out that these attempts at enriching the foundations of Keynesian economics have led to some interesting ideas about how economic agents may behave while at disequilibrium. Nevertheless, we also note that we have failed as yet to capture the essence of the workings of such an economy. Although it may seem disappointing to conclude our analysis at such an uncertain point, we at least can appreciate the complexity of attempting to analyze an economy once one abandons the artificial assumption that economic plans are always satisfied and that markets function only when they have cleared.

STUDY QUESTIONS

1. List three different explanations for the labor market's failure to work in the classical sense. What does each imply for the labor market model? (That is, how can each explanation be illustrated with a labor supply and demand diagram?)

2. The unemployment rate is high. What is likely to happen if the wage rate is lowered in a model in which (a) the unemployment was caused by a general deflation with wages slow to fall and (b) the unemployment was caused by layoffs due to inadequate financial capital on the part of firms?

3. How does the relation between labor and commodity markets differ under (a) the dual decision hypothesis and (b) the Walrasian general equilibrium model. (*Hint:* You may wish to re-read the Chapter 4 discussion of the Walrasian model and the Chapter 9 discussion of the dual decision hypothesis.)

4. Compare and contrast the ideas of the following economists with respect to the workings of the labor and commodity markets:

    a) Clower   d) Barro-Grossman
    b) Patinkin   e) Walras
    c) Feldstein   f) Keynes

(*Hint:* Review Chapters 4 [Walras and Keynes], 9 [Clower], and 3 and 25 [Feldstein]).

5. Discuss the ideas of Keynes and post-Keynesians with respect to the workings of the macroeconomy.

REFERENCES

Barro, Robert and Herschel Grossman, *Money, Employment and Inflation.* London: Cambridge University Press, 1976.

Clower, Robert W., "The Keynesian Counter Revolution: A Theoretical Appraisal," in F. H. Hahn and F. P. R. Brechling (eds.), *The Theory of Interest Rates.* London: Macmillan & Co., 1965.

Grossman, Herschel, "Aggregate Demand, Job Search and Employment," *Journal of Political Economy*, Vol. 81, No. 6 November/December 1973, pp. 1353-1369.

Patinkin, Don, *Money, Interest and Prices*, 2nd ed. New York: Harper and Row, 1965.

Phelps, Edmund, et al., *Microeconomic Foundations of Employment and Inflation Theory*. New York: W. W. Norton, 1970.

INFLATION FROM PHILLIPS TO RATIONAL EXPECTATIONS

part VIII

Inflation, public enemy number 1, seems to be the curse of modern industrial market economies. The liberal administrations of Lyndon Johnson and Jimmy Carter and the conservative administrations of Richard Nixon and Gerald Ford were unable to stop it. From 1965 to 1980 inflation gradually accelerated from 3-4 percent to 10-15 percent. Why?

Inflation, a continuing tendency for prices to rise, is the central subject of this section. In Chapter 21 we begin to analyze the causes of inflation. First, we build a simple model of price and wage increases, and then we discuss the linkage between this wage-price model and our comparative static models of aggregate demand and supply. This framework allows us to examine the causes of inflation analytically. We then turn to a careful study of inflation in the extreme—using the hyperinflation studies of Phillip Cagan. We see that hyperinflation is a pure monetary phenomenon which receives its impetus from money expansion by the central monetary authority.

In Chapter 22 we develop models of the price and wage process integrating expectations of the type used by Cagan. Expectations appear to be the mechanism through which inflation is transmitted throughout the economy. The idea of expectations based upon knowledge of economic structure is next developed. This idea, developed by Robert Lucas of Chicago has greatly advanced our understanding of the inflation process. It suggests that a more sensitive analysis of macroeconomic policy is necessary.

How bad is inflation? What are its costs? Who suffers the most? We analyze the consequences of inflation in Chapter 22, first, under the assumptions that inflation is anticipated, and second, when it is a surprise. Full discussion of anti-inflation policy waits until Chapter 25, but we outline some approaches to the problem at the end of Chapter 22.

The council of Economic Advisers to the President of the United States wrote in 1973: "By the end of 1972 the American anti-inflation policy had become the marvel of the rest of the world." Six months later, prices were rising in the United States at an annual rate of over 25 percent. As this unfortunate experience indicates, our inability to control inflation has been a perplexing problem of modern domestic political economy. Furthermore, it is not simply a political problem. Understanding the causes of inflation and the processes through which it influences the economy has been the central problem confronting modern economic theory. Inflation is to economics what cancer is to medicine. Economists devote considerable energy to studying inflation, and they have produced numerous explanations based upon a variety of complex and elaborate theories. Over the decade of the 1970s, no topic in economics received as much research attention as inflation. A wide variety of policy prescriptions

21

Inflation I:
A Theoretical Appraisal
of its Causes

were recommended, including stringent monetary contraction, presidential jaw-boning, voluntary wage-price guidelines, wage and price controls, tax-based incomes policies, and wage insurance programs. Each of these policy prescriptions when based on some economic model appears to be sound and effective. The surgery always seems to come off without a hitch. But, alas, the patient invariably fails to heal!

Why are economists unable to deal adequately with inflation? What is inflation? What are its causes? What are the consequences of inflation? What policy remedies are likely to rid the economy of inflation? We shall address these questions in the next two chapters.

This chapter is devoted primarily to a theoretical analysis of the causes of inflation. To develop an understanding of inflation, we employ two tactics. First, in Section A of this chapter we will examine the implications for inflation of the theoretical models we developed earlier. Our theoretical analysis will provide us with considerable insight into the causes of inflation. Within this part of this chapter, we will first examine the basis for inflation and will then attempt to elaborate on our theoretical structure in order to better understand the processes of inflation. As a result of this analysis, we will be able to draw several important conclusions about the general nature of inflation. Although these conclusions will not answer all the questions we have, they will help us debunk a number of myths.

The tactic utilized in Section B is to study special historical episodes in which inflation was the dominant characteristic of the economy. We shall examine Philip Cagan's theoretical analysis of seven European war and interwar period hyperinflations. Cagan's study of these periods with their astronomical inflation rates provides us with more insights into the nature of the inflation process and its underlying causes.

A ● What Do Our Macro Models Imply for Inflation?

Most of our attention in this book so far has been devoted to comparative static models of aggregate economic behavior. A comparative static model, it will be recalled, is one in which we first derive a set of equilibrium conditions; second, we consider exogenous changes in the economy which will produce a new equilibrium, and third, we compare the different equilibrium points. Starting back in Chapter 5, continuing through Chapters 12 through 14 and culminating in Chapters 18 through 20, we developed two comparative static models. Figure 1 illustrates these two models. Figure 1(a) depicts the neoclassical model, in which the rate of wage adjustment is assumed to be the same as the rate of price adjustment so that the economy comes to equilibrium at a natural rate of employment and a natural rate of output. Recall that this natural rate of output and employment is determined by the particular structural characteristics of the real sector of the economy and need not be what Keynesians mean by full employment (nonzero unemployment according to national statistics).

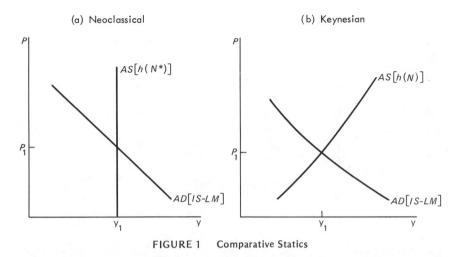

FIGURE 1   Comparative Statics

Figure 1(b) contains the modern Keynesian version of the macroeconomy in which the aggregate supply schedule is not perfectly inelastic because the rate of wage adjustment is assumed to be slower than the rate of price adjustment, so that the economy does not have a natural rate of production nor a natural rate of unemployment. Both models are depicted as being in equilibrium at output level y_1 and price level P_1.

We also presented briefly in the text two different models that compare the rate of change of the price level to the rate of unemployment. Figure 2(a) contains the natural rate hypothesis, and Figure 2(b) contains the traditional Phillips curve. Notice that the neoclassical comparative static model and the natural rate hypothesis are both depicted in Figure 1(a) and 2(a), respectively, while the Keynesian comparative static model and the Phillips curve are depicted in Figures 1(b) and 2(b). The modern battleground between Keynesians and monetarist economists has shifted from the comparative static models to the relation between the rate of price change and the rate of unemployment. In addition to drawing a vertical line representing the long-run natural unemployment rate in Figure 2(a), we have drawn several short-run sloped Phillips curves. The reason for this is that many monetarists believe that in the short run, pairs of unemployment and inflation may be represented by a Phillips curve. They argue, however, that these are not points of dynamic equilibrium but are only temporary points of disequilibrium, and that the economy will always revert to the natural rate of unemployment on the long-run vertical line. We have also drawn relatively flat short-run curves in Figure 2(b) as well as a steeper long-run Phillips curve. Keynesians also believe that in the short run the trade-off between the inflation rate and the unemployment rate is greater than it is in the long run, but that nevertheless a long-run tradeoff exists.

It may seem that economists should be able to reconcile relatively easily these two positions. After all, they do not appear to be that far apart. However, the

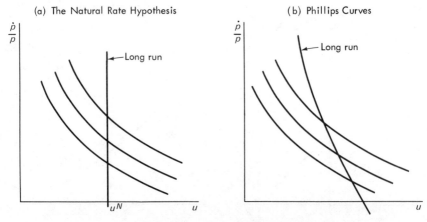

FIGURE 2   Dynamic Models

underlying analysis of inflation and unemployment is much more complex than is suggested by Figures 1 and 2. Figure 3 compares actual experience in the United Kingdom over the early post WWII years with a Phillips curve fitted to data running over the longer period from 1861 to 1913. This curve is the original work of Phillips, after whom the curve was named. Phillips curve evidence is represented for the U.S. in Figure 3(b). The U.S. figures run from 1950 through 1978. Visual inspection of the Phillips diagram for the U.S. should convince most readers that the relationship between the rate of increase in wages and the rate of unemployment is more complex than can be depicted by a simple Phillips diagram.

Let us pause at this point and consider the number of problems we have to resolve. First, we need to carefully specify what we mean by inflation. Second, we need to link the comparative static models of Figure 1 to their dynamic counterparts in Figure 2. Third, we need to use our models to explore the implications for the causes of inflation. Fourth, we need to examine historically the evidence on the causes and processes of inflation.

First, we define the rate of inflation. The term *inflation* is used very carelessly in the press, and we shall try to be more precise. The rate of inflation is the average rate at which some general index of the prices of a wide range of commodities is rising over a reasonably long period of time. While this definition is admittedly somewhat vague and rather general, it does rule out several important situations. Suppose, for example, that an economy is hit with a sudden, one-time shock, such as a severe winter blizzard which reduces supply and production for a month; then if the result is a large, one-time increase in prices, we would not consider this to be inflation, because inflation is a *persistent* tendency for prices to rise. As a second example, suppose the prices for a small group of commodities are rising over time. We would not consider this to be inflation, either. Specifically, suppose impending shortages of oil imply that the prices of petrochemical

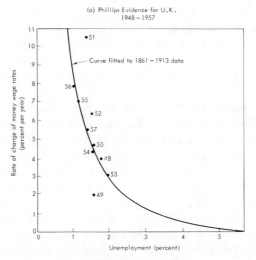

(a) Phillips Evidence for U.K.
1948 – 1957

Source: A. W. Phillips (1958).

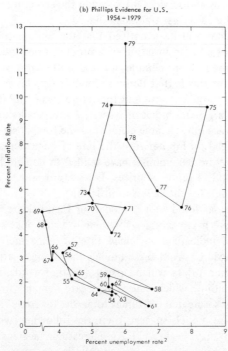

(b) Phillips Evidence for U.S.
1954 – 1979

Source: U.S. Department of Commerce and U.S. Department of Labor
1 Percentage Change in the GNP Implicit Price Deflator.
2 Percent of Civilian Labor Force.
Latest date allotted: 1977

FIGURE 3   Actual Inflation-unemployment Pairs for U.K. and U.S. in Select Years

products, relative to other prices, will be rising steadily over several years. One would probably not consider this to be an inflationary episode, because it represents an increase in only one set of prices relative to those of other goods, and, therefore, a change in the price structure rather than the price level. For inflation to take place, prices of a very broad range of products must be rising over a long period of time.

As a practical matter, therefore, we usually select some index of the prices of a large bundle of goods to represent the price level. For example, in the United States a commonly used index of inflation is the Consumer Price Index (CPI). This index, as will be recalled from our discussion of indices in Chapter 3, measures the average price of goods consumed by the typical consumer as defined by the Bureau of Labor Statistics. However, at other times we may be concerned not with the CPI but with some index of prices paid by producers, such as the Producer Price Index (PPI) in the U.S. Perhaps the best general indicator of the inflation rate for an economy would be an index of a broader range of products. The index used in the National Income Accounts to deflate gross national product, called the GNP deflator, is just such an index. Since GNP contains all final goods and services produced in the economy in a year, an index to deflate it would be a very general index indeed.

The cautious reader will have noticed that the Phillips relation depicted in Figure 3(a) does not contain inflation of a product price index on the vertical axis at all. Rather, the rate of unemployment is plotted against a rate of wage increase. The reason for this is that Phillips himself began his analysis with a comparison of the unemployment rate and the rate of wage inflation. (That is, the rate of increase of a general index of wages.) As we shall show more carefully later, because the wage bill is a large element of the total costs of most products, we expect a close relationship between the rate of wage increase and the rate of price increase. Therefore, economists have tended to depict Phillips curves both in terms of wages and in terms of prices. Let us turn now to examining the implication of our models for the causes of inflation.

The aggregate demand and supply models of Figure 1 are comparative static models, and therefore it is necessary for them to reach price stability at equilibrium. They cannot indicate a sustained rate of price increase—an inflation. Nevertheless, it is evident from these models that if aggregate demand exceeds aggregate supply, then prices will be rising. In other words, if some change or shock hits the economy which causes aggregate demand to exceed aggregate supply, and the gap so created continues to persist for some time, then inflation will take place. These models suggest, then, the following two possible ways in which an inflation may begin: (1) An increase in aggregate demand above the current level of production creates an inflationary gap, and prices begin to rise. (2) An inflationary gap is created by a reduction in aggregate supply. If the aggregate supply curve shifts to the left, then the equilibrium price level will be above the original level, and prices will begin to rise. Reductions in supply produce not only an increase in the equilibrium price but also a decrease in equilibrium output. In fact, in both the neoclassical and Keynesian models, if the supply curve shifts to the left, then the equilibrium output level will fall as the price level rises. In other words, a reduction in aggregate supply implies an increase in the equilibrium price and a reduction in output. This observation suggests that an inflation-recession, such as that experienced by the U.S. economy in 1974-75, can be initiated by a downward supply shock. Such experiences, inflation accompanied by recession, are, however, historically uncommon. Of course, if aggregate demand rises faster than aggregate supply, then prices will be rising even though aggregate supply is increasing.

History of business cycles in capitalist economies reveals that inflations are typically experienced in boom periods. That is, when economies are growing rapidly and expanding toward their productive capacities, inflation begins to set in. The history of capitalism before the post-World War II period is, to some extent, one of economic fluctuations in which boom periods are accompanied by rising prices and slumps are accompanied by falling prices. For example, in the first three years of the Great Depression, from the end of 1929 to 1933, the U.S. price level fell by 50 percent as real production fell 25 percent.

A famous historical inflation episode was that suffered by the U.K. at the end of the eighteenth century under the leadership of Prime Minister Pitt. At that time, England was at war with Napoleon. (At the same time, England was engaged in a rather minor police action in the American colonies.) This war, like many others, was accompanied by a substantial inflation. Galbraith (1975) tells us, "Wheat, which was 6s., 9p. a bushel at Michaelmas in 1797 and at the same level a year later, went to above 11s. in 1799 and to 16s. the following year. Bread went up accordingly." The inflation continued throughout the next decade. A great debate over the cause of the inflation followed, and this debate makes the episode of interest to us today. As usual, inflation had been associated with expansion, and expansion had been associated with increases in the supply of hand to hand currency and coins. On one side of the debate was a famous British economist David Ricardo. Ricardo held the view that excessive expansion of currency by the Bank of England was the primary cause of the inflation. In other words, Ricardo argued the monetarist position, though he did not call it that. As was often to be the case later, while Ricardo's position won the theoretical debate, it was unacceptable to the political leadership of his country, and the Prime Minister, to finance his navy, continued to extract loans from the central bank, which resulted in further expansions in the money supply. It was not until 1821, when the war was over, that the expansions of currency by the central bank were stopped. The other side of the debate, supported by bankers, was that the endogenous force of economic change did not originate with the central bank but with internal economic expansion, which drew increases in the money supply along with it. This classic debate was continued right down to the modern day: The issue now is between monetarists and Keynesians: Does money cause inflation or does expansion cause money to expand? All we may conclude at this point is that, historically, rapidly rising aggregate demand has been associated with periods of inflation, and inadequate demand has been associated with recessions and with periods of deflation.

Unfortunately, since World War II, inflation has appeared to take on a somewhat different form in industrialized economies: Rather modest rates of inflation have taken place in the presence of historically large levels of domestic unemployment. This postwar phenomenon was first identified as *creeping inflation* in the 1950s and has since been referred to as *stagflation*—because the economy is relatively stagnant while inflation is taking place. It is this evident change in the characteristic of inflation that has caused the modern disagreements between monetarists and Keynesians about the importance of the structure of the economy as a causal mechanism in inflation. In order to assess this issue, it is necessary to establish a conceptual link between the comparative static theoretical frameworks developed earlier and depicted in Figure 1 to the dynamic frameworks depicted in Figure 2. In Figure 4 we illustrate the Keynesian comparative static model and the Keynesian Phillips curve. After establishing a linkage between these two models, we will be able to draw some tentative but important conclusions about the inflation process.

Figure 4 depicts the Keynesian models in equilibrium at initial price level P_1, output level y^*, employment level N^*, and unemployment level U^* at point A. To begin linking the comparative static to the dynamic model, we may ask under what conditions will the inflation rate depicted by $\dot{p}$ be equal to zero? In order to answer this question, we need a story that will relate the inflation rate to the economy; this story must begin with an equation describing how pricing policies are established. The simplest pricing policy we might begin with would be one in which price per unit of output is set as a constant markup factor over cost per unit of output. However, we shall be even simpler than that by assuming

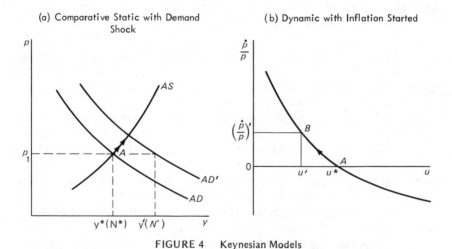

(a) Comparative Static with Demand Shock

(b) Dynamic with Inflation Started

FIGURE 4   Keynesian Models

that prices are marked up simply over the labor cost per unit of output. We represent unit labor costs by *ULC*. In symbols,

$$p = m(ULC) \tag{1}$$

where m is the markup factor over unit labor cost. Unit labor cost may be described in the following equation:

$$ULC = WN/y \tag{2}$$

Equation (2) simply states that labor cost per unit of output is calculated by dividing the wage bill by the number of units of output sold. From this expression, by dividing the numerator and denominator on the right-hand side of equation (2) by N, the number of units of labor, we see that unit labor costs are equal to the ratio of the wage rate to the level of output per laborer:

$$ULC = W/(y/N) \tag{3}$$

If producers change their prices in percentage terms by the same rate at which unit labor costs are changing, then, if we let an overdot represent a percentage change, we have

$$\dot{p} = m[\dot{W} - \dot{y/N}] \tag{4}$$

The last expression in equation (4), $(\dot{y/N})$, stands for the percentage rate of change of output per man-hour, or the percentage rate of change in average *labor productivity*. Equation (4), then, simply states that the rate of price increase will equal the markup factor times the rate at which wage increases exceed the rate of productivity change. In other words, if wage increases are just enough to offset productivity increases, then the rate of price increase will be zero. We shall use the symbol $\dot{\eta}$ to represent the percentage rate of change of labor productivity; then we may write equation (4) as

$$\dot{p} = m(\dot{W} - \dot{\eta}) \tag{5}$$

Equation (5) is our first version of the price equation, and it forms one of the central equations in linking the dynamic Phillips curve to the comparative static Keynesian model. Equation (5) also links the wage Phillips curve Figure 3(a) to the price curve in Figure 3(b). While this price equation is based on a very simple idea of markup policies on the part of producers, it can be derived from more complex policies of price behavior, including competitive models of production.

We now need to develop a relationship between the rate of inflation, or the rate of price increase, and conditions in the labor market which produce the rate of unemployment. This connection is established with a wage equation. The theory behind the wage equation was developed by Richard Lipsey (1960). Lipsey and other economists reasoned in the 1960s that, because wages and prices were rising even though the economy was not at full employment, the rate of money wage increase would depend upon the difference between the demand for labor and the supply. We may depict Lipsey's hypothesis as follows:

$$\dot{W} = [(N^d - N^s)/N] \tag{6}$$

In other words, wage adjustments are proportional to the percentage of excess demand in the labor market. Ignoring job vacancies, the rate of wage increase is inversely related to the rate of unemployment. Thus, we may compress equation (6) above as follows:[1]

$$\dot{W} \doteq f[-U/N] = f(-u) \doteq f(1/u) \tag{7}$$

or

$$\dot{W} = b_0 + b_1(1/u) \tag{8}$$

where b_0 and b_1 are positive algebraic constants and where equation (8) simply states that the rate of wage increase is inversely related to the rate of unemployment.

We now combine the wage equation represented in equation (8) and the price equation depicted in equation (5). First, however, we should note that in more complex theories of pricing behavior the markup coefficient over wage increases may not be the same as the coefficient for productivity increases, so we rewrite equation (5) as

$$\dot{p} = a_0 + a_1\dot{W} - a_2\dot{\eta} \tag{5'}$$

where a_0, a_1, and a_2 are positive algebraic constants. We now substitute the wage equation (8) for the term $\dot{W}$ into price equation (5') to derive the following expression:

$$\dot{p} = a_0 + a_1b_0 + a_1b_1(1/u) - a_2\dot{\eta} \tag{9}$$

Equation (9) simply states that the rate of inflation will be equal to the difference between the rate of wage increase as a result of the degree of tightness in the labor market and the rate at which prices may be held down by percentage increases in labor productivity. We can now conclude from equation (9) that the equilibrium position at which $\dot{p} = 0$ depicted in the Figure 4(b) model as point A comes about when the rate of wage increase is just sufficient to offset the rate of productivity increase so that the rate of inflation can be zero. In other words,

[1] It will be seen to be convenient to replace $-U/N$ with $1/u$, where $u = U/N$.

when wage increases are just sufficient to offset productivity increases, they do not lead to price increases. Let us now examine how this model works when the economy of Figure 4 starts at A and is hit with a shock creating an inflationary gap.

Figure 4(a) depicts a rightward shift in the aggregate demand curve which drives the economy away from equilibrium. An increase in demand over supply will produce a depletion of inventories and therefore an increase in inventory demands. Production will rise and unemployment will fall. As u falls, $\dot{p}$ rises as in equation (9). As prices rise, they drive the real wage rate down. The reduction in real wages tightens the labor market by reducing the level of unemployment. This results in a movement up the aggregate supply curve, as depicted by the arrows in Figure 4(a). However, with the Lipsey hypothesis, we now see that the rate of wage increase will rise because the labor market has tightened. Initially the rate of wage increase was just sufficient to offset the rate of productivity increase so that $\dot{p}$ was zero.[2] Since unemployment has now fallen below the original rate, say from u^* to u', the rate of wage increase will now be more rapid than it was before. This result is represented by the following expressions:

$$u' < u^* \Rightarrow (W)' = b_0 + b_1\left(\frac{1}{u'}\right) > (W)^* \tag{10}$$

Given a lower rate of unemployment, equation (9) indicates that the rate of price increase will now be greater than it was originally. Figure 4(b) depicts the movement of the economy from its original equilibrium point of price stability and unemployment at level u^* to a lower unemployment level u' and a higher rate of inflation $(\dot{p}/p)'$. The economy has moved from point A in Figure 4(b) on the Phillips curve up to point B.

Now as prices rise and wages rise, the important question we must ask is will the economy stay at point B or will it return to unemployment rate u^* and price stability, $\dot{p} = 0$? Put another way, as the economy moves toward a higher price level, will the demand pressures fall off and thus eliminate the inflationary gap? To some extent, the answer to this question depends upon whether we are dealing with a neoclassical or a Keynesian model. The neoclassical model has a vertical aggregate supply curve so that the new equilibrium position in the comparative static model must return the economy to the original level of employment N^* and therefore to the original unemployment level u^* unless authorities accept a still higher rate of inflation. Furthermore, the economy returns to price stability, but if the aggregate demand curve remains shifted upward, the new price stability will be at a higher price level.

The Keynesian model is different with respect to the results in the labor market. Because the aggregate supply curve is not vertical, the economy moves

[2]Even though, with the comparative static model of the labor market in Figure 5, we illustrate the initial conditions as having a constant wage rate and a constant marginal product of labor, the dynamic model is in terms of the value of marginal product of labor rising with productivity at the same rate at which wages are rising.

permanently (or at least for a long time) to a lower level of unemployment and a higher level of employment. However, the economy, which was exacerbated by the aggregate demand increase, will achieve a new point of rest at which prices will stabilize above the original level unless the gap between aggregate demand and aggregate supply persists. Both of these models imply a very important conclusion about the inflation process: Regardless of how the original shock takes place, if an excess demand generates an inflation, the increase in prices will automatically begin to choke off the excess demand. Recall that this choking-off of excess demand as a result of inflation takes place because the real purchasing power of money M/P is automatically decreased as prices rise. This contraction of the real money supply will then always choke off inflationary pressures unless the inflationary gap is maintained and accommodated by money supply increases that offset the compressing effects of the price level increases.

The model we have developed above is incomplete in several respects. Most important, we have made no allowance for how the behavior of economic agents may change when prices begin to rise for long periods of time. Nevertheless, the analysis above allows us to draw several somewhat tentative but extremely important conclusions:

1. If aggregate demand rises faster than aggregate supply, then prices will rise.
2. Increases in aggregate demand can be initiated in several ways:
   a. increases in the money supply
   b. increases in government deficit spending, which can be brought about by increases in government spending financed by borrowing from the public or from the central bank, or by reductions in the rate of taxation at the existing level of government expenditures, or by some combination of these fiscal measures (an inflationary gap can be caused by government deficits only in a model in which the LM curve is not vertical)
   c. increases in aggregate demand from the private sector, which can take the form of investment booms or increases in private consumption
3. Reductions in aggregate supply or slowdowns in its rate of expansion can be brought about in several ways as well: Depressive supply shocks could come from outside the economy if certain critical products such as oil become suddenly less available to the production process. In this situation, we might represent that shock by a downward shift in the level of output associated with each employment level according to the production function. This downward shift would correspond to a leftward shift in the aggregate supply schedule. A change in the structure of the labor market (if it caused the marginal product of labor schedule to shift to the left) would also generate a leftward shift in the aggregate supply schedule.
4. Regardless of how it is initiated, an inflationary gap will be choked off by the inflation itself via the reduction in the real money supply unless the nominal money supply is expanded in order to accommodate the inflationary gap.

We end this section with a fifth point, which is not a result but a major question we have yet to resolve: Namely, can the economic structure impinge upon the ability of the economy to close the inflationary gap? In other words, is it possible that its structure makes the economy susceptible to inflationary pressures when it is hit with certain exogenous shocks?

We turn now to an analysis of several episodes of economic history in which the dominant feature characterizing the economy was inflation.

B ● An Analysis of Hyperinflation

Perhaps the most famous study of hyperinflations appeared in the late 1950s in a collection of essays about the modern quantity theory of money. Phillip Cagan studied the hyperinflations of Europe following World Wars I and II. He thought that we could learn a great deal about the inflationary process if we studied it in the extreme cases. Furthermore, since the inflations he was studying were accompanied by rather small changes in real output, he reasoned that we could study these inflationary episodes without regard to the nagging debate between the monetarists and Keynesians over the extent to which monetary phenomenen may be dichotomized from the real sector. In other words, there was little action in the real sector, so one could essentially analyze this hyperinflation as if a pure monetarist model applied. In each of the episodes Cagan studied, seven European hyperinflations altogether, he observed one prevalent characteristic: "The astronomical increases in prices and money dwarf the changes in real income and other real factors."

Table 1 contains some select monetary statistics of the seven hyperinflations studied by Cagan. From row 1 we can see that these inflation periods tended to last for about a year, although the Russian inflation lasted twice that long. The monthly average rate of price increases ranged from a low of 46% in the Hungarian revolution of the 1920s to 19,800% in Hungary at the end of World War II. The corresponding percentage increases in the volume of hand-to-hand currency in circulation averaged from 30.9% in Austria up to 12,200% in Hungary. A prevalent characteristic of all of these hyperinflations is the ratio of M to P, which we shall depict as m, the real money supply. The value of m had a tendency to decline over the period. That is, M increased less than P, as seen in row 4.

Cagan sets out to explain why m tends to decline during hyperinflations. The reason Cagan focuses on this question is that it is a widely held view that hyperinflations become self-perpetuating. A self-perpetuating inflation is one which in driven by the desire on the part of the private sector to flee from money at such a pace that the rate at which money changes hands becomes so astronomical as to generate a rapid increase in prices, which exceeds the increase in the quantity of money and drives the inflation independently. The alternative point of view is that the inflation which results from the monetary expansion does not become a self-perpetuating process. Rather, inflation continues, even throughout these extreme cases, to depend upon the rate of monetary expansion. Essentially, then, Cagan is addressing the question: Is a hyperinflation self perpetuating, or is it caused by the rate of monetary expansion?

Table 1
Select Monetary Characteristics of Seven Hyperinflations

	AUSTRIA	GERMANY	GREECE	HUNGARY	HUNGARY	POLAND	RUSSIA
(1) Rough period of Hyperinflation	10/1921-8/1922	8/1922-11/1923	10/1943-11/1944	3/1923-2/1924	8/1945-7/1946	1/1922-1/1923	12/1921-1/1924
(2) Average monthly percentage price rise ($\dot{p}/p$)	47.1	322.0	365.0	46.0	19,800	81.4	57.0
(3) Average monthly percentage rise in currency ($\dot{M}/M$)	30.9	314.0	220.0	32.7	12,200	72.2	49.3
(4) (2) ÷ (3)1/($\dot{m}/m$)	1.52	1.03	1.66	1.41	1.62	1.13	1.16

We shall analyze Cagan's theory in terms of our theoretical framework for monetary analysis. We may represent the money market with the following three equations:

$$M^s = M_0 \tag{11}$$

$$M^d = PL(y, W, R, \text{etc.}) \tag{12}$$

$$M^s = M^d \tag{13}$$

Equation (11) states that the nominal money supply M^s is exogenous. In other words, it is assumed that the central monetary authority controls the volume of hand-to-hand currency that it places in circulation M but does not control the price level P. Equation (12) states that the nominal demand for money is equal to the product of the price level and the liquidity preference function L, which, it will be recalled, is the demand for real cash balance. The L function depends upon a set of variables which would include y, output; W, wealth; R, rate of interest, and any other variables which may influence the demand for money schedule. Equation (13) states that in equilibrium the nominal supply of money must be equal to the nominal demand for money. (Recall Chapter 14 on money demand.) It is straightforward to show that the real supply of money is equal to the demand for real cash balances:

$$M_0/P = m = L(y, W, R, \text{etc.}) \tag{14}$$

We may now express [with the use of equation (14)] Cagan's central question in different form. Reductions in the volume of real cash balances m, which occur when M is rising, can come about either if there is a structural shift in the real liquidity preference schedule $L(\cdot)$ or if there is a change in a variable that appears in the liquidity preference function, both of which imply an increase in P. If the real demand for money falls dramatically as a result of a structural shift in liquidity preference function, then we may say that there has been a general flight from money, that the rate of inflation is being induced by the demand side of the money market, and that inflation has, therefore, become a self-perpetuating process. If, on the other hand, the reduction in the demand for real cash balances results from a change in a variable that appears in the demand schedule, rather than from a change in people's underlying preferences for cash, and if we can show that the change in this variable has resulted from changes in the nominal supply of money, then it is reasonable to conclude that the inflation is not a self-perpetuating process but one that is driven by the supply side of the market, implying that it is driven by the monetary authorities.

Cagan's central thesis is that a key variable in the demand for money function caused a reduction in demand for real cash balances. That variable is the *expected rate of inflation.* Cagan argues that as expansions of the money supply became rampant, and the currency's value depreciated, people developed expectations of inflation which reduced their demand for real cash balances. Had the rate of monetary expansion been slowed down, then the rate of anticipated inflation would have declined and the demand for money would have begun to rise once again, indicating that no change in tastes and no general flight from cash had occurred. He says that a reduction in the demand for money takes place as long as money is expected to continue to depreciate in value.

Cagan finds that, when he estimates the demand for real cash balance function over these hyperinflation periods, the past changes in the rate of inflation operating through the expected inflation term dominate variations in the demand for money schedule. In his words,

> For the periods of hyperinflation covered the results indicate that an exponentially weighted average of past rates of change in prices adequately accounts for movements in real cash balances.

Thus, Cagan provides evidence to support his contention that the most active changing variable in the money demand expression is the expected rate of inflation. He then goes on to provide evidence that the inflation was not a self-perpetuating process. Again, in Cagan's words: "In view of the actual price rises that occurred therefore, none of the hyperinflations appears to have been self-generating." To state this conclusion in yet another way, if the combined effects of inflation on inflationary expectations and of these expectations on the demand for money were greater than one in percentage terms, then a hyperinflation would be an explosive self-perpetuating process. However, in the episodes studied this was not the case at all. Therefore, in Cagan's view inflation could have been stopped if the rate of monetary expansion had been brought down.

Cagan concluded that the central cause for hyperinflations in each of the episodes he studied was expansion of the money supply by the monetary authority. This conclusion, of course, raises the question of why a monetary authority (such as a central bank) would generate and perpetuate a hyperinflation. Cagan argues that the expansions of the money supply were used to finance government deficits. He goes on to explain why in these situations governments found it necessary to finance their deficits by monetary expansions. In each case, it seems that the government was unable to collect sufficient taxes or to borrow sufficient funds from the private sector in order to support its level of spending. The governments then financed their expenditures by printing money and producing rapid inflation. Inflation then drove down the purchasing power of cash balances held in the hands of the public. Consequently, Cagan views this method of government finance as an implicit tax imposed on the holdings of cash balances. As the money supply is increased and the value of money begins to depreciate through inflation, individuals rationally reduce their holdings of money, and the rate of inflation begins to exceed the rate of monetary expansion. As a result, the value of real cash balances begins to decline as wealth is, in effect, extracted from cash balance holders in order to finance the government's activity. However, as the value of currency is depreciated, it becomes necessary for the government to issue even more money each period in order to finance its same level of real government expenditures. (The government's tax base is essentially declining.) Thus the government finds itself on a treadmill in which it must accelerate its rate of monetary expansion in order to maintain its level of revenue collection.

We may now draw several important conclusions from Cagan's analysis.

1. Hyperinflations are caused by monetary expansion.
2. The hyperinflations studied were not self-perpetuating processes but depended upon the continued expansion of currency.
3. The money supply was expanded as a means of financing government deficits when the governments were either unable or unwilling to finance their expenditures by taxation or direct borrowing.
4. Because printing money depreciated the currency, the rate of monetary expansion had to continually accelerate in order for the bank to collect the same revenue.

Similar studies of hyperinflations in Latin America and elsewhere have tended to support the main thrusts of Cagan's analysis. We must, however, be cautious in extrapolating these conclusions to more modest periods of inflation. Episodes in which real variables as well as monetary variables are changing are analytically much more complex than pure hyperinflations.

STUDY QUESTIONS

1. Define inflation and explain intuitively why it is ordinary pro-cyclical.

2. How did the inflation-unemployment experience of the 1970s differ from that of the 1950s and early 1960s?

3. Illustrate, with aggregate demand and supply curve and with a wage-price model (geometric), an economy at equilibrium (with price stability). Show, using your model, the consequence of a once-and-for-all increase in the money supply.

4. What causes hyperinflation, according to Cagan? How can hyperinflation be stopped?

5. Summarize our analytic knowledge of the causes of inflation. Write a brief essay about some historical episode of inflation explaining what you believe to be the primary cause. How would you have dealt with it?

6. Starting at equilibrium in an aggregate supply and demand model, trace the response of an economy to a leftward shift (drop) in aggregate supply (say, due to a slowdown in labor productivity). (Use wage and price equations to illustrate the process.)

7.   a) Using an AD-AS model, trace the response of the economy to a reduction

in the average product of labor. (*Hint:* Treat the average product reduction as a downward shift in the total product curve.)

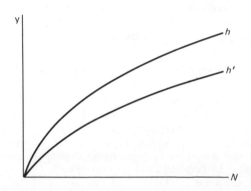

b) Use wage and price equations to illustrate the process by which wages and prices respond to the exogenous shock.

c) How would a decrease in the money supply affect the outcome of the response to the shock in part a: (1) If wages and prices are perfectly flexible? (2) If wages are rigid downward?

8. Suppose firms set prices by a mark-up policy in which price is a fixed proportion mark-up over unit-labor-costs. Derive an equation for the rate of price change from this decision rule.

REFERENCES

Bailey, Martin J., "The Welfare Cost of Inflationary Finance," *Journal of Political Economy,* April 1956.

Barro, Robert J., "Inflationary Finance and the Welfare Cost of Inflation," *Journal of Political Economy,* September/October 1972.

Board of Governors of the Federal Reserve System and Social Science Research Council, *The Economics of Price Determination Conference,* October 30-31, 1970, Washington, D.C., June 1972.

Bosworth, Barry, "Phase II: The U.S. Experiment with an Incomes Policy," *Brookings Papers on Economic Activity,* No. 2, Washington, D.C., 1972.

Cagan, Phillip, "The Monetary Dynamics of Hyperinflation," in Milton Friedman (ed.), *Studies in the Quantity Theory of Money.* Chicago: University of Chicago Press, 1956.

Foster, Edward, *Costs and Benefits of Inflation.* Federal Reserve Bank of Minneapolis, March 1972.

Friedman, Milton, *The Optimum Quantity of Money and Other Essays.* Chicago: Aldine Press, 1969.

————, "The Role of Monetary Policy," *American Economic Review,* March 1968.

Galbraith, John Kenneth, *Money, Whence It Came and Whence It Went.* Boston: Houghton Mifflin Co., 1975.

Gibson, William, "Interest Rates and Monetary Policy," *Journal of Political Economy,* May/June 1970.

———and George Kaufman, *Monetary Economics: Readings on Current Issues.* New York: McGraw-Hill, 1971.

Hall, Robert E., "Prospects for Shifting the Phillips Curve through Manpower Policy," *Brookings Papers on Economic Activity,* No. 3, Washington, D.C., 1971.

Johnson, Harry G., *Further Essays in Monetary Economics.* Cambridge, Mass.: Harvard University Press, 1973.

Keynes, John Maynard, "Inflation (1919)," in *Essays in Persuasion.* New York: W. W. Norton, 1963.

Lipsey, Richard, "The Relation Between Unemployment and the Rate on Money Wage Rates in the United Kingdom, 1952-1957: A Further Analysis," *Economica,* February 1960.

Mundell, Robert, "Inflation and Real Interest," *Journal of Political Economy,* June 1963.

Phelps, Edmund S., et al., *Microeconomic Foundations of Employment and Inflation Theory.* New York: W. W. Norton, 1970.

Phillips, A. W., "The Relation Between Unemployment and the Rate of Change of Money Wages in the United Kingdom, 1861-1957," *Economica,* November 1958.

Samuelson, Paul A., and Robert M. Solow, "Analytical Aspects of Anti-Inflation Policy," *American Economic Review,* May 1960.

Sargent, Thomas, "The Fundamental Determinants of the Interest Rate: A Comment," *Review of Economics and Statistics,* August 1973.

Stein, Jerome, "Monetary Growth Theory in Perspective," *American Economic Review,* March 1970.

Tobin, James, "Inflation and Unemployment," *American Economic Review,* March 1972.

Weidenbaum, M., et al., "Symposium: The Future of U.S. Wage-Price Policy," *Review of Economics and Statistics,* August 1972.

The fact that nominal prices and wages tend to rise more rapidly at the peak of the business cycle than they do in the trough has been well recognized from the time when the cycle was first perceived as a distinct phenomenon. The inference that permanent inflation will therefore induce a permanent economic high is no doubt equally ancient, yet it is only recently that this notion has undergone the mysterious transformation from obvious fallacy to cornerstone of the theory of economic policy.

Robert Lucas in Brurmer and Meltzer (1976)

Even though we have learned a good deal about inflation, a number of important problems and questions still remain. Perhaps the most important is: To what extent is a modest inflation a nonmonetary phenomenon? In other words, how far can one take the lessons of Cagan's analysis of hyper-inflations? A second important question is: Can we improve upon the expectations analysis suggested by Cagan? Cagan's treatment of expectations as being simply adapted from past rates of inflation is rather simple. Perhaps the development of expectations is more sophisticated. Understanding this development should help us in understanding the inflation process. A third important question is closely related to the first one above: Upon what kinds of analytic issues does the debate over the natural rate hypothesis hinge? Monetarists argue that the economy has a natural rate of unemployment. Keynesians argue that the rate of unemployment will vary, depending upon the rate of inflation. Who is correct? Finally, we shall conclude this chapter with a study of the consequences of inflation and with a brief discussion of the policy remedies suggested for dealing with it.

22

Inflation II:
Wage-Price Dynamics
and Consequences

A ● Is inflation a purely monetary phenomenon?

To what extent is inflation a purely monetary phenomenon? While the main thrust of historical evidence indicates that inflation is associated with monetary expansion, the character of inflations in the modern industrialized economies since World War II has differed from previous experience. For example, the U.S. has experienced two types of inflation which suggest to many economists that inflation of the late 1950s, in which the inflation rate varied from 2 to 3.5 percent while the economy appeared to be stagnating with real growth at about 2-2½ percent suggested to many that inflation was *not* a result of excess aggregate demand created by monetary expansion. Second, the accelerating inflation experience of the 1970s, especially 1975-1979, took place in a period in which U.S. unemployment was high by historical standards (6 to 9 percent). This experience also implied that inflation has changed its character.

The Two Views: Despite these apparent differences in the character of inflation since World War II, monetarists argue that the central cause of inflation is, as always, monetary in nature. Specifically, they claim that the Federal Reserve Bank in the U.S. causes inflation by excessive expansion in the money supply. Monetarist economists, led by Carl Brunner and Alan Meltzer, have even formed a Shadow Open Market Committee to monitor the actions of the Federal Reserve System's Open Market Committee. Generally this monetarist group advocates less expansionary policy than that undertaken by the U.S. Federal Reserve. They argue that most economic slowdowns in the U.S. economy have resulted from sudden and unnecessarily abrupt monetary contractions. These contractions, the Shadow Open Market Committee economists argue, are so severe that they are followed by a return to overly expansionary policy as the FED overreacts and underwrites excessively expansionary policy in order to allow the government to continue to support deficit spending without driving interest rates up and crowding out private expenditures. In other words, the monetarist position is very similar to the Cagan description of the underlying causes of hyperinflation: M expansion is excessive in order to support government deficits. However, as pointed out by some monetarists, such as Laidler and Parkin (1975), the political analysis of why governments allow the rate of inflation to persist has not been sufficiently studied.

Nonmonetarists take the position that inflation in the postwar period is, to a great extent, a result of structural imperfections in the economic systems of industrialized economies. These "structuralists" argue that a number of characteristics of markets reduce the adaptability of the economy to exogenous shocks. They argue that the economy, so constrained, can absorb exogenous shocks only by responding with inflation. Examples of the types of structural causes of inflation which some nonmonetarists propose include

1. Concentration in labor and product markets: powerful trade unions which are able to resist reductions in the real wage and powerful oligopo-

lies which are able to administer price increases without regard to demand conditions.

2. Government regulation of particular industries, which works to support prices, for example, agricultural policies and regulation of the trucking industry.

3. Legal impediments that prevent downward flexibility of wages and prices, such as minimum wage laws and various agricultural price controls.

4. Various impediments that prevent or impinge upon changes in the structure of relative prices, such as escalator clauses in wage contracts and ceiling prices on oil products.

5. Pressure imposed by Congress upon the central bank which in effect constrains the latter from resisting inflationary pressures with contractionary monetary policy.

6. Government resistance to currency depreciation on international markets, which prevents the rapid domestic inflation from shifting high demand from the domestic to the foreign sector, and thus exporting some of the inflation.

7. The greater prevalence of government employment in which the workers' salaries are resistant to downward flexibility.

The structuralists argue that these various types of impediments to the workings of a capitalist economy cause it to be more susceptible to inflation than one in which these impediments do not exist. Furthermore, they argue that the industrialized economies of the postwar period have tended to worsen with respect to most if not all of these kinds of impediments.

Expectations and the Long-run Phillips Curve: Corresponding to the two points of view about the extent to which inflation is a monetary phenomenon and about the central cause of inflation in today's economies are the two dynamic models which we began to develop in Chapter 21. Our objective now is to elabo-

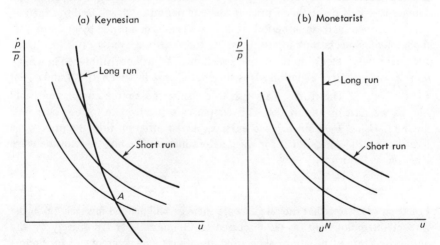

FIGURE 1   Inflation-Unemployment: Two Views

rate on these models in order to show how different conclusions about the causes of inflation are couched in different bodies of analysis. Figure 1 depicts the two central positions about the relationship between inflation and unemployment. Figure 1(a), depicting the Keynesian short- and long-run Phillips curves, corresponds to the structuralist position that inflation is influenced by the structure of the economy and that it is not, therefore, a purely monetary phenomenon. Figure 1(b), which contains the long-run vertical Phillips curve and the natural rate of unemployment hypothesis, corresponds to the monetarist position that the inflation process is a purely monetary phenomenon. To develop the algebraic models which correspond to these two dynamic positions, we begin by reproducing the price and wage equations from Chapter 21:

$$\dot{p} = a_0 + a_1 \dot{w} - a_2 \dot{\eta} \tag{1}$$

$$\dot{w} = b_0 + b_1 (1/u) \tag{2}$$

Recall that $\dot{p}$ and $\dot{w}$ refer to percentage changes. We saw from the Cagan analysis that an important element of the inflation process is the development of inflationary expectations. Our first task now is to integrate a very simple model of inflationary expectations into our price-wage equation framework. The simplest form of the *adaptive expectations* model has the current rate of expected inflation depend upon the realized rate of inflation in the previous period. In symbols:

$$\dot{p}_t^e = \dot{p}_{t-1} \tag{3}$$

Where $\dot{p}_t^e$ represents the expected rate of inflation for period t and is seen to depend upon the realized rate of inflation in period $t - 1$.

A somewhat more sophisticated version of an expectations model than equation (3) would be $\dot{p}_t^e = d\dot{p}_{t-1}$, where d is some constant term. Equation (3) assumes $d = 1$. If $d < 1$ then a price increase in period $t - 1$ will lead to expectations of a price increase in period t but one which is dampened by $d < 1$. $d > 1$ implies that expectations for future price increases are even greater than post price increases. Later a more complex version of $\dot{p}_t^e$ will be introduced in which $\dot{p}_t^e = \sum_{i=1}^{\infty} d_i \dot{p}_{t-i}$. Here equation (3) is the special case in which $d_1 = 1$ and $d_i = 0$ for $i = 2, \ldots$. The reader may wish to consider these more complex possibilities as we develop the model. This simple case is adequate for our purposes, however. Using equation (3), we enter expected inflation into the price wage model through equation (2) for wage determination. We now rewrite the wage equation as follows:

$$\dot{w}_t = b_0 + b_1 (1/u_t) + b_2 \dot{p}_t^e \tag{4}$$

Equation (4) states that the rate of wage increase will depend inversely upon the rate of unemployment, as we discussed in Chapter 21, and positively on the anticipated rate of inflation taken from equation (3). The argument in support of introducing expected inflation into the wage equation is the idea that wage negotiations are likely to be influenced by the rate at which people expect prices to rise in the future; i.e., unions and employers are concerned about real wages. Rewriting the price equation, we have

$$\dot{p}_t = a_0 + [a_1 \dot{w}_t - a_2 \dot{\eta}_t] \tag{5}$$

Our model now consists of three equations, (3), (4), and (5), which are the *price expectation equation*, the *wage equation*, and the *price equation*, respectively. The joint solution to these three equations is

$$\dot{p}_t = (a_0 + a_1 b_0) + a_1 b_1 \left(\frac{1}{u_t}\right) + a_1 b_2 \dot{p}_{t-1} - a_2 \dot{\eta}_t \tag{6}$$

In equation (6) we have simply substituted equation (3) for the price expectations term in the wage equation, and we have then substituted equation (4) for the rate of wage change into equation (5). Equation (6) illustrates that the rate of inflation in period t will depend upon three factors: first, the unemployment rate, which represents the balance of aggregate demand and supply as measured by the degree of tightness in the labor market; second, the last period's inflation rate, which represents the rate of anticipated inflation in the current period; third, the rate of productivity increase, which represents the extent to which improvements in product efficiency can offset the inflationary effects of wage increases.

We are now prepared to distinguish between short-run and long-run Phillips curves with the use of equation (6). Suppose that the rate of productivity change is constant. Given the rate of price increase in period $t - 1$, we can then rewrite equation (6) as follows:

$$\dot{p}_t = (a_0 + a_1 b_0) + [a_1 b_2 \dot{p}_{t-1} - a_2 \dot{\eta}_t] + a_1 b_1 \left(\frac{1}{u_t}\right) \tag{7}$$

Equation (7) is the short-run Phillips curve equation. The terms in square brackets in equation (7) are constant for period t, and their values determine the position of the short-run Phillips curve. For example, a *ceteris paribus* one-shot drop in the rate of productivity change, $\dot{\eta}_t$, will raise the inflation rate associated with every unemployment rate without altering the steepness and shape of the Phillips curve. Similarly, if the past rate of inflation were higher, then again the Phillips curve would be in a higher position but would not have a steeper shape. The steepness of the short-run Phillips curve is determined by the product of the constant coefficients a_1 and b_1. From the price equation, equation (5), we can see that a_1 represents the extent to which wage increases are *ceteris paribus* transmitted into price increases, and from the wage equation (4) we can see that b_1 represents the extent to which changes in the unemployment rate induce changes in the rate of wage adjustment.

It is comparatively straightforward now to derive a long-run Phillips curve schedule, such as the one depicted in Figure 1, from (7), the equation for the short-run Phillips curve. By the long run, we mean a situation in which the rate of inflation has become stable. In this model we can depict that situation to be one in which the rate of inflation stays the same from one period to the next, or, specifically, a situation in which $\dot{p}_t = \dot{p}_{t-1}$. If the rate of inflation is constant over two subsequent periods, then we may derive the following expression from equation (7):

$$\dot{p}_t(1 - a_1 b_2) = (a_0 + a_1 b_0) - a_2 \dot{\eta}_t + a_1 b_1 \left(\frac{1}{u_t}\right) \tag{8}$$

If the product of the two terms $a_1 b_2$, both of which are positive algebraic constants, is less than one, then we may write:

$$\dot{p}_t = \frac{(a_0 + a_1 b_0 - a_2 \dot{\eta}_t)}{1 - a_1 b_2} + \frac{a_1 b_1}{(1 - a_1 b_2)} \left(\frac{1}{u_t}\right) \tag{9}$$

Equation (9) represents the long-run Phillips curve. The intercept is a constant, given the rate of productivity increase, and the steepness of the long-run Phillips curve is represented by the slope parameter expression $a_1 b_1 /(1 - a_1 b_2)$.[1] Figure 1(a) depicts these short- and long-run Keynesian inflation models based on the above Phillips analysis. The short-run schedule corresponds to the short-run Phillips curve, equation (7), and the steeper long-run schedule corresponds to the long-run Phillips curve, equation (9).

It is useful at this point to make several observations about the relationship between the short- and long-run Phillips curves and about their location parameters. First, the implication of the derivation of the long-run Phillips schedule from the short-run curve is that while the trade-off in the short run between unemployment and the rate of inflation may be represented by a comparatively flat Phillips curve, in the long run, once the inflation rate settles down to a constant rate, the terms of the trade-off will be much steeper. The steeper long-run trade-off between inflation and unemployment reflects the fact that economic agents eventually accommodate to inflation by adjusting their expectations so that their wages and prices reflect this higher rate of expectations without altering real conditions, such as unemployment.

Second, the long-run Phillips curve, equation (9), was derived contingent on the assumption that the product $a_1 b_2$ be less than 1. If this product is equal to

---

[1] We are dealing with nonlinear equations, rectangular hyperbolas; however, it is convenient to refer to the parameters as slope parameters, even though the slopes are obviously not constant; i.e., the derivatives at each unemployment rate differ.

1, then equation (9) breaks down, because we cannot divide by zero. The term a_1 is from the price equation and reflects the extent to which wage increases, *ceteribus paribus*, lead to price increases. In other words, if wage increases, which exceed increases in labor productivity, are fully transmitted to price increases, than a_1 would equal 1. The term b_2 represents the extent to which inflationary expectations lead to wage increases. If wage increases fully accommodate expected inflation, then b_2 would also equal 1. If both a_1 and b_2 equal 1, then the long-run Phillips curve does not exist! Put another way, the more anticipated inflation generates wage increases and these cost increases generate price increases, the steeper will be the long-run Phillips curve.

Third, notice that the sign of productivity increase in the long-run Phillips curve equation is negative: $-a_2$. This negative coefficient indicates that increases in the rate of productivity advancement will reduce the rate of inflation for a given degree of tightness in the labor market. In other words, if the rate of productivity increase rises, then both the long- and short-run Phillips curves would be shifted inward. Conversely, of course, slowdowns in the rate of productivity increase will result in rightward shifts in the long- and short-run Phillips curves.

The Natural Rate Hypothesis: Monetarists believe that the long-run Phillips curve is vertical, so, regardless of stabilization policy measures, the economy will tend to gravitate toward one unemployment rate, which they call the natural rate of unemployment. In the preceding paragraphs we derived the long-run Phillips curve, equation (9), under the assumption that the product $a_1 b_2$ was less than 1. Now consider the implications of the alternative possibility, namely, that the product $a_1 b_2$ equals 1. As we noted above, this assumption corresponds to the condition that anticipated inflation is completely converted into effective rates of wage increase and that these wage increases are effectively transmitted into inflation. This condition is a dynamic version under uncertainty of the Walrasian assumption that markets clear in the sense that agents' expectations work to achieve equilibrium. We say this because when the product $a_1 b_2$ equals 1, we have a situation in which price expectations feed through the model perfectly into actual increases in prices. If $a_1 b_2$ equals 1, then we can derive the following expression from equation (7):[2]

$$\dot{p}_t - \dot{p}_{t-1} = -a_2 \dot{\eta}_t + a_1 b_1 \left(\frac{1}{u_t} \right) \tag{10}$$

or, more generally, if we reintroduce $\dot{p}_t^e$, we may write

$$\dot{p}_t - \dot{p}_t^e = -a_2 \dot{\eta}_t + a_1 b_1 \left(\frac{1}{u_t} \right) \tag{10'}$$

Up until now our analysis of expected inflation has rested on the assumption

[2]We drop the intercept terms, since they do not alter the analysis.

that the rate of price increase expected for period t was equal to the previous period's realized rate of inflation. Suppose we relax this assumption by assuming instead that the expected rate of inflation in period t, $\dot{p}_t^e$ be a weighted average of past periods' rates of inflation. (This assumption is the one used by Cagan in his historial studies of hyperinflation.) Here we assume the following:

$$\dot{p}_t^e = \sum_{i=1}^{\infty} \omega_i \dot{p}_{t-i} \tag{11}$$

Equation (11) states that the rate of inflation expected for period t is a weighted average of past periods' rates of inflation. We might assume that the weights ω_i decline as i increases. In this case, the expectations for inflation are seen to adapt over time to experience. This expectation model is called the *adaptive expectations* model.

Equation $(10')$ may now be used to derive a very important conclusion about the performance of an economy in the long run under a constant rate of inflation: when the economy reaches a state of steady inflation, or long-run equilibrium, the actual rate and the expected rate must be equal. This result implies that the left-hand side of equation $(10')$ is, in the long run, equal to zero, and therethe right-hand side must be equal to zero also. Given that the rate of change of labor productivity, represented by the term $\dot{\eta}_t$, is predetermined, we may solve the right-hand side of equation $(10')$, which is set equal to zero, for the only unknown in the expression, the rate of unemployment. The solution to this equation is u_t^n, *the natural rate of unemployment*. It is important to observe that the solution to equation $(10')$ for the natural rate of unemployment will be the same, regardless of the rate of inflation, as long as that rate is a constant and as long as the realized rate and expected rate are equal. In words, this result means that the Phillips curve must be vertical in the long run. That is, under the assumption that the product $a_1 b_2$ equals 1, the Phillips curve analysis leads us to the conclusion that one and only one rate of unemployment is consistent with equilibrium or with a nonaccelerating rate of inflation. The rate of unemployment which solves equation $(10')$, the natural rate, depends upon the values of the various parameters in the model. Figure 2 depicts the natural rate hypothesis.

It may be helpful at this point to describe the workings of this natural rate hypothesis model. Suppose the economy begins period t at point A in Figure 2 in which the unemployment rate is at the natural rate u_t^n and in which the inflation rate is at $\dot{p}_A$. The short-run Phillips curve is the one in which the expected rate of inflation is equal to $\dot{p}_A$. The equation which corresponds to this Phillips curve would be similar to equation (10) above in which the expected rate of inflation was $\dot{p}_{t-1}$ rather than $\dot{p}_A$. Suppose, as a result of an increase in aggregate demand, the economy is moved along the short-run Phillips curve from A to B. In the short run this means that the economy moves to a higher inflation rate $\dot{p}_B$ but a lower unemployment rate u_1. The story told by the natural rate hypothesis theorists using adaptive expectations is that since the expected rate of

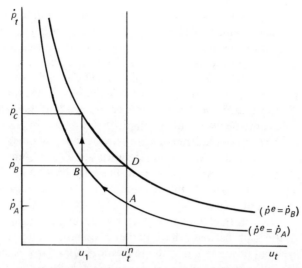

FIGURE 2   The Natural Rate Hypothesis

inflation is adapted from past experience, people will come to expect the higher rate of inflation. Wage contracts, price policies, and so forth will then adjust to the new higher expected rate of inflation, and the short-run Phillips' curve will shift up. Now if the stabilization authority wishes to hold unemployment at u_1, it must now "accept" a higher rate of inflation, $\dot{p}_c$. However, if it accepts $\dot{p}_c$, expectations will again adjust and the Phillips curve will shift up again. In this model if the stabilization authorities want to permanently lower the unemployment rate below the natural rate, the result is continual increases in the rate of inflation.

This result leads this model to be called the *acceleration hypothesis*. The stabilization authority accepts the higher rate of inflation by printing money to prevent the *LM* curve from shifting to the left and choking off the inflation and raising unemployment. Even higher rates of inflation require even larger increases in M. The stabilization authority could choose to fight inflation by slowing the rate of growth of money or even by contracting M. In this case, the inflation will reduce the real money supply, the *LM* curve will shift left, income will fall, unemployment will rise, and the economy will move back toward u_t^n. If the stabilization authority sticks to its guns and holds the rate of increase in M down, the economy will end up at u_t^n with a rate of inflation consistent with the chosen rate of growth of M and rate of growth of potential output as determined by labor force growth and by changes in labor productivity. How long it will take to get back to u_t^n and whether the economy must cycle around u_t^n depends upon the specifics of how price expectations are formed and exactly how the stabilization authority manages the changes in M. This analysis implies that in order to maintain an unemployment rate below the natural rate, the stabilization authority cannot merely accept a higher rate of inflation but must accept accelerating inflation.

Of course, the logic which implies that a higher rate of inflation cannot permanently hold unemployment below the natural rate also implies that even a permanent acceleration of inflation would not hold the unemployment rate below the natural rate. If economic agents are able to anticipate the rate of inflation and act according to their anticipations, then why would they not also be able to anticipate the rate of acceleration of inflation and adapt that into their plans as well? In short, the natural rate hypothesis implies that there is no lasting or permanent trade-off between either inflation or the rate of acceleration in inflation on the one hand and the rate of unemployment on the other. This result follows from the assumption that economic agents are able to eventually recognize the effects on their plans of changes in the price level and in the rate of inflation and are able to translate this recognition into effective action in wage-price and other types of policies.

We have now two distinct though closely related bodies of analysis which bear on the relationship between the inflation rate and the rate of unemployment. The Keynesian position is that the long-run Phillips curve is steeper than the short, but still not vertical; most monetarists believe the natural rate hypothesis position that the long-run Phillips curve is perfectly vertical. The two positions depend upon the value of the product $a_1 b_2$. Unfortunately, the empirical evidence on this issue is difficult to assess, very complicated to explain, and subject to dispute. James Tobin, in a volume edited by Otto Eckstein, *A Conference on Wage and Price Determination* (1972), argued that the evidence clearly indicates that the product $a_1 b_2$ is less than 1. However, as noted by other authors [see, for example, R. J. Gordon (1976)], as new evidence has been gathered over the years, the product $a_1 b_2$ appears to be converging on 1 as the rate of inflation increases. Furthermore, Lucas in Eckstein (1972) and others argue that the Phillips curve coefficients $a_1 b_2$ may appear to be less than one even when the long run is characterized by a vertical schedule. Keynesians counter attack with other points: One, if expectations take a long time to adjust, say a decade or so, then the shorter-run schedule will have short-run policy relevance. Two, a potential advantage of running a high-pressure economy for a while may be that it will induce positive changes in the economy which improve the natural unemployment rate. For example, marginal workers may be taught better work habits and skills.

It is interesting to notice that the two positions held each follow a long tradition in economic thought. Milton Friedman in his Nobel lecture (1977) indicates that he introduced the phrase the *natural rate of unemployment* in order to parallel his thinking to the work by an earlier economist, Knut Wicksell, who believed that there was a "natural rate of interest." Friedman's idea is indeed very close to the classical principle of the dichotomy, because he argues that the unemployment rate is naturally determined by "real" factors as opposed to monetary phenomena. James Tobin, on the other hand, in his American Economic Association Presidential Address in 1972 and in his Western Economic Association address in 1977 explains that the modern Phillips curve analysis takes as its ancestry the work of Lord Keynes.

Rational Expectations: Up until now we have considered models in which the expected rate of inflation is determined solely from past inflation rates. A very novel and interesting concept introduced in recent years approaches expectations in a more comprehensive way. We begin by assuming that equation (10') is essentially correct: The difference between the rate of inflation and the expected rate is zero when the unemployment rate is equal to the natural rate. This equation also implies that if actual inflation exceeds the expected rate, then unemployment is less than the natural rate. This result implies a new relationship between actual inflation and expected inflation. How, we might ask, may unemployment be held below the natural rate? The unemployment rate u_t may be less than the natural rate for two types of reasons: (1) There may be systematic causes which hold the realized inflation rate consistently above the expected rate, or (2) there may be random shocks which temporarily drive u_t below the natural rate. (Examples of such shocks may be sudden shifts in labor market activity, such as productivity changes, changes in labor participation rates and so forth, or unexpected changes in monetary or fiscal policy.) We may represent these two different types of causes by a simple modification of equation (10') above, in which we assume that the relationship between unemployment's deviation from the natural rate and inflation's deviation from the expected rate is in a simpler, linear form than that expressed in equation (10'). We do this as follows:

$$u_t - u_t^n = -\alpha[\dot{p}_t - \dot{p}_t^e] + \epsilon_t^s \tag{12}$$

Equation (12) states in symbols what we stated in the above paragraph—namely, that the difference between unemployment and the natural rate is negatively and systematically related to the difference between the actual and expected rate of inflation, and is also influenced by a random element represented by ϵ_t^s. The symbol ϵ_t^s simply depicts the idea that an economy may be hit with unexpected shocks, including shocks from policy, which cause the unemployment rate to suddenly rise or suddenly fall without regard to any systematic trend in prices.

The crucial question we shall address with equation (12) is: Can the stabilization authorities systematically hold u_t below the natural rate? Equation (12) implies that unemployment may be held below the natural rate only if inflation is held above the expected rate. We shall now show that if expectations are formed in a rather sophisticated way, then the stabilization authorities will be unable to systematically hold inflation below the expected rate. This result was developed by a number of economists, the most important of whom are John Muth (1961), Robert Lucas in Eckstein (1972), and Sargent and Wallace (1975) and (1976). Muth (1961) developed the basic idea of a rational expectations framework. However, he does not seem to have recognized its full potential. Lucas was among the first to recognize the broader implications of Muth's ideas. Sargent and Wallace applied the idea of rational expectations to monetary policy.

The basic concept behind the Muth-Lucas rational expectations model is that the rate of expected inflation in any single period is based upon all the information available to individuals. This information includes the past record of the economy and expectations of future policies likely to be undertaken by stabilization authorities. Suppose that economic agents utilize all the knowledge about the economy available to them, as of period $t - 1$, in developing their expectations about prices in period t. If these economic agents are rational in the sense used here, then they will organize this information in the same systematic way that it would be organized by the stabilization authorities. Furthermore, the economic agents would include in their forecasts about the future rate of inflation any systematic information which they can devise about the potential performance of the stabilization authorities. In other words, economic agents can include in their forecasts about the expected rate of inflation anything systematic which the stabilization authorities themselves may do in trying to influence the future course of economic events. Muth and Lucas show that if expectations are so devised—rationally—then although economic agents may make mistakes in predicting future inflation, they will *on average* forecast the correct rate. In other words, all that will be missing in their forecasts will be unexpected random shocks that hit the economy in the current period.

This assumption about expectations is radical indeed: Economic agents will include in their forecasts the systematic behavior of the stabilization authorities. Put yet another way, forecasters may be wrong about the future rate of inflation, but they will not ignore trends in policy or fixed rules undertaken by policy makers.

We can apply this new concept about expectations to the Phillips analysis. This application draws from a number of sources, especially from R. J. Gordon (1976). To illustrate the implications for stabilization policy and the relationship between inflation and unemployment of the rational expectations model, we use a simple example. Suppose that the factors which influence the period-t rate of inflation can be divided into two sets: The first set, representing actions of the stabilization authorities, are depicted by increases in the money supply, and the second set, representing unexpected increases or decreases in aggregate demand from sources other than the stabilization authorities, is depicted by a random variable:

$$\dot{p}_t = \dot{m}_t + \epsilon_t^d \tag{13}$$

The variable $\dot{m}_t$ represents the rate of monetary expansion undertaken by the monetary authority, and the variable ϵ_t^d represents random shocks and has two important properties: First, the expected value of ϵ_t^d is zero. This property means that some random shocks will cause the rate of inflation to be larger than that associated with the rate of monetary expansion, and some random shocks will cause the rate of inflation to be less than the rate of monetary expansion, but on average the rate of inflation will equal the rate of monetary expansion.

The second property of ϵ_t^d is that its value in any period t cannot be systematically related to any information available in period $t - 1$. (In statistical terms, ϵ_t^d in period t is uncorrelated with any information available to stabilization authorities or economic agents in period $t - 1$.)

Under rational expectations, economic agents would set their expectations of the period-t rate of inflation equal to the rate of expected monetary expansion for period t. According to equation (13), monetary expansion actually determines inflation. Rational expectations implies that economic agents are assumed to understand the economy's structure, as represented by equation (13). This leads us to the following expression for price expectations:

$$\dot{p}_t^e = \dot{m}_t^e \tag{14}$$

Now if we subtract (14) from (13), we get

$$\dot{p}_t - \dot{p}_t^e = \dot{m}_t + \epsilon_t^d - \dot{m}_t^e \tag{15}$$

Equation (14) implies that forecasts of prices will depend on forecasts of $\dot{m}$, so we next must determine the origin of the expected rate of monetary expansion. In other words, how do economic agents determine $\dot{m}_t^e$? To answer this question, we must first consider how the monetary authority behaves when it determines $\dot{m}$. Suppose that the central bank tries to follow a simple rule in setting the rate of monetary expansion. That rule might take the following form. The rate of monetary expansion consists of a constant average rate $\dot{m}_0$ plus an adjustment factor that depends on the extent to which unemployment in the previous period deviated from the natural rate plus an additional random factor. If the central bank observes such a decision rule, then the *actual realized* rate of monetary expansion will be the sum of three terms: the average rate of growth of the money supply, the adjustment factor for deviations between unemployment and the natural rate, and a random factor which represents random fluctuations in the rate of monetary growth uncontrollable by the central bank. In symbols:

$$\dot{m}_t = \dot{m}_0 + \beta[u_{t-1} - u_{t-1}^n] + \epsilon_t^m \tag{16}$$

where $\dot{m}_0$ represents the average rate of monetary expansion, β is the adjustment factor in the monetary growth rate in response to deviations in the unemployment rate from the natural rate, and ϵ_t^m represents the random component in the rate of growth in the money supply.

An important implication of the rational expectations hypothesis is that in considering forecasts of $\dot{m}$, economic agents will study the behavior of stabilization authorities and use this information to predict the systematic components of the central bank's policies. (Of course, the idea that economic agents' can predict the systematic behavior of the central bank can be extended to their predicting any systematic policy.) By studying the performance of the central bank, economic agents would expect the rate of monetary growth to consist of the systematic portions of equation (16). This would lead us to the following equation:

$$\dot{m}_t^e = \dot{m}_0 + \beta[u_{t-1} - u_{t-1}^n]$$ (17)

Equation (17) simply states that the expected rate of monetary expansion for period t is determined by the average growth rate of the money supply plus the rule used by the central bank to adjust that average rate. Of course, forecasts will not be perfect because of the random element ϵ_t^m. The term ϵ_t^m represents random shocks as a result of the inability of the central bank to completely control monetary magnitudes, vagaries of the membership of the Board of Governors, unexpected changes in the structure of the financial system, random (unexpected) pressures from Congress, and so on. If we now replace the expected rate of monetary expansion in equation (15) with equation (17) we have the following:

$$\dot{p}_t - \dot{p}_t^e = [\dot{m}_0 + \beta(u_{t-1} - u_{t-1}^n)] + \epsilon_t^m + \epsilon_t^d - [\dot{m}_0 + \beta(u_{t-1} - u_{t-1}^n)]$$ (18)

Therefore,

$$\dot{p}_t - \dot{p}_t^e = \epsilon_t^m + \epsilon_t^d$$ (19)

Equation (19) states that the difference between the actual rate of inflation in period t and the expected rate is equal the sum of two random terms—unexpected variations in monetary expansion and unexpected exogenous demand shocks. In other words, the actual and the expected inflation rates do not differ in any systematic way if expectations are determined rationally. In simple hueristic terms, the central bank cannot systematically alter the difference between the inflation rate and that which is expected by economic agents, because the public learns what the FED knows and how the FED behaves!

Further striking results can be unearthed by returning to equation (12), which showed that under the natural rate hypothesis the unemployment rate can differ from the natural rate systematically only if the inflation rate systematically differs from the expected inflation rate. If we now substitute equation (19), which summarizes our results on inflation forecasting into equation (12), we obtain the following extraordinary result:

$$u_t - u_t^n = -\alpha[\epsilon_t^m + \epsilon_t^d] + \epsilon_t^s$$ (20)

Equation (20) shows that deviations between u_t and u_t^n equal a sum of purely random elements. In other words, the unemployment rate will differ from the natural rate only because of random elements in monetary expansion, ϵ_t^m, random shocks to aggregate demand ϵ_t^d and random shocks to aggregate suppy, ϵ_t^s. Equation (20) implies that stabilization authorities cannot systematically force the unemployment rate away from the natural rate, because all systematic elements of stabilization policy are eventually learned by the public and built into their expectations and, therefore, into their behavior. We have now formally seen the full logic of the natural rate hypothesis and the rational expectations model.

The logic, very briefly, is that if economic agents are well informed and perfectly rational, then, given enough time, they can avoid any planned attempts by the stabilization authorities to utilize policies that will drive the economy away from its natural rate of unemployment and by implication from its natural rate of production. This result is extremely powerful and very important, because it implies that rational economic agents will force the economy to a particular solution, regardless of systematic attempts by the stabilization authorities to woo the economy to some other point.

We should emphasize that the results of the rational expectations model follow from strong assumptions about how economic agents analyze the economy. They are assumed to be able to gather information and analyze the performance of stabilization authorities with a high degree of accuracy and precision. Furthermore, economic agents are able to translate their expectations into suitable wage contracts and into suitable pricing policies so that the natural rate of unemployment is maintained.

It is not clear whether this model will be important over a reasonably long period of time in an economic environment in which the rate of inflation is difficult to predict and highly variable. More importantly, it is unclear whether these results will hold up in an economy in which there are legal and other restraints on the ability of economic agents to convert their expectations into effective wage and price policies. In his 1977 Nobel lecture, Professor Milton Friedman pointed out that it may take decades before the economic system is able to adapt to a situation of sustained inflation. Furthermore, analysis by a number of economists, summarized in R. J. Gordon (1976), suggests that the time needed for monetary expansion to lead to price increases and for price increases to lead into subsequent wage increases may be quite long. These various lags can run anywhere from one to four years. Since economic agents are, of course, forced to continue undertaking transactions, these transactions may lead to deviations in actual economic performance from the optimal paths suggested by the rational expectations model. It may be, in other words, that the economy fails to converge on the path suggested by the rational expectations model. As indicated earlier in this chapter, there are numerous imperfections in modern industrialized economies, (imperfections in the sense that these economies do not correspond to Walrasian market processes), because we have various degrees of concentration, government regulation and intervention, various kinds of resistance to changes in relative price structures, and various legal constraints to flexibility in prices and wages.

William Poole (1976), Benjamin Friedman (1979), and others have raised critical questions about the rational expectations model. Rational expectations involves two crucial assumptions: (1) Forecasts are rational, given information, in the sense that the entire set of information is included in the calcualtion of the forecast. (2) Agents know the model which determines the course of economic events. Friedman questions the second assumption. After all, he reasons, economists' views of how the economy works have been changing over time, and surely these views will continue to change. In the meantime, although individuals may behave rationally with the information they have, they, like economists, have limited information. In the short run, therefore, individuals' behavior should, in Friedman's view, reflect a learning process as they attempt to learn how the economy and the policy maker works. We might add to this point that the structure of the economy itself changes over time. For example, the government sector is much larger now than it was in the 1920s and 1930s. Transfers such as social security are much more important today than they were in the 1950s. Imports and exports play a bigger role today than they did in the 1950s, and there are many other changes as well. Thus, economic agents are learning about a changing structure. While the learning process is going on, individuals cannot act rationally in the sense of Muth, Lucas, Sargent, and Wallace, because individuals do not yet know the true structure. In the meantime, policy makers may have leeway to implement effective systematic policy.

Poole raises an even more telling point. He notes that business cycles are a persistent feature of the economic landscape and he questions the ability of the rational expectations model, when applied to complete information, to explain business cycles. Thus Poole believes that constraints on behavior must exist which somehow dilute the importance of rational expectations. For example, in an uncertain world with persistent cycles, employees may wish to be "insured" against fluctuations in incomes with an average wage held constant over the cycle. Employers may be willing to provide such "insurance" in order to maintain a stock of contented satisfied workers. In some instances these insurance policies may take the forms of contracts, legally binding documents. In others, these policies may be implicit. In both cases, economic agents are tied to prior wage commitments. (The same may occur for product prices when customers' loyalty is important.) Such prior commitments create short-run periods over which people cannot (or choose not to) act "rationally" in the Muth-Lucas sense. Again, policy has a period over which it can have systematic effects.

We end our discussion of the causes of inflation with an evident paradox. Economists seem to fall into two distinct groups when they discuss inflation and unemployment. On the one hand, we have the neoclassical-monetarist story, which culminates with the rational expectations model. This story attributes all but temporary random fluctuations in the rate of inflation to the stabilization authorities, especially to the central bank. The unemployment rate, except for temporary deviations as a result of random shocks to the economy, hovers around a natural level which is caused by the structure of the economy.

While the neoclassical-monetarist camp attributes unemployment to structure, the Keynesians attribute inflation to structure. The Keynesians, (referred to by some as *structuralists*), argue that unions and oligopolies, government regulations, agricultural policies, resistance to changes in price structure, control of the central bank by Congress and the political system, minimum wage laws and so forth, cause the economy to be inflation prone. They argue that, rather than attributing the cause of inflation to the central bank, the central bank is often forced by political pressures to accommodate to endogenous inflation. See, for example, Robert Solow (1975). The Keynesians also argue that because the economic system is imperfect, in the sense that it does not correspond closely to a Walrasian market mechanism, the labor market does not always clear, so there is, therefore, no natural rate of unemployment. This position is held, for example, by Tobin [(1973) and (1977)]. Furthermore, the Keynesians believe that the unemployment rate which the economy achieves in the short run can be influenced by the stabilization authorities. In short, Keynesians believe that the inflation rate is heavily influenced by structure and that unemployment may be set by the stabilization authorities.

Although these two different points of view may seem quite far apart, there is a broad area of consensus. First, hyperinflations are quite clearly purely monetary phenomena. When the rate of inflation is substantial, it invariably is accompanied by a massive rate of increase in money. Second, an important element of the inflationary process clearly involves the way in which economic agents develop expectations and the ways in which economic agents are able to convert their expectations into actual performance. Third, it is also clear that the structure of the economy has a significant influence on the way in which the economy adjusts in labor markets and product markets to disequilibrium forces. Whether these impediments to the structure of the economy cause a high natural rate of unemployment or whether they cause variability in the rate of unemployment but not around any natural level is still subject to some dispute. What is not subject to dispute, however, is that much unemployment in the economy is a result of these various imperfections in structure.

Fourth, both the neoclassical-monetarist position and the Keynesian position can be analyzed within the framework of the price and wage models that we have been developing. This fact suggests that the *process* of inflation, if not the cause, is being captured by our analysis, even though different economists have different views about precisely how this process works. Finally, it seems evident that past debates and arguments among economists over whether inflation is caused by cost-push factors or demand-pull factors or whether inflation is caused by the central bank or by decisions by private economic agents were somewhat fruitless. It is now evident that accommodation of inflationary pressures by the monetary authority is necessary for a sustained inflation. It is equally evident that the central authority itself is, and has always been, unable to withstand the tremendous political pressures placed on it when inflationary forces are in the economy. It now seems evident that wage policies by aggressive unions, which some have called the cause of inflation, are really part of the inflationary transmission mechanism. Similarly, while one may think of the central bank as causing inflation, one can also think of the central bank as being an actor in the economic environment and its behavior as also being part of the inflation transmission mechanism.

B ● The Consequences of Inflation and Suggested Remedies

While inflation has long been recognized to be a social evil, governments of capitalist economies have had, in recent decades, a very difficult time in slowing it down. One reason for this apparent policy failure may be that the precise consequences of inflation are difficult to determine and assess. In order to facilitate an understanding of the consequences of inflation, it is helpful to distinguish between two types of inflation—those anticipated and those unanticipated. As discussed above at some length, economists now believe that if a steady rate of inflation persists long enough, then economic agents will develop inflationary expectations and adjust their behavior according to these expectations. If, however, inflation is unexpected, then individuals cannot anticipate and adjust their behavior accordingly. When an inflation is fully anticipated, individuals will adapt their behavior to the inflation process. This adaptation means that people will be able to allow for inflation as they make contractual arrangements, monetary agreements, and so forth in order to protect their financial status from the inflationary process.

In countries where inflation has occurred at relatively rapid and steady rates for long periods of time, there is evidence that contractual arrangements indeed adjust to allow for anticipated inflation. For example, in some Latin American countries in which inflation has become a normal state of affairs over many years, interest rate charges in financial contracts tend to be larger than the inflation rate: If the inflation rate runs at 70 percent, then it is not uncommon for the rate of interest to run 75 percent. Inflation expectations are also built into wage contracts in these economies. For example, minimum wages are often automatically increased with the rate of inflation on an annual basis. In general, then, inflationary expectations become built into fixed money contracts by increasing the money rate of return by the level of expected inflation. When these adjustments are made, the consequences of inflation are quite different than when they are not.

In this section, we shall first discuss the consequences of inflation under special circumstances—in which all economic agents are able to fully anticipate the rate of inflation. We hasten to mention several caveats before entering into this analysis. To say that an inflation is fully anticipated implies both that economic agents are aware of what the future inflation rate will be and also that they are able to act on the basis of these expectations. This assumption would be quite strong when applied to the U.S. economy in the 1970s and 1980s. Even though high rates of inflation had been persistent for ten years or so by the middle of 1970s, economic agents were in many cases unable to fully adjust their behavior even though they may have had accurate expectations. This was so because of legal constraints placed on the behavior of some institutions and some individuals. For example, the rates of interest offered on the deposits at financial institutions were controlled by laws which prevented individuals from receiving higher rates of interest, even if higher rates were agreed to by both parties. Also, the political system was rather slow to adapt to inflation. For example, the U.S. tax system is still based on money income rather than on the underlying purchasing power of income.

A second caveat refers to the ability of economic agents to predict the rate of inflation when it becomes rapid. Evidence for the U.S. from the 1960s and 1970s indicates, for example, that as the inflation rate gradually increases, so does the variability of the rate of inflation. This tendency suggests that even though an inflation may be accelerating, on average, over many years, economic agents have a difficult time anticipating the future rate because the variability of inflation grows with the average rate itself. Thus, while we shall now analyze the consequences of inflation under the assumption that it is fully anticipated, we realize that economic agents may find it difficult to anticipate inflation.

Anticipated Inflation: In order to analyze the consequences of a fully anticipated inflation we first show that inflationary expectations will lead individuals to alter the terms of monetary contracts. Recall the definition of a bond: An I.O.U. in which a fixed dollar return is to be paid to the lender. In other words, a bond is a fixed money contract which specifies the dollar payments and the period of those payments into the future. (In some situations, it is possible for bonds to be issued which are variable money contracts. Such bonds are called, when they vary according to the inflation rate, *indexed bonds*. Also, mortgage loans can have variable rate terms, as can business loans.)

Since at the moment we are assuming that inflation is fully and accurately anticipated, it is reasonable to assume that both the borrower and the potential lender agree about the expected rate of inflation. If this is the case, the nominal return on fixed money contract bonds would have to take into account the reduction in purchasing power of future dollars in order to offer the lender a positive real return. Put another way, suppose that a borrower and a lender agree that when neither parts expects inflation that the lender should receive a rate of return of 5 percent. Then if both come to expect a 2 percent inflation rate, they should logically agree to a 7 percent nominal rate of interest. In other words, if we let $\dot{p}^e$ represent the agreed-to expected rate of inflation and if we let ρ represent the rate of return which they would agree to when there is no inflation, then the rate of interest they would agree to under expected inflation is approximately the sum of ρ and $\dot{p}^e$. (We are abstracting there from taxes and other special circumstances which complicate the relation between ρ and R.) We might think of ρ as representing the real rate of return on physical capital; i.e., ρ depicts the return on capital after deducting the rate at which the monetary unit is expected to erode. The sum of the real rate of return on capital, and the expected rate of inflation is called the nominal rate of interest and is represented by R. The relationship between ρ and R is

$$\rho = R - \dot{p}^e \tag{21}$$

Equation (21) states that the real rate of return equals the nominal rate of interest minus the rate of expected inflation. (Note that p is an *ex ante* rate of return. Only if $\dot{p} = \dot{p}^e$ will the real *ex post* rate of return equal $R - \dot{p}^e$.)

To give yet another example, suppose that a producer wishes to undertake a capital project which he knows will provide him a real rate of return after inflation of 4 percent. (This 4 percent return is assumed to include a normal rate of profit.) Suppose he also expects the rate of inflation to be 3 percent. Under these circumstances he would be willing to borrow money in order to finance this project at a nominal rate of 7 percent. He is willing to pay 7 percent in order to receive a real yield of 4 percent, because he knows that over the period during which he has borrowed the money, the value of the dollar will depreciate 3 percent, so the dollars he will be repaying will be worth 3 percent less than the dollars he borrowed.

The comparative static effects of this increase in anticipated inflation will depend upon the detailed characteristics of the model. In a neoclassical model, an increase in expected inflation decreases money demand and this creates an excess money supply and, therefore an inflationary gap. The real rate of interest will not change, and the level of equilibrium income will be the same. However, since the price level has increased, the real volume of cash balances held will be less than those that were held at the original equilibrium. Since the volume of real cash balances held at equilibrium is now less as a result of the increase in the equilibrium price level, there has been a real cost to expected inflation. That cost has taken the form of a reduction in the average holdings of real cash balances.

Of course, we cannot adequately analyze the consequences of inflation in a comparative static context. Fortunately, the spirit of the dynamic framework for analyzing inflation is really rather simple now that we have learned that the effect of an increase in expected inflation is to reduce the real quantity of money. Dynamic models which incorporate expected inflation were developed earlier to describe adaptive and rational expectations. Under either rational or adaptive expectations, the expected rate of inflation eventually becomes the same as the realized rate of inflation except for random disturbances to the latter. The adjustment is rapid under rational expectations and slower under adaptive expectations. Under rational expectations, in a model in which the rate of monetary expansion determines the rate of inflation, the rate of expected inflation is derived from the rate of monetary expansion. But in both cases, the rate of monetary expansion and the rate of inflation will have to be the same after an initial allowance has been made for the expected rate of inflation in the demand for money schedule. Consequently, the reduction in real cash balance holdings as a result of inflation which becomes fully expected is a one-time reduction.

In the long run, dynamic equilibrium is characterized by a constant rate of monetary expansion, a constant rate of inflation (which are the same), and a constant rate of expected inflation. The constant rate of expected inflation has the effect of permanently shifting the liquidity preference schedule to the left and thus reducing the equilibrium quantity of real cash balances. Edward Foster (1972) utilizes such a dynamic analysis of the effects of fully anticipated inflation to show that the cost of fully anticipated inflation is the cost incurred by economic agents as they reduce their average real cash balance holdings in response to expected inflation. (More recent analysis is discussed in the policy chapter, Chapter 25.) As we argued above, real consumption, income, investment, and interest are all unaffected by inflation when it becomes fully anticipated. Thus, optimizing economic agents are able to insulate themselves and the economy from any perverse effects of inflation by fully anticipating it and reducing their average holdings of cash balances in response to the rate at which those cash balances are expected to depreciate.

It is possible to measure the costs to economic agents of avoiding cash balances. That is, we can measure the cost of changing the structure of portfolios away from liquid assets. To do so, however, we would have to turn to methods used in welfare economics, which are beyond our scope here. [See Milton Friedman, *The Optimum Quantity of Money* (1969).] Intuitively, the social costs consist of all the trouble which results from holding fewer cash balances, i.e., more shopping trips, more time lost transferring money into bonds and commodities, and so on. The important point is that inflation, even when fully anticipated, has a social cost.

The neoclassical model suggests that the only cost of inflation comes about because people are forced to economize on cash balances once they are able to fully anticipate the inflation. However, in different models inflation has still other consequences even when fully anticipated. For example, in a Keynesian model in which aggregate output is not predetermined from the labor market, the attempt by economic agents to economize on cash balances has the effect of increasing aggregate demand, which in turn increases output. The permanent effect on interest rates is that the real rate will fall.

A similar result is achieved with a different model by Robert Mundell (1962). Mundell argues that if the demand schedule for commodities, represented by the *IS* curve, depends in part upon the volume of real cash balances, then the lower real cash balances which occur as a result of the anticipated inflation will shift the *IS* curve to the left and bring about a new equilibrium in which the real rate of interest is lower than it was originally. Both of these models—

Keynesian and Mundell's—imply that the initial effect of anticipated inflation will be to reduce the real rate of interest. Economists have long argued about the permanent effects of expansionary monetary policy on real interest rates.

The neoclassical model suggests that expansions in the money supply which produce inflation will not permanently alter the real rate of interest but will raise the money rate of interest by the rate at which prices are expected to increase; thus the money rate of interest will rise with monetary expansion and the real rate of interest will stay the same. The Keynesian and Mundell analyses on the other hand, suggest that monetary expansion which generates an inflation and in return an expected inflation will increase the money rate of interest above the original equilibrium rate but will lower the real rate of interest. The upward effect upon the money rate of interest which results from an increase in the rate of anticipated inflation is called the *Fisher effect*. The Fisher effect indicates that expansionary monetary policy will increase money rates of interest. The reduction in the real rate of interest which initially results from monetary expansion is called the *Keynes effect*. Feldstein (1979) argues that taxes will augment the Fischer effect. In conclusion, we cannot be certain on the basis of purely theoretical arguments whether the real rate of interest falls or not with monetary expansion. However, it seems evident that with sustained monetary expansion the money rate of interest will rise, given the eventual increase in the rate of expected inflation. Since our primary objective here is to examine the consequences of inflation, we conclude that when fully anticipated the primary cost of inflation is probably that associated with the necessity to economize on the use of cash balances.

Unanticipated Inflation: The social costs of unanticipated inflation are far more complicated and severe than the costs associated with anticipated inflation. For this reason, economists often argue that variations in the rate of inflation can be more troublesome for private economic planning than inflation itself. When variations in the rate of inflation are small, economic agents are more likely to learn how to anticipate it, and consequently the social costs are only those associated with conservation of the monetary unit. When, on the other hand, inflation is erratic, the public cannot anticipate and hedge against it. In this situation the evils of inflation are those reported in the popular press. These disruptive consequences of inflation may be organized under two general headings— (1) the redistribution effects of inflation and (2) the uncertainty effects of inflation.

It is difficult to generalize about the redistribution consequences of inflation, because these effects depend upon the extent to which various groups in the economy are able to anticipate inflation and insulate themselves against it. When price level increases are greater than expected, then those individuals and groups who are net creditors in the economy find that their repayments will be in units of a depreciated currency. Consequently, one important redistribution effect of an unexpected inflation is a redistribution of real wealth from creditors to debtors. In other words, those economic agents who are in a net debt position when an unexpected inflation takes place are net winners. The reason for this is that debtors will be repaying their monetary contracts in depreciated currency and thus creditors will be receiving an inadequate return.

Aside from one's net credit or debt position, whether one wins in an unexpected inflation also depends on whether one's money income changes more or less than inflation. A fixed money contract position is a position in which an economic agent is unable to alter the money terms of his contracts. People on fixed incomes are naturally susceptible to great losses when an unanticipated inflation takes place. The poor, wage earners, and the aged are generally thought to be groups who have fixed incomes, and who therefore suffer a great deal. While it appears to be the case that the poor are less able than other economic groups to alter their contractual arrangements when inflation takes place, careful studies of the relative positions of the aged and those on wage incomes indicate that a number of public social and private measure can, and in the U.S. often are, undertaken which minimize the burden of inflation on these groups.

Some economists have even argued that the poor and the aged tend to gain as a result of inflation rather than to lose. For example, public assistance in the form of increases in social security took place a number of times throughout the inflation period of the 1960s and 1970s, i.e., in 1965, 1968, 1973, and 1977. This form of public assistance is now automatic because it is *indexed* to increase automatically with the inflation. Second, Foster (1972) reports a University of Wisconsin Poverty Institute study which shows that fixed nominal return pensions were in fact a very small fraction of the pension income earned by the aged. Finally, throughout the 1960s and 1970s, transfer payments, especially medical benefits, increased considerably to improve the lot of those usually thought to be on fixed incomes.

Perhaps the major redistribution consequence of inflation has not been that from the poor to the rich but has been from the private sector to the public sector. Although a number of adjustments were made in the tax structure in the 1960s and 1970s, the U.S. federal tax system and most state and local tax systems are progressive in their structure. As a result, people are driven at the margin by inflation into higher tax brackets. Higher tax brackets imply that the ratio of taxes to income rises without a voted increase in the tax rate. Consequently, the public sector extracts a greater tax burden on the private sector.

Uncertainty effects of inflation may be even more substantial than the redistribution effects. In recent years, as the business community has tried to adjust to an inflation environment, they have begun to alter their accounting procedures to obtain profit measures which are not distorted by inflation. This modification in business practices suggests that when inflation was unanticipated, firms miscalculated the true values of their inventories and profits and may have misunderstood their true economic position. Furthermore, when inflation is taking place and firms are uncertain about the future price level, this additional degree of uncertainty complicates their planning. Uncertainty may have a direct cost by forcing firms to curtail marginal investment projects.

Theory suggests that when inflation is anticipated economic agents tend to economize on liquid assets and to hold less liquid portfolios in order to avoid the burden imposed by a depreciating currency. However, in the 1970s it appears that individuals moved toward more liquid portfolios. One explanation for this rather surprising shift in the composition of portfolios was suggested by Phillip Cagan and Richard Lipsey (1978): Increasing uncertainty causes people to move toward more liquid portfolios in the presence of rapid inflation rather than toward less liquid portfolios.

While we have listed some of the consequences of inflation, it is quite clear that this discussion is somewhat tentative. The reason for this is that inflation, especially when unanticipated, has a variety of consequences which depend not only on abstract economic theory but also upon the reactions of various individuals to an uncertain environment and upon the structure of the economy which is hit with the inflation.

Policies for Slowing Inflation: A fully developed policy discussion of inflation, unemployment, and the like will be undertaken in Chapter 25, after we have completed analysis of growth and international economics. It is, nevertheless, helpful to examine now some of the policy implications of our analysis of domestic inflation. An economist's policy prescriptions derive, of course, from this theory as well as from his normative judgments. We shall not consider here issues of the choice between various objectives, but rather we shall focus on policy measures for dealing directly with inflation. Because economists disagree about the causes of inflation,they hold different views about counterinflationary policies. First consider the policy recommendations for dealing with inflation from the monetarist viewpoint.

Basically, monetarists believe that the economy is dichotomized into a real and a money sector, and since, in their view, the rate of inflation is determined by the rate of monetary expansion, the primary policy recommendation is to slow the rate of money growth. Because the unemployment rate, the level of output, and the real wage are all in the long run independent of the money market, they will be unaffected by declines in the rate of monetary expansion. Even if one holds a nonmonetarist view of the structure of the economy, it is clear that inflation could be halted by slowing the rate of monetary expansion. Still, many nonmonetarists believe that such a measure would take a long time and would have devastating short-term effects on the real sector of the economy.

Historical experience of the late 1960s and early 1970s suggests that when the economy is above the natural rate of unemployment, slowing inflation may not be an easy task. The Chairman of the Board of Governors of the Federal Reserve System in the late 1960s and early 1970s was Arthur Burns. Arthur Burns, himself an economist and a close friend and teacher of Professor Milton Friedman, the guru of modern monetarism, oversaw the FED throughout a period when the rate of inflation gradually *accelerated*. Judging from Burns's public statements, he thought that inflation was a serious social problem. He frequently lectured Congress about its evils. Why, then, did the rate of inflation continue to accelerate throughout his term at the FED. It may be that the central bank was politically and perhaps even mechanically unable to slow the rate of monetary expansion.

In fact, throughout Burns's tenure and that of his successor, G. William Miller, the Federal Reserve System in the U.S. was under considerable pressure by the Congress to avoid contractionary monetary policies. The Congress adopted a number of new regulations requiring the FED to justify its policies frequently, and more exactly, to the Congress. Furthermore, throughout this period several innovations in financial markets made the job of monetary control of the economy more difficult. The commercial banks, whose liabilities are money, were able to insulate themselves from contractionary pressures by the FED by borrowing on the Eurodollar market or by borrowing short-term excess funds from one another. They borrowed these excess funds on the federal funds market, a market which was originally developed as banks with excess reserves sought to put them to work. In addition, other financial institutions throughout this period began to expand into new markets. In particular, they began to issue liabilities which were payable on demand—nearly perfect substitutes for bank money. These new types of money were issued by money market mutual funds, credit unions, savings and loan associations, and savings banks. It appears, therefore, that political pressures and endogenous responses by the private sector impose constraints on the ability of the central bank to control the rate of money expansion.

As noted earlier, slowing the rate of money growth may damage the real sector of the economy. In the late 1960s and early 1970s, a number of structural changes in the financial sector caused severe repercussions to take place when the central bank attempted to contract the money supply. As explained in chapter 10, a complex maze of regulations was created to control the interest rates that financial institutions pay their depositors. When monetary contraction increased interest rates on bonds, sudden outflows of deposits from these financial institutions took place. Financial institutions were unable to raise their rates in response to the higher rates on private and government bonds due to controls. Private savers, finding the higher rates on bonds more attractive than the low, controlled rates offered by financial institutions, withdrew deposits. The result was a contraction in deposits at financial institutions and a drying-up of funds for borrowing.

Despite these problems, monetarists argue that the only reliable solution to inflation is to slow the rate of monetary expansion. The view held by some monetarists is that monetary contraction is difficult because expansion supports the ability of governments to run deficits. The question not yet resolved in the monetarists' analysis of inflation is why governments tend to finance deficits by monetary expansion in the face of inflation. In other words, why do governments run permanent deficits? Keynes proposed deficits but only as a temporary measure against cyclical slumps and not as a policy of long-run government finance.

The question is why do governments persist in running deficits even as they attempt to slow excess-demand inflation? It may be that government actions reflect the inability of the very complex and amorphous representative groups and coalitions to agree about the legitimate objectives of the society. For example, our evidence on government finances in Chapters 6 and 7 indicates a trend for large increases in the rate of transfer expenditures. Throughout this same period, taxes did not increase as rapidly as expenditures and transfer payments. For example, Vietnam was the first war fought by the United States which was not accompanied by a tax rate increase even though social expenditures were very high. Also, through the late 1960s and early 1970s, a number of reforms of the federal tax system resulted in reducing average tax rates. In other words, while the need for taxes was rising, because of war finance and social transfers, tax rates were not increased accordingly. Running persistent deficits eventually requires financing from the public, and much of this finance in fact took the form of printing money by borrowing from the central bank.

Perhaps the set of pressure groups in America which control the expenditure and transfer systems of the government favor increases in expenditures, while the pressure groups which control the collection system want to lower taxes. In other words, suppose that transfer recipients have the most influence in determining spending, whereas taxpayers have the greatest influence in tax policy. In this case, it is possible for a wedge to be driven between the expenditures plans and revenues plans.

Keynesian economists, of course, hold a different view of the nature of inflation. They believe that inflation is caused by excess aggregate demand induced by economic structure. They argue that the economy responds to expansionary shocks by creating inflationary pressures. These pressures are then accommodated by the central bank as a part of the inflationary process. Many Keynesians argue politically for creating inflationary pressure because they believe there is a trade-off between the inflation rate and the unemployment rate and that the relative social costs favor holding unemployment down. Keynesian analytic views call for a change in structure as a means of slowing the rate of inflation. These views also call for an attempt to "cheat" the Phillips curve by reducing the inflation rate associated with each rate of unemployment. Keynesians have, consequently, suggested a number of measures which are designed to reduce the susceptibility of the economy to inflation and thus to improve the trade-off.

Generally speaking, Keynesian proposals fall under two different headings: First are the conventional stabilization measures designed to move the economy from one point on the Phillips curve to another. These policies follow from the Keynesian view that there is a long-run trade-off between unemployment and inflation. Second are measures designed to shift the Phillips curve downward toward the origin. These policies are designed to alter the economic structure. While conventional stabilization policies are analytically straightforward, they slow inflation only at the expense of increasing unemployment. The second type of measure proposed by Keynesians, however, reduces the rate of inflation associated with any given level of unemployment. Some of these measures operate directly on the inflation rate, and others operate directly on the unemployment rate. We shall comment here only on the proposals designed to reduce inflation.

If the central force which causes inflation is endogenous to the economy, then the rate of inflation must be slowed by reducing the internal pressures. The main focus of policies for doing this is on the rate of expected inflation. The Keynesians suggest we attack this component of the transmission mechanism of inflation in a number of ways. They attempt to reduce the rate at which prices are expected to rise by imposing constraints on the ability of various economic agents to raise their wages and raise their prices. Some measures which are designed to reduce the expected rate of inflation by reducing the rate at which wages and prices can be increased are (1) moral suasion by the government's leaders, especially presidential jawboning, (2) established guidelines suggesting rates at which wages and prices can be increased without being inflationary, (3) wage and price controls and so on.

In recent years, Keynesian economists have suggested a number of new, imaginative programs for dampening the rate of wage and price increases. Wage-price policies are often euphemistically called "incomes policies." One of the more interesting proposals of recent years is a tax-based incomes policy program called TIPS. TIPS was to be an incomes policy program based on the concept of enforced guidelines on wage and price increases. The enforcement aspect of the TIPS program was that tax policy was to be tied to wage and price decisions of private institutions. Industries in which wage increases and price increases were modest were to receive tax breaks, and those with excessive increases were to suffer tax surcharges. Another proposal, this one endorsed by the Carter administration, was to institute a *wage insurance* program. The idea of wage insurance was that the government would request compliance with its guidelines. If inflation exceded government forecasts, then individuals who had complied and then been cheated by the inflation would receive revenues or tax breaks from the government.

Other structural changes in the economy have been suggested by both Keynesian and non-Keynesian economists as a means of making the economy generally less susceptible to inflation and in part also as a means of reducing the natural unemployment rate. Generally speaking, these structural changes take the form of reducing government intervention in private markets. These measures include (1) less regulation, (2) increased competition, (3) fewer government price supports, and (4) weaker minimum wage laws. Proposals such as these are made on a number of grounds. With respect to inflation, they are hoped by their advo-

cates to have two effects. They should reduce, one time, the level of prices, be-
because they tend to reduce the costs of doing business. They also may alter the
economy's structural response to exogenous shocks by making it better able to
accommodate changes in the relative price structure. When a shock (which
requires a substantial change in relative prices) hits the economy, then, if the
structure of the economy prohibits prices and wages from falling, the relative
price system can adjust only through increased inflation. The greater extent to
which structure impeded reductions in prices, the greater will have to be the
inflation to accommodate any given shock requiring a change in relative prices.

STUDY QUESTIONS

1. Discuss the implications for modest inflation of Cagan's hyperinflation
analysis.

2. Analyze the role of each of the following in the inflation process:
   a. Aggressive unions employing escalator clauses.
   b. Stabilization authorities' attempts to hold u below the natural rate u^n.
   c. Rational expectations.
   d. Increases in labor productivity.

3. "Inflation is everywhere and always a monetary phenomenon." Comment.

4. What structural features of an economy make it, in the view of Keynesians,
susceptible to inflation?

5. To what extent do monetarists and Keynesians agree about inflation?

6. Evaluate the effects on each of the following groups of a high-pressure economy with high inflation and low unemployment:
   a. Retired people on social security.
   b. Taxpayers.
   c. Poor marginal workers.
   d. Homeowners.
   e. Corporations in debt.
   f. Financial institutions with existing mortgages.

7. Compare the costs and benefits of inflation: (a) when it is anticipated and
(b) when it is unanticipated.

8. Model: (1) $\dot{p}_t = a_1 \dot{w}_t - a_2 \dot{n}_t$
   (2) $\dot{w}_t = b_1(1/u_t) + b_2 \dot{p}_t^e$
   a) Solve for the short-run Phillips curve.
   b) If $\dot{p}_t^e = \dot{p}_{t-1}$, then solve for the long-run Phillips curve.
   c) Plot for each case below the short-run Phillips curve:

case 1: $a_1 = a_2 = 1$ case 2: $a_1 = a_2 = 1$
$\qquad b_1 = 0.1$ $\qquad\qquad b_1 = .1$
$\qquad b_2 = 0$ $\qquad\qquad b_2 = .5$
$\qquad \dot{p}^e = .03$ $\qquad\qquad \dot{p}^e = .03$

case 3: $a_1 = a_2 = 1$ case 4: $a_1 = a_2 = 1$
    $b_1 = 0.1$ $b_1 = .1$
    $b_2 = 1$ $b_2 = .5$
    $\dot{p}^e = 0.03$ $\dot{p}^e = 0$
     case 5: $a_1 = a_2 = 1$
        $b_1 = 0.1$
        $b_2 = 0.5$
        $\dot{p}^e = 0.1$

 d) Illustrate the effect on the short-run Phillips curve of case 5 if $\dot{\eta}$ increases from $\dot{\eta}_t^1$ to $\dot{\eta}_t^2$.

9. What is the difference between the "real" and the "nominal" rate of interest? How are these rates affected by an increase in the expected rate of inflation? By an increase in the realized rate of inflation?

10. Discuss the ability of the FED to control the U.S. money supply.

11. Use a model with rational expectations to illustrate the effectiveness of monetary expansion to alter real variables, such as unemployment.

12. Critically assess the rational expectations model. Be sure to consider (a) timing and (b) policy effectiveness.

REFERENCES

Cagan, Phillip and Robert E. Lipsey, *The Financial Effects of Inflation*. Cambridge, Mass.: NBER, 1978.

Eckstein, Otto (ed.), *The Economics of Price Determinations* Conference, October 30-31, 1970, Board of Governors of the Federal Reserve System, Washington, D.C., June 1972.

Feldstein, Martin S., "The Welfare Cost of Permanent Inflation and Optimal Short-Run Economic Policy," *Journal of Political Economy*, August 1979.

Foster, Edward, *Costs and Benefits of Inflation*. Federal Reserve Bank of Minneapolis, March 1972.

Friedman, Benjamin, "A Critique of Rational Expectations Theory," *Journal of Monetary Economics*, February 1979.

Friedman, Milton, *The Optimum Quantity of Money and Other Essays*. Chicago: Aldine Press, 1969.

————, "Nobel Lecture: Inflation and Unemployment," *Journal of Political Economy*, June 1977.

————, "The Role of Monetary Policy," *American Economic Review*, March 1968.

Gordon, Robert J., "Recent Developments in the Theory of Inflation and Unemployment," *Journal of Monetary Economics*, April 1976.

Lucas, Robert E. Jr., "Econometric Policy Evaluation: A Critique," in Brunner, Karl and Allan H. Meltzer (eds.), *The Phillips Curve and Labor Markets,* Vol.

1, Carnegie-Rochester Conference Series on Public Policy. Amsterdam, The Netherlands: Holland Press, 1976.

Modigliani, Franco, "The Monetarist Controversy or, Should We Forsake Stabilization Policies?," *American Economic Review*, March 1977.

Mundell, Robert, "Inflation and Real Interest Rates," *Journal of Political Economy*, June 1963.

Okun, Arthur M., "Inflation: Its Mechanics and Welfare Costs," *Brookings Papers on Economic Activity*, No. 2, 1975.

Poole, William, "Rational Expectations in the Macro Model," *Brookings Papers on Economic Activity*, No. 2, 1976.

Sargent, Thomas J. and Neil Wallace, "Rational Expectations, the Optimal Monetary Instrument, and the Optimal Money Supply Rule," *Journal of Political Economy*, April 1975.

Solow, Robert N., "The Intelligent Citizen's Guide to Inflation," *The Public Interest*, Winter, 1975.

Stein, Jerome L. (ed.), *Monetarism*. New York: North Holland Press, 1976.

Tobin, James, "Inflation and Unemployment," *American Economic Review*, March 1972.

———, "How Dead is Keynes?" *Economic Inquiry*, October, 1977.

GROWTH, TRADE, and MACRO POLICY ANALYSIS

part IX

We have now completed the core of macroeconomic modelling and studied the major domestic economic problem of stabilization in an economy with unemployment and inflation. This last part of macroeconomics, Part IX, applies our analysis to three areas of general interest: growth, trade, and policy. We are now broadening the scope of our analysis in three new directions: First, in chapter 23, we broaden the time horizon of our analysis. We no longer focus only on the short run—quarterly, annual, and perhaps three- to five-year horizons—we now turn to the long run—five years to a decade and even longer. The analysis changes somewhat along with our perspective but the tools developed so far will serve us well.

Second, we move out from our national perspective to an international view of aggregate economics. The models developed so far will be extended and modified in chapter 24 to accommodate questions of trade and stabilization, of international monetary arrangements, and of economic interdependence.

Finally, we bring it all together in the last chapter to analyze U.S. policy issues. How are these models we have developed used? How does one attack complex multiple objective problems? How can competing needs for the economy be reconciled? How do we measure the relative importance of various policy problems? What are economists trying to do about inflation, unemployment, low productivity, high oil prices, scarcities, etc.? What do monetarists, rationalists, Keynesians, neoclassicists, and others actually propose for these practical problems? These and other practical issues of great political importance are the subjects of our policy analysis in Chapter 25.

The Okun Diagram, Figure 8 of Chapter 1, depicted the actual and potential GNP paths of the U.S. economy. The main issues of the text so far have dealt with the actual path. Effort was devoted to conveying an understanding of the determinants of the major components of actual GNP, the level of output, and the effect on output of various stabilization policies. We now turn our attention to the potential GNP path rather than the actual. To illustrate, suppose that stabilization measures could be undertaken to bring the actual GNP path in line with the potential at each point in time. Economic growth deals with the issue of where the potential GNP path would then take the economy.

Figure 1 depicts several alternative outcomes that could be in prospect for an economy in the long run. From t_1 to t_2 the economy is shown converging on potential GNP. Earlier chapters discussed various issues relating to such a convergence. In Figure 1, from t_2 to t_3 the economy is on the potential GNP path. At time t_3 some alternative scenarios for potential GNP are represented. Paths 1 and 2 represent the possibility that the economy could veer off its path either into a depression or a hyperinflation—some explosion upward or downward. While economies have, of course, been known to suffer periods of rapid inflation and periods of slump, there is

23

Long-Run Economic Growth

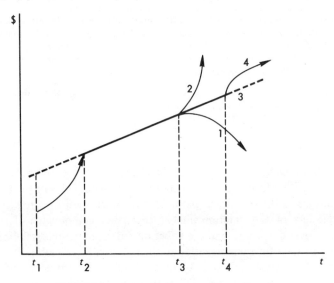

FIGURE 1   Long-run Prospects for an Economy

little evidence to suggest that modern industrialized economies will explode or collapse. Path 3 depicts an economy growing along a smooth path at a constant rate. A path such as path 3 is called a *steady state*.

Let us briefly review the postwar growth record of the U.S. economy. U.S. economic performance has been comparatively admirable. From 1947 to 1960 the average annual rate of economic growth in private domestic output was 3.7%. From 1960 to 1973 economic growth was even higher: 4.3 percent per year. The cumulative effects of these average annual rates of growth from 1947 to 1973 was an increase in gross domestic product of approximately 250 percent. Subject to caveats which will be discussed below, this 250 percent increase in production implies a substantial potential welfare increase. Despite this successful performance and the improvement in U.S. living standards which it has implied, there has been much concern in recent years over the possibility of a slowdown in the trend rate of economic growth.

George Perry, of the Brookings Institution, noted in (1977): "The 1974-75 recession and its aftermath have sparked reestimates of potential GNP that are substantially lower than the previous official estimates and that anticipate a slower growth of potential in coming years than previous official projections." Perry goes on to identify one of the causes in his judgment of the slowdown in growth potential: . . . "(One element) in the CEA revisions is the observed weakness in productivity since 1973. Output per hour in the (nonresidential, nonfarm) business sector declined by 3.5 percent in 1974, the first decline of any size in the post war years . . . ." Later, in its January 1979 *Report to the President*, the Council of Economic Advisors observed, "Between 1948 and 1965 productivity growth in the private nonfarm sector averaged 2.6 percent per year. In 1965-73 this rate declined to 2.0 percent. Since 1973, private nonfarm productivity growth was averaged less than 1 percent per year." The Council goes on to conclude that "this latest deterioration in productivity . . . adds to the accumulating evidence that the secular trend in productivity growth may be considerably less than 2 percent per year." Finally, they state, "Taken together these components imply a growth in potential output over the 1978-83 period of 3 percent annually, the same as the revised estimate for 1973-78." This 3 percent annual rate of growth is down even lower than the earlier estimate of 3.35%. Thus while the record since World War II of economic growth has been admirable, there is considerable concern about the future.

The term "steady state" is analogous to the concept of equilibrium in comparative statics. The *steady state* is a situation in which the crucial variables are moving along some smooth path; their values are not necessarily constant, but their growth rates are. Growth economics deals with questions which focus attention on the nature and existence of steady states: Under what circumstances will a steady state path exist? Will an economy stay on a steady state path once there? Is the steady state *stable* in the sense that an economy, if driven away from it, will return? Can an economy move from one steady state to another and if so, how? Figure 1 depicts the possibility at time t_4 of an economy moving from steady state path 3 to a new steady state path at a higher level of output but the same rate of growth, path 4.

While analysis of the steady state consists of dealing with a set of very abstract theoretical issues, economists are obviously also concerned with the practical growth issues of trying to establish the determinants of the growth path. What is the engine of economic growth? To what extent can the rapid growth in the U.S. economy after World War II, and in other industrialized economies as well, be attributed to growth in the capital stock? Or are these rapid growth rates attributable to growth in the size of the labor force or to quality improvements in human capital? Yet a third possibility is that growth can be attributed to what economists call productivity change. *Total factor productivity change* is the residual after one has attributed as much as possible to growth in the capital and labor factor inputs. Such productivity changes may come about because of improvements in organization and managerial techniques, shifts in sectoral emphasis from less productive to more productive industries, changes in the scale of operations, and so on. It may be possible, once we can attribute economic growth to various sources, to develop policies to alter the stationary state. It may even be possible to determine, given certain initial conditions, whether or not there is an optimal steady state path—one which we should attempt to achieve.

In the lead quote of this chapter by Robert Solow of MIT, he suggests that growth theory is little more than a parable. This is uncharacteristic trepidation for an economist. Why is this so? Growth theory deals with long-run macroeconomics. Any student who has studied microeconomic theory knows how complicated it can be. Macro, as the aggregate of microeconomic systems, adds one more degree of complexity to the micro models. Growth compounds the difficulties one more step by adding a new problem: that of dealing with long-run activity. One of the basic themes of this text has been that an essential ingredient to effective economic analysis is the confrontation of economic theories with actual empirical evidence. It is on the basis of actual observed phenomena that we have been able to modify some theories and weed out others. This continual interplay of economic theory with empirical evidence permitted new directions of study and a greater degree of confidence about economic policy prescriptions. Confronting growth theories with empirical evidence requires long-run time series data on many major components of economic performance at a national level.

The construction of national income and product accounts was not begun until the advent of World War II. While some economists have devoted considerable energy to reconstructing data for earlier periods, the evidence available for economic performance before the turn of the century is rather scattered and somewhat unreliable. Simon Kuznets reconstructed national income accounting data for the U.S. economy back as far as 1889. The very difficult task of constructing capital stock and wealth data was undertaken by Raymond Goldsmith in the 1950s for the U.S. economy in the postwar period. Perhaps the most important organization, assisting Goldsmith and others who constructed national income and product and capital stock data, is the National Bureau of Economic Research (NBER). The study of economic growth is so complicated and requires the simultaneous analysis of so many economic variables that most empirical research dealing with economic growth is focused on the period in which the data are most reliable—namely the post-World War II era. For international comparisons, economists have tended to focus on the industrialized countries in Europe as well as on Japan and the United States. We shall discuss some of this evidence later in the chapter.

While the point of departure for much of the work in this text was the work of Lord Keynes, he said little about economic growth. Yet Keynes's ideas were transformed to a growth context by his colleague, Sir Roy Harrod. The MIT economist Evsy Domar extended the Harrod framework, and today the work of Harrod and Domar is often presented as the Harrod-Domar model. This model builds on the Keynesian notions of the marginal propensities to consume and save, but focuses attention on the existence and stability of a stationary state. The Harrod-Domar model provides the conditions under which steady state growth is possible. While the model successfully characterizes a steady state, it raises the possibility that steady state growth is unstable. Within the conceptual framework, the slightest deviation from steady state conditions leads to the economy careening off into oblivion—either collapsing into catastrophic depression or exploding into hyperinflation.

The evidence for developed countries over the last 35 years does not suggest such severe instability. Consequently, one of the central tasks that growth economists set for themselves, after the work of Harrod and Domar, was to establish more flexible models in which steady state conditions could exist, and in which small deviations from the steady state would not drive the economy permanently away but allow it to move back.

This chapter consists of three sections. Section A contains analysis of the Harrod and Domar model. This model specifies the steady state and serves as a departure point for subsequent analysis. In Section B, a more elaborate conceptual framework is developed. This model is a neoclassical growth model of the type which has dominated the literature in recent years. Neoclassical economists attempt to explain existing evidence. In 1958, the British economist Nicholas Kaldor identified six facts which he called "stylized facts." These stylized facts were designed to characterize the observed patterns of economies, and therefore it has been the objective of growth models to attempt to approximate these facts.

The facts consist of the paths which certain crucial variables, such as output per man-hour or the capital output ratio, seem to have followed. Section C contains reports of an empirical study of the performance, since World War II, of several European economies and those of the U.S., Canada, and Japan. This study attempts to attribute economic growth to its various sources: increases in the labor force, increases in the stock of capital and improvements in quality.

The neoclassical models, more flexible than the Harrod-Domar framework, allow for substitution between labor and capital factors in determining any given level of output. As a result, these models come closer to fitting the stylized facts and to suggesting useful policies for growth. Additional suggestions may be gleaned from the empirical studies of various countries over the postwar period. Nevertheless, one must be cautious in the field of growth about recommending policy, for policy tastes can change rapidly and dramatically. Over the last 20 years, for example, national consensus in the U.S. seems to have undergone three major transformations in growth objectives. In the early 1960s economic growth was a strongly supported national objective. Widespread support for rapid growth led to numerous proposals advanced by President Kennedy and his economists. The importance of sustained growth in the U.S. derived, no doubt, from the evident stagnation of the U.S. economy throughout the 1950s compared to the unusually rapid growth of other industrialized countries, especially Japan, France, Italy, and Germany. Furthermore, and perhaps more important, the Soviet Union appeared to be advancing more rapidly than the U.S. The Premier of the Soviet Union, Nikita Khrushchev, was fond of reminding Americans of this fact by threatening to bury capitalism by rapid growth of his socialist system.

The very success of the U.S. economy through the 1960s led to some deemphasis of growth as an objective. Of equal importance was increasing public awareness of and concern for the negative ecological and environmental effects of industrialization. By the early 1970s the objective of economic growth was nearly reversed, and some went so far as to propose zero economic growth as a national objective. Just ten years before, the debate had been whether the target rate should be 3 percent or 4 percent. This sudden reversal of the growth objective was accompanied by and complicated by the fear that limited supplies of exhaustible resources (oil, etc.) place an irrevocable limit on growth.

To some extent, a reexamination of social objectives is both healthy and warranted. First, fresh air, clean water, and pleasant surroundings are surely utility-producing commodities which market systems tend to undervalue. Only through public policy can society attain the appropriate levels of these resources whose valuation is external to the private market. Second, irreversibilities of ecological systems force us to be cautious to protect the natural environment which, under our system of ownership, is also undervalued by the market mechanism. Third, the location, extraction, and production of alternatives to exhaustible resources can be quite time-consuming and costly, and the economic system therefore would require long periods of time to adapt to new technologies.

While concern about the side effects of industrialization and growth is welcome, it can lead to misunderstanding and to counterproductive proposals. Perhaps the most severe example of a misdirected proposal is the call for zero economic growth. While a first simplistic glance at the economy may suggest that economic growth and environmental quality are at odds, a careful definition of terms and consideration of the meaning of growth will indicate that growth can be compatible with, and perhaps even essential to, attainment of environmental quality. As indicated above, clean water, fresh air, and pleasant surroundings are commodities which should be included in measures of economic welfare. To some extent, recent shock about the poor quality of these goods indicates the failure of many to realize that the quantities of these scarce resources had been dwindling. To reconcile these resources with traditional growth targets based upon the measure of GNP, Nordhouse and Tobin (1972) suggest an alternative target index which they call a *Measure of Economic Welfare.*

To increase consumption of undervalued resources, such as air and water, requires costs. These costs are difficult to incur when the economy is stagnant. In a static economy, the imposition of these costs requires sacrifice of other objectives—high employment, for example. Such conflicts in goals can result in a terribly acrimonious debate. On the other hand, under balanced growth, these "environmental" costs are easier to absorb socially and politically. The costs incurred in cleaning up the environment include not only resources directly involved in reducing environmental destruction and pollution but also the costs incurred in developing whole new technologies that are "environment proof." Finally, the effect on growth of the consumption of exhaustible resources is an important scientific question. The extent and speed with which exhaustible resources can be replaced by alternatives has in the past been enhanced by technological innovation. The role to be played by innovation in the future cannot now be known.

Growth policy took in the late 1970s yet another turn. Because of long-suffered inflation since the 1960s, economists have studied the system carefully to discover why it is so susceptible to inflation. One important set of facts which have been uncovered is that the rate of output from labor was growing at a much slower rate in the 1970s than it had been. This slowdown in "labor productivity" growth concerned a number of public officials and renewed interest in economic growth. For example, the Chairman of the U.S. Federal Reserve Board, Arthur Burns, testifying in 1973 before the Senate Finance Committee, warned of the lack of growth of productivity in many critical industries. The council of Economic Advisors through the late 1970s published consistently more pessimistic figures on potential GNP. While there is little consensus as to the causes of the slowdown in productivity and even less on what should be done about it, concern about the growth objective has returned.

A • Harrod-Domar Growth Model

In short-run comparative static models, both Keynesian and neoclassical, variations in employment lead to variations in output, under the assumption that the capital stock is fixed. Fixing the capital stock in the short run is a convenient fiction allowing us to focus attention on employment in the short run. It was logically inconsistent, we now confess, to assume in the same model that net investment is positive and that the capital stock is constant. To study growth, it is necessary to examine the effects of capital accumulation, net investment, upon the productive potential of an economy. The Harrod-Domar model, which is Keynesian in spirit, allows for the effects of variations in the size of the capital stock. We shall now develop the Harrod-Domar model in three stages. The first step is to develop the aggregate demand conditions. Second, we shall study the supply side of the economy, and third, we shall establish the condition for equilibrium.

Aggregate demand in the Harrod-Domar model is a simple Keynesian consumption function with exogenous investment. Consumer behavior is characterized by a proportional consumption function and may, therefore, be expressed by a proportional savings schedule:

$$S(t) = sY^d(t) \tag{1}$$

The term s in equation (1) is, of course, the familiar marginal propensity to save. If we set savings equal to investment, and solve the resultant equation for income, demand Y^d, then we determine the level of income compatible with aggregate demand:

$$Y^d(t) = (1/s)I(t) \tag{2}$$

Equation (2) states that income is the product of the multiplier, $1/s$, times the rate of investment. Equation (2) is the Harrod-Domar demand condition.

Turning now to aggregate supply, we begin by recognizing that the Harrod-Domar framework assumes fixed proportions between capital and labor. This implies that the productive potential of the economy (potential output) is constrained by the size of the capital stock. This condition may be expressed as follows:

$$Y^s(t) = \alpha K(t) \tag{3}$$

Equation (3) states that output and capital are proportional to each other. The term α in equation (3), the factor of proportionality, is equal to one over the capital output ratio. The assumption, expressed in equation (3), that the capital output ratio is an exogenously determined constant, suggests a severely restricted type of technology: Output can only be varied by changing the capital stock. This implies that the rate of capacity utilization of the capital stock is a constant. Furthermore, it suggests that if the capital stock increases at some constant percentage rate, then the percentage rate of growth of output must adapt to that capital growth rate. (α may appear familiar to readers who will recall from the investment theory in Chapter 10 that the factor of proportionality between output and the capital stock was the *accelerator*.)

From the definition of α in equation (3), and remembering the development of the accelerator in Chapter 10, we can derive the following expression:

$$Y^s(t+1) - Y^s(t) = \alpha[K(t+1) - K(t)] \tag{4}$$

Defining net investment in t as the period-t change in the capital stock, we see that a constant capital output ratio implies that the time rate of change of output potential must be proportional to the rate of net investment. In symbols,

$$\dot{Y}^s(t) = \alpha I(t) \tag{5}$$

(We adopt the convention that a time rate of change in a variable is represented by an overdot.) If we were to solve equation (5) for the rate of net investment, $I(t)$, we would see that it equals the capital output ratio times the rate of increase in output.

Equilibrium, in this model, is determined by equating output potential $Y^s(t)$ to the level of output compatible with aggregate demand, $Y^d(t)$. Replacing aggregate demand with equation (2) and solving (5) for investment produces the following set of results:

$$Y^s(t) = (1/s)I(t) = (1/s)(1/\alpha)\dot{Y}^s(t) \tag{6}$$

We may solve the equation consisting of dividing the left-hand expression in equation (6) into the far right-hand expression in equation (6) in order to obtain the percentage rate of change of productive potential over time. The result is

$$\dot{Y}^s(t)/Y^s(t) = s\alpha \tag{7}$$

Equation (7) contains the first major result of the Harrod-Domar model of economic growth. We see that the rate of growth of productive potential is determined by two terms: the marginal propensity to save, s, and the capital-output ratio, $1/\alpha$. In words, the rate of growth of output is determined by the savings rate (which leads in turn to a rate of capital accumulation) times the ratio of capital to output.

We may also determine, in this model, the rate of change of investment expenditures. We begin with the left-hand expression in equation (6) and the middle expression in equation (6). If we take first differences from one time period to the next of both terms, we have

$$\dot{Y}s(t) = (1/s)\dot{I}(t) \tag{8}$$

Dividing (8) by the respective terms in equation (6) yields the result that the percentage rate of growth of output and the percentage rate of growth of investment expenditures must be proportional in equilibrium. This means that the rate of investment expenditures must also equal the product of MPS and the capital-output ratio: $s\alpha$.

We have now seen that in the Harrod-Domar model the percentage rate of growth and the percentage rate of investment are determined by the product of two exogenous parameters: the marginal propensity to consume and the capital-output ratio. The Harrod-Domar model also contains another exogenous parameter which determines the rate of economic growth. The additional parameter is the rate of growth of the labor force, n. Since Harrod and Domar assume that the labor to output ratio is a fixed constant; just as the capital output ratio was assumed to be a fixed constant, the rate of growth of productive potential, $\dot{Y}/Y$ must grow at the same rate as the labor force. Combining this result with equation (7), we have: $n = s\alpha$.

The variable most likely to show short-run variations among the three in this statement of equilibrium is the marginal propensity to save, s. Therefore, we express the necessary condition for steady state economic growth as:

$$s = n/\alpha \tag{9}$$

Equation (9) is the famous Harrod-Domar condition for *steady state economic growth*: An economy will grow at a steady and constant rate equal to the product of s and α; investment will grow at this same rate, as will the labor force, if and only if the marginal propensity to save equals the product of the growth rate in the labor force and the capital-output ratio. This result has proved most important in growth theory, because it establishes the characteristic condition which must be met by a growing economy in a steady state. It stresses that in a steady state, an economy must have compatibility among the savings rate, the rate of investment spending, the rate of growth of the labor force, and the underlying technology which determines the relationship between capital and output.

Unfortunately, in the Harrod-Domar model, the steady state condition is an equality containing three exogenous parameters. What, one might ask, is the likelihood that a condition such as equation (9) will be met? To illustrate the problem, suppose that the savings rate falls short of n/α. In other words, suppose that savings falls short of the rate of growth of the labor force times the capital-output ratio: $s < n/\alpha$. What will happen? Recall that in this model, the savings rate is assumed to determine the multiplier effect on demand of the rate of investment. Consequently, if the savings rate is lower than n/α, then the multiplier will be large and the rate of capital accumulation will not be sufficient to keep up with demand. The result is that capital becomes scarce! Since the savings rate is determined exogenously, it remains below the labor force and the capital-output ratio determined growth rate. Given the constant capital-output ratio, inadequate capital becomes continually more scarce, and the growing labor supply finds itself without jobs. Increasing levels of unemployment are the result, and this result would appear to worsen without end. Excessive savings does not, on the other hand, solve the problem because if savings are too large, the multiplier is too small and then excessive capacity will generate pressure to overutilize limited labor and the economy will boom with an unending investment expansion.

Sir Roy Harrod defined the steady state growth rate which was consistent with n/α to be the "warranted rate of growth." Harrod thought of n/α as warranting a particular rate of economic growth. He argued that if savings was less than that warranted, then the realized or actual demand would outstrip capacity. The economy would be spiraling upward with no end in sight. At the other extreme, if the saving rate were excessive, this would lead to excess capacity and idle resources. The economy would spiral downward. The implication of the Harrod-Domar model is that, since the key parameters are all exogenous, then if there is even slight deviation in the savings rate from the warranted rate, the economy will explode away from the steady state path. Consequently, the Harrod-Domar steady state is extremely unstable: Small deviations from the path drive the economy away from it. Because the Harrod-Domar model contains no mechanism by which an economy may be stabilized either via return to its original steady state or movement to a new one, it is called a "razor's edge" steady state model. As long as the economy remains exactly on the edge of the razor (determined by the steady state condition), it will grow along a steady state path. If, however, the savings rate deviates slightly in either direction, the economy careens into oblivion.

The Harrod-Domar model was a major contribution in economic theory because it established the conditions for a steady state and because it developed a model in which such a steady state exists. However, it clearly suffers a number of important defects, and these have led to the development of new models. First of all, empirical evidence does not show capitalist economies tending to explode away from steady state growth. There are episodes of economic instability, but we do not observe the wild fluctuations of a razor's edge. Second, the Harrod-Domar restrictions on technology implied by a fixed capital-output ratio and a fixed labor output ratio are quite unsatisfactory. One of the important objectives of growth model builders since Harrod-Domar has been to relax these restrictions on technology. Finally, while the Harrod-Domar model provides us with a set of important parameters for studying economic growth, the rate of growth of the labor force, the savings rate, and the capital output ratio, it would be preferable to try to explain some of these parameters endogenously.

Though the early classical economists did not develop such sophisticated mathematical models in which they specified steady state conditions, much of their economic analysis did deal with growth. The focus of much classical growth analysis was on the rate of growth of the labor force. It was the view of a number of classical economists that labor growth was the crucial variable, which adjusted internally, to achieve what we now call the Harrod-Domar steady state. For example, consider the analysis of Parson Malthus. Suppose savings and therefore investment fall short of productive capabilities. While the immediate result may be increased unemployment and a lower wage rate, Malthus suggested that such conditions would produce a reduction in the rate of growth of the population and, therefore, that the product n/α would, by virtue of the reduction in the rate of growth of population, converge to the new low rate of savings. The rate of growth of the labor force is treated by most modern economists as a very slowly moving variable which is not closely linked to current economic activity. Demographers, of course, devote their energies to studying the rate of population growth. However, economists have in recent years been prone to treat the rate of population growth as an uncontrollable parameter, and their focus has been on the variables largely ignored by the early classical economists: the capital to output ratio and the savings rate.

B • Neoclassical Economic Growth Theory

Stylized Facts of Growth: Nicholas Kaldor, Cambridge, England, developed a set of facts which he believed characterized modern, growing industrialized economies. Because empirical evidence on growth is somewhat difficult to develop, these facts are not to be taken as conclusive. For this reason, Kaldor referred to them as "stylized" facts. They do provide a factual backdrop upon which growth models might be built. Here are the key stylized facts provided by Kaldor:

1. Real output per man-hour, $Y/N = y_n$, grows at a relatively steady rate in the long run. Total output growth can be attributed to growth in two factors: either y_n or n. Again using the notation that a dot on top of a variable represents its time rate of change, we may express this stylized fact as follows:

$$\dot{y}_n = \text{constant} > 0 \qquad\qquad (10)$$

For the U.S. economy, $\dot{y}_n$ appears over the postwar period to have hovered around 3 percent. (As we will discuss later, there is considerable concern that this term has slowed to around 1 percent in recent years.) $\dot{y}_n$ is referred to as the rate of growth of *labor productivity*. If the rate of growth of labor productivity is 3 percent and if the labor force grows at a rate of about 1 percent per year, then total output, y, can grow at around 4 percent per year.

2. The capital stock, in constant prices, appears to grow at a relatively constant rate which is faster than the rate of growth of the labor force. This means that the stock of capital available per worker has been increasing. In symbols, we let $k_n = K/N$ be the per capita capital stock. $\dot{k}_n$ is positive:

$$\dot{k}_n = \text{constant} > 0 \qquad (11)$$

Evidence for the U.S. appears to suggest that $\dot{k}_n$ has been about 4 percent per year. Even though the average rates of growth of capital per unit of labor and output per unit of labor appear to have been around 4 percent, variations in both of these terms are large. Furthermore, these facts are based on very broad aggregative measures which are quite unreliable and controversial. Recent studies suggest that $\dot{k}_n$ for the U.S. may have fallen to 3% in recent years.

3. The capital output ratio varies from period to period and from economy to economy and does not appear to have any particular trend.

$$K/Y = 1/\alpha \qquad (12)$$

Evidence by Edward Dennison (1967) suggests that variations in the capital-output ratio across countries are quite large but that the trends in the capital-output ratio in various countries are quite different. We conclude that while α may vary, we cannot be certain of the direction of its variation.

4. Profit, by which is meant in this context the rate of return on capital, appears to have no systematic growth rate trend. Evidence on profit is probably even less reliable than on other measures discussed above.

Robert Solow (1970), whose model we shall study next, draws the following inference from the stylized facts: "The key ratios are not stable, as the literal steady state picture would demand, but they move slowly and sometimes change direction."

A Neoclassical Model: The main elaboration of the neoclassical growth models over Harrod and Domar deals with the relationship between the labor and capital inputs on the one hand and the level of output on the other. We saw in the Harrod-Domar model that the capital-output and labor-output ratios had to be constant. This means that capital and labor had to be combined in fixed proportions in order to produce output. The neoclassical models begin with a production function relating the quantities of factor inputs to output:

$$Y = F(K, N) \qquad (13)$$

Equation (13) simply expresses the idea that the aggregate quantity of capital and the aggregate quantity of labor combine in some technological way to yield an aggregate level of output. In the model employed by Robert Solow the functional relationship between the inputs and output is restricted by the assumption of constant returns to scale. (Production functions were encountered earlier in this text in the discussion of the neoclassical investment theory of Chapter 11.) It may be recalled that *constant returns to scale* means that if all the inputs are changed in the same proportion, then the level of output will be changed in the same proportion. This assumption rules out increasing returns to scale: If all inputs are doubled, then output can more than double. Decreasing returns to scale are also ruled out. If technology is restricted to constant returns to scale, then one can fix the level of one input, and explore the relationship between output and the remaining inputs at that fixed level. Whatever results are obtained would also maintain for the relationship between output and the varied inputs at every other level of the fixed input. For example, if we fix the capital stock, K, in equation (13), then observe the way in which output varies in response to variations in the quantity of labor, then the results we find will also apply at other levels of capital.

We shall establish this result mathematically and then illustrate it with an algebraic production function as an example. A constant return to scale production function must obey the following condition:

$$F(\lambda K, \lambda N) = \lambda F(K, N) = \lambda Y \qquad (14)$$

Equation (14) states that if each factor input is multiplied by the same constant, so that the scale of production is changed but the ratios of the inputs all remain the same, then the effect on output will be that it will increase by the same scale. In this example the scale parameter is some constant λ. If λ takes on the special value one over the capital stock, $1/K$, then we have

$$F(K/K, N/K) = Y/K \qquad (15)$$

or because K/K is one, letting y_k be output per unit of capital and letting n_k be labor per unit of capital, we can rewrite equation (15) as

$$y_k = f(n_k) \qquad (16)$$

Put another way, output per unit of capital is a function only of the quantity of labor per unit of capital and not of the level of economic activity.

We may further illustrate the important idea of constant returns to scale with a specific production function. The most convenient function to use is the one employed in Chapter 11, the Cobb-Douglas production function:

$$Y = AK^\alpha N^\beta \qquad (17)$$

Suppose that we change the quantity of capital and labor both by constant amount λ; then we have

$$A(\lambda K)^\alpha (\lambda N)^\beta = \lambda^{(\alpha+\beta)} A K^\alpha N^\beta = \lambda^{(\alpha+\beta)} Y \tag{18}$$

Output will be increased in this case by $\lambda^{(\alpha+\beta)}$. Constant returns to scale imply that output must increase by λ. This result applies if and only if $\alpha + \beta = 1$. Constant returns to scale in the case of a Cobb-Douglas production function then requires that the unknown coefficients $\alpha + \beta = 1$. We may under these circumstances rewrite the Cobb-Douglas production function, assuming constant returns to scale as:

$$Y = AK^\alpha L^{1-\alpha} \tag{19}$$

If we now divide both sides of equation (19) by the quantity of capital, we will be able to establish the result expressed in equation (16) that output per unit of capital depends only upon the quantity of labor per unit of capital and not the level at which production is taking place.

$$\frac{Y}{K} = AK^{\alpha-1}N^{1-\alpha} = A(N/K)^{1-\alpha} \tag{20}$$

or

$$y_k = An_k^{1-\alpha} \tag{21}$$

This now completes our illustration of the fact that the assumption of constant returns to scale allows us to focus on one level of economic activity and to be able to draw inferences from that level to any other level of activity.

The Cobb-Douglas production function may be used to illustrate the relationship between y_k and n_k. An increase in the quantity of labor per unit of capital will lead to an increase in output per unit of capital. This result follows as long as the parameter α is a positive fraction. However, an increase in one input, given another input fixed, will lead to diminishing returns. These two results imply that the marginal product of labor is positive but declining. In mathematical terms, this means that the first derivative of the expression in equation (21) must be positive and the second derivative negative:

$$\frac{\partial x_k}{\partial n_k} = (1-\alpha)An_k^{-\alpha} > 0 \tag{22}$$

$$\frac{\partial^2 x_k}{\partial n_k^2} = -\alpha(1-\alpha)An_k^{-(\alpha+1)} < 0 \tag{23}$$

To summarize, the neoclassical restriction on technology of fixed proportions for the factor inputs is no longer required; technology obeys constant returns to scale and diminishing marginal returns. At each level of capital, then, the relationship between output and the variable input, labor, is represented by an increasing line with a decreasing slope, as indicated in the top curve of Figure 2. While technology is more sophisticated in this model than it was in the Harrod-Domar model, the relationship between investment and the demand for output is the same as in the Harrod-Domar framework. In particular, investment is assumed to be a constant proportion of output, and the constant is the savings rate, s. If we divide both investment and the quantity of output by the capital stock, then the proportionality between investment and output yields

$$i_k = s y_k \tag{24}$$

In words, the rate of capital accumulation per unit of capital is a constant fraction (the savings rate) of the level of output per unit of capital. Because the saving rate is obviously less than one, the savings schedule will lie below the production function, as illustrated in Figure 2. In other words, savings grows at a diminishing rate with the growth in labor per unit of capital.

An intuitive explanation of the workings of the model is helpful. At any point in time the existing capital stock is a predetermined fact of history. Given this capital stock, then, we have Figure 2. Investment is determined by the exogenous savings rate in a similar fashion to the story told by Harrod and Domar. From the savings rate, s, and from the resultant rate of investment, one may determine the level of output by utilizing the standard Keynesian multiplier analysis. These relationships are illustrated in Figure 2 by beginning at the point

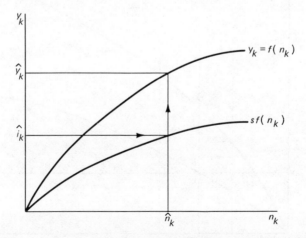

FIGURE 2   Production Function with Fixed Capital and Variable Labor

$\hat{i}_k$ which represents the exogenous rate of investment spending. From the rate of investment spending and the rate of saving one can determine the level of output on the graph to be $\hat{y}_k$. From the level of output per unit of capital, one can in turn determine the level of employment, which on the graph is quantity $\hat{n}_k$. Note that since in the analysis the quantity of capital is historically fixed, variations in output produce variations in the employment level.

The Steady State: Let us now examine the nature of the model in terms of the steady state condition established by Harrod-Domar. Like Harrod and Domar, Solow assumes that the rate of growth of the labor force, $\dot{n}$, is an exogenous datum. In Figure 3, we reproduce the production function and savings-investment schedule from Figure 2. In addition, $\dot{n}$ is represented by a horizontal line since the rate of growth of the labor force is exogenous. Consider the characteristics of the model at point b. $\dot{n}$ equals $sf(n_k)$. In words, the rate of growth of the labor force equals the product of the marginal propensity to save, s, and the ratio of output to capital, y_k. But this equality is exactly the Harrod-Domar steady-state condition: $\dot{n} = sf(n_k) = sy_k$. The rate of capital accumulation, i_k, exactly equals the rate of population growth, $\dot{n}$, because $i_k = sf(n_k)$. In short, a steady-state position exists in the model: should the economy be at point b it will stay there.

Consider movements of the economy should it not be in the steady state. Suppose historical conditions have placed the economy at point c in Figure 3. At c, the rate of capital accumulation will be the vertical distance to $sf(n_k)$ which exceeds the rate of growth of the labor force. Suppose employment policies

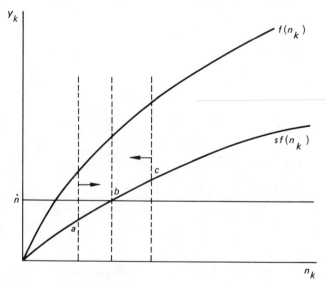

FIGURE 3   Steady-state Growth

maintain the employment rate growing at the same rate as the labor force—perhaps full employment policies are maintained. Then i_k greater than $\dot{n}$ means that n_k is falling, since $n_k = N/K$. Capital will be rising faster than the rate of employment, and the economy will move toward more capital-intense production to the left of c toward b. If the economy were starting to the left of b, at a point like a, labor growth in excess of the rate of capital accumulation would drive the economy to the right—toward b, and as it did so the returns to labor would diminish and the economy would converge to the steady state.

The outcome is that the economic system depicted in the neoclassical model tends toward the steady state. In the steady state, the rates of growth of employment, output, and capital are all equal. This rate of growth is determined by $\dot{n}$, which is taken as exogenous. Consequently, unless the rate of population growth changes, the steady-state rate of growth cannot change.

Suppose, to illustrate the dependency of the rate of growth on the growth rate of the labor force, that the rate of savings rises from s. At the original steady-state point b, the new higher savings rate suddenly creates excess capital accumulation. If the existing unemployment level is maintained, then employment will continue to rise at the constant rate $\dot{n}$. This labor force and employment growth rate is less than the new rate of capital accumulation. The excess capital accumulation will, therefore, reduce the ratio of labor to capital and because of diminishing marginal product will reduce the level of output per unit of capital as well. A falling labor-to-capital ratio and falling output-to-capital ratio implies that the economy is coming to rest at a new steady state to the left of point b. Because the labor force growth rate is occurring at the same level as before, the new steady state must be on the same horizontal line $\dot{n}$. Consequently, the rate of capital accumulation returns to again being equal to $\dot{n}$; thus the rate of output growth is the same as in the original steady state. The economy has, however, undergone changes, because the transition period which resulted from an increased savings rate produced temporary excessive capital accumulation. This excessive capital accumulation increased the quantity of capital per worker and therefore the level of output per worker. Put another way, the economy has moved from one growth path such as path 3, Figure 1, to another, path 4, characterized by the same growth rate but at a different level. This example illustrates that the savings rate can change the level of the growth path but not the rate of ascent when the rate of labor force growth is constant. In this example, the upward shift in the growth path came about at the expense of an increase in the rate of capital accumulation and by implication at the expense of a reduction in current consumption.

Optimal Consumption: Let us now consider the implications of this growth model for consumption. What happens to consumption as the economy moves from one steady state to another? Is there some ratio of labor to capital which produces an optimal level of per capita consumption? We have seen that if the long-run savings rate changes, this will cause a change in the rate of capital accumulation. Is there a target level of capital accumulation, given the rate of growth of the labor force, which one might attempt to attain to achieve some social optimum? First, we shall use the diagram to measure per capita consumption. We reproduce in Figure 4 the production function and savings schedule. The steady state is at point a on the savings schedule. In steady state, the distance from the horizontal axis to the production function measures total output per unit of capital. This total output is allocated between savings and consumption; thus the distance from the savings schedule, at point a to the production function is consumption per unit of capital or, in symbols:

$$c_k = C/K.$$

The horizontal distance from point a to the vertical axis, along the ray $\dot{n}$, measures N/K. Consequently, the ratio of the vertical to the horizontal distance, which is the slope of a ray from the point $\dot{n}$ on the vertical axis to the stationary state point on the production function, is the ratio of consumption per unit of labor:

$$c_k/n_k = C/N$$

In other words, we may measure per capita consumption at any steady state as the slope of the ray from the steady-state point on the production function to the intersection of the labor force growth rate and the vertical axis.

Now suppose we use this measure of per capita consumption, the slope of such a ray, to observe the effect on per capita consumption of varying the steady state by adjusting the savings rate. In other words, we choose the steady state (by adjusting the savings rate) which will produce the optimal level of consump-

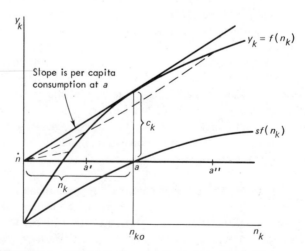

FIGURE 4   Per Capita Consumption and the Steady State

tion. We do so by selecting that steady state for which the ray is the steepest. The optimal steady state, from the point of view of maximum per capita consumption, is the one for which the ray is exactly tangent to the production function. In Figure 4, it is the ray associated with steady state a. Note that the rays represented by the dotted lines all have lower slopes than the tangency ray.

That the steady state with optimal consumption is associated with a ray tangent to the production function has an interesting economic interpretation. At steady state a, per capita consumption is at a maximum. To the right of this steady state, the savings rate would have to be lower, so with a lower rate of capital accumulation, inadequate capital would be available to labor and diminishing returns to the labor input would be incurred. Consequently, per capita consumption would be low. Similarly, to the left of steady state a, say at a', excessive capital accumulation has taken place, so the capital input suffers from diminishing returns. Again, per capita consumption falls because the mix of the factor inputs is not at an optimum. How might an economic policy maker select the optimum steady state? The answer to this question has to do with the economic interpretation of the tangency to the production function. The slope of the production function $f(n_k)$ is the marginal physical product of labor, for it tells us the ratio of the increase in physical product per unit of additional labor. At the tangency steady state, the rate of consumption per worker, the slope of the tangent, equals the marginal product of labor. If an economy operates competitively, then the wage rate is set equal to the marginal product of labor. In other words, the wage bill, the total return to the labor input, is exactly equal to total consumption. Thus the optimal steady state corresponds to the steady state achieved under competitive economic conditions when factor inputs are paid according to their marginal products. Because this model assumes constant returns to scale, the competitive equilibrium steady state, which produces optimal consumption, is also associated with the condition that the profit rate equals the marginal product of capital. This rate of profit can also be shown to equal, by the tangency condition, the natural rate of growth.

C • The Sources of Economic Growth: Study of Productivity

The Facts Versus the Theory: We have now developed a neoclassical growth model. While it is mathematically rather sophisticated, the model is a terribly skeletal version of an economy. Though the model does not require rigid adherence to the stylized facts, a characteristic stable steady state does exist which seems to fit the facts reasonably well. Unfortunately one aspect of the stylized facts, which seems to fit empirical evidence reasonably well, appears to be inconsistent with the implications of the model. The rate of growth of output and capital exceed the rate of growth of the labor force. Output per worker and capital per worker, in the post-World War II period, tend to be rising. Yet, in the model, capital and output growth must always return at the steady state to the rate of growth of the labor force. Put another way, if we attempted to predict the rate of economic growth from the rate of growth of the labor force and the capital stock, we would have a growth rate that is less than the rate actually observed. It is to this apparent enigma that economists have in recent years directed their attention. How does one explain the phenomenal period of growth since World War II? Although this problem is a very difficult one, it will be interesting to explore some empirical evidence on actual growth performance. Let us begin by illustrating, in a diagram similar to the ones used in the Solow growth model, the nature of the enigma. We construct in Figure 5 below a production function in which we have measured output and capital both per unit of labor. (This is analogous to the Solow diagrams, in which we divided through by the capital stock.) The analysis begins on the production function 1. The economy begins at point A on this production function, producing output level y_A with capital k_A, both measured in labor units, i.e., $y = Y/N$ and $k = K/N$. After a period of time has elapsed, the economy is at point B. The question economists would like answered is how the economy moved from point A to point B.

Econometric studies which estimate the change in the capital stock and the change in the labor force can explain an increase in output per capita up to point C. However, since the economy moved all the way to B, some changes other than those identified with the factor inputs must have taken place. This unexplained portion of economic growth is called total factor productivity. Some students of economic growth refer to this as a measure of our ignorance. Others consider it to be a result of a technological change, of computerization, of organizational amd managerial improvements, or of shifts from less productive to more productive sectors. In any case, our objective here is to review a specific attempt to measure, empirically, the actual growth performance of several countries from the end of World War II until the late 1970s. As Figure 5 suggests, in order for the economy to have moved from A to B, the production function

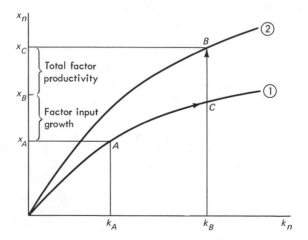

FIGURE 5   The Enigma of Post-World War II Growth

must have shifted upward. This increase in total factor productivity explains some proportion of economic growth. The objective of econometric studies of growth has been to decompose the move from A to B into two parts: first, the movement from A to C–growth in factor inputs; second, the movement from C to B–total factor productivity. (We should clarify that even though our figure holds the quantity of labor fixed by deflating output and capital by the quantity of labor, total factor productivity is the residual which is left over after we attribute as much growth in output as possible to growth in all factor inputs, including labor.)

The econometric study we shall review here was undertaken by Christiansen, Cummings, and Jorgenson (1980). First, let us briefly develop the theoretical model which underlies the measures of economic growth developed by Christiansen, Cummings, and Jorgenson (CCJ). The analysis begins with a production function not unlike that used in the Solow growth model:

$$Q = AF(K, L) \qquad (25)$$

Equation (25) states that output Q is equal to a constant times the production function which depends upon the quantities of capital and labor used in the production process. The constant term, A, represents the technological changes which cause production to be larger than that explained by the increases in the quantities of capital and labor. The constant term A in equation (25) is referred to as a *Hicksian index of technological change*. With some fairly straightforward calculus, one can produce a measure of productivity change by studying the effect on equation (25) of changes in all variables over time. (If the mathematics in the following paragraphs is too difficult, the student should concentrate only on the logic of the result in equation (28).) Letting an overdot represent a change in a variable over time, we can attribute the total change in output to the sum of two terms, the first the total change in the technology parameter A and the second, the total change in the function which depends in turn on the total changes in capital and labor. In symbols:

$$\dot{Q} = \dot{A}F(K, L) + [Q_K \dot{K} + Q_L \dot{L}] \qquad (26)$$

The terms in brackets simply represent the total change in the production function as a result of the time rate of change of the capital stock and the time rate of change of the labor force. In other words, the total change in the production function F is the sum of the marginal physical product of capital times the rate of change of the capital input plus the marginal physical product of labor times the rate of change in the labor input. Dividing equation (26) by Q and making some appropriate adjustments produces

$$\frac{\dot{Q}}{Q} = \frac{\dot{A}}{A} + \left[Q_K \frac{K}{Q} \left(\frac{\dot{K}}{K} \right) + Q_L \frac{L}{Q} \left(\frac{\dot{L}}{L} \right) \right] \qquad (27)$$

At this point CCJ make two critical assumptions in their analysis. They assume that the production function satisfies constant returns to scale and that the economy can be characterized by competitive equilibrium. This last conclusion means that each factor input is paid the value of its marginal product. From this result, as we have seen earlier both in this chapter and in Chapter 11, the following two results hold:

$$Q_K = c/p \quad \text{and} \quad Q_L = w/p$$

where c represents the cost of capital, p the product price, and w the wage rate. Substituting the real cost of capital and the real wage for the respective marginal products in equation (27) and rearranging terms, we have

$$\frac{\dot{Q}}{Q} = \frac{\dot{A}}{A} + \left[\left(\frac{cK}{pQ}\right)\frac{\dot{K}}{K} + \left(\frac{wL}{pQ}\right)\frac{\dot{L}}{L} \right] \tag{28}$$

Equation (28) forms the theoretical basis for the econometric work of CCJ. Equation (28) states that the percentage change in real output may be attributed to the sum of the percentage change in productivity plus the change in output attributed to changes in factor inputs. To understand the measurement of these latter two terms, note that the terms in parentheses in the brackets are respective factor shares. The term cK is the total cost of capital and wL is the total wage bill. Under constant returns to scale, when an economy is in competitive equilibrium, the returns to all factor inputs will exhaust total output. Consequently, the terms in parentheses represent the respective shares in total revenue of the individual inputs. Thus, the effect on output of changes in capital and labor depend upon their relative shares in total product. Letting v_k and v_l represent the shares of total revenue of capital and labor respectively, we may now indicate that the percentage rate of change in total factor productivity is equal to the difference between the percentage rate of change of output and the share-weighted percentage rates of change of the factor inputs. Letting lowercase letters represent percentage rates of change, we have

$$\dot{a} = \dot{q} - [v_k \dot{k} + v_l \dot{i}] \tag{29}$$

The first set of results is contained in Table 1, the average annual percentage rates of change in real output for five countries: the United States, Canada, Germany, Japan, and the United Kingdom. In each case, the data are divided into two subperiods: (1) from the end of World War II (which varies a bit from country to country) to 1960, and (2) 1960 through 1973. These two subperiods are roughly of equal length, and the average annual percentage rates of change may be compared across them. The first observation one may draw from Table 1 is that the U.S. had moderate growth, whereas Japan's growth was quite miraculous. Japan's growth rate per year was 8.1 percent in the earlier period and 10.9

TABLE 1

Select Growth Rates (Average Annual Percentage Rates of Change)

| COUNTRY | PERIOD ENDING 1960 [1] | | | 1960-1973 | | |
	OUT-PUT [2]	IN-PUTS	PRODUC-TIVITY	OUT-PUT	IN-PUTS	PRODUC-TIVITY
U.S.A.	3.7	2.3	1.4	4.3	3.0	1.3
Canada	5.2	3.5	1.7	5.1	3.3	1.8
Germany	8.2	3.6	4.7	5.4	2.4	3.0
Japan	8.1	4.7	3.4	10.9	6.4	4.5
U.K.	3.3	1.8	1.5	3.8	1.8	2.1

[1] The beginning of the period differs by country: 1947 for U.S.A. and Canada, 1950 for Germany, 1952 for Japan, and 1955 for the U.K.
[2] *Output* refers to real product; *Input*, to total factor input; Productivity, to total factor productivity.

Source: Table 11, p. 51, Christensen, Cummings, and Jorgenson (1980).

percent in the later period. While Germany's economic growth was high, it had fallen from the first period to the second. The U.K., whose economic growth was positive, was small by the standards of the other countries. There is sufficient variation over time and across countries to allow some detailed analysis of the sources of economic growth.

The first major conclusion come to by CCJ is that growth of output is closely associated with growth in the factor inputs. In other words, growth cannot be explained by productivity alone; it must be accompanied by increases in the quantities of inputs. For example, the increase in Japan's growth rate from 8.1 percent to 10.9 percent across the periods was associated with an input growth rate from 4.7 percent to 6.4 percent. Germany, in contrast, incurred a decline in its rate of economic growth from 8.2 to 5.4 percent, and its factor inputs declined from 3.6 to 2.4 percent across the periods. Finally, the smallest rates of economic growth for the U.K. are associated with the smallest growth rates in inputs.

We can examine the relationship between economic growth and rates of growth of the individual inputs by referring to Table 2. Table 2 contains the value share of capital in each country at each point in time and the individual rates of growth of capital and labor. On the basis of this evidence, CCJ draw a number of conclusions: (1) The capital share is relatively stable across countries, varying from 35 percent for Japan to 45 percent for Canada. (2) Capitals' share is increasing from the first period to the second period, and the rate of capital growth exceeds the rate of labor growth in all countries except Japan during the earlier period. (3) Perhaps most important, high economic growth requires a high growth rate in both factor inputs. Conversely, slow growth is associated with slow growth in both factor inputs. For example, the U.K.'s slow growth (3.3 and 3.8 percent) is associated with only modest capital growth (4.5 and 4.6 percent) but with near zero growth in the labor factor (0.2 and 0 percent). Capital growth

Table 2

Value-Shares of Capital and Growth Rates of Capital and Labor

	PERIOD ENDING 1960			1960-1973		
	K-SHARE	*Growth Rates of* CAPITAL	LABOR	K-SHARE	*Growth Rates of* CAPITAL	LABOR
U.S.A.	39.3	4.5	1.0	41.4	4.0	2.2
Canada	42.0	6.8	1.1	44.9	4.9	2.0
Germany	36.7	6.9	1.6	40.1	7.0	−0.7
Japan	35.2	4.5	4.8	41.5	11.5	2.7
U.K.	38.0	4.5	0.2	38.7	4.6	0.0

Source: Column 1, Table 12, p. 51; columns 2 and 3, Table 11, p. 55 in Christensen, Cummings, and Jorgenson.

in the U.S. is also modest (4.5 and 4 percent), but higher labor growth (1 and 2 percent) produced a higher rate of economic growth. Germany also provides an interesting example. While its capital growth remained constant across the two periods (from 6.9 to 7.0 percent), its labor factor growth declined from 1.6 to −0.7 percent, and its rate of economic growth as seen in Table 1 declined from 8.2 to 5.4 percent. Japan's growth, which increased the most over time, was accompanied by comparatively rapid growth in both its factor inputs (4.5 to 11.5 percent for capital and 4.8 to 2.7 percent for labor). These were the largest in each case compared to the other countries. Finally, an example of a country whose labor input grew but whose capital input did not: Canada's labor input grew from the early to the later period from 1.1 to 2 percent. However, output growth remained roughly the same, 5.2 to 5.1 percent. The capital factor's growth rate declined from 6.8 to 4.9 percent. It is evident from these comparative figures that the growth of *both* factor inputs must occur in order to support economic growth.

One final conclusion from Table 2 is that the changes in the rate of growth of one factor tend to move in the opposite direction from the changes in the rate of growth of the other factor. For example, when the rate of capital growth rises (Japan from 4.5 to 11.5 percent), that of labor falls (4.8 to 2.7 percent). When the capital growth rate declines (Canada from 6.8 to 4.9 percent), that of labor rises (1.1 to 2.0 percent). This result indicates a high degree of substitution between the labor and capital inputs.

The last body of evidence we take from the Christiansen, Cummings, and Jorgenson analysis of growth in different countries appears in Table 3. Table 3 provides an analysis of the sources of economic growth, for it presents the percentage of contributions to total growth of capital, labor, and total factor productivity. It is interesting to note that the contributions to growth of the labor and capital factors vary greatly over time and across countries. Even though, as we saw in the earlier tables, rapid growth requires growth in both inputs and even though the share of total product which goes to capital is comparatively constant, the percentage contributions of the different factors vary substantially. Capital accounted for less than 20 percent of Japan's growth in the earlier period and nearly 55 percent of Canada's growth. While labor contributed 38 percent to the growth of Japan before 1960, it contributed less than 15 percent in the later period, and the labor contribution to Germany and the U.K. in the latter period was actually negative. We should note that the underlying growth rates in the individual factor inputs, seen in Table 2, are consistent with the results on the relative contributions of the factor inputs. Finally, note from Table 3 that total factor productivity, the term which embodies technological change, accounts for from one-third to over half of economic growth!

One should be cautious not to conclude from this last observation that technological change has, *on its own*, caused a 30 percent increase in the rate of economic growth. As Hulten (1979) pointed out, even though we can partition the growth process to the capital factor and the labor factor, each weighted by their respective shares and to a residual for total factor productivity, the growth process may require growth in the capital factor in order for technological change to be large because technology often comes on line with new capital.

We have now completed our analysis of the remarkable period of economic growth appreciated in the U.S., Canada, Germany, Japan, and the U.K. We have seen that substantial economic growth requires growth in both capital and labor inputs, and yet a substantial proportion of growth is still attributed to total factor productivity, which means that it cannot be explained strictly on grounds of growth in the capital and labor factor inputs. We turn now to a brief discussion of the slowdown in the rate of economic growth in the U.S. in the 1970s compared to the 1960s.

We presented earlier the views of various presidential councils that the growth rate of potential GNP was slowing continually in the late 1970s. Why was this slowdown in growth taking place? Statistical evidence from the Department of Labor on the rate of growth of output per unit of labor input both in manufacturing, for which statistics are reasonably good, and for the economy at large,

TABLE 3

Value-Share of Capital and Sources of Growth

Country	Period Ending 1960 % Contribution of			1960-1973 % Contribution of		
	K^1	L	A	K	L	A
U.S.A.	46.9	16.0	77.5	39.3	30.6	30.1
Canada	54.9	12.7	32.5	43.0	20.9	36.1
Germany	31.0	12.0	56.8	52.0	-7.4	55.6
Japan	19.7	38.0	42.1	43.7	14.7	41.4
U.K.	44.5	4.2	51.3	53.8	-0.6	46.8

[1] K is real capital input; L is real labor input; A is total factor productivity.

Source: Table 12, p. 55, Christensen, Cummings, and Jorgenson (1980).

indicates that the rate of growth of output per labor input has declined rather substantially from a high of around 3 percent in the 1960s to 1 percent or to 1.5 percent in the 1970s. Why? There is some evidence that both the quality of the labor input and the quantity of the capital input have failed to grow as rapidly in the 1970s as they had in earlier years. First, the composition of the labor force shifted towards primarily younger workers with a massive influx of teenagers. Many of these younger workers were high school dropouts, and younger workers in general have a lower level of skills than more experienced workers. This explains in part the deterioration in the labor input. Many economists also attribute the slowdown in labor productivity to a slowdown in the rate of capital accumulation in the late 1960s and early 1970s. Bosworth and Duesenberry (1976), for example, argue that the U.S. is entering into a period of severe capital shortages as a result of inadequate capital accumulation in the past.

However, a capital shortage, if one exists, only raises the question of why did it occur? Different economists have provided different answers to this question. Arthur Burns, for example, attributed some of the blame for the slowdown in the growth to environmental concerns and to the constraints therefore placed on industry attempting to acquire new capital. Monetarists and free market economists attribute the slowdown in capital accumulation to excessive government deficits which place pressure on financial markets and crowd out private domestic investment. Tax economists tend to attribute the slowdown in capital accumulation to tax burdens. Holland, for example, in a publication by the American Enterprise Institute (1978) argued that the tax burden on capital was excessive. R. J. Gordon, on the other hand, attributes the slowdown in productivity to a slowdown in the rate of technological change. Gordon claims that the rate of technological change had slowed abruptly from the mid-1960s to the mid-1970s. Finally, Feldstein argues that the slowdown in capital accumulation can best be explained by the dampening effects on the savings which come from ill-conceived social plans such as Social Security. It should be evident from this discussion that the causes of slowdowns in economic growth are very difficult to determine. Many plausible explanations are available, and, while each of the above views may have an element of truth to it, it is difficult to determine which is the most important factor.

STUDY QUESTIONS

1. Construct the Harrod-Domar model and illustrate the necessary and sufficient condition for a stationary state. Why, in the context of this model, does a stationary state appear unlikely?

2. What does it mean to say the Harrod-Domar steady state is unstable?

3. Define and either illustrate or give an example of each of the following terms:

warranted rate of growth   constant returns to scale
rate of time preference   the razor's edge
stylized facts   embodied technological change

4. Why do economists believe that the razor's edge characteristic of the Harrod-Domar model is a weakness of the model? How do the neoclassicists reconcile the problem of instability in their models?

5. Construct a neoclassical growth model. Show that the steady state exists and is stable.

6. Trace the effects on the various economic magnitudes of the neoclassical model in Question 5 of an increase in the savings rate.

7. Derive geometrically the stationary state for which consumption per capita is a maximum. (Utilize the model developed in Question 5 above.)

8. Explain as carefully as you can the factors which you would consider in determining whether to increase or decrease the savings rate over the long run.

9. How does one reconcile the fact that an increase in the savings rate in a growth model can lead to an increase in consumption with the paradox of thrift?

10. Is growth compatible with "the quality of life?"

11. Assuming a constant returns production function and competitive product and factor markets, show that if technology is represented by A, where output Y is $Y = AF(K,L)$, where K, L are capital and labor respectively, that the rate of technological change is the difference between the rate of growth of output and the share-weighted growth of the inputs.

12. List three empirical observations one may draw from the Cummings, Christensen, and Jorgenson results on growth summarized in Tables 1, 2, and 3. Discuss policy conclusions which you believe follow from these empirical observations.

13. Analyze the causes of the slowdown in productivity reported in the table below. You may wish to consider the role of (a) the labor force, (b) savings, (c) taxes, (d) industrial composition, (e) capital formation, (f) technological change, (g) stabilization measures, and (h) government. (An answer merely listing possible causes without some notion either of their relative importance or of the process by which they reduce productivity change would be insufficient.)

Average Annual Growth of Productivity*

	Private non-farm	*Manufacturing*
1948-65	2.8%	3.1
1965-73	2.0	2.5
1973-78	1.1	1.7

*Source: "Editors' Summary" #2, 1979, *Brookings Papers on Economic Activity*, Arthur Okun and George Perry (eds.).

REFERENCES

Allen, R. G. D., *Macroeconomic Theory*. London: MacMillan, 1968. Chaps. 10, 11, 14, 15.

Christensen, Laurits R., Dianne Cummings, and Dale W. Jorgenson, "Economic Growth, 1947-1973: An International Comparison," in J. W. Kendrick and B. N. Vaccara (eds.), *New Developments in Productivity Measurement and Analysis*. Chicago, Ill.: University of Chicago Press, 1980.

Davidson, Paul, "Money, Portfolio Balance, Capital Accumulation and Economic Growth," *Econometrica*, 1968.

Denison, Edward F., assisted by Jean-Pierre Poullier, *Why Growth Rates Differ: Postwar Experience in Nine Western Countries*. Washington, D.C.: Brookings Institution, 1967.

Domar, Evsy, "Expansion and Employment," *American Economic Review*, 1947.

Foley, Duncan, and Miguel Sidrauski, *Monetary and Fiscal Policy in a Growing Economy*. New York: Macmillan, 1971.

Gordon, Robert A., and Lawrence Klein, *Readings in Business Cycles*. London: George Allen and Unwin, 1966.

Hahn, F. H., and R. C. D. Matthews, "The Theory of Economic Growth: A Survey," *Surveys of Economic Theory*, American Economic Association and the Royal Statistical Society, 1967.

Harrod, Roy, *Toward a Dynamic Economics*. London: MacMillan, 1948.

Hulten, Charles R., "On the 'Importance' of Productivity Change," *American Economic Review*, March 1969, pp. 126-36.

Johnson, Harry, "Money in a Neo-Classical One-Sector Growth Model," *Essays in Monetary Economics*. London: George Allen and Unwin, 1966.

Jorgenson, Dale W., "Growth and Fluctuations: A Causal Interpretation," *Quarterly Journal of Economics*, August 1960.

————, and Zvi Griliches, "The Explanation of Productivity Change," *Review of Economic Studies*, May 1969.

Levhari, D., and Don Patinkin, "The Role of Money in a Simple Growth Policy," *American Economic Review*, 1968.

Nordhaus, William, and James Tobin, "Is Growth Obsolete?" *Economic Growth*, Fiftieth Anniversay Colloquium, Vol. 5, National Bureau of Economic Research. New York: Columbia University Press, 1972.

Robinson, Joan, *The Accumulation of Capital*. Homewood, Ill.: Richard D. Irwin, 1956.

Sen, A., *Growth Economics*. Baltimore: Penguin Press, 1970.

Shell, Karl, *Essays on the Theory of Optimal Economic Growth*. Cambridge, Mass.: MIT Press, 1967.

Sidrauski, Miguel, "Rational Choice and Patterns of Growth in a Monetary Economy," *American Economic Review*, May 1967.

Solow, Robert, *Growth Theory: An Exposition*. Oxford and New York: Oxford University Press, 1970.

————, "A Contribtuion to the Theory of Economic Growth," *Quarterly Journal of Economics*, 1956.

————, "Technical Changes and the Aggregate Production Function," *Review of Economics and Statistics*, 1957.

Stein, Jerome, "Money and Capacity Growth," *Journal of Political Economy*, 1968.

Tobin, James, "A Dynamic Aggregative Model," *Journal of Political Economy*, 1955.

_____, "Money and Economic Growth," *Econometrica*, 1965.

It does not strain reality very much to describe the world economy we seek to achieve as one in which (1) there is complete freedom in the international movement of goods and capital, (2) exchange rates are fixed, and (3) individual countries are free to use monetary and fiscal policy—primarily the former—to attain their domestic price and employment goals. And the system is subject to the constraint that each country possesses a limited supply of reserves with which to cover deficits in its balance of payments. The trouble with this system is that it is basically inconsistent.

Warren L. Smith (1965)

While the net contribution of the foreign sector to GNP in the U.S. is generally quite small—usually less than 1 percent—international trade, investment, and monetary exchange play an extremely important role in the U.S. economy. For example, while exports minus imports, the net contribution to GNP, in 1978 was negative, −$10.3 billion, gross exports were $207.2 billion. Foreign markets are extremely important to the U.S. economy. They represent a larger share of U.S. production than do federal purchases, $152.6 billion in 1978, including expenditures for national defense. In the same year, the U.S. was importing $217.5 billion worth of goods and services.

Anyone living through the decade of the 1970s realizes the extreme im-

24

International Trade
and
Domestic Stabilization

portance of foreign products to the U.S. standard of living. The most dramatic example was petroleum. Sudden dramatic price increases imposed by the OPEC cartel several times in the 1970s produced traumatic dislocations in the U.S. domestic economy. Furthermore, the volume of petroleum products imported to the U.S. grew enormously over this period: from $2 to $2.5 billion per year in the late 1960s to $45 billion of petroleum products in 1977. The U.S. imports about 3 billion barrels of crude oil per year or 8.2 million a day!

The U.S. economy interacts with foreign economies through financial capital flows as well as through the exchange of goods and services. Foreign direct investment in the U.S. grew dramatically over the last decade: from $200 million in 1972 to $5.6 billion in 1978, for example. Meanwhile, U.S. direct investment abroad in 1978 was $15.4 billion. These massive financial capital flows reflect the increasing extent to which world financial markets have become integrated.

Substantial trade and capital flows by the late 1970s between the U.S. and the rest of the world were accompanied by large fluctuations in the rates of exchange between foreign currencies and the dollar. Figure 1 provides an illustration of the purchasing power of the dollar in terms of foreign currencies. Figure 1 graphs the intertemporal movements from 1970 through 1978 of the "weighted-average exchange value of the U.S. dollar," which is a general index of dollar movements against ten major currencies. (The weights for each of these currencies are the total 1972-1976 multilateral trade shares for each country.) When the value of the index is above 100, this indicates that foreign currencies (on average the ones which are most important for U.S. trade) have become

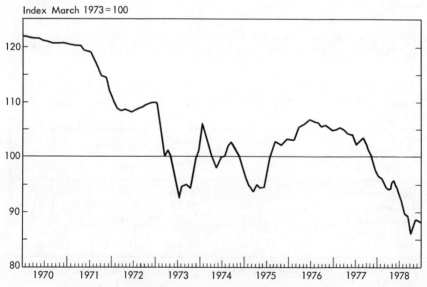

FIGURE 1   Weighted-Average Exchange Value of the U.S. Dollar
Source: Economic Report of the President, January, 1979.

more expensive, and when the index falls below 100, foreign currencies are comparatively inexpensive. As Figure 1 indicates, in the middle of 1973 and from late 1975 to mid-1977 the dollar deteriorated relative to other major currencies. While the exchange value of the dollar improved to 94.8 in 1978, the balance on current account for the U.S. was −$16 billion, and official reserve transactions indicate a foreign reserve increase of $34 billion. The largest single component of this foreign reserve increase into the U.S. reflected the purchase by foreign central banks, primarily those of our major trading partners, of $24 billion in short-term U.S. government securities. These official central bank and government financial transactions in late 1977 and in 1978 indicate that governmental intervention was undertaken in order to improve the position of the dollar and in order to stabilize the U.S. balance of payments.

Since 1971, international monetary arrangements have basically involved a system of partially managed floating rates of exchange. This means that the exchange ratios between currencies are partly allowed to fluctuate automatically. It is misleading under this arrangement to evaluate a country's international transactions performance solely on the basis of its balance of payments figures. Nevertheless, the U.S. clearly had some balance of payments problems: We were importing $10.9 billion more goods and services than we were exporting, and the U.S. balance on current account was negative: −$16 billion. Furthermore, as we noted above, foreign reserves in the U.S. were increased by $34 billion. A more complete picture of the U.S. international transactions position can be obtained by combining this information from the U.S. balance of payments with other information, such as the foreign exchange rate between the dollar and other major currencies.

Table 1, contains the cost of select foreign currencies in terms of the dollar as well as the weighted average exchange value of the dollar for select years. From 1977 to 1978 the dollar's ability to purchase foreign currencies had, in

TABLE 1

Foreign Exchange Rate

Currency	¢/F* (1973 = 100) March			
	1973	1975	1977	1978
Canadian dollar	100.30	100.00	95.10	88.80
Japanese yen	0.38	0.35	0.36	0.43
German mark	35.50	43.10	41.80	49.20
U. K. pound	247.20	241.80	171.40	190.60
Average	100.00	93.90	105.20	94.80

*The index measures the ratio of American cents per unit of foreign exchange, in the base period 1973.

Source: *Economic Report of the President*, January 1979.

general, improved considerably, because, even though the Japanese yen and the Deutschmark had become more expensive, the general cost of foreign exchange had fallen from an index number of 105.2 to 94.8. Unfortunately, this relative improvement in the value of the dollar undoubtedly reflects to a great extent the active interventionist policies established in 1977 by the U.S. government and the central bank. While the actual transactions undertaken in foreign currencies by the central bank are kept confidential, it is known that foreign central banks, especially the German, agreed to buy large volumes of U.S. government short-term securities with their reserves, which the U.S. could then use to purchase back American dollars on international markets. The increased purchases of U.S. dollars on the international market by the U.S. itself tends, of course, to bolster the dollar.

The 1977 interventionist policies of the U.S. to support the dollar are an interesting example of policy actions taken in order to foster international trade and exchange. In fact, international monetary instability has been a feature of the economic landscape for quite some time and has often produced stabilization reactions. Lawrence Krause (1970) estimated that the international monetary system founded at Bretton Woods in 1944 had from 1967 to 1970 undergone at least five major crises. By 1971 the U.S.' balance on goods and services was nearly zero. A negative U.S. trade balance had, up until then, not occurred since 1893. Concerned with the erosion of the U.S. balance of payments position in 1971, President Nixon imposed, in August of that year, a comprehensive and dramatic set of new measures which were designed to slow aggregate demand, freeze domestic wages and prices, suspend convertibility of the dollar into gold, and constrain trade by temporary import surcharges. While the Nixon measures forced a change in the nature of international monetary arrangements, the international balance picture for the U.S. does not appear to have improved permanently.

Table 2 summarizes U.S. international transactions in some select years. The table indicates a continued deterioration of the balance of payments on current account in the 1970s. Both 1972 and 1974 were years of current account deficits. 1975, the reader may recall, was a year in which the U.S. suffered a severe recession. The 1975 recession produced such a reduction in domestic demand that we had a large balance of payments surplus on goods and services of $16 billion. The late 1970s are another story altogether. The U.S. continued to run large current account deficits and to bring in large volumes of foreign official assets.

It is by no means clear that these balance of payments figures represent a dangerous situation for the U.S. The position of the U.S. in international economic affairs is unique. Not only is trade with the U.S. essential to most of her trading partners, but the U.S. also functions as the banker for the rest of the world. The U.S. is in this position mainly because it is a major super power whose dollar is the central reserve currency used in most international transactions.

TABLE 2

U.S. International Transactions Summary (Select Years)

| Year | Balance of Payments | | O.R.T.* | |
	Goods and Services	Current Account	U.S.	Foreign
1960	4.0	1.7	2.1	1.3
1970	2.9	− .4	2.5	7.4
1972	− 6.0	− 9.8	0.0	10.7
1974	3.6	− 3.6	−1.4	11.0
1975	16.3	11.7	−0.6	6.9
1977	−10.5	−15.3	−0.2	37.1
1978	−10.9	−16.0	0.9	34.0

* O.R.T.: Official Reserve Transactions
  U.S.: U.S. official reserve assets [increase/capital outflow (−)]
Foreign: Foreign official assets in the U.S.[increase/capital flow (+)]

Sources: *Survey of Current Business*, June 1976, 1979; and *Economic Indicators*, May 1979, J.E.C.

In summary, international economic activity is important, even to a large economy such as the U.S., for a number of reasons:

1. Foreign markets have become increasingly important to the U.S. The ratio of exports to GNP increased from 5 percent in 1950 to 10 percent in 1978.
2. Imports of particular goods and services, such as petroleum products, are essential to the U.S.
3. Financial capital markets have become nearly fully integrated, so financial transactions are becoming as important as commodity and the U.S. is a central monetary market force.
4. Stabilization authorities, both central banks and government economic agencies, often respond dramatically to real or perceived problems in balance of payments positions.

The purpose of this chapter is to incorporate international trade and financial activity into our macro comparative static models. The first step is to introduce the direct effects on the commodity market of exports and imports. The second, and more complex, task is to introduce international financial activity into the models. This task requires two steps: (1) development of a theoretical model of international exchange, and (2) development of the interaction between the domestic economy and international monetary transactions. This new model may be used to study potential conflicts between domestic stabilization objectives and balance of payments problems, the relative effectiveness of fiscal and monetary policies, various theoretical views as to the importance of international monetary activity, and finally the transmission of inflation across international boundaries.

A • Imports and Exports in Commodity Market Equilibrium

The inclusion of trade in the commodity market will be developed in two stages. First, consider the income-expenditure model in which the domestic economy is characterized by the following system of five equations, each expressed in real terms:

$$c = c_0 + by_d \tag{1}$$

$$i = i_0 + fy \tag{2}$$

$$g = g_0 \tag{3}$$

$$\tau = t_0 + ty \tag{4}$$

$$y = c + i + g \tag{5}$$

An economy such as that represented in equations (1) through (5) is called a *closed economy* because it contains no economic interaction with other systems. The algebraic solution for income, it will be recalled, is

$$\overline{y} = \frac{c_0 + i_0 - bt_0 + g_0}{1 - [b(1 - t) + f]} \tag{6}$$

To introduce the "rest of the world" into the commodity market model, let z and j represent the deflated real values of exports and imports, respectively. To avoid at this point complications resulting from price level changes, suppose that the domestic price level and the "rest of the world" price level always change in exactly the same proportion. Given the assumption that relative price levels remain fixed, we may add two equations to the model. First, exports of U.S. products would depend upon phenomena in the rest of the world and will therefore be treated as exogenous:

$$z = z_0 \tag{7}$$

Imports, on the other hand, represent demand by U.S. individuals for foreign products. Because imports may be viewed as merely a special type of consumer demand and producer demand, they, (much like consumption) will depend on domestic economic factors. Imports may be considered dependent on real disposable income:

$$j = j_0 + qy_d \tag{8}$$

Equation (8) states that real imports are a linear function of real disposable income. j_0 is a constant exogenous factor and q is the marginal propensity to import out of disposable income. The equilibrium condition, equation (5), is now:

$$y = c + i + g + z - j \tag{9}$$

A comment about equation (9) is necessary for clarification. $y + j$ equals the total supply (from both domestic and foreign sources) of goods and services to the domestic economy. $c + i + g + z$ is aggregate demand for these goods and services, again domestic and foreign. Thus, (9) is merely a revised version of the statement that supply equals demand.

The new model consists of equations (1) through (4) and (7) through (9). The algebraic solution to equilibrium income is determined in the usual fashion by substituting the relevant schedules into (9):

$$\overline{y} = \frac{c_0 - (b - q)t_0 + i_0 + g_0 + z_0 - j_0}{1 - [(b - q)(1 - t) + f]} \tag{10}$$

Exogenous exports increase aggregate demand while exogenous imports decrease aggregate demand. Furthermore, q, the marginal propensity to import, will alter the multipliers.

Figure 2 illustrates that the foreign sector changes both the intercept and the slope of the aggregate demand curve. The intercept is increased by $z_0 - j_0 + qt_0$. z_0 is exogenous foreign demand for U.S. products and j_0 is the loss in domestic demand as replaced by imports. qt_0 indicates that a portion of consumer tax liability will detract from demand for foreign goods, not domestic. If $z_0 - j_0 + qt_0 > 0$, the AD curve will shift upwards as depicted in Figure 2. The slope of the AD curve was formerly $[b(1 - t) + f]$, the sum of the marginal propensity to consume out of disposable income and the marginal propensity to invest. The slope is now $[(b - q)(1 - t) + f]$, which is smaller by $q(1 - t)$. q $(1 - t)$ represents the induced increases in imports from increases in income. Rising imports in this model detract from domestic aggregate demand. Thus increases in AD from a given increase in y are moderated by rising import demand: the slope of AD is smaller.

Equilibrium income in the closed economy and open economy may be compared with the use of Figure 2. As drawn here, the foreign sector increases equilibrium income from y_1 to y_2. At the new equilibrium level of income the distance between the old AD curve and the new one represents the difference $z - j$: the distance from y_2 to the AD (open economy) line is c plus i plus g at income level y_2 plus $z - j$. The trade balance $z - j = B_p$ is a surplus because exports exceed imports at y_2. However, the result need not be so. Equilibrium income could be below what it would have been had the economy been closed. The trade balance is then negative and GNP is actually reduced by excessive imports over exports.

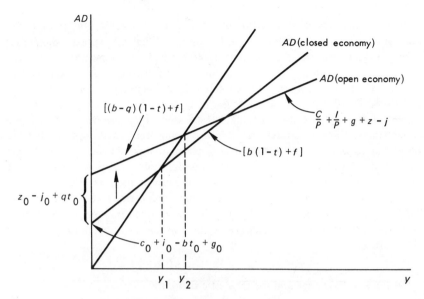

FIGURE 2   Commodity Market: Open Economy

As indicated above, the foreign sector alters the slope of the aggregate demand curve. Consequently the impact upon y of any exogenous change will be altered by the trade relationships. Specifically, the marginal propensity to import alters the multipliers. Consider the government expenditure multiplier k_g computed from Equation (10):

$$k_g = \frac{1}{1 - [(b - q)(1 - t) + f]} \tag{11}$$

Recall that b, the marginal propensity to consume, and k_g, the government expenditure multiplier, are positively correlated. A large MPC results in a larger government multiplier. The introduction of q, the marginal propensity to import, is analogous to lowering b, because now an additional dollar of income partly goes to foreign demand as well as to increases in domestic consumption. Since increases in import demand do not directly induce domestic production and income increases, the multipliers are now smaller. Thus the marginal propensity to import has the effect of reducing multipliers. The economy is stabilized by the import function.

The model may now be extended to allow for the effects upon investment of interest rate variations. The investment schedule is:

$$i = i_0 + fy - v_0 R \tag{12}$$

What of imports and exports? It is difficult to imagine the import function varying much with domestic interest rates, except to the extent that the durable goods model applies to durable goods imports. What of exports? Generally, exports of goods and services are thought to depend upon conditions in foreign countries. One would not expect a decision to add to the German capital stock to depend directly upon income in the U.S. However, some influences may be felt. What of interest rates? Investment depends on interest within the Keynesian lexicon because marginal efficiencies of capital are compared to interest rates. Viewing interest rates as the opportunity cost suggests that the willingness to undertake investment projects may well depend upon financing opportunities. But these are financial considerations which will have to be determined in a more complex model. Let us suppose for now that the effects upon exports of domestic interest rate variations are small enough to ignore. The locus of commodity market equilibria for an open one-sector economy is unchanged from the earlier model. Next, the international monetary system will be introduced.

B ● Foreign Exchange and the Domestic Economy

Exchange Rate Mechanisms: In order for trade to occur between parties in two different countries, currencies must be exchanged. The exporter needs to receive, and pay his inputs, in one currency, while the importer wishes to buy products with another. Therefore, some international monetary arrangement must be devised by which the purchaser of foreign goods and services can obtain the foreign currency which the seller must receive. Toward the end of World War II, the U.S., Britain, and other allied countries met at Bretton Woods in 1944 to establish international monetary arrangements which would foster trade after the war. The result was the famous Bretton Woods Agreement, characterized by a system of fixed rates of exchange between currencies. The Bretton Woods system served the western world and much of the developing world from the end of World War II until the end of 1971. As the result of financial instability and international crises in the late 1960s and early 1970s, the Bretton Woods system eventually fell apart. The 1970s was characterized by a less well-defined and more flexible system in which exchange rates were allowed to vary subject to periodic intervention by various central banks. This system is called the system of *managed float* or by some "dirty float". We shall now develop a model which we can use to describe and evaluate both the Bretton Woods system and the system of managed float.

We shall start by building a model representing trade between one country and the rest of the world. For convenience of exposition the country will be the U.S., using the dollar as its currency. The rest of the world's currency will be represented by the symbol F for foreign exchange. In order to purchase American exports, foreigners must be able to purchase American dollars with their foreign exchange. Thus, we may think of an export demand function as corresponding to both a demand for dollars schedule and a supply of foreign exchange schedule. Letting the symbol π represent the dollar price of a unit for foreign exchange, we assume that export demand, the supply of foreign exchange, will be positively related to π. (Expensive foreign exchange, say $10 per unit of F, corresponds to a relatively inexpensive American dollar for foreigners, $10 for F. Consequently, at high foreign exchange prices export demand will, *ceteris paribus*, be high. High export demand corresponds to a high supply of foreign exchange.) Figure 3 depicts the market for F. The curve S represents the supply line for foreign exchange as a function of the exchange rate π. Corresponding to this supply schedule is the export demand function, which is now modified from equation (7) to be

$$z = z_0 + \eta_1 \pi \tag{13}$$

η_1 is a positive constant representing the positive relationship between exports z and the exchange rate for dollars π.

Just as U.S. exports supply foreign exchange to international markets, U.S. imports correspond to a supply of U.S. dollars and a demand for foreign exchange in international markets. *Ceteris paribus*, the demand for foreign exchange will be inversely related to π. Figure 3 also contains the demand curve for foreign exchange, D_F. The algebraic expression corresponding to this schedule is the equation for import demand. We modify equation (8) to allow for the negative relationship between imports j and the foreign exchange rate π:

$$j = j_0 + q y_d - \eta_2 \pi \tag{14}$$

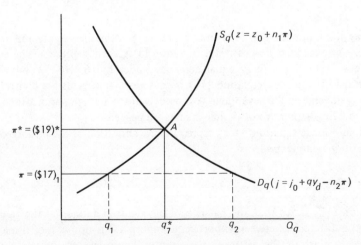

FIGURE 3   Market for Foreign Exchange

Equation (14) states that imports j are positively related to domestic disposable income y_d and negatively related to the rate of exchange.

Suppose that the price of π is exactly π^* in Figure 3. At this exchange rate the supply and demand for foreign exchange are equal. The volume of imports is q_F^* and exactly equals the volume of exports from the U.S. We represent this equilibrium exchange rate by the symbol π^*. At π^* the market for foreign exchange clears, and there need be no financial flows of capital from one country to another because imports and exports are exactly offsetting. Under the Bretton Woods system the exchange rates between various currencies were all pegged in terms of their purchasing price of gold. The result was, of course, that the rate of exchange between any two currencies was also pegged.

To depict this Bretton Woods system, suppose $\overline{\pi}$ represents the fixed or pegged exchange price of foreign currency for U.S. dollars. Under the Bretton Woods regime of fixed exchange rates, we have an additional equation for the foreign sector:

$$\pi = \overline{\pi} \tag{15}$$

After 1971, the Bretton Woods exchange rate system was replaced by a system in which exchange rates were partially allowed to float. Under a system of purely flexible exchange rates, with no central bank management, shifts in supply and demand for foreign exchange would, in theory, produce variations in the exchange rate until that rate moved to the new equilibirium point, such as point A in Figure 3 at which the supply and demand of foreign exchange are equal so that exports equals imports. In order to depict this situation, we replace equation (15) with

$$j = z \tag{16}$$

We may think of equations (13) and (14) as representing the supply and demand for foreign exchange, respectively. Equation (16), then, represents the equilibrium condition that supply equal demand. Under the Bretton Woods system equation (15) replaced equation (16) because exchange rates are controlled at the pegged value $\overline{\pi}$. We have, then, two models of the foreign sector which differ according to whether or not exchange rates are pegged.

An additional equation which represents the definition of the balance of payments in this simple model is

$$B_P \equiv z - j \tag{17}$$

Equation (17) states that the balance of payments is defined as the trade balance, the difference between exports and imports. This simple model may now be used to illustrate the nature of the Bretton Woods system and to compare it to a flexible exchange rate system.

Under the Bretton Woods system, it was obviously possible for the authorities to inadvertantly peg rates at which exchange markets would not clear. Such a case is illustrated in Figure 3. At the exchange rate $\bar{\pi}$, the demand for foreign exchange exceeds the supply. In other words, the cost of foreign exchange is too low, and the dollar is an overvalued currency. When we substitute the value for the exchange rate from equation (15) into the export demand and import demand equations (13) and (14), respectively, the value of imports j will exceed the value of exports, z. The result will be a negative trade balance, a deficit in the balance of payments. Two corrective mechanisms were available under the Bretton Woods system for dealing with a deficit form of external imbalance. The particular mechanism employed depended upon whether or not the imbalance was thought to be temporary.

Under the Bretton Woods system of fixed exchange rates, very small changes in the exchange rates were allowed to occur if there were tiny external shortages of exchange. Larger temporary external shortages of foreign exchange were provided by the domestic monetary authority out of its holdings of official international reserves. The logic of the Bretton Woods mechanism was that if the imbalance was temporary, then at some later date the shortage would be offset by a surplus, so foreign central banks would return the foreign currencies to the original monetary authority. As long as the temporary imbalances were small enough and short enough to be supported by the flows of reserves held by the central banks, this system provided an adequate cushion for deviations in supply and demand about the pegged rates.

If central banks had inadequate supplies of foreign currency, they could purchase more with gold or other acceptable international claims. Since most trading countries undertook exchange in U.S. dollars, the American dollar served as the international currency. This placed the United States in a special position in international monetary affairs, because when it needed foreign exchange it was able to purchase it, with its own currency, American dollars. As long as the demand for American dollars by the rest of the world was no larger than the supply made available by U.S. deficits, the Bretton Woods system continued to work reasonably well.

When an external imbalance was thought to be permanent, the Bretton Woods' adjustment mechanism called for devaluation of its currency by the deficit country. Devaluation of a currency consists of raising the price of all foreign exchange by raising the currency's gold price. In our illustration, Figure 3, devaluation of the dollar corresponds to raising the price of foreign exchange above $\bar{\pi}$. Devaluation tends to reduce the demand for foreign exchange (to reduce imports) and to increase the supply of foreign exchange (to increase exports). As one can see from equation (13), (14), and (17), an increase in π will increase exports, reduce imports, and reduce the balance of payments deficit. Throughout the late 1960s, the U.S. balance of payments position continued to approach deficits, so this period witnessed a substantial increase in American currency held on international markets. Eventually, the U.S. Federal

Reserve Bank felt compelled to provide foreign exchange and gold to foreign central banks. Thus, it appeared evident that a devaluation of the U.S. dollar would eventually be necessary.

Unfortunately, devaluation is not a very useful corrective device, because it is generally viewed as a measure to be avoided. First, a country which permits its currency to become overvalued is considered to have instituted irresponsible domestic policies. For example, the need for devaluation may come about because the country has allowed excessive domestic inflation. As its domestic prices have been rising with respect to those in the rest of the world, its import demand has risen while its export demand has fallen creating a worsened deficit. A deficit is viewed, therefore, by many as a signal of policy failure. Second, devaluation means that foreigners holding the currency to be devalued will lose purchasing power. Since holders of your currency are those who have expressed confidence in you, they are precisely the ones whom you do not wish to hurt. Third, once a currency has devalued several times, there is some fear that it will be viewed as an unreliable means of storing value. It may lose its effectiveness, therefore, as a medium of international exchange. Finally, importers and domestic consumers will find the costs of foreign products rising when the currency is devalued. This prospect is not attractive to most politicians. Consequently, devaluation was long viewed with considerable distaste and often was not employed under the Bretton Woods system unless absolutely unavoidable. It was, therefore, typical that devaluations occurred only after a crisis had developed. Governments were then able to blame the crisis environment, rather than the underlying causes, for the need to devalue.

Rather than devaluation, as our models indicate, yet another method may be used to resolve a balance of payments deficit. From equations (9) and (17), which represent the equilibrium conditions and the balance of payments expression, we see that

$$B_p = y - (c + i + g) \tag{18}$$

Equation (18) states that the balance of payments equals the difference between output and domestic aggregate demand. It should be clear from equation (18) that downward pressure on domestic aggregate demand will contract imports and reduce the balance of payments deficit. Consequently, contradictory domestic stabilization policies may be employed to solve, without resorting to devaluation of the currency, the balance of payments deficit problem.

Like devaluation, however, slowing the domestic economy is an unattractive option. Consequently, a final set of measures to resolve an external balance of payments deficit has been all too popular. This set involves direct restrictions on and intervention in trade itself, including import quotas, tariffs, export subsidies, adjustments in military foreign aid, and so on. Although our models indicate that trade restrictions effectively reduce imports and stimulate exports and help the balance of payments deficit, economists dislike such measures because these measures tend to constrain trade and reduce worldwide allocative efficiency. Such restrictive trade policies reduce competition, curtail world income, and hamper international trade rather than foster it.

A flexible exchange rate system, like the Bretton Woods system, can also be illustrated with the help of Figure 3 and the equations we developed above. We replace equation (15), a fixed exchange rate, with equation (16), which states that exports must equal imports in order for the foreign exchange market to clear. Under this system, the balance of payments will always be zero, and no mechanism is required in response to imbalances in foreign exchange. Devaluations become unnecessary, because exchange rates are not pegged, and they float automatically to eliminate any balance of payments surpluses or deficits. Some economists question whether exchange rates might not fluctuate too much, under a regime of flexible rates, creating a new type of instability in trade. The evidence for the 1970s is difficult to assess, because exchange rates were not allowed to float freely but were managed with occasional intervention by central banks. When a central bank felt its currency was falling too rapidly, it purchased its own currency with foreign exchange in order to prevent the price of the currency from falling too much. Naturally, under such a system, when the exchange rates are not allowed to float freely, imbalances in trade can occur.

A Three-market Model–IS-LM-BP: We are now prepared to build a more complete model of the foreign sector and to combine such a model with the *IS-LM* framework. First we shall summarize the features of the domestic markets, depicted by the familiar *IS-LM* curves. The behavioral equations for the commodity market are equations (1), (3), (4), and (12), and the export and import equations are (13) and (14). Substituting these equations into the equilibrium condition for the commodity market, equation (9), yields

$$y = \frac{c_0 + i_0 - bt_0 + g_0 + z_0 - j_0 + (\eta_1 + \eta_2)\pi - vR}{1 - [(b - q)(1 - t) + f]} \qquad (19)$$

Equation (19) is simply an *IS* curve in which export and import functions are included. The equation for money market equilibrium, represented by an *LM* curve under the same types of models we were dealing with in earlier chapters, is

$$R = \frac{M_0}{mp} + \frac{k}{m}y \qquad (20)$$

This money market equilibrium equation represents equilibria between domestic money supply and domestic money demand.

It is now necessary to add one complication to the market for foreign exchange. As indicated earlier, in transactions between countries, financial capital flows which represent investments and payments across national boundaries are as important as commodity trade. Two modifications are needed in order to introduce these financial capital flows to our model. First, we replace the definition of the balance of payments, equation (17) above, with

$$B_p = z - j - F \tag{21}$$

where F is defined as the net volume of financial capital to flow *out* of the domestic country. Equation (21) states that the total balance of payments is the trade balance minus the volume of net capital outflows. Financial capital flows from the U.S. abroad when U.S. investors wish to make investments in foreign countries. Foreigners, of course, also make considerable investments in the United States.

Given the high degree of sophistication in international financial capital markets, it appears reasonable to assume that the value of financial capital outflows will be an endogenous variable. Capital flows will depend upon the differential between the rates of interest available in the domestic economy (the U.S.) and those available in the rest of the world. We shall assume that the rates of interest in the rest of the world are exogenous to our model, so that the volume of capital outflows depends upon the domestic rate of interest only. (In a more sophisticated model we would have to take *stock* equilibrium conditions into account as well as flow equilibrium but such a model is beyond our scope here.) A high domestic rate of interest would indicate a reduction in the volume of net capital outflows, because financial capital would tend to be attracted to the U.S. If the U.S. rate of interest is low relative to that in the rest of the world, then we would expect capital outflows to rise. Consequently, we have

$$F = F_0 - \xi R \tag{22}$$

Equation (22) depicts the negative relationship between net capital outflows and the domestic rate of interest. The symbol ξ represents the elasticity of capital outflows with respect to the domestic rate of interest R. (R, which the domestic rate, is really a proxy variable for the difference between U.S. rates and world rates.)

We have now completed construction of the equations necessary for the integration of the domestic model with a model of the balance of payments. First, in order to understand the workings of this model, suppose that the exchange rates are fixed at $\bar{\pi}$. Given $\bar{\pi}$, the *IS-LM* schedules may be solved jointly for domestic income y and the domestic rate of interest R. In other words, the domestic economy will determine its own point of equilibrium in terms of the values of the rate of interest and the level of output. (For convenience, we are assuming a Keynesian *IS-LM* framework.) Given R from the *IS-LM* solution the level of capital flows is determined by equation (22). Given $\bar{\pi}$ and the domestic determination of output, both exports and imports are also determined so that we have a determinant solution to the balance of payments equation (21). However, the value of B_p may not be zero, given the values of y and R from the *IS-LM* solution. The *IS* curve represents commodity market equilibrium, and the *LM* curve represents money market equilibrium; thus we can similarly construct a curve for balance of payments equilibrium by setting equation (21) for B_p equal to zero. Substituting the expressions for exports, equation (13), imports, equation (14), and capital flows, equation (22), into this equilibrium equation results in

$$R = \frac{F_0 - z_0 + j_0 - qt_0 - (\eta_1 - \eta_2)\pi}{\xi} + \frac{q(1 - t)}{\xi} y \qquad (23)$$

Equation (23) represents the locus of equilibrium points for the balance of payments.

The three sets of equilibrium conditions, one corresponding to each market, equations (19), (20), and (23), are depicted in Figure 4. The *IS* and *LM* schedules are straightforward and have been studied at great length earlier. The balance of payments equilibrium line is upward sloping. The logic of the positive slope is that as output increases and aggregate demand increases as well, the balance of payments would deteriorate were it not offset by increased interest rates which attract financial capital from abroad. Because, as we saw in the preceding paragraph, the domestic economy may be solved for R and y without regard to the value of balance of payments, the balance of payments locus of equilibrium need not intersect the domestic equilibrium, for example, E_1 in Figure 4. In fact, while the domestic economy is in equilibrium at (R_1, y_1), the balance of payments must be in surplus. The balance of payments is clearly greater than zero at E_1, because E_1 lies above the locus of points for which B_p equals zero. In other words, at income level y_1, the high rate of interest R_1 is

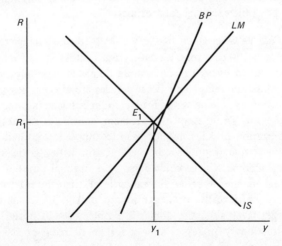

FIGURE 4   An Open Economy: Internal and External Balance

attracting enough excess foreign currency to create a balance of payments surplus.

A surplus in the balance of payments implies that the combination of U.S. exports plus investments into the U.S. by foreigners exceed U.S. imports plus financial flows abroad. Consequently, the amount of money flowing into the United States exceeds that flowing out in international transactions. In order to avoid an expansion of the money supply, in excess of that which generates the *LM* equilibrium, the Federal Reserve would have to institute federal open market sales of U.S. government securities in order to absorb the flow of money into the U.S. Such an action is called *sterilization* of money from foreign markets. Alternatively, one could employ domestic stabilization policies to reduce domestic interest rates.

If we drop the assumption that the rate of exchange is fixed at $\bar{\pi}$, then balance of payments surpluses and deficits are eliminated by automatic adjustments in the rates of currency exchange. In this case, the equilibrium equation for the foreign exchange market becomes

$$z = j + F \tag{24}$$

Equation (24) simply states that this market will clear when exports are exactly offset by the sum of imports plus net outflows of financial capital. Since the exchange rate is now assumed to adjust whenever the balance of payments is in surplus or deficit, it is now necessary for the *BP* line to cut through the equilibrium point of the *IS-LM* schedules, point E_1. Put another way, *BP*, the balance of payments, must be zero regardless of the pairs of R and y, because the exchange rate will always adjust until the balance of payments is zero. Let us now employ the model to analyze domestic stabilization policies for dealing with internal problems and balance of payment problems simultaneously under both fixed and flexible exchange rate regimes.

Stabilization Policies in an Open Economy: With fixed exchange rates, when an external balance becomes severe, a country must either curtail its international trade, devalue its currency, or contract its domestic economy with stabilization policies. Since monetary and fiscal policies are also employed to stabilize the domestic economy, the potential for a conflict between internal and external objectives is present. To illustrate this problem, consider a Keynesian economy in which stabilization policies may be used to choose an optimal point on the long-run Phillips curve. (Suppose the central authorities settle upon a target level of money income which would imply the optimal point on the Phillips curve.) If actual income is below the target level, then the internal problem is unemployment, which calls for expansionary policy. If actual income were above the target level, then the domestic problem would be inflation, which calls for contractionary policy. Under a system of fixed exchange rates, the balance of payments could either be in deficit or surplus; consequently an external imbalance may be present as well as the internal imbalance. Table 3 depicts the possible cases of internal and external imbalance with the appropriate policies called for in each case.

TABLE 3
Internal and External Objectives of Stabilization Policy

Case	Internal Balance	External Balance	Prescribed Policy		
			Internal	External	Solution
1	Unemployment	Surplus	Expand	Expand	Expand
2	Inflation	Surplus	Contract	Expand	Conflict
3	Unemployment	Deficit	Expand	Contract	Conflict
4	Inflation	Deficit	Contract	Contract	Contract

As an example consider Case 3: the domestic problem is unemployment and the balance of payments problem is a deficit. The internal problem calls for expansion, while the foreign deficit calls for contraction. A conflict in objectives is evident. While expansionary policies will reduce unemployment, expansion will also, through the import demand schedule, aggravate the demand for foreign exchange and exacerbate the payments deficit. Furthermore, since domestic expansion will move the economy up the long-run Phillips curve, the more rapid domestic inflation may also contract exports and further exacerbate the payments deficit. This more pronounced external imbalance will increase pressures for foreign trade controls or for devaluation. Consequently, stabilization authorities will be confronted with an increasingly difficult conflict of objectives.

Figure 5 depicts this case of conflict in internal and external policy objectives. The IS-LM schedules intersect at income level y_1, an unemployment level of income. The balance of payments equilibrium schedule indicates that at y_1 with the interest rate at R_1, the balance of payments will be in deficit. Expansionary domestic policies will aggravate the balance of payments and contraction will aggravate domestic unemployment. Let us now analyze the effects of monetary and fiscal policies in Case 3 to illlustrate their different impacts when internal and external balance objectives are in conflict.

If monetary policy were employed to reduce unemployment, the excess aggregate demand caused by an expansion of the money supply would be accompanied by a reduction in domestic interest rates. In an open economy, we must consider, in addition to domestic effects, the consequences of excess aggregate demand on the foreign sector. Excess demand, operating through two channels, will tend to enlarge the payments deficit. First, excess demand will increase domestic income, which in turn will induce an increase in imports. Second, as excess demand produces increases in the domestic price level, imports will in-

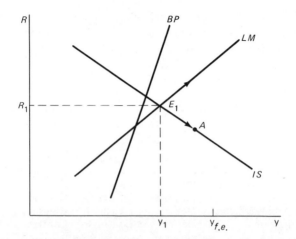

FIGURE 5   Internal and External Imbalance (Case 3, Table 4. Unemployment and BP deficit)

crease as foreign products are substituted for more expensive domestic products, and, for the same reason, exports will tend to decrease. In terms of Figure 5, expansionary monetary policy shifts the *LM* curve outward to the right, and the domestic equilibrium exacerbates the balance of payments disequilibrium by driving the domestic equilibrium point on the *IS* curve even farther from the B_p equilibrium line from E_1 toward A.

Recall that increases in the money supply create excess aggregate demand by lowering domestic interest rates. Lower domestic interest rates, in the model we are using, will have an independent influence on the balance of payments. Domestic interest rates, driven below world rates, give investors added incentive to supply financial capital to the higher rate available in world markets. If we assume that the country in question is small enough relative to the rest of the world that world rates remain the same, and if we assume that there are no constraints on financial capital flows, then financial capital will flow out of the domestic country toward the rest of the world. In other words, monetary expansion, in this model, has the effect of driving the domestic money supply abroad. As long as the interest rate differential persists, the domestic money supply will contract as investors send financial capital abroad. Since the interest rate differential cannot persist, monetary policy has no permanent expansionary effect on the domestic imbalance. The net comparative static change in the domestic money supply is zero, and thus in this model the monetary authority essentially has no stabilization power.

If we moderate the assumption that the country is small with respect to the rest of the world, then the conclusions we have just drawn must also be modified. The financial capital that leaves the domestic country, if that country is large, may result in downward pressure on world interest rates. In this case, the expansion in the domestic money supply may maintain lower rates of interest not just in the domestic country but abroad as well. Furthermore, in this case, the monetary authority will have some effect on expanding the domestic economy.

Suppose stabilization authorities had tried expansionary fiscal policy to alleviate the unemployment in the above example. Expansionary fiscal policy would generate excess aggregate demand, as did monetary policy. But fiscal policy is different in that interest rates rise with the expansion rather than fall. As was the case with monetary policy, the excess demand itself will stimulate the domestic economy and aggravate the foreign exchange imbalance. However, with interest rates higher, financial capital will be attracted to the domestic economy rather than abroad. Financial capital attracted to the expanding country will reduce the foreign exchange outflow [as seen in equation (21)], and will improve the payments deficit. Under the assumptions that the economy in question is small with respect to the rest of the world and that financial capital flows are unconstrained, expansionary fiscal policy will produce automatic increase in the domestic money supply via increased financial flows into the domestic economy. The expansionary fiscal policy, then, is automatically reinforced by monetary expansion.

Robert Mundell (1971), employing analysis similar to that presented above, argues that if monetary and fiscal policies are mixed in the appropriate way, then they can be complementary to one another and resolve the apparent conflicts between internal and external imbalances. In particular, faced with domestic unemployment and a balance of payments deficit, expansionary fiscal policy may be employed to reduce unemployment while contractionary monetary policy may be employed to raise interest rates and reduce the balance of payments deficit by encouraging financial flows to the domestic country. It is straightforward to show that, if faced with domestic inflation and a balance of payments surplus, the appropriate stabilization measures would be deflationary fiscal policy and expansionary monetary policy. Of course, a corollary to Mundell's solution (that there is an appropriate mix of monetary and fiscal policy) is that if the authorities select the wrong blend of policy measures, the balance of payments and the domestic imbalance both will be worsened.

Mundell's analysis applies to a world of flexible exchange rates as well. In a world of flexible exchange rates, the balance of payments cannot be in deficit or in surplus, but exchange rates can be changed by shifts in supply and demand for foreign goods and by financial capital flows. Consider again a country confronted with unemployment and a payments deficit. In this model expansionary fiscal policy, for dealing with unemployment, will again drive up domestic interest rates. The higher interest rates will attract financial capital to the domestic country, but in this model the increased supply of foreign exchange will drive down the exchange rate. When the exchange rate falls, the value of the domestic currency is increased, which stimulates imports and curtails exports. (These effects are captured in equation (19) by the presence of the exchange rate, π, on the right-hand side of the IS equilibrium equation.) The reduced exchange rate will shift the *IS* curve to the left and offset the expansionary fiscal policy! Paradoxically, monetary policy will be an effective domestic stabilization device. Expansionary monetary policy will reduce domestic interest rates and stimulate the demand for foreign exchange. The result will be an increase in the rate of exchange and a stimulus to domestic demand. Table 4 summarizes the appropriate mix of stabilization measures for dealing with internal and external disequilibria, which is suggested by Mundell's analysis.

TABLE 4

Appropriate Mix of Policy Instruments for Internal and External Imbalances

Exchange Rate System	Stabilization Policy Measure Focus	
	Monetary	*Fiscal*
(1) Fixed	External	Internal
(2) Flexible	Internal	External

The World Monetarists: The analysis of financial capital flows and interest rate differentials by Robert Mundell in 1968 and 1971 along with the work on the balance of payments by Harry Johnson in 1973 has been combined in recent years with the neoclassical and monetarist analysis of the domestic economy to produce a *world monetarist* view of international economic activity. This view, while controversial, has produced some interesting suggestions about the international monetary system now operating which explain the trend toward more rapid rates of inflation around the industrialized world. World monetarists combine four sets of assumptions, all by now familiar to us, in their analysis: The domestic economy is represented by (1) a neoclassical-type model in which the labor market is assumed to clear and (2) by a classical dichotomy in which monetary activity leaves real variables fixed. (3) The world economy is assumed to be integrated to the extent that it works well in the sense of a Walrasian auctioneer dominating the relative price system. (4) Each country is assumed to be small relative to the rest of the world. Under these four sets of assumptions, it is fairly straighforward to show that output will be fixed, the rate of interest in the domestic country will be tied to the world rate, the relative price structures in various countries will be independent of monetary flows, and the rate of inflation in one country must be tied to world inflation rates subject to the rules which govern the degree of flexibility in exchange rates.

Under these circumstances, the demand for money schedule must be fixed and the *real* money supply must adjust to the real demand for money. This means that increases in the money supply lead eventually to increases in world inflation. Thus, one may view the world as a fully integrated economy in which the world money supply determines the world inflation rate. In this analysis, the position of the U.S. is unique: Its currency is the money for world exchange and its trade dominates world markets. The U.S. is thus the central banker for the world. The primary source of inflation is, then, expansionary monetary policy of the U.S. central bank.

While the set of assumptions which lead to this world monetarist conclusion are obviously extreme and while they would not pertain in a short-run situation, they may lead to a reasonable approximation of the very long run. One interesting result which follows from this world monetarist view is that changes in exchange rates have no permanent effect on real supplies and demands of goods and services. This result follows from the assumptions that relative scarcities determine relative prices and that exchange rate variations result only in offsetting adjustments in relative inflation rates. Consequently the real underlying relative price systems will be uninfluenced.

Just as Cagan's pure monetarist analysis of hyperinflations assisted us in understanding the inflation process, the world monetarist model is helpful in understanding the mechanisms through which inflation is transmitted from one country to another. Suppose, to make the argument simple, that the U.S. central bank is the world banker and that expansion of the U.S. domestic money supply produces a U.S. inflation. How might this inflation be transmitted to the rest of the world? Robert Gordon in (1977) explains the four central channels of inflation across international boundaries: (1) The *direct price effect*. As U.S. product prices rise, U.S. citizens increase their demand for the less expensive foreign products, and non-Americans purchase at home rather than from the U.S. Thus the demand for product prices in other countries is increased by the U.S. inflation. This process, called *commodity market arbitrage*, results both in an increase in the price of foreign goods and an increase in the costs of inputs used to produce foreign goods. (2) *The balance of payments surplus effect*: as U.S. income rises faster than that in the rest of the world, other economies will have, relative to the U.S., payment surpluses. Payment surpluses for a country cause increases in domestic income and, therefore, create inflationary pressures through excess demand. (3) The *Bretton Woods monetization channel:* the U.S. payments deficit created by domestic expansion must be financed, within the fixed exchange rate model, by increases in U.S. financial flows abroad. Thus world monetary expansion exceeds that in the U.S. because financial capital is sent abroad. (4) *Inflationary expectations effect:* As we have seen in our analysis of inflation, it breeds expectations of inflation, which in turn lead to further price and wage increases.

STUDY QUESTIONS

1. Utilizing a one-sector model of an open U.S. economy, illustrate the effects on equilibrium income of:

    a. A boom in exports of goods and services.

    b. A quota on imports.

    c. A private decision by U.S. consumers to buy American.

2. (a) Build an algebraic one-sector model of an economy, including an endogenous import function and exogenous exports.

(b) Compute the government expenditure, tax, and investment multipliers. How do these compare to their counterparts in a closed income-expenditure model?

3. Trade occurs with fixed exchange rates. The economy is characterized by domestic unemployment and a balance of payments deficit. Select the appropriate mix of monetary-fiscal policy measures for dealing with both internal and external balance. Defend your choice.

4. Construct a three-sector model of an open economy. Assume a domestic inflation which exceeds foreign rates of inflation. If exchange rates are flexible, trace the effects on the system of contractionary fiscal policy.

5. The following system of equations depicts the commodity market of an economy:

$$c = c_0 + by_d$$

$$j = j_0 + qy_d - \eta_2 \pi$$

$$i = i_0 + fy$$

$$g = g_0$$

$$\tau = \tau_0$$

$$z = z_0 + \eta_1 \pi$$

$$y = c + i + g + z - j$$

a. Derive the expression for equilibrium income y.

b. Draw the supply of foreign exchange schedule z.

c. Draw the aggregate demand schedule and show the algebraic expression for the slope and intercept.

d. Let $B = z - j$ be the balance of payments equation and assume that $\pi = \bar{\pi}$.

1) Derive the effect upon the equilibrium income level of an increase in g.
2) What will be the effect upon B?
3) Suppose $B < 0$. What fiscal actions can be taken to balance the balance of payments (i.e., set $B = 0$)? What will these measures do to y?
4) Derive the balanced budget multiplier.
5) How will an increase in $\bar{\pi}$ to $\bar{\pi}'$ affect y and B?

e. Let $B = z - j$ and assume that the foreign sector is allowed to clear so that equation $\pi = \bar{\pi}$ is replaced in part d with $z = j$. What will be the effect on y, π, z, and j of a tax cut?

6. The equations below represent an economy:*

$c = c_0 + b y_d$ $z = z_0 + \eta_1 \pi$

$j = j_0 + q y_d - \eta_2 \pi$ $y = c + i + g + z - j$

$i = i_0 - v_0 R$ $m^s = M_0 / P$

$g = g_0$ $m^d = ky - m_0 R$

$\tau = \tau_0$ $m^s = m^d$

$B = z - j - F$ (balance of payments) $P = P_1$

$F = F_0 - \xi R$ (financial capital flows)

a. Derive the equation for the *IS* curve, the *LM* curve (at $P = P_1$), and for balance of payments equilibrium ($B = 0$) under the assumption of fixed exchange rates ($\pi = \bar{\pi}$).

b. Assume all three markets are in equilibrium initially at $\bar{\pi}$. Show graphically the effects upon the economy (y, R, BP, etc.) of each of the following exogenous actions:

   1) An increase in g.
   2) A decrease in M.
   3) A decrease in $\bar{\pi}$.

*Very enterprising students may wish to replace parameters, such as c_0, b, etc., with actual numerical values and then solve for equilibrium.

REFERENCES

Board of Governors of the Federal Reserve System, *Federal Reserve Bulletin*, April 1978.

Economic Report of the President, January 1979. Washington, D.C.: U.S. Government Printing Office.

Gordon, Robert J., "World Inflation and Monetary Accomodation in Eight Countries," *Brookings Papers on Economic Activity*, No. 2, 1977, pp. 409-477.

Johnson, Harry G., *Further Essays in Monetary Economics*. Cambridge, Mass.: Harvard University Press, 1973.

_____ and A. R. Nobay (eds.), *Issues in Monetary Economics*, Proceedings of the 1972 Money Study Group Conference. Oxford: Oxford University Press, 1974.

Krause, Lawrence B., "Recent International Monetary Crises: Causes and Cures," in W. L. Smith and R. L. Teigen (eds.), *Readings in Money, National Income, and Stabilization Policy*, revised ed. Homewood, Ill.: Richard D. Irwin, 1979.

————, *Sequel to Bretton Woods*. Washington, D.C.: Brookings Institution, 1971.

Meade, J. E., "The International Monetary Mechanism," in M. G. Mueller (ed.), *Readings in Macroeconomics*, 2nd ed. New York: Holt, Rinehard and Winston, 1971.

Mundell, Robert A., "Capital Mobility and Stabilization Policy under Fixed and Flexible Exchange Rates," *Canadian Journal of Economics and Political Science*, November 1963.

————, *International Economics*. New York: MacMillan, 1968.

————, "The Appropriate Use of Monetary and Fiscal Policy for Internal and External Stability," *International Monetary Fund Staff Papers*, March 1962.

————, *Monetary Theory*. Pacific Palisades, Cal.: Goodyear Publishing, 1971.

Smith, Warren L., "Are There Enough Policy Tools?", *American Economic Review*, May 1965.

Teigen, Ronald L., "International Finance," in R. L. Teigen (ed.), *Readings in Money, National Income and Stabilization Policy*, 4th ed. New York: Richard D. Irwin, 1978.

Triffin, Robert, *Our International Monetary System: Yesterday, Today, and Tomorrow*. New York: Random House, 1968.

Whitman, Marina V. N., "Global Monetarism and the Monetary Approach to the Balance of Payments," in R. L. Teigen (ed.), *Readings In Money, National Income and Stabilization Policy*, 4th ed. New York: Richard D. Irwin, 1978.

The application of policy requires a shrewd blend of science, guesswork, normative judgment, and political savvy. Stabilization policy has two main branches: monetary and fiscal. In addition, macroeconomic policy includes manpower policies, incomes policies, and numerous other select policy measures, such as regulation Q, indexation and margin requirements. In the U.S., stabilization policy is undertaken by two different organizations. Fiscal policy, which consists of government expenditures, taxes, and transfers, is implemented by the federal government with the executive usually taking the initiative. The chairman of the President's Council of Economic Advisors (CEA) is ordinarily the chief architect of fiscal policy. However, the CEA must work closely with other organizations and individuals in the executive branch, such as the Director of the Office of Management and Budget, the Secretary of the Treasury, and the Director of the Wage-Price Board.

Monetary policy, consisting primarily of open market operations, reserve requirements, and the discount rate, is implemented by the Board of Governors of the quasi-public Federal Reserve System. The Board, consisting of seven governors, is not directly accountable to the President. Unlike members of his cabinet, the Board of Governors may not be fired by the President once appointed. However, the Federal Reserve System is a creation of Congress, and the Board is answerable to several Congressional Committees. The most important policy-making organization of the FED is the Federal Open Market Committee (FOMC). The FOMC has twelve members: the seven governors plus five directors taken on a rotating basis from the various branches of the FED. Thus stabilization policy is determined by two independent organizations: The CEA is under the leadership of the President, and the FED is under the leadership of the Chairman of the Board of Governors.

25

Macroeconomic Policy in Action

Coordination of monetary and fiscal policies can be difficult, especially when the FED chairman and the President disagree about appropriate policy. Other policies with macroeconomic implications are implemented by still other organizations. Income policies, for example, are established by the executive branch under the Carter Administration in the Council on Wage and Price Stability. Manpower policies are organized by the Department of Labor. The most important manpower program of the 1970s, The Comprehensive Employment and Training Act (CETA), was primarily implemented by state and local government agencies, especially those of nonbank financial institutions. Commercial banks are under the direct control of the FED; savings and loans, mutual savings banks, and credit unions each have their own central regulator. In addition to different implementation organizations for policy, there are congressional offices with considerable influence over macroeconomic policy. The government budget is evaluated regularly by the Congressional Budget Office (CBO). The Government Accounting Office (GAO) examines and evaluates various aspects of policy. Many government reorganizations are frequently undertaken to alter the responsibilities of various groups. Consequently, for better or worse, a wide variety of organizations interact in the determination of macroeconomic policy. When discussing and evaluating the appropriate blend and mix of macroeconomic policies from our vantage point as scholars, we should bear in mind this complex array of political institutions which must mesh and coordinate their efforts in setting policy.

In Figure 1 below we illustrate the nature of macroeconomic policy making. In the abstract, we may think of policy making as a matching of instruments to targets in order to maximize some objective function such as "social welfare." The essence of the macroeconomic policy problem is to implement actions in order to achieve normative goals. To the left of Figure 1 we see a set of instruments available to policy makers. In this simple illustration, the instruments consist of a rate of change of the quantity of money, a rate of government expenditures, a tax rate, and a discount rate. These instruments operate through the structure of the economy in order to achieve certain values for the targets. In our example, the targets consist of the rate of inflation, the rate of unemployment, the rate of output growth, and balance in foreign exchange payments. In Figure 1, the structural system of the economy, as depicted in the middle of the figure, is being struck by outside shocks. In the table below the figure we list some shocks which alter the course of the structural system. The actual implementation of policy is made difficult by the presence of these unexpected outside shocks to the system.

In order to illustrate the policy maker's problem of selecting instruments to achieve target values, think of a student at the end of the fall term preparing to drive home for the Christmas holidays. The student has two targets in mind: (1) He would like to reach home. (2) He would like to get there in time for Christmas. Thus he has a particular path to follow and a particular speed to attain in reaching home. His car has two instruments: a steering wheel and a gas pedal. He matches the steering wheel to the path target so that he steers his car

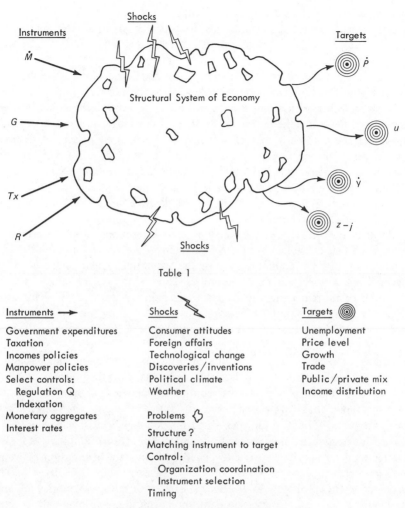

FIGURE 1   The Policy Problems

home, and he adjusts the gas pedal to achieve the speed target for reaching home by Christmas. (An especially wealthy student has an airplane. He has an additional target, namely, a minimum altitude needed to pass over a mountain between the university and his home. Fortunately, his airplane has an altimeter, the additional instrument needed for achieving the additional target value.)

Policy makers similarly have a variety of instruments with which to achieve a variety of target values. For example, suppose that policy makers wish to achieve certain values for the following three targets: the balance of payments, nominal money income, and the mix between private and public expenditures. Assume that policy makers have already determined the target values: reduce the balance of payments deficit by \$2 billion, increase nominal income by \$20 billion, and decrease public expenditures to 18 percent of total GNP. Their problem is to select the appropriate mix of instruments to achieve these three target values. We learned in Chapter 24 that if the rate of exchange between currencies is pegged, then the appropriate mix between fiscal and monetary policies for achieving both external and internal balance calls for monetary policy to achieve the balance of payments target and fiscal policy to achieve the domestic objective. Based upon this theoretical result, then, policy makers use monetary policy to reduce the external deficit. Fiscal policy is then used to achieve the other two targets. The magnitude of the government deficit determines the nominal income target value and the level of government expenditures, and given the deficit, therefore, the level of taxes will determine the public and private mix. In other words, policy makers can achieve all three targets by the appropriate match of instruments to targets.

In fact, of course, the actual policy problem is far more complicated than our example. First, as indicated in the figure above, the effects of various policies operate through the complex maze of the structural system of the economy. Second, one is uncertain about the initial values of the targets, not to mention direction of movement in the targets while policy is germinating. This uncertainty is illustrated in the Figure by the shocks hitting the structure. Third, not only is the structure subject to exogenous shocks, but the form of the structure itself may unexpectedly change over time. These changes occur because of reactions to policy changes, because of prior policy changes, and because of changing social, political, and legal arrangements. Fourth, policy is not fully coordinated. Fifth, policy makers' control of specific instruments is limited. (For example, the FED cannot control all the monetary aggregates.) Sixth, policy requires normative judgments and the consequences of achieving specific values for targets are not always fully understood. (For example, it is no easy matter to determine the costs and benefits of the rate of inflation.) Seventh, policy implementation requires political consensus. This difficulty alone has rendered many proposals ineffective. (For example, to the dismay of many economists, political leaders seem bent upon achieving continual balance in the federal budget as a target. While such a target has clear political appeal, it does not have widespread support in the economics profession as a means of clearly advancing social welfare.)

In this chapter we shall analyze the problems encountered by policy makers. The first problem is that of assessing the current state of the economy and of forecasting the future. The forecasting problem may be further decomposed into three issues: (1) What is the structure of the economy? (2) What are the major sources of uncertainty in this structure and what does this uncertainty imply for forecasts? (3) What methodology should be employed in determining the forecast? We shall discuss each of these three issues in turn.

The second general problem we shall assess in this chapter is the control problem. The control problem involves two distinct issues: (1) Are the policy-making bodies well organized to achieve their objectives? Is the independence of the FED from the executive worth the cost of uncoordinated policies? As a corollary to this second question, it may be that monetary policy should be thought of as a by-product to government expenditure plans. In this spirit, recent research on the government budget restraint has indicated that the financing of government deficits either through debt issue or borrowing from the FED can be important in determining the viability of fiscal and monetary policy. (2) How should policy instruments be selected? As we shall see, the best policy instrument depends upon the degree of control, predictability, and significance of alternate choices of instruments.

The third general topic in this chapter is the appropriate selection of targets and target values. Because the selection of optimal values for policy targets is clearly normative, economists have been rather slow to apply formal quantitative and analytical tools to this issue. However, in recent years some effort has been made to assess the social welfare implications of various values for certain targets.

This general discussion of macroeconomic policy outlined above comprises Section A. In Section B we shall analyze the specific measures which certain groups of economists might propose. Economists are disagreed as to the structure of the economy; therefore, they disagree about the selection of policy instruments and targets. We shall discuss policy proposals, therefore, in two stages. We examine first the policies which might be recommended by monetarists/rationalist economists, and second, the policies of Keynesian/structuralists. We end this chapter with an assessment of the state of knowledge on policy issues.

A ● Forecasting and the Structure of the Economy

The focus of this book has been on analyzing the structural system of the economy. We looked at a number of comparative static and dynamic models and developed two general theoretical points of view about the workings of the system. While it would be impossible to present a list of boxes in which a student could place each economist he might encounter, we did examine schools of thought. Some economists are monetarists, and some are fiscalists. Some are Keynesians. Some economists are rationalists and Walrasian; some are non-Walrasian, nonmarket economists. One Group will attribute some phenomena to structural characteristics, while others explain them by policy. Some are accelerationists, and some are not. And so it goes. Thus, the first question one must resolve in determining the effects of policy is the nature of the structure with which one is dealing. This text has been eclectic so that the reader could decide which structure best suits the economy. Whether the economy is fundamentally neoclassical or whether the economy is Keynesian is still subject to considerable dispute. Nevertheless, in order to analyze policy proposals, one must make a professional judgment about the nature of the system.

As if a wide variety of opinion about structure were not enough, structuralists and rationalists have presented us with an even more troublesome specter. Both argue that structural components which we had thought fixed may, in fact, vary over time. For example, in Keynesian analysis the marginal propensity to consume (*MPC*) is constant. Friedman, however, suggested the *MPC* may vary depending upon the perceptions of consumers. Endogeneity of *MPC* makes the concept far less useful as an anchor to the system. Structuralists claim that the system itself is different today from the one Keynes studied. Today, after over a decade of accelerating inflation, our monetary system is quite different from the earlier one of controlled commercial banks. The nature of union contract agreements in recent years is also very different than they were in the past. Escalator clauses, in which future wage increases in response to future price increases are written in, are more prevalent. The role of the federal government has increased dramatically over the past 25 years, so in peace time government expenditures now account for over 20 percent of GNP. Furthermore, the government is engaged in a substantial transfer system. The most important component of this transfer system is the massive Social Security system. Social Security and other transfer mechanisms have changed the fortunes of individuals whose incomes used to be buffeted by cyclical fluctuations. Consequently, one should expect the structure system of the economy to respond differently to changes in instruments than it did years ago.

In addition to long-term trends in changes in structure, the system may change in response to short-term instrument changes. This is the view held by rationalists. Recall from Chapter 22 the rationalists' view that economic agents include and discount the decision rules of policy makers. When this is done, policy decisions, when based upon rules, become endogenous to the system. This means that we cannot forecast the economy under the assumption that policy is an exogenous force. Furthermore, if policy is endogenous, can it alter the course of the system? Rationalists say no. The possibility that "fixed parameters" of the system are in fact endogenous is troublesome, because it deprives us of a fixed structural system through which the instruments are operating.

Even if we could settle on structure, there are numerous sources of uncertainty which make forecasting tenuous. We place these sources of uncertainty into two groups: (1) outside shocks and (2) the values of the parameters of the system. In the table below Figure 1 there is a list of sources of outside shocks which strike the structure of the economy. Any one of these outside shocks can unexpectedly drive the economy off its anticipated path. For example, if consumer attitudes suddenly turn pessimistic, the level of national income could drop. At the University of Michigan, its Survey Research Center surveys consumer attitudes in order to minimize the uncertainty of dealing with consumer behavior. Business attitudes are also subject to unexpected variations which must be analyzed. The McGraw-Hill Surveys attempt to forecast investment plans. By far the most dramatic shock to an economy is an unexpected war. Because economists are aware of the damage done to any forecast of such catastrophic events, they always present forecasts with caveats such as "All bets are off in the event of war!" In other words, unexpected changes in the weather conditions, the political climate, foreign events, technological change, discoveries, inventions, and the like can cause enormous errors in forecasting.

In the judgment of economists who believe that the private economy is self-stabilizing, the primary sources of uncertainty come from government and the central bank, and for these economists forecasting the behavior of policy makers becomes of paramount importance. The Claremont Economic Institute (CEI), for example, devotes most of its forecasting energy to studying the political system and behavior of the monetary and fiscal authorities.

Perhaps the most dramatic shocks to strike the U.S. economy through the 1970s came from foreign political and economic events. Twice in the decade of the 1970s the U.S. economy was struck with enormous increases in the price of oil products. In 1973 the Organization of Petroleum Exporting Countries (OPEC) quadrupled the price of crude oil. This massive increase in all prices caused substantial shocks and large price increases in a wide variety of producer and consumer products. In the same year, crop failures in the Soviet Union and protein shortages in South America produced a severe strain on the U.S. agricultural system. Thus 1973, 1974, and 1975 were years in which food and oil-related product prices increased considerably. These outside shocks had a substantial effect on the course of economic events. In 1979 OPEC once again instituted dramatic increases in oil prices: These prices were doubled in one year. Furthermore, in 1979 the collapse of the regime of the Shah Reza Pahlevi produced a sudden unexpected shock to the U.S. economy. Iranian oil production fell considerably, and Iran had been the world's second largest oil exporter. Substantial exogenous shocks such as the ones described here destroy any economic forecast. And, in fact, forecasts for 1974 and forecasts for 1979 and 1980 were far from the mark. Forecasters have little choice but to hedge their predictions with caveats. However, it seems apparent that instability in the third world, the source of many raw materials, can be expected to continue. Furthermore, there is reason to expect instability from the Soviet agricultural system in the future. Consequently, some of these irregular events will occur in the future and should in some way be built into forecasts.

Parameters of the System: Even among economists who agree about structure, considerable debate takes place over the values of the parameters. For example, what is the value of *MPC*? What is the interest elasticity of investment expenditures? How responsive will money demand be to a ten basis point change (0.10%) in the rate of interest? Answers to questions such as these will determine the values of the multipliers through which changes in stabilization instruments influence the structure of the economy. The magnitude of multipliers and the speed with which policy actions operate on the economy must be known by policy makers in order to predict the consequences of their actions. Two basic methodologies have been employed in order to estimate fiscal and money multipliers. The first method is to build macroeconometric models based upon structural equations, derived from economic theory. The parameter values of each equation are based upon econometric studies. The large-scale model then consists of a set of individual equations, each with coefficients based on actual empirical investigation. The large scale model is used to estimate the multipliers by simulation, that is, by tracing effects upon the economy of specific instrument changes. The second method of estimating multipliers is to begin with an algebraic system of equations, such as the *IS/LM* model, and to solve this system for its solution. The solution to such a system is called the *reduced form*.

Table 1 contains estimates of money and fiscal multipliers according to five different studies. Two of them, those by Friedman and Meiselman and by Anderson and Jordan, used reduced form techniques. The other three used large-scale econometric models. While each study employed different measures of M, T, and G, it is interesting to see some estimates of the multipliers. Friedman and Meiselman used M_2, cash plus demand deposits and time deposits issued by commercial banks, as their measure of the money supply, while Anderson and Jordan used a measure of the monetary base. The three econometric models each used unborrowed reserves to indicate the monetary instrument. Their measures of fiscal policy also varied because they have different views about control of the federal budget. Estimates of money multipliers vary from 3 to 20. The three econometric models seem to produce a consensus range of value for k_G of 2.7 to 2.9. The tax multiplier was around -1.2 to -2.5 for the large-scale models.

TABLE 1

Monetary and Fiscal Policy Multipliers Estimated from Various Studies

Study	Dates	k_M	k_G	k_T
Friedman-Meiselman	1945-58	2.94	1.06	-1.06
Anderson-Jordan	1952-68	16.01	-0.54	0.51
Wharton School Model	Postwar	2.90	2.90	-2.40
Brookings Model	Postwar	8.20	2.70	-1.20
FRB-MIT Model	Postwar	20.60	2.70	-2.50

Source: The numbers in this table were taken from "The Usefulness of Monetary and Fiscal Policy as Discretionary Stabilization Tools," by Edward Gramlich *The Journal of Money, Credit, and Banking* (May 1971).

Tobin (1972) cautioned us against concluding that a small k_G and a large k_M mean that monetary policy is more effective than fiscal policy. As Tobin points out, "Any comparison of the effectiveness of two medicines requires a common metric for the dosages." To properly assess monetary and fiscal policy we must examine the costs and side effects of the measures and not merely the size of the impact of a one billion dollar change in each.

The large differences between multipliers estimated from econometric models and those from reduced form equations are somewhat disturbing. Especially troublesome are the perverse signs of the multipliers for fiscal actions found by the Anderson and Jordan reduced form study. Their study, as that of Friedman and Meiselman, has been subject to considerable dispute and evaluation. One of the difficulties with the Anderson and Jordan study is that their reduced form estimated was presented without actually deriving the system of structural equations.

In a study, critical of the reduced form approach, Steven Goldfeld and Alan Blinder (1972) examined the implications of having stabilization policy formulated by two independent agencies. Their study has implications both for reduced form estimation and for the implementation of policy by uncoordinated agencies.

Goldfeld and Blinder show that if the monetary authority but not the fiscal authority reacts to erroneous forecasts, then their reaction will reduce the estimated size of the fiscal multiplier when reduced form methods are used. For example, if the fiscal authority reacts to deviations in income, then any given monetary action which might otherwise have fallen short could be enhanced by supportive fiscal policy reactions. Estimated money multipliers from reduced forms will overstate the potency of monetary policy. At the same time, if a fiscal action is undertaken and if the monetary authority reacts with a poor forecast, not taking into account the fiscal action, then fiscal policy will appear to be ineffective. Goldfeld and Blinder point out that reduced form estimates may tell us less about multipliers than they do about the degree of cooperation between the FED and the executive.

The Relative Stability of Various Sectors: In addition to disagreement about the values of parameters, and about the relative importance of various shocks, economists disagree about the relative stability of various sectors. Fiscalists tend to believe that the commodity market, the *IS* schedule, is relatively stable, while monetarists think the *LM* curve is more stable. William Poole in "Optimal Choice of Monetary Policy in a Simple Stochastic Macro Model," (1970) points to the relationship between the selection of instruments by the FED and the relative stability of the *IS* and *LM* curves. Poole asks the following question: Which instrument should the FED employ, the money supply M or the rate of interest R? In the models we have built so far, all equations are deterministic. However, in fact, structural equations contain some randomness. In statistical terminology, for example, the consumption equation is not determinstic but is stochastic. In deterministic models, the FED can either fix the money supply and therefore the position of the *LM* curve or adjust the money supply so as to fix the rate of interest. Given the money demand schedule as a structural equation, the FED cannot simultaneously set R and M. Figure 2 depicts these two choices confronting the policy maker. (We assume here for simplicity that the FED has complete control of M or R. We will discuss shortly the problem confronting policy makers when they do not have complete control of their instru-

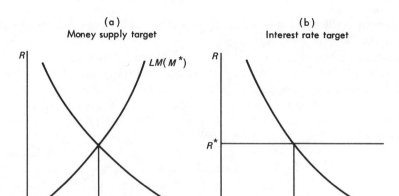

FIGURE 2   Choice of Monetary Policy Instrument in Deterministic Model

ments.) In Figure 2(a) the central bank chose M, its instrument variable, to be M^*. Having selected M^* the FED produced income level Y^*. (We are ignoring fiscal policy in this problem.) Thus the FED chose LM curve $LM(M^*)$. In Figure 2(b) the central bank chose to fix R at level R^*. To do so the FED must adjust the LM curve to hold R at R^*. Consequently, the money market locus of equilibria will not be any particular LM curve but the horizontal line R^*. Now in a deterministic model, in Figure 2, it does not appear to matter whether the FED fixes R or M because in each case target Y^* is realized. However, in a more realistic stochastic world with uncertainty, the problem is more difficult.

Economists have for years debated the relative stability of the money and commodity markets. Monetarists argue that the demand for money schedule is the stable anchor. This implies that the LM curve is stable. Monetarists, especially Friedman, argue at the same time that the IS curve is unstable. (Recall Friedman's attack on the marginal propensity to consume.) Suppose that the monetarists are correct and that the IS curve is unstable due to large random shocks while the LM curve is perfectly stable. This would imply the situation depicted in Figure 3: the LM curve is located exactly, once a value for the money supply instrument is determined, but the IS curve may fall anywhere within a shaded band. Let the target income level be Y^*. If the FED attempts to reach this target by setting the R instrument to R^*, then it will succeed in bringing income into the range Y_4-Y_1 about Y^*. That is the best it can do. What if the FED had used a money supply instrument instead? Had the FED chosen M^*, it would have restricted the money market to curve $LM(M^*)$ and the range of equilibrium income levels would have been narrowed to $(Y_3$-$Y_2)$. Thus the money supply instrument is more precise than the interest rate.

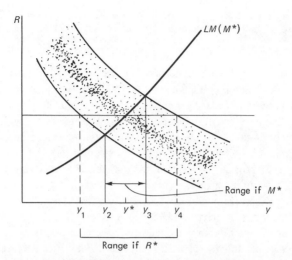

FIGURE 3   Money Supply Instrument vs. Interest Rate Instrument when There is Uncertainty in Commodity Market

If the monetarists are incorrect, however, and the commodity market is relatively stable, then if the FED sets the interest rate instrument at R^*, it hits the income target Y^*.

Forecasting Methods: Given the difficulty in determining structure, of choosing unknown values for parameters, and of foreseeing the major outside shocks, how can we expect forecasters to give us reliable estimates of the future? The candid answer is that we cannot. Nevertheless, this fact has not stopped economists and others from attempting to foresee the future. Forecasters are concerned with the future values of GNP, the rate of inflation, the rate of unemployment, and the many other macroeconomic magnitudes. While evaluation of these statistics as discussed in earlier chapters is fraught with difficulty, they are an essential input to both public and private decisions. Alas, economic forecasting, which some call crystal ball gazing, is one of the less reliable aspects of economics. Serious economic forecasters utilize three different types of methods: (1) surveys of anticipations, attitudes, and plans, (2) leading indicators, and (3) large-scale model forecasts. It must be confessed at the outset that none of the three methods is highly reliable as a purely predictive device.

Attitudinal surveys are taken by the Office of Business Economics and the Securities and Exchange Commission (OBE-SEC). Their interest is in assessing the prospects for fixed business investment. As noted earlier, McGraw-Hill undertakes surveys of planned business investment, and attitudinal surveys of consumers are undertaken by the Michigan Survey Research Center. Economists tend to be somewhat skeptical of their value. The logic of the poor predictive power of consumers is explained by Evans in 1969:

Since the average individual is probably not a very good forecaster, the future state of the economy in his mind probably is closely related to the present state.

The second commonly employed method of economic forecasting is to utilize leading indicators. Leading indicators are economic series, such as new orders for durable goods, five hundred common stock prices, and corporate profit after taxes, which seem to lead the general pace of economic activity. The National Bureau of Economic Research (NBER) has devoted enormous resources to empirical formulation, compilation, and evaluation of series of economic magnitudes for the U.S. economy. NBER holds the view that economic activity tends to occur over time in a roughly cyclical pattern, rising to a peak, then falling off to a trough, and then rising again. While the long-run trend of the economy may be upward, economic activity tends to cycle about this upward secular trend. NBER attempts to identify major cycles by observing points in time when economic activity peaks and troughs. *Ex post*, NBER identifies a reference cycle by these peaks and troughs. The major determinants of the cycle are money GNP, real GNP, and the index of industrial production. Since economic series tend to move somewhat erratically, it is difficult to spot a cycle turning point, peak, or trough, *ex ante*. However, NBER has identified reference cycles historically. Table 2 indicates some general features of reference cycles observed by NBER in the U.S. They run generally about three-and-a-half to four years long with the expansion phase roughly twice the contraction phase, the former usually a little longer than two years, the latter a little longer than one year.

TABLE 2
General Characteristics of Reference Cycles

| | Duration in Months | | | |
| | | | Entire Cycle | |
Average, All Cycles	*Contraction Peak to Trough*	*Expansion Trough to Peak*	*Trough to Trough*	*Peak to Peak*
26 cycles 1954-1961	19	30	49	49
10 cycles 1919-1961	15	35	50	54
4 cycles 1945-1961	10	36	46	46
Average peacetime cycles				
22 cycles 1854-1961	20	26	45	46
8 cycles 1919-1961	16	28	45	48
3 cycles 1945-1961	10	32	42	42

Source: Michael K. Evans, *Macroeconomic Activity* (New York: Harper & Row, 1969), p. 447; all figures are taken from *Business Cycle Developments*.

Having identified the reference cycles, NBER then identifies about seventy series as either *leading series*, those which tend to precede the reference cycle, *coincident series*, or *lagging series*. For purposes of forecasting, the leading series are the most interesting. If they could give us some notice of when the reference cycle is about to change direction, we could adjust stabilization measures accordingly. Unfortunately, careful analysis of the leading indicators suggests that they cannot be very helpful for prediction. It is one thing to select a leading indicator for a reference cycle *ex post*. It is quite another to predict a reference cycle from leading indicators. Evans studies the predictive power of thirty leading indicators for the postwar U.S. economy. After rejecting several as too erratic or as turning too close to the reference cycle to be useful for predictions, Evans finds that "Only two of the series are useful for predicting both peaks and troughs: accession rate and the change in unfilled orders. This is not a very impressive record." After considering the possibility of a leading indicator indicating a false turning point, Evans is even more pessimistic. He concludes:

> Clearly the set of thirty leading indicators considered together cannot be used to forecast turning points, because the lead time is either too short or too erratic, and too many false recessions are signaled.

Hymans (1973) evaluated the "composite index of leading indicators" (CLI), which consists of a weighted average of twelve leading indicators, as a predictor of the composite index of coincident indicators (CCI) which closely tracks the reference cycle. Hymans evaluates the performance of the CLI against a straw-man alternative:

> Thus a "naive" forecaster who never said anything but [No change] would have made 64 errors, an error rate of 22 percent, compared with 50 errors, an error rate of 18 percent, resulting from use of the CLI.

The tendency to predict peaks when none occurs is strong for the CLI; 49.1 percent of the predicted peaks were false. Hymans says, "When the CLI signals a peak, flip a coin! And that is a serious indictment of the indicator." The general conclusion then is that leading indicators are not terribly useful as predictive devices. This result does not imply that studies of cyclical series is not helpful for many purposes but they are not yet reliable forecasting tools.

The third device for forecasting the state of the economy is the econometric model. The models are based upon theories of aggregate economic behavior like those developed in the text. The model developed for the Brookings Institution, for example, contains five equations for consumption expenditures. Consumption is determined much as it was discussed in Chapters 8 and 9. The Data Resources Incorporated (DRI) macromodel utilizes concepts about investment behavior such as those developed in Chapters 10 and 11. The Penn-MIT-FED model depicts interaction between the monetary and real variables much like the relations developed in Parts IV and V. In general, these large-scale macromodels are attempts to quantify, elaborate, and unify the macrotheory models in order to interpret, estimate, measure, and predict actual U.S. data.

Econometric models have several advantages over a collection of series that is not based on *a priori* reasoning and over surveys of opinions and plans. Econometric models forecast interrelations between sectors as well as information on a variety of sub-elements of the economy—output by sector, prices, unemployment, and so on. Furthermore, the large-scale models permit one to provide forecasts conditional on various policy actions. Consequently, the FED could consider three alternative forecasts: one assuming the FED does not change its behavior from the previous period, one assuming the FED is more expansionary, and one assuming it is contractionary. Finally, the models should conceptually provide information about the nature of errors. If the models are carefully designed, errors in particular equations should show up as poor forecasts in those sectors. However, the existing models really appear to be too large and complex for analysis by anyone but a committee of economists. Nonetheless, forecasts are needed to formulate policy and policy makers use many pieces of information, including large-scale macromodel forecasts.

Organization and Coordination of Stabilization Policy: The necessity of matching instruments to targets is evident from our earlier discussion. The unique structure of the institutions charged with implementing stabilization policy in the U.S. presents several problems. First, armed with traditional American skepticism about the potential abuses of power, Congress created a central bank which was independent of the executive branch of government. In fact, the FED was not originally designed to be a central bank at all and only evolved into a central bank gradually as the Board of Governors gained more control over monetary policy. The necessity to coordinate financing of the huge federal deficits during and immediately after World War II forced close coordination between the FED and the U.S. Treasury. However, in 1951, over a disagreement with President Truman, the Board of Governors achieved a break with the executive branch to once again establish its independence. The advantages and disadvantages of independence of the FED have been debated among economists for many years. In most western economies, the central bank is headed by a member of the government in power. As governments change hands, so does the leadership of the central bank. In the 1970s, as inflation has become a more prominent economic problem and as the conduct of monetary policy has come under closer public scrutiny, the issue of the independence of the FED has shifted slightly. In the late 1970s the issue became less whether the FED should be folded into the executive branch and more whether the FED should be accountable to congress. In part this shift in emphasis reflected the noneconomic forces in government for power to shift away from the executive toward congress. In part, however, it also reflected the trend toward demanding greater accountability on the part of the practitioners of monetary policy. The FED is now required to explicitly state target-values for monetary policy instruments. Howevery, the FED still remains independent of the executive branch.

A second set of issues dealing with the efficiency of the stabilization institutions has to do with the organizational structure of each institution itself. Is the budgetary process efficiently organized to institute countercyclical fiscal policy?

Fiscalists have long complained that the budgetary process is ponderous, requiring complex interaction between both houses of Congress as well as coordination among the Treasury, the Bureau of the Budget, the Council of Economic Advisors, and so on. Conventional wisdom among fiscalists seems to be that fiscal policy is a poor fine-tuning instrument, especially with the disintegration of party control in the congressional branch. Similar questions about the efficiency of the FED have been raised.

For example, James Pierce (1979), questions the wisdom of giving the directors of the branch banks of the FED influence over national monetary policy as members of the FOMC. He and others also question the wisdom of voluntary membership in the FED by banks. Also, it is now evident that the liabilities of a variety of financial institutions are very similar to demand deposits at commercial banks. Since nonbank financial institutions are under the control of different regulatory agencies, the institution of monetary policy might well be severely diluted. These political and institutional issues are important in assessing the efficiency and effectiveness of stabilization policies.

The Budget Restraint: Despite the political independence of the FED and the Council of Economic Advisors, recent research into the implementation of fiscal and monetary policies implies that it may be more constructive to view them as an integral part of a coherent budget process. For example, Carl Christ (1979) argues that if one views the issuance of money as an integral part of the federal budget process, then one's thinking about the implementation of policy changes considerably. If the central bank were part of the executive, we might naturally realize that federal deficits can be financed by issuing either interest-bearing debt or money. To illustrate the nature of the government budget restraint, we shall use the following list of symbols:

G: government expenditures	r: interest rate on federal debt
T_x: federal taxes	$\dot{B}$: new federal bonds sold to public
T_r: federal transfer payments	$\dot{M}$: rate of change of monetary base
D: outstanding federal debt	

The government deficit is the difference between total outlays and total income. Total outlays consist of government expenditures on goods and services plus transfer payments plus interest paid on the debt, and income consists of taxes. Thus the deficit is $G + T_r + rD - T_x$. This deficit must be financed by either new bond issues or new issues of money or some combination. Consequently, the government budget restraint is

$$G + T_r + rD - T_x = \dot{B} + \dot{M}$$

This budget restraint must be satisfied by government finance at all times. Several important points follow from analysis employing this budget restraint.

First, it is obvious that we cannot change just one variable in the equation alone. At least two variables must be changed by any policy action. For example, when we think of monetary policy, we are usually thinking in terms of open market operations. An open market expansion of the money supply consists of increasing M and simultaneously reducing B by the same amount. When we talk in terms of an increase in government expenditures as a pure fiscal action, we think of this increase in government expenditures as being financed by an increase in the sale of new bonds. In this pure fiscal action, then, we changed both G and $\dot{B}$.

Since the FED, when it undertakes open market operations, purchases or sells U.S. government securities on the open market, it is undertaking management of the federal debt. It adjusts the amount held in the hands of the public. The FED can change not only the volume of this debt but also its composition when buying or selling bonds of different maturities. Since one of the central financial tasks of the U.S. Treasury is management of the federal debt, we clearly have two separate agencies—the Treasury in the executive branch and the quasi-public FED—instituting management of the federal debt. Again, it would seem evident that some degree of coordination between these agencies is essential.

One of the most interesting points Christ makes in his analysis of stabilization policy and the government budget restraint is that a rather popular, well-known policy proposal may be subject to stability problems. Christ quotes Milton Friedman:

> The right policy—not alone for this episode but as a general rule—is to let the quantity of money increase at a rate that can be maintained indefinitely without inflation (about 5 percent per year) and to keep taxes and spending at levels that will balance the budget at high employment.

As Christ points out, a low rate of monetary expansion may require, in an economy with high unemployment, continual expansion of the federal debt. But as this debt expands, interest payments of the debt will continue to expand and the deficit will automatically worsen. In other words, Friedman's proposal would have to be very carefully tuned and modulated. The increasing interest payments needed to sustain payments on the increased debt would have to be offset by continual reductions in the rate of government expenditures. The lesson of this analysis of budget restraints is that neither monetary nor fiscal policy is an independent process and that any policy proposals must be carefully analyzed in the context of their full implications for the federal budget.

Instrument Control: Another set of practical issues confronted by policy makers has to do with their ability to control the instruments of policy. While it is simple for us to talk about the FED setting the value of M, it is apparent to those who take monetary policy seriously that the central bank has a difficult time controlling monetary aggregates. Twice in the 1970s, the monetary aggregates most often proposed by monetarists, M_1, (cash plus demand deposits issued by commercial banks) and M_2 (M_1 plus savings and time deposits issued by commercial banks) altered their courses of expansion unexpectedly. From late 1974 through 1977, M_1's growth rate was unexpectedly slow. In late 1978 and early 1979 the rate of expansion of M_1 again slowed unexpectedly.

A related problem in the 1970s has been the creation of new financial instruments which are close substitutes for M_1 and M_2. Negotiable-orders-of-withdrawal (NOW) accounts began to be issued by New England thrift institutions, and share drafts were issued by credit unions across the country in the mid-1970s. Furthermore, the ability of depositors to transfer funds from savings accounts to checking accounts changed considerably in the 1970s with the introduction of automatic transfer systems (ATS). Other highly liquid assets which are close substitutes for demand deposits were issued by commercial banks and by even nonfinancial institutions: namely, money market funds and money market certificates. In general, with the acceleration of inflation in the late 1970s the extent of cash management both by corporations and by individuals intensified considerably. This intensification of cash management, as shown by Porter, Simpson, and Mauskopf (1979) was a product of high interest rates from nonfinancial institutions, tight regulatory control of financial institutions, and the technological innovations represented by ATS and the like.

As Klein (1979) warns, however, the control problem for monetary aggregates may be irresolvable. Even the narrowest monetary aggregate, M_1, is subject to considerable measurement error. Statistical revisions are common and often involve large adjustments due to errors in reporting or errors in concept. For example, as Klein tells us, revisions reported in 1976 produced M_1 adjustments which were as large as $2 billion going back as far as 1970 to 1971. Furthermore, with the advent of many different types of financial assets, the predictability of various component parts of the monetary aggregates becomes quite difficult. Many banks are not members of the Federal Reserve System; nor are nonbank financial intermediaries. Thus even if the central bank could measure and predict broadly defined monetary aggregates, their ability to control them is subject to doubt. Finally, the monetary aggregates which the central bank can control and those which it can predict may not be the ones which are the most important from the point of view of economic performance. That is, the best instrument from the point of view of affecting the course of the economy may not be the one which the monetary authorities can control.

The central bank is not the only stabilization authority which has a difficult time determining exactly which instrument to employ. Whenever the executive branch considers implementing discretionary fiscal policy, the choice of exactly how to do so is hotly debated. For example, when considering a tax cut, the Council of Economic Advisors invariably encounters difficulties on Capitol Hill. Proposed tax cuts must go through the Congress's House Ways and Means Committee. Invariably, this committee concerns itself with all the issues of equity and efficiency in addition to the issue of stability. As a result, the implementation of tax cuts is often dependent upon issues unrelated to stabilization: What will be the incidence of the cut? Will the new rules be fair? What will happen to the relative price structure? To resource reallocation? The process of instituting a tax cut can be very cumbersome, awkward, and slow. It may be possible to earmark some instruments of tax policy as common stability instruments. These could be used frequently and, therefore, with more ease. Two examples would be investment tax credits and wage subsidies.

Targets and Norms: In Figure 1 we presented a partial list of policy targets. Of course, macroeconomic policy has many primary targets and is constrained by a great many secondary targets. Stabilization authorities must take into account the impacts on special critical industries such as housing or automobiles. They must be constantly concerned with the interests of unions and the protection of labor rights. They must be concerned with the distribution of income, with the social effects on various subgroups of poverty, and with unemployment. The list could be continued. And how does one determine the relative importance of achieving various values for these targets? In other words, given the state of the economy and forecasts of its future, the stabilization authority must establish norms against which he can compare actual performance. In the most aggregative terms the selection of a target begins with determination of potential money GNP. One could select that level for which a social welfare function, incorporating and weighting the costs and benefits associated with both inflation and unemployment, is a maximum. The resultant level of GNP would then become the target income level. Of course, a number of additional problems would remain: the optimal mix of income between public and private expenditures and between current consumption and capital accumulation, the reconciliation of internal and external balance, and the appropriate magnitude and speed of policy implementation are just a few. However, let us first consider the selection of target income. In Chapter 22, the welfare costs of inflation when anticipated and when unanticipated were discussed. The welfare costs of unemployment may now be considered.

The pathbreaking work on estimating the social costs of unemployment was undertaken over a decade ago in 1962 by Arthur Okun (1970), then chairman of the CEA. Estimating the incremental costs of 5 percent rather than 4 percent unemployment, Okun (in 1973) reconfirmed his earlier finding: For each 1 percent reduction in the rate of unemployment, GNP will increase by 3 percent. Three percent of a $1.3 trillion economy represents a $30 to $40 billion loss in social welfare. Consider the forgone houses, schools, social programs, automobiles, and hospitals represented by a loss of $30 to $40 billion. As Okun emphasized, the incremental 1 percent increase from 4 to 5 percent unemployment is "merely the tip of the iceberg that forms in a cold economy."

Okun estimated the percentage rate of change of unemployment from the percentage rate of change of GNP, assuming a linear relation and utilizing quarterly data from 1947-II to 1960-IV. His result:

$$\dot{u} = 0.3 - 0.3\dot{y} \tag{9}$$

where $\dot{u}$ is the percentage rate of change over the quarter of unemployment and $\dot{y}$ is the quarterly percentage rate of change of real GNP. Consider the implication of these parameters. If real GNP fails to grow for one quarter, the rate of unemployment will increase by 3 percentage points. The unemployment rate will rise because the labor force is growing, productivity is increasing, and capital is accumulating, so that while more workers are available, fewer are actually needed. These estimated parameters indicate that to prevent unemployment from rising, GNP must grow by 1 percent per quarter.

Synthesizing the results from a number of statistical techniques, such as the one outlined above, Okun settled on the following relation between potential GNP $y(P)$ and actual GNP $y(A)$:

$$y(P) = y(A)[1 + .032(u - 4)] \tag{10}$$

Utilizing equation 10 one can easily estimate potential GNP from readily available statistics on actual GNP and on the rate of unemployment. As equation (10) indicates, at 4 percent unemployment, actual and potential GNP are equal. In other words, Okun selects 4 percent as the target level of unemployment for computing target GNP. However, presumably one can compute GNP associated with 5, 4.5, 3.5, and 3 percent unemployment levels as well and compare the GNP losses from each 0.5 percent of unemployment to the gains from the lower inflation rate computed from the Phillips curve. But we are getting ahead of ourselves.

Where does the 3 percent increase in output come from when unemployment falls from 5 to 4 percent? In his first development of this idea, now called *Okun's Law*, Okun did not address this question formally. However, in 1973 he does estimate the sources of new output. These estimates, while clearly only approximations, give some idea of the information in the unemployment iceberg submerged below the surface of the cold economy. Three types of increases in labor input, when u falls from 5 to 4 percent, increase real output by 2.10 percent:

Component	%
Jobs for the unemployed	1.05
Lengthened workweek	0.40
Increase labor force participation	0.65

Source: Arthur Okun, "Upward Mobility in a High-Pressure Economy," *Brookings Papers on Economic Activity*, No. 1 (1973), p. 211. ©1973 by The Brookings Institution, Washington, D.C.

In addition, then, to the newly employed who increase output by 1.05 percent, those previously employed work longer hours on the average and others, unidentified by the statistics on unemployment, join the labor force. The second major component contributing to the increase in GNP is the increase in output from increased productivity. Okun argues that as the labor market tightens, laborers are bumped up the ladder to jobs utilizing their various skills more efficiently. This additional productivity increases the 2.1 percent from increases in labor input to about 3 percent—thus the final increase in real GNP per 1 percent drop in the unemployment rate is 3 percent.

R. J. Gordon and others have argued that, with the productivity slowdown of the 1970s, a 1 percent drop in the unemployment rate now produces an increase in real GNP of 2 percent rather than Okun's 3 percent. Since the rate of productivity increase is likely to also change in the 1980s, additional econometric research would be necessary to determine the actual quantitative magnitude of the dollar cost of unemployment. The main force of Okun's analysis, however, is that the social costs of unemployment are incurred by the society at large in foregone output. Some economists quarrel with the implication of Okun's analysis that one can gain permanent benefits by pressuring the economy to a point at which the unemployment rate is low. Recall the position of the advocates of the natural rate hypothesis that any attempt to reduce the unemployment rate with stabilization policy below its natural rate will produce only temporary gain and a permanent increase in the rate of inflation. Furthermore, scientific attempts at measuring the welfare costs of inflation and unemployment are relatively primitive. We have Okun's law and we have the attempts by Foster, discussed in Chapter 22, for measuring the costs of conserving cash balances in the face of inflation. Gramlich (1979) points out that while economists have long enumerated the nature of the social costs of inflation and unemployment, they have made little headway in quantifying the relative costs of these social evils. Gramlich attempts to estimate the marginal rate of substitution between unemployment and inflation by estimating the slope of the Phillips curve in the range of current economic performance. But this effort must be viewed as tentative.

B • Policy proposals for the 1980s

The Monetarist-Rationalist View: Let us turn now to the nature of policy proposals which one might expect to come from economists representing the two major divisions of economic thought in the U.S. Suppose a monetarist-rationalist (MR) was confronted with the problem of recommending policies for dealing with the U.S. economy in the early 1980s: the inflation rate is 13 percent, and the unemployment rate 6 percent. How might these economists approach the policy problem? Figure 4 illustrates the monetarist-rationalist view of the short-run and long-run set of inflation-unemployment choices. In the long run, the MR thinks the Phillips curve is vertical: the natural rate hypothesis. It would be his view that the economy had reached point *A* as a result of historical attempts to drive the unemployment rate below the natural rate:

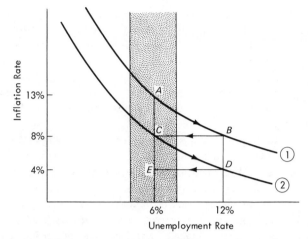

FIGURE 4   Monetarist-Rationalist View of Inflation-Unemployment Choices

6 percent. Since it is the MR view that the unemployment rate is independent of stabilization policy in the long run, stabilization would be used exclusively to achieve a target value for inflation.

Thus, first MR economists would determine the optimal target value for inflation. To these economists the costs of inflation are associated with the loss in efficiency incurred as a result of attempts to economize on cash balances. Economic agents economize on cash balances to avoid the erosion of their wealth that would accompany inflation if they were holding money. Foster, Friedman, and others argue that the *optimal rate of inflation* is that rate which is small enough so that the opportunity cost of holding cash balances is zero (zero being the return on money). In an economy in which cash bears zero interest, the return will be positive only if the inflation rate is negative. This means that a *deflation* is necessary for the return on cash to equal its opportunity cost. The optimal rate of deflation must be equal to the real rate of return. Since it seems unrealistic in a world with 13 percent inflation to expect the inflation rate to be converted to a 4-5 percent rate of deflation, let us suppose that MR economists are content to reduce the average rate of inflation to the 3-5 percent range. (In fact, given inherent biases in the typical price indexes we employ, it may not be unrealistic to think of 3 to 5 percent as representing zero inflation in a perfect index.) Given an optimal inflation target, MRs would then propose reducing the rate of monetary expansion to that rate which is consistent with the target rate of inflation.

In the short run, such a proposal amounts to moving along the short-run Phillips curve labeled 1 in Figure 4 from point A toward point B. Of course, MRs are well aware that a risk of slowing the rate of monetary expansion will be to create a recession. The central bank may panic and reverse its policy. Consequently, suppose that as a gradual intermediate step these economists set an intermediate inflation target of 8 percent and reduced the rate of monetary expansion from, say, 13 percent to around 8 percent. The short-run effect on the economy would be to move it from point A to point B on the short-run Phillips curve in Figure 4. At point B the average inflation rate is 8 percent and the unemployment rate has increased from the initial rate of 6 percent to, say, 12 percent. (In order to determine how much the unemployment rate would rise from the initial rate of 6 percent, one must estimate the shape of the short-run Phillips curve.)

How would MRs justify a recession in order to reduce the rate of inflation? Three arguments seem to be commonly employed in the defense of generating a short-run recession: (1) Some economists argue that a recession is a cleansing process. This was the view held, for example, by the great economic historian, Joseph Schumpeter. In recent years economists from the American Enterprise Institute have made the same argument. Recessions, it is believed, purge the economy from poor decision makers and allow only the efficient to survive. (2) The economy has built-in mechanisms to protect the unemployed so that the pain of unemployment is diminished: Unemployment compensation, food stamps, aid to families with dependent children, and so on. (3) The more rapid the rate of inflation, the longer the recession needed in order to return to price stability. The choice, therefore, is whether we can have a short, mild recession now or a deeper, longer recession later.

Given the analytic position of the MR, unemployment will not be sustained at 12 percent, because this is not the natural rate of unemployment. The economy would eventually return to 6 percent unemployment, because that is long-run equilibrium. (Presumably, the same economists would propose again shifting down the new short-run Phillips curve to point D and eventually bringing the economy to rest at point E, which would be 6 percent unemployment and the optimal inflation of, say, 4 percent.)

MRs do not ignore the unemployment rate, but they feel that stabilization policies are best suited to achieving a target value for the inflation rate. How, then, one might ask, do they deal with unemployment? Perhaps the best work from this ideological stance on reducing unemployment is that of Martin Feldstein, President of the National Bureau of Economic Research. Feldstein suggests a variety of proposals for permanently reducing the unemployment rate. First, let us ask what is the actual value of the natural unemployment rate? Economists have known for some time that the demographic composition of the labor force changed dramatically from the 1960s to the 1970s. Recessions in 1969-70 and 1973-75 were unusual in that they were accompanied by acceleration in the inflation rate over previous years. Econometric evidence compiled by George Perry (1970) and by R. J. Gordon (1971, 1972) indicated that the Phillips curve had shifted upward. More recently, analysts believe that the Phillips curve has continued its upward drift. Both Gordon and Perry attributed much of the shift in the Phillips curve to changes in the composition of the labor force. These changes tended to be from highly employable 25- to 64-year-old white males to the traditionally difficult-to-employ teenagers, minorities, and female workers. Perry considers both the change in composition of the labor force and the increased inability of the female and teenage workers to obtain employment. Perry constructs an index of unemployment dispersion to obtain an indicator of labor market tightness sensitive to age-sex composition. The inclusion of the *Perry Dispersion Index*, in estimates of the Phillips curve, reduces the unemployment rate associated with a given rate of inflation by about 1½ to 2 percent.

Modigliani and Papademos (1975), utilizing unemployment figures adjusted for changes in the composition of the labor force a la Perry, argue that, if the adjusted unemployment rate is reduced below 4 percent, acceleration in the inflation rate is extremely likely. They conclude that "Policy makers should vigorously avoid [an adjusted unemployment rate of 4 percent] because it leads to increasing inflation." For Modigliani and Papademos the unemployment rate at which inflation will not accelerate falls between 5½ and 6 percent.

Robert E. Hall (1974) also points to the effect on unemployment statistics of changes in the composition of the labor force. Hall points out, "In 1974, an official unemployment rate of 6 percent indicates the same degree of tightness as 5.4 percent did in 1964." Hall found that the equilibrium unemployment rate, at which the labor market would clear without wage inflation, was about 5.5 percent, with a range of from 4.9 to 6.1 percent. Edward Gramlich (1979) produced an adjusted unemployment rate for price stability of around 4.5 percent. This, Gramlich points out, "corresponds to a noninflationary official unemployment rate of 6.2 percent in 1968, which is approximately what other investigators such as Hall, Modigliani and Papademos, Wachter and Cagan, have found." Thus, a consensus seems to have emerged that reducing the unemployment rate in the late 1970s below around 6 percent would produce an accelerating inflation. Thus stabilization policy is ruled out by these economists as a means of reducing the unemployment rate.

Feldstein, however, examined the unemployment figures in some detail and prepared in (1973) a set of proposals for dealing with unemployment. Feldstein argued that "the major problem to be dealt with is not a chronic, aggregate shortage of jobs but the instability of individual employment." Feldstein decomposed the labor force into submarkets and explained much of current unemployment by various inefficiencies in the component markets. Feldstein suggested numerous proposals for improving the flow of job market information such as computerized "job banks," for reducing the "average duration of unemployment." Feldstein argued that the unemployment rate could be reduced by 1½ percentage points simply by reducing the average duration of unemployment by one month from the postwar average of about three months. Feldstein also proposes a number of changes for dealing with the high level of teenage unemployment including a "youth employment scholarship paid to young workers as a supplement to their wage income." Such programs would avoid the depressing effects on the demand for jobs of programs such as the minimum wage. Feldstein also proposed reform of the unemployment compensation system, because it has the effect of producing a very high marginal tax rate on the income one would earn by becoming employed. Taxing unemployment compensation and increasing the tax on firms which perennially sustain long periods of employee layoffs would reduce the incentives for long durations of unemployment and would reduce the marginal tax rate on earned income of returning to work. These and other proposals by MR economists for dealing with the high natural rate of unemployment are, of course, all structural in nature and not of the stabilization type.

In addition to introducing proposals for reducing inflation toward the optimal rate and for reducing the natural unemployment rate, monetarist/rationalists also propose insulating the private economy against the ravages of rapid unexpected inflation. These measures fall under the heading of *indexation*. Two major structural proposals are made in the spirit of indexation. One is to index the federal tax system so that the effect of moving tax payers, both individuals and businesses, into higher tax brackets via inflation can be offset. In a thorough study of the tax system and inflation, edited by Henry Aaron (1976), a group of Brookings economists studied the relationship between inflation and the U.S. tax structure. An interesting conclusion of this study was that viewed in retrospect, with allowance for the congressional tax reform acts, the federal tax system appeared to be relatively well indexed. In other words, the experience of inflation in the late 1960s and early 1970s did not produce an average increase in most taxpayer's tax rates. Furthermore, it would prove very difficult, as a practical matter, to avoid introducing new distortions into the tax system when indexing.

The second proposal for insulating the private sector from inflation is to eliminate Regulation Q because it prevents financial institutions from paying interest on checking accounts and restricts the interest rates paid on time and savings accounts. One of the most troublesome costs of rapid inflation has been the extent to which private voluntary saving is discouraged by the failure of interest rates on checking and savings accounts to keep pace with the inflation.

The Keynesian-Structuralist View: How would Keynesian-structuralist economists (KS) attempt to deal with the same policy problem confronted by the monetarist/rationalists above? Figure 5 illustrates the KS view of the inflation-unemployment trade-off in both the short and long runs. KS believe that there is a long-run trade-off between inflation and unemployment. It is the KS view that deceleration of inflation does not require a recession induced by monetary contraction. Even though continual inflation requires monetary expansion, it is the structuralist view that the inability of the economy to respond to external shocks is the underlying cause of inflation. Consequently, KS recommend changes in structure to insulate the system from external shocks. A more responsive system is less likely to require monetary expansion. In addition to rejecting recession induced by monetary contraction, KS argue that it is very undesirable

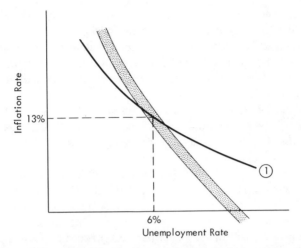

FIGURE 5   Keynesian-Structuralist View of the Inflation-Unemployment Trade-off

to slow the economy down. (Though it is clearly a matter of degree and normative judgment, MR seem more willing to incur the costs of recession to reduce
inflation than do KS.)

KS present two arguments in their defense of rejecting a policy-induced
recession: (1) They estimate the costs to the economy of a recession by employing Okun's Law and find those costs to be large. Some argue that a one percent
reduction in inflation from 13 percent by an induced recession would cost the
U.S. economy $200 billion! They say that a $200 billion tax would not be voted
by the public if that were the explicit price of reducing inflation by 1 percent.
(2) These economists argue that some inflation is essential to maintaining har-
mony in the social fabric. When the economy is struck with depressive exogenous
shocks, such as the 1979 doubling of oil prices by OPEC, the reduction in
money incomes in a noninflating economy would have to be so large that it
would rip apart the social fabric as various groups fought to maintain their
relative positions. Consequently, the KS ordinarily recommend utilizing stabilization policies to prevent the unemployment rate from falling below the 6 percent range of the nonaccelerating inflationary rate. They then turn to structural
measures for dealing with inflation. These structural measures may be placed
into three categories: (1) manpower policies, (2) incomes policies, and (3) other
structural measures.

Manpower policies focus on the unemployment problem. The unemployed
are not a randomly selected group of individuals from the entire labor force. On
the contrary, they tend to represent distinct subgroups, in particular, minorities,
women, and teenagers. For example, the teenage black unemployment rate is
four times the average white unemployment rate. Manpower policies are aimed
at reducing unemployment of these groups. The most famous manpower policies

were those introduced in the early 1930s to combat the high levels of unemployment during the Great Depression. The largest of these programs was the Works Progress Administration (WPA). The WPA program alone cost the federal government over $10 billion and at its peak employed over 3,000,000 workers. Despite the magnitude and apparent necessity of these programs, their effectiveness has always been questioned by academics.

Again, in the 1980s we find ourselves questioning the value of manpower policies in which federal expenditures are used to directly finance the employment of individuals who are unable to obtain jobs on their own from the private sector. The reason for this skepticism on the part of academics is the fear that while these programs are employing individuals, they may be doing so at the expense of private employment of other individuals. This idea is called the *displacement principle*. Suppose, to illustrate the idea, that the government collects one dollar in taxes to finance one dollar in government expenditures for a WPA employment project. Will the taxpayer reduce his expenditures and thus reduce the private demand for labor enough to offset the force on total employment of the government employment program? The effectiveness of the manpower programs is the central issue raised in John L. Palmer's *Creating Jobs* (1978). This collection of articles analyzes the effectiveness of various types of direct job creation (DJC) programs. DJC has two characteristics: (1) Federal funds are granted to public and private employers for employing certain individuals. (2) Eligibility for employment using these funds is restricted to people who are ordinarily unemployable, such as those with low incomes, welfare dependency, youth, previous unemployment, or residence in high unemployment areas.

Martin N. Bailey and James Tobin analyze the effectiveness of DJC by asking under what circumstances the multiplier effect of government expenditures to finance these programs would be larger than any other types of government expenditures. We know from our analysis of fiscal policy that multipliers work by operating through the after-tax marginal propensities to consume of those receiving the government expenditures. After the first stage in a multiplier process, we could expect the subsequent multiplier effects to be the same regardless of the original impact of government expenditures. However, the first-stage effects of a DJC program may be more (or less) substantial than the first-stage effects of a different type of government expenditure program. Because the poor are likely to have large marginal propensities to consume and low marginal tax rates, one would expect the initial impact of a DJC program to be large. However, we should bear in mind that operating against this effect is the fact that if a poor individual is employed by a DJC program, he must give up any transfer payments he may have been receiving from other programs. Thus, the loss in income from reduced transfers may offset some of the initial expansion effect as a result of the increase in wage income.

Baily and Tobin also suggest another reason for some skepticism about the effectiveness of DJC programs. First, it may be that some of these public programs are not as socially desirable. Work done elsewhere, either in the public or private sector, may be socially more desirable. Second, one form in which these programs are being undertaken is through subsidized jobs by state and local governments. There is some evidence that these organizations have utilized the grants to support employment that they would otherwise have been undertaken anyway. In these cases, the net effects of DJC programs would be near zero, since they would be offset by reduced state and local government expenditures. On a more optimistic note, Bailey and Tobin also point out that by raising the demand for the types of labor for which there seems to be considerable slack rather than for labor in general, DJC programs can move along a relatively flat Phillips curve for these specific labor types. Thus, the wage inflation pressures will be small relative to what they would be if pressure were placed on all labor markets.

A different perspective on DJC programs may be to view them as a supplement to an overburdened educational system. Through the late 1960s and early 1970s the number of teenagers grew dramatically because of the high reproduction rates following World War II. There is considerable evidence to support the view that the secondary school system in the United States, especially in the center cities, was unable to absorb so many pupils efficiently. This fact, and the availability of a relatively high minimum wage, drove many teenagers out of the school system. DJC programs may have served the purpose of providing federal funding to educate and train these individuals in state and local government agencies and in private businesses.

Incomes Policies: In addition to manpower programs, KS have proposed a wide variety of incomes policies for reducing the average rate of inflation associated with each level of unemployment. These programs are, in theoretical terms, designed to shift the Phillips curve mapping inward toward the origin. The most aggressive, visible, and controversial attempt to reduce inflation without increasing unemployment was the imposition of wage and price controls by the Nixon Administration from 1971 to 1973. A careful, systematic evaluation of controls, particularly the strict Phase II controls following the freeze, was undertaken by Brookings Institution economist Barry Bosworth (1972, 1973). At the conclusion of the ninety-day wage-price freeze in mid-November 1971, Phase II of tightly controlled, but not frozen, wages and prices was begun. The objective of the program was to reduce the rate of inflation to 2.5 percent without increasing the 5.9 percent rate of unemployment. To accomplish this target, price and wage control measures had to be reconciled with one another and with the rate of growth of productivity. Otherwise controls would interfere with resource allocation which might actually drive down the level of output.

Table 3 indicates the performance of wages and of the consumer price index before, during, and after the program. Critics of controls have placed considerable emphasis on the apparent slowdown in the rate of increase of the CPI prior to the freeze from 5.9 percent in 1969 and 1970 to 3.8 percent in late 1970 and early 1971. Bosworth, however, disaggregates the CPI and discovers that the components which fell the most could be explained by purely transitory phenomena such as removal of the automobile excise tax and the rise in mortgage interest rates from the tightening of monetary policy. Consequently, he sees no clear trend for prices to fall prior to August 1971.

TABLE 3

Price and Wage Performance and Controls

	1969-1970	Prefreeze	Freeze	Phase II	1973
Prices*	5.9	3.8	1.9	3.4	8.8
Wages**	7.1	7.4	—	5.3	10.7

  *Consumer Price Index.
**Employee compensation per manhour, nonfarm private sector.

Source: The figures in the table, compiled by the author, were extracted from Barry Bosworth, "Phase II: The U.S. Experiment with an Incomes Policy," *Brookings Papers on Economic Activity*, No. 1 (1972), pp. 346-47; and "The Current Inflation: Malign Neglect?" *Brookings Papers on Economic Activity*, No. 1 (1973), p. 165. © 1972 and 1973 respectively by The Brookings Institution, Washington, D.C.

The price and wage performances of Phase II are not unimpressive. Wages rose at 5.3 percent which "came into line with the Pay Board standard of 5.5 to 6 percent." Prices rose at 3.4 percent compared to the prefreeze 1969-1970 rate of 5.9 percent. Bosworth observes: "A significant slowing of inflation is evident in the behavior of most major price indexes." Furthermore, the rapid increase of prices after the controls were greatly relaxed suggests that controls had indeed been effective in holding down prices.

However, one must ask two questions which Bosworth fails to address fully. First, the counterfactual question: What might have happened had controls not been employed? Second, did controls merely suspend price increases temporarily without having any permanent effect upon underlying causes of inflation? If controls merely capped inflationary pressures temporarily, they may have actually fed inflationary pressures by constraining resource allocation and disguising excess demands.

Tax-based Income Policies: After the perceived failure of the Nixon wage-price control system, politicians have been unwilling to impose anything stronger than voluntary wage-price control mechanisms. However, many economists work to develop effective modifications to wage-price controls. The most interesting of these proposals is the tax-based incomes policies first suggested by Henry C. Wallich and Sydney Weintraub in (1971). The first version was that wage-price guidelines would be established for firms and labor and that firms which failed to comply with the *wage* guidelines would be required to pay higher tax rates. Later, in (1977) Arthur Okun suggested lowering the corporate tax rate for firms which offer wage increases below the guidelines. The idea behind both of these programs was to provide financial incentive so that firms will negotiate more effectively with unions in settling modest wage agreements. Implicit in both of these programs is the view that when unconstrained employers can offer high wages increases with the knowledge that they can pass them on in price increases. Price increases, in turn, will not reduce demand, because high demand will be sustained by expansionary stabilization policies.

Seidman proposes employing both tax rate increases for firms which fail to comply and tax rate reductions for firms which offer lower than target wage increases. Seidman (1979) justifies these tax-based incomes policies (TIP) in the following way. Many imperfections in the labor market, such as minimum wage laws, aggressive unions, and government programs requiring taxes, make the labor market inefficient, so unemployment is large. The public policy measures which are attempting to reduce unemployment generate inflation. While these "inefficiencies" in the labor market may well advance social welfare, the accelerating inflation brought about by stabilization policies designed to reduce the high unemployment is an external *dis-economy*. In other words, the "public bad" of accelerating inflation is a byproduct of the "imperfections" in the labor market. It is the intention of TIP programs to internalize to the firm and the labor union the external costs (dis-economy) of inflation. Seidman integrates a TIP program into a model of wages and prices such as ours in Chapter 22. He shows that, if TIP succeeds in reducing the wage inflation, monetary contraction is more feasible. Figure 6 illustrates the paths that inflation and unemployment would take if a gradual monetary contraction is introduced both with and without a TIP program. The solid lines are without TIP and the dashed lines are with TIP. In Seidman's example he reduces the rate of monetary expansion from an initial rate of 7 percent to 1 percent, and this is assumed with or without TIP to

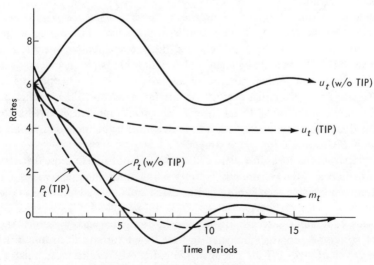

FIGURE 6   TIP in a Monetarist Model

permanently reduce the inflation rate from 6 percent to zero. Notice that without TIP unemployment increases substantially in the short run. It may be this bulge in unemployment which prevents, as a practical political matter, the imposition of contractionary monetary policy. The TIP program eliminates this bulge and permanently reduces the unemployment rate associated with any given rate of inflation.

Another innovative incomes policy was proposed by Abba Lerner. Lerner calls his plan the wage increase permit plan (WIPP). The plan works as follows: All employers receive from the government a set of permits which reflect the size of their labor force. If they hire more workers, they receive more permits; if they lay off workers they receive fewer permits. Each permit allows the employer to raise wages just enough to meet the national average rate of productivity increase. The number of permits issued assures Lerner that the average wage rate for the economy will rise at the national rate of productivity increase and no faster. To be sure that wage increases can be more rapid in high productivity industries than in low productivity industries, Lerner allows permits to be traded openly on the market, much as a share of IBM is traded on the stock exchange. Lerner's idea is that in industries for which wage increases are most necessary, firms will purchase extra permits on this open market. In industries where wage increases are not as essential, firms will sell wage permits. Lerner would also allow employers who reduce their wage bills to qualify for additional permits. Thus the national average rate of wage increase would be tied to the national average rate of productivity increase, and yet differences in wage increases could take place in different industries. Lerner argues that his WIPP program would, by tying the average wage increase to the average productivity increase, eliminate price inflation and still leave relative wages free to be determined by individuals and collective bargaining.

While these innovative incomes policies are interesting, it seems quite unlikely that they will be adopted. Their design is to place teeth in the incomes policy programs. However, it seems unlikely that the public would be likely to tolerate teeth so sharp. What would happen to the relationship between an employer and his employees were workers to observe the boss selling his wage permits on the open market for substantial profits? As one famous Nobel Prize winner put it, "If the public were forced to take the loss in wealth implied by outside shocks such as doubling of oil prices without the sleight of hand implied in double digit inflation, blood would run in the streets."

Other structural measures suggested by KS are not unlike those discussed by non-Keynesians. Many economists prefer eliminating minimum wages for the highly unemployable teenagers in center cities, and many advocate relaxation or elimination of Regulation Q controls. In addition, KS advocate cushioning the domestic economy's susceptibility to shocks from the energy sector. Another set of structural proposals designed to have long-term impact on the inflation-unemployment trade-off are stimulants for domestic capital accumulation. As noted in Chapter 23, the productivity slowdown in the 1970s from around 3 percent to around 1½ percent can in part be attributed to the reduced rate of capital accumulation. Consequently, a number of economists propose tax incentives to stimulate investment spending.

Synthesis of the Two Views: We have now seen two general approaches to dealing simultaneously with high inflation and high unemployment. While it may appear as if economists are disagreed about this important problem, we should realize that there is some agreement among them on these very fundamental issues. While economists will always disagree about the relative costs and benefits of social objectives such as high employment and price stability, they do agree on a number of analytic points. We should, of course, always expect disagreement among **reasonable** men when dealing with normative policy issues, but we should also bear in mind that when positive analysis can throw light on analytic points, we must take positive analysis into consideration.

The accumulated evidence of the last decade and a half has suggested to economists that stabilization policies may be used to establish a short-run level of nominal income but that in the long run the rate of monetary expansion will produce an approximately proportional rate of increase in the price level. Given the nature of the monetary and fiscal weapons, many economists seem now to believe that monetary expansion ought to be used to determine the average rate of increase of money income and that government fiscal actions, both expenditure and tax policy, may best be employed to determine the public-private mix of total GNP and other ancillary social objectives.

We should also realize that below some (natural?) unemployment level, the economy will start to have accelerating inflation. This result, as Modigliani and Papademos showed, is consistent with both the vertical and the nonvertical views of the long-run Phillips curve. A by-product of this point is that to reduce unemployment at each inflation rate, one must turn to nonstabilization devices. Two types of devices are worth considering: (1) Devices designed to improve the structure of the labor market. These include proposals such as Feldstein's for making the unemployment compensation system more efficient and proposals to reduce the prevalence of minimum wages in highly unemployed sectors. (2) Manpower policies. Finally, many economists are agreed that the nature of regulatory programs must be examined very carefully to eliminate the inflationary bias in the effected industries. Regulation Q is perhaps one of the worst offenders. By holding interest rates down in the face of accelerating inflation, Regulation Q only serves to discourage private saving and therefore to discourage capital accumulation and investment. Thus there is widespread agreement among economists that to improve the unemployment-inflation trade-off we are going to have to use nonstabilization measures and that these measures are likely to include a number of regulatory reforms.

STUDY QUESTIONS

1. You have been asked by the chairman of the CEA to assess the current state of the economy and to forecast its activity over the coming year. Do so.

2. Comment carefully on each of the following as forecasting and measurement devices:

    a. Composite leading indicator.

    b. Consumer price index.

    c. Large-scale macromodels.

    d. Consumer attitudinal surveys.

    e. Unemployment statistics.

3. Why might the U.S.'s Phillips curve have shifted upward from the mid 1960s to the present? What policies could be employed to shift it downward?

4. Under what circumstances would you recommend wage and price controls? Evaluate their costs and benefits.

5. What is potential GNP? Why does a 1 percent reduction in the rate of unemployment lead to a 3 percent increase in real GNP according to Okun's Law?

6. Suppose the economy is at 3 percent inflation and 5 percent unemployment. Suppose stabilization measures could bring the economy to 4 percent inflation and 4 percent unemployment. Evaluate carefully the costs and benefits of such a move.

7. The FED wishes to increase income to some target level. Under what type of relative uncertainty in the commodity and money markets should the FED select the money supply as its instrument variable rather than the interest rate? Defend your answer.

8. Suppose the CEA and the FED implement fiscal and monetary policy endogenously be reacting to deviations from target income. Will reduce-form equations treating stabilization policies as exogenous accurately estimate multipliers?

9. Compare and contrast monetary and fiscal policies as stabilization devices. Consider economic theory and empirical evidence in developing your answer.

10. Based upon your study of stabilization policy, what reforms of U.S. monetary and fiscal institutions would you propose? Support your proposals.

11. a. Define Okun's Law and illustrate the relationship, according to the Law, between output and the unemployment rate.

    b. Use a comparative static model (AD-AS) to analyze the types of changes which will produce an Okun's Law relationship.

    c. Give three examples of shocks that will cause the economy to deviate from Okun's Law.

12. Analyze three nonstabilization measures for improving the unemployment-inflation trade-off. (Be as specific as you can.)

13. Compare and contrast the Keynesian-structuralist and the monetarist-neoclassical views of the unemployment-inflation short- and long-run trade-off.

14. What are two possible explanations for a deterioration in the unemployment-inflation trade-off? What policy is suggested by each?

15. a. Specify a model (AD-AS and price and wage equations) that you think roughly characterizes the economy.

b. List four major potential sources of shocks for the economy over the next year and forecast best-case, worst-case, and best-guess outcomes for each source.

c. Combine parts a and b to forecast output, unemployment, inflation, interest rates, and the mix between C, I, G and $(Z - J)$.

*16. a. Collect some historical data on planned goverment expenditures, taxes, and some monetary aggregate measure. Use a reduced IS-LM form model to estimate money GNP. What are k_g, k_T and k_M, the values of the multipliers?

b. Show how a government or central bank reaction function can bias your answers.

*(This problem is a computer problem requiring regression analysis.)

17. Suppose the interest elasticity of money demand is small and suppose that the commodity market is far less stable than the money market. Should the monetary authorities use a monetary aggregate or interest rate instrument? Defend your answer.

18. Briefly assess each of the following forecasting approaches:
    a. surveys of opinions
    b. leading indicators
    c. econometric models
    d. reduced form models

19. Analyze the implications for open market operations and for Treasury debt finance of the budget restraint analysis of Carl Christ.

20. How would the recommendations of monetarists-rationalists for reducing unemployment differ from those of Keynesian-structuralists?

21. Why did unemployment statistics help imply deterioration in the 1970s of the relation between u and $\dot{P}$? Discuss Feldstein's proposals for permanently reducing unemployment?

22. Define and state the significance of each of the following:

    the natural unemployment rate
    monetary aggregates
    reduced form equations
    composite leading indicator
    Okun's Law
    monetarist-rationalist model of u and $\dot{P}$.
    TIPs and WIPP

23. Analyze with a wage-price equations model either TIPs or WIPP.

24. Assess the contributions to economic policy of each of the following economists:

Arthur Okun
Martin Feldstein
Friedman and Meiselman
Goldfeld and Blinder
Abba Lerner

REFERENCES

Aaron, Henry J. (ed.), *Inflation and the Income Tax*. Washington, D.C.: The Brookings Institution, 1976.

Andersen, Leonall C., and Jerry L. Jordan, "Monetary and Fiscal Actions: A Test of Their Relative Importance in Economic Stabilization," *Federal Reserve Bank of St. Louis Review*, November 1968.

Baseman, R. L., "The Brookings Quarterly Econometric Model: Science or Number Mysticism?" in Karl Brunner (ed.), *Problems and Issues in Current Econometric Practice*. Columbus, Ohio: Ohio State University, 1972.

Bosworth, Barry, "Phase II: The U.S. Experiment with an Incomes Policy," *Brookings Papers on Economic Activity*, No. 2, 1972.

————, "The Current Inflation: Malign Neglect," *Brookings Papers on Economic Activity*, No. 1, 1973.

Christ, Carl, "On Fiscal and Monetary Policies and the Government Budget Restraint," *American Economic Review*, September 1979, pp. 526-538.

Council of Economic Advisers to the President, *Economic Report*, January 1974.

Evans, Michael K., *Macroeconomic Activity, Theory, Forecasting and Control*. New York: Harper & Row, 1969.

Feldstein, Martin, "The Economics of the New Unemployment," *The Public Interest*, No. 33, Fall 1973, pp. 3-42.

Fellner, William, "Discussion of 'Upward Mobility in a High Pressure Economy,'" by Arthur Okun, *Brookings Papers on Economic Activity*, No. 1, 1973.

Friedman, Benjamin M., "Optimal Economic Stabilization Policy: An Extended Framework," *Journal of Political Economy*, September/October 1972.

Friedman, Milton, and David Meiselman, "The Relative Stability of Monetary Velocity and the Investment Multiplier in the United States, 1897-1948," *Stabilization Policies*, Commission on Money and Credit. Englewood Cliffs, N.J.: Prentice-Hall, 1963.

Fromm, Gary, and Paul Taubman, *Policy Simulations with an Econometric Model*. Washington, D.C.: Brookings Institution, 1968.

Goldfeld, Stephen M., and Alan S. Blinder, "Some Implications of Endogenous Stabilization Policy, " *Brookings Papers on Economic Activity*, No. 3, 1972.

Gordon, Robert A., and Lawrence R. Klein, *Readings in Business Cycles*, London: George Allen & Unwin, Ltd., 1966.

Gordon, Robert J., "Inflation in Recession and Recovery," *Brookings Papers on Economic Activity*, No. 1, 1971.

————, "Wage-Price Controls and the Shifting Phillips Curve," *Brookings Papers on Economic Activity*, No. 2, 1972.

Gramlich, Edward M., "The Usefulness of Monetary and Fiscal Policy as Discretionary Stabilization Tools," *Journal of Money Credit and Banking*, May 1971.

————, "Macro Policy Responses to Price Shocks," *Brookings Papers on Economic Activity*, No. 1, 1979, pp. 125-179.

Hall, Robert E., "Prospects for Shifting the Phillips Curve through Manpower Policy," *Brookings Papers on Economic Activity*, No. 3, 1971.

Hymans, Saul H., "On the Use of Leading Indicators to Predict Cyclical Turning Points," *Brookings Papers on Economic Activity*, No. 2, 1973.

Klein, Lawrence R., and A. S. Goldberger, *An Econometric Model of the United States, 1929-1952*. Amsterdam: North Holland, 1969.

————, "Money Supply Hard to Control," *Los Angeles Times*, Nov. 27, 1979, p. 3, Part IV.

Lerner, Abba P., "A Wage-Increase Permit Plan to Stop Inflation," *Brookings Papers on Economic Activity*, No. 2, 1978, pp. 491-505.

Modigliani, Franco and Lucas Papademos, "Targets for Monetary Policy in the Coming Years," *Brookings Papers on Economic Activity*, No. 1, 1975.

Okun, Arthur M., "The Great Stagflation Swamp," *Challenge*, Vol. 20, November/December, 1977.

————, *The Political Economy of Prosperity*. Washington, D.C.: Brookings Institution, 1970.

————, "Upward Mobility in a High Pressure Economy," *Brookings Papers on Economic Activity*, No. 1, 1973.

Palmer, John L. (ed.), *Creating Jobs: Public Employment Programs and Wage Subsidies*, Washington, D.C.: Brookings Institution, 1978.

Perry, George L., "Changing Labor Markets and Inflation," *Brookings Papaers on Economic Activity*, No. 3, 1970.

Pierce, James L., "A Case for Monetary Reform," *American Economic Review*, May 1979, pp. 246-250.

Poole, William, "Rules of Thumb for Policy," in *Open Market Policies and Operating Procedures—Staff Studies*, Board of Governors of the Federal Reserve System, July 1971.

Porter, Richard D., Thomas D. Simpson, and Eileen Mauskopf, "Financial Innovation and the Monetary Aggregates," *Brookings Papers on Economic Activity*, No. 1, 1979, pp. 218-230.

————, "Optimal Choice of Monetary Policy in a Simple Stochastic Macro Model," *Quarterly Journal of Economics*, May 1970.

Rasche, Robert, and Harold T. Shapiro, "The FRB-MIT Econometric Model: Its Special Features," *American Economic Review*, May 1968.

Seidman, Lawrence, C., "The Role of a Tax-Based Incomes Policy," *American Economic Review*, May 1979, pp. 202-206.

Theil, Henri, *Applied Economic Forecasting*. Amsterdam: North Holland, 1966.

Tobin, James, *The New Economics One Decade Older*, The Eliot Janeway Lectures delivered in 1972. Princeton: Princeton University Press, 1974.

Wallich, Henry C. and Sidney Weintraub, "A Tax-Based Incomes Policy," *Journal of Economic Issues*, June 1971.

Acceleration hypothesis, 397
Accelerator and inventory cycles, 177-81
Accumulation account, 21
Ackley, Gardner, 137
Adapted expectation, 157
Adaptive expectations model, 396
AD curve, downward sloping, 311
Adjustment, speed of, 154
Aggregate consumption, 74
Aggregate demand, 76-77, 78, 79, 81, 90
Aggregate demand-aggregate supply, 332, 340
    workings of neoclassical, 315-21
Aggregate supply, 311
    when wages and prices are flexible, 316
American Enterprise Institute, 446
Andersen, Leonall, 293, 482
Annual time series, 127, 131
Arbitrage, 172, 278
Auctioneer, 57, 61
Automatic transfer systems (ATS), 491
Average propensity to consume (APC), 121, 132, 133

Bailey, Martin N., 500-501
Balanced budget multiplier, 99
Balance of payments surplus effect, 471
Banks, and money supply, 265-70
Barro, Robert, 361, 363
Baumol, William, 280
Baumol's transactions, 297
Bischoff, Charles, 196
Blinder, Alan, 483
Bond(s):
    consols, 276, 298
    coupon value, 276
    indexed, 407
Bosworth, Barry, 446, 501, 502
Brainard, William, 175, 176, 199

Bretton Woods, international monetary system, 453, 460, 461, 471
Brookings Institution, 422, 501
Brunner, Carl, 390
Brunner, Karl, 298
Budget restraint, 489
Budget studies, 123-26
    cross-section in U.S., 125
Bureau of Census, 45
Bureau of Economic Analysis (BEA), 40
Bureau of Labor Statistics (BLS), 41-42, 45, 123, 374
Burns, Arthur, 412, 427, 446
Business cycles, 8

Cagan, Phillip, 381, 384, 385, 412, 471, 497
    theory of, 383
Capacity utilization theory, 193
Capital:
    accumulation, 163
        optimal rate of, 191
    essence of, 186
    interest rates, 171-74
    marginal efficiency of (MEC), 169-70, 171, 174
    user cost of, 188
    vintage of, 186
Capital theory to investment theory, 186-92
Carter, Jimmy, 3
Carter administration, 415
Cash balances, real, 148-49
Chain-link indexes, 40
Chicago School, 22, 279
Chow, Gregory, 298
Christiansen, Laurits, R., 441, 444
Circular flow of income, 12-15
Claremont Economic Institute (CEI), 481
Clower, Robert W., 3, 61, 138, 150-51, 344, 362, 363

Index

Cobb-Douglas production function, 189-90, 433, 434
Coefficient of determination, 129
Commerce, U.S. Department of, 22, 24, 27, 40
Commodity market, 233, 316
  arbitrage, 471
  open economy, 457
Composite index of leading indicators (CLI), evaluation of, 487
Comprehensive Employment and Training Act (CETA), 476
Conference on Wage and Price Determination, A, 398
Congressional Budget Office (CBO), 476
Consol(s), 298
  defined, 276
Constant returns to scale, 433
Consumer Price Index (CPI), 42, 43, 374
Consumption, optimal, 437-39
Consumption analysis, advanced, 137-62
Consumption anchor, Keynesian, 119-36
Consumption expenditures, 75
  determination of, 119
Consumption 1929-1951, actual and predicted, 132
Contractionary monetary policies, 4
Control(s):
  price and wage, 88
  variables, 89
Coolidge, Calvin, 24
Council of Economic Advisors (CEA), 4, 6-7, 89, 111, 248, 422, 475, 491
Countercyclical fiscal policies, 105
Creating Jobs, 500
Crouch, Robert, 298
Cummings, Dianne, 441, 444
Cybernetic Revolution, 6

Data Resources Incorporated (DRI), 487
Deferred payment, standard of, 259
Deflation, 495
  in money and labor markets, 338
Deflationary gap, 318-20
  effects of, 332

Demand for money function, 278-79
  motives, 279-85
  speculative, 281
Depression assumptions vs. a more flexible model, 215-17
Derived demand for labor, 314
Dichotomy, classical, 56-66, 334
Direct job creation (DJC) programs, 500, 501
Direct price effect, 471
Discretionary fiscal policy versus automatic stabilizers, 104-16
Disequilibrium, 356
Disequilibrium analysis, Barro and Grossman's, 361, 362
Displacement principle, 500
Disposable income, derivation and allocation 1978, 32
Dolde, Walter, 150
Domar, Evsy, 424
Domestic investment, gross private, 26-27
Domestic private market economy, 75
Downward shock to aggregate demand, 357
Dual decision hypothesis, Clower's, 360-61
Duesenberry, James, 125, 143, 146, 264, 446
  relative income hypothesis, 117, 144
Durable goods and speed of adjustment, 151-58
Dynamic model(s), 372
  production lag, 84
Dynamics, short-run, 344-65

Eckstein, Otto, 398
Eclectic nonnormative aggregate economics, 11
Econometric model, 193-94
Econometrics, 130
Economic growth:
  long-run, 421-49
  neoclassical theory, 431
  sources of, 439-46
Economic performance:
  comparing, 36-49
  measuring, 18-35
Economic welfare, measure of, 426
Economists, classical, 15
Economy, long-run prospects of, 422

Economy, forecasting and structure of, 479-94
  parameters of system, 481-83
  stability of various sectors, 483-85
Edgeworth, Francis V., 59
Eisner, Robert, 165, 193
Employed persons, 45
Employment, full, 314
Employment and unemployment, 42-46
  comparison chart, 44
Employment and Unemployment Statistics, Committee to Appraise, 44
Endogenous investment and income-expenditure approach, 208-15
Endogenous net taxes, effect of, 108, 115
Equilibrium, market clearing, 349
Equilibrium level, 79
Equilibrium values, 77-78
Exchange, medium of, 258
Exchange rate mechanisms, 458-63
Exogenous increase in aggregate demand, 328
Exogenous money demand shift, 333
Expansionary fiscal policy in a monetarist model, 296
Expansionary monetary policy:
  in liquidity trap, 291
  in monetarist model, 296
Expansion or contraction, 247-48
Exports of goods and services, net, 27-28

Fand, David, 293
Federal budget:
  taxes, 110
  transfers, 110
  See also Government
Federal Deposit Insurance Corporation, 167
Federal Home Loan Bank Board, 167
Federal Open Market Committee (FOMC), 248, 249, 455, 489
Federal Reserve Board, 167
Federal Reserve notes, 217, 264, 266, 295
Federal Reserve System, 224, 230, 232, 244, 248, 260
Feldstein, Martin, 46, 112, 197, 410, 496, 497

Fiat money, 260, 264, 265
Fiscal activists, 100
Fiscal dividend, 111
Fiscal drag, 111
Fiscal policy:
  discretionary, 111
  dynamics of lag in, 112-15
  lags in, 105-6
  pure, 244
  speed of, 105
  theory of, 87-103
Fisher, Franklin M., 36, 40
Fisher, Irving, 184
Fisher effect, 410
Fisherian approach, 63
Flexible accelerator, 190-91
  competing theories, 192-93
Float, managed, 458
Ford, Gerald, 3, 5, 107
Forecasting methods, 485-88
Foreign exchange:
  and domestic economy, 458-71
  market for, 459
  rate of, 452
Foster, Edward, 409, 411
Friedman, Benjamin, 404
Friedman, Milton, 3, 21, 54, 69-70, 101, 104, 117, 138, 143, 146, 157, 208, 218, 219, 262, 273, 274, 279, 287, 345, 398, 403, 412, 480, 482
Full employment equilibrium, 327
Funds transfer, electronic, 263

Galbraith, J. K., 25, 369, 375
General Theory of Employment, Interest and Money, The, 21, 54, 56, 66, 67-71
Goldfeld, Steven, 298, 483
Goldsmith, Raymond, 424
Gordon, R. J., 398, 400, 403, 446, 471, 494, 496
Gordon Committee, 44-45
Government:
  expenditures, 89-92
  fiscal action, 88-89
  purchases of goods and services, 28
  spending model, 191
Government Accounting Office (GAO), 476
Government expenditure multiplier, 91-92, 97, 113, 210

Gramlich, Edward, 101, 494
Grossman, Herschel, 355, 361, 363
Gross National Product (GNP), 8, 29
    actual, 10
    in current and constant prices, 22
    definition of, 22
    deflator, 22
    by major use, 23
    1978, 24
    potential, 8, 9, 10
    real, 22
        slowdown in, 107
Growth rates, select, 443

Haavelmo, T., 184
Hall, Robert E., 497
Hansen, Alvin, 73
Harrod, Roy, 166, 424
Harrod-Domar growth model, 425,
    427-31
Heller, H. R., 298
Heller, Walter, 87, 101, 111
Hess, Alan, 151
Hicks, John, 63, 205, 223, 228, 273
    index of technological change, 441
    IS-LM diagram, 235
Horizon, 140
Households, economic activities of, 12
Hulten, Charles R., 197, 445
Husby, Ralph, 122
Hymans, Saul H., 487
Hyperinflation, 220, 251, 390
    analysis of, 381-85
    select monetary characteristics of,
        382

Implicit rental price, 152-54
Implicit service prices, 152
Imports and exports in commodity
    market equilibrium, 455-58
Import surcharges, 88
Income(s):
    disposable, 138, 305
    expected, 140
    past-peak, 143-45
    permanent, 140
    personal and disposable, 30-32
    policies, 501
    transitory, 140
    wealth and wage, 145-48

Income determination:
    in neoclassical macroeconomics,
        326-35
    neo-Keynesian, 335-42
Income-expenditure approach, 68
Income-expenditure model(s)
    dynamic, 81
    Keynesian, 73-86, 290
Income-expenditure theory, 11, 16
Income or wealth, 143
Income tax cut, 7
Indeterminancy, 304-11
Indexes, price, 36, 43, 374
Index numbers, 37-42
    theory of, 39-40
Inflation, 3, 10
    accelerating, 390
    anticipated, 407-10
    causes of, 369
    consequences and suggested
        remedies, 406
    creeping, 376, 390
    expected rate of, 383-84
    implications of macro models for,
        370
    Keynesian models, 376
    in money market, 330
    optimal rate of, 495
    policies for slowing, 412
    as purely monetary phenomenon,
        389-406
    rate of, 372
    structural causes of, 390-91
    two types of, 406
    unanticipated, 410-12
    wage-price dynamics and conse-
        quences, 389-417
Inflationary expectations effect, 471
Inflationary gap, 327, 330
Inflation-unemployment, two views,
    391
Inflation-unemployment pairs for U.K.
    and U.S., 373
Inflation-unemployment trade-off,
    250-52
    Keynesian-structuralist view of, 499
Information, perfect, 349
Initial equilibrium and reduction in
    demand, 338
Instrument control, 490-92
Interest inelasticity of investment,
    290-92, 341

Interest rates, term structure of, 172
Internal and external imbalance, 468
    mix of policy instruments for, 470
International trade and domestic
    stabilization, 450-74
Investment, 81, 165-82
    analysis, 166-68
    expenditures, 75
        private domestic, 74
    marginal efficiency of (MEI), 173,
        210
    realized, 84
IS curve, comparative statics in, 326-31
IS-LM curves, 232-39
    significance of, 236
    at unemployment output, 289
IS-LM model:
    deficiency of, 250
    moderate, 298
    price level changes in, 304-11
    with price level variable, 310

Job search and employment acceptance
    analysis, 348-56
Johnson, Harry G., 53, 470
Johnson, Lyndon, 3, 7
Jordan, Jerry L., 482
Jorgenson, Dale W., 18, 183, 184-203,
    441, 444
    investment theory, critiques of, 199

Kahn, Alfred, 53
Kaldor, Nicholas, 425, 431
Kennedy, John F., 7, 44
Keynes, John M., 16, 54, 279
    and classical economists, 53-72
    consumption anchor, 119-36
    consumption theory, 120-26
        empirical evidence for, 122-34
    investment multiplier, 80-81
    investment theory, 169-77
    monetarist views synthesis of, 297
    speculative demand, 297
Keynes effect, 410
Keynesian model one, 74-79
Keynesian-Structuralist (KS) view,
    498-501
Khrushchev, Nikita, 425
Klein, Lawrence, 491
Koyck, L. M., 154, 156, 157, 158, 184
Krause, Lawrence, 453

Kuznets, Simon, 133, 140, 144, 181

Labor force, 45
Labor market, 315
    equilibrium, 314
    response to price level increase, 329
    traditional analysis, 360
Labor productivity, 377
Lag(s):
    decision, 105
    distributed, 154
    earnings, 82
    expenditure, 82
    production, 82
    recognition, 105
Laidler, David, 262, 390
Laspeyres index, 37-42
    quantity index numbers, 38-39
Least-squares line, consumption evi-
    dence 1929-1941, 131
Least-squares method, 127-31
Leijonhufvud, Axel, 54, 67, 303
Lerner, Abba, 73, 504
Life cycle hypothesis (LCH), 145, 147,
    148, 150
Linear homogeneity, 278
Lipsey, Richard, 378, 412
    hypothesis, 378, 379
Liquidity, 263
Liquidity constraints and the dual
    decision hypothesis, 149-51
Liquidity preference function, 281
Liquidity preference schedule, 229
Liquidity trap, 291, 339-41
LM curve, 228
Long-run time series, 133-34
Lord, H. M., 111
Lucas, Robert, 398, 399, 404

Macroeconomics:
    in action, 3-11
    policy, 475-509
    scope of, 3-17
    targets and norms, 492
Malthus, Parson, 431
Manpower policies, 499
Marginal propensity to consume
    (MPC), 81, 92, 120, 130, 150
Marginal utility function, diminishing,
    283
Marshall, Alfred, 63

Marxists, 68
Mauskopf, Eileen, 491
Measures, analytically constructed,
    46-47
Meiselman, David, 482
Meltzer, Alan, 390
Meltzer, Allen, 298
Metzler, Lloyd, 168, 177
    inventory cycle, 177-81
Michigan Survey Research Center, 485
*Microeconomic Foundations of Em-
    ployment and Inflation Theory,* 348
Microeconomics, 54, 305, 311
Miller, G. William, 413
Mixed policies, 249-50
Modigliani, Ando, and Brumberg
    (MAB) theory, 145
Modigliani, Franco, 497
    life cycle hypothesis, 117
Monetarism, 292-95
    defined, 292
    and Keynes, 288-90
    synthesis and evidence, 296-98
Monetarist(s), 15
    approach, 217-20
    and Keynes, 287-300
    rationalist view, 494-98
    world, 470
Monetary expansion, actual realized
    rate of, 401
Monetary and fiscal policy multipliers,
    482
*Monetary History of the United States,
    A,* 220
Monetary policy, 247
    contractionary, 332
    lags in, 248-49
Monetary policy instrument in deter-
    ministic model, choice of, 484
Money:
    alternative approach to, 263-64
    commodity, 259
    demand for, 273-86
    full-bodied, 259
    functions of, 258
    lagged effect on prices, 345
    in a macromodel, 223-42
    quantity theory of, 11, 15, 63-66,
        69, 274-79
    sterilization of, 466
    supply instrument vs. interest rate
        instrument, 485
    traditional approach to, 259-63

Money, Employment and Inflation, 361
Money, Interest and Prices, 356
Money demand:
    decrease in, 233
    schedules, 227
Money market, 224-32, 234, 315-18
    equilibrium, 228, 229, 309
    need for, 207-22
    parameter changes, 229-32
    price levels P_1 and P_2, 309
    shifts, 331
Money wages, sticky, 335-39
Multiplier(s), 96
    defined, 80
    impact, 156
Mundell, Robert, 409, 469, 470
Muth, John, 399, 404
Muth-Lucas rational expectations
    model, 400

National accounts, conceptual basis
    for, 19-22
National Bureau of Economic Research
    (NBER), 424, 486, 496
National income:
    and consumption expenditure, 133
    expenditure, and product accounts,
        22-32
    1978, 29, 30
National income account, 21
National product and expenditure
    accounts, 21
Natural rate hypothesis, 395-98
Negotiable orders of withdrawal (NOW)
    accounts, 260, 262, 491
Neoclassical growth model, 432-36
Neoclassical investment model and tax
    policy, Jorgenson's, 183-203
Neoclassical model, implications of,
    334-35
Net national product (NNP), 28, 29
    and national income, 28-30
Nixon, Richard M., 3
Nixon administration, 501
Non-Walrasian economy, 354
Nordhouse, William, 426
Numéraire, 258

Office of Business Economics and the
    Securities and Exchange Commission
    (OBE-SEC), 485

Okun, Arthur, 8, 101, 104, 492, 502
Okun Diagram, 8, 10, 421
Okun's Law, 47, 493
Open economy, internal and external balance, 465
Open market operations, 267
Optimum quantity of money, 409
Organization of Petroleum Exporting Countries (OPEC), 451, 481
Oughtred, William, 73

Paasche index, 38-42
Palmer, John L., 500
Papademos, Lucas, 497
Patinkin, Don, 61, 362, 363
    coexistence theorem, 356
    disequilibrium analysis, 358
    view of Keynes, 356-60
Pearson, Gail, 264
Per capital consumption and steady state, 438
Permanent income hypothesis (PIH), 117, 138-43, 158
    policy implicatons and reservations, 142
Perry, George, 4, 7, 422, 496
Perry dispersion index, 497
Personal consumption expenditures, 25-26
Personal income from national income, 1978, 31
Phillips analysis, 400
Phillips curve, 371, 372, 377, 379, 414, 415, 493, 494
    analysis, 398
    long-run, 391, 394, 395, 466, 505
    short-run, 393, 394
Pierce, James, 489
Pigou, A. C., 148, 217
    real balance effect, 149
    wealth effect, 148
Pitt, William, 375
Policy problems, 477
Policy proposals for the 1980s, 494-505
Poole, William, 404, 483
Porter, Richard D., 491
Portfolio, assets in, 275-78
Post-World War II growth, enigma of, 440
Precautionary demand, 282
Price:
    equation, 393

expectation equation, 393
implicit rental, 152-54
implicit service, 152
indexes, 36
level, 275
    changes, effect on inflation, 305
    indexes, 276
takers, 349
and wage controls, 88
and wage performance and controls, 502
Private domestic investment expenditures, 74
Production and aggregate supply, Keynesian, 337
Production function with fixed capital and variable labor, 435
Production-labor market, 311-15
Profit maximization, 186-88
Pure fiscal policy, defined, 244
Putty clay model, 196

Q regulation, 167
Quasi-equilibrium, 347

Ratchet effect, 145
Real cash balances, 148-49
Recession, 5, 375
Reference cycles, general characteristics of, 486
Regulation Q, 498, 505
    ceilings, 167
Reimer, R., 298
Relative income hypothesis (RIH), 117, 144
Resource allocation, 247
Ricardo, David, 375
Risk averter, 283, 284
Robinson, Joan, 168-69
Roosevelt, Franklin, 107
Rothschild, Michael, 197

Samuelson, Paul, 73, 297
Sargent, Thomas J., 399, 404
Savings, 76-77
    definition of, 94
    gross, 32
    and investment, 12-13
    and investment 1978, 32
Say, J. B., 61
Say's Law, 60, 61, 66

Say's principle, 58, 59, 60
Schumpeter, Joseph, 166, 173, 496
Schwartz, Anna, 208, 218, 219
Seidman, Lawrence C., 503
Series:
    coincident, 498
    lagging, 487
    leading, 486
Shadow Open Market Committee, 390
Shadow price, 188
Shell, Karl, 36
Short run disequilibrium analysis,
    Keynesian economics, 356
Shultze, Charles, 111
Siebert, C. D., 203
Simpson, Thomas D., 491
Smith, Warren, 261, 287, 450
Smithies, Arthur, 126
Solow, Robert, 137, 405, 421, 423
Stabilization policy, 243-54
    internal and external objectives,
        467
    in open economy, 466-70
    organization and coordination of,
        488-89
Stabilizers, automatic, 107-12
    defined, 110
Stagflation, 6, 7, 11, 376
Stagnation, 6
Standard error of coefficient, 130
Starleaf, Dennis R., 298
Statics, comparative, 81, 371
Steady state, 422, 423, 436-37
Steady-state growth, 436
Stein, Herbert, 101
Sticky real wages, 341-42
    in labor market, 336
Strotz, R. H., 193
Structuralists, 405
Stylized facts of growth, 431-32
Supply and demand, 65, 69, 383
    analysis, 55, 68
    and labor market, 314
    money theories, 234

Taste and quality, changes, 40-42
Tatonnement process, 58, 59
Taxation, defined, 92
Tax-based incomes policies (TIP), 502,
    503, 504
Taxes:
    and transfers, 92

    new model, 93-96
    and user costs, 197-98
Tax policy and investment, 196-200
Teigen, Ronald, 298
Theobald, Robert, 6
Three-market model, 319, 463-66
    disequilibrium, 320
    price level increase in, 331
Tobin, James, 54, 70, 71, 150, 174,
    176, 177, 264, 268, 280, 282, 325,
    398, 405, 426, 482, 500, 501
    precautionary demand, 297
    q-theory, 174
Total factor productivity change, 423
Traditional labor market analysis, 360
Transactions demand, 280-82
Transfer payments, 28, 97
    defined, 92
Transfers, 111
Transfers of money, direct, 31
Treasury bills, 263

Unemployed, 45
Unemployment:
    involuntary, 68, 355, 356
        defined, 314
    natural rate, 396, 398
    rate of, 495
Unemployment Act of 1946, 42
United of account, 258
United States dollar, weighted-average
    exchange value of, 451
User-cost, 152-54

Value, store of, 259
Value added, 27
Value shares of capital and growth
    rates of capital and labor, 444
Value-shares of capital and sources of
    growth, 445
Voluntary wage-price guidelines, 6

Wage equation, 393
Wage increase permit plan (WIPP), 504
Wage insurance, 415
Wage and Price Commission, Office of,
    476
Wage-price flexibility, 303-24
Wage price freeze, 5, 88
Wage price guideposts, 7

Wallace, Neil, 399, 404
Wallich, Henry C., 502
Walras, Leon, 149
  general equilibrium model, 56-63
Walrasian economy, 351
Walras's Law, 59, 60, 61
Wealth account, 20
Weighted unemployment rate, 146
Weintraub, Sydney, 502

White, William H., 184
Wholesale Price Index (WPI), 374
Wicksell, Knut, 398
Wisconsin Poverty Institute, University of, 411
Workers, discouraged, 45
Works Progress Administration (WPA), 500
Wykoff, Frank C., 197